'Encompassing a diverse range of scholarly perspectives, this timely volume offers a panoptical overview of European Business. It is ideal as a core text for taught postgraduate courses in European Business as well as providing reference material for graduate research students and researchers in International Business.'

— *Louis Brennan*, Trinity Business School, Trinity College Dublin, Ireland

'This excellent volume provides one of the most comprehensive treatments of regionalisation in European business to date. It offers a single repository on the current state of knowledge and debates as well as future research agendas on Europe as a distinct region. The contributions offer an engaging read by covering different disciplinary fields and multiple perspectives including firm, national and supra-national levels of analysis. This essential reference book speaks to a broad audience of both junior and more seasoned researchers in business as well as management educators in the field. I can warmly recommend it.'

— *Rebecca Piekkari*, Aalto University, School of Business, Finland

THE ROUTLEDGE COMPANION TO EUROPEAN BUSINESS

International Business is a well-established research field, in which regionalisation has recently gained significant prominence. Europe comprises marketplaces characterised by unique patterns of highly advanced economic integration. No other marketplace in the world has progressed to the same levels of harmonisation across sovereign countries and economies.

European Business is a subject in its own right with its own research momentum. Contemporary research evidences that firms view Europe as a challenging, mostly – yet not entirely – mature market location. Yet this location, often seen from a multi-country perspective, is subject to complexities revealing strategic corporate strengths and weaknesses. Theory, concepts and models known from International Business hence often vary in their applicability and relevance in this business environment.

This comprehensive reference volume brings together a global team of contributors to analyse and overview the key issues, themes and phenomena that affect business in Europe. With interdisciplinary perspectives, the book covers crucial themes that any European Business research needs to acknowledge, including business cultures and identity, entrepreneurship and innovation, M&A and institutional trends, European HRM, migration, climate change issues, Brexit and more. The selection of authors, from 17 countries worldwide, reflects the international scope of this research field and its agenda.

A unique resource, this book provides an essential guide to researchers, research students and scholars of business and the social sciences, as well as the informed business community.

Gabriele Suder, PhD, is Professor and Professorial Fellow at The University of Melbourne and its Melbourne Business School. She is also trade and investment expert at the EU, UNCTAD and the Australian Government, business advisor and an entrepreneur.

Monica Riviere, PhD, is Assistant Professor of International Business Strategy at ISC Business School Paris. She co-manages the Master of Science – Innovation in European Business – with the University College Cork, Ireland and the University of Applied Sciences Utrecht, the Netherlands.

Johan Lindeque, PhD, is Senior Research Associate at the University of Applied Sciences and Arts Northwestern Switzerland, and affiliated with the University of Amsterdam Business School.

ROUTLEDGE COMPANIONS IN BUSINESS, MANAGEMENT AND ACCOUNTING

Routledge Companions in Business, Management and Accounting are prestige reference works providing an overview of a whole subject area or sub-discipline. These books survey the state of the discipline including emerging and cutting edge areas. Providing a comprehensive, up to date, definitive work of reference, Routledge Companions can be cited as an authoritative source on the subject.

A key aspect of these Routledge Companions is their international scope and relevance. Edited by an array of highly regarded scholars, these volumes also benefit from teams of contributors which reflect an international range of perspectives.

Individually, Routledge Companions in Business, Management and Accounting provide an impactful one-stop-shop resource for each theme covered. Collectively, they represent a comprehensive learning and research resource for researchers, postgraduate students and practitioners.

Published titles in this series include:

THE ROUTLEDGE COMPANION TO EUROPEAN BUSINESS

Edited by Gabriele Suder, Monica Riviere
and Johan Lindeque

Routledge
Taylor & Francis Group

LONDON AND NEW YORK

First published 2019
by Routledge
4 Park Square, Milton Park, Abingdon, Oxon OX14 4RN
and by Routledge
605 Third Avenue, New York, NY 10017

First issued in paperback 2022

Routledge is an imprint of the Taylor & Francis Group, an informa business

Publisher's Note
The publisher has gone to great lengths to ensure the quality of this reprint but points
out that some imperfections in the original copies may be apparent.

British Library Cataloguing-in-Publication Data
A catalogue record for this book is available from the British Library

Library of Congress Cataloging-in-Publication Data
Names: Suder, Gabriele G. S., editor. | Riviere, Monica, editor. |
Lindeque, Johan, editor.
Title: The Routledge companion to European business / edited by
Gabriele Suder, Monica Riviere and Johan Lindeque.
Description: Abingdon, Oxon ; New York, NY : Routledge, 2018. |
Series: Routledge companions in business, management and accounting |
Includes bibliographical references and index.
Identifiers: LCCN 2018003547 | ISBN 9781138226586 (hardback) |
ISBN 9781315397306 (ebook)
Subjects: LCSH: Business enterprises–Europe. | Business literature–Europe.
Classification: LCC HD62.65 .R68 2018 | DDC 338.7094–dc23
LC record available at https://lccn.loc.gov/2018003547

ISBN 13: 978–1–03–247609–4 (pbk)
ISBN 13: 978–1–138–22658–6 (hbk)
ISBN 13: 978–1–315–39730–6 (ebk)

DOI: 10.4324/9781315397306

Typeset in Bembo
by Out of House Publishing

CONTENTS

FIGURES

TABLES

LIST OF CONTRIBUTORS

Editors

Johan Lindeque, PhD, is Senior Research Associate at the University of Applied Sciences and Arts Northwestern Switzerland and affiliated with the University of Amsterdam Business School. His research focuses on the relationship between international business and government and is published in journals including the *Journal of World Trade* and *Journal of Common Market Studies*.

Monica Riviere is Assistant Professor of International Business Strategy at ISC Business School Paris. She co-manages the Master of Science – Innovation in European Business. Her research interests focus on the role of internationalisation in the firm's ability to maintain competitive advantages, with publications for example in *International Business Review*.

Gabriele Suder is Professor/Professorial Fellow at The University of Melbourne's Melbourne Business School, and expert at the EU, UNCTAD, JETRO and the Australian Government. She is author of award-winning international business books, including *Doing Business in Europe*, SAGE, 2007, and scholarly and media papers. She is Editorial Board member of the *Journal of International Business Policy* and *International Business Review*.

Contributors

Björn Ambos is Chaired Professor of Strategic Management and Managing Director of the Institute of Management of the University of St. Gallen. His research focuses on regional headquarters, the headquarters–subsidiary relationship in multinational enterprises, strategic management and innovation. His work has been published in journals such as *Strategic Management Journal*, *Organizational Science* and *Journal of World Business*.

Cordula Barzantny is Professor of Human Resource Management at Toulouse Business School with a focus on European, international and intercultural management and global leadership. She is also involved in AeroSpace business and management education development. Cordula is an associate editor of the *European Journal of International Management* and on several editorial boards.

Edgar Bellow is Associate Professor of International Management and Sustainable Business at NEOMA Business School, and academic and research representative for corporate social responsibility and sustainable development goals at NEOMA Business School. He provides sustainability consulting and teaches in various University in China and Europe.

Maureen Benson-Rea is Associate Professor in Management and International Business, University of Auckland Business School. She previously held roles with the Confederation of British Industry, where she advised companies, developed policy and represented the views of British business in Whitehall, Westminster and Brussels. Maureen was the founding co-Director of the University of Auckland Europe Institute.

Alan Butt-Philip taught at the University of Bath for 40 years until 2016, latterly as Reader in European integration. He was also Jean Monnet Chair. His research interests span the role of EU interest groups and policy-making, structural funds, the single market and the implementation of EU law.

Regis Coeurderoy is Professor in Strategic Management and Innovation, ESCP Europe, France. A Doctor in management (HEC France), he is Director of i7 – Institute for Innovation and Competitiveness (ESCP Europe). Before joining the academic world, Regis worked as a business economist at Bank of France and the European Commission.

Cheryl Marie Cordeiro is Researcher at the Centre for International Business (CIBS), School of Business, Economics and Law at the University of Gothenburg, Sweden. She has a PhD in general linguistics and is a Flexit scholar with the Bank of Sweden Tercentenary Foundation researching human use and acceptance of new technologies in European-founded multinational enterprises.

Peter Enderwick is Professor of International Business at Auckland University of Technology, Auckland, New Zealand. His research interests cover emerging markets, global factory systems and theory of the firm. He is an editor of *International Business*, Oxford University Press, 2018.

Anna Gerke is Associate Professor at Audencia Business School in Paris in the Department of Management. Her research focuses on organisational theory, innovation and economic geography, notably in the context of sport organisations. Anna is head of the specialised master of management of sport organisations.

Elisa Giuliani is Professor, Economics and Management, at University of Pisa, and 2017–2018 visiting professor at MIT Sloan School of Management. Her research focuses on understanding how the private sector shapes the world where we live, published for example in *Cambridge Journal of Economics, Journal of Business Ethics*.

Terrence R. Guay is Clinical Professor of International Business in the Smeal College of Business at The Pennsylvania State University, USA. His publications include seven books and over 25 articles and chapters on Europe's business environment, the global defence industry, transatlantic relations, NGOs and corporate social responsibility.

Lotfi Hamzi is Associate Professor of Geopolitics and International Relations at NEOMA Business School and Head of the Economics and International Affairs Department. He was a lawyer specialising in public business law and intellectual property rights, and teaches at various universities in China, Europe and the Middle East.

Sara Melén Hånell, PhD, is a Research Fellow at the Department of Marketing and Strategy, Stockholm School of Economics. She conducts research on the internationalisation of small and medium-sized European enterprises and has published her research amongst others in the *Journal of World Business*.

Karin Jõeveer is Associate Professor at the Department of Economics and Finance at the Tallinn University of Technology. She has broad research interests in the field of financial economics. Among other things, she has studied firms' financial decisions and financial institutions' efficiency.

Anna John, PhD, is a lecturer in Strategic Management at the Open University Business School, UK. Her research interests include approaches to, and performance of, cross-border mergers and acquisitions in Europe and the relationship between non-market activity and foreign direct investments.

Andreas Kaplan is Professor of Marketing and Dean at ESCP Europe, Berlin, Germany. His research focuses on social media and the digital world. He has more than 100 publications, the majority in leading journals including *Business Horizons*, and is highly cited. He also publishes on higher education.

Andreas Kornelakis, PhD LSE, is Senior Lecturer in International Management at King's College London, King's Business School, UK. His research interests dwell on the changing European political–economic and business environment, industrial relations and human resources management. He has published in journals including the *European Journal of Industrial Relations*.

Marina Latukha is Doctor of Economics and Associate Professor of Organisational Behaviour and Human Resources Management at the Graduate School of Management, Saint Petersburg State University, and also the lead researcher at the Centre for the Study of Emerging Market and Russian Multinational Enterprises.

Thomas Lawton, PhD, FRSA, is Professor of Strategy and International Business and Head of the Department of Strategy and Entrepreneurship at Surrey Business School, University of Surrey in the UK. He is Visiting Professor of Business Administration at the Tuck School of Business at Dartmouth in the USA. His research focuses on nonmarket strategy, particularly corporate political activity in an international.

Chiara Macchi, PhD, is a postdoctoral research fellow and lecturer in international human rights law and in business and human rights at the Sant'Anna School of Advanced Studies (Pisa, Italy). She completed her PhD in international human rights law.

Maureen Meadows is Professor of Strategic Management at the Centre for Business in Society (CBiS) at Coventry University, UK. She is co-leader of a research cluster on 'Data, Organisations and Society'. Key research themes include the relationship between data and organisational strategy, and the impact of data sharing on privacy and trust.

Natalie Solveig Mikhaylov is Assistant Professor of International Business at Pontificia Universidad Javeriana, Cali, Colombia. She has a PhD in Management and Organization from Turku University and ten years of professional experience in human resources management in the USA and Europe. She is engaged in research on international human resources management.

Øystein Moen is Professor at the Norwegian University of Science and Technology. One of his key research areas is the internationalisation processes of small and medium-sized firms. Currently, his work focuses on the renewable energy sector with involvement in several large research programmes.

Emilia Rovira Nordman, PhD, is a Research Fellow at the Department of Marketing and Strategy, Stockholm School of Economics. Her research investigates the internationalisation of small European enterprises and Born Globals. Her research has been published in *International Business Review* and *Entrepreneurship and Regional Development*.

Kalle Pajunen is a Professor of Strategic Management at University of Jyväskylä, Finland. His research related to international business and institutions is published for example in *Journal of International Business Studies*, *Journal of Management Studies* and *Research in the Sociology of Organizations*.

Nicholas Parry is a PhD candidate at the Australian-German Climate and Energy College at the University of Melbourne, Australia. His research focuses on the politics of the energy transition with a particular focus on Europe.

Anita Pelle, PhD in Economics (2010), is working as Associate Professor and Jean Monnet Chair at the University of Szeged, Hungary. Her teaching and research cover the economy of the EU, the EU internal market and, most recently, the EU internal divide.

Elfriede Penz is Associate Professor at WU Vienna. Her research is on international marketing and consumer behaviour; especially, Dr Penz investigates sustainable consumption, online consumer behaviour and aspects regarding counterfeits and the sharing economy. She has published in refereed international journals and presented at international conferences.

Áron Perényi, PhD, is Lecturer in International Business at Swinburne University, Melbourne, Australia. Dr Perényi was born and educated in Hungary, and completed his PhD in Australia. His research interests include entrepreneurship, economic diplomacy, policy, development and international business in Central and Eastern Europe.

Alex Rialp-Criado is Associate Professor at Universitat Autònoma de Barcelona, Spain, and Adjunct Professor at the Norwegian University of Science and Technology. His research covers international business and entrepreneurship, with a focus on the internationalisation of new ventures and established small and medium-sized enterprises, and international entrepreneurship in the renewal energy sector.

Barbara Stöttinger is Dean of the WU Executive Academy and Associate Professor of International Marketing at WU Vienna. She has extensive experience as a educator in North America, Europe and Asia. Her research in international marketing issues (e.g., exporting and consumer behaviour) is published in leading journals.

Sonja A. Sackmann is Professor at the Bundeswehr University Munich's EZO Institute for Developing Viable Organizations in Neubiberg, Germany. Her research focuses on leadership, corporate/organisational culture, personal, team and organisational competence and development in national and multinational contexts, published in journals such as *Administrative Science Quarterly*.

Daniel Tolstoy, PhD, is a Research Fellow at the Department of Marketing and Strategy, Stockholm School of Economics. He is currently involved in projects that focus on international retailing and global sourcing. He has published his research in *Journal of Small Business Management and Technovation*.

Louise van Weerden is Associate Professor, SMEs in International Business at Saxion University of Applied Sciences, the Netherlands. She has a background in linguistics and business. Her focus is on curriculum development, project development in international business and traineeships and research on international competencies.

Michail Veliziotis, PhD University of Essex, is Lecturer in Human Resource Management at University of Southampton, Southampton Business School, UK, and focuses his main research on the fields of employment studies, industrial relations and labour economics. He publishes in *The International Journal of HRM, European Journal of Industrial Relations* and others.

Martin Wainstein is a PhD researcher at the Australian-German Climate and Energy College, University of Melbourne, Australia. He has a background in biological sciences from the University of Southern California, and several years of experience as a sustainability entrepreneur in Argentina. He provides ongoing consultancy on innovative business strategies.

Marjo Wijnen-Meijer is Associate Professor Health Professions Education and she works at University Medical Center Utrecht, the Netherlands. She has a background as an educational scientist. Her focus is on curriculum development, quality assurance of education, training in didactics and educational research.

Bruce Wilson is Director, European Union Centre and Professor at RMIT University, Australia. He leads a research programme on comparative regional policy in Europe, Australia and Asia, on interventions to promote innovative economic development and human capability that improves the living and working conditions of people in city regions.

Nina Zobel is a PhD Student at the University of St. Gallen as well as consultant at the Boston Consulting Group. Her research interest lies in the areas of regionalisation, headquarters–subsidiary relationships, organisational justice and envy.

ACKNOWLEDGEMENTS

We very sincerely thank our families for their great morale and intellectual support and their patience, and the inspiration they provide.

We also acknowledge the support provided by our respective universities.

In particular, we thank the chapter contributors for their excellent work and collaborations.

1

INTRODUCTION

Development of the discipline and trends

Gabriele Suder, Monica Riviere and Johan Lindeque

This *Routledge Companion to European Business* provides you with a timely, authoritative overview of the current state of European business literature from an academic perspective and as a field of practice. It is a prestige reference work that offers graduate students, PhD candidates and international business (IB) researchers an introduction to current scholarship in the expanding discipline of European business, and in-depth analyses to advance further research in this field.

We refer to European business as the act of doing business in Europe, whether conducted by European-owned or non-European-owned organisations.

This volume

- reviews and analyses the literature that is relevant in the field of European Business,
- provides theoretical, sectoral, functional and case-driven contributions that advance research, and
- discusses future research avenues.

International business is a highly related and well-established research field, in which regionalisation has gained prominence in the last decade. The study of European business has gained its role within this literature and in its own name for two main reasons:

One, Europe is a market that shows specific patterns of highly advanced formalised market integration. In particular, firms view Europe as a challenging, mostly – yet not entirely – mature market location that is subject to complexities that help reveal strategic corporate strengths and weaknesses. Also, Europe – and its many sub-locations – represents a location that undergoes frequent and rapid change due to its geoeconomic and geopolitical position, reflecting the concurrent significant integration, at times partial fragmentation, and simultaneous isolated de-integration processes. It provides the perfect research ground to explore region – and country – specific advantages and conditions within the internationalisation discussion that supports further development of IB theory and practice.

Two, the study of regionalisation has gained significant momentum worldwide. Due to its advanced patterns of regionalisation, Europe is increasingly scrutinised on an international, comparative level in literature that explores the underlying factors that drive regionalisation, ranging from the political economy to geography to global value chain effects. Reflecting its unique characteristics, European Business literature provides for a subject in its own right and with its own research momentum.

This volume provides essential reading. It aims to foster better in-depth understanding of this business environment and the complex challenges that accompany its development and impact business strategey and internationalisation in Europe. This is the first single text on the state of current research knowledge on European business or which offers a comprehensive guide to research students and academics on the subjects of Europeanisation: we offer you a single repository on the current state of research knowledge, current debates, relevant literature and future research agendas.

The remainder of the book reflects a rich research agenda. It is organised into the following seven thematic parts:

A. *European business research: Review of literature and state of affairs*
B. *International business theory and evidence in Europe: Origins and evolutions*
C. *Culture, identity and European business*
D. *The political economy of doing business in advanced regionalisation*
E. *Managing people in Europe*
F. *Functional and sectorial perspectives*
G. *Complex challenges: European society and the natural environment*

Each of the chapters, organised according to the above themes, provides you with a balanced overview of the current literature, research and knowledge, identifying issues and relevant debates related to its focus, and concludes with an outlook into future research themes. Much theory building remains to be done and the volume endeavours to provide a solid theory extension and a basis for more such work. As a result, you will find that the style of the chapters is purposefully analytical and engaging, and that the authors reflect on where the research agenda is likely to advance in the future.

Our selection of authors is international by origin and professional career and drawn from institutions located in 17 countries, including Austria, Australia, Colombia, Estonia, Finland, France, Germany, Hungary, Italy, Russia, Sweden, Switzerland, the Netherlands, New Zealand, Norway, the United Kingdom and the USA. This reflects not only the diversity of the European business environment and its literature but also its international reach in terms of influence and relevance.

We now provide a synopsis of the thematic parts and their constituent chapters that you will find in this book, so as to help you focus your reading.

A. European business research: Review of literature and state of affairs

The first part includes two review chapters. In the first, Áron Perényi addresses the intersection of international business and European business research. The second showcases Nina Zobel and Björn Ambos adopting a corporate strategy perspective to focus on the common interest in regionalisation of both the international and European business literatures.

Chapter 2 provides an extensive and systematic review of the European business literature, which reveals the diversity and centrality of European geographic foci in this body of work and diverse disciplinary origins, with a particularly strong presence of studies in the disciplines of ethics (including corporate social responsibility (CSR) and sustainability), entrepreneurship and innovation. Collectively, the research shares an emphasis on cross-country, cross-cultural and cross-institutional adaptation of the business sector actors.

Chapter 3 draws on the centrality of Europe and the European Union (EU) as a regional spatial phenomenon to explore from a corporate strategy perspective how the regional nature of (European) business can be explained. Both the 'regional embeddedness' and the regional organisation of firms to maximise the benefits derived from a regional focus are discussed, with the highly interrelated nature of these two explanations for the phenomenon of regionalisation.

B. International business theory and evidence in Europe: Origins and evolutions

Part B includes four contributions with a focus on the relevance of established international business theoretical/conceptual approaches to understanding European business, respectively on the contributions of internalisation theory, the Uppsala model of internationalisation, the institutional embeddedness and born global streams of research to understanding European business.

Peter Enderwick in Chapter 4 emphasises firm-specific and location-specific advantages to highlight how internalisation theory can help understand ongoing diversity at the country level, with respect to research and development (R&D) and entrepreneurial activities, within the overarching EU Single Market (SEM) integration efforts.

Cheryl Marie Cordeiro's Chapter 5 investigates research on the ongoing process of market integration and fragmentation that features the European business environment, and focuses on the Götheborg IV (G4) model. This is developed on the basis of the Uppsala model of internationalisation, thereby enabling a visualisation of a unified systemic perspective of firm–institution co-evolution.

Kalle Pajunen's Chapter 6 continues the focus on the institutional embeddedness of European business to explore Europe as a location, featured through ongoing institutional heterogeneity, within the significant progress with creating unified economic and political rules in the largest part of the European marketplace, the EU.

Finally, Øystein Moen and Alejandro Rialp-Criado take a European perspective in Chapter 7 to understand the relevance of the born global phenomenon for European business and argue that European Born Globals (or Born-Europeans) tend to be home-region oriented and smaller in size compared to those from other regions.

C. Culture, identity and European business

Part C comprises three chapters that address the related foci of European culture and identity in relation to business. Regis Coeurderoy considers the link between European national cultures and innovation, while Sonja A. Sackmann puts the development of European cultures and their consequences for business into historical context. Andreas Kaplan then proceeds with a case study to provide an account of how a European business culture is reproduced today through the institutions of higher education .

Chapters 8 and 9 hence address the adaptability and innovativeness of European business in contemporary and historical perspective in relation to the changing and growing European business environment. A common theme that emerges is the contribution of the diversity of the European national cultures to sustaining ongoing innovation by and growth of European businesses.

As the European business environment has increasingly become economically integrated into the global economy, the uniqueness of the European approach to business and its education is reflected and discussed in Chapter 10.

D. The political economy of doing business in advanced regionalisation

Part D includes four chapters with a focus on the EU as a unique example of advanced regionalisation.

Bruce Wilson in Chapter 11 addresses the EU regional development policy, highlighting its intricate relationship to the Single European Market policy process and its changing nature as the EU moves towards a knowledge-driven digital economy.

Chapter 12, by Maureen Benson-Rea and Anna Gerke, then considers the historic and ongoing evolution, and incomplete nature, of the Single European Market, and its relevance in extant literature. Terrence Guay then in Chapter 13 addresses the international expansion/ projection of Europeanisation via free trade and regional trade agreements. Finally, Alan Butt-Philip puts these institutional integration efforts into context in Chapter 14. He discusses the evolving institutions of the EU, the largest market regulator in Europe, which implement, shape and lead the process undergone by this unique marketplace.

E. Managing people in Europe

The five chapters in Part E investigate how people management is shaped within European business, and how this is reflected in research. In Chapter 15, Andreas Kornelakis and Michail Veliziotis explore the relationship between EU regulations and policies for job quality and national human resources management strategies and practices, which emphasises the role of national employment systems. Cordula Barzantny then provides a broader assessment of human resources management and European business in Chapter 16, while Louise van Weerden and Marjo Wijnen-Meijer in Chapter 17 address the role of higher education graduates for small and medium-sized enterprise (SMEs), and provide insight into international relation competences in a Dutch context.

Chapter 18 by Natalie Mikhaylov studies research on human resources management practices with a sub-regional approach, and reveals the relevance of multicultural European regional clustering. Finally, Marina Latukha's Chapter 19 provides insights into the opportunities and challenges European businesses face when seeking to transfer human resource management policies and practices to the transitioning member countries of the Commonwealth of Independent States (CIS), the successor entity of the former Soviet Union.

F. Functional and sectorial perspectives

Part F addresses European business from functional, corporate and sectorial perspectives. In their Chapter 20, Elfriede Penz and Barbara Stöttinger focus on European business marketing, studying the complexity of the EU single market as an international marketing environment. Sara Melén Hånell, Emilia Rovira Nordman, and Daniel Tolstoy follow with Chapter 21, which explores the innovative foundations of the success of international SMEs in the Swedish life-sciences industry, as an example of factors for European business survivals. In Chapter 22, Karin Jõeveer then discusses the extant knowledge on firm capital structure and adopts a comparative approach to highlight the effects of regionalisation of financial markets in shaping convergence.

Anna John, Thomas Lawton and Maureen Meadows then move the discussion with Chapter 23 to the corporate strategy of cross-border mergers and acquisitions within Europe, focusing on the EU from an institutional, resource-based and firm–environment perspective.

The two final chapters of this part, Chapters 24 and 25, address the broader categories of manufacturing and service sectors. First, Edgar Bellow and Lotfi Hamzi provide research focus through a single case study of the large manufacturing firm BASF, to show how innovation, entrepreneurship and business growth are inextricably linked to the European geopolitically oriented economic policy environment. Anita Pelle's chapter turns our research attention to the services sector in relation to EUn efforts to implement a single market for services. Chapter 25 also provides a detailed account of public policy on regulated professionals, retail and business services, construction services, financial services and posted workers.

G. Complex challenges: European society and the natural environment

The final part of the book opens the researcher's mind further to the unique and complex challenges facing Europe and the EU in particular, along with the inevitable leadership role that the EU, its member countries and businesses have taken on these issues. In Chapter 26, Nicholas Parry and Martin Wainstein explore literature that helps focus on the recognised international policy leadership role of the EU and its member states in responding to the mitigation of climate change. They explore the promotion of innovation and broader effects on European industries and businesses, finding European business is well placed to embrace the challenges of responding to climate change and contribute to leading the transition to a low-carbon future. Finally, in Chapter 27, Chiara Macchi and Elisa Giuliani investigate a global leadership of the EU in the protection and promotion of human rights, and extend research through a discussion of a controversial case, the Ilva Pteel case from Taranto, Italy, calling for further European business research into the limits of governments' abilities to guarantee strict adherence to human rights by European businesses, particularly under conditions of economic crisis.

We will then conclude this reference book outlining research relevance and future European business research avenues, aiming to pave the way even further into this promising, challenging and growing field. We trust that you will find the readings and references of this handbook not only useful but inspiring.

PART A

European business research
Review of literature and state of affairs

2

EUROPEAN BUSINESS

A literature review

Áron Perényi

Introduction

A review of literature on the topic of '*European* business' is a sizable task the boundaries of which need to be specified clearly to ensure a meaningful outcome. In order to conduct research that *makes a difference* (Busi, 2013), that results in an *interesting* outcome (Davis 1971), *relevant* in the fields of *business and management* (Bartunek et al. 2006), and specific to Europe, the scope and robustness of the methodology both need careful attention.

Firstly, the definition of what constitutes European business needs to be clarified. This is probably the question subject to most debate. European is identified along dimensions of politics (and specifically the European Union (EU) and integration), European history, nationality, culture, arts, languages, political ideology and geography (Checkel and Katzenstein 2009).

Johnson and Turner (2006) argue that business environments and strategies are shaped by culture, traditions, economies and institutional frameworks, creating a diverse global, national and regional level mosaic. The unique specificity of *European* business implies further geographical, ideological, linguistic and religious dimensions to the focus of the literature review. This review focuses on research that self-identifies as 'European', regardless of past and current ideological barriers or political affiliations. The focus on Europe means selection of European journal outlets, European research topics and studies involving European countries. On the other hand, it does not include research done by European authors on topics other than the above, or studies that do not self-identify as European. Identification as 'European' therefore is primarily recognised through the language used in the articles, by the authors, including titles, keywords, subject terms or in the text of the articles.

Subsequently, the definition of the field of international business is necessary to clearly specify the discipline areas within business explored in the review of European business. The *Journal of International Business Studies* defines six sub-domains of international business:

> (1) the activities, strategies, structures and decision-making processes of multi-national enterprises; (2) interactions between multinational enterprises and other actors, organizations, institutions, and markets; (3) the cross-border activities of firms [...]; (4) how the international environment [..] affects the activities, strategies, structures and decision-making processes of firms; (5) the international dimensions of

organizational forms […] and activities […]; and (6) cross-country comparative studies of businesses, business processes and organizational behavior in different countries and environments.[1]

Future areas of relevancy in the field of international business include (1) macro level, (2) industry specific (3) firm/organisational, (4) functional, (5) manager/entrepreneur level and (6) process level (Zettinig and Vincze 2011). The publication of Johannson and Vahlne (1977) marks the beginning of the era of studying international business. This expanded over time to cover (1) explaining foreign direct investment flows; (2) activities and strategies of multinational enterprises and (3) understanding and predicting the internationalisation of firms and developments of globalisation (Buckley 2002).

The multidisciplinary nature of international business as a field implies that the review of literature in European business will be multidisciplinary and therefore highly complex. Measures taken to reduce this complexity in this chapter are a clear selection of research contributions by discipline affiliation, and a systematic process of identification and analysis of the current body of knowledge. These ultimately allow for the inclusion of relevant research topics and outcomes into the review.

Finally, I argue that it is appropriate to consider European business as a combination of European and international business. Within international business, the need for stronger contextualisation of research has emerged (Michailova 2011), based on an emerging desire to engage stakeholders for impact (Collinson et al. 2011) and to bring together research results from across countries as well as disciplines (Zettinig and Vincze 2011).

The study of international business in a European context lies at the intersection of the issues of geographical specificity and interdisciplinary collaboration. This chapter therefore endeavours to provide a review of international business literature focusing on Europe, with a view to classifying disciplinary fields of research and map their occurrence, proliferation and interactions.

The chapter proceeds as follows. The methodology of the systematic review of literature is introduced. This is followed by the explanation of the findings of the article search and various metrics of the search outcome. Finally, the articles reviewed are grouped in terms of their theoretical affiliations, topic areas and geographical alignment. The chapter is concluded by a summary of findings regarding the body of international business literature focusing on Europe, as represented in peer-reviewed journal publications, and suggestions for further research directions.

Methods and data analysis

The systematic literature review methodology was selected for conducting a review of European business literature. As defined earlier, international business literature involving Europe was considered relevant for this exercise. It is recognised that there is comprehensive work available on the domain in book format, such as the two editions of Suder (2008, 2011), the three editions of Johnson and Turner (2006, 2016), the four volumes of Kaplan (2015), the edited volumes of Cassis, Colli and Schröter (2016) and Dana et al. (2008), and further books by Harris and McDonald (2004) and Mercado et al. (2001), Harris (1999) and Nugent and O'Donnell (1994). However, research published in peer-reviewed academic journals is also available in great abundance. Traditional methods of literature reviewing can only capture a fragment of this vast body of knowledge. Therefore, a systematic literature review method has been selected, which has the capability of handling literature available in great abundance and diversity. This method is a powerful and comprehensive way of capturing the knowledge base in this topic.

Systematic review methodology

A systematic review enables the researchers to (1) catalogue state-of-the-art research on the phenomenon (European business), (2) systematically explore and evaluate the themes and areas of discussion in the research and (3) suggest emerging fields of research to be pursued. A systematic review procedure was devised based on the instructions of Tranfield et al. (2003) and following the example of Jones et al. (2011). The specification of the search and evaluation procedure is described in the Appendix.

Peer-reviewed scholarly journal articles were extracted from the EBSCO academic journal databases using the search engine. The search phrases 'international business' AND 'Europe*' were used, to capture international business literature labelled with European relevancy. After an initial examination of search results, criteria were established for exclusion of certain articles. Editorials, conference and book reviews, and commentaries were excluded because they may be relevant to the topic, but they are not scholarly content. Furthermore, articles not concerning Europe or not touching on the domain of business or economics were also removed. The complete list of articles extracted from the search engine was reviewed and items not corresponding to the search criteria were removed from the list. The remaining articles provided the basis for analysis.

Descriptive analysis of articles search results

The analysis of the 2,650 articles identified to be relevant in terms of the search and exclusion criteria proceeded with firstly extracting key information about the article from the database and secondly with labelling every article by geographical focus and subject topic area.

Key information about the articles included journals, year of publication, keywords (author supplied), subject terms and geographical locations. For the 2,650 articles, there were 6,048 keywords, 16,726 subject terms and 2,055 geographical locations listed. However, some individual articles had as many as 15 keywords, subject terms or geographical locations listed, with a significant proportion of articles not providing keywords or geographical locations. Figure 2.1 displays the number of publications over time. The diagram also shows the expansion of the EU, which undoubtedly contributed to the growth of the European identity, and therefore the expansion of the number of articles published on European business research.

Articles had several subject terms associated with them, with on average 6.3 subject phrases per article. These subject phrases often described the theoretical domain, the subject matter or the method and also the geographical focus of the article. Figure 2.2 displays a word cloud with the most frequent subject terms appearing in largest print. (Even though the word cloud is displayed in the format of the map of Europe, the locations of the words on the map do not correlate to the particular word displayed in that location.) The word cloud suggests that economics, business, law, ethics, policy, investment, trade, managers, accounting, interest rates, industries, finance, trade and investment were the key areas of interest.

The records also contained author-supplied keywords. Of the 2,650 articles, 1,451 have no keywords noted, with an average number of 2.3 keywords per article. Figure 2.3 provides the word cloud made up of these keywords. The word cloud highlights that, while the focus of the research was European, other countries such as the USA and particular regions of Europe, such as Central and Eastern Europe (CEE), and individual countries like Poland, Greece or the UK have gained frequent mentions. As for topic-related keywords, International Financial Reporting Standards (IFRS), innovation, entrepreneurship, research and development, trade, investment, ethics and culture can be highlighted, suggesting key topics of the articles.

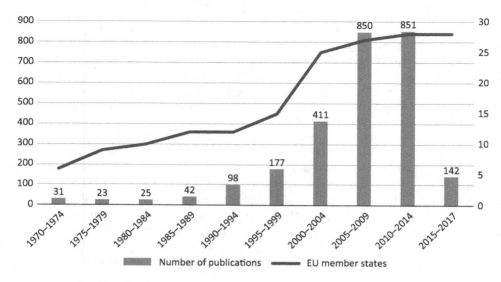

Figure 2.1 Number of publications over time in literature on European business

Figure 2.2 Subject term word cloud for literature review on European business

Figure 2.3 Keyword word cloud for literature review on European business

And finally, location information was also listed for the articles. Of the 2,650 papers, 1,223 had none listed, with an average of 0.8 locations per paper. Figure 2.4 provides a word cloud showing all locations listed in the database. Not surprisingly, the largest location term is Europe. There are a surprising lot of studies on Romania, in comparison to Germany, France, Great Britain or Italy. This can also be attributed to one particular journal published by a university in Romania, which altogether provided 7.3% of all articles in the search output, and overwhelmingly published studies about Romania.

The articles were published in 390 different journals. Table 2.1 lists all journals with more than 20 publications listed in the systematic review search. Key journal topics include economics, finance, accounting, ethics, law, regional studies, business, management, marketing and history. When contrasting this to the topics discussed in the books published on European business, the overlap in areas and focus is shown, which validates the systematic search results.

Thematic evaluation of article search results

Manual identification of the geographical scope and key topic coverage of the articles was made necessary by the generally high proportion of papers lacking keywords or geographical location identification. The large number of subject terms also made it difficult to identify the key topic or subject area of the articles. Therefore, based on the keyword, subject term and geographical

Figure 2.4   Geographical location word cloud for literature review on European business

Table 2.1 Most frequently recorded journals in literature on European business

Journal	# of studies	Journal	# of studies
Accounting in Europe	34	*International Review of Applied Economics*	25
Annals of the University of Oradea, Economic Science Series	193	*International Studies of Management and Organization*	42
Applied Economics	54	*Journal of Business Ethics*	54
Business Ethics: A European Review	50	*Journal of Business Finance and Accounting*	23
Business History	52	*Journal of Common Market Studies*	25
Eastern European Economics	43	*Journal of International Marketing*	28
European Accounting Review	73	*Northwestern Journal of International Law and Business*	35
European Financial Management	38	*Regional Studies*	27
European Planning Studies	81	*Review of International Economics*	24
International Advances in Economic Research	25	*Small Business Economics*	22
International Journal of Human Resource Management	112	*Strategic Management Journal*	22
International Journal of Production Research	34	*Thunderbird International Business Review*	44
International Journal of the Economics of Business	31	*World Economy*	39

Note: The journals listed are those that have contributed over 20 articles to the systematic review.

Table 2.2 Most frequently recorded journal focus in literature on European business

Geographical focus	Frequency	Per cent
CEE	354	13.4
EU	578	21.8
Europe	374	14.1
Europe comparative	146	5.5
Global	570	21.5
SEE	98	3.7
West Europe	530	20
Total	2,650	100

location data, the title and abstract of the articles, the papers were classified into primary topic and geographical focus categories, as described in the appendix.

In approximately half the cases, an actual screening of the article text was necessary to identify these classification categories, as sufficient information was lacking, or the different pieces of information recorded was incongruent. This made the process rather time consuming.

The articles were grouped into seven geographical focus categories. Table 2.2 displays the frequency of the different geographical foci identified. Central and Eastern Europe (CEE) includes the transitional countries from Hungary to Russia, but excludes the Nordic countries or South-Eastern Europe (SEE). Articles classified as SEE focused on one or more countries from the former Yugoslavia, Albania, Turkey, Malta or Cyprus. West Europe consists of highly developed countries in West, North of South Europe, including non-EU countries. The EU is defined as its current (28) member states, including the UK, and is used to identify articles which focused on one or more of the member states, or the EU itself. Articles labelled Europe were the ones that focused on countries together from different regions of Europe. Europe comparative papers compared various parts of Europe with countries or regions from the rest of the world. Global articles had one or more European country, or complete regions of Europe included as components or reference points of the study. Studies focusing on Western Europe and the EU member states are as abundantly present as studies with a global outlook. CEE and extended European papers, comparative European papers and articles focusing on SEE are much less frequent. The proportion of CEE- and SEE-focused papers has grown over time from below 10 per cent to nearing 20 per cent, demonstrating the shift in focus of research interests. On the other hand, the proportion of studies targeting the EU or Europe (including the Europe comparative studies) has been stagnating at around 40 percent since the 1980s, which suggests that the European identity and interest in business research has been dominant since the 1980s.

A similar, manual classification has been implemented to identify the primary topic focus of the articles. A total of 33 primary conceptual areas were identified based on the review of the data at hand (see Appendix) which was consolidated into eight broad topics. Table 2.3 displays the number of articles for the eight primary topic areas identified. Accounting and finance studies concentrate on accounting, finance, banking and taxation-related topics. About half the papers in this category are about finance, and many of those are related to the Euro. Economics papers consist of general economics articles, economic development and competitiveness-related articles, with the majority falling into the general economics

Table 2.3 Most frequently recorded primary topic areas in literature on European business

Topic area	# of articles
Accounting and finance	453
Economics	464
Entrepreneurship and innovation	223
Ethical business issues	113
International business	400
Management	396
Marketing	116
Public sector	485

category. Entrepreneurship and innovation is a diverse topic area, with the majority of the articles originating from the field of innovation and research and development, but there are also several entrepreneurship, small and family business management studies. Studies on ethical business issues focus on corporate social responsibility (CSR) and ethics as key topics. International business studies discuss foreign trade, investment, firm internationalisation and cross-culture research. Management was by far the most fragmented topic, consisting of general management, corporate governance, human resources management (HRM), information systems, logistics and supply chain management, production management, quality management, strategy and tourism and hospitality management. Marketing was relatively under-represented in the sample. Public-sector-related topics included education, industrial relations, law, migration, politics, policy and regulation. The latter constituted the majority of the articles in the topic area.

Discussion

It is important to understand how the findings of the systematic review correspond to the a priori definitions of European business. This will firstly validate the definition employed to identify European business, subsequently providing grounds to establish the legitimacy of the findings of the review (the key areas identified), and finally allow for identification of research directions available for further exploration.

What defines European business today?

The term European can be defined in geographical, ideological, language and religious dimensions. Results of the geographical focus classification as displayed in the word cloud (Figure 2.4) are specified further in Table 2.4. Discounting the global location references (North America, USA, Asia, Japan) and the countries otherwise often considered peripheral to Europe (Russia, Turkey) from the list, geographical focus of the European identity still rests within the term 'Europe' or the 'EU'. The other half of the most frequently listed geographical terms are specific European countries. The emerging presence of Central and Eastern Europe as a region in the listing is notable.

The listing of most frequently used keywords (see Table 2.5) also confirms the emergence of a European identity and the role of the EU in it, these terms providing the most frequently used keywords by the authors. Ideological or religion-related keywords did not make it onto the top listing, except for 'globalisation', which remains the basis for the study of international business

Table 2.4 Most frequently recorded geographical locations in literature on European business

Country	# of studies	Country	# of studies
Asia	21	Italy	28
Europe	611	Japan	29
Europe, Central	50	Netherlands	26
Europe, Eastern	83	North America	22
European Union countries	98	Poland	26
France	30	Romania	80
Germany	70	Russia	23
Great Britain	128	Spain	50
Greece	26	Turkey	23
Hungary	23	United States	153
Ireland	22		

Note: The geographical locations are those that have been noted more than 20 times in the systematic review.

Table 2.5 Most frequently recorded keywords in literature on European business

Keyword	# of studies	Keyword	# of studies
Asset pricing; trading volume; bond interest rates	11	Firm performance: size, diversification, and scope	12
Central and Eastern Europe	13	Foreign direct investment	18
Competitiveness	16	Globalisation	13
Corporate governance	13	IFRS	12
Corporate social responsibility	18	Innovation	28
Aconomic growth	13	International financial markets	17
Economic Integration	13	Multinational firms; international business	15
Entrepreneurship	19	Performance	14
EU and European Union	33	R&D	16
Europe	20	Regulation	11
Financing policy; financial risk and risk management; capital and ownership structure; value of firms; goodwill	12		

Note: The keywords listed are those that have been noted more than ten times in the systematic review.

altogether. Even though the search was restricted to English language papers (for practical reasons of language processing capacity limitations) some articles still presented non–English language keywords. Languages in which keywords were also supplied included Lithuanian, Turkish, German, Spanish, French and Croatian, illustrating the role of language in the definition of a European identity.

Table 2.6 shows that across the most frequently cited subject terms, none is location, religion or language specific. From the domain of ideology, globalisation and social

Table 2.6 Most frequently recorded subject terms in literature on European business

Subject term	# of studies	Subject term	# of studies
Accounting	60	Globalisation	158
Accounting standards	62	Industrial management	118
Business cycles	63	Industrial relations	80
Business enterprises	174	International business enterprises	385
Business ethics	66	International economic integration	111
Business planning	64	International economic relations	94
Competition	77	International markets	90
Competition (economics)	62	International relations	66
Consolidation and merger of corporations	63	International trade	228
Economic development	183	Investments	73
Economic indicators	111	Personnel management	112
Economic policy	80	Research	147
Economics	68	Social responsibility of business	84
Financial statements	75	Strategic planning	92
Foreign investments	177	Technological innovations	63

Note: The subject terms listed are those that have been noted 60 times or more in the systematic review.

responsibility emerge. Theoretical subject-specific keywords such as competitiveness, economics, accounting, finance, business, internationalisation, technology and research are dominating the list, suggesting a deep anchoring in economic liberalism and the prevalence of market coordination (Kornai 2000).

In conclusion, the domain of European business literature still remains primarily defined by the European identity, which is supported by globalisation as a key driver, and the ideological supremacy of the liberal market economy. These findings are also confirmed by the classification of articles into primary topic (Table 2.3) and geographical focus (Table 2.4) categories.

How does European business align with the broader domain of international business?

Johnson and Turner (2006) suggest that due to the variety of factors shaping European business, a review of literature needs to be multidisciplinary and complex. The strong multidisciplinary character of the systematic review presented is reflected in the journals (Table 2.1), the keywords (Table 2.5) and the subject terms (Table 2.6) listed in the review.

In Table 2.7, the primary topics identified during the review of systematic search results are matched with the matrix of the components of the definition of the *Journal of International Business Studies* of topics of international business and the levels of international business analysis proposed by Zettinig and Vincze (2011). It is demonstrated that the primary topics extracted from the literature search cover the topic areas and levels of analysis of international business comprehensively.

Even though the topics of CSR and ethics are present, the proposal of Collinson et al. (2011) for stronger engagement of stakeholders for impact is not represented in research at the

Table 2.7 Subject areas of European business fitting with the matrix of international business topics

Journal of International Business Studies definition of international business	Areas of relevance in the field of international business (Zettig and Vincze, 2011)					
	Macro level	Industry specific	Firm/organisational	Functional	Manager/entrepreneur level	Process level
The 'internal workings' of MNEs	Banking Finance and tax Foreign inv. and trade	Accounting Banking Finance and tax	Accounting Banking Corporate governance Ethics	Accounting Finance and tax HRM Logistics and supply chain man. (SCM) Marketing and comm. Prod. and qual. man.	Entrepreneurship Ethics Family business Prod. and qual. man.	Accounting Finance and tax Firm intern. Prod. and qual. man.
MNEs and their relation to the world	Finance and tax Policy and regulation	CSR Finance and tax	CSR Ethics	Logistics and SCM Marketing and comm. Prod. and qual. man.	CSR Ethics	Accounting Finance and tax Prod. and qual. man.
Cross-border activities	Economics/development Finance and tax Policy and regulation Politics and law	Foreign inv. and trade Firm intern.	Corporate governance Ethics	Accounting Finance and tax HRM Logistics and SCM Marketing and comm. Prod. and qual. man.	Family business SME management Prod. and qual. man. Tourism and hosp.	Accounting Finance and tax Prod. and qual. man.
International environment and its impact	Competitiveness and prod. Economics/development Finance and tax Foreign inv. and trade Policy and regulation Politics and law	Accounting Foreign inv. and trade Firm intern.	CSR Ethics	Accounting Finance and tax HRM Logistics and SCM Marketing and comm.	Entrepreneurship Prod. and qual. man. Tourism and hosp.	Accounting Finance and tax Prod. and qual. man.

(continued)

Table 2.7 (Cont.)

Journal of International Business Studies definition of international business	Areas of relevance in the field of international business (Zettinig and Vincze, 2011)					
	Macro level	Industry specific	Firm/organisational	Functional	Manager/entrepreneur level	Process level
International organisation forms	Banking Policy and regulation	Education Firm intern.	Corporate governance Firm intern.	Accounting; Finance and tax; HRM Logistics and SCM Marketing and comm.	Prod. and qual. man.	Accounting Finance and tax Prod. and qual. man.
Cross-country comparative studies	Competitiveness and prod. Economic development Finance and tax Foreign inv. and trade Migration Policy and regulation Politics and law	Education Ethics Firm intern.	Cross-culture research Ethics Firm intern.	Accounting Education Finance and tax HRM Logistics and SCM Marketing and comm.	Cross-culture research Entrepreneurship Ethics Prod. and qual. man. Tourism and hosp.	Accounting Finance and tax Prod. and qual. man.

functional level, and sparsely implemented in the context of MNEs. This points out room for further research.

The contributions of European business research to the domain of international business can be captured in eight core disciplines, which cover 33 different conceptual areas (see Appendix).

Accounting and finance: 453 articles were classified in this discipline. Key conceptual areas in this discipline include accounting (140 papers), banking (49 papers), finance (232 papers) and taxation (32 papers).

Harmonisation of accounting and reporting has been on the European business research agenda since the acceleration of European integration in the 1990s (e.g. Thorell and Whittington, 1994), and led to a substantial body of research on international accounting standards harmonisation (e.g. Moldovan 2014). Research about banking in Europe initially focused on market integration (e.g. Forbes 1993) and progressed into exploring systemic (e.g. Vallascas and Keasey 2013) and operational (e.g. Lozano-Vivas and Weill 2012) aspects of cross-border banking activities. Research on market integration (Herwartz and Siegel 2009) and international regulation (Carbó-Valverde 2007) also contributed to the body of European business knowledge. A substantial proportion of finance studies dealt with the Euro, as currency (e.g. Kaikati 1999), as capital market (e.g. Kearney and Potì 2008) and a vehicle of economic integration (e.g. Hardouvelis et al. 2006). Sovereign risk and associated public finance implications (e.g. Georgoutsos and Migiakis 2013) dominated research in the domain of government-related studies. From the business perspective, capital-related topics (e.g. Bancel and Mittoo 2009) were researched. Taxation-related research in European business was about tax policy (e.g. Morris 2007) and its business implications (e.g. Overesch and Wamser 2009), in particular tax optimisation (e.g. Gravelle 2009).

Economics: 464 articles were classified in this discipline, presenting research on conceptual areas of competitiveness and productivity (101 papers), economic development (98 papers) and economics (265 papers). European research in economics primarily discussed convergence (e.g. Polanec 2004), performance of various markets (e.g. Weinrich 2016) and foreign balances (e.g. Chen et al. 2013). Papers focusing on economic development broadly deal with sustainability and economic growth issues of European nations (e.g. Cuestas et al. 2015). Papers discussing competitiveness and productivity either have a specific industry focus (e.g. Wijnands et al. 2008), test particular competitiveness models at the firm level (e.g. Naldi et al. 2014), or pertain to policies enhancing competitiveness (e.g. Zemanek 2012).

Entrepreneurship and innovation: 223 studies cover conceptual domains of entrepreneurship (32 papers), family business research (6 papers), research, technology development and innovation (169 papers), and SME management (16 papers). SME, family business and entrepreneurship research features topics such as entrepreneurship–innovation ecosystems (e.g. Groth et al. 2015), the development of European family firms (e.g. Niedermeyer et al. 2010) or various aspects of entrepreneurial activities and characteristics across Europe (e.g. Freytag and Thurik 2007). Innovation studies in European business discuss issues around protection of intellectual property (e.g. Kim and Clarke 2013), systemic aspects of innovation (e.g. Castellacci 2009) and the utilisation of research results (e.g. Festel and Rittershaus 2014).

Ethical business issues: 113 articles focus on areas of ethical business, in particular corporate social responsibility (58 papers) and more general ethics (55 papers). Papers on general ethics primarily discuss corruption (e.g. Moran 1999), the informal economy (e.g. Kapelyushnikov et al. 2012), ethics of trade and investment (e.g. Maitland 1998) and business ethics culture or comparative studies (e.g. Rausch et al. 2014). Corporate social responsibility is studied from the perspectives of frameworks or institutions (e.g. van Marrewijk and Hardjono 2003), socially responsible funding or investment (e.g. Leite and Cortez 2014), and relationships with business partners or other stakeholders (e.g. Leppelt et al. 2013).

International business: 400 articles cover international business. Its conceptual areas are cross-culture research (56 papers), firm internationalisation studies (157 papers), foreign investment (103 papers) and foreign trade (84 papers). Foreign trade-related articles discuss Europe's position in global trade (e.g. Paas et al. 2008), trade in specific sectors (e.g. Marel and Shepherd 2013), and trade between particular members of the EU (Ghatak et al. 2009). An overwhelming proportion of foreign investment studies focuses on emerging economies, and in particular Central and Eastern Europe (e.g. Gorynia et al., 2007). Further foreign investment studies explore the relationships between decisions investment and other economic factors (e.g. Cardamone and Scoppola 2012), or investment location choices (e.g. Yavan 2010). Firm internationalisation was first studied in European businesses (e.g. Gullander 1976), and entry mode (e.g. Brouthers and Brouthers 2000) and location choices (e.g. Rugman and Ok 2013) have been heavily investigated in the European context later as well. Cross-culture studies in European business explored national differences within European nations (e.g. Kaasa et al. 2014) and across the world (e.g. DeDee and Frederickson 2004).

Management: The field of management encompasses 396 articles in the review, and provides the most diverse collection of conceptual areas in literature. The conceptual areas include: corporate governance (29 papers), human resource management (104 papers), information systems (18 papers), logistics and supply chain management (57 papers), general management (61 papers), production management (19 papers), quality management (32 papers), strategic management (52 papers), and tourism and hospitality management (24 papers). Research topics reviewed include the evaluation of European practices of corporate governance (e.g. Eklund and Poulsen 2014), European national (Minbaeva and Muratbekova-Touron 2013) and comparative international (e.g. Zeira and Harari 1979) human resource management practices, business (e.g. Genius et al., 2014) and government (e.g. Otjacques et al. 2007) application of digital systems, green supply chains (e.g. Blome et al. 2014), the European Qualify Framework (e.g. Sadeh et al. 2013), and strategic adaptation in an internationalising EU context (e.g. Iversen and Larsson 2011).

Marketing: The domain of marketing and communication research in European business consisted of 116 articles in the sample. Notable contributions include research in export marketing (e.g. Diamantopoulos et al. 1990), European consumer culture (e.g. Kale 1995), and social media marketing (Singh et al. 2012).

Public sector research The topics explored in the 485 articles in this category include education (32 papers), industrial relations (60 papers), law (44 papers), migration (20 papers), policy and regulation (277 papers), and politics (52 papers). Notable topics in education are ethics education (e.g. Crane and Matten 2004), and comparative qualification frameworks and systems (e.g. Thomas et al 2014). Research in industrial relations discusses labour market negotiations (e.g. Roberts 1973) and social partnership institutions (e.g. Egels-Zandén 2009) in a European context. Studies examining legal aspects of European business are centred around the practice of legal harmonisation and institutional architecture (e.g. Kurylo and Maffei 2007). Migration is discussed primarily from the perspective of the European labour market impact (e.g. Raess and Burgoon 2015). Political articles in European business question globalisation and discuss geo-politics (e.g. Lippert 2007). However, the majority of articles – not surprisingly – research, review and theorise the vast variety of areas within the European political and economic integration itself (e.g. Batory and Cartwright 2011).

Conclusions and suggestions for further research

The purpose of this chapter was to deliver a review of literature on European business. It was proposed that European business is a component of the broader topic area of international business, and is identified by geographical, ideological, language and religious barriers. A systematic search of literature allowed for the creation of an extensive database of peer-reviewed academic journal articles and their associated geographical, subject and keyword associations to be analysed. The primary driver for European identification was found to be geography, with a largely homogenous ideological setting within globalisation, market economy and European integration.

The key topics and levels of analyses within international business were covered by the articles contributing to European business. It was also shown that European business has moved beyond single country studies of European markets, and provided ample discussion on issues pertinent to developing the economies of European countries, such as integration, social responsibility, innovation and entrepreneurship.

Conceptually, the main contributions of European research to international business covered a wide variety of specific domains and theories. In the banking and finance sectors, international standardisation (e.g. IFRS), banking and finance contributed to creating the infrastructure of economic integration through trade and investment. Economics and public sector research focused on the process and outcome of European economic and political integration, providing a policy basis and empirical background to institutional decisions shaping the business environment in the Single Market. It is within this context that European international business research explored behaviours in marketing, international business and management, which allowed for the testing and development of theories pertaining to cross-country, cross-cultural and cross-institutional adaptation of the key participants of the business sector. It is particularly interesting that the disciplines of ethics (including CSR and sustainability), entrepreneurship and innovation found a fertile ground in European research, identifying two key dimensions of development. In a developing country context, ethical issues become a key avenue of socially responsible development, both within and outside the market. At the same time, the conceptual infiltration of entrepreneurship and innovation into European business research resulted in the exploration of key ideas in terms of facing the changing global economic environment. Enabling business actors to participate in innovation and fostering entrepreneurial development paves the road to the future development of the European economy.

There was a magnitude of articles specifically articulating that the researchers had received support from EU funding, or that the source of the research presented in the article was an EU-funded project. This demonstrates the substantial involvement of the public sector in Europe supporting European business research.

Note

1 As described on the website of the *Journal of International Business Studies* http://link.springer.com/journal/41267 (accessed 2 November 2016).

References

Bancel, F. and Mittoo, U.R. (2009), 'Why do European firms go public?' *European Financial Management*, vol. 15, no. 4, pp. 844–884.

Bartunek, J.M., Rynes, S.L. and Ireland, R.D. (2006), 'What makes management research interesting, and why does it matter?' *Academy of Management Journal*, vol. 49, no. 1, pp. 9–15.

Batory, A., and Cartwright, A. (2011), 'Re-visiting the partnership principle in cohesion policy: The role of civil society organizations in structural funds monitoring', *Journal of Common Market Studies*, vol. 49, no. 4, pp. 697–717.

Blome, C., Hollos, D. and Paulraj, A. (2014), 'Green procurement and green supplier development: Antecedents and effects on supplier performance', *International Journal of Production Research*, vol. 52, no. 1, pp. 32–49.

Brouthers, K.D. and Brouthers, L.E. (2000), 'Acquisition or greenfield start-up? Institutional, cultural and transaction cost influences', *Strategic Management Journal*, vol. 21, no. 1, p. 89.

Buckley, P.J. (2002), 'Is the international business research agenda running out of steam?' *Journal of International Business Studies*, vol. 33, no. 2, pp. 365–373.

Busi, M. (2003), *Doing Research that Matters*, Bingley, UK, Emerald Group Publishing Limited.

Carbó-Valverde, S. (2007), 'Implications of Basel II for different bank ownership patterns in Europe', *Atlantic Economic Journal*, vol. 35, no. 4, pp. 391–397.

Cardamone, P. and Scoppola, M. (2012), 'The impact of EU preferential trade agreements on foreign direct investment', *World Economy*, vol. 35, no. 11, pp. 1473–1501.

Cassis, Y., Colli, A. and Schröter, H.G. (eds) (2016), *The Performance of European Business in the Twentieth Century*, Oxford, Oxford University Press.

Castellacci, F. (2009), 'The interactions between national systems and sectoral patterns of innovation', *Journal of Evolutionary Economics*, vol. 19, no. 3, pp. 321–347.

Checkel, J.T. and Katzenstein, P.J. (2009), *European Identity*, Cambridge, Cambridge University Press.

Chen, R., Milesi-Ferretti, G.M., and Tressel, T. (2013), 'External imbalances in the eurozone', *Economic Policy*, vol. 28, no. 73, pp. 101–142.

Collinson, S., Doz, Y., Kostkova, T., Liesch, P. and Roth, K. (2011), 'The domain of international business and AIB', *AIB Insights*, vol. 13, no. 1, pp. 3–9.

Crane, A. and Matten, D. (2004), 'Questioning the domain of the business ethics curriculum', *Journal of Business Ethics*, vol. 54, no. 4, pp. 357–369.

Cuestas, J.C., Gil-Alana, L.A. and Regis, P.J. (2015), 'The sustainability of European external debt: What have we learned?' *Review of International Economics*, vol. 23, no. 3, pp. 445–468.

Dana, L.P., Welpe, I.M., Han, M. and Ratten, V. (eds) (2008), *Handbook of Research on European Business and Entrepreneurship: Towards a theory of internationalization*, Cheltenham, UK, Edward Elgar.

Davis, M.S. (1971), 'That's interesting: Towards a phenomenology of sociology and a sociology of phenomenology', *Philosophy of the Social Sciences*, vol. 1, no. 4, pp. 309–344.

DeDee, J.K. and Frederickson, P. (2004), 'Poland: What U.S. managers need to know', *Thunderbird International Business Review*, vol. 46, no. 3, pp. 293–316.

Diamantopoulos, A., Schlegelmilch, B.B. and Allpress, C. (1990), 'Export marketing research in practice: A comparison of users and non-users', *Journal of Marketing Management*, vol. 6, no. 3, pp. 257–273.

Egels-Zandén, N. (2009), 'Transnational governance of workers' rights: Outlining a research agenda', *Journal of Business Ethics*, vol. 87, no. 2, pp. 169–188.

Eklund, J.E. and Poulsen, T. (2014), 'One share–one vote: Evidence from Europe', *Applied Financial Economics*, vol. 24, no. 7, pp. 453–464.

Festel, G. and Rittershaus, P. (2014), 'Fostering technology transfer in industrial biotechnology by academic spin-offs in Europe', *Journal of Commercial Biotechnology*, vol. 20, no. 2, pp. 5–10.

Forbes, W.P. (1993), 'The integration of European stock markets: The case of the banks', *Journal of Business Finance and Accounting*, vol. 20, no. 3, pp. 427–439.

Freytag, A. and Thurik, R. (2007), 'Entrepreneurship and its determinants in a cross-country setting', *Journal of Evolutionary Economics*, vol. 17, no. 2, pp. 117–131.

Genius, M., Koundouri, P., Nauges, C. and Tzouvelekas, V. (2014), 'Information transmission in irrigation technology adoption and diffusion: Social learning, extension services, and spatial effects', *American Journal of Agricultural Economics*, vol. 96, no. 1, pp. 328–344.

Georgoutsos, D.A. and Migiakis, P.M. (2013), 'European sovereign bond spreads: Financial integration and market conditions', *Applied Financial Economics*, vol. 23, no. 20, pp. 1609–1621.

Ghatak, S., Silaghi, M.P. and Daly, V. (2009), 'Trade and migration flows between some CEE countries and the UK', *Journal of International Trade and Economic Development*, vol. 18, no. 1, pp. 61–78.

Gorynia, M., Nowak, J. and Wolniak, R. (2007), 'Poland and its investment development path', *Eastern European Economics*, vol. 45, no. 2, pp. 52–74.

Gravelle, J.G. (2009), 'Tax havens: International tax avoidance and evasion', *National Tax Journal*, vol. 62, no. 4, pp. 727–753.

Groth, O.J., Esposito, M. and Tse, T. (2015), 'What Europe needs is an innovation-driven entrepreneurship ecosystem: Introducing EDIE', *Thunderbird International Business Review*, vol. 57, no. 4, pp. 263–269.

Gullander, S. (1976), 'Joint ventures in Europe: Determinants of entry', *International Studies of Management and Organization*, vol. 6, no. 1/2, pp. 85–111.

Hardouvelis, G.A., Malliaropulos, D. and Priestley, R. (2006), 'EMU and European Stock Market Integration', *Journal of Business*, vol. 79, no. 1, pp. 365–392.

Harris, N. (1999), *European Business*, UK, Macmillan Education.

Harris, P. and McDonald, F. (2004), *European Business and Marketing*, London, SAGE Publications.

Herwartz, H. and Siegel, M. (2009), 'Development and determinants of systemic risk in European banking – an empirical note', *Applied Economics Letters*, vol. 16, no. 4, pp. 431–438.

Iversen, M.J. and Larsson, M. (2011), 'Strategic transformations in Danish and Swedish big business in an era of globalisation, 1973–2008', *Business History*, vol. 53, no. 1, pp. 119–143.

Johanson, J. and Vahlne, J. (1977), 'The internationalization process of the firm – A model of knowledge development and increasing foreign market commitments', *Journal of International Business Studies*, vol. 8, no. 1, pp. 23–32.

Johnson, D. and Turner, C. (2006), *European Business*, New York, Routledge.

Johnson, D. and Turner, C. (2016), *European Business*, 3rd edn, New York, Routledge.

Jones, M.V., Coviello, N. and Tang, Y.K. (2011), 'International entrepreneurship research (1989–2009): A domain ontology and thematic analysis', *Journal of Business Venturing*, vol. 26, no. 6, pp. 632–659.

Kaasa, A., Vadi, M. and Varblane, U. (2014), 'Regional cultural differences within European countries: Evidence from multi-country surveys', *Management International Review (MIR)*, vol. 54, no. 6, pp. 825–852.

Kaikati, J.G. (1999), 'The euro versus the U.S. dollar: An overview', *Journal of World Business*, vol. 34, no. 2, p. 171.

Kale, S.H. (1995), 'Grouping Euroconsumers: A culture-based clustering approach', *Journal of International Marketing*, vol. 3, no. 3, pp. 35–48.

Kapelyushnikov, R., Kuznetsov, A. and Kuznetsova, O. (2012), 'The role of the informal sector, flexible working time and pay in the Russian labour market model', *Post-Communist Economies*, vol. 24, no. 2, pp. 177–190.

Kaplan, A. (2015), *European Business and Management*, London, SAGE Publications.

Kearney, C. and Potì, V. (2008), 'Have European stocks become more volatile? An empirical investigation of idiosyncratic and market risk in the euro area', *European Financial Management*, vol. 14, no. 3, pp. 419–444.

Kim, Y.J. and Clarke, G. (2013), 'Determinants of inter-firm technology licensing in the EU', *Applied Economics*, vol. 45, no. 5, pp. 651–661.

Kornai, J. (2000), 'What the change of system from socialism to capitalism does and does not mean', *Journal of Economic Perspectives*, vol. 14, no. 1, pp 27–42.

Kurylo, L.V. and Maffei, S.J. (2007), 'Understanding the legal status of the world's largest business market: The European Union', *Review of Business*, vol. 27, no. 3, pp. 56–63.

Leite, P. and Cortez, M.C. (2014), 'Selectivity and timing abilities of international socially responsible funds', *Applied Economics Letters*, vol. 21, no. 3, pp. 185–188.

Leppelt, T., Foerstl, K. and Hartmann, E. (2013), 'Corporate social responsibility in buyer-supplier relationships: Is it beneficial for top-tier suppliers to market their capability to ensure a responsible supply chain?' *Business Research*, vol. 6, no. 2, pp. 126–152.

Lippert, B. (2007), 'The EU Neighbourhood Policy + profile, potential, perspective', *Intereconomics*, vol. 42, no. 4, pp. 180–187.

Lozano-Vivas, A. and Weill, L. (2012), 'How does cross-border activity affect EU banking markets?' *European Financial Management*, vol. 18, no. 2, pp. 303–320.

Maitland, G. (1998), 'The ethics of the international arms trade', *Business Ethics: A European Review*, vol. 7, no. 4, pp. 200–204.

Marel, E. and Shepherd, B. (2013), 'Services trade, regulation and regional integration: Evidence from sectoral data', *World Economy*, vol. 36, no. 11, pp. 1393–1405.

Mercado, S., Welford, R. and Prescott, K. (2001), *European Business*, 4th edn, Harlow, Financial Times/ Prentice Hall.

Michailova, S. (2011), 'Contextualizing in international business research: Why do we need more of it and how can we be better at it?', *Scandinavian Journal of Management*, vol. 27, no. 1, pp. 127–139.

Minbaeva, D.B. and Muratbekova-Touron, M. (2013), 'Clanism', *Management International Review*, vol. 53, no. 1, pp. 109–139.

Moldovan, R. (2014), 'Post-implementation reviews for IASB and FASB standards: A comparison of the process and findings for the operating segments standards', *Accounting in Europe*, vol. 11, no. 1, pp. 113–137.

Moran, J. (1999), 'Bribery and corruption: The OECD Convention on Combating the Bribery of Foreign Public Officials in International Business Transactions', *Business Ethics: A European Review*, vol. 8, no. 3, pp. 141–150.

Morris, W.H. (2007), 'European tax policy', *International Tax Journal*, vol. 33, no. 2, pp. 35–68.

Naldi, L., Wikström, P. and Von Rimscha, M.B. (2014), 'Dynamic capabilities and performance', *International Studies of Management and Organization*, vol. 44, no. 4, pp. 63–82.

Niedermeyer, C., Jaskiewicz, P. and Klein, S.B. (2010), '"Can't get no satisfaction?" Evaluating the sale of the family business from the family's perspective and deriving implications for new venture activities', *Entrepreneurship and Regional Development*, vol. 22, no. 3/4, pp. 293–320.

Nugent, N. and O'Donnell (1994), *The European Business Environment*, UK, Macmillan Education.

Otjacques, B., Hitzelberger, P. and Feltz, F. (2007), 'Interoperability of e-government information systems: Issues of identification and data sharing', *Journal of Management Information Systems*, vol. 23, no. 4, pp. 29–51.

Overesch, M. and Wamser, G. (2009), 'Who cares about corporate taxation? Asymmetric tax effects on outbound FDI', *World Economy*, vol. 32, no. 12, pp. 1657–1684.

Paas, T., Tafenau, E. and Scannell, N.J. (2008), 'Gravity equation analysis in the context of international trade', *Eastern European Economics*, vol. 46, no. 5, pp. 92–113.

Polanec, S. (2004), 'Convergence at last?' *Eastern European Economics*, vol. 42, no. 4, pp. 55–80.

Raess, D. and Burgoon, B. (2015), 'Flexible work and immigration in Europe', *British Journal of Industrial Relations*, vol. 53, no. 1, pp. 94–111.

Rausch, A., Lindquist, T. and Steckel, M. (2014), 'A test of U.S. versus Germanic European ethical decision-making and perceptions of moral intensity: Could ethics differ within Western culture?' *Journal of Managerial Issues*, vol. 26, no. 3, pp. 259–285.

Roberts, B. (1973), 'Multinational collective bargaining: A European prospect', *British Journal of Industrial Relations*, vol. 11, no. 1, pp. 1–19.

Rugman, A.M. and Oh, C.H. (2013), 'Why the home region matters: Location and regional multinationals', *British Journal of Management*, vol. 24, no. 4, pp. 463–479.

Sadeh, E., Arumugam, V.C. and Malarvizhi, C.A. (2013), 'Integration of EFQM framework and quality information systems', *Total Quality Management and Business Excellence*, vol. 24, no. 1/2, pp. 188–209.

Singh, N., Lehnert, K. and Bostick, K. (2012), 'Global social media usage: Insights into reaching consumers worldwide', *Thunderbird International Business Review*, vol. 54, no. 5, pp. 683–700.

Suder, G. (2008), *Doing Business in Europe*, London, SAGE Publications.

Suder, G. (2011), *Doing Business in Europe*, 2nd edn, London, SAGE Publications.

Thomas, L., Billsberry, J., Ambrosini, V. and Barton, H. (2014), 'Convergence and divergence dynamics in British and French business schools: How will the pressure for accreditation influence these dynamics?' *British Journal of Management*, vol. 25, no. 2, pp. 305–319.

Thorell, P. and Whittington, G. (1994), 'The harmonizing of accounting within the EU', *European Accounting Review*, vol. 3, no. 2, pp. 215–239.

Tranfield, D.R., Denyer, D. and Smart, P. (2003), 'Towards a methodology for developing evidence-informed management knowledge by means of systematic review', *British Journal of Management*, vol. 14, pp 207–222.

Vallascas, F. and Keasey, K. (2013), 'The volatility of European banking systems: A two-decade study', *Journal of Financial Services Research*, vol. 43, no. 1, pp. 37–68.

van Marrewijk, M. and Hardjono, T. (2003), 'European corporate sustainability framework for managing complexity and corporate transformation', *Journal of Business Ethics*, vol. 44, no. 2/3, pp. 121–132.

Weinrich, M. (2016), 'Europe: House price development', *Housing Finance International*, Spring, p. 8.

Wijnands, J.M., Bremmers, H.J., van der Meulen, B.J. and Poppe, K.J. (2008), 'An economic and legal assessment of the EU food industry's competitiveness', *Agribusiness*, vol. 24, no. 4, pp. 417–439.

Yavan, N. (2010), 'The location choice of foreign direct investment within Turkey: An empirical analysis', *European Planning Studies*, vol. 18, no. 10, pp. 1675–1705.

Zeira, Y. and Harari, E. (1979), 'Host-Country Organizations and Expatriate Managers in Europe', *California Management Review*, vol. 21, no. 3, pp. 40–50.

Zemanek, H. (2012), 'How governments should support the adjustment of competitiveness in the euro area – and how they should not', *Economic Affairs*, vol. 32, no. 3, pp. 78–84.

Zettinig, P. and Vincze, Z.S. (2011), 'The domain of international business: Features and future relevance of international business', *Thunderbird International Business Review*, vol. 53, no. 3, pp. 337–349.

APPENDIX: Methodological procedures for search, selection and exclusion

A. Criteria for defining European business as a field of study and delineating its parameters
  1. Find consensus on the definition of European business
     - Domain of international business
     - Self-identifies as Europe-related or European
     - Outcomes pertaining to Europe or European economies
  2. Peer-reviewed scholarly journal articles only
  3. Include *empirical* AND *conceptual* articles/studies
B. Exclusion criteria by theoretical relevance
  1. Editorials and commentaries
  2. Case studies – without conceptualisation and analysis
  3. Conference and book reviews
  4. Articles not relating to business or economics
  5. Articles not concerning Europe
C. Search method and scope – Stage I
  1. Full search of articles across academic journals relevant to the field, from 1970 to 2017
  2. Admittance criteria by general keyword search using EBSCO (Business Source Complete, n=3,428) database.
  3. Initial focus on: a) citation and abstract, and b) title
  4. Keywords:
     a. International business
     b. Europe★ (which allows for Europe or European)
  5. Types or articles included in the search:
     a. Scholarly/peer-reviewed journal articles
     b. Articles with full text available in the database
D. Search method and scope – Stage II
  1. Extraction of key reference information from search results, namely:
     a. Bibliographic information: title, year published, journal name, number of authors
     b. Content information: abstract, keywords (author supplied), subject terms, industry, geographical focus
     c. Technical information: search sequence identifier, length of record (number of fields), permanent link to database
  2. Manual reading/checking by investigator of all papers included in the search outcome to exclude erroneous or inaccurate records, based on information extracted. In case relevant information was unavailable, the full article was viewed to identify/extract relevant details. Of the 3,428 articles identified in the search,
     a. missing information was identified for 1 record in the subject field, 1,929 records in the keyword field, 7 records in the author field, 1,595 records in the geographical focus field, and 996 records in the industry field.
     b. 73 records were identified as not being actual peer-reviewed journal articles, but rather conference overviews, book reviews, country information publications, editorials or duplicates.
     c. 699 records were identified as not relating to Europe at all.
     d. 6 records were identified as not relating to any specific field in business or economics.

3. 2,650 of the 3,428 records were considered relevant for further analysis. Manual classification of these articles according to primary field of research and geographical focus was conducted.

   a. 33 primary field of research topic categories identified as follows:

Accounting	*Family business*	*Management*
Banking	*Finance*	*Marketing and communication*
Competitiveness and productivity	Firm internationalisation	Migration
Corporate governance	Foreign investment	Policy and regulation
Cross-culture research	Foreign trade	Politics
Corporate social responsibility (CSR)	HRM	Production management
Economic development	Industrial relations	Quality management
Economics	Information systems	SME management
Education	Innovation, R&D	Strategy
Entrepreneurship	Law	Taxation
Ethics	Logistics and supply chain management (SCM)	Tourism and hospitality

   b. Seven areas of geographical focus were identified, namely:

Central and Eastern Europe (CEE), – Central and Eastern European transitional countries
European Union (EU) – any one or more of the current EU 28, including the UK
Europe – broad geographical area, not elsewhere classified or including several countries across different parts of Europe
Europe comparative – Europe or European countries as basis of comparison to one or more other geographical regions globally
Global – any European country as part of a global analysis
South Eastern Europe (SEE) – including any ex-Yugoslav state, Greece, Turkey, Cyprus and Malta
West Europe – including highly developed, Northern and Southern European countries

Full list of articles and other details of analysis are available upon request.

3

EUROPEAN BUSINESS RESEARCH IN PERSPECTIVE

The focus of regionalisation in the international business literature

Nina Zobel and Björn Ambos

Introduction

Globalisation has been a key topic in recent decades with many scholars, politicians and economists predicting that the world would become increasingly integrated on a global basis (cf. Friedman 2005, Ghemawat 2005, Economist 1997). Nonetheless, a renewed interest in the phenomenon of regionalisation and increasing scepticism about globalisation can be observed in the international business (IB) literature (cf. Rugman and Hodgetts 2001, Dunning et al. 2007). In fact, the world is not as global as previously believed. For example, many multinational corporations (MNCs) operate regionally rather than globally. Prominent studies by Alan Rugman and his peers (cf. Rugman and Hodgetts 2001, Dunning et al. 2007, Flores and Aguilera 2007, Rugman and Verbeke 2004) largely build on the argument that firms' operations are not scalable beyond regional boundaries. These studies show that MNCs manage their businesses regionally. For example, more than 70 per cent of large European MNCs' sales and assets are concentrated in Europe (Oh and Rugman 2012). Other scholars, who postulate that MNCs seek a form of 'semi-globalization' (Ghemawat 2003), propose an intermediate version of MNCs' global integration in which global and national strategic advantages are balanced (Yip 1989). Consequently, the call for more research into the more common type of MNCs – home-region-oriented MNCs – has become louder (Sammartino and Osegowitsch 2013).

At the same time, the topic of organisational structures and management has become popular as a potential means for firms to cope with the complexities of global business. Organisational mid-layers, such as regional headquarters (RHQ) (Lasserre 1996, Nell et al. 2011) or regional management centres (Enright 2005), have been proposed as a better way to manage units in host regions. Regional management allows for the development of regional strategies (Schütte 1997), helps in the sensing of local business opportunities and innovation (Hoenen et al. 2014) and reduces management complexity by dividing authority between MNCs' headquarters and their subsidiaries (Paik and Sohn 2004).

These two literature streams address the issue of *why regionalisation occurs*. The first stream argues that MNCs are region-bound due to the limited scalability of their operations, while the second regards regional management as a way to better manage a global organisation. While the two streams have been kept separate thus far, we draw on corporate strategy literature to argue that they are linked. We show that the tendency to regionalise reflects the interplay between the boundaries of a firm's scope and its capabilities to manage it. As Europe – especially the European Union (EU) – represents one of the most advanced forms of integration of regional organisations (Johnson and Turner 2006, p. 60), we use it as an exemplary region in this chapter.

A corporate strategy perspective on regionalisation

Organisations constantly face corporate-level issues, which can be grouped into the categories of scope and value creation (Johnson et al. 2008). On the one hand, firms need to decide which products to sell and where to sell them. On the other hand, they need to determine how to create maximum value, which parenting role to assume and how to manage their business portfolios. Issues of scope pertain to a firm's products and its international diversity. Issues of value creation are concerned with the role of headquarters and the management of dispersed business operations, which are essentially questions of organisational structure. Consequently, a regional focus among MNCs can be motivated by two factors – scope and structure. The former refers to what and where to sell, while the latter pertains to value creation through organisational structure (Figure 3.1).

Figure 3.1 summarises the two distinct but complementary streams of literature that have evolved around regionalisation. The first is concerned with MNCs *operating* regionally and the second focuses on MNCs *organising* regionally. As such, the first stream touches on the question of scope and analyses MNCs' tendencies to regionally limit their operations. The second stream centres on the question of structure and focuses on organisational mid-layers, such as RHQs, as additional regionally focused management and control bodies.

The magnitude of regionalisation

Scholars have long shown an interest in the magnitude of globalisation and regionalisation, and the scope of MNCs' operations. Ohmae (1987, p. 17) postulated that global competition

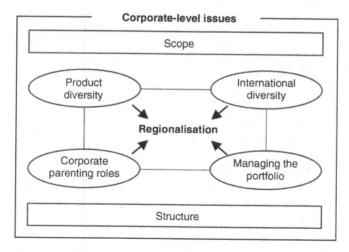

Figure 3.1 Framework corporate-level issues related to regionalisation

occurred in a tetrahedral world in which 85 to 90 per cent of all value-added, high-technology products were manufactured and consumed in only three regions – the United States, Europe and Japan. Research by Michalak and Gibb (1997, p. 266) supported these results and showed that intra-regional trade accounted for 38 per cent of merchandise imports and exports, while inter-regional trade represented only 10 per cent. The study by Rugman and Hodgetts (2001) of trade data from 1997 also provided strong evidence for triad-shaped world trade. Rugman (2005, p. 11) further revealed that 84.2 per cent of firms in his sample made more than half of their sales in their home region of the triad (Europe, North America, Asia). As such, Rugman (2005) was the first to provide evidence of MNCs' home-region orientation and to illustrate the limits of the scalability of a firm's operations and, thereby, its scope. Only 6.6 percent of the companies in his sample generated less than 50 per cent of sales in their home region and at least 20 per cent in two regions (including the home region), which made them bi-regional (Rugman 2005, pp. 12–13). The author characterised only nine of these firms as truly global, thereby refuting the prominent assumption that MNCs generally operate on a global basis. In general, firms prefer to internationalise within their home regions before moving into new territories (UNCTAD 2007). Firms' assets also show patterns of regionalisation as around 80 per cent of MNCs' assets are deployed in their home region (Rugman and Verbeke 2008, Rugman and Oh 2012), confirming that most MNCs are not global but regional in scope. Large European MNCs are mostly home-regional, as less than 30 per cent of their sales and assets are outside Europe (Oh and Rugman 2012, p. 495). Syed and Colleen (2011) highlighted an increasing trend towards regionalisation and reported a significant increase in intra-regional trade within Europe. Intra-regional exports in the EU increased by 163 per cent from 1,910 billion euros in 2002 to 3,115 billion euros in 2016 (Eurostat 2017).

Banalieva and Dhanaraj (2013) went in a different direction. These authors analysed which MNCs were the most prone to being home-region oriented, and found that European MNCs were more home-region oriented than MNCs from the USA or Japan. The authors suggested that this finding was the result of comparably low institutional diversity in Europe, which can be attributed to the presence of the EU – the most advanced level of regional integration in the world (Blevins et al. 2016).

All of these studies aim to improve our understanding of MNC scope, which is a key issue in strategy research (Johnson et al. 2008). Whether there is a relationship between multinationality and performance has been intensively discussed (Cardinal et al. 2011), but the results are inconclusive (Verbeke and Forootan 2012). A variety of multinationality-performance relationships, including positive, negative, curvilinear, S-shaped, M-shaped and W-shaped, have been proposed (Powell 2014). Despite their divergence, all of these studies view multinationality as a continuum ranging from no multinationality to global coverage, thereby ignoring limits to multinationality arising from regional confines. The scope literature on regionalisation opposes this view, as it regards multinationality as a set of stages in which each stage relates to a certain region. Essentially, a firm's spread is argued to be region-bound and its scope is limited by regional boundaries.

What defines a region?

A region is a collective term referring to neighbouring countries or markets. As such, a regional orientation reflects a firm's deliberate choice to enter close, attractive markets in order to strengthen its competitive position (Sammartino and Osegowitsch 2013). Regional clusters draw homogeneous countries closer together (Schlie and Yip 2000). The meaning of the term 'closer' depends on the chosen distance dimension(s): geographical, administrative, economic and cultural (Ghemawat 2001). A region combines markets with low distance among them (Sammartino and Osegowitsch 2013) based on one or more distance dimensions.

Aguilera et al. (2007, pp. 8–9) argue that 'physical immediacy is a precondition for a sense of unity or shared properties'. The most prominent geography-based regional classification pattern is the triad-concept introduced by Ohmae (1985), which was initially composed of the United States, Europe and Japan, and later extended to a 'broad triad' including North America, Europe and Asia Pacific (Rugman and Oh 2012). Time zones are another aspect of geographical distance often used by firms to efficiently organise their operations (e.g. facilitate correspondence (Nan et al. 2009) or allow for closer monitoring (Elango 2004)). Regional classification patterns that minimise administrative and economic distance are often manifested in regional trade agreements (RTAs) (e.g. EU, NAFTA, ASEAN) (Fratianni and Oh 2009) that minimise institutional diversity. Notably, MNCs strive for maximum uniformity in their institutional environments (Banalieva and Dhanaraj 2013) in order to facilitate administrative work, increase efficiency, support regional scalability and simplify organisational control. Along these lines, RTAs lead to the formation of regional economic areas that bring about economic proximity, tax and familiarity benefits; reduce tariff and non-tariff barriers; and facilitate governmental and business coordination (Hejazi 2007). This regional focus, or regionalism (Suder 2015), often gives rise to a trade bias for RTA-based regions (Fratianni and Oh 2009). It is important to remark, however, that RTAs do not necessarily require geographic proximity (Suder 2015), although that is often the case. Rather, an alignment in institutional matters is the key focus of RTAs, which allows them to span large geographical distances and facilitate trade among geographically distant countries (Suder 2015). The EU, which is the most far-reaching attempt at regional integration among independent nations in modern times, includes economic, social and political elements (Kolk et al. 2014). The EU not only encompasses a common European market, including uniform tariffs and trade regulations, but also a common governmental body (the European Commission), a political agenda and a common currency (at least in part) (Blevins et al. 2016), which further reduce perceived distance (Verbeke and Asmussen 2016).

Cultural clusters that minimise (perceived) cultural distances are another way to define a region (Banalieva and Dhanaraj 2013). They often share the same or similar languages as language is an antecedent of national culture (Ronen and Shenkar 2013). Dunning et al. (2007) confirmed the existence of culturally induced regions in a study on foreign direct investment.

There is little agreement on what determines a region or how it can best be operationalised (Dunning et al. 2007). We understand 'region' as a spatial concept that combines proximate markets in terms of geographical, administrative, economic or cultural distance, where geography is the most prominent determinant (Banalieva and Dhanaraj 2013). When they decide on their region(s) of operation, firms choose their spatial scope and a corresponding set of boundary conditions (Verbeke and Asmussen 2016). Therefore, the perceived compound distance across distance dimensions within the region is lower than the distance to any area outside the region's border. In other words, a region's 'outsiders' are characterised by a greater distance relative to a region's 'insiders' (Verbeke and Asmussen 2016). On the basis of salience theory, which suggests that the choice of a subject or referent partly depends on the relative salience of the objects (Tversky 1977), we challenge this view. Salience theory predicts firms to choose their regions of operations based on a few firm-specific requirements that are salient compared to others. This argument is supported by distinctiveness theory, which asserts that individuals focus on aspects that are more peculiar than others (McGuire and Padawer-Singer 1976). The degree of peculiarity then influences the relative importance of certain features (Mehra et al. 1998).

Observing firms with operations in Europe, this idea is confirmed. European-based MNCs are seen as the strongest inter-organisational regional networks (Cantwell and Janne 1999). They prefer to internationalise their R&D activities in this region due to its attractiveness in terms of knowledge base, industry-specific and cluster-based spillovers, and technological specialisation (Cantwell and Piscitello 2002). Cantwell and Piscitello (2002) assert an increased regional focus based on technological advancement. Along these lines, due to a favourable regulatory framework within the EU, automobile supply chains are clustered intra-regionally (Rugman and Oh 2012). Service activities are also more local than global (Rugman and Oh 2012) and are likely to be clustered regionally. Within Europe, service firms tend to group their operations according to language. For example, Bain and Company, in parts, internally combines the markets of Austria, Germany and Switzerland, which all share German as the dominant language. In such situations, a common language appears as the most salient factor for setting operational boundaries.

In this respect, changes in the regulatory environment and language barriers appear to be natural fault lines that induce the splitting of groups (Lau and Murnighan 2005). In other words, one or more distinguishing factors align in their uniqueness and form distinct schisms (Li and Hambrick 2005) that then determine the boundaries of a subgroup. Therefore, while the European continent itself offers a natural regional definition, firms select certain factors that they find most salient given their needs and then determine their operational space accordingly. Thus, regional fault lines depend on the characteristics of an individual firm and its operational requirements (e.g. technological know-how, regulatory environment, common language). Rather than being determined by firms, a region can be seen as an induced 'space' limited by schisms in the proximity of firm-specific, salient, regional denominators. These denominators form the same regional outer boundary. Therefore, regions do not always form based on a single factor but can be the result of the interplay among similar specificities and a number of factors.

Why does regionalisation occur?

Multinational corporations are encouraged to 'design strategies and adopt structures that focus on markets close to their countries-of-origin' (Goerzen and Asmussen 2007, p. 66). Although MNCs often do so, they may also operate in host regions. In the European region, it is important to distinguish between European home-region MNCs and European host-region MNCs. Given that firms face corporate-level issues that are concerned with either the firm's scope (i.e. strategy) or structure (Figure 3.1), we aim to explain why many firms confine their operations to Europe or smaller regions therein.

Scope

In their commentary on Alan Rugman's theory of the regional multinational, Oh and Li (2015) summarise that Rugman describes the regional multinational as an organisation whose business activities are mainly limited to the home region. An MNC's corporate advantage is based on a combination of firm- and country-specific advantages unique to a country (Rugman et al. 2012). The majority of companies follow regional strategies and remain in their home regions (Filippaios and Rama 2008), where they build on (home-) region-specific advantages (Suder 2015, Lee and Rugman 2012), such as (a combination of) location-bound firm-specific advantages (Rugman et al. 2012) and country-specific advantages that are similar among countries within the region. This results in a home-region bias (Rugman and Oh 2012) or home-region effect (Oh and Rugman 2007), which pertain to the MNC's strength, especially in the home region. In Europe, this effect has been termed 'Europeanisation', which implies a regional economic concentration in Europe and refers to the rise of firms that operate on a truly European basis, such as EADS (European Aeronautics, Defence and Space). These firms build their competitive advantage on the region's characteristics and capabilities (Suder 2011).

Consequently, a decision to expand into another region would be based on the combination of extant resources with host-country (Verbeke and Asmussen 2016) or host-region resources. As Osegowitsch and Sammartino (2007, p. 46) note, 'in an age of purported globalization, many of the world's largest firms appear to have barely ventured beyond the confines of their home region'. Verbeke and Asmussen (2016) argue that a company's regional focus is largely induced by significant, noticeable discontinuities at the regional boundaries. Intra-regional distance is generally perceived as lower than inter-regional distance, and anything outside a region entails a 'spike' in distance (Rugman et al. 2011). The firm's spatial scope, as marked by its regional boundaries, determines its barriers to resource combination. This implies that the deployment of firm-specific advantages is facilitated in markets located within a region.

A firm's adherence to a region is further supported by the liability of foreignness (Zaheer 1995) that firms face outside their home region due to a lack of local knowledge, which represents a competitive disadvantage. The liability of foreignness increases as the perceived distance between markets increases. As such, it is higher outside a region's boundaries. This is also termed the 'liability of regional foreignness' (Rugman and Verbeke 2007).

As such, an MNC's geographical scope is determined by its ability to redeploy its firm-specific advantages and link them to location-specific advantages in another country, where the benefits should outweigh the costs of redeployment associated with local adaptation (Rugman and Verbeke 2005). MNCs can avoid these costs by simply sticking to their home region (Li 2005). Therefore, regionalisation is essentially selectivity in internationalisation (Rugman and Verbeke 2005) and aims to achieve a balance between the scalability and efficiency of a firm's operations.

One topic that ties in with this view are global value chains (GVCs), which organise value-chain activities in such a way that an MNC's location and transaction costs are reduced. In other words, although these MNCs focus on their region, they source internationally outside their home region (Hernández and Pedersen 2017). GVCs thus allow firms to operate within their regional boundaries while benefiting from the advantages of sourcing globally. GVC-based firms build on their region-specific advantages. According to Buckley (2016), MNCs within a GVC or 'global factory' are part of a network of independent and interconnected firms that contributes to a context of trust and power within a volatile environment. This can most likely be attributed to the MNCs' regional specialisation and uncontested regional dominance within the GVC.

In summary, this literature stream builds on the idea that MNCs strive for 'regional embeddedness' in which business operations are managed and organised on a regional basis in order to capture economies of regionalisation (Yeung et al. 2001). In this regard, Europe is seen as one of the three regional building blocks in which production is concentrated (Baldwin and Lopez-Gonzalez 2013). For example, in the Netherlands, 55 per cent of outsourcing is domestic and 34 per cent is from within the EU, while only 11 per cent is from global markets (Rugman et al. 2009, p. 388).

Structure

The second stream explaining the phenomenon of regionalisation bases its arguments on aspects of organisational structure. Structure-related corporate-level issues include decisions regarding the role of headquarters and how to manage the portfolio of subsidiaries in order to add maximum value to subsidiaries (Figure 3.1). The parenting literature suggests that headquarters' main purpose is to add value to the MNC's portfolio of subsidiaries (Nell and Ambos 2013) – in other words, to settle on a particular parenting strategy (Goold 1996). Essential to

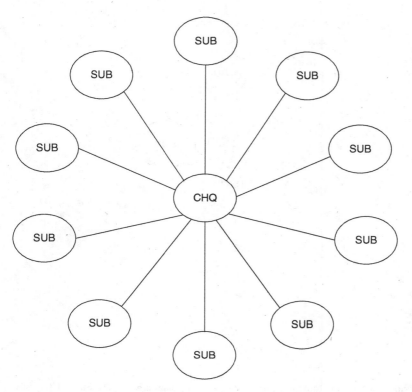

Figure 3.2 Organisation of MNC without regional structures/RHQs

the right parenting strategy is the fit between the parent's characteristics and the subsidiary's parenting needs, as well as the parent's familiarity with the subsidiaries (Goold et al. 1994). A suitable organisational structure is therefore crucial. In this respect, hierarchical structures, especially RHQs, are undergoing a revival (Nell et al. 2011) (e.g. the number of European RHQs increased by 76 per cent from 2000 to 2010 (Ambos and Schlegelmilch 2010)).

RHQs are relatively autonomous units (Enright 2005) responsible for managing a firm's operations in a host region (Yeung et al. 2001). As such, RHQs are a phenomenon limited to MNCs' host regions. As intermediaries between headquarters and subsidiaries, RHQs face the constant challenge of responding to both parties. Two main control relationships result – one between headquarters and RHQs and one between RHQs and the regional subsidiaries (see Figures 3.2 and 3.3). Thus, an RHQ limits a headquarters' sphere of control by taking on the task of subsidiary oversight.

RHQs are believed to have intra-regional and inter-regional effects. As Yeung et al. (2001) observe, RHQs have a mandate to exercise control over subsidiaries that require local management despite assumed regional market homogeneity. As MNCs need to simultaneously be locally responsive and globally integrated in order to benefit from global efficiencies (Doz and Prahalad 1984), management from a distance may be inappropriate. An RHQ is a control unit that manages the subsidiaries in its realm (Yeung et al. 2001), balances the conflicting demands of globalisation and localisation as an intermediary unit (Paik and Sohn 2004) and makes simultaneous exploitation possible (Schlie and Yip 2000). RHQs serve as 'two-way conduits of influence' (Kriger and

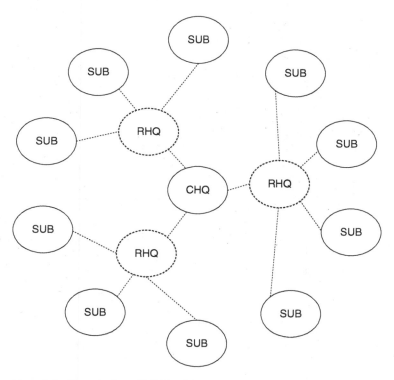

Figure 3.3 Organisation of MNC with regional structures/RHQs (adapted from Johnson et al. (2008))

Rich 1987, p. 45) or 'strategic mid-way houses' (Yeung et al. 2001, p. 165) with the purpose of implementing a firm's global strategies on a regional level. Regionalisation can thus be seen as 'a half-way house that meets these balancing and often conflicting pressures' (Khan 2010, p. 28).

In Europe, RHQs were introduced by many MNCs to manage operations and carry out headquarters' functions in Central and Eastern Europe (CEE) after the fall of the Iron Curtain (Schuh 2013). The main benefits of setting up an RHQ in CEE were regional knowledge bundling, adaptation of global strategies to a regional level, headquarters' complexity reduction and synergy creation (Schuh 2013), as well as RHQs' positive nurturing effect for core competencies (Filippaios and Rama 2008). RHQs enable MNCs to leverage synergies across countries in a host region (Werth 2006). Moreover, they serve as a coordinating body for host-region operations that bundles supporting services for subsidiaries, thereby reducing costs (Mori 2002). They also support knowledge transfer between headquarters and subsidiaries (Asakawa and Lehrer 2003). Overall, RHQs are an organisational solution for maximising the value added to subsidiaries. While headquarters are restricted in their parenting resources, RHQs can execute the headquarters' role on a regional level. As such, they can play an important part in coordinating GVCs with internationally dispersed, but regionally focused value-chain activities that are inherent to a single MNC.

Ghemawat (2005) critically reflects on the role of RHQs and challenges the view that RHQs are the enabling unit in regional strategies. While RHQs can help in the realisation of regional strategies, it is far more essential for MNCs to determine how they plan to add value to their subsidiaries in a region. Regional organisational structures may be useful, but a fit between the parent's intention to add value and the roles and capabilities of the RHQ is essential.

In sum, this literature stream views regionalisation as motivated by the desire to add maximum value to subsidiaries by means of regional organisational structures. RHQs provide MNCs with a means to limit headquarters' span of control and manage a region from a distance (Yeung et al. 2001). Furthermore, RHQs are host-region bound – they are established because they better understand the local environment (Lasserre 1996) and, therefore, allow for regional synergy realisation. However, as Ghemawat (2005) stresses, RHQs should not necessarily be regarded as the best method for implementing regional strategies. Rather, they are one of several alternatives.

Discussion – a holistic view on regionalisation

MNC regions are defined in terms of regional denominators, such that markets within a region are perceived as closer than markets outside that region. The firm-specific saliency of certain regional denominators is likely to induce fault lines that determine regional boundaries. The formation of regions is explained in two streams of the IB literature centring on arguments of scope and structure. We posit that an integration of not only these two streams, but also other views on what defines a region would help answer the question of why regionalisation occurs, and lead to a holistic understanding of the phenomenon of regionalisation and its contingencies. We have identified two areas in which we see considerable potential benefits from such an integration.

First, a firm's scope and structure are interrelated. Whether firms regionalise and to which degree is dependent on two main corporate-level issues (see Figure 3.1) – decisions regarding scope (i.e. which products to sell where) and decisions regarding structure (i.e. which parenting role to choose and how to manage the portfolio of subsidiaries). Given the principle of 'structure follows strategy' (Chandler 1962, p. 314), the chosen organisational structure (i.e. headquarters' decision on its parenting role/how to manage the portfolio of subsidiaries) must fit the chosen strategy as reflected in the choice of firm scope. Therefore, both perspectives must be taken into account. A firm's regional choice reflects a compromise between the maximum feasible scope from a strategic perspective and the maximum complexity that an organisation can handle.

Second, the phenomenon of regionalisation is evident in both home and host regions. Even though the majority of MNCs are predominantly oriented towards their home regions, bi-regionally oriented firms do exist (Rugman 2005). In this respect, an analysis of the phenomenon from both the home- and host-region perspectives is beneficial. Arguments that certain firm-specific advantages do not qualify for redeployment beyond regional confines may also apply to advantages associated with host regions. As in a home region, host-region countries can be assumed to be homogeneous (e.g. the European market as a host region consists of proximate countries on a variety of distance dimensions, such as regulatory environment or geography). When explaining home-region orientation, ignoring host-country scope-related issues in the debate about RHQs or arguments about organisational structure and control can lead to certain biases. Clearly, both home- and host-region orientations exist. They should therefore be analysed jointly rather than in isolation.

Conclusion

In drawing from corporate strategy, this chapter offers a better understanding of the phenomenon of regionalisation by discussing and challenging popular perspectives on the topic found in the IB literature. While regionalisation seems to be well explained on an abstract level, these explanations leave significant room for clarification. We are forced to acknowledge that the extant research does not offer a clear answer as to why regionalisation occurs. Therefore, we call for more research on this topic.

References

Aguilera, R.V., Flores, R. and Vaaler, P.M. (2007). 'Is it all a matter of grouping? Examining the regional effect in global strategy research'. https://papers.ssrn.com/sol3/papers.cfm?abstract_id=981187 (accessed 17 March 2018).

Ambos, B. and Schlegelmilch, B.B. (2010). *The New Role of Regional Management*, Basingstoke, UK, Palgrave Macmillan.

Asakawa, K. and Lehrer, M. (2003). 'Managing local knowledge assets globally: The role of regional innovation relays', *Journal of World Business*, vol. 38, 31–42.

Baldwin, R. and Lopez-Gonzalez, J. (2013). 'Supply-chain trade: A portrait of global patterns and several testable hypotheses', *The World Economy*. https://doi.org/10.1111/twec.12189 (accessed 28 March 2018).

Banalieva, E.R. and Dhanaraj, C. (2013). 'Home-region orientation in international expansion strategies', *Journal of International Business Studies*, vol. 44, 89–116.

Blevins, D.P., Moschieri, C., Pinkham, B.C. and Ragozzino, R. (2016). 'Institutional changes within the European Union: How global cities and regional integration affect MNE entry decisions', *Journal of World Business*, vol. 51, 319–330.

Buckley, P.J. (2016). 'The contribution of internalisation theory to international business: New realities and unanswered questions', *Journal of World Business*, vol. 51, 74–82.

Cantwell, J. and Janne, O. (1999). 'Technological globalisation and innovative centres: The role of corporate technological leadership and locational hierarchy', *Research Policy*, vol. 28, 119–144.

Cantwell, J. and Piscitello, L. (2002). 'The location of technological activities of MNCs in European regions: The role of spillovers and local competencies', *Journal of International Management*, vol. 8, 69–96.

Cardinal, L.B., Miller, C.C. and Palich, L.E. (2011). 'Breaking the cycle of iteration: Forensic failures of international diversification and firm performance research', *Global Strategy Journal*, vol. 1, 175–186.

Chandler, A.D., Jr. (1962). *Strategy and Structure: Chapters in the history of the industrial enterprise*, Oxford, England, M.I.T. Press.

Doz, Y. and Prahalad, C.K. (1984). 'Patterns of strategic control within multinational corporations', *Journal of International Business Studies*, vol. 15, 55–72.

Dunning, J.H., Masataka, F. and Nevena, Y. (2007). 'Some macro-data on the regionalisation/globalisation debate: A comment on the Rugman/Verbeke analysis', *Journal of International Business Studies*, vol. 38, 177–199.

Economist, The (1997). 'One world?' 16 October.

Elango, B. (2004). 'Geographic scope of operations by multinational companies: An exploratory study of regional and global strategies', *European Management Journal*, vol. 22, 431–441.

Enright, M.J. (2005). 'The roles of regional management centers', *MIR: Management International Review*, vol. 45, 83–102.

Eurostat (2017). *EU28 trade by SITC product group* [Online]. European Commission. http://appsso.eurostat.ec.europa.eu/nui/show.do?dataset=ext_lt_intertrd&lang=en (accessed 28 March 2018).

Filippaios, F. and Rama, R. (2008). 'Globalisation or regionalisation? The strategies of the world's largest food and beverage MNEs', *European Management Journal*, vol. 26, 59–72.

Flores, R.G. and Aguilera, R.V. (2007). 'Globalization and location choice: An analysis of us multinational firms in 1980 and 2000', *Journal of International Business Studies*, vol. 38, 1187–1210.

Fratianni, M. and Oh, C.H. (2009). 'Expanding RTAs, trade flows, and the multinational enterprise', *Journal of International Business Studies*, vol. 40, 1206–1227.

Friedman, T.L. (2005). *The World is Flat: A brief history of the twenty-first century*. New York: Farrar, Straus and Giroux.

Ghemawat, P. (2001). 'Distance still matters. The hard reality of global expansion', *Harvard Business Review*, vol. 79, 137–147.

Ghemawat, P. (2003). 'Semiglobalization and international business strategy', *Journal of International Business Studies*, vol. 34, 138–152.

Ghemawat, P. (2005). 'Regional strategies for global leadership', *Harvard Business Review*, vol. 83, 98.

Goerzen, A. and Asmussen, C.G. (2007). 'The geographic orientation of multinational enterprises and its implications for performance', in M. Rugman (ed.), *Regional Aspects of Multinationality and Performance*. Emerald Group Publishing Limited.

Goold, M. (1996). 'Parenting strategies for multibusiness companies', *Long Range Planning*, vol. 29, 419–421.

Goold, M., Campbell, A. and Alexander, M. (1994). 'How corporate parents add value to the stand-alone performance of their businesses', *Business Strategy Review*, vol. 5, 33–56.

Hejazi, W. (2007). 'Reconsidering the concentration of US MNE activity: Is it global, regional or national?' *MIR: Management International Review*, vol. 47, 5–27.

Hernández, V. and Pedersen, T. (2017). 'Global value chain configuration: A review and research agenda', *BRQ Business Research Quarterly*, vol. 20, 137–150.

Hoenen, A.K., Nell, P.C. and Ambos, B. (2014). 'MNE entrepreneurial capabilities at intermediate levels: The roles of external embeddedness and heterogeneous environments', *Long Range Planning*, vol. 47, 76–86.

Johnson, G., Scholes, K. and Whittington, R. (2008). *Exploring Corporate Strategy: Text and cases*, Essex, Pearson Education.

Johnson, D. and Turner, C. (2006). *European Business*, London, Routledge.

Khan, O.J. (2010). 'The regionalization vs. globalization debate on internationalization: An analysis and direction for future research', *Global Partnership Management Journal*, vol. 1, 25–36.

Kolk, A., Lindeque, J. and Buuse, D.V.D. (2014). 'Regionalization strategies of European Union electric utilities', *British Journal of Management*, vol. 25, S1

Kriger, M.P. and Rich, P.J.J. (1987). 'Strategic governance: Why and how MNCs are using boards of directors in foreign subsidiaries', *Columbia Journal of World Business*, vol. 22, 39.

Lasserre, P. (1996). 'Regional headquarters: The spearhead for Asia Pacific markets', *Long Range Planning*, vol. 29, 30–37.

Lau, D.C. and Murnighan, J.K. (2005). 'Interactions within groups and subgroups: The effects of demographic faultlines', *Academy of Management Journal*, vol. 48, 645–659.

Lee, I.H. and Rugman, A.M. (2012). 'Firm-specific advantages, inward FDI origins, and performance of multinational enterprises', *Journal of International Management*, vol. 18, 132–146.

Li, J. and Hambrick, D.C. (2005). 'Factional groups: A new vantage on demographic faultlines, conflict, and disintegration in work teams', *Academy of Management Journal*, vol. 48, 794–813.

Li, L. (2005). 'Is regional strategy more effective than global strategy in the US service industries?' *MIR: Management International Review*, vol. 45, no. 1, 37–57.

Mcguire, W.J. and Padawer-Singer, A. (1976). 'Trait salience in the spontaneous self-concept', *Journal of Personality and Social Psychology*, vol. 33, 743.

Mehra, A., Kilduff, M. and Brass, D.J. (1998). 'At the margins: A distinctiveness approach to the social identity and social networks of underrepresented groups', *Academy of Management Journal*, vol. 41, 441–452.

Michalak, W. and Gibb, R. (1997). 'Trading blocs and multilateralism in the world economy', *Annals of the Association of American Geographers*, vol. 87, 264–279.

Mori, T. (2002). 'The role and function of European regional headquarters in Japanese MNCs', The European Institute of Japanese working paper.

Nan, N., Espinosa, J.A. and Carmel, E. (2009). *Communication and Performance across Time Zones: A laboratory experiment*. United States, AIS Electronic Library (AISeL).

Nell, P.C. and Ambos, B. (2013). 'Parenting advantage in the MNC: An embeddedness perspective on the value added by headquarters', *Strategic Management Journal*, vol. 34, 1086–1103.

Nell, P.C., Ambos, B. and Schlegelmilch, B.B. (2011). 'The benefits of hierarchy? – Exploring the effects of regional headquarters in multinational corporations', in C. Asmussen, T. Pedersen, T. Devinney and L. Tihanyi (eds), *Dynamics of Globalization: Location-specific advantages or liabilities of foreignness*. Bingley: Emerald Group.

Oh, C.H. and Li, J. (2015). 'Commentary: Alan Rugman and the theory of the regional multinationals', *Journal of World Business*, vol. 50, 631–633.

Oh, C.H. and Rugman, A.M. (2007). 'Regional multinationals and the Korean cosmetics industry', *Asia Pacific Journal of Management*, vol. 24, 27–42.

Oh, C.H. and Rugman, A.M. (2012). 'Regional integration and the international strategies of large European firms', *International Business Review*, vol. 21, 493–507.

Ohmae, K. (1985). *Triad Power. The coming shape of global competition*, New York, NY Free Press.

Ohmae, K. (1987). 'The triad world view', *Journal of Business Strategy*, vol. 7, 8–19.

Osegowitsch, T. and Sammartino, A. (2007). 'Exploring trends in regionalisation', in *Regional Aspects of Multinationality and Performance*. Bingley: Emerald Group Publishing Limited, pp. 45–64.

Paik, Y. and Sohn, J.H.D. (2004). 'Striking a balance between global integration and local responsiveness: The case of Toshiba Corporation in redefining regional headqaurters' role', *Organizational Analysis*, vol. 12, 347–359.

Powell, K.S. (2014). 'From m–p to ma–p: Multinationality alignment and performance', *Journal of International Business Studies*, vol. 45, 211–226.

Ronen, S. and Shenkar, O. (2013). 'Mapping world cultures: Cluster formation, sources and implications', *Journal of International Business Studies*, vol. 44, 867–897.

Rugman, A.M. 2005. *The Regional Multinationals: MNEs and "global" strategic management*, Cambridge, Cambridge University Press.

Rugman, A.M. and Hodgetts, R. (2001). 'The end of global strategy', *European Management Journal*, vol. 19, 333–343.

Rugman, A.M., Li, J. and Oh, C.H. (2009). 'Are supply chains global or regional?' *International Marketing Review*, vol. 26, 384–395.

Rugman, A.M. and Oh, C.H. (2012). 'Why the home region matters: Location and regional multinationals', *British Journal of Management*, vol. 24, 463–479.

Rugman, A.M., Oh, C.H. and Lim, D. (2012). 'The regional and global competitiveness of multinational firms', *Journal of the Academy of Marketing Science*, vol. 40, 218–235.

Rugman, A.M. and Verbeke, A. (2004). 'A perspective on regional and global strategies of multinational enterprises', *Journal of International Business Studies*, vol. 35, 3–18.

Rugman, A.M. and Verbeke, A. (2005). 'Towards a theory of regional multinationals: A transaction cost economics approach', *MIR: Management International Review*, vol. 45, 5–17.

Rugman, A.M. and Verbeke, A. (2007). 'Liabilities of regional foreignness and the use of firm-level versus country-level data: A response to Dunning et al. (2007)', *Journal of International Business Studies*, vol. 38, 200–205.

Rugman, A.M. and Verbeke, A. (2008). 'A new perspective on the regional and global strategies of multinational services firms', *Management International Review*, vol. 48, 397–411.

Rugman, A.M., Verbeke, A. and Nguyen, P.C.Q.T. (2011). 'Fifty years of international business theory and beyond', *Management International Review*, vol. 51, 755–786.

Sammartino, A. and Osegowitsch, T. (2013). 'Dissecting home regionalization: How large does the region loom?' *Multinational Business Review*, vol. 21, 45–64.

Schlie, E. and Yip, G. (2000). 'Regional follows global: Strategy mixes in the world automotive industry', *European Management Journal*, vol. 18, 343–354.

Schuh, A. (2013). 'Do regional headquarters for Central and Eastern Europe have a future?' *Central European Business Review*, vol. 2, no. 1, 53–54.

Schütte, H. (1997). 'Strategy and organisation: Challenges for European MNCs in Asia', *European Management Journal*, vol. 15, 436–445.

Suder, G. (2011). *Doing Business in Europe*, 2nd edn, London, SAGE Publications.

Suder, G. (2015). 'Regional trade agreements: Non-market strategy in the context of business regionalization', in T.C. Lawton and T.S. Ragwani (eds), *Routledge Companion to Non-market Strategy*, New York, Routledge, pp. 332–347.

Syed, H.A. and Colleen, B. (2011). 'An empirical note on regionalization and globalization', *Multinational Business Review*, vol. 19, 26–35.

Tversky, A. (1977). 'Features of similarity', *Psychological Review*, vol. 84, 327.

UNCTAD (2007). *World Investments Prospects Survey 2007–2009*. New York and Geneva, United Nations.

Verbeke, A. and Asmussen, C.G. (2016). 'Global, local, or regional? The locus of MNE strategies', *Journal of Management Studies*, vol. 53, 1051–1075.

Verbeke, A. and Forootan, M.Z. (2012). 'How good are multinationality–performance (m-p) empirical studies?' *Global Strategy Journal*, vol. 2, 332–344.

Werth, A. (2006). *EU Regional Headquarters: Implications for host countries and skills of domestic labor force*, diplom. de.

Yeung, H.W.C., Poon, J. and Perry, M. (2001). 'Towards a regional strategy: The role of regional headquarters of foreign firms in Singapore', *Urban Studies*, vol. 38, 157–183.

Yip, G.S. (1989). 'Global strategy… In a world of nations?' *MIT Sloan Management Review*, vol. 31, 29.

Zaheer, S. (1995). 'Overcoming the liability of foreignness', *Academy of Management Journal*, vol. 38, 341–363.

PART B

International business theory and evidence in Europe

Origins and evolutions

4

INTERNALISATION THEORY AND EUROPEAN BUSINESS

Peter Enderwick

Introduction

This chapter examines the theory of internalisation as applied to the multinational enterprise (MNE) and, in particular, to European business. Internalisation theory is the pre-eminent explanation for the existence of MNEs and for more than four decades has remained relevant in the face of changes in the strategy and structure of international businesses. The theory has evolved to explain internationalisation across a range of industry sectors, types of firm and governance modes.

Internalisation theory is highly relevant to the European experience in part because of the long history of European business and its early internationalisation, as well as the fact that Europe provided the crucible for many of the major developments in the theory and its testing. I focus on three key issues. First, in the following section I provide a brief overview of internalisation theory and its relationship to other relevant explanatory frameworks such as transaction cost economics and the resource-based view of the firm. I consider the role of firm-specific and locational advantages that underpin internalised transactions. Second, I examine the internationalisation of European business, considering Europe as both a source (home region) and a destination (host region) for international business activities. My focus is on a Europe comprising the 28 members of the European Union, the five accession or candidate countries, as well as key European economies that are not members of the EU (Switzerland, Norway, Iceland). Our discussion highlights the interdependencies between locational conditions, the creation of firm-specific advantages and their cross-border transfer and protection. The final substantive section evaluates some of the current debates around internalisation and their implications for European business.

Internalisation theory

The importance of internalisation theory is critically linked to its centrality in explaining one of the key institutions of the contemporary global economy, the MNE. I define an MNE as a firm that owns and/or controls value-creating assets in more than one country (Buckley and Casson 2009). At the heart of this definition is the cross-border dimension of business; the MNE operates in more than one country. While the existence of such firms is undisputed, providing a theoretical explanation for their persistence is no simple matter. The difficulties encompass two issues: the existence of firms per se, and of international firms in particular. Where markets are incomplete or inefficient, transactions may be more efficiently coordinated by managerial fiat; in effect, a firm is created. This is the process of internalisation. The boundaries of the firm are determined by the relative efficiencies of the market and of administrative structures.

The second difficulty, the existence of multinational firms, is more subtle and arises from the expectation that foreign firms should not be able to survive in overseas markets; they should be outcompeted by local firms that enjoy advantages of familiarity with local conditions. In addition, operating facilities at a distance add to communication and control costs faced by international firms undertaking foreign direct investment (FDI), the so-called 'liabilities of foreignness' (Zaheer 1995).

Answers to the puzzle of how international firms can be successful originated with the recognition that FDI involved the international transfer of a package of resources (capital, technology, management skills) under the control of the international firm (Hymer 1976). Such assets served to provide an advantage to the foreign investor, an advantage that could offset the liabilities of foreignness.

Subsequent work on the nature of advantages such as brand names, technology and marketing knowledge highlighted their international mobility and value when combined with locational advantages (markets, specialist skills, natural resources etc.) in the host country (Caves 1971; Kindleberger 1969). Critical to continuing foreign involvement is maintenance of firm-specific advantages. If local firms are able to replicate the advantages enjoyed by MNEs then competitive advantage is transient. Explanations for the continuation of competitive advantage by MNEs identified a number of ways in which this could be achieved.

One, the resource-based view of the firm, focused on the characteristics of firm advantages. Such advantages were seen as difficult to replicate because of so-called isolating mechanisms (Rumelt 1984) creating a barrier to competitors (Barney 1991).

A second explanation focused on the challenges of acquiring such advantages, where assets are embedded within a target firm (Chen 2010). Difficulties in undertaking market-based transactions for assets (Chen and Hennart 2004) suggest that such resources may be best accumulated internally (Dierickx and Cool 1989; Madhok 2002).

A third explanation focused on the dynamic nature of firm-specific assets and their continuous production and reproduction (Buckley and Casson 1976). This dynamic conception of firm-specific advantage has been generalised by Teece (2007) highlighting the orchestration capabilities of MNEs in combining their internationally mobile resources with location-bound country-specific assets. Combining the internalisation of transactions with selection of the least-cost overseas location provided a rigorous but parsimonious explanation of the MNE.

Table 4.1 shows the major transactional hazards or frictions that can arise when exchange occurs externally, through the market and the price mechanism. The table provides a brief explanation of the nature of each hazard and how internalisation (bringing transactions under common governance within the firm), can mitigate such hazards. In addition, the seminal works in each of these areas are provided.

The internationalisation of European firms

Europe's extensive history and international political ambitions mean that its global involvement has long been significant. European firms have a considerable history of internationalisation, and Europe has been at the very centre of theory development on the MNE with the classical application of internalisation thinking (Buckley and Casson 1976), the OLI framework

Table 4.1 Overview of internalisation as a response to transactional frictions

Transactional Issue	Nature of the Issue	Internalisation Responses	Seminal Sources
Asset specificity	Problem of holdup	Provides opportunities for aligning incentives and a range of administrative controls	Williamson (1975) Riordan and Williamson (1985) Whyte (1994)
Contentious negotiations	Need to resolve disagreements and conflict	Opportunities for frequent, cooperative adaptation	Klein et al. (1978) MacNeil (1978) Poppo and Zenger (2002)
Need for contractual safeguards	Adds to transaction costs and inhibits trust	Can be reduced or replaced by trust and shared objectives	Ring and Van den Ven (1992) Woolthius et al. (2005) Teece (1986)
Opportunism	Self-interest-seeking with guile	Familiarity of partners in exchange. Shared goals and residual claimancy. Security of relationship discourages opportunism	Williamson (1993) Moschandreas (1997) Verbeke and Greidanus (2009)
Uncertainty	Increases number of possible contingencies and communication costs. Benevolent preference reversal. Hinders coordination	Common governance may facilitate identification of contingencies. Employment contracts provide flexibility and adaptation. Familiarity reduces communication costs and likelihood of over-commitment or reprioritisation. Coordination facilitated by common governance, alignment of incentives and resolution of conflict	Carson et al. (2006) Williamson (1975)
Output and quality measurement difficulties	Observability hazards and cheating	Authority centralisation facilitates monitoring and measurement of outputs	Barzel (1982) Demsetz (1988) Holmstrom (1979)
Appropriability	Loss of value	Vertical integration protects intellectual property, facilitates efficient exploitation and protects knowledge transfer. Accentuates causal ambiguity	Oxley (1997) Madhok and Tallman (1998) Gottschalg and Zollo (2007)
Knowledge transfer	Problems arising from tacit resources and buyer uncertainty	Vertical integration helps overcome buyer uncertainty and knowledge transfer costs.	Kogut and Zander (1993) Grant (1996) Foss (1996)
Firm scope	Breadth of expertise and knowledge absorption	Greater ease of transferring tacit knowledge Greater scope facilitates transfer and application of new knowledge	Klein et al. (1978) Grossman and Hart (1986)
Co-specialisation of resources	Need to coordinate asset creation and investment	Facilitated under common governance	Teece (2007)
Pricing in imperfect markets	Need to assign shadow prices	Opportunities for transfer pricing (through central fiat, independent internal negotiation, arms-length pricing).	Hirshleifer (1956) Eden (1985)

(Dunning 2000) and process models (Johanson and Vahlne 1977) all originating from European-based scholars.

Explaining the internationalisation of European firms within an internalisation framework requires an understanding of the influence of two factors: location-specific and firm-specific advantages. It is the combination of these two sets of assets, typically under the common governance of the MNE, that explains the internationalisation process.

Location advantages

Modern thinking on the MNE highlights the importance of both home and host locational factors as key to understanding the behaviour of MNEs (Andersson et al. 2014; Rugman and Verbeke 2001). The environment in the home country provides the conditions for the creation of globally mobile firm-specific advantages that can be applied and augmented in host country locations. In addition, the multinationality of the firm strongly influences the opportunities for applying advantages and the ease with which they can be transformed from location-bound country-specific advantages (CSAs), to globally mobile firm-specific advantages (FSAs) (Hennart 2009).

Europe, with its considerable diversity, offers a variety of locational conditions that help explain the internationalisation of its firms. Porter's (1990) model of national competitiveness, for example, highlights four key determinants: consumer demand; factor market conditions; competition; and rivalry and supporting sectors. Europe has a sizeable population, with many enjoying high income levels, and is characterised by a large number of discerning consumers who drive the high quality standards achieved by European producers in sectors as diverse as fashion, ceramics, motor vehicles, pharmaceuticals, and food and beverages.

Europe's considerable diversity of member states provides a variety of factor market conditions. The EU in particular benefits from having a stable political, legal, and regulatory environment, underpinned by strong institutions. There is access to highly skilled labour in many member countries, but lower cost labour is available in parts of Central and Eastern Europe and through offshore sourcing.

Europe scores highly in a range of indices of economic success, competitiveness and innovation. For example, Europe contains four of the ten largest economies in the world, 11 of the 20 most competitive countries in 2016 were European (WEF 2016), with European countries among the globally most innovative, and the number of European companies in the Fortune 500 having declined only slightly, from 158 in 2001 to 143 in 2017 (Fortune 2017).

However, these aggregate data conceal the considerable diversity that exists within Europe. For example, levels of national competitiveness vary significantly, with the Nordic countries (Denmark, Finland, Sweden, and Norway) being by far the most competitive. They are followed by Western European economies, with Southern and Eastern European countries being the least competitive, particularly Greece, Romania and Bulgaria. Interestingly, accession and candidate countries, with the possible exception of Iceland, would appear to contribute little to improving overall competitiveness of the EU. The basis of Europe's competitiveness also differs from that of other blocs, with a strong commitment to inclusiveness and sustainability, at the expense of newer technologies and higher value added (WEF 2016).

While Europe represents one of the three triad blocs that dominate innovation, the rise of Asia has been at the expense of Europe with more than 70 per cent of knowledge creation now occurring outside Europe (Stierna and Rangelova 2013). Also noteworthy are differences in the types of innovation occurring within the triad regions. When compared with competitor regions, Europe has a broader technology profile, one that focuses on industries of traditional advantage such as transport, construction, food and agriculture. In contrast, North American and Asian research is more likely to target enabling and transformative technologies, areas that are likely to underpin emerging sectors.

Regional diversity is also apparent in innovation and R&D spending. Spending on R&D has reached the EU target of 3 percent of GDP only in the Nordic countries; in some of the countries of Central and Southern Europe it is less than 1 per cent. The lower-spending countries are also over-dependent on public R&D investment. Comparable disparities are also apparent in the areas of digital skills and number of people engaged in knowledge-intensive activities (Eurostat 2016). Innovative activities that encourage concentration and the creation of regional clusters tend to favour already strong regions benefiting from the presence of strong academic institutions and high levels of knowledge spillover.

Equally worrying is evidence of similar inequalities in entrepreneurial activity, with Northern Europe outperforming Central and Southern Europe (Kontolaimou et al. 2016), particularly in the framework conditions for entrepreneurial activities (Szerb et al. 2013). Also of interest is the finding that Europe scores more strongly in internal entrepreneurship (the creation of new ideas and technologies within existing businesses) than other regional economies. This may encourage internalisation both through the continuous creation of new technologies that are best exploited internally, and a lower rate of new business start-ups contributing to the pool of contract suppliers (Szerb et al. 2013). The finding that much entrepreneurial activity in the weaker economies is driven by necessity (limited employment opportunities), rather than opportunity identification, also impedes technological catch-up (Kontolaimou et al. 2016).

There is some evidence to suggest that Europe may be losing some of its locational attractiveness, certainly to global investors as competition from other regions, and particularly from within Asia, increases. For example, in 2015 only two European nations (the United Kingdom and Germany) made the top ten ranked locations in one major study of MNE locational decisions (IBM-PLI 2016). However, while Europe may not perform as strongly in terms of total inward investment and the number of jobs created, it is able to attract a disproportionate share of the highest quality investments, in part because of its highly competitive metropolitan areas (IBM-PLI 2016).

Firm-specific advantages (FSAs)

Locational conditions are critical for the creation of firm-specific advantages by local firms. As discussed earlier, many European nations enjoy strong institutions and secure environments that are conducive to the creation of advantages. Research identifies two key determinants of the ability to create CSAs: local environmental conditions; and market dynamics (McCann and Mudambi 2005; Rugman and Verbeke 2001).

Local environmental conditions capture the institutional, regulatory, technological and entrepreneurial conditions of home markets. Sound institutional and regulatory structures are conducive to economic growth and development. Technological capability, the result of investment in human capital and R&D, determines the pace and direction of technological innovation. Opportunities for the creation of local competences also depend on the level of entrepreneurial activity. All other things equal, higher rates of entrepreneurship bring greater opportunities for all firms, local and foreign, to contribute to, and benefit from, asset creation. The rate of resource and competence creation will also be affected by government policy (supported, for example, by investment in education, research institutes and programmes), the level of research specialisation and supporting structures (industrial clusters, strong digital infrastructure, encouragement of complementary sectors), for example. Local competences can be technological, but also organisational, where home conditions encourage the development of innovative management processes and business models (Andersson et al. 2014).

The pace of asset creation is strongly affected by local market and competitive dynamics (Zander 1998). Strong competitive pressure, the result of both market structures and regulatory policy, encourages innovation and the opportunity to develop and apply new competences (Jenkins and Tallman 2010). The Single Market has stimulated competition with the number of businesses increasing from 12 million in 1999 to more than 21 million in 2015 (BusinessEurope 2015). European competitiveness policy is seen as effective in controlling anticompetitive mergers and agreements as well as abuse of market power. However, competition policy appears less effective at the local level, where detailed regulations impair incentives to upgrade (Vetter 2013).

International business within Europe

Location and inward FDI

Europe is both a source for, and a host region to, MNEs. Foreign multinationals invest within Europe to take advantage of many of the same locational advantages that stimulate the founding of local firms. Reflecting three of Dunning's (1998) FDI motives, foreign investors are attracted by the existence of large numbers of affluent consumers (market-seeking FDI), as well as strong technological capability (resource-seeking FDI). Recently, a number of emerging market MNEs from countries such as China and India have targeted strategic assets within European-based firms, often through acquisition (strategic asset-seeking FDI). Examples include the purchase of Volvo by China's Geely and of Jaguar/Land Rover by India's Tata Motors. The rise of emerging economies such as India and China is reflected in changing patterns of inward investment into the European region. Recent years have seen a sharp rise in Chinese FDI targeting high-tech European firms, for example the 2016 acquisition of Germany's robot manufacturer Kuka by China's Midea (Hanemann and Huotari 2015). One of the key locational advantages of Europe, however, is not simply its size or resource endowment, but its high level of regional integration, particularly within the EU.

The Single Market and FDI

There is a vast literature examining the impact of regional economic integration (REI) on FDI (Blomström and Kokko 1997; Chen 2009; Feils and Rahman 2011; Medvedev 2012). The consensus of this work is that REI may be expected to increase inward FDI following integration (Dunning 1997), but that the impacts are complex, varied, and difficult to generalise. Regional integration increases market size, may improve overall efficiency, and through a possible growth stimulus, add to market attractiveness. Opportunities to access new locations (e.g. the further enlargement of the EU after 2004), increase scale,and incentives to rationalise production all encourage internalisation. Traditionally, Europe has been both a major source of, and host for, FDI. At the end of the last century the region was attracting more than half of total global inflows and accounting for 70 per cent of outflows (Gestrin 2014). A number of studies focusing on the various stages of European integration report positive effects on FDI, particularly extra-European FDI (Barrel and Pain 1999; Dunning 1997; Pain 1997).

In recent years Europe's share of FDI flows has decreased substantially, with the key change the sharp decline in intra-European FDI. This may reflect a reduction in intra-regional transaction costs and increasing opportunities for internal trade. An increasing share of Europe's (now lower) volume of inward investment comes from outside the region and increasingly, in the form of cross-border mergers and acquisitions. Over the period 2010–15, European firms were the target for 43 per cent of international asset sales, while cross-border asset purchases by European firms were around half this level (United Nations 2016). It would be naive to interpret such changes as simply a reflection of declining European competitiveness; rather they may be a response to the changing structure of the world economy (Gestrin 2014). Future economic growth will occur predominantly outside Europe, much of it in Asia, and European firms need to internationalise through trade, investment or outsourcing if they are to participate in future opportunities.

The Single Market and competitiveness

The creation of the Single Market has added to the competitiveness of European firms. It has lowered transaction costs through mutual recognition of standards, increased competitive pressure and enhanced regional labour mobility. In addition, financial transaction costs are reduced for companies operating within the Euro area. The large integrated market also facilitates the achievement of economies of scale. The elimination of barriers within the Single Market has undoubtedly encouraged regional specialisation and the development of regional value chains, reflected in growing levels of intra-regional trade, particularly vertical trade in intermediate components (Frensch et al. 2016; Kawaecka-Wyrzkowska 2009). Regional chains facilitate the adoption of just-in-time production and distribution systems, an increasingly important competitive edge in a global economy. An example is provided by the car parts sector. A BMW Mini crankshaft is likely to cross the English Channel at least three times before completion. The raw crankshaft is cast by a French supplier before being shipped to a BMW plant in Warwickshire UK, for drilling and milling. It then travels to Munich for insertion into the engine. The engine is then shipped back to the UK for insertion into the Mini body (Ruddick and Oltermann 2017).

Size and integration also provides a bargaining advantage when EU members are pursuing external trade agreements, the benefits of which are enjoyed by all member firms (Vetter 2013). The empirical evidence is generally supportive of these expectations with integration contributing to growth, employment and trade (Boltho and Eichengreen 2008; Ilzkovitz et al 2007).

However, the benefits are not shared equally. Economies with a high share of intra-EU trade and which have dismantled high protectionist barriers are likely to enjoy greater benefits. Similarly, small economies with high trade intensity and those that enjoy competitive advantage in sectors offering significant economies of scale also benefit more. Deeper integration of the Single Market could bring additional competitive advantage to European firms. Further gains seem achievable in a number of areas including trade in goods and services, public procurement and the digital economy (Pataki 2014).

Internalisation and European business: An evaluation

Our discussion has highlighted the centrality of internalisation theory in understanding the emergence and strategy of MNEs. A clear strength of internalisation theory is that it offers a general explanation of the internationalisation of the firm (Buckley 2016). This is important for European business, because it is applicable to a wide range of different types of firm characteristic of the region, including state-owned enterprises, small firms, Born Globals, family business and non-hierarchical businesses. Similarly, the theory can be applied to both technology and marketing-led firms (Buckley and Casson 1976; 2011).

A further strength is the dynamism of internalisation. With the rise of the networked multinational, internalisation thinking has been applied to such firms both in terms of bundling FSAs and CSAs (Hennart 2009) and in the form of the global factory (Buckley 2009; 2011). European firms have responded to these changes by increasingly targeting emerging markets, offshore sourcing activities, and the sale of assets through restructuring. For example, the Spanish clothing brand Zara undertakes just over half of all manufacturing internally, outsources a quarter to Europe and North Africa, and 20 per cent, focusing on basic designs, to Asia. Internalisation theory highlights the need to control key activities such as knowledge transfer, but the opportunity to outsource and re-integrate more peripheral tasks. Such flexibility is of considerable importance to a region such as Europe, sometimes criticised for inflexibilities in policy and the operation of labour and capital markets.

Significant future changes that are likely to impact on international business can also be modelled within internalisation theory. For example, new information and communications technologies (Chen and Kamal 2016) and 3D printing technologies (Laplume et al. 2016) will impact scale, location and the ability to protect intellectual property. Fragmented production systems, facilitated by improved coordination technologies, can provide an alternative to internalisation in the protection of FSAs (Gooris and Peters 2016). The dynamism of internalisation thinking is also relevant to changes in European integration. The impact of Brexit, and any possible future de-integration, can be modelled in terms of market size, locational advantage and incentives for rationalisation of supply chains, providing valuable insights into possible strategy and spatial shifts.

Conclusions

In this chapter I have examined internalisation theory and its applicability to European business. Its consideration of both firm-specific and location advantages is invaluable in understanding European business. Location advantage helps us appreciate how firm competencies are created, and why foreign MNEs are attracted to the European region.

Internalisation theory helps in understanding new opportunities for the creation of competitive advantages. For example, growing servitisation, the addition of value creating services to products, offers new opportunities for European business (Vandermerwe and Rada 1998). Further reform of both the European services and digital sectors could add significantly to firm competitiveness in a rapidly evolving market space. There is a similar case for the emerging sharing economy underpinned by new business models and competitive strategies. This is an area where significant policy reforms are a prerequisite to success and the Single Market may be uniquely placed to effect such changes in a coherent fashion (BusinessEurope 2015).

Internalisation thinking has important policy implications that are relevant to the European experience. Internalisation theory brought a policy acceptance that MNEs do not simply exploit monopoly power, but contribute to growth and development (Casson 2015). Similarly, internalisation thinking provided an extension of competitive diamond thinking from a single (home country) view to that of multiple linked diamonds (Rugman 2005), opening up opportunities for regional specialisation and the development of clusters (Dunning and Lundan 2008). It also makes clear the types of locational factors that governments – local, national, and regional – should be supporting and investing in.

However, despite the aims of a single integrated region, performance differences between European nations appear likely to persist. Divisions in innovation and national competitiveness between Northern and Western Europe and areas of Central and Southern Europe seem likely to persist despite significant and targeted policies (WEF 2016).

Because of its ability to adapt to changing environmental conditions internalisation theory has value in understanding the likely impact of any slowing or reversal of globalisation. It suggests that given the complexity of modern global value chains, increases in protectionism and nationalism are unlikely to attract jobs to a particular location; rather, such changes will disrupt and reconfigure global value chains, probably to the detriment of more protectionist regions. This may present an opportunity for European firms, which must continue to internationalise to take advantage of new business opportunities outside their home region, particularly the dynamic Asian region (Alliance for a Competitive European Industry 2015).

References

Alliance for a Competitive European Industry (2015), *Shifting Gears for a New EU Industrial Partnership: A Manifesto,* Brussels, Alliance for a Competitive European Industry.

Andersson, U., Dellestrand, H. and Pedersen, T. (2014), 'The contribution of local environments to competence creation in multinational enterprises', *Long Range Planning,* vol. 47, no.1–2, pp. 87–99.

Barney, J.B. (1991), 'Firm resources and sustained competitive advantage,' *Journal of Management,* vol. 17, no. 1, pp. 99–120.

Barrel, R. and Pain, N. (1999), 'Domestic institutions, agglomerations and foreign direct investment in Europe,' *European Economic Review,* vol. 43, no. 4, pp. 925–934.

Barzel, Y. (1982), 'Measurement cost and the organization of markets,' *Journal of Law and Economics,* vol. 25, no. 1, pp. 27–48.

Blomström, M. and Kokko, A. (1997), 'Regional integration and foreign direct investment', Stockholm School of Economics, Working Paper in Economics and Finance No.172, Stockholm.

Boltho, A. and Eichengreen, B. (2008), 'The Economic Impact of European Integration', CEPR Discussion Paper 6820, London.

Buckley, P.J. (2009), 'Internalisation thinking: From the multinational enterprise to the global factory', *International Business Review,* vol. 18, no.3, pp. 224–235.

Buckley, P.J. (2011), 'International integration and coordination in the global factory', *Management International Review,* vol. 51, no. 2, pp. 269–283.

Buckley, P.J. (2016), 'The contribution of internalisation theory to international business: New realities and unanswered questions,' *Journal of World Business,* vol. 51, no. 1, pp. 74–82.

Buckley, P.J. and Casson, M.C. (1976), *The Future of the Multinational Enterprise,* London, Macmillan.

Buckley, P.J. and Casson, M.C. (2009), 'The internalisation theory of the multinational enterprise: A review of the progress of a research agenda after 30 years', *Journal of International Business Studies,* vol 40, no. 9, pp.1563–1580.

Buckley, P.J. and Casson, M.C. (2011), 'Marketing and the multinational: Extending internalisation theory', *Journal of the Academy of Marketing Science,* vol. 39, no. 4, pp. 492–508.

BusinessEurope (2015), 'Building a True Single Market for Europe – Business' Priorities', BusinessEurope Strategy Paper 28 September, Brussels.

Carson, S.J., Madhok, A., and Wu, T. (2006), 'Uncertainty, opportunism, and governance: The effects of volatility and ambiguity on formal and relational contracting', *Academy of Management Journal,* vol. 49, no. 5, pp. 1058–1077.

Casson, M.C. (2015), 'Coase and international business: The origin and development of internalisation theory', *Managerial and Decision Economics,* vol. 36, no. 1 pp. 55–66.

Caves, R.E. (1971), 'Industrial corporations: The industrial economics of foreign investment', *Economica,* vol. 38 no. 149, pp 1–27.

Chen, M.X. (2009), 'Regional economic integration and geographic concentration of multinational firms', *European Economic Review,* vol. 53, no. 3, pp. 355–375.

Chen, S.-F. (2010), 'A general TCE model of international business institutions: Market failure and reciprocity', *Journal of International Business Studies,* vol. 41, no. 6, pp. 935–959.

Chen, S.-F. and Hennart, J-F. (2004), 'A hostage theory of joint ventures: Why do Japanese investors choose partial over full acquisitions to enter the United States?' *Journal of Business Research,* vol. 57, no. 10, pp. 1126–1134.

Chen, W. and Kamal, F. (2016), 'The impact of information and communication technology adoption on multinational firm boundary decisions', *Journal of International Business Studies,* vol. 47, no.5, pp. 563–576.

Demsetz, H. (1988), 'The theory of the firm revisited', *Journal of Law, Economics, and Organization*, vol. 4, no. 1, pp. 141–161.

Dierickx, I. and Cool, K. (1989), 'Asset stock accumulation and sustainability of competitive advantage', *Management Science,* vol. 35, no. 12, pp. 1504–1511.

Dunning, J.H. (1997), 'The European internal market programme and inbound foreign direct investment,' *Journal of Common Market Studies* vol. 35. no. 1, pp. 1–30.

Dunning, J.H. (1998), 'Location and the multinational enterprise: A neglected factor?', *Journal of International Business Studies*, vol.29, no.1, pp. 45–66.

Dunning, J.H. (2000), 'The eclectic paradigm as an envelope for economic and business theories of MNE activity', *International Business Review* vol. 9, no. 2, pp. 163–190.

Dunning, J.H. and Lundan, S.M. (2008), *Multinational Enterprises and the Global Economy,* Cheltenham, Edward Elgar.

Eden. L. (1985), 'The microeconomics of transfer pricing', in A.M. Rugman and L. Eden (eds), *Multinationals and Transfer Pricing*, London and New York, Croom Helm, pp. 13–46.

Eurostat (2016), *Regional Yearbook 2016*, Luxembourg, Eurostat.

Feils, D. and Rahman, M. (2011), 'The impact of regional integration on insider and outsider FDI', *Management International Review,* vol. 51, no.1, pp. 41–63.

Fortune (2017), 'The Fortune global 500', *Fortune Magazine*, New York, Time Inc.

Foss, N.J. (1996), 'More critical comments on knowledge-based theories of the firm', *Organization Science,* vol. 7, no. 5, pp. 519–523.

Frensch, R., Hanousek, J. and Kocenda, E. (2016), 'Trade in parts and components across Europe', *Czech Journal of Economics and Finance,* vol. 66, no. 3, pp. 236–262.

Gestrin, M. (2014), *International Investment in Europe: A canary in the coal mine?* Paris, OECD Investment Insights, November.

Gooris, J. and Peeters, C. (2016), 'Fragmenting global business processes: A protection for proprietary information', *Journal of International Business Studies,* vol. 47, no. 5, pp. 535–562.

Gottschalg, O. and Zollo, M. (2007), 'Interest alignment and competitive advantage', *Academy of Management Review*, vol. 32, no. 2, pp. 418–437.

Grant, R.M. (1996), 'Toward a knowledge-based theory of the firm', *Strategic Management Journal*, vol. 17, no. 2, pp. 109–122.

Grossman, S.J. and Hart, O.D. (1986), 'The costs and benefits of ownership: A theory of vertical and lateral integration', *Journal of Political Economy*, vol. 94, no. 4, pp. 691–719.

Hanemann, T. and Huotari, M. (2015), *Chinese FDI in Europe and Germany: Preparing for a new era of Chinese capital*, Berlin, Mercator Institute for Chinese Studies/Rhodium Group.

Hennart, J.-F. (2009), 'Down with MNE-centric theories! Market entry and expansion as the bundling of MNE and local assets', *Journal of International Business Studies*, vol. 40, no. 9, pp. 1432–1454.

Hirshleifer, J. (1956), 'On the economics of transfer pricing', *The Journal of Business*, vol. 29, no. 3, pp. 172–189.

Holmstrom, B. (1979), 'Moral hazard and observability', *The Bell Journal of Economics*, vol. 10, no. 1, pp. 74–91.

Hymer, S.H. (1976), *The International Operations of National Firms: A study of direct foreign investment,* Cambridge, MA, MIT Press.

IBM-PLI (2016), *Global Location Trends: 2016 annual report,* New York, IBM.

Ilzkovitz, F., Dierx, A., Kovacs, V. and Sousa, N. (2007), *Steps Towards a Deeper Economic Integration: The internal market in the 21st century,* Contribution to the Single Market Review European Economy No 271, Brussels, European Commission.

Jenkins, M. and Tallman, S.B. (2010), 'The shifting geography of competitive advantage: Clusters, networks and firms', *Journal of Economic Geography*, vol. 10, no. 4, pp. 599–618.

Johanson, J. and Vahlne, J.E. (1977), 'The internationalization process of the firm – a model of knowledge development and increasing foreign market commitment', *Journal of International Business Studies,* vol. 8, no. 1, pp. 23–32.

Kawecka-Wyrzkowska, E. (2009), *Evolving Patterns of Intra-industry Trade Specialisation of the New Member States (NMS) of the EU: The case of the automotive industry,* European Commission Economic Papers 364, March, Brussels.

Kindleberger, C.P. (1969), *American Business Abroad*, New Haven, CT, Yale University Press.

Klein, B., Crawford, R.G. and Alchian, A. (1978), 'Vertical integration, appropriable rents, and the competitive contracting process', *Journal of Law and Economics,* vol. 21, no. 2, pp. 297–326.

Kogut, B. and Zander, U. (1993), 'Knowledge of the firm and the evolutionary theory of the multinational corporation', *Journal of International Business Studies*, vol. 24, no. 4, pp. 625–645.

Kontolaimou, A., Giopoulos, I. and Tsakanikas, A. (2016), 'A typology of European countries based on innovation efficiency and technology gaps: The role of early-stage entrepreneurship', *Economic Modelling*, vol. 62, no. B, pp. 477–484.

Laplume, A., Petersen, B. and Pearce, J.M. (2016), 'Global value chains from a 3D printing perspective', *Journal of International Business Studies*, vol. 47, no. 5, pp. 595–609.

Macneil, I.R. (1978), 'Contracts: Adjustment of long-term economic relations under classical and neoclassical, and relational contract law', *Northwestern University Law Review*, vol. 72, no. 5, pp. 854–905.

Madhok, A. (2002), 'Reassessing the fundamentals and beyond: Ronald Coase, the transaction cost and resource-based theories of the firm and the institutional structure of production', *Strategic Management Journal*, vol. 23, no. 6, pp. 535–550.

Madhok, A. and Tallman, S.B. (1998), 'Resources, transactions and rents: Managing value through interfirm collaborative relationships', *Organization Science*, vol. 9, no. 3, pp. 326–339.

McCann, P. and Mudambi, R. (2005), 'Analytical differences in the economics of geography: The case of the multinational firm', *Environment and Planning*, vol. 37, no. 10, pp. 1857–1876.

Medvedev, D. (2012), 'Beyond trade: The impact of preferential trade agreements on FDI inflows', *World Development*, vol. 40, no. 1, pp. 49–61.

Moschandreas, M. (1997), 'The role of opportunism in transaction cost economics', *Journal of Economic Issues*, vol. 31, no. 1, pp. 39–57.

Oxley, J.E. (1997), 'Appropriability hazards and governance in strategic alliances: A transaction cost approach', *Journal of Law, Economics and Organization*, vol. 13, no. 2, pp. 387–409.

Pain, N. (1997), 'Continental drift: European integration and the location of UK foreign direct investment', *The Manchester School Supplement*, vol. LXV, pp. 94–117.

Pataki, Z. (2014), *The Costs of Non-Europe in the Single Market: 'Cecchini Revisited'*, Brussels, European Parliamentary Research Service.

Poppo, L. and Zenger, T. (2002), 'Do formal contracts and relational governance function as substitutes or complements?' *Strategic Management Journal*, vol. 23, no. 8, pp. 707–725.

Porter, M.E. (1990), *The Competitive Advantage of Nations*, New York, Free Press.

Ring P.S. and van de Ven, A.H. (1992), 'Structuring cooperative relationships between organizations', *Strategic Management Journal*, vol. 13, no. 7, pp. 483–498.

Riordan, M.H. and Williamson, O.E. (1985), 'Asset specificity and economic organization', *International Journal of Industrial Organization*, vol. 3, no. 4, pp. 365–378.

Ruddick, G. and Oltermann, P. (2017), 'A Mini part's incredible journey shows how Brexit will hit the UK car industry', *The Guardian*, 3 March.

Rugman, A.M. (2005), *The Regional Multinationals: MNEs and 'global' strategic management*, Cambridge, Cambridge University Press.

Rugman, A.M. and Verbeke, A. (2001), 'Subsidiary-specific advantages in multinational enterprises', *Strategic Management Journal*, vol. 22, no.3, pp. 237–250.

Rumelt, R. (1984), 'Towards a strategic theory of the firm', in R.B. Lamb (ed.), *Competitive Strategic Management*, Englewood Cliffs, NJ: Prentice-Hall, pp. 556–570.

Stierna, J. and Rangelova, G. (2013), *Europe's Competitive Technology Profile in the Globalised Knowledge Economy*, Innovation Union Competitiveness Papers 2013/3, Luxembourg, European Commission.

Szerb, L.A., Acs, Z. and Autio, E. (2013), 'Entrepreneurship and policy: The national system of entrepreneurship in the European Union and in its member countries', *Entrepreneurship Research Journal*, vol. 3, no. 1, pp. 9–34.

Teece, D. (1986), 'Transaction cost economics and the multinational enterprise: An assessment', *Journal of Economic Behavior and Organisation*, vol. 7, no. 1, pp. 21–45.

Teece, D.J. (2007), 'Explicating dynamic capabilities: The nature and microfoundations of (sustainable) enterprise performance', *Strategic Management Journal*, vol. 28, no. 13, pp. 1319–1350.

United Nations (2016), *World Investment Report 2016: Investor nationality: Policy challenges*, Geneva and New York, UNCTAD.

Vandermerwe, S. and Rada J. (1998), 'Servitization of business: Adding value by adding services', *European Management Journal*, vol. 6, no. 4, pp. 314–324.

Verbeke, A. and Greidanus, N.S. (2009), 'The end of the opportunism vs trust debate: Bounded reliability as a new envelope concept in research on MNE governance', *Journal of International Business Studies*, vol. 40, no. 9, pp. 1471–1495.

Vetter, S. (2013), *The Single European Market 20 Years on*, Frankfurt, EU Monitor Deutsche Bank.

WEF (World Economic Forum) (2016), *The Global Competitiveness Report 2016–2017*, Geneva, World Economic Forum.

Whyte, G. (1994), 'The role of asset specificity in the vertical integration decision', *Journal of Economic Behavior and Organization*, vol. 23, no. 3, pp. 287–302.

Williamson, O.E. (1975), 'Markets and hierarchies: Analysis and antitrust implications', New York, Free Press.

Williamson O.E. (1993), 'Opportunism and its critics', *Managerial and Decision Economics*, vol. 14, no. 2, pp. 97–107.

Woolthuis, R.K., Hillebrand, B. and Nooteboom, B. (2005), 'Trust, contract and relationship development', *Organization Studies*, vol. 26, no. 6, pp. 813–840.

Zaheer, S. (1995), 'Overcoming the liability of foreignness', *Academy of Management Journal*, vol. 38, no. 2, pp. 341–368.

Zander, I. (1998), 'The evolution of technological capabilities in the multinational corporation: Dispersion, duplication and potential advantages from multinationality', *Research Policy*, vol. 27, no. 1, pp. 17–35.

5

ON THE BASIS OF THE UPPSALA MODEL

Evolution of European research models and frameworks

Cheryl Marie Cordeiro

The European business environment: Uncertain, complex and dynamic

Economic development is increasingly dependent on the development of advanced institutions, where the co-evolution of multinational business enterprises (MBEs) and the institutions pertaining to the broader contextual business environment is needed to cope with the uncertainties of a dynamic socio-economic ecology (Cantwell, Dunning and Lundan 2010; Volberda and Lewin 2003). Strategic socio-economic and geopolitical decisions taken at supranational level can be consequential for Europe, and in particular the European business environment (EuBE). The EuBE, which includes the European Union (EU) member states on whiuch this chapter will focus, is part of the global business environment (GloBE). It features various levels and degrees of market integration and fragmentation. Interconnected and interdependent, Europe's economic integration efforts work, amongst other objectives, towards the lowering of economic barriers in forming regional groupings or preferential trading agreements in order to leverage larger markets and economies of scale so that it can remain competitive on the global platform (Lawton and Rajwani 2015; Dreger and Heene 2013). More about macro-regionalisation and the influencing forces of EU institutions on the EuBE can be found in chapters 11 and 14 by Bruce Wilson and Alan Butt Philip, respectively.

Purpose and focus of chapter

There is broad scholastic agreement that firms co-evolve with socio-political and economic institutions (Peng, Wang and Jiang 2008). Scholars generally agree that a firm's strategy is composed of integrated market and non-market srategies (McGuire et al. 2012; Aggarwal 2001; Baron 1995a, 1995b), yet there remains no unified theory or literature stream that explores the phenomena of firm-institution co-evolution (Feinberg, Hill and Darendeli 2015; Peng et al. 2008) and non-market strategy remains comparatively under-researched in IB studies compared to market strategies (McGuire et al. 2012). The previous chapter by Peter Enderwick discussed internalisation theory as applicable to European business. This chapter focuses on research methodology and takes an integral (unified) systems perspective of firm internalisation theory, incorporating macro-level political (national/regional/global), meso-level economic stakeholder influence (firm, inter-firm) and micro-level group level (intra-firm) perspectives. In particular, the elements of the Uppsala model (UM) are presented and expanded upon in the multi-levelled context of the EuBE. The chapter illustrates how an application of the perspectives of the Pronoun Reference System found in language in use (Halliday and Matthiessen, 2014; Wilber 2006) in the elements of the UM can help broaden the UM's application to the multifaceted, multi-levelled context of the EuBE in studying integrated firm strategy.

As a step towards applying the elements of the UM in a more comprehensive, dynamic EuBE context, the pronoun system of *I (You)*, *We (They)*, *It* and *Its* in language is applied to the elements of the UM that renders a four-quadrant perspective that results in different types of knowledge zone of the firm internationalisation processes. The re-perspectivising of the elements of the UM into a four-quadrant knowledge map by applying the Pronoun Referencing System is labelled the Götheborg IV model or the G4 model. The Götheborg IV model is an open and adaptive visualisation that enables the unified, systematic mapping of relative perspectives in research design. Depending on individual research design and launching perspective, the application limitations and future directions of the use of both the UM and the G4 model are discussed towards the end of the chapter.

European business environment theoretical frameworks and research models

There are several theories that students and researchers can draw upon when studying the business environment in Europe that include neofunctionalism, intergovernmentalism and multi-level governance (MLG). These theoretical frameworks reflect how interacting actors situated at different governance levels help shape the EuBE.

Neofunctionalism

Neofunctionalism, whose foundations from the late 1950s (Lindberg 1963; Haas 1958) postulated an autopoiesis of integration, occurs when the processes of integration can create and gain their own momentum, the value of which evolves beyond the sum of governmental political calculations and strategies. Processes of integration are forward looking, each progression evolves from previous levels of endeavours, encompassing previous effects and efforts to new levels of integration. The theory, although acknowledged in academic literature to be nuanced, has endured in its ideas because it can explain how the various state and non-state actors influence each other ('spillover' effects), organising themselves into a more efficient practical framework of cooperation and coexistence. Neofunctionalism is a theory that endeavours to lend voice to all interest groups. Business groups are viewed as prominent actors in European integration because they are seen as primary agents of change. Given the economic agenda of the EU, the theory works with the assumption that business enterprises and trade associations would be actors who would influence and shape regional socio-economic strategies and policies. As no theory can explain all practicalities, the main critique of neofunctionalism is that it has difficulty explaining intra-EU institution dynamics, in terms of which institution (the Council, Parliament or European Court of Justice) has the greatest influence in addressing objections from sovereign nations and bringing the region into deeper integration.

Intergovernmentalism

Similar to neofunctionalism, intergovernmentalism is a macro-level theory that explains deepening European integration. Taking a different perspective to neofunctionalism, however, intergovernmentalism (Hoffman 1966) postulates that national governments, not business enterprises or interest groups, are the primary influencers in shaping deeper European integration and steering the region's international activities. Hoffman's main critique of neofunctionalism lies in the limitations of the foundations of the functional method, arguing that the diversity of interests of national governments and their tight management of uncertainty superseded the spillover effects that neofunctionalism proposed (Moga 2009). The difficulties of accession of some member countries whose governments made clear that they would resist any gradual transfer of sovereignty to the community led to the beginnings of foreign policy coordination between the countries. Intergovernmentalism, which gives agency to states and national governments as main actors of regional integration in part explains how such coordinated national efforts led to the forming of the European Council in the 1970s (Bergmann and Niemann 2015; Wallace et al. 2010).

A variation of intergovernmentalism, liberal intergovernmentalism, was developed following the realist tradition of emphasising sovereign states as primary influencers of deepening European integration (Moravcsik 1993). This theory proceeds in two steps. The first is that it considers domestic interest groups as influencers shaping the preferences of national governments. Second, it analyses the outcome of deepening European integration efforts of intergovernmental negotiations. This perspective views the supranational institution of the EU as an instrumental creation of intergovernmental collaboration, working to strengthen individual national sovereignty and interests rather than weaken them.

Multi-level governance (MLG)

Scholars have noted that the presence or absence of independent organisations with some autonomous powers to enforce trade rules alter the contextual fabric and possibilities of outcomes that affect negotiation behaviour between various institutions (Yarbrough and Yarbrough 1992).

> Once states created an international organization with independent powers, they have brought to life a creature that is, because it possesses autonomy, not entirely under their control. An IO with autonomous powers of enforcement can shape the interpretation and application of the rules, which is to say it makes rules' (Sandholtz 1996, p. 408).

The institution of the EU is more nuanced in its practical workings than perceived by intergovernmentalism or liberal intergovernmentalism. When the Commission declares a nation state to have infringed upon the rules, it can demand that sovereign state respond in argument based on the rules. It is such observations of institutional behaviour that led scholars to call for a more nuanced theoretical approach to European integration (Bergmann and Niemann 2015; Mérand, Hofmann and Irondelle 2011).

In view of the fact that international organisations can become actors that have political influence based on their network collaborations and strategies, a more comprehensive framework that allows for multi-level analysis was developed (McGuire et al. 2012; Marks et al. 1996; Marks 1993). The focus of MLG is to study and understand the complexity of European integration efforts and its various actors, pegged at multiple levels of analysis. Multi-level governance views supranational institutions, national institutions and local actors such as companies and special interest groups as working together to shape policies and regulations, often in overlapping contexts.

The challenge of European business environment research

The myriad of interrelated actors situated at different levels coupled with the different theories that scholars use to study and analyse the EuBE context indicates the complexity of the fabric of reality, not least when placed in the context of rising global protectionism (Enderwick 2011). Viewed from a network perspective, the EuBE is a dynamic grid of relationships mapped in a complex variation of patterns. Research into the social network of international business (IB) studies indicates that MBEs are increasingly embedded in social exchanges, where the main activity of the MBE is the process of trade (Pinho and Pinheiro 2015; Agndal et al. 2008; Coviello 2006; Ellis 2000; Turnbull 1987). Business enterprises that operate in the context of the European market will need to consider the regional regulatory integration policies (including the EU, European Free Trade Area and European Economic Area) to adapt both market and non-market strategies that require (and are shaped by) interaction with governments, regulatory institutions and labour groups as well as non-governmental organisations (NGOs) (Suder 2015; Guay 2014; Kolk et al. 2013; McGuire et al. 2012). Just as there exists no grand trajectory theory of studying the EuBE context that can explain all processes and outcomes at once, neither are business internationalisation theories that encompass regionalisation processes all-encompassing in their scope. What can be addressed is the manner in which internationalisation theories are applied as tools of perspectivising and studying change in the EuBE in a context of uncertainty and complexity.

Ontology of the Uppsala model of firm internationalisation

While there are several theories and models of internationalisation within the field of IB studies, the most prominent is the UM, proposed by Johanson and Vahlne in 1977. The UM is a process-focused model that remains the most cited and critiqued in the field of IB (Welch et al. 2016; Carneiro et al. 2008; Oviatt and McDougall 1994; Andersen 1993). It was developed on the assumption that knowledge was lacking about the processes and operations of business enterprise internationalisation. This gap in knowledge was seen as necessary and essential in order to understand the two directions of firm internationalisation: the increasing involvement of the enterprise in a foreign country, and the continued establishment of operations in new countries (Johanson and Vahlne 1977).

Evolutionary economics

In the past decades, theories on the EuBE have become progressively comprehensive in perspective, moving away from dichotomous frameworks of analyses (Piattoni 2009; Dosi and Malerba 2002; Aggarwal 2001; Baron 1995a). Current theories of European integration tend to consider the complexity of activities and outcomes at multiple levels in a longitudinal frame. The evolutionary perspective encompasses and highlights an organic behavioural aspect to firm development and processes over time. These theoretical developments in integration theories are compatible in foundational thought to the UM in its original form, being a model in which 'the same basic mechanism can be used to explain all steps in the internationalization [process]' (Johanson and Vahlne 1977, p. 26). Nelson and Winter (1982) observed a change in connotations of 'profit maximization' as a standard assumption of business motivation. Neoclassical economic theory could not account for non-equilibrium conditions of the developments of the firm. As such, the UM was launched with the understanding that the firm evolves in a manner of progressive learning through a long period of time (Nelson and Winter 1982, 2002; Johanson and Vahlne 1977).

Organisation discourse and research on the interrelated elements of stability and change have interested scholars since the 1950s (March et al. 1958). The topic has been studied from various perspectives including social psychology (Weick 1979), organisation learning (March 1991), operations productivity (Adler et al. 2009), organisational adaptation research (Gupta et al. 2006), renewal capability and strategies (Riviere and Suder 2016), and ambidextrous dynamic capabilities of the firm (Vahlne and Jonsson 2017). It is also assumed that at any point in time, the organisation works with the best possible information available at that particular state of internationalisation in order to make decisions and create policies and operation strategies (Riviere and Suder 2016; Johanson and Vahlne 1977). Current European integration theories and the UM have an interacting double-helical approach in understanding firm internationalisation processes. The state (or context of situation) of the enterprise and its business environment will inform and influence the decisions taken for its continued development, and its development will in turn influence its context of situation. These theories work with the assumption that business environments, consisting of various processes, exist and evolve in a fairly stable state of disequilibrium.

Multi-faceted, multi-levelled

Knowledge and relations develop with the firm over time in its learning capacity, creating in effect, a heterogeneous landscape of firm operations (Wernerfelt 2013; Penrose 1959). Although the original perspective of the UM was meant to address firm-level analysis, where the establishment chain and psychic distance were identified from over 2,000 subsidiaries in a study of Swedish multinational enterprises during the 1960s and early 1970s (Welch et al. 2016), its process ontology grounded in behavioural sciences foregrounds the study of heterogeneous organisational dynamics (Dopfer, Potts and Pyka 2016; Dopfer and Potts 2008; Dosi and Marengo 2007). This allows for the UM to be applied from a variety of perspectives. The firm encompasses not only a widely dispersed engagement in foreign markets (defined as 'internationalisation') but has a network of differentiated units that can potentially exploit advantages of specialisation on location (Ghoshal and Bartlett 1990). This knowledge- and relations-based perspective makes specific firm boundaries arbitrary, dependent upon its network relations and contextual surroundings at a specific point in time (Johanson and Vahlne 2009; Coviello 2006). Fluidity in process dynamics and the emergent nature of organisational practices particularly highlight the temporal–relational dimension in firm processes (Ericson 2014).

The heterogeneous fabric within which firm processes operate, coupled with a knowledge network perspective, was reflected in the 2011 development and application of the UM unto the concept of globalisation. The typology for 'internationalisation' as used in the UM was aligned with a similar typology for 'globalisation', so that the UM could now reflect both internationalisation and globalisation processes (Vahlne et al. 2011; Ohmae 1985). The authors believed that 'the mechanisms of the Uppsala model are sufficiently general to allow for them to be used for all managerial processes that are characterised by uncertainty, ambiguity and complexity' (Vahlne et al. 2011, p. 2).

The elements of the UM include market knowledge (the extent of 'insidership'), market commitment, commitment decisions and current activities (learning, innovation and operations), placed in two broad dimensions that are interdependent in their influences on each other, classified as *state* and *change* aspects, as shown in Figure 5.1. The two state variables influence each other to the extent that knowledge is considered a resource upon which the firm can act to either increase or decrease commitment to the market. There are also different types of knowledge. Experiential knowledge, for example, is associated with particular market conditions

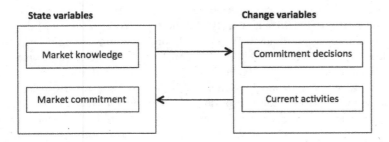

Figure 5.1 The basic mechanisms of internationalisation – state and change aspects (Johanson and Vahlne 1977, p. 26)

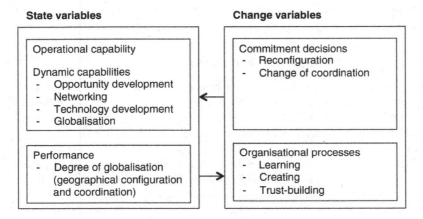

Figure 5.2 The Uppsala globalisation process model, adapted from Vahlne and Ivarsson (2014, p. 242)

and is non-transferrable to other markets (Penrose 1959). The change variables influence each other to the extent that the continuous activities of the firm will determine strategic decisions and commitment of the firm to the market. Figure 5.2. shows the Uppsala globalisation process model, in which the state and change dimensions are shown in greater detail.

Using the pronoun system to map knowledge zones of the Uppsala model

The UM was described by Johanson and Vahlne (1977) as a model of knowledge development for the firm increasing its foreign market commitments. The main tenet would be to identify knowledge gaps in the processes of firm internationalisation, 'knowledge [being] vested in the decision-making system' (Johanson and Vahlne 1977, p. 26). Knowledge zones within the internationalisation process, the dimensions and elements of the UM can be re-perspectivised by applying the deictic ('pointer') function of pronouns used in language.

Three-quarters of the world's language typology includes a *subject, verb* and *object* in its sentence construction (Crystal 1997; Francis and Crystal 1990). The pronoun perspectives of *I (You), We (They), It* and *Its* fulfil a reference function that directs the attention of the user towards a certain perspective. These perspectives, if continuously pursued as a form of inquiry, will render a type knowledge (singular/plural, subjective/inter-subjective, objective/inter-objective)

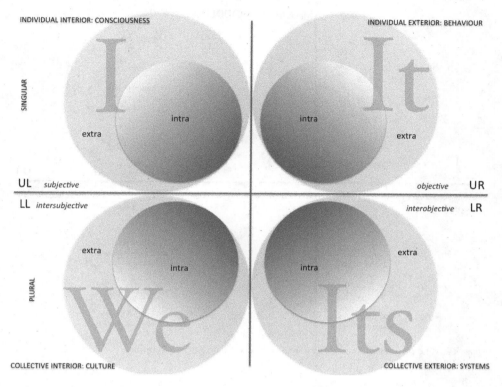

Figure 5.3 The four perspectives of the pronoun system 'I', 'We', 'It' and 'Its', adapted from Wilber (2000)

and knowledge zone. The difference in perspective is reflected in the functional use of language. Language helps users get things done. As such, inherent in the structure of language are its multiple levels of construct reflected in its patterns of use for various human activities and social purposes (Bache 2010). Language is also its own meta-language, where it can be applied to the study of other subjects (Halliday and Matthiessen 2014). In language, the use of noun, noun-phrases and pronouns in subject position renders the various perspectives of actors or doers of an action, while noun, noun-phrases and pronouns in object position denotes who is affected by the action of a verb in a sentence. These perspectives can be mapped in a four-quadrant model illustrated in Figure 5.3.[1]

The perspectives from the quadrants are holons, moving from narrower to broader perspectives, with each broader perspective encompassing the narrower perspectives. The Individual Interior perspective is expressed in the Upper Left quadrant (UL, *subjective*), which is *I (intra)/You (extra)*. The Collective Interior perspective is expressed in the Lower Left quadrant (LL, *intersubjective*), which is *We (intra)/They (extra)*. It is in the LL quadrant that many anthropological and ethnographical research studies of culture are designed and framed. Crossing diagonally over from bottom left to top right, the Individual Exterior perspective is expressed in the Upper Right quadrant (UR, *objective*), which is *It (intra)/It (extra)*. Many statistical empirical studies on culture in IB would fall in this quadrant in research design and framing, of which the dimensional theory of culture can be efficiently applied. In this quadrant of research frameworks, scholars/students can, for example, study from an objective point of view the combined effects

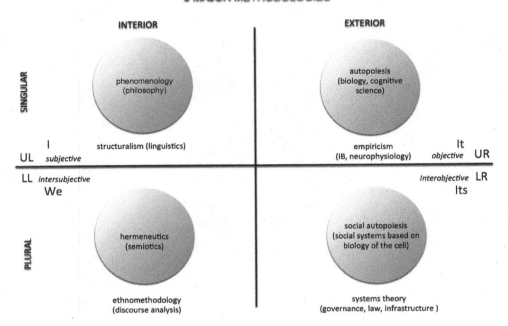

Figure 5.4 The primordial knowledge zones produced by pronoun system inquiry (Wilber 2006, pp. 36–40)

of elements from the UL and LL quadrants in terms of human behaviour exhibited in relation to their environment. If one were interested in studying systems or networks of behaviours, then this could be framed in the Collective Exterior perspective, expressed in the Lower Right (LR, *interobjective*) quadrant. The LR quadrant would be the broadest perspective, encompassing all other perspectives.

Figure 5.3 not only maps various perspectives, but the quadrants render four different types of knowledge zones. Taking into account that each perspective can have an intra- or extra-, singular or plural positioning, eight knowledge zones result and the dominant methodologies can be mapped onto a four-quadrant model as shown in Figure 5.4 (Wilber 2006, pp. 36–40). Figure 5.4 shows some examples of disciplines or knowledge paradigms that broadly define and are defined by the methodologies in the four quadrants. IB studies for example tend to be heavily oriented towards empiricism.

The unfolding of knowledge zones by applying the pronoun system of perspectives allows likewise for an unfolding of the dimensions of the UM so that it can in turn be situated in the various context of EuBE studies. In order to disambiguate the departure from the UM, the reperspectivised model is called the Götheborg IV or G4 model (Cordeiro 2016) illustrated in Figure 5.5. The G4 model can be described as an applied linguistics perspective of the elements of the UM. Using the meta-capacity of language, it does two things: first, it disambiguates the words 'firm as a whole' and 'firm' in the context of illustration, and second, it uncovers the knowledge zones in which the dialogic processes of internationalisation occur. The following sections will explain in greater detail the workings of these two aspects of the G4 model.

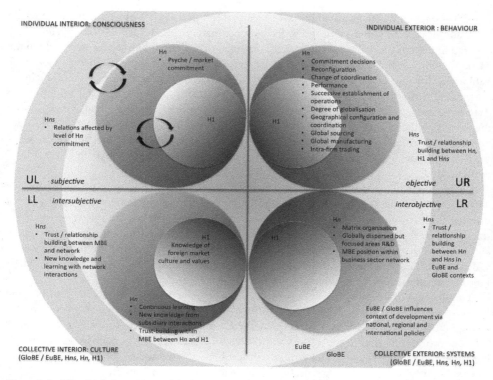

Figure 5.5 The Götheborg IV model: Illustrating elements of the Uppsala model in the context of the European and global business environments

The Götheborg IV model: Integrating elements of the Uppsala model and the European business environment

The process ontology of the UM implies that the models as reflected in Figures 5.1. and 5.2. could in effect be applied to different research perspectives, depending upon research design, method used and types of question asked. The complexity and dynamics of the UM between an enterprise, its subsidiaries and its network relations can also be contextualised in relation to integration theories of the EuBE. Having uncovered the knowledge zones of the UM, a further unfolding of its elements set within the context of the EuBE can be effected by a visual disambiguation of an MBE and its subsidiaries.

The Götheborg IV model

According to Johanson and Vahlne (1977, p. 23), the internationalisation (which includes regionalisation) process has two directions, '[the] increasing involvement of the firm in the individual foreign country, and successive establishment of operations in new countries'. Implicit in this context is the ambiguous manner in which the word 'firm' is used. Depending on context, the word 'firm' can either refer to the collective enterprise as a single unit, or to a single unit/subsidiary within the collective enterprise. The same context-dependent meaning of the use of the word 'firm' is found in Johanson and Vahlne (2009), where the word 'firm' can refer to the 'internationalizing firm' (p. 1411) as a single unit, or as its subsidiaries, illustrated in 'networks of relationships in which firms are linked to each other' (p. 1411). Within the literature of the UM, subsidiaries are also understood to have differentiating roles to play for the greater MBE. Located in foreign countries, subsidiaries are expected to have local knowledge upon which the MBE as a whole can leverage and benefit due to its geolocational embeddedness (Suder 2015; Vahlne and Johanson 2013; Vahlne et al. 2011). For MBEs to grow and improve their efficiency, they might 'reconfigure their widely dispersed value chains and develop their coordination systems to make the different units specialize, integrate and operate towards the overall best for the firm as a whole' (Vahlne and Ivarsson 2014, p. 227). The two directions of internationalisation inherent in the UM indicate a need for a non-ambiguous use and illustration of the word 'firm' where instances of the word when used in context could either refer to 'firm as a whole' or 'firm-level' (Vahlne and Ivarsson, 2014, p. 227).

By disambiguating the use of the words 'firm as a whole' (MBE) and 'firm' (a unit within the MBE), the G4 model shown in Figure 5.5 makes explicit the duo directions of the processes of internationalisation pegged at different levels of activities and analysis. A business enterprise as referred to by the UM model is denoted as H in the G4 model. Since an enterprise can contain an unknown number of units (denoted by n) within its network, the MBE or 'firm as a whole' is denoted as Hn. The 'firm', denoted by H1, is a singular example of a unit within the MBE, Hn. The business network in which both Hn and H1 exist is denoted as Hns.

The dialogic of interaction that occurs in a constant state of flux between H1 and Hn, and Hn to its business network of Hns illustrates the dynamicity of the influence between state and change variables in the UM. As with the UM, the G4 model works with the assumption that all relations evolve with time. Time in the G4 model is thus not a zone of knowledge to be studied, but rather, Time exists in the background fabric of the internationalisation and globalisation processes. Without Time, there would be no internationalisation processes.

Taking the firm and the enterprise as singular holons, labelled Hn for enterprise, and H1 for firm, the eight perspectives rendered by the G4 model are derived mainly from the interior and exterior Hn and H1 perspectives of the internationalisation processes, placed in four quadrants. Figure 5.5. shows the knowledge zones and perspectives of the G4 model. The G4 model can be described as an applied linguistics (*I(You)*, *We(They)*, *It/Its*) perspective of the Uppsala model of internationalisation processes, enabling a unified perspective of various levels of interactants, both firms and institutions. All entities exist in a network of relationships between each other in context. The circular arrows crossing unit boundaries indicate the dialogic of the relations and collaborations where learning and exchange take place. This exchange takes place in all four quadrants, even if only illustrated in the upper left quadrant in Figure 5.5. The process elements as well as units of analysis (firm level, network level) are set in the European business environment (denoted as EuBE in Figure 5.5) and the global business environment (denoted as GloBE in Figure 5.5).

Units and contexts of analysis can occur at various levels, as illustrated in Figure 5.5. The subsidiary, the collective MBE and even contextual units of analysis such as the EU MBEs within the EuBE, can be designated to be singular entities for analysis, depending on research design and question. The pedagogic value of the G4 model lies in that it enables a more systematic mapping of knowledge gaps in the UM by the use of the four quadrants in helping to visualise the relative perspectives.

The Upper Left (UL, *subjective*) quadrant is the zone of the MBE (Hn) and example subsidiary (H1) knowledge pertaining to their interior enterprise consciousness and ideology. This quadrant is where the 'Commitment' behind the 'Commitment decisions' thus enacted from the UM is represented in the G4 model. The Lower Left (LL, *intersubjective*) quadrant is the zone of knowledge of Hn and H1 pertaining to the collective interiors of enterprise and subsidiary culture. These interior knowledge zones are then expressed in the exterior quadrants, the material actions of which can be observed exteriorly in behaviour. The Upper Right (UR, *objective*) quadrant is the zone of H*n* and H1 knowledge pertaining to individual exteriors of enterprise and firm behaviour. The Lower Right (LR, *interobjective*) quadrant is the zone of H1 and H*n* knowledge pertaining to collective exteriors of enterprise and firm structures and systems. The business network H*ns* is the largest holon or contextual fabric within which all enterprise H*n* and firm H1 processes occur. All units of analysis are situated in national, regional (EuBE) and international (GloBE) contexts, reflected in Figure 5.5 as the outward radiating circles from the four quadrants. Elements from the theories of European integration that include neofunctionalism, intergovernmentalism and MLG will fall in the knowledge zone of the EuBE.

Application and use of the Götheborg IV model

Practitioner questionnaires and surveys can be designed by using the quadrant structure as a tool that can help identify knowledge gaps and systematically target the quadrant of knowledge needed for the level of analysis required. In scholastic research, most studies intending to understand the EuBE processes of internationalisation (and regionalisation) are likely to adopt a wide systemic perspective, although some studies reflected in this book, such as the chapters covering culture in the EuBE, could be said to span between the LL and LR quadrants. Such studies would thus encompass an analysis of the processes and activities of the interior and exterior perspectives of the MBE H*n* and its example subsidiary H1 in relation to regional policy influences. In the G4 model, factors that affect the inter-relationship between these units in a continuous dialogic synchrony towards the sustained development of the MBE can be mapped, listed and investigated in detail. This approach can also be used to scope literature within a specific knowledge zone.

Challenges and limitations of the Götheborg IV model

There exists no perfect model to express or illustrate all complexities and inter-relations of EuBE and GloBE networks. While the G4 model is illustrated here as a means to expand upon the contextual use of the UM in support of integrated firm strategies, the myriad perspectives on strategic internationalisation as outlined by Riviere and Suder (2016) remain. Their article also provides useful insight into future directions of EuBE research with regards to strategic internationalisation. Due to the various perspectives reflected in the G4 model, what becomes fundamental in its use in research design is for users to disambiguate and scope their own use of concepts. To that extent, the G4 model is abstract. Without the scoping of research design and concepts, the G4 model can instead create a too ambitious project scope in the hopes of studying 'everything' and 'anything'.

Conclusion

Increasing complexity in the EuBE requires a systematic and systemic method of study. Noting the under-researched topic of an integrated (unified) firm strategy (Riviere and Suder 2016; Feinberg et al. 2015; McGuire et al. 2012), this chapter has broadly outlined European integration theories and traced the thought evolution of the UM and presented a unified systemic perspective of firm-institution co-evolution in a conceptual visualisation framework labelled the Götheborg IV (G4) model. Following the foundations of the UM, this chapter illustrates how the application of the pronoun reference system in language can help reperspectivise elements of the UM into the four quadrants of the G4 model, which map the various knowledge zones to internationalisation. The G4 model can be seen as a research framework and tool in aid of research design and approach. Rather than being prescriptive in how empirical studies might be conducted, this chapter has taken on a complementary perspective of discussing the relativity of elements of the UM and how they might be applied to the specific context of the deepening integration of the EuBE. The open and adaptive G4 model is abstract in its visualisation, and the manner in which it is applied will depend upon the researcher perspective and research design.

Note

1 The works of Ken Wilber entitled *Sex, Ecology, Spirituality: The Spirit of Evolution* and the formulation of Integral Theory gives a comprehensive description and diagrammatic illustration of the different perspectives that relate to interior consciousness of the human mind to exterior material states of the human environment (Wilber 2000, p. 446).

References

Adler, P.S., Benner. M., Brunner, D.J., MacDuffie, J.P., Osono, E., Staats, B.R., Takeuchi, H., Tushman, M.L. and Winter, S.G. (2009), 'Perspectives on the productivity dilemma', *Journal of Operations Management*, vol. 27, pp. 99–113.

Aggarwal, V.K. (2001), 'Corporate market and nonmarket strategy in Asia: A conceptual framework', *Business and Politics*, vol. 3, no. 2, pp. 89–108.

Agndal, H., Chetty, S. and Wilson, H. (2008), 'Social capital dynamics and foreign market entry', *International Business Review*, vol. 17 no. 6, pp. 663–675.

Andersen, O. (1993), 'On the internationalization process of firms: A critical analysis', *Journal of International Business Studies*, vol. 24, no. 2, pp. 209–231.

Bache, C. (2010), 'Hjelmslev's glossematics: A source of inspiration to systemic functional linguistics?', *Journal of Pragmatics*, vol. 42, no. 9, pp. 2562–2578.

Baron, D.P. (1995a), 'Integrated strategy: Market and nonmarket components', *California Management Review*, vol. 37, no. 2, pp. 47–65.

Baron, D.P. (1995b), 'The nonmarket strategy system', *Sloan Management Review*, vol. 37, no. 1, pp. 73–85.

Bergmann, J. and Niemann, A. (2015), 'Theories of European integration', in K.E. Jørgensen, A.A. Kalland and E. Drieskens (eds), *The Sage Handbook of European Foreign Policy*, Vol. 1, Los Angeles, CA, London, New Delhi, Singapore, Washington DC, Boston, MA, SAGE, Publications, pp. 166–182.

Cantwell, J., Dunning, J. and Lundan, S. (2010), 'An evolutionary approach to understanding international business activity: The co-evolution of MNEs and the institutional environment', *Journal of International Business Studies*, vol. 41, no. 4, pp. 567–586.

Carneiro, J., Rocha, A.D. and Ferreira da Silva J. (2008), 'Challenging the Uppsala internationalization model: A contingent approach to the internationalization of services', *Brazilian Administration Review*, vol. 5, no. 2, pp. 85–103.

Cordeiro, C.M. (2016), 'The Götheborg IV (G4) model and the function of language in the globalization process of the firm: The case of Swedish MNEs', in M. Khan (ed.), *Multinational Enterprise Management Strategies in Developing Countries*, Hershey, PA, Business Science Reference, pp. 215–236.

Coviello, N. (2006), 'The network dynamics of international new ventures', *Journal of International Business Studies*, vol. 37 no. 5, pp. 713–731.

Crystal, D. (1997), *English as a Global Language*, Cambridge, Cambridge University Press.

Dopfer, K. and Potts, J. (2008), *General Theory of Economic Evolution*, London, Routledge.

Dopfer, K., Potts, J. and Pyka, A. (2016), 'Upward and downward complementarity: The meso core of evolutionary growth theory', *Journal of Evolutionary Economics*, vol. 26, no. 4, pp. 753–763.

Dosi, G. and Malerba, F. (2002), 'Interpreting industrial dynamics twenty years after Nelson and Winter's evolutionary theory of economic change: A preface', *Industrial and Corporate Change*, vol. 11, no. 4, pp. 619–622.

Dosi, G. and Marengo, L. (2007), 'On the evolutionary and behavioural theories of organizations: A tentative roadmap', *Organization Science*, vol. 18, no. 3, pp. 491–502.

Dreger, J. and Heene, A. (2013), 'European integration and Europeanization: Benefits and disadvantages for business', Bruges European Economic Policy Briefings (BEEP), no. 29, 16 September 2013. http://bit.ly/2hQg4UZ (accessed 6 November 2017).

Ellis, P. (2000), 'Social ties and foreign market entry', *Journal of International Business Studies*, vol. 31 no. 3, pp. 443–469.

Enderwick, P. (2011), 'Understanding the rise of global protectionism', *Thunderbird International Business Review*, vol. 53, no. 3, pp. 325–336.

Ericson, M. (2014), 'On the dynamics of fluidity and open-endedness of strategy process toward a strategy-as-practicing conceptualization', *Scandinavian Journal of Management*, vol. 30, no. 1, pp. 1–15.

Feinberg, S., Hill, T.L. and Darendeli, I.S. (2015), 'An institutional perspective on non-market strategies for a world in flux', in T.C. Lawton and T.S. Rajwani (eds), *The Routledge Companion to Non-market Strategy*, New York, Routledge, pp. 29–46.

Francis, W. and Crystal, D. (1990), 'The English language', *Language*, vol. 66, no. 4, pp. 861–862.

Ghoshal, S. and Bartlett, C.A. (1990), 'The multinational corporation as an interorganizational network', *The Academy of Management Review*, vol. 15, no. 4, pp. 603–625.

Guay, T. (2014), *The Business Environment of Europe: Firms, governments and institutions*, Cambridge, Cambridge University Press.

Gupta, A.K., Smith, K.G. and Shalley, C.E. (2006), 'The interplay between exploration and exploitation', *The Academy of Management Journal*, vol. 49, no. 4, pp. 693–706.

Haas, E. (1958), *The Uniting of Europe: Political, social and economic forces, 1950–1957*, Stanford, CA, Stanford University Press.

Halliday, M. and Matthiessen, C. (2014), *Halliday's Introduction to Functional Grammar*, 4th edn, Abingdon, Oxon; New York, Routledge.

Hoffman, S. (1966), 'Obstinate or obsolete? The fate of the national state and the case of western Europe', *Daedalus*, vol. 95, no. 3, pp. 862–915.

Johanson, J. and Vahlne, J.-E. (1977), 'The internationalization process of the firm: A model of knowledge development and increasing foreign market commitments', *Journal of International Business Studies*, vol. 8, no. 1, pp. 23–32.

Johanson, J. and Vahlne, J. (2009), 'The Uppsala internationalization process model revisited – from liability of foreignness to liability of outsidership', *Journal of International Business Studies*, vol. 40, no. 9, pp. 1411–1431.

Kolk, A., Lindeque, J. and Van den Buuse, D. (2013), 'Regionalization strategies of European Union electric utilities', *British Journal of Management*, no. 25, pp. S77–S99.

Lawton, T.C. and Rajwani, T.S. (eds) (2015), *The Routledge Companion to Non-market Strategy*, New York, Routledge.

Lindberg, L.N. (1963), *The Political Dynamics of European Economic Integration*, Stanford, CA, Stanford University Press.

March, J.G. (1991), 'Exploration and exploitation in organizational learning', *Organization Science*, vol. 2, pp. 71–87.

March J.G, Guetzkow, H. and Simon, H. (1958), *Organizations*, New York, John Wiley and Sons.

Marks, G. (1993), 'Structural policy and multi-level governance in the EC', in A.W. Cafruny and G.G. Rosenthal (eds), *The State of the European Community*, vol. 2, Boulder, CO, Lynne Rienner, pp. 391–410.

Marks, G., Scharpf, F., Schmitter, P.C. and Streeck, W. (1996), *Governance in the European Union*, London, Sage.

McGuire, S, Lindeque, J. and Suder, G. (2012), 'Learning and lobbying: Emerging market firms and corporate political activity in Europe', *European Journal of International Management*, vol. 6(2), no. 3, pp. 342–362.

Mérand, F., Hofmann, S. and Irondelle, B. (2011), 'Governance and state power: A network analysis of European security', *Journal of Common Market Studies*, vol. 49, no. 1, pp. 121–147.

Moga, T.L. (2009), 'The contribution of the neofunctionalist and intergovernmentalist theories to the evolution of the European integration process', *Journal of Alternative Perspectives in the Social Sciences*, vol. 1, no. 3, pp. 796–807.

Moravcsik, A. (1993), 'Preferences and power in the European community: A liberal intergovernmentalist approach', *Journal of Common Market Studies*, vol. 31, pp. 473–524.

Nelson, R.R. and Winter, S.G. (1982), *An Evolutionary Theory of Economic Change*, Cambridge, MA, Harvard University Press.

Nelson, R.R., and Winter, S.G. (2002), 'Evolutionary theorizing in economics', *The Journal of Economic Perspectives*, vol. 16, no. 2, pp. 23–46.

Ohmae, K. (1985), *Triad Power: The coming shape of global competition*. New York, Free Press.

Oviatt, B. and McDougall, P. (1994), 'Toward a theory of international new ventures', *Journal of International Business Studies*, vol. 25, no. 1, pp. 45–64.

Peng, M.W., Wang, D.Y. and Jiang, Y. (2008), 'An institution-based view of international business strategy: A focus on emerging economies', *Journal of International Business Studies*, vol. 39, no. 5, pp. 920–1036.

Penrose, E.T. (1959), *The Theory of the Growth of the Firm*, Oxford, Blackwell.

Piattoni, S. (2009), 'Multi-level governance: A historical and conceptual analysis', *Journal of European Integration*, vol. 31 no. 2, pp. 163–180.

Pinho, J.C. and Pinheiro, M.L. (2015), 'Social network analysis and the internationalization of SMEs: Towards a different methodological approach', *European Business Review*, vol. 27, no. 6, pp. 554–572.

Riviere, M. and Suder, G. (2016), 'Perspectives on strategic internationalization: Developing capabilities for renewal', *International Business Review*, vol. 25, no. 4, pp. 847–858.

Sandholtz, W. (1996), 'Membership matters: Limits of the functional approach to European institutions', *Journal of Common Market Studies*, vol. 34 no. 3, pp. 403–429.

Suder, G. (2015), 'Regional trade agreements: Non-market strategy in the context of business regionalization', in T.C. Lawton and T.S. Ragwani (eds), *Routledge Companion to Non-market Strategy*, New York, Routledge, pp. 332–347.

Turnbull, P.W. (1987), 'A challenge to the stages theory of the internationalization process', in P.J. Rosson and S.D. Reid (eds), *Managing Export and Expansion*, New York, Praeger, pp. 21–40.

Vahlne, J.-E., Ivarsson, I. and Johanson, J. (2011), 'The tortuous road to globalization for Volvo's heavy truck business: Extending the scope of the Uppsala model', *International Business Review*, vol. 20, pp. 1–14.

Vahlne, J.-E. and Ivarsson, I. (2014), 'The globalization of Swedish MNEs: Empirical evidence and theoretical explanations', *Journal of International Business Studies*, vol. 45, no. 3, pp. 227–247.

Vahlne, J.-E. and Johanson, J. (2013), 'The Uppsala Model on evolution of the multinational business enterprise: From internalization to coordination of networks', *International Marketing Review*, vol. 30, no. 3, pp. 189–210.

Vahlne, J.-E. and Jonsson, A. (2017), 'Ambidexterity as a dynamic capability in the globalization of the multinational business enterprise (MBE): Case studies of AB Volvo and IKEA', *International Business Review*, vol. 26, no. 1, pp. 57–70.

Volberda, H.W. and Lewin, A.Y. (2003), 'Guest editors' introduction: Co-evolutionary dynamics within and between firms: From evolution to co-evolution, *Journal of Management Studies*, vol. 40, no. 8, pp. 2111–2136.

Wallace, H., Pollack, M.A. and Young, A.R. (2010), *Policy-making in the European Union*, 6th edn, Oxford; New York, Oxford University Press.

Weick, K.E. (1979), *The Social Psychology of Organizing*, 2nd edn, Reading, MA, Addison-Wesley.

Welch, C., Nummela, N. and Liesch, P. (2016), 'The internationalization process model revisited: An agenda for future research', *Management International Review*, vol. 56, pp. 783–804.

Wernerfelt, B. (2013), 'Small forces and large firms: Foundations of the RBV', *Strategic Management Journal*, vol. 34, no. 6, pp. 635–643.

Wilber, K. (2000), *Sex, Ecology, Spirituality: The spirit of evolution*, 2nd edn, Boston, MA; London, Shambhala.

Wilber, K. (2006), *Integral Spirituality: A startling new role for religion in the modern and postmodern world*, Boston, MA, Integral Books.

Yarbrough, B.V. and Yarbrough, R.M. (1992), *Cooperation and Governance in International Trade: The strategic organizational approach*. Princeton, NJ, Princeton University Press.

6

THE INSTITUTIONAL HETEROGENEITY OF EUROPE AS A REGIONAL MARKET

Kalle Pajunen

Introduction

Europe, and in particular the European Union, has integrated both politically and economically over recent decades (see Butt-Philip, Chapter 14 in this volume). However, it remains a continent consisting of 50 sovereign states with their distinct institutional characteristics. This institutional heterogeneity can impose major challenges for firms entering or operating in different European locations (cf. Jain et al. 2016; Kim and Aguilera 2016). Indeed, researchers have demonstrated that, in general, the performance of international firms is dependent on the surrounding institutional conditions and on their ability to adapt to different locations (e.g. Christmann et al. 1999; Makino et al. 2004; Chan et al. 2008). In this chapter, I discuss the institutional heterogeneity of Europe as a market area by building on complementary streams of literature on the subject. In so doing, I shall specify a related set of challenges for firms' international activity in Europe.

In addition to drawing on the growing body of research in the field of international business (e.g. Rugman and Verbeke 2004; Jackson and Deeg 2008; Peng et al. 2008; Schneider et al. 2010; Holmes et al. 2013; Kolk et al. 2014), I build on research in the fields of organisational sociology, economics and political science. It is beyond the scope of a single review to capture the developments in these various bodies of literature, which display multiple theoretical angles and analytical approaches. However, the commonly agreed argument is that business organisations are always embedded within institutional contexts that both constrain and enable their activities. According to North (1990), for example, the formal and informal rules of the institutional environment provide a fundamental incentive structure for economic actors. Neo-institutional research in organisation theory, for its part, has shown that at the organisation level, the institutional environment can create specific pressures of legitimacy as well as related processes towards isomorphic behaviour as firms try to ensure their survival by aligning themselves with the environment (e.g. DiMaggio and Powell 1991; Scott 2008). However, research on institutional entrepreneurship (e.g. Battilana et al. 2009), institutional work (e.g. Lawrence et al. 2009), and institutional logics (e.g. Thornton et al. 2012) has indicated that organisations and individual actors do also have the capacity to induce changes to the prevailing institutional settings (cf. Lamberg and Pajunen 2010).

This chapter is constructed as follows. First of all, because the institutional infrastructure of a country may have considerable influence on the activities and performance of firms, I discuss how research on comparative institutional analysis (cf. Ahmadjian 2016; Morgan et al. 2010) has approached this topic, and how it has attempted to capture the socio-political heterogeneity of European countries. Second, I shall consider the features and implications of this heterogeneity from an organisational point of view, seeking to provide a more fine-grained understanding of how firms may evaluate appropriate locations for their activities within Europe. Third, I consider what the differences in European locations imply for multinational firms, not only in terms of maximising profits, but also in their endeavours to fulfil the role of a good citizen in a given host country. Finally, I outline questions for future research.

The institutional diversity of European locations

Research on comparative institutional analysis (e.g. Ahmadjian 2016; Morgan et al. 2010) has explicitly addressed the institutional complexity of nation states. This field of research also includes the impactful discussions on *Varieties of Capitalism* (Hall and Soskice 2001) and *National Business Systems* (Whitley 1999). Altogether, these accounts provide an appropriate starting point for considering the particularities and commonalities of Europe, with its patchwork of nation states, as a market area.

The Varieties of Capitalism (VoC) approach of Hall and Soskice (2001) emphasises that the performance of firms is dependent on how they engage with other actors in a given political economy. The central questions involve how firms are able to raise finance, how wages and working conditions are regulated, how to ensure the necessary skills of employees, how to secure access to inter-firm inputs and technology, how market competition regarding the product is regulated, and how interfirm cooperation is arranged. On the basis of notable variations in these (institutional) domains of economic activity, two basic types of capitalist economies have been proposed, namely the *liberal market economy* (LME) and the *coordinated market economy* (CME). The core difference between these systems involves the dominant mechanism of *coordination*. In the case of LMEs, such coordination is based on market mechanisms, whereas in the case of CMEs, the coordination is based on more strategic interactions with stakeholders.

The archetype of the LME is the United States, but European countries such as the United Kingdom and Ireland are also typically considered to be examples of LMEs (Hall and Gingerich 2009). According to Hall and Soskice (2001), in LME countries, the shareholding of large firms is dispersed, and access to external financing depends heavily on measurable criteria such as stock valuation models. Due to relatively weak levels of unionisation and employment protection, the labour markets in LMEs are fluid, and wage setting occurs between employers and workers without strong external regulative coordination. This, in turn, creates incentives for workers to acquire general and transferable skills.

Although it is possible to identify LMEs in Europe, the continent has more examples of CMEs (for example the Nordic countries, Belgium, the Netherlands, Switzerland), with Germany providing an archetypal case (Hall and Gingerich 2009). In these European CMEs, the ownership of large firms is more heavily controlled by networks of cross-shareholding, with the employer and industry associations having a pivotal role in the interfirm cooperation and governance structures of the nation as a whole. The role of the employer associations is strong in terms of coordinating wage setting and defining standards for industry-specific skills. These institutional characteristics require relatively stable interaction between different spheres of the economy and society, and may also promote the emergence of consensual decision making.

The VoC approach also includes the explicit statement that institutional conditions are often complementary, meaning that the enhancement of one institutional condition assists the provision of another. This complementarity can be one reason behind the greater extent of capitalistic models in Europe. In line with this, Whitley (1999) focused on dominant patterns of economic organisation and control. He proposed the existence of six different types of national business systems (fragmented, coordinated industrial district, compartmentalised, state organised, collaborative, highly coordinated). Empirical validation for this notion was provided by Hotho (2014), who showed that while these distinct business systems could be regarded as ideal types, examples closely approximating to them can be found in Europe. In addition to the above, open economies in Northern Europe, such as those of Denmark, Sweden and Finland, seem to constitute a distinct Nordic business system (Amable 2003; Hotho 2014).

While the Nordic countries have not been immune to the financialisation and competitive pressures that require a relatively flexible labour force, this increasing flexibility has been at least partly complemented by the high skills of employees, the high level of social protection, and at least a moderate level of employment protection. It appears that the distinct institutional environments in Nordic countries may still be supportive of knowledge-intensive business activities, even if transformations within these countries have brought them closer to the market-based model.

Currently, the CME model in continental Europe appears to be under pressure. In line with this, the importance of banks in the German financial system has weakened, and some elements of the shareholder-value model have strengthened relative to the previously dominant stakeholder orientation. This development can be seen as making Germany internally more heterogeneous (Jackson and Sorge 2012). However, since the financial crisis of 2008, there have been political tendencies working in favour of more regulated forms of capitalism. These may support the renewal of some elements that are typical of CMEs in continental Europe.

Currently, despite the fact that most European nation states have continued to move in the direction of a liberal, market-based system, one can see opposing tendencies involving protectionist and nationalistic voices. These have taken the form of, in particular, strong public criticism of the European Union (as seen in the Brexit referendum in the United Kingdom), resistance towards the Transatlantic Trade and Investment Partnership and the increasing popularity of populist and even extreme right-wing parties throughout Europe. These may have the potential to act as a brake on market liberalisation. Indeed, from the economic point of view, a likely consequence of Brexit is that the amount of free trade in Europe will diminish, with a potentially negative effect on economic growth. From a political point of view, the claims presented by nationalistic populists may also push governmental decision makers to reconsider the appropriate form of capitalism in their respective countries.

How is the diversity of European locations important to firms and managers?

The institutional logics of interpretation

To gain a deeper understanding of what the heterogeneity of European locations means for specific types of economic activity, one must consider the issue from the organisational and managerial point of view. The complexity of the institutional environment creates challenges for firms even in their home country contexts. However, understanding how shared norms and values constrain or enable organisational activities is critical when the firm enters new host countries (cf. Kim and Aguilera 2016; Marano et al. 2016; see also Cordeiro, Chapter 5 in this volume). Researchers focused on neo-institutional organisation theory have paid notable attention to consider this issue in general.

A core concept in this discussion has been that of institutional logics. Thornton and Ocasio (1999, p. 804) have defined these as 'the socially constructed, historical patterns of material practices, assumptions, values, beliefs and rules by which individuals produce and reproduce their material subsistence, organize time and space, and provide meaning to their social reality'. Thus, by definition, if the managers of firms do not have any knowledge of the prevailing institutional logics, they can be largely adrift regarding how to interpret matters and behave in contextually bounded social situations. This may of course have critical influence on the success of their international operations.

With increasing European integration, there could exist certain institutional logics that are shared throughout the entire European market area (McGuire et al. 2012; Butt-Philip Chapter 14 in this volume). However, the core features of institutional logics are that they are historically contingent, and that they operate at multiple levels of analysis (Thornton et al. 2012). This means that generally speaking, logics are culturally, politically and cognitively embedded, and relatively slow to change. A firm that has always been embedded in a particular institutional context may take the prevailing institutional logics for granted, fitting its organisational routines and practices round those logics of the home country. As a result, if this firm tries to internationalise, it will almost inevitably face a host location that possesses its own, historically contingent, cultural and cognitive rules for social interaction. This new location may not provide a perfect fit with organisational routines and practices that have been unquestioningly reproduced in the home location of the firm. Similarly, if the founders of Born Global or Born-European (Suder 2011) firms do not have prior experience of the country in which they start their operations, they are likely to face the same situation, at least to some extent.

Recent accounts of institutional complexity (e.g. Greenwood et al. 2011) have emphasised that firms may encounter heterogeneity regarding institutional logics of action, even within a single location; and that this heterogeneity, while historically contingent, may not be stable over time. Thus, when one takes into account the institutional variety that exists in Europe, one can anticipate that even within the borders of a single nation state, the management of institutional complexity may pose a real challenge for multinational and internationalising firms.

Industry-level analyses of institutional conditions

For multinational firms, it is crucial to find an appropriate location for business activities. Correspondingly, it is important for nation states to attract investment from foreign firms. The institutional infrastructures of countries may have an important role in such investment decisions. Pajunen (2008) has shown the ability to attract foreign direct investment (FDI) does not depend on a single institutional factor, but rather on specific combinations of institutional conditions. Furthermore, even among a relatively homogeneous set of European countries, there can be several paths to the same outcome. For example, if we consider countries located in Central and Eastern Europe, a country may improve its FDI attractiveness relative to its peers by ensuring political rights and civil liberties, political stability and at least one of the following conditions: favourable taxation, a fair and independent judicial system and property rights. Political instability is a strong deterrent to FDI. Moreover, among the nation states of Europe, corruption – combined with either inflexible labour regulation or an unfavourable taxation system – creates institutional conditions that make a country unattractive for FDI inflows.

Firms also need to understand how the institutional conditions of political economies specifically relate to the competitive forces prevailing in their industry. This can impel them to take a pragmatic, firm-based approach in seeking out an appropriate location for their business activities. Usually, this begins by evaluating the conditions within a country that may be critical for the industry in which the firm operates. A study by Pajunen and Airo (2013) sheds some light on this issue. The researchers focused on the location-specific conditions for a successful generic medicines industry within European countries. They found that even if the drivers of a firm's performance are always various, the generic medicine industry provides an example of an industry in which firm performance is typically explained by country-specific features. Here, one must bear in mind that generic medicine, by definition, is produced without patent protection (because the original patent has expired). This means that the type of regulative system in a given country is likely to have a fundamental effect on the success of the industry. The primary issue in this case is whether the country has established a reference price system. The industry may also benefit from an institutional environment that supports small-scale improvements in the production processes. In fact, this condition appears to be a typical feature in CMEs overall (Hall and Soskice 2001). Furthermore, the level of public healthcare expenditure and the demographics of the population constitute important factors influencing the demand for generic medicines. Altogether, European countries are far from homogeneous regarding all these conditions.

In line with the view that institutional conditions are often complementary, no single location-specific condition on its own is necessary for the presence or absence of a high-performance generic medicine industry (Pajunen and Airo 2013). Finding a suitable country for the industry thus requires an examination of the interdependent and complementary effects of the various institutional conditions. This means, first of all, that the causal relationships between country-specific conditions and industry performance can be complex. Secondly, there can be different configurations of conditions that lead to the same outcome.

The findings of Pajunen and Airo (2013) indicate that there are two sufficient configurations of conditions supporting the existence of a high-performance industry. First of all, a favourable environment for the generic medicine industry includes a country location with CME characteristics, a high level of public healthcare expenditure and price regulation via a reference price system. The Nordic countries, such as Denmark and Iceland, are prime examples of this type of location. As an alternative path, a clearly different set of Southern European countries provides an advantageous environment for this industry. The conditions in this case comprise a CME, a price reference system, a high proportion of elderly people and a relatively low national income. Thus, the political economy of CMEs and the regulative environment manifested as a price reference system are important country-specific conditions that in part explain the success of a generic medicine industry. Nevertheless, these are not, as separate conditions, sufficient to guarantee the success of the firms.

Overall, earlier accounts on comparative institutional analysis have provided theoretical understanding of how country-related conditions enable or restrict business activities, and have also offered more practical, industry-related implications concerning the institutional conditions that matter for specific types of business. This kind of analysis is important for a multinational company that is evaluating appropriate country locations for its operations, whether these are related to innovative products and services or to bulk products. Altogether, while increasing EU integration has worked to harmonise institutional structures among the member countries, it is likely that the attractiveness and market potential of different European locations varies with the industry in question.

Societal norms and values from an ethical point of view

Beyond consideration of the market potential provided by different European locations, firms need to consider the *societal legitimacy* of their activities. Basically, this is related to how far firms take note of ethical and responsibility-related issues reflecting societal norms and values. While one might assume that Europe is a relatively homogeneous area in terms of practices related to *corporate social responsibility* (CSR), previous research has indicated that this may not be the case (Aguilera et al. 2007; Matten and Moon 2008). In fact, according to a study by Gjølberg (2009), there are striking differences between 16 European nations regarding the CSR activity of the companies they host.

Using a CSR index, Gjølberg (2009) found that relative to the size of the economy, countries such as Switzerland, Norway, Finland, Sweden and Denmark are the most over-represented in terms of CSR; in contrast, Greece, Italy, and Ireland are strongly under-represented in this dimension. As a point of comparison, the USA scores negatively in all the different variations of the index. This finding is interesting, given that the USA is often seen as the originator of CSR practices. One explanation for this result relates to the fact that the indicators within the index do not include philanthropy (Gjølberg, 2009), which has been a traditional manifestation of CSR in the USA.

In considering the implications of heterogeneity in CSR, it is crucial to understand that CSR takes on different meanings in different institutional environments (Aguilera et al. 2007; Matten and Moon 2008; Brammer et al. 2012). The common definitions of CSR emphasise the centrality of voluntary activity that 'further[s] some social good, beyond the interests of the firm and that which is required by law' (McWilliams and Siegel 2001, p. 117). Indeed, seeing CSR as something that goes beyond legal requirements allows different types of activities to be included under the label of CSR in different institutional settings (Brammer et al. 2012). Matten and Moon (2008) recognise this issue. Building on notions of national business systems and the VoC approach, they argue that there are two distinct manifestations of CSR, which can be termed *explicit* and *implicit*.

Explicit CSR encompasses openly-declared voluntary programmes and strategies on the part of corporations. Activities in this domain, relying on corporate discretion, can be driven by instrumental, relational, and moral motivations (Aguilera et al. 2007). They typically combine social and business interests. Sometimes explicit and instrumentally motivated CSR can be fully subjugated to the strategic goals of the corporation. Implicit CSR, for its part, refers to the ways in which corporations are embedded in the institutional environment of the society in question. Basically, the values, norms and rules of society (both informal and formal) impose mandatory and customary requirements for companies regarding how far they should consider the claims of different stakeholders in a collective manner, rather than in relation purely to the firm (Matten and Moon 2008). Seen in this light, the role of corporations is to follow and adapt to the institutionally established practices of legitimate and responsible business activity.

Explicit and implicit CSR also lead to different forms of linguistic usage related to CSR. According to Matten and Moon (2008), firms practising explicit CSR use the language of CSR in stakeholder communication. However, this is not typical in the case of firms practising implicit CSR. Despite this, the institutional embeddedness of implicit CSR does not indicate that corporations are less active in their responsibility-related behaviour. In fact, as shown by Gjølberg (2009), it is likely that the opposite is the case.

Regarding the basic types of capitalistic economies in Europe, the findings of Jackson and Apostolakou (2010) suggest that companies within LME countries follow explicit CSR practices as a substitute for formal institutions. In CMEs, for their part, the institutionalised and societally regulated practices related to the social responsibilities of companies do not seem to require the same kind of explicit CSR activity. The findings of Kang and Moon (2012) also show that in LMEs, the manifestations of CSR are predominantly competitive, complementing shareholder-value thinking.

On the basis of the studies mentioned above, I would argue that in doing business in different locations in Europe, companies need to consider their views on what is legitimate and ethically acceptable corporate behaviour, relative to the institutional frameworks of the countries in which they operate. This can be a particularly important issue if a firm is extending its operations from one type of national business system to another. Here, one must also bear in mind that the heterogeneity of European institutional environments ranges beyond the 'ideal' types of political economy discussed above. Moreover, there are likely to be industry-specific concerns related to the appropriate forms of CSR to be followed (Jackson and Apostolakou 2010). Because of this, we can assume that the variety of ethical standards across (and within) country contexts will bring considerations of appropriate CSR practices strongly to the fore, wherever the firm has business activities (Mantere et al. 2009). This is underlined by recent empirical research indicating that multinational corporations (MNCs) are likely to encounter a notable level of institutional complexity related to CSR practices in different countries (Marano and Kostova 2016).

Altogether, there can also be possible downsides in the institutional awareness of MNCs. In particular, it can lead to a situation identified by Surroca et al. (2013), in which firms use internationalisation as an instrument to transfer their socially irresponsible practices to the locations of their subsidiaries, in order to 'window-dress' their behaviours within their headquarter countries. Europe cannot be seen immune to this issue.

Conclusion

The development of the European Union has to a large extent unified economic and political rules in Europe for the member states. Thus, from the perspective of non-European – and even European firms – the continent exemplifies several attributes of a regional market. In this chapter, however, I suggest that Europe is still institutionally heterogeneous. This variety among nation states generates both notable opportunities and challenges for multinational and internationalising firms. Indeed, it is important to be aware that the 'psychic distance paradox' suggested by O'Grady and Lane (1996) seems to be valid also from a pan-European point of view. One could go so far as to say that institutional heterogeneity is a core idiosyncrasy of Europe as a regional market area.

Although multidisciplinary literature regarding this topic has advanced during recent years, the discussion in this chapter indicates a clear need for continuing research. In particular, I consider that there is a need for a better understanding of the multi-level effects and relationship dynamics between different socio-political systems and interpretation systems at firm level. I shall conclude by considering some questions related to these issues.

First of all, more empirical research is needed on how the different forms of capitalism and national business systems in Europe influence actual corporate behaviour. For example, we may consider that in Germany or in Nordic countries, the relatively strong heritage of stakeholder involvement, the central role of bank-based financing, and the underlying welfare ideology have created systemic institutional logics supporting long-term development and investment activity on the part of firms. This course has been followed as an alternative to corporate strategies for the maximisation of short-term earnings and shareholder value – aspects that are emphasised in typical liberal market economies (Aspara et al. 2014). However, we do not have much knowledge (Kolk et al. 2014) of whether and to what extent current market liberalisation and financialisation developments within the European economies may have actually changed the institutional logics influencing managerial behaviour.

On a related topic, while our understanding of institutional logics has accumulated during recent years, we do not know much about how firms are able to modify attention structures and cognitive frames. This is especially the case when firms enter foreign locations and face local actors that follow certain logics of behaviour based on certain cultural and material practices of that country. It would be reasonable to assume that individuals and organisations in new host locations will tend to act and to give meaning to their social reality primarily on the basis of the logics learned in their home country. In line with this, previous research has underlined the importance of home country institutions in the location choices made by firms (e.g. Kolk et al. 2014). Here one can point to an example providing anecdotal evidence: the stock of investments from Sweden to (institutionally close) Finland is more than five times higher than the stock of investments from Sweden to France, even though the French economy is ten times larger than the economy of Finland.

At the same time, at the firm level, one can also predict that those firms that have successfully managed institutional complexity in their home locations will be at an advantage in terms of learning about and adapting to the institutional logics prevailing in foreign locations. Thus, further research is needed on the cognitive capabilities of managers in terms of dealing with institutional complexity. I consider that examination of this issue could also advance the capabilities perspective on internationalisation (see e.g. Sapienza et al. 2006).

Furthermore, research at the firm level could examine how firms have localised their CSR and ethical practices in Europe, and how the measures taken may have influenced their legitimacy in different countries, and among their customers. Here, it would be of interest to examine how the variety of implicit and explicit CSR practices in Europe has created cognitive challenges for the managers of multinational firms. Studies in this domain would also consider how managers orchestrate their responsibility activities, and how they seek to communicate with different stakeholders concerning these activities.

References

Aguilera, R.V., Rupp, D.E., Williams, C.A. and Ganapathi, J. (2007), 'Putting the S back in corporate social responsibility: A multilevel theory of social change in organizations', *Academy of Management Review*, vol. 32, no. 3, pp. 836–863.

Ahmadjian, C.L. (2016), 'Comparative institutional analysis and institutional complexity', *Journal of Management Studies*, vol. 53, no. 1, pp. 12–27.

Amable, B. (2003), *The Diversity of Modern Capitalism*, Oxford, Oxford University Press.

Aspara, J., Pajunen, K., Tikkanen, H. and Tainio, R. (2014), 'Explaining corporate short-termism: Self-reinforcing processes and biases among investors, the media and corporate managers', *Socio-Economic Review*, vol. 12, no. 4, pp. 667–693.

Battilana, J., Leca, B. and Boxenbaum, E. (2009), 'How actors change institutions: Towards a theory of institutional entrepreneurship', *Academy of Management Annals*, vol. 3, pp. 65–107.

Brammer, S., Jackson, G. and Matten, D. (2012), 'Corporate social responsibility and institutional theory: New perspectives on private governance', *Socio-Economic Review*, vol. 10, no. 1, pp. 3–28.

Chan, C.M., Isobe, T. and Makino, S. (2008), 'Which country matters? Institutional development and foreign affiliate performance', *Strategic Management Journal*, vol. 29, pp. 1179–1205.

Christmann, P., Day, D. and Yip, G.S. (1999), 'The relative influence of country conditions, industry structure, and business strategy on multinational corporation subsidiary performance', *Journal of International Management,* vol. 5, pp. 241–265.

DiMaggio, P.J. and Powell, W.W. (eds) (1991), *The New Institutionalism in Organizational Analysis*, Chicago, University of Chicago Press.

Gjølberg, M. (2009), 'Measuring the immeasurable? Constructing an index of CSR practices and CSR performance in 20 countries', *Scandinavian Journal of Management*, vol. 25, no. 1, pp. 10–22.

Greenwood, R., Raynard, M., Kodeih, F., Micelotta, E.R. and Lounsbury, M. (2011), 'Institutional complexity and organizational responses', *Academy of Management Annals*, vol. 5, pp. 317–371.

Hall, P.A. and Gingerich, D.W. (2009), 'Varieties of capitalism and institutional complementarities in the political economy: An empirical analysis', *British Journal of Political Science*, vol. 39, no. 3, pp. 449–482.

Hall, P.A. and Soskice, D. (2001), 'An introduction to Varieties of Capitalism', in P.A. Hall and D. Soskice (eds), *Varieties of Capitalism: The institutional foundations of comparative advantage*, Oxford, Oxford University Press, pp. 1–70.

Holmes, R.M., Miller, T., Hitt, M.A. and Salmador, M.P. (2013), 'The interrelationships among informal institutions, formal institutions, and inward foreign direct investment', *Journal of Management*, vol. 39, pp. 531–566.

Hotho, J.J. (2014), 'From typology to taxonomy: A configurational analysis of national business systems and their explanatory power', *Organization Studies*, vol. 35, no. 5, pp. 671–702.

Jackson, G. and Apostolakou, A. (2010), 'Corporate social responsibility in Western Europe: An institutional mirror or substitute?', *Journal of Business Ethics*, vol. 94, pp. 371–394.

Jackson, G. and Deeg, R. (2008), 'Comparing capitalisms: Understanding institutional diversity and its implications for international business', *Journal of International Business Studies*, vol. 39, no. 4, pp. 540–561.

Jackson, G. and Sorge, A. (2012), 'The trajectory of institutional change in Germany, 1979–2009', *Journal of European Public Policy*, vol. 19, no. 8, pp. 1146–1167.

Jain, N.K., Kothari, T. and Kumar, V. (2016), 'Location choice research: Proposing new agenda', *Management International Review*, vol. 56, no. 3, pp. 303–324.

Kang, K. and Moon, J. (2012), 'Institutional complementarity between corporate governance and Corporate Social Responsibility: A comparative institutional analysis of three capitalisms', *Socio-Economic Review*, vol. 10, pp. 85–108.

Kim, J.U. and Aguilera, R.V. (2016), 'Foreign location choice: Review and extensions', *International Journal of Management Reviews*, vol. 18, pp. 133–159.

Kolk, A., Lindeque, J. and Buuse, D. (2014), 'Regionalization strategies of European Union electric utilities', *British Journal of Management*, vol. 25, no. S1, S77–S99.

Lamberg, J.A. and Pajunen, K. (2010), 'Agency, institutional change and continuity: The case of the Finnish Civil War', *Journal of Management Studies*, vol. 47, no. 5, pp. 814–836.

Lawrence, T.B., Suddaby, R. and Leca, B. (2009), *Institutional Work: Actors and Agency in Institutional Studies of Organizations*, Cambridge, Cambridge University Press.

Makino, S., Isobe, T. and Chan, C.M. (2004), 'Does country matter?' *Strategic Management Journal*, vol. 25, pp. 1027–1043.

Mantere, S., Pajunen, K. and Lamberg, J.A. (2009), 'Vices and virtues of corporate political activity: The challenge of international business', *Business and Society*, vol. 48, no. 1, pp. 105–132.

Marano, V. and Kostova, T. (2016), 'Unpacking the institutional complexity in adoption of CSR practices in multinational enterprises', *Journal of Management Studies*, vol. 53, no. 1, pp. 28–54.

Marano, V., Arregle, J.L., Hitt, M.A., Spadafora, E. and van Essen, M. (2016), 'Home country institutions and the internationalization-performance relationship: A meta-analytic review', *Journal of Management*, vol. 42, no. 5, pp. 1075–1110.

Matten, D.A. and Moon J. (2008), 'Implicit and explicit CSR, a conceptual framework for understanding of corporate social responsibility', *Academy of Management Review*, vol. 33, no. 2, pp. 404–424.

McGuire, S., Lindeque, J. and Suder, G. (2012), 'Learning and lobbying: Emerging market firms and corporate political activity in Europe', *European Journal of International Management*, vol. 6, no. 3, pp. 342–362.

McWilliams, A. and Siegel, D. (2001), 'Corporate social responsibility: A theory of the firm perspective', *Academy of Management Review*, vol. 26, no. 1, pp. 117–127.

Morgan, G., Campbell, J.L., Crouch, C., Pedersen, O.K. and Whitley, R. (2010), 'Introduction', in G. Morgan, J.L. Campbell, C. Crouch, O.K. Pedersen and R. Whitley (eds), *The Oxford Handbook of Comparative Institutional Analysis*, New York, Oxford University Press, pp. 1–14.

North, D.C. (1990), *Institutions, Institutional Change and Economic Performance*, New York, Cambridge University Press.

O'Grady, S. and Lane, H.W. (1996), 'The psychic distance paradox', *Journal of International Business Studies*, vol. 27, no. 2, pp. 309–333.

Pajunen, K. (2008), 'Institutions and inflows of foreign direct investment: A fuzzy-set analysis', *Journal of International Business Studies,* vol. 39, no. 4, pp. 652–669.

Pajunen, K. and Airo, V. (2013), 'Country-specificity and industry performance: A configurational analysis of the European generic medicines industry', *Research in the Sociology of Organizations,* vol. 38, pp. 255–278.

Peng, M.W., Wang, D.Y.L. and Jiang, Y. (2008), 'An institution-based view of international business strategy: A focus on emerging economies', *Journal of International Business Studies,* vol. 39, pp. 920–936.

Rugman, A.M. and Verbeke, A. (2004), 'A perspective on regional and global strategies of multinational enterprises', *Journal of International Business Studies*, vol. 35, no. 1, pp. 3–18.

Sapienza, H.J., Autio, E., George, G. and Zahra, S.A. (2006), 'A capabilities perspective on the effects of early internationalization on firm survival and growth', *Academy of Management Review*, vol. 31, no. 4, pp. 914–933.

Schneider, M.R., Schulze-Bentrop, C. and Paunescu, M. (2010), 'Mapping the institutional capital of high-tech firms: A fuzzy-set analysis of capitalist variety and export performance', *Journal of International Business Studies,* vol. 41, pp. 246–266.

Scott, W.R. (2008), *Institutions and Organizations*, London, Sage.

Suder, G. (2011), *Doing Business in Europe*, 2nd edn, London, Sage.

Surroca, J., Tribó, J.A. and Zahra, S.A. (2013), 'Stakeholder pressure on MNEs and the transfer of socially irresponsible practices to subsidiaries', *Academy of Management Journal*, vol. 56, no. 2, pp. 549–572.

Thornton, P.H. and Ocasio, W. (1999), 'Institutional logics and the historical contingency of power in organizations: Executive succession in the higher education publishing industry, 1958–1990', *American Journal of Sociology*, vol. 105, no. 3, pp. 801–843.

Thornton, P.H., Ocasio, W. and Lounsbury, M. (2012), *The Institutional Logics Perspective: A New Approach to Culture, Structure, and Process*, Oxford, Oxford University Press.

Whitley, R. (1999), *Divergent Capitalisms: The Social Structuring and Change of Business Systems*, Oxford, Oxford University Press.

7

EUROPEAN SMEs AND THE BORN GLOBAL CONCEPT

Øystein Moen and Alex Rialp-Criado

Introduction

Newly established firms with early involvement in international markets have received considerable attention during the past 25 years. These firms have been labelled 'Born Globals' (Rennie 1993), 'International New Ventures' (McDougall et al. 1994), 'Instant Internationals' (Preece et al. 1999) or 'Global Start-ups' (Jolly et al. 1992), while the research stream has often been defined as International Entrepreneurship (McDougall and Oviatt 2000; Peiris et al. 2012). We will use the term 'Born Global', referring to firms with significant international sales within a short time of inception.

Originating both from Europe and outside Europe, we now have a number of papers focusing on Born Global firms. In addition, there have been several literature reviews, for example by Rialp et al. (2005), Aspelund et al. (2007), Jones et al. (2011) and Kiss et al. (2012).

The size of the home market, geographical and cultural distance to export markets as well as the industrial context and environment in which a firm is established may all be factors contributing to differences between Born Global firms. Knight et al. (2004) found US Born Globals to be more than three times larger than Danish Born Globals in terms of both annual turnover and number of employees. Andersson et al. (2015) suggested that the role of the government is more important for Chinese Born Globals than it is for Born Globals established in Western countries. While some studies, for example in Norway (Moen 2002), questioned the concept of internationalisation as a gradual learning process, Zou and Ghauri (2010) presented case studies of high-tech new ventures from China and identified gradual learning and expansion processes. Bjørgum et al. (2013) showed that in the emerging wave and tidal energy industry, firms selected location and moved activities between countries in their early development phase in order to maximise resource access.

All these elements indicate that location may be important for Born Global firms. Few studies have compared Born Global firms based on the country in which they are established, and there are hardly any previous studies comparing Born Globals established in Europe with Born Globals from other parts of the world. We will focus on four distinct issues highly relevant to our understanding of Born Global firms within a European business context:

(a) How common are Born Global firms in Europe?
(b) Why are Born Global firms important?

(c) What are the most important characteristics and marketing strategies of European Born Global firms?

(d) Are European Born Globals different from Born Globals from other parts of the world?

We will identify some of the most relevant and important empirical studies focusing on European Born Global firms and present the key results from these studies with regard to characteristics, marketing strategies and performance.

How common are Born Global firms in Europe?

Moen and Servais (2002) based their study on samples of exporting firms with less than 250 employees from Norway, Denmark and France. They found that 'In Norway, France, and Denmark, 38.8%, 34.3%, and 30.7% of the exporting firms commenced their export activities within two years of establishment. This means that there are large numbers of newly established exporting firms' (Moen and Servais, p. 69). They further concluded that 75% of these firms had an export share higher than 25%. If a Born Global firm is defined as starting with export within two years from establishment and having more than 25% export share, then about 35% of small- and medium-sized exporting firms in these three countries may be defined as Born Globals. Moen (2002) used data from Norway and France, adding also a criterion related to year of establishment (i.e. after 1990). He found that 52.2% and 63.7% of exporting firms in Norway and France, respectively, were Born Globals.

Knight et al. (2004) introduced a related criterion in addition to export share (more than 25%) and exporting within two years from establishment, where the firms should have been established sometime during the past 20 years. Based on this, they described a large Danish survey with 57% Born Globals.

In Spain, Rialp and Rialp (2007) analysed a large sample (n=1102) of exporting manufacturing firms. They defined Born Global firms as having started with export within two years of establishment and having more than the sample average of approximately 40% export share. In their data, almost 23% of the firms were Born Globals. Their results also identified an increasing number of Born Global firms.

In Finland, Kuivalainen et al. (2007) selected exporting firms with more than 50 employees. Out of the 783 firms included in the final sample, 185 had started exporting within three years with more than 25% export share, equalling 23.6% Born Globals according to this slightly different definition. Jantunen et al. (2008) also focused on Finland and identified 12.5% Born Globals based on similar criteria as Kuivalainen et al. (2007).

Choquette et al. (2016) used public register data from all Danish manufacturing firms established between 1994 and 2008. In this large sample (n=23,201), Born Globals (defined as those exporting within three years from birth, with more than 25% export share) represented 5% of the total sample. Accordingly, of the 24% of firms with export involvement, Born Globals represented 20.8%. Using data (n=35,184) from the National Bank of Belgium, Sleuwaegen and Onkelinx (2014) defined global start-ups as those exporting within five years of establishment to at least five countries and two regions (at least one outside Europe). In this large dataset, 21% of exporting firms were identified as global start-ups.

Based on these results, it appears that the percentage of Born Globals in a regular sample of exporting firms is between 12.5 and 25.0%; but if we only consider firms established later (in the past 20 years/after 1990), the percentage found is 20.8–63.7%. Rialp and Rialp (2007) and more recently Choquette et al. (2016) found Born Globals in all manufacturing sectors.

Preece et al. (1999) described an increasing number of Born Global firms in Canada. However, Choquette et al. (2016) did not find increasing percentages from 1994 to 2008 in Denmark, and it is possible that the percentage of Born Global firms is not increasing further in small, open economies.

Differences in selection criteria and samples appear to contribute to variation in the percentages of Born Globals observed, but it seems reasonable to conclude that Born Global firms make up a small fraction of all established firms, but a significant share of newly established exporting firms. They are present both in nations with limited domestic markets and also, as described by Cavusgil and Knight (2015), in large economies such as the USA and China.

Why are Born Global firms important?

Young firms are considered important in general. The Kauffman Foundation reported that about two-thirds of new jobs in the USA come from young firms (Kane 2010). Cavusgil and Knight (2015) found that empirical evidence from around the world suggests that Born Global firms 'account for a substantial portion of export growth' (p. 4).

In a report from the European Union entitled: '*Born Global: The potential of job creation in new international business*' (Eurofound 2012), the importance of Born Global firms for economic development and employment is widely discussed, with strong attention on the need for policy development. The OECD (2013) further described how Born Global firms were important in the recovery from the 2007/2008 financial crisis; a similar conclusion was reported from Israel by Almor (2011). Analysing public register data in Denmark, Choquette et al. (2016, p. 458) concluded that Born Globals '[e]xhibit superior performance in terms of turnover levels, employment levels and market reach compared to all other start-ups'.

It is known that a limited number of firms represent most of the growth potential in many economies; this is supported by the meta-analysis by Henrekson and Johansson (2010). It is expected that many of the firms with the highest growth potential will be Born Globals. The perceived growth potential is also the most important reason for researchers, policymakers and investors focusing on these firms.

Selection of important empirical studies focusing on European Born Global firms

In this part, we first identify important and relevant papers published in international journals. Google Scholar, SCOPUS and ISI Web of Science were used as search engines. We used the terms Born Global/Born Globals/International New Venture/International New Ventures and International Entrepreneurship and manually checked the results for empirical studies based on European samples (n>30), published in journals and using statistical analysis. First, we limited the search to studies with more than 100 citations; this resulted in only 11 papers. Second, we searched further for relevant studies, with particular attention to geographical areas not well covered by the first 11 papers. We added another seven papers based on a subjective evaluation of relevance, and these total of 18 papers represent the starting point of our presentation of current empirically based knowledge on Born Global firms in Europe.

Table 7.1 provides an overview of the selected papers. The samples originated from Denmark (4), Norway (3), Finland (3), Spain (3), Germany (2), the UK (2) as well as Italy, Belgium and France. Two studies were developed building on public registered data (Sleuwaegen and Onkelinx 2014; Choquette et al. 2016) while the others collected data via surveys of managers.

Table *7.1* Selected Europe-based empirical studies of Born Global firms

Authors	Year	N*	Sample data from	Authors from
Moen and Servais	2002	677	Norway (335), Denmark (272), France (70)	Norway, Denmark
Moen	2002	405	Norway (335), France (70)	Norway
Knight, Madsen and Servais	2004	292	USA (186), Denmark (106)	USA, Denmark
Aspelund and Moen	2006	335	Norway	Norway
Madsen, Rasmussen and Servais	2006	272	Denmark	Denmark
Luostarinen and Gabrielson	2006	89	Finland	Finland
Rialp and Rialp	2007	1,102	Spain	Spain
Kuivalainen, Sundqvist and Servais	2007	185	Finland	Finland, Denmark
Acedo and Jones	2007	216	Spain	Spain, UK
Mudambi and Zahra	2007	275	UK	USA, UK
Jantunen, Nummela, Puumalainen and Saarenketo	2008	299	Finland	Finland
Sommer and Haug	2011	116	Germany	Germany
Dimitratos, Voudouris, Plakoyiannaki and Nakos	2012	162	UK (91), USA (71)	UK, Greece, USA
Harms and Schiele	2012	65	Germany	the Netherlands
Baronchelli and Cassia	2014	53	Italy	Italy
Sleuwaegen and Onkelix	2014	35,184	Belgium	Belgium
Rodriguez-Serrano and Martin-Velicia	2015	102	Spain	Spain
Choquette, Rask, Sala and Schoder	2017	23,201	Denmark	Denmark, Germany

* Sample size includes the total number of firms included in the study; in some cases, this included only Born Global firms; in other cases, all types of manufacturing firms (both exporting and non-exporting) were included.

Key results from the selected studies

Aspelund and Moen (2001) divided firms into three generations based on year of establishment: the traditional exporters, the flexible specialists and the Born Globals. Their results suggest that Born Globals are technologically advanced, use niche strategies and have strong customer orientation compared to other exporting firms. A key result of the study was the support for an idea of generations of firms with distinct and unique characteristics. Moen (2002) used the same dataset from Norway but also added responses from a sample of firms in France that had answered a translated version of the survey. The idea of generations of firms was further developed, and it was found that Born Global firms evaluated the home market as unattractive (poor demand conditions) while export markets were regarded as more favourable. This suggests that market-related perceptions might also influence the degree of international focus. Moen and Servais (2002) combined the data from Norway and France with a survey from Denmark. A key result was found in terms of how firms with rapid international involvement outperformed firms starting to export with a longer timespan from establishment. They concluded, 'The results indicate that the future export involvement of a firm is, to a large extent, influenced by its behavior shortly after establishment' (p. 49).

Knight et al. (2004) used data from both the USA and Denmark. When we consider the results based on Danish firms, the firms were found to have rapid international growth and customer orientation, and marketing competence was strongly related to international performance.

Rialp and Rialp (2007) used a resource-based view in order to build their analyses of a large sample of Spanish exporting firms. Their results show that intangible resources characterise Born Global firms, more specifically this is reflected in the existence of an export department, the percentage of employees with higher training/studies or more positive perceptions of export profitability among managers.

Acedo and Jones (2007) built their study on a sample of small- and medium-sized firms in Spain. Speed of international activity is an important element in international entrepreneurship research, and the authors focused on how psychological aspects (cognition) influence speed. One important result is that risk perception has a strong impact on internationalisation speed.

Kuivalainen et al. (2007) used a sample of Finnish firms. They divided Born Global firms into two groups: 'true Born Global' and 'Born International' based on market/country distance and export turnover. The results show that true Born Globals 'performed better than their less international counterparts on all three measures (sales, profit and sales efficiency)' (p. 264).

Jantunen et al. (2008) also used a dataset from Finland and looked at the importance of the strategic orientation of managers of Born Global firms. All Born Global firms had high scores for entrepreneurial orientation, while an important and significant difference between Born Globals and other firms was that there was more focus on learning orientation among Born Globals.

Sommer and Haug (2011) studied small- and medium-sized German firms. They used the theory of planned behaviour to analyse intentions, knowledge and experience. The results showed that the most important impact on international intentions was related to perceived behaviour control (to what extent the individual perceived himself being able to perform the behaviour); this was followed by significant influence also from experience and knowledge. These results, like that of several others (Acedo and Jones 2007; Zahra 2005) point towards the importance of cognitive aspects when attempting to understand the behaviour of Born Global firms.

Harms and Schiele (2012) built their sample on German finalists in an 'Entrepreneur of the Year' contest. They used effectuation and causation approaches to understand the choice of entry modes. The results suggest that experienced entrepreneurs use effectuation (emergent strategies) rather than causation (rational planning) approaches. Further, if the entrepreneurs used causation approaches they tended also to select exporting as the entry mode. The study was built on a limited sample in terms of firms included (n=65), but represents a promising approach investigating how different approaches to decision-making processes are linked to actual strategy choices among Born Global firms.

Dimitratos et al. (2012) used data from medium-sized firms (50–249 employees) in the UK and the USA. They focused on measurement development, contributing with a new opportunity-based instrument to measure international entrepreneurship. The study found support for a significant relationship between international entrepreneurial culture and international performance.

Baronchelli and Cassia (2014) collected data from Italian SMEs (n=53) and investigated determining antecedents of Born Global firm performance defined as export share. They found four significant positive factors (market and segments knowledge, firm innovativeness, access to networks and being part of a niche-oriented industry), while dynamism of the industry apparently had a negative impact on export share.

Rodríguez-Serrano and Martín-Velicia (2015) investigated absorptive capacity among Spanish Born Global firms. They found that market orientation had a strong impact on absorptive capacity, and that such absorptive capacity is a key success factor for Born Global firms.

Sleuwaegen and Onkelinx (2014) and Choquette et al. (2016) used different types of data, although both studies used large public registered datasets to analyse the Born Global phenomenon. Choquette et al. (2016) concluded that Danish Born Globals have significantly higher turnover, levels of employment and job growth rates compared to other firms. From Belgium, the data presented by Sleuwaegen and Onkelinx (2014) identified the highest growth rates in Born Global firms, but also the highest failure rates.

What are the most important characteristics and marketing strategies of European Born Global firms?

When we summarise the results of the studies presented, Born Global firms in Europe may be generally described as follows.

They are very proactive in international markets from inception or shortly thereafter. Most of these firms start exporting as their first and primary foreign entry mode. They tend to export their products and/or services within two or three years of inception and sell more than one-quarter of their production abroad. Some of them also develop other, more committed ways of internationalisation, collaborating with foreign partners and even undertaking foreign direct investments and operating in a wide variety of markets around the world.

They are characterised by limited financial and tangible resources. Due to their young age, most Born Global firms tend to be of rather small size. Therefore, their level of endowment of tangible, financial and human resources is usually small compared with large multinational firms. Nevertheless, international activities are a feasible and profitable option for Born Globals largely due to their possession or accessibility to more knowledge-based and/or knowledge-intensive resources (intangibles).

They can be identified in a wide variety of industrial sectors. While many researchers have tended to consider that the Born Global phenomenon is highly concentrated in high-tech activities, there is evidence of this phenomenon also in more traditional, mature and even low-tech sectors (Madsen and Servais 1997; McAuley 1999; Moen 2002).

Their founders and managers show a high level of international entrepreneurial orientation. Born Global firm management tends to perceive the world as their natural marketplace from the very beginning. Many Born Globals are created by international entrepreneurs and/or managers with a high entrepreneurial orientation that overcomes the borders of the home market and allows them to identify and exploit international opportunities in foreign markets. Such an international entrepreneurial orientation (Covin and Miller 2014) is highly associated with a global vision and international experience, as well as with a risk-taking and proactive competitive attitude with a clear orientation towards innovativeness in the form of new products and/or processes.

They often emphasise a differentiation/focused competitive strategy based on quality and technological leadership. Born Global firms typically emphasise product differentiation strategies offering unique and highly distinctive products and/or services with a better design and superior quality compared to their competitors, which provides them with consumer loyalty on a global scale. They are often highly innovative companies recognised for technological leadership in their product category. The combination of differentiation and niche focus strategies becomes

especially suitable for Born Global firms due to their resource scarcity and relative specialisation and also because such target market niches become a relevant source of opportunities for
small-sized firms. Their high-quality products and services are especially adapted to meet the
specific needs of a given market segment, stimulating client loyalty. In fact, many of these firms
are established based on the innovative development of new products and/or technological
processes.

They exploit the potential of ICTs. New technologies, such as the internet, for example, allow
Born Global firms, even the smallest ones, to obtain and process information very efficiently
and to communicate with suppliers, customers or partners around the world and at marginal
cost. Such technological improvements in information systems are changing the traditional
limits between firms and help them manage much better business models widely distributed
in geographic terms. Many Born Global firms also take advantage of ICTs to conduct proper
market segmentation and focus on meeting the highly specialised needs of specific market
niches identifiable in different countries on a global scale.

They leverage intermediaries in foreign markets. Most Born Global firms leverage independent
intermediaries and/or distributor resources located abroad to properly promote and channel
their foreign sales. By directly exporting through allied networks of foreign distributors, their
operations abroad can become more flexible, entering and leaving some countries relatively
easily and rapidly. Occasionally, these local intermediaries are those who identify a profitable
market opportunity that they channel towards a given foreign supplier. Most experimented
Born Global firms may combine export activities with other entry and development strategies
in foreign markets, such as joint ventures or foreign direct investments. However, the lower
cost and level of operational risk associated with exporting combined with the possibility of
taking advantage of foreign partners' resources makes exporting the most adequate foreign entry
strategy.

Discussion

Part 1: Are Born Globals in Europe different from Born Globals in other parts of the world?

In order to understand the establishment and development of Born Global firms from
European countries, it is highly relevant to address their potential differences to Born Global
firms established in other parts of the world. Our presentation of empirical results suggests that
European Born Globals have many similar characteristics to Born Globals in other parts of the
world (for example, internationally proactive, exploiting ICT-based opportunities). One reason
may be the distribution of the existing studies, where there are many from European countries and few originating from developing countries. Further, as described by Andersson et al.
(2015), studies from developing countries often adopt concepts and focus similar to studies from
Western countries without adjusting for the local context. In this section, we will address the
possible differences in more detail.

First, when considering growth, Knight et al. (2004) used similar selection criteria in
Denmark and the USA, targeting firms with at least 25% export share and established during
the past 20 years. They found that the US Born Globals were larger, having on average 213
employees compared to 63 in Denmark, while average turnover was $36 million in the USA
compared to $10 million in Denmark. Export share was higher in Denmark (71%) than in the
USA (47%). The geographical distribution of sales was different: 89% of the Danish firms stated
that another European country was their most important export market, while the US Born

Globals had more variation (Europe, 38%; Japan, 29%; other Asian countries/Australia, 21%). In both countries, high export growth rates were observed. Empirical evidence is limited, but we note that in this study with similar selection criteria, the US Born Globals appear to be three times larger than their Danish counterparts.

Second, one factor that may influence the higher growth potential of US-based Born Globals is the difference in access to funding. Venture capital firms play an important role in both the establishment and growth processes. Wikipedia lists the major venture capital firms in the world and their locations, with 79 out of 89 of the largest venture capital funds (equalling 88.7%) being located and based in the USA, while only seven are based in Europe. With regard to hedge funds, *Business Insider* reports that 18 of the largest 20 are located in the US (equalling 90%) and the remaining two are located in the UK.

A highly successful Born Global firm is Tesla Company, established in California in 2003. In 2015, about 50% of sales came from international markets. In April 2016, Tesla showed higher stock market value than General Motors and was the most valuable US automaker. We will highlight two important questions: First, do European countries have the venture capital and funding resources necessary in order to develop this kind of company? Second, if a company such as Tesla had been established in a European country, would it have been acquired by non-European investors and maybe relocated? The empirical evidence is scarce, but there is a need for more insight into how funding, mergers and acquisitions influence the development of Born Global firms.

Third, the internationalisation process and strategies may be different when examining Born Globals from developing countries. Zou and Ghauri (2010) stated there is limited research on the internationalisation of firms from developing countries, and they argue that high-tech new ventures from emerging markets will follow an incremental and gradual internationalisation process. Based on three case studies from China, they observed a gradual internationalisation process, leading them to suggest that cultural differences and the need for learning may explain this result. Later, Andersson et al. (2015) discussed differences between Western and Chinese Born Globals and suggested that the latter would be more often established in traditional/ mature industries and more likely to use a cost advantage or low price strategy compared to Born Globals in Western countries. We note examples of highly successful Born Globals from China, such as the mobile phone and electronics producer Xiaomi. Founded in 2010, the company launched its first phone in 2011 and is now valued at US$46 billion. While its main market is China, it also exports to countries in Southeast Asia and is targeting expansion into countries such as Russia, India and Brazil. Xiaomi could be regarded as an example of a successful Chinese Born Global firm following a low-cost strategy, selling its products at a price about half of that of iPhones but with similar specifications.

Part 2: What do we not know about European Born Globals?

Based on the previous sections, we lack knowledge about differences between European and non-European Born Global firms with regard to growth rates, strategies and access to funding. Moen et al. (2008) found that business angels investing in Born Globals were significantly different from business angels investing in other firms. We need much more information about who invests in these firms at different development phases and how this influences Born Global firms.

In addition, we will point to several important areas with limited insight in need of more research. Few studies have focused on how acquisitions and mergers relate to Born Global firms. Henrekson and Johansson (2010) state that mature firms basically grow through mergers and acquisitions; as such, Born Globals may be important for industrial renewal and represent a growth opportunity for established industrial firms. Also, more focus is needed on the extreme examples of successful Born Global firms. Several questions need to be asked about these firms, such as where in the world were they started? How did they develop and grow? What were the defining decisions? How did they gain access to resources? The extreme cases are particularly important, because it is possible that even among Born Global firms, a very small fraction may be drivers of a large part of increased employment and value creation within an economy.

Further, what are the public policy initiatives that may stimulate the establishment of these firms and contribute to their positive development when once established? In this context, how important are pre-establishment processes, taxation systems, individual motivation or know-ledge access, and how would these firms be assisted best from a policy perspective? Especially in Europe, a critical component of the economic integration in this region, the Single European Market, that represents the enactment of the economic goals of the EU (Benson-Rea and Gerke, Chapter 12 of this volume), may have significant impact on European businesses' international business strategy. In future research, the role of EU integration, as well as the role of large research initiatives such as Horizon 2020 and processes related to Brexit need to be addressed as the political, regulatory and economic environment may influence both the establishment of and development of Born Global firms. In their longitudinal study of the various factors that concur to the long-term survival and organic growth of internationalising and innovative SMEs in the Swedish life-science industry, Hånell et al. in Chapter 21 of this volume discuss the importance of policy initiatives. Suder (2011) uses the term *Born Europeans*; many of these may take advantage of the EU single market with more open borders and harmonisation of regulations. Further research on all these issues would be greatly welcomed.

Final remarks

Henrekson and Johansson (2010) performed a meta-analysis of studies focusing on firm growth. They concluded 'The survey of existing studies clearly shows that a small number of high-growth firms are particularly important for net job creation' (p. 240). We expect that Born Global firms constitute an important share of these high-growth firms. This reflects studies more than two decades ago, when for example Rennie (1993) described Born Global firms as strikingly competitive, emerging in increasing numbers and being highly important for job creation. These conclusions still appear valid, and we have much better knowledge of these firms thanks to the large number of research studies. From a society perspective, Born Globals are particularly important as they are the new generation of firms meeting the most competitive environment with high failure rates while also being the few firms with the highest growth potential.

References

Acedo, F.J. and Jones, M.V. (2007), 'Speed of internationalization and entrepreneurial cognition: Insights and a comparison between international new ventures, exporters and domestic firms', *Journal of World Business*, vol. 42, no. 3, pp. 236–252.

Almor, T. (2011), 'Dancing as fast as they can: Israeli high-tech firms and the great recession of 2008', *Thunderbird International Business Review*, vol. 53, no. 2, pp. 195–208.

Andersson, S., Danilovic, M. and Huang, H. (2015), 'Success factors in Western and Chinese Born Global companies', *iBusiness*, vol. 7, no. 1, p. 25.

Aspelund, A., Koed Madsen, T. and Moen, Ø. (2007), 'A review of the foundation, international marketing strategies, and performance of international new ventures', *European Journal of Marketing*, vol. 41, no. 11/12, pp. 1423–1448.

Aspelund, A. and Moen, Ø. (2001), 'A generation perspective on small firm internationalization: From traditional exporters and flexible specialists to born globals', in C.N. Axinn and P. Matthyssens (eds), *Reassessing the Internationalization of the Firm (Advances in International Marketing vol. 11)*, Amsterdam, JAI/Elsevier Inc., pp. 197–225.

Baronchelli, G. and Cassia, F. (2014), 'Exploring the antecedents of born-global companies' international development', *International Entrepreneurship and Management Journal*, vol. 10, no. 1, pp. 67–79.

Bjørgum, Ø., Moen, Ø. and Madsen, T.K. (2013), 'New ventures in an emerging industry: Access to and use of international resources', *International Journal of Entrepreneurship and Small Business*, vol. 20, no. 2, pp. 233–253.

Cavusgil, S.T. and Knight, G. (2015), 'The born global firm: An entrepreneurial and capabilities perspective on early and rapid internationalization', *Journal of International Business Studies*, vol. 46, no. 1, pp. 3–16.

Choquette, E., Rask, M., Sala, D. and Schröder, P. (2016), 'Born globals—is there fire behind the smoke?' *International Business Review*, vol. 26, no. 3, pp. 448–460.

Covin, J.G. and Miller, D. (2014), 'International entrepreneurial orientation: Conceptual considerations, research themes, measurement issues, and future research directions', *Entrepreneurship Theory and Practice*, vol. 38, no. 1, pp. 11–44.

Dimitratos, P., Voudouris, I., Plakoyiannaki, E. and Nakos, G. (2012), 'International entrepreneurial culture—toward a comprehensive opportunity-based operationalization of international entrepreneurship', *International Business Review*, vol. 21, no. 4, pp. 708–721.

Eurofound (2012), *Born Global: The potential of job creation in new international businesses*, Luxembourg, Publications Office of the European Union.

Harms, R. and Schiele, H. (2012), 'Antecedents and consequences of effectuation and causation in the international new venture creation process', *Journal of International Entrepreneurship*, vol. 10, no. 2, pp. 95–116.

Henrekson, M. and Johansson, D. (2010), 'Gazelles as job creators: A survey and interpretation of the evidence', *Small Business Economics*, vol. 35, no. 2, pp. 227–244.

Jantunen, A., Nummela, N., Puumalainen, K. and Saarenketo, S. (2008), 'Strategic orientations of born globals—do they really matter?' *Journal of World Business*, vol. 43, no. 2, pp. 158–170.

Jolly, V.K., Alahuhta, M. and Jeannet, J.P. (1992), 'Challenging the incumbents: How high technology start-ups compete globally', *Strategic Change*, vol. 1, no. 2, pp. 71–82.

Jones, M.V., Coviello, N. and Tang, Y.K. (2011), 'International entrepreneurship research (1989–2009): A domain ontology and thematic analysis', *Journal of Business Venturing*, vol. 26, no. 6, pp. 632–659.

Kane, T. (2010), 'The importance of startups in job creation and job destruction', *Kauffman Foundation Research Series: Firm Formation and Economic Growth*, Kansas City: Ewing Marion Kauffman Foundation.

Kiss, A.N., Danis, W.M. and Cavusgil, S.T. (2012), 'International entrepreneurship research in emerging economies: A critical review and research agenda', *Journal of Business Venturing*, vol. 27, no. 2, pp. 266–290.

Knight, G., Koed Madsen, T. and Servais, P. (2004), 'An inquiry into born-global firms in Europe and the USA', *International Marketing Review*, vol. 21, no. 6, pp. 645–665.

Kuivalainen, O., Sundqvist, S. and Servais, P. (2007), 'Firms' degree of born-globalness, international entrepreneurial orientation and export performance', *Journal of World Business*, vol. 42, no. 3, pp. 253–267.

Madsen, T.K. and Servais, P. (1997), 'The internationalization of born globals: An evolutionary process?' *International Business Review*, vol. 6, no. 6, pp. 561–583.

McAuley, A. (1999), 'Entrepreneurial instant exporters in the Scottish arts and crafts sector', *Journal of International marketing*, vol. 7, no. 4, pp. 67–82.

McDougall, P.P. and Oviatt, B.M. (2000), 'International entrepreneurship: The intersection of two research paths', *Academy of Management Journal*, vol. 43, no. 5, pp. 902–906.

McDougall, P.P., Shane, S. and Oviatt, B.M. (1994), 'Explaining the formation of international new ventures: The limits of theories from international business research', *Journal of Business Venturing*, vol. 9, no. 6, pp. 469–487.

Moen, Ø. (2002), 'The born globals: A new generation of small European exporters', *International Marketing Review*, vol. 19, no. 2, pp. 156–175.

Moen, Ø. and Servais, P. (2002), 'Born global or gradual global? Examining the export behavior of small and medium-sized enterprises', *Journal of International Marketing*, vol. 10, no. 3, pp. 49–72.

Moen, Ø., Sørheim, R. and Erikson, T. (2008), 'Born global firms and informal investors: Examining investor characteristics', *Journal of Small Business Management*, vol. 46, no. 4, pp. 536–549.

OECD (2013), 'Fostering SMEs' participation in global markets: Final report', Organisation for Economic Co-operation and Development.

Peiris, I.K., Akoorie, M.E. and Sinha, P. (2012), 'International entrepreneurship: A critical analysis of studies in the past two decades and future directions for research', *Journal of International Entrepreneurship*, vol. 10, no. 4, pp. 279–324.

Preece, S.B., Miles, G. and Baetz, M.C. (1999), 'Explaining the international intensity and global diversity of early-stage technology-based firms', *Journal of Business Venturing*, vol. 14, no. 3, pp. 259–281.

Rennie, M.W. (1993), 'Born global', *The McKinsey Quarterly*, vol. no. 4, pp. 45–53.

Rialp, A. and Rialp, J. (2007), 'Faster and more successful exporters: An exploratory study of born global firms from the resource-based view', *Journal of Euromarketing*, vol. 16, no. 1–2, pp. 71–86.

Rialp, A., Rialp, J. and Knight, G.A. (2005), 'The phenomenon of early internationalizing firms: What do we know after a decade (1993–2003) of scientific inquiry?' *International Business Review*, vol. 14, no. 2, pp. 147–166.

Rodríguez-Serrano, M.Á. and Martín-Velicia, F.A. (2015), 'The role of absorptive capability on born-global performance', *Journal of Promotion Management*, vol. 21, no. 4, pp. 447–458.

Sleuwaegen, L. and Onkelinx, J. (2014), 'International commitment, post-entry growth and survival of international new ventures', *Journal of Business Venturing*, vol. 29, no. 1, pp. 106–120.

Sommer, L. and Haug, M. (2011), 'Intention as a cognitive antecedent to international entrepreneurship—understanding the moderating roles of knowledge and experience', *International Entrepreneurship and Management Journal*, vol. 7, no. 1, pp. 111–142.

Suder, G. (2011), *Doing Business in Europe*, 2nd edn, Lonson, SAGE Publications.

Zahra, S.A. (2005), 'A theory of international new ventures: A decade of research', *Journal of International Business Studies*, vol. 36, no. 1, pp. 20–28.

Zou, H. and Ghauri, P.N. (2010), 'Internationalizing by learning: The case of Chinese high-tech new ventures', *International Marketing Review*, vol. 27, no. 2, pp. 223–244.

PART C

Culture, identity and European business

8

INNOVATION CAPACITIES AND NATIONAL CULTURES

Drawing a cartography of the European landscape

Regis Coeurderoy

Introduction

One of the European Union's key objectives is to be an economic area that remains at the cutting edge of innovation and moreover ensures a standard of living through innovation policies (European Council 2000). In order to implement that strategy, the European Council launched the Lisbon Strategy,[1] subsequently revised in 2006, in particular with the purpose of increasing research investment to 3% of GDP. After ten years, the outcomes were, however, mixed (Figure 8.1): only two countries (Sweden and Finland) reached the 3% goal and only five other countries (Denmark, Austria, Germany, France and Belgium) were above the EU average. The EU average remained virtually the same for almost a decade, only rising from 1.85% to 1.90% (European Commission, 2010). A new strategy for the decade 2010–2020 was launched, called 'Europe 2020', with a strong focus on research and innovation. The new innovation framework does not really change the previous targets and maintains the 3% of EU GDP to be invested in R&D (European Commission 2017a).

A typical first reaction to these results is of course to speak of economic growth. It is true that economic growth would give public and private actors greater flexibility to invest in R&D. But economic research considers that innovation is a driver rather than a consequence of economic growth (Aghion and Howitt 2010). It is thus key to enact reforms that would unleash the creativity, initiative-taking and entrepreneurial spirit that are powerful engines of innovation – and not only rely on R&D budget expenditures and patent counting. As pointed out by Philippe Aghion (2006, p. 3),

> it would be naive to assume that patent protection and R&D subsidies would be sufficient to foster innovation and productivity growth. It is not enough to invest more in R&D here and there to get the economy to grow faster. In the same way that R&D becomes essential when an economy develops, it becomes vital to create the micro and macro-economic conditions for innovation-based growth.

Basically, innovation must be more globally understood as related to the set of norms, behaviours, beliefs and customs that exist within the population of a sovereign nation – what we call a national culture (Hofstede 2001).

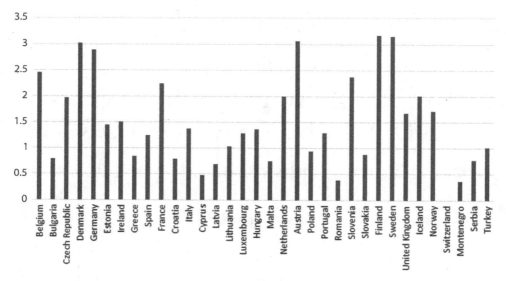

Figure 8.1   Gross domestic expenditure on R&D (GERD), % of GDP, 2014
Source: Figure elaborated from data provided by Eurostat (2017).

Although a link is to be expected between national culture and innovation performance at country level, the topic remains relatively unexplored, as discussed below. For that reason, the objective of this chapter is to shed light on the impact of national cultures on the innovation capacities of European countries. In the next section, I set out some facts and figures that provide first insights on the issue in Europe. This is followed by a review of the literature with a special focus on empirical research articles. I then describe my methodology and provide key results – including regression analysis and cartography. I conclude with some key implications of these findings for possible reforms in Europe.

Facts and figures on national cultures and innovation in the EU

A comparison of the current situations of EU countries in terms of innovation reveals significant and persisting diversity. The Innovation Scoreboard published by the European Commission (2016) shows a 1:4 ratio between the most innovative country in Europe (Switzerland, or second-placed Sweden if only EU member states are considered) and the least innovative country, which is Bulgaria (Table 8.1). In its annual report (European Commission 2016), the European Commission identifies four main groups of countries, which I have reproduced in this table: (1) innovation leaders; (2) strong innovators; (3) moderate innovators; and (4) modest innovators. This ranking manifests the disparities between Northern Europe and Southern and Eastern Europe. The EU member countries ranked as 'innovation leaders' are Sweden, Denmark, Finland, Germany and the Netherlands (2015 values). The current situation is not new: the 2008 figures exhibit the same group of leaders, apart from the Netherlands, which managed to join the group more recently (conclusion drawn from European Commission 2017b).

This ranking is not confined to a few innovation performance indicators ('outputs'), but also evaluates the infrastructures that have been put in place in these countries ('enablers') and the innovation activities undertaken by companies ('firm activities'). It thus offers an overview of a country's long-term innovation capacity. That is the main reason why the positions in the

Table 8.1 Classification of European countries by innovation group

Types of innovators	Countries
(1) innovation leaders	*Switzerland*, Sweden, Denmark, Finland, Germany, Netherlands
(2) strong innovators	Ireland, Belgium, United Kingdom, Luxembourg, Austria, *Iceland*, France, Slovenia, *Norway*
(3) moderate innovators	Cyprus, Estonia, Malta, Czech Republic, Italy, Portugal, Greece, Spain, Hungary, Slovakia, Poland, Lithuania, Latvia, Croatia
(4) modest innovators	Bulgaria, Romania

Source: Classification derived from data provided in European Commission (2016, p. 7). EFTA countries added by the author (in italics).

ranking remain stable through time. The innovation performance index is a composite measure of 25 indicators, computed from an unweighted average (European Commission 2016, p. 12).[2]

A literature review of empirical studies on national cultures and innovation

In the academic literature, relatively few research articles have tackled the relations between innovation and culture at country level. In a seminal article, Scott Shane (1992) raised the question 'Why do some societies invent more than others?' In his paper, the author explores the extent to which the cultural features of one country influence its propensity to innovate. He draws two main conclusions from his empirical research findings. First, the results show that the extent to which a society stresses social hierarchy tends to decrease inventiveness. The main reasons are that bureaucracy limits creativity and that hierarchisation inhibits communication between superiors and subordinates. Moreover, hierarchy goes alongside centralisation and reduces employees' incentives. Hierarchical societies place greater emphasis on regulation than on trust and may be more reluctant to accept radical changes challenging established positions. Shane (1992) also provides evidence that individualistic societies tend to be more inventive. They value freedom more than collectivist societies and provide more individual rewards for initiatives and inventions. Last but not least, individualistic societies encourage more independence and non-conformity, which are both powerful drivers for innovation. These key findings are based upon the measure of the per capita number of invention patents granted to nationals of 33 countries (in 1967, 1971, 1976 and 1980). The cultural values are the measures developed by Hofstede (2001) from a large survey of 88,000 employees at IBM throughout the world.

These first findings were confirmed by Scott Shane (1993) in another paper on a related topic. In that article, Shane (1993) directly assesses the effect of cultural values on national rates of innovation for the same group of 33 countries (in 1975 and 1980). He finds that rates of innovation are clearly associated with uncertainty acceptance and, to a lesser degree, related to power distance and individualism. Shane (1993) concludes from this research that, first, 'culture matters' in innovation issues at country level. Innovation is not just a question of spending money but also, if not more, a question of societal values. These influential values are no surprise to researchers involved in innovation studies. A reluctance to accept uncertainty inhibits innovativeness, because innovation involves risk and change, while individualism and lack of power distance are associated with innovation (Shane 1992). In a more recent article, Rinne et al. (2011) revisit the study by Shane (1993). They also find a strong negative relation between power distance and innovation, at a national level, and a strong positive relation between individualism and innovation. By contrast, they do not find any relation between uncertainty avoidance and innovation.

Taylor and Wilson (2010) explore in greater depth the influence of individualism on innovation rates. They analyse data on 62 countries spanning more than two decades and test several measures of individualism. They confirm that most measures of individualism have a strong, significant and positive effect on innovation. They show, however, that a certain type of collectivism – patriotism and nationalism – can also foster innovation.

Methodology, data analysis and key findings

Based on these previous findings, the precise aim of my empirical investigation is to determine whether the EU countries ranked among the most innovative are culturally distinct from the other European countries. To do this, I base my analysis on the national cultural dimensions identified and analysed by Geert Hofstede (2001) and previously used in the first assessments of the links between culture and innovation (Shane 1993, 1995; Tellis et al., 2009; Taylor and Wilson 2010). I test the impact of the following three cultural dimensions (Hofstede 2017), all of which have been previously studied: (1) power distance – which is the degree to which the 'less powerful members of a society accept and expect that power is distributed unequally'; (2) individualism versus collectivism – individualism being the 'preference for a social framework in which individuals are expected to take care of only themselves and their immediate families'; and (3) uncertainty avoidance – which expresses 'the degree to which the members of a society feel uncomfortable with uncertainty and ambiguity' (Hofstede 2017).

I assess the impact of these dimensions on the innovation capacity of European countries as measured in the above-mentioned European Commission (2016) report. I run regression analysis to assess the impact of cultural features on the innovation performance of countries during the 2011–2015 period (Table 8.2).

For the rest of the analysis I keep only those European countries that are integrated into the European Union or those maintaining long and close relationships, by which I mean European Free Trade Area (EFTA) countries. This includes Iceland, Norway and Switzerland. Data on Liechtenstein are not available. Note also that, for the case of Cyprus, I have taken the decision to replicate the Greek values. This is something that can be considered as an acceptable approximation because the figures are for the Republic of Cyprus only. I run the analysis on a panel of 31 countries for five years (155 observations). Because the three significant cultural dimensions are closely correlated (Table 8.3), I also create a synthetic factor (through principal component analysis), which summarises the three cultural dimensions. The low values of this factor stand for countries supporting rather individualistic behaviours, sharing power and accepting risk-taking. I regress innovation capabilities on the three values of national culture, but also introduce GDP per capita (thousands of current US$) as a control variable.

In this regression model, I thus assess the direct effect of national cultures on innovation performance. Following Williamson's framework on the economics of institutions, culture can be considered as a key component of social embeddedness. This level is taken as given and changes very slowly – in the order of centuries (Williamson 2000, p. 597). In that perspective, cultural dimensions can be considered as exogenous and stand-alone. Nonetheless, it would be fruitful to further explore the diffusion of cultural dimensions in other sub-level strata.

Regression results significantly confirm the power of cultural values on the capability of countries to perform in innovation in the European context, with an explained variance close to 50 per cent when measured alone. The most discriminating variable is power distance,

Table 8.2 Regression analysis of cultural values on innovation performance

	Model 1	Model 2	Model 3	Model 4
Power distance	−0.324	−0.143		
	(9.48)★★	(3.79)★★		
Individualism	0.156	0.113		
	(1.98)★	(1.98)★		
Uncertainty avoidance	−0.171	−0.115		
	(3.85)★★	(3.26)★★		
Synthetic factor of national cultures			−12.928	−7.259
			(14.79)★★	(6.57)★★
GDP per capita		0.326		0.329
		(5.38)★★		(5.62)★★
Constant	66.034	43.523	21.188	34.790
	(8.36)★★	(6.61)★★	(11.18)★★	(17.13)★★
R^2	0.48	0.65	0.47	0.64

$N = 155$ observations; ★ $p < 0.05$; ★★ $p < 0.01$.

Table 8.3 Correlation between the cultural dimensions for EU and EFTA countries

	Power distance	*Individualism*	*Uncertainty avoidance*	*GDP per capita*
Power distance	1.00			
Individualism	−0.57★★	1.00		
Uncertainty avoidance	0.62★★	−0.59★★	1.00	
GDP per capita	−0.59★★	0.43★★	−0.47★★	1.00

$N = 155$
★★ $p < 0.01$.

followed by uncertainty avoidance and, slightly behind that, individualism. These results confirm that European societies where power is distributed unequally among individuals strongly inhibit their innovation capacities. A taste for collectivism apparently does nothing to foster innovation capacity, while a dose of individualism tends to favour it, maybe because it may more easily unleash entrepreneurial initiatives, which are a powerful engine of innovation at present. A reluctance to accept uncertainty and ambiguity, and a desire to regulate change produce a similar effect on innovation in Europe. Innovation initiatives do indeed generally require test-and-try initiatives and actions whose outcomes can remain unknown for a long while. Finally, it should be noted that in these three cases the results exhibit significant explanatory power, in particular for power distance. Note also that the cultural synthetic indicator can be seen as a clear signal in favour of the influential role of culture to differentiate innovation capacities in Europe. This suggests that, although the relations between culture and innovation are obviously not directly observable, they are nevertheless very likely to be closely linked.

Although I can give evidence on the relations between national cultures and innovation performance, I do not know the specific situation of each country. For that reason, I pursue the analysis with a cartographic approach. I create a graph in which the cultural dimension derived from the synthetic factor is plotted along the x-axis, while the y-axis indicates innovation capacities,

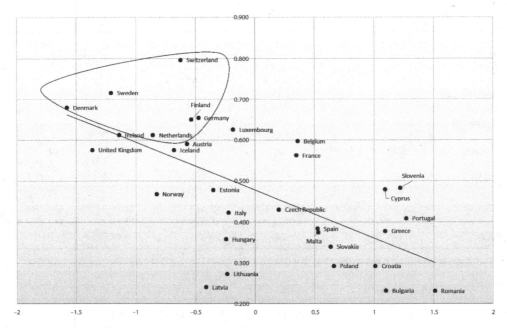

Figure 8.2 The cultural space of EU innovation capacities
X axis = cultural dimension derived from the factorial analysis of the three measures – power distance, individualism and uncertainty avoidance.
Y axis = innovation capability on a 0–1 scale.
EU and EFTA countries included.

using the innovation performance values calculated for the EC report (European Commission 2016), computed as averages for the period 2011–2015.[3] Note that these are unweighted values, so for example Germany and Malta have equal weight. The reason for this choice is that I am seeking to compare national cultures independently of their economic or demographic weight. Nevertheless, one should bear in mind these proportions when studying the graphs.

Some clear conclusions can be drawn from this synthetic graph (see Figure 8.2). First of all, it is quite visible that the most innovative EU countries, according to the European scoreboard, are located in the top-left quadrant of the graph. Narrowing this down, the top most innovative countries ('the innovation leaders') can be grouped together in a specific zone that I will call the 'cultural space of innovation'.

In contrast to this zone, I observe that the least innovative countries are mainly located in the bottom-right quadrant – indicating opposite characteristics to the first group. As a particular case, note the situation of Luxembourg, which shows a good performance level on average (2011–2015) but left the group of innovation leaders in 2015. It remains that Luxembourg, like Austria and the United Kingdom, is very close to this cultural space. It can thus be expected that these countries are not likely to have strong cultural barriers against innovation and could easily trigger a catch-up process.

Another sub-group can also be detected, which exhibits relatively low innovation capacity levels but exhibits cultural features that are not so different from the leading group: the three Baltic countries, plus Italy and Hungary. Even though there is a gap which is not trivial, it seems that these countries benefit from cultural patterns that are quite favourable for unleashing more innovation-driven policies and can then expect a catch-up process in innovation performance in the medium run. The remaining singular case is Norway (not an EU member state), which is not an innovation leader but is a special case in Europe owing to its oil revenues, which may dampen the incentive to innovate. For the other countries, it can be derived from the analysis that entering into what many call an 'innovation-driven society' would require triggering strong cultural changes. On the basis of this synthetic cultural factor, their positioning shows that entering an innovation-driven society is a big challenge.

Of course, the analysis developed in this chapter is a national-level analysis and hence provides an assessment of relations on an average basis. It introduces explanatory dimensions for understanding why some societies may generate more innovation than others. There remain, however, limitations in this exploratory perspective. Innovation performance can also be driven by sub-groups in one population and – on some occasions – transformations can be unleashed by minorities, and this could be termed a 'revolution'.

Conclusion

The cultural analysis of innovation capacity shows that, although there is no such thing as an 'innovation culture' per se, innovation is more likely to thrive in certain cultural spaces. In particular, accepting a more egalitarian distribution of power (according to the power distance indicator) and refusing to regulate the future (according to the uncertainty avoidance indicator), will help to create favourable conditions for innovation in Europe. Furthermore, a 'loosely-knit' structure of relations between individuals seems to be more favourable to innovation.

These cultural questions are seldom taken into account in structural reform programmes, as efforts are generally focused on regulatory dimensions and on incentive schemes, without really considering how these regulatory changes are integrated by actors from the normative and cognitive perspectives. Working from the above results, it is possible to sketch out the foundations of other reforms – 'cultural reforms' – in order to build an environment that would be more conducive to innovation in countries that are deficient in this regard. Concerning the question of power distance, it is important to encourage the countries that are most strongly attached to this principle to implement policies that will foster the development of more egalitarian relations. At the interpersonal level, these actions should begin with educational policy, starting from an early age and carrying on through to higher education. In the working world, significant efforts should be made towards a form of decentralisation that would reduce the number of hierarchical echelons and also lessen vertical interdependence between people.

Concerning the question of uncertainty, it is also important to encourage the more reluctant countries to face up to uncertainty and to pursue policies that promote its acceptance. This would entail implementing policies based on experimentation and the evaluation of results and, as far as possible, circumscribing any debates that focus on general principles or laying down rules. It would also involve curtailing the existence of established positions or statuses that tend to paralyse efforts towards change. Last but not least, it would be useful in some countries to introduce reforms helping individual initiatives to be launched and rewarded. This would enhance risk-taking behaviours in these societies.

These reforms would certainly release significant innovation potential in those countries. But there is one point, one difficulty that must not be overlooked and that can be expressed in the following question: How can we change culture? Obviously, we cannot change a country's history and it would be an illusion to think we can ignore the historical foundations upon which a society is built. We also must be wary of undertakings aimed at 'cultural revolution'. Our memory of the past century and certain current events should cause us to exercise great caution in this area.

It is nevertheless possible to gradually introduce a process of transformation in order to move in the intended direction, even though the effects of these changes will only be felt in the medium to long term. Perhaps it would be better to say 'it is important to introduce a transformation process quickly in order to move in the intended direction because the effects will only be felt in the medium to long term'.

Notes

1 The Lisbon Strategy recommended six main initiatives to boost innovation: (1) developing networking activities and joint research programmes; (2) improving the business environment to foster R&D investments; (3) better coordinating and monitoring the national efforts; (4) developing the infrastructures in information technologies to better circulate scientific knowledge; (5) removing mobility barriers for researchers and crafting policies to attract research talents in Europe; and (6) moving towards patent protection at the community level.
2 'Enablers' is the first pillar evaluating country performances across three dimensions: human resources; open, excellent research systems; and finance and support. 'Firm activities' is the second pillar with three dimensions: firm investments; linkages and entrepreneurship; and intellectual assets. 'Outputs' is the third pillar with two dimensions: innovators; and economic effects. The full methodology is described in European Commission (2016).
3 Other graphs with each cultural value were also made but only the synthetic one is presented here for the sake of parsimony. Graphs and analysis are available upon request.

References

Aghion, P. (2006), 'A Primer on Innovation and Growth', Bruegel Policy Brief, October, no. 6.
Aghion, P. and Howitt. P.W. (2010), *The Economics of Growth*, Cambridge, MA, London, MIT Press.
European Commission (2010), *Lisbon Strategy Evaluation Document*. http://ec.europa.eu/archives/growthandjobs_2009/pdf/lisbon_strategy_evaluation_en.pdf (accessed 6 November 2017).
European Commission (2016), *European Innovation Scoreboard 2016*. http://ec.europa.eu/growth/industry/innovation/facts-figures/scoreboards_en (accessed 6 November 2017).
European Commission (2017a), *Europe 2020 Strategy*. https://ec.europa.eu/info/strategy/european-semester/framework/europe-2020-strategy_en (accessed 6 November 2017).
European Commission (2017b), *European Innovation Scoreboard 2017*. http://ec.europa.eu/growth/industry/innovation/facts-figures/scoreboards/ (accessed 6 November 2017).
European Council (2000), *Presidency Conclusions, Lisbon European Council, 23 and 24 March 2000*. www.consilium.europa.eu/media/21038/lisbon-european-council-presidency-conclusions.pdf (accessed 28 March 2018).
Eurostat (2017), *Science, Technology and Innovation – Database*. http://ec.europa.eu/eurostat/web/science-technology-innovation/data/database (accessed 6 November 2017).
Hofstede G. (ed.) (2001), *Culture's Consequences: Comparing Values, Behaviors, Institutions and Organizations across Nations*, 2nd edn, SAGE Publications.
Hofstede G. (2017), *The 6-D Model of National Culture*. http://geerthofstede.com/culture-geert-hofstede-gert-jan-hofstede/6d-model-of-national-culture/ (accessed 6 November 2017).
Rinne, T., Steel G. and Fairweather J. (2012), 'Hofstede and Shane revisited: The role of power distance and individualism in national-level innovation success', *Cross-cultural Research*, vol. 46, no. 2, pp. 91–108.
Shane S. (1992), 'Why do some societies invent more than others?' *Journal of Business Venturing*, vol. 7, no. 1, pp. 29–46.
Shane S. (1993), 'Cultural influences on national rates of innovation', *Journal of Business Venturing*, vol. 8, no. 1, pp. 59–73.
Shane S. (1995), 'Uncertainty avoidance and the preference for innovation championing roles', *Journal of International Business Studies*, vol. 26, no. 1, pp. 47–68.
Taylor, M. and Wilson, S. (2010), 'Does culture still matter? The effects of individualism on national innovation rates', *Journal of Business Venturing*, vol. 27, no. 7, pp. 234–247.
Tellis, G., Prabhu J. and Chandy R. (2009), 'Radical innovation across nations: The preeminence of corporate culture', *Journal of Marketing*, vol. 73, no. 1, pp. 3–23.
Williamson, O. (2000), 'The new institutional economics: Taking stock, looking ahead', *Journal of Economic Literature*, vol. 38, no. 3, pp. 595–613.

9

CULTURE AND EUROPEAN BUSINESS ENVIRONMENT

Past, present and future

Sonja A. Sackmann

Introduction

As one of the old world's settlements, Europe has 'a richness of cultures and languages unparalleled anywhere else in the world' (Hill 1993, p. 9) including a long business tradition that has co-evolved over time. Important shapers of culture in Europe and in business are its history of the various nations and regions, its ethnicities, various societal groups and their predominant Christian religion. Most frequently, Europe is implicitly or explicitly associated with the countries that belong to the European Union (EU) including the countries that belong to the European Free Trade Association as well as the Schengen Treaty comprising the nations of Iceland, Liechtenstein, Norway and Switzerland. Moreover, each one of these European countries has regional differences that may surface in the form of different languages or dialects, region-specific products and customs. As research has shown, regional cultural differences may be stronger than national differences (Kaasa et al. 2014).

Nevertheless, Halecki (1957, p. 5) argues that Europe came together as a historical unity, because many very different peoples joined to cooperate on the basis of common cultural understanding, traditions and principles without giving up their characteristics and without uniting politically. In the process of passing on these cultural understandings, the related beliefs, values, norms and practices to new generations, some of them remained rather stable over time while others changed.

The following sections will examine how culture in Europe co-evolved with European business ideologies and practices in the context of specific societal and political constellations due to a number of drivers for change. The discussion focuses on six different 'ages': the late Middle Age; the Age of the Commercial Revolution; the Industrial Revolution; World War I and II; the period of Europeanisation; and Europe today with its current and future challenges.

Table 9.1 provides an overview of these six ages in terms of their political and societal context with the predominant values of different societal groups being important regarding business at that time. It includes the co-evolving business ideologies and the nature of business with some of its customs, practices and markets as well as the driving forces for change in this evolutionary and at times revolutionary process.

The following discussion is based on Table 9.1, providing richer contextual information for each age. Despite all the driving forces for cultural change in European society and

Table 9.1 Overview of major factors influencing European business culture in different ages

	Middle Ages	Age of Commercial Revolution	Age of Industrialisation	Age of Changing World Order	Age of Europeanisation	Europe today and tomorrow
	> 15th century	Late 13th–18th centuries	18th–19th centuries	1914–1945	1946–2000	Present – Future
Political and Societal Context	Monarchies and Clergy (Patriarchal system); many fiefdoms and small towns	Monarchies and clergy; many fiefdoms and small towns; emergence of nation state	Monarchies; developing democracies; nation states on the basis of monarchies	Democracies replacing most monarchies; changing borders of nation states	Democratic nation states; few representational monarchies	Democratic nation states; few representational monarchies
Predominant Societal Values	Reigning Class: power, materialism; Peasants: survival; work is duty; Craftsmen: quality, recognition, achievement, materialism	Reigning class: power, materialism, discovery; Peasants: survival; Craftsmen: quality, recognition, achievement, materialism; Calvinism: work is duty	Reigning class: power, materialism, dominance; Business owners: materialism, achievement, status; Workers: survival; emerging democratic values (Liberté, Égalité, Fraternité)	Democratic values; materialism; achievement; status; survival; work is duty	Democratic values; entrepreneurship; independence; status; materialism; emerging post-materialistic values (interdependence, life-balance, personal development; ecological balance)	Democratic values; post-materialistic and materialistic values
Predominant business ideology	Feudalism	Mercantilism	Capitalism	Capitalism, evolving socialism and Marxism	Social capitalism	Social capitalism
Nature of Business, Customs and Practices	Agriculture (land owned by nobility); Town-based guilds of skilled freemen; hierarchical apprentice system	Agriculture (land owned by nobility); Trade; Town-based guilds; developing cottage industries	Trade; Agriculture (land owned by nobility); Town-based industry organised in factories (beginning of mass production)	Industry: mass- and customised production; trade; agriculture (increasingly owned by farmers)	Mass- and customised production; trade; entrepreneurship; service-based industries; agriculture	Service-based industries; Trade; Mass- and customised production

Markets	Small protected town-based markets; monopolies of guilds	Trade with colonies → large protected markets within kingdoms	Large protected markets (nation-based tariffs)	Nation-based protected markets	Development of unified EU-based market; free movement of goods and labour	Unified EU-based market; free movement of goods and labour
Drivers for Change	Increasing importance of guilds and accumulation of wealth of craftsmen	Inventions (navigation, shipbuilding, cartography) Need for natural resources; Reforms in banking and accounting; ideological changes due to reformation and renaissance	Inventions re. production methods (mass-production); French and Glorious Revolutions	Economic crisis World Wars I and II: changing world order; Emigration; Revolutions; multi-national agreements	Reconstruction; multinational agreements; founding of EEA and EU; introduction of common currency in most EU countries; deregulation; information technology/internet	Economic crisis → re-regulation; Immigration; Refugees; Digital transformation

business, some of the underlying values and themes remain, such as the quest for freedom and democracy.

Culture and European business in the late Middle Age

The Middle Age in Europe was characterised by the ideology of feudalism – a hierarchical structure regulating the distribution of land and wealth, of rights and responsibilities in all spheres of life including business. Emperors and kings had most power; they owned the land, made laws, and imposed taxes on their citizens, who they also had to take care of. Dukes ruled provinces; knights were mostly vassals protecting their lord and his land. Even though over 90 per cent of the population were peasants, they had the lowest social rank, struggling for survival with work being a duty. While some were freemen and could own a small piece of land, most were serfs having neither political rights nor land. They were at the disposal of the vassal who had to take care of them.

In towns, higher social status could be achieved by joining a guild – either a craft guild or a merchant guild. Each craft had its own guild. Guilds were founded as a form of collective protection from the excessive tax raises of the royals. Each guild created its own guild law regulating the competition among members by determining and thus limiting the number of craftspeople, journeymen and masters, by regulating prices, quality of goods and workmanship. The guild law regulated working hours and conditions, protected members when travelling, helped with funeral expenses and regulated admission and apprenticeship. They also prevented outside traders from selling goods in their town or forced them to pay tolls for being allowed to conduct business in their town (Webster 1919). As such, guilds were early monopolies, educational institutions, insurance providers and quality control institutions at the same time.

Guild members, in turn, had civic duties such as protecting the town as well as helping when building a church. Admission to a guild was only possible for freemen fulfilling certain criteria. An apprenticeship lasted between three and six years. Becoming a master was rather restricted for journeyman and involved, among other things, money to finance their masterpiece, paying for citizenship and other items such as a large meal with several courses for the masters (Schulz 2010). With increasing industrialisation and globalisation of trade, the power and importance of guilds declined towards the nineteenth century.

Even though feudalism ended with the emergence of the nation state in the late eighteenth century, some of its underlying values and elements, such as hierarchical structures, collective organisation and social welfare, as well as rules regulating apprenticeship, workmanship and quality of products remained important cultural characteristics of European business. Zurich still has an active guild tradition, limited today, however, to social activities. Guild apprenticeships represented some early roots of the dual education system typical of Germany, Austria and Switzerland and recently considered a possible means to help reduce unemployment among young people in countries such as Spain, Portugal and Greece (Lübke 2013). The pride in good workmanship, quality, innovation and perseverance may also be one of the reasons of the success of the so-called European hidden champions (Simon 2009). These are medium-sized companies with annual revenues under $4 billion being world market leaders in their respective industries and niches.

The commercial revolution – the age of discovery, colonialism and mercantilism

The commercial revolution spanned the time from the late thirteenth century until the end of the eighteenth century (Lopez 1971). This was a period of European political and business expansion characterised by colonialism and increasing mercantilism, motivated by a spirit of exploration and the need for resources. The venturing out into the new world was enabled by inventions in shipbuilding, navigation instruments and cartography as well as in banking and insurance helping to finance the ventures. The result was an exploration and domination of substantial parts of the globe, an accumulation of wealth in Europe through global trade, increasingly formalised rules of conducting business and the emergence of the modern nation state. Europe became the dominant player in world trade. Present implications of colonialisation include migration from former colonialised regions and, as a result, increasing cultural diversity within Europe and its workforce.

Modern colonialism began with striving for discovery. Marco Polo, a Venetian merchant, paved the way with his travel to China in the thirteenth Century. During colonial times, several major powers emerged on the European continent due to their specific knowledge, skills and resources: Portugal and Spain followed by England, France, the Dutch empire and Sweden. All these kingdoms were skilled seafarers. Increasing knowledge and formal arrangements, their resources and skills allowed them to explore the world across the oceans, develop a better understanding of the world and set out to acquire natural resources in the 'new' world, thus dominating business in Europe and in their colonies.

The need for natural resources such as silver and gold for printing coins, and spices and silk as well as trade difficulties with the Ottoman Turks motivated a Portuguese expedition to search for a seaway to India in the fifteenth century (Newitt 2005). Portugal became the first world empire and the longest-lasting colonial empire of Europe, ending in 1999 with the return of Macau to the People's Republic of China. The Portuguese expedition started along the African coast creating so-called factories serving as trading outposts to secure the trade route and eliminate competition. With their discovery of the seaway to India, landing in Calicut in 1498, Portugal became the leading trade and naval power in the fifteenth and sixteenth centuries. Supported by the Catholic Church who wanted to missionise heathen people, the Portuguese crown acquired colonies in South America, Africa, Arabia, India, South-East Asia and China (Russell-Wood 1998).

While the Portuguese expedition to India was motivated by the desire to open up a new trade route for securing needed resources, the following wave of colonialisation was predominantly motivated by mercantilism, trying to gain and accumulate as much wealth as possible and thus gain power on the European continent. England, France and Holland soon followed with their expansions into Asia, taking over most of the Portuguese colonies. Spain and later Britain ventured across the Atlantic exploring and conquering the Americas.

The colonies provided raw materials, customers and investment opportunities. They had to benefit the mother countries, which prohibited them from developing their own commerce and imposed their respective administration systems. With a shortage of people in the colonies due to the massive die-off of indigenous people, a triangular trade was established. Slaves were exported from Africa to the Americas, raw materials were imported from the Americas to Europe, and finished goods were exported from Europe to the Americas.

Reforms in banking and accounting such as double bookkeeping had spread from Italy throughout Europe. Lending with interest was now allowed and the first stock exchanges opened in Amsterdam and London refining the financial systems. To share the risks of the trade across the oceans, emerging insurance practices were formalised. Lloyd's of London started to publish news from different parts of the world, which underwriters used to assess the risk of a particular trading ship with its cargo. All these developments enabled and supported trade, which enhanced the emergence of nation states based on existing monarchies.

The age of industrialisation

Scientific discoveries and developments gave rise to the age of industrialisation that had tremendous impact on European business, societies, their structure and way of life due to new production methods based on radical inventions. The first industrial revolution started about 1760 in England. Important inventions such as the spinning frame, steam-powered engines, machine tools and the production of chemicals took place in Great Britain giving rise to entrepreneurial behaviour. While absolutist forms of power were still dominant on the European continent, the Glorious Revolution in 1688 in England with the bill of rights and the King-in-parliament provided a business-friendly legal and cultural framework. England united with Scotland provided a market without tolls so that trade and entrepreneurship could blossom. In the early nineteenth century, mechanised forms of production spread to continental Europe and the second industrial revolution with steam-powered transportation including railways and ships and, eventually, the motor car took off.

Industrialisation started to change all spheres of life – the way of production, the nature of work, living standards, as well as legal frameworks, social structures and the economy. The invention of the affordable spinning jenny gave rise to the cottage industry and mainly women formerly active in farming now became involved in the textile industry working at home. With mass production due to the invention of costly spinning mules and power looms, new kinds of factories developed owned by capitalists. This form of concentrated production fostered urbanisation. People who previously had worked in agriculture, then in a cottage industry, now had to move into the cities and the industrial areas for work, thus separating work from home. Important industrial areas in England were London and Manchester, Wallonia in Belgium and the Ruhr Valley in Germany. Since Germany still consisted of 36 politically separate and independent states at that time, industrialisation started later, taking off after its unification in 1871. France, weakened by its Revolution and Napoleon's wars, was also delayed in the industrialisation process (Trebilcock 1998, p. 52).

Because of the factories and urbanisation, the population density in these areas increased, resulting in slums with poor living conditions. These gave rise to severe criticism from Marx (1992) and Engels (2009) and other socialists and communists. While some economists suggest that standards of living for the ordinary people underwent sustained growth with industrialisation (Lucas 2002) probably due to the fast-growing GDP, others argue that many workers' living standards declined in the first phase of capitalism (Feinstein 1998). Trade unions developed to try and help improve working conditions. The first law against child labour was passed in 1844 in England prohibiting children's work before the age of nine and during nights, limiting workdays to 12 hours for those under the age of 18.

With industrialisation, the social structure also changed. The middle class grew including a new group of professionals such as businessmen, entrepreneurs, engineers, clerks and foremen as well as those who had accumulated wealth either through trade or through mass production. These 'nouveaux riches' and professionals became more powerful, achieved recognition and status while reducing the social power and influence of the nobility.

After the Napoleonic wars, Europe experienced a long peaceful period. In the 1880s, the international gold standard was introduced and the value of Europe's major currencies became fixed in relation to each other. All these factors contributed to flourishing trade, representing one-third of world production between 1800 and 1913, with Europe accounting for almost two-thirds of global trade and even more of global investments, which had grown 20 times between 1855 and 1914 (Stevenson 2014). With the achievements of the French Revolution, the combined values of freedom, equality and solidarity spread, fostering increasingly democratic values. Having to struggle for survival was still dominant among the labour work-force consisting of both men and women. Work being a duty was an important value especially among Calvinistic professionals and businessmen – both groups being reserved for men while their wives managed the family and their societal life. The predominant business ideology was capitalism with materialistic values being important for all social groups.

Changing world order and power due to World Wars I and II

Both World Wars changed the distribution of world and business powers, including national borders, leading to major social and cultural changes. The defeated empires of Germany, Russia and Austria-Hungary as well as the Ottoman Empire were partially dissolved and several new countries were created in Eastern Europe. The socialist and communist ideas of the Russian Revolution in 1917 spread to Western Europe, especially to Germany and Hungary. Among the ideas were calls for the destruction of the power of capitalists, the redistribution of power and wealth, and the introduction of equal rights and pay not only between men and women but also between highly skilled professionals and workers.

In combination with starvation and the flu pandemic, these influences contributed to the German Revolution in 1918–1919 creating the Weimar Republic. Democracies, however fragile, replaced most monarchies in Central Europe. The treaties created after World War I offended many citizens and allies partially due to the redistribution of land, wealth and people, forming new states with national minorities resulting in a large wave of migration.

Reparation payments after World War I created hyperinflation in Germany followed by deflation after the collapse of the New York Stock exchange in 1929 spurring the world economic crisis (Blaich 1985). In Europe, businesses were destroyed, many people lost their fortune and many more lost their jobs. The great depression with high unemployment and feelings of unjust treatment strengthened socialist ideas and prepared the ground for nationalistic ideas and the rise of strong leaders such as Hitler, Mussolini, Franco and Salazar, promising betterment especially regarding the economy of their countries. This led to the next major destruction of Europe, migration and again a redistribution of land, wealth and people redrawing national boundaries. Many intellectuals, business people and professionals emigrated to the Americas. The power between states shifted again, and Europe became divided into Western Europe, with its business and culture influenced by (social) democratic ideas and Eastern Europe influenced by the socialist and communist ideas of the Union of Soviet Socialist Republics (USSR), founded in 1922. With the destruction of many European economies including their industries and businesses, the economic supremacy of Europe had vanished by the end of World War II.

The United States helped rebuild Western Europe's economy with the European Recovery Plan (Milward 1987), providing loans, food, natural resources and goods. During the four-year programme (1948–1952), the US supported Europe's economic recovery with about US$13 million. The money was distributed with the help of the newly founded Organisation for European Economic Co-operation (OEEC) that evolved into the OECD in 1961. The US goals were helping people in need, containing the USSR and communism, and creating a market for US goods.

In the late 1940s, several multinational institutions were founded and agreements negotiated to stabilise countries and their economies and to secure peace. Among them are the United Nations and the General Agreement on Tariffs and Trade, the latter evolving into the World Trade Organization in 1994. The International Monetary Fund (IMF) was founded in 1944 to stabilise economies, introducing the Bretton Woods System of exchange rate bands in combination with the gold standard, which was abandoned in the early 1970s.

In March 1957, Belgium, France, Italy, Luxemburg, the Netherlands and the Federal Republic of Germany founded the European Economic Community, which evolved into the European Union in 1993, thus creating a common European market with increasingly common standards.

The age of Europeanisation

After World War II, the relationship between the two world powers, the USA and USSR, evolved into the Cold War. The ideological conflict between capitalism and communism dominated foreign, security and business policies on both sides for the second half of the twentieth century. The demarcation line ran through Germany due to the American, French, British and Soviet occupation separating the newly founded Federal Republic of Germany from the German Democratic Republic under Soviet influence. Increasing tensions between the two world powers led to the Soviet's order for the construction of the Berlin Wall in 1961. With its history of industrialisation and solidarity, capitalism in Europe received a social interpretation with a concern for the well-being of workers and citizens expressed in collective agreements, labour laws and welfare systems shared in EU countries to different extents (Gerhards 2005). The formerly strong hierarchical and patriarchal structures in business and societies softened, starting participatory business practices such as co-determination in Germany.

The reconstruction of Europe and the newly created political and economic frameworks stimulated most economies in Western Europe. After years of destruction and deprivation, the dominant values became materialistic combined with a general entrepreneurial spirit. Europeans were optimistic looking forward, trying to rebuild their homes and improve their living conditions. This resulted in the *Wirtschaftswunder* (economic miracle) of the 1960s in Germany as well as other countries of Western Europe (Eichengreen 1996). Western European countries conducted business with the West based on predominantly social-capitalistic ideals, values and practices while Eastern European countries conducted business with the USSR and other communist countries based on communist ideology, values and respective practices.

The US civil rights movement in the 1960s spilled over to Western Europe, leading to civil and values conflicts. Demonstrations especially among students culminated in 1968, starting a democratisation process in all phases of life including European business and its work organisations. The results are less hierarchical systems, aspiring to gender equality with women no longer being only part of the labour force but also entering into professional, managerial and leadership roles. As a result of a combination of increasing prosperity, liberalisation and ecological problems due to intense industrial production, the establishment of the Club of Rome (Meadows et al. 1972) and the oil shock of 1973, post-materialistic values started to evolve, replacing materialistic and work as duty values especially among the younger generation with a focus on life and ecological balance, personal development and interdependence.

Gorbachev's Perestroika and Glasnost, a lagging economy, the nuclear catastrophe of Chernobyl and the growing quest for more freedom created a climate of change in the USSR leading to the peaceful break-down of the Berlin Wall on 9 November 1989. Overnight, the demarcation line between the Western and the Eastern world, between capitalism and communism was gone. Germany became reunited and (social) capitalist ideas penetrated formerly Eastern bloc countries. More and more states declared their independence marking the official end of the USSR on 31 December 1991. Hence, additional markets opened for Western goods and thoughts as well as business values and practices. In addition, Eastern European countries provided lower-cost production opportunities and a highly motivated workforce wanting to improve their standard of living, thus creating new business opportunities in an enlarged open market.

The founding and enlargement of the EU have strongly influenced today's European business. An increasing number of European countries joined in several rounds of enlargement, with UK, Ireland and Denmark joining in 1971. Greece, Spain and Portugal followed in the 1980s, Sweden, Finland and Austria in 1995. With the fall of the Iron Curtain, the formerly communist states Estonia, Latvia, Lithuania, Poland, the Czech Republic, Slovenia, Slovakia and Hungary joined in 2004 as well as the island of Malta and the Greek part of Cyprus. In January 2007, Romania and Bulgaria were accepted and Croatia in 2013. The citizens of Norway and Switzerland voted against membership. Official candidates for joining sometime in the future are Turkey, Macedonia, Montenegro, Albania and Serbia. Depending on their GDP, member states pay a contribution to the EU or receive support. As such, the EU is a means of fostering the development of less-developed European nations, securing peace and providing a large common market.

When the Schengen Treaty was passed in 1985, borders between EU nations opened, easing travel and business across borders. The Treaty of Maastricht in 1992 turned the EEC into the independent legal entity the European Union (EU) headquartered in Brussels with the European Court located in Strasbourg. The EU treaty guarantees free movement of people regarding work and residency, of trade and services as well as capital and payments with certain restrictions for newly joined members (Suder 2012). Information technology and the spread of the internet enables virtual business opportunities and practices.

Over the course of its existence, the EU's competencies have increased, addressing mutual issues such as foreign, security, labour, legal, ecological and digital policies as well as research funding. Of the current 28 members, 19 form an economic and currency union. In 2000, the euro was introduced as a common currency while leaving fiscal policies to the nations. This has all contributed to a large common market in Europe with goods, services and labour moving freely based on democratic, materialistic as well as post-materialistic values. As the research of Inglehart and Baker (2000) shows, economic development in Europe 'is associated with shifts away from absolute norms and values toward values that are increasingly rational, tolerant, trusting, and participatory' (p. 19). These values have influenced European business policies and practices with nation-, region-, industry- and firm-size-specific interpretations surfacing in their implementation.

Europe today and tomorrow

While the common economic policies, enlarged common free market and information technologies have enabled Europe to prosper and raise living standards for most of its nations and people, the financial and subsequent economic crisis in 2008 tested some of its achievements. Faced with economic and social problems such as slow growth, high numbers of unemployed and refugees, many EU member states tend to see their nation's or regional business interests as more important. Being part of Denmark but autonomous, Greenland left the EU in 1985 and Great Britain officially turned in its formal motion to exit the EU on 31 March 2017 after 51.9 per cent of its citizens had decided against EU membership in 2016. Other member countries have political parties that also support an exit from the EU arguing that they will fare better economically on their own.

What has happened to the *Aufbruchstimmung*, the idea and spirit of a united common market and Europe? Despite the efforts to ease the movement of trade, business and people within EU member states, despite common EU laws, policies, symbols and a common currency, there seems to be some EU fatigue among citizens of the 28 EU nations. To what extent does a European identity exist and what are its chances of surviving next to national and other cultural identities? Some of the social and political movements have shown that cultural boundaries and identifications do not necessarily coincide with national boundaries (Sackmann and Phillips 2004; Phillips and Sackmann 2015). Examples are the break-up of the USSR, the troubles in Ireland, Catalonia and the Basque region striving for more independence in Spain, the Lega Nord trying to separate from Southern Italy and the differences between England and Scotland. In their desire to stay in the EU, Scotland and Northern Ireland are even considering leaving the UK. Gerhards' (2005) comparison of social values between EU member states and EU candidate countries shows considerable cultural differences especially regarding democratic ideas, the importance of religion and gender roles.

Some European countries are still suffering from the aftermath of the financial crisis. There are ongoing discussions about a Europe of 'two speeds', a strong and a weak euro currency or even abandoning the common currency. The long-term consequences of the high unemployment rates even among well-educated young people especially in Southern European countries are unclear in terms of a lost generation (Froymovich 2013). In addition, increasing life expectancies will strain social welfare systems and consequently will put strains on the European business environment.

The recent waves of migrants and refugees trying to find a new home in the EU do not only place logistic and financial strains on the EU and its member states but also social and especially cultural strains based on different social values and religions. As discussed above, the EU member states have undergone a democratisation process in all spheres for a long period including gender roles. Their values are predominantly rooted in Christianity and most of them consider religion a personal and thus private matter. As stated in the preamble to the EU treaty, it drew 'inspiration from the cultural, religious and humanistic inheritance of Europe, from which have developed the universal values of the inviolable and inalienable rights of the human person, freedom, democracy, equality and the rule of law'. Many refugees and immigrants share neither this history nor religion, with views on, for example, the role of women that differ from the EU ideal (Gerhards 2005).

Despite all these challenges, Europe has experienced one of the longest periods of freedom and the member countries of the EU have reached a higher living standard compared to their situation at joining. Europe represents a market of about 500,000 million people providing ample business opportunities. Most European citizens have received advanced education and solid work qualifications. They can work and travel within a Europe with no boundaries. Educated and skilled refugees may help to tackle Europe's problems with its social security system due to its aging population and the shortage of skilled labour and experts.

Europe's culture has always been diverse, consisting of many facets that have influenced its business culture and practices. The overarching values of democracy, equality, freedom and solidarity have led to European business policies providing common symbols and common frameworks (Suder 2012). Nevertheless, their interpretation and translation into business practices still vary between nations, regions, industries as well as firm size and organisation. Examples are differences in jurisdictions influencing taxation, working hours, pay systems, benefits, and management and leadership practices including the interpretation of gender equality. Northern and some Western European countries as well as younger industries tend to practise, for example, participatory leadership with equal opportunities for men and women including few status differences and informal interactions. Leadership practices in Southern European countries still tend to be more patriarchal, formal and status oriented including dress codes as documented in many publications (e.g., Bosrock 2006; Gannon and Pillai 2012; Hofstede et al. 2010; Kessler and Wong-MingJi 2009; Trompenaars and Hampden-Turner 2012). Given a history in which hierarchy played an important role with men dominating business, many European countries still have fewer women in managerial and leadership positions, and those who have made it these positions are often paid less than their male colleagues.

The framework and values of the EU provide a basis for embracing cultural differences. As the EU Preamble states, 'United in diversity, Europe offers them [the peoples of Europe] the best chance of pursuing, with due regard for the rights of each individual and in awareness of their responsibilities toward future generations and the Earth, the great venture which makes of it a special area of human hope'. With the tolerance acquired on its long route to freedom and democracy, European business has become increasingly diverse and it may have to add a few facets to its diversity, turning it increasingly into a multicultural fabric. In addition, European citizens of all ages should remain aware of how far Europe has come in its present social, democratic, economic, legal and ecological accomplishments, so that the idea of solidarity does not get lost when faced with social and economic problems.

References

Blaich, F. (1985), *Der schwarze Freitag. Inflation und Weltwirtschaftskrise,* Munich, Deutscher Taschenbuch-Verlag.

Bosrock, M.M. (2006), *European Business Customs and Manners: A Country-by-Country Guide to European Customs and Manners,* Minnetonka, MN, Meadowbrook.

Eichengreen, B. (1996), 'Mainsprings of recovery in post-war Europe', in B. Eichengreen (ed.), *Europe's Post War Recovery,* Cambridge, Cambridge University Press, pp. 3–38.

Engels, F. (2009), *The Condition of the Working Class in England,* reissued edn, Oxford, Oxford University Press.

Feinstein, C. (1998), 'Pessimism perpetuated real wages and the standard of living in Britain during and after the Industrial Revolution', *Journal of Economic History,* vol. 58, no. 3, pp. 625–658.

Froymovich, R. (2013), *End of the Good Life: How the Financial Crisis Threatens a Lost Generation – and What We Can Do About It,* New York, Harper Perennial.

Gannon, M.J. and Pillai, R.K. (2012), *Understanding Global Cultures: Metaphorical Journeys Through 34 Nations, Clusters of Nations, Continents, and Diversity,* 6th edn, Thousand Oaks, CA, Sage.

Gerhards, J. (2005), *Kulturelle Unterschiede in der Europäischen Union: Ein Vergleich zwischen Mitgliedsländern, Beitrittskandidaten und der Türkei,* Wiesbaden, VS Verlag für Sozialwissenschaften.

Halecki, O. (1957), *Europa, Grenzen und Gliederung seiner Geschichte,* Darmstadt, Hermann Gentner Verlag.

Hill, R. (1993), *We Europeans,* 4th ed., Brussels, Europublications.

Hofstede, G., Hofstede, J. and Minkov, M. (2010), *Culture and Organizations: Software of the Mind,* 3rd edn, New York, McGraw Hill.

Inglehart, R. and Baker, W.E. (2000), 'Modernization, Cultural Change and the Persistence of Traditional Values', *American Sociological Review,* vol. 65, no. 1, pp. 19–51.

Kaasa, A., Vadi, M. and Varblane, U. (2014), 'Regional Cultural Differences within European Countries: Evidence from Multi-Country Surveys', *Management International Review,* vol. 54, no. 6, pp. 825–852

Kessler, E.H. and Wong-MingJi, D.J. (2009), '*Cultural Mythology and Global Leadership,* Part II: Europe', Cheltenham, UK and Northampton, MA, Edward Elgar.

Lopez, R.S. (1976), *The Commercial Revolution in the Middle Ages, 950–1350,* New York, Cambridge University Press.

Lübke, F. (2013), *Ein deutsches Modell macht Schule.* (accessed 13 September 2017).

Lucas, R.E., Jr. (2002), *Lectures on Economic Growth,* Cambridge, MA, Harvard University Press.

Marx, K. (1992), *Capital: Volume 1: A Critique of Political Economy,* reprinted edn, London, Penguin Classics.

Meadows, D.H., Meadows, D.L., Randers, J. and Behrens, W.W. III. (1972), *The Limits of Growth: A Report of the Club of Rome's Project on the Predicament of Mankind,* New York, Universe Books.

Milward, A.S. (1987), *The Reconstruction of Western Europe, 1945–51,* rev. edn, New York and London, Routledge.

Newitt, M. (2005), *A History of Portuguese Overseas Expansion, 1400–1668,* London: Routledge.

Phillips, M.E. and Sackmann, S.A. (2015), 'Cross cultural management rising', in N. Holden, S. Michailova and S. Tietze (eds), *The Routledge Companion of Cross-Cultural Management,* London, Routledge, pp. 8–18.

Russell-Wood, A.J.R. (1998), *The Portuguese Empire, 1415–1808: A World on the Move,* Baltimore, MD, Johns Hopkins University Press.

Sackmann, S.A. and Phillips, M.E. (2004), 'Contextual influences on culture research: Shifting Assumptions for new workplace realities', *International Journal of Cross-Cultural Research*, vol. 4, no. 3, pp. 371–392.

Schulz, K. (2010), *Handwerk, Zünfte und Gewerbe. Mittelalter und Renaissance,* Darmstadt, Wissenschaftliche Buchgesellschaft.

Simon, H. (2009), *Hidden Champions of the Twenty-First Century: The success strategies of unknown world market leaders*, Heidelberg, Springer.

Stevenson, D. (2014), 'Europe before 1914', The British Library Newsletter. www.bl.uk/world-war-one/articles/europe-before-1914 (accessed 20 March 2017).

Suder, G. (2012), *Doing Business in Europe,* 2nd edn, Thousand Oaks, Sage.

Trebilcock, C. (1998), 'The industrialization of modern Europe, 1750–1014', in T.C.W. Blanning (ed.), *The Oxford Illustrated History of Modern Europe*, Oxford, Oxford University Press, pp. 40–46.

Trompenaars, F. and Hampden-Turner, C. (2012), *Riding the Waves of Culture*, 3rd edn, New York, etc., McGraw Hill Education.

Webster, H. (1919), *Medieval and Modern History*, Boston, MA, Heath and Co.

10

TOWARDS A THEORY OF EUROPEAN BUSINESS CULTURE

The case of management education at the ESCP Europe Business School

Andreas Kaplan

European culture today: Maximum diversity – minimum distance

Europe is characterised by 'maximum cultural diversity at minimal geographical distances' (Kaplan 2014, p. 532). With around 50 nations and over 60 distinct languages, the European continent is the epitome of cultural variety. The high heterogeneity of European cultures leads to a correspondingly high diversity of business, management and working styles. Therefore, one can reasonably question whether it is truly possible to define a unified concept of European business culture.

In order to discuss European business and management from a theoretical perspective, it is necessary to begin by examining the institutions where the European approach to management is developed and taught – namely, European business schools. Accordingly, this book chapter starts with a brief reassessment of the history of business schools, with an emphasis on how European institutions differ from their counterparts in the USA (cf. Kaplan 2014, 2015).

Consequently, we apply the following definition for the European approach to management: 'a cross-cultural, societal management approach based on interdisciplinary principles' (Kaplan 2014, p. 529). This definition implies that a successful European manager needs to possess cultural intelligence, consider societal factors in his or her decisions, and be highly adaptable to contextual diversity, which entails being informed by a variety of disciplines and understanding the interdependencies among them.

Building on this definition, this chapter takes a closer look at how European management is currently conceptualised and disseminated at one of the most quintessential European business schools: ESCP Europe. ESCP Europe Business School has six different campuses across Europe – in Berlin, London, Madrid, Paris, Turin and Warsaw – and students study on different campuses over the course of their studies. To be European is part of the school's DNA, and is proclaimed as such in ESCP Europe's mission statement. We investigate how the key elements of European management, as defined above, are perceived by different ESCP Europe students as well as by young alumni.

A potential definition of European management, theoretically derived from the history of European business schools

To derive a theory-based characterisation of business culture that is distinctly European, it is useful to look at the differences between US and European business schools – i.e., the places where management education and styles are institutionalised and disseminated (cf. Kaplan 2014). Such an approach is in line with the work of Berger and Luckmann (1966), who explain that contexts are socially constructed, and that the socialisation of people in general occurs within cultural contexts and in nationally rooted educational systems.

Higher management education differs between European and US institutions in both approach and content. McNulty (1992), for example, states that in contrast to their US counterparts, European business schools show a stronger preference for action learning methods, learning via practical internships and professional endeavours. Kipping et al. (2004) point out that, for many years, European business schools rejected the case study method invented by Harvard University and adopted widely in US business schools. Indeed, since its establishment in 1819 in Paris, the ESCP Europe Business School has preferred to rely on pedagogical simulation games for teaching purposes (Antunes and Thomas 2007; Blanchard 2009).

US and European business schools differ substantially not only in their teaching methods but also in their approaches to research activities. European researchers frequently adopt a qualitative and more exploratory approach to scientific research, whereas US scholars tend to focus more on quantitative and confirmatory research (Welter and Lasch 2008). These divergent approaches are manifested in the known discussion on rigour versus relevance (Lehmann et al. 2011).

A look at the general history of business schools can provide a deeper understanding of the differences between European and US institutions. The history and evolution of business schools started in 1819 with the establishment of ESCP Europe, the world's first business school, and can be divided into three distinct periods. The first is the Founding Period, spanning the years between 1819 and 1944. During this period, three rather independent models of business schools emerged: the US model, the French–Belgium 'South European' model, and the German 'North European' model (Kaplan 2014). The second period, referred to herein as the Assimilation Period, started in 1945, with a general post-World War II Americanisation of business schools across Europe. The final and third period in the history of European business schools, i.e., the Emancipation Period, started in 1997 with the founding of EQUIS, the European accreditation label of the European Foundation for Management Development (EFMD). EQUIS constituted a counterweight to the US accreditation agency AACSB and was effectively a move towards European independence from US standards.

During the Founding Period, the establishment of ESCP Europe in France inspired several business schools to be founded in southern Europe, especially in Italy. A second development was led by Germany, with the establishment of the Handelshochschule in Leipzig in 1898 (Kieser 2004), which primarily influenced the evolution of higher management education in Northern Europe, particularly in Scandinavia. In the USA, the movement started with the founding of the Wharton School of Finance and Commerce in 1881 and the Harvard Business School in 1908.

During the Founding Period, it was already possible to observe that European and US business schools differed in terms of their international perspective. While schools in North America did not promote an international or cross-cultural approach during their early years, both European streams, i.e., the Southern as well as the Northern models, were international in nature. More than one-third of ESCP Europe's student body represented nationalities other than France, with 15 different countries represented in the school from the first classes onwards.

In addition, these students were offered foreign language courses in ten different languages (Renouard 1999). In contrast, this was not the case at the Wharton School, in line with the aim of Joseph Wharton, the school's founding father, 'to create a liberally educated class of leaders for American society' (Sass 1982, p. 20).

Scholars such as Geert Hofstede (1980) have since shown that European countries have specific cultural characteristics that impact business and management. Accordingly, the European manager – to a greater extent than businessmen in other regions of the world – needs skills that enable him or her to adjust rapidly to different cultures and cultural contexts. This idea is confirmed by Calori and de Woot (1994, p. 237), who observe that such skills include 'international experience, competence in at least three languages, geographical mobility and global thinking'.

Alongside the cross-cultural component of the European approach to management education, a strong societal element can be identified. Neo-classical economist Jean Baptiste-Say, one of ESCP Europe's co-founders, ensured that the school's approach to business education would be social as well as demand-oriented in scope (Forget 1999). Similarly, the economist Eugen Schmalenbach, a prominent figure in the founding period of the North European (German-oriented) model of business schools, emphasised that business schools should aim to foster common social well-being rather than serve solely to promote individual interests (Kieser 2004). US business schools focused less on societal aspects, because, at the time of Wharton's founding, Taylorism and the theories of Adam Smith were omnipresent. Accordingly, Wharton's main objective was to enhance financial efficiency, particularly via an increase in work productivity (Wren and Van Fleet 1983). Years later, Wallace Donham (1933), former Harvard Business School Dean, would point out US schools' shortfall of consideration of economic issues within their broader societal environment.

More current scientific research demonstrates the continuing importance of societal notions in the European approach to management (Calori et al. 1995). For example, Pudelko and Harzing (2007) point out that, in comparison to the US management style, European management is characterised by a more balanced approach between financial objectives and societal considerations. In addition, Europe puts more weight on the public administration sector, whose broader aim is to guarantee the prosperity of society at large (Kaplan and Haenlein 2009), which could be considered as proof of the societal emphasis inherently present in European business cultures. It is important to acknowledge that societal considerations are not exclusive to European management – managers from other global macro regions deal with such concerns as well. It is, however, reasonable to suggest that business and management approaches in Europe have traditionally emphasised these factors to a greater extent compared with those of other world regions (Kaplan 2014).

Another difference that one detects when analysing the foundations of business schools in Europe and the USA concerns interdisciplinary aspects. While European schools proposed curricula with a large variety of study areas, including economics, foreign languages, geography, history, humanities and law (Meyer 1998; Renouard 1999), the Wharton School's approach was, again, inspired by Frederick Taylor, who desired to create a veritable management science 'resting upon clearly defined laws, rules, and principles, as a foundation' (Taylor 1911, p. 7). Consequently, Wharton's curricula were less interdisciplinary, with a focus on courses in business and finance.

The structure of the European business education system provides additional evidence that interdisciplinary aspects constitute a distinguishing feature of European management research. Whereas US schools were integrated early on into the university system, the first European business schools were set up independently, outside a collegiate system. Integration within universities made it necessary for US business schools to establish a clearly-defined scientific management discipline. Such 'scientisation' led to focusing on a single discipline only, whereas in Europe a more interdisciplinary approach was and still is possible. Indeed, an analysis by Welter and Lasch (2008) suggests that European scientists apply more descriptive and qualitative methodologies than do their US colleagues, and that, generally speaking, scientific research in Europe is more contextual compared with research in the USA.

As indicated above, European management can therefore be defined as 'a cross-cultural, societal management approach based on interdisciplinary principles' (Kaplan 2014, p. 529).

It should be noted that the differences between US and European business schools diminished during the Assimilation and Americanisation period of the history of business schools; however, they began to re-emerge during the Emancipation Period, as European business schools grew more independent and established a stronger focus on their founding characteristics. This evolution towards a distinct European style of management and management education has been strengthened by a number of EU decisions, such as the 1999 Bologna Agreement, which seeks to promote common standards for higher education quality across Europe, and to simplify the mobility of students in Europe. Moreover, as mentioned above, the founding of the European quality label EQUIS by the EFMD has further fostered 'European independence' in this regard. Compared with the US accreditation system (AACSB), EQUIS puts more emphasis on accredited schools' internationalisation, general strategy and differentiation attempts. Of course, such European efforts did not completely stop the Americanisation and Globalisation of business school practices, which continues in different forms across the world (cf. Juusola et al. 2015).

European management from the practical perspective of students and recent graduates of ESCP Europe Business School

Kaplan's (2014) theoretical definition of European management implies that European managers need to have three characteristics, which are referred to herein as the '3Cs' of European managers: they must display Cross-cultural intelligence, integrate Corporate social responsibility into their decisions and be able to adapt quickly to Contextual diversity. To achieve the latter, an interdisciplinary approach to management education should be pursued.

In what follows, after briefly elaborating on the meaning of each of the 3Cs, we will show how these aspects are perceived and developed in practice at a quintessential European business school: ESCP Europe, whose mission is to form future European managers in a globalised world in line with the school's slogan, 'European Identity, Global Perspective'.

Methodology

For this study, a qualitative research design was preferred over a quantitative approach. Specifically, a series of 21 in-depth interviews were conducted in English, with an average time span of 35 minutes each. This number of respondents is consistent with the work by Guest et al. (2006). In selecting interview partners, we considered two different groups, i.e., students and young alumni, with an attempt to achieve maximum diversity in the interviewees' nationalities. As soon as interviewees agreed to take part, interviews were carried out according to a semi-structured approach, in which the 3Cs of European management were emphasised.

The following Table 10.1 presents each interviewee's profile. Actual names are anonymised, and each interviewee has been assigned a 'name' that represents his or her profile. Specifically, each alumnus has been given a first name starting with an A, and each student's name begins with an S. Names are also representative of the interviewees' nationalities and genders; e.g.,

Table 10.1 Overview of European business culture interview respondents

name	type	nationality	gender	age
Aarav	Alumni	Indian	Male	29
Adalina	Alumni	Swedish	Female	30
Alberta	Alumni	Italian	Female	28
Alejandra	Alumni	Spanish	Female	27
Aleksander	Alumni	Polish	Male	30
An	Alumni	Chinese	Male	33
Andreas	Alumni	German	Male	31
Antonia	Alumni	German	Female	28
Samira	Student	Moroccan	Female	23
Sandrine	Student	French	Female	23
Sandro	Student	Italian	Male	23
Sarah	Student	French	Female	24
Sergei	Student	Russian	Male	21
Sheng	Student	Chinese	Male	23
Shu	Student	Chinese	Female	24
Simon	Student	German	Male	25
Sixtine	Student	French	Female	21
Sneha	Student	Indian	Female	26
Soan	Student	French	Male	21
Stefanie	Student	German	Female	24
Stéphane	Student	French	Male	23

Antonia represents a female German alumna, and Sergei represents a male Russian student. The sample comprised 52 per cent women, the average age was 26, and respondents represented ten different nationalities.

The interviews led to more than 60 pages of interview transcripts. Using these transcripts as a basis, we applied the standard six-step process for the study of qualitative notes (e.g., LeCompte 2000; Spiggle 1994): categorisation, abstraction, comparison, dimensionalisation, integration and iteration. Interview transcripts were first catalogued, labelled and reviewed along the three elements of European management. Then, they were categorised on the individual interviewee level to pinpoint passages or topics that portrayed the same common phenomena. In a last step, the empirically detected categories were grouped into broader conceptual groups, which resulted from the comparison of several interviews. Overall, this procedure was repeated to consider all results from the 21 interviews, until no additional alterations were required.

Our analysis relies on verbatim statements obtained from interviews held with several ESCP Europe students and recent graduates. It has to be noted that the case setting and interviewees chosen for this study represent a somewhat specific and idiosyncratic sample. First, ESCP Europe is doubtlessly a rather advanced example for business school Europeanisation. Furthermore, all respondents are part of the community of one of the best management institutions in Europe. This has to be considered when interpreting the results mentioned below.

General perceptions of the tenets of European management

Before being questioned specifically about the three defining elements of European management discussed above, interviewees were asked to provide their own general definitions and descriptions of 'European business culture(s)' and of the 'European style of management'. Almost all respondents clearly referred to the cross-cultural component. Simon, for example, stated that 'European management includes knowledge of diverse cultures and celebrates the differences between the different countries'. Stéphane also felt that European management is about the diversity in cultures, and that there is not one homogenous European style of management: 'In my opinion, business cultures differ among nations; a German business culture or a French business culture have stronger identities than an overarching European one. A European business culture would be more likely to be defined in contrast to other large powers such as China, US or Russia'. Notably, interview partners from outside the European Union extended the notion of doing business across cultures to countries outside Europe: 'European management is closely related to cultural integration, including the countries outside the EU … In particular, it is about understanding cultural nuances across the globe' (Sergei). In addition to referring to the cross-cultural aspect, respondents also mentioned the ability to speak several languages: 'European management accounts for diversity in cultures and languages' (Sneha), which 'includes being fluent in at least three languages and being historically and culturally [fluent] in a number of European cultures so as to be truly able to manage companies and groups across European borders' (Simon).

The societal aspect was also clearly described as a defining characteristic of European business and management: 'I would say that the respect and protection of workers, [white-collar] or not, are a common trait in most of the European countries' (Sarah); 'Respect for the employees; respect for the environment' (Sandro); 'European management is about the well-being of all stakeholders' (Sneha). Interviewees were particularly likely to emphasise the societal aspect when comparing European business cultures to the US approach to doing business: '[European managers are] more respectful of people. Less aggressive in terms of business' (Sarah); '[European] employees have more rights. Companies respect the environment to a greater extent' (Sandro); 'The European approach is, I guess, more open to others and more willing to collaborate with others' (Shu).

Respondents also mentioned the importance of an interdisciplinary perspective and contextual diversity, albeit not necessarily in a straightforward manner, but rather within discussions of the cultural and societal dimensions of European management: 'European business and management encompasses a variety of political environments, as well as social and economic dimensions' (Samira); 'Of course legal frameworks differ from country to country' (Andreas). Notably, one alumna working in the field strongly emphasised this dimension, pointing out that 'In Europe you cannot be only specialised in management. You need to have knowledge about the legal and political frameworks. Public administration and the public sector play a vital role in European countries. History and social sciences are important to understand why different cultures behave like they do' (Alberta).

Some respondents mentioned additional elements as important characteristics of a European style of management. Several mentioned the significance of product quality: 'A high level of quality and quality assurance' (Sneha); 'Quality of products and services' (Sandro). Others (Sneha, Sandrine) pointed out the importance of a good work–life balance. Finally, some of the interviewees defined European management as being open, interpersonal and friendly.

Cross-cultural intelligence

Cross-cultural intelligence can be described as a manager's capacity to function effectively in culturally distinct environments (Earley and Ang 2003). Cultural diversity is regularly said to be a source of added value, as it can encourage creativity, new ideas and innovation (West and

Anderson 1996; Thomas and Ely 1996). Research indicates that the effectiveness of a manager's approach to business and management is strongly linked to the cultural environment in which the manager is acting (e.g., Calori and Dufour 1995; Tixier 1994). Institutions can 'teach' their students cultural intelligence by having them live abroad for a significant period of time, while simultaneously educating them with courses on cross-cultural matters (Eisenberg et al. 2013). Ideally, the student body and faculty should come from culturally diverse backgrounds (Kedia and Harveston 1998).

At ESCP Europe, students of all programmes pursue their studies in a minimum of two countries, most often in those where the school's own six campuses are located. For example, in the full-time MBA programme, which is one year long, students spend each semester in a different country. The school's Bachelor in Management programme is designed along the lines of 'three years – three countries – three languages', with students moving from one campus to another on an annual basis. Furthermore, students are strongly encouraged to do their mandatory internships in different countries during the course of their studies. For programmes with a duration of over one year, students need to achieve trilingualism, which is tested via external certification bodies such as TOEFL, the Goethe Institut and others.

Interviewees clearly believed that their cross-cultural intelligence had developed as a result of studying on various campuses, participating in internships in different countries and learning different languages. Antonia, for example, explicitly stated that cross-cultural abilities are increased by 'Having different campuses and encouraging students to study on them; learning different languages; internships everywhere in the world'. Many of the respondents indicated that, in their view, cultural intelligence is not developed in specific courses but rather is learned through experience: 'The most efficient way of developing cultural intelligence is to let students work in and experience different cultures. This is done at ESCP Europe by allowing students to study on our different campuses and exchange patterns. Cultural intelligence cannot be taught in a classroom but [can] only be learned through personal experience' (Aleksander); 'At ESCP Europe, students learn [cultural intelligence] in group works in their courses. Not particularly taught, but experienced, I think this is the most efficient and most effective way to develop this skill' (Simon). In particular, respondents emphasised the intermingling of students coming from different cultures in their various team assignments: 'I believe that ESCP Europe ensures that students develop cultural intelligence by mixing for instance people from different backgrounds, getting them to work on the same project' (Samira).

The interviewees also pointed to areas where ESCP Europe might further enhance its cross-cultural focus. Some expressed a desire to acquire more theoretical insight into cross-cultural management; Sergei, for example, recalled 'distinct frameworks from organisational behaviour and psychology courses that can be used to analyse cultural features ... I would welcome more detailed focus on those frameworks in the courses.' Many respondents suggested that the scope of multinational teamwork should be expanded: 'More projects should be assigned to multicultural teams' (An); 'Students must be automatically put in cross-cultural teams with each teamwork done by one Italian, one German, one French, and two other nationalities. Additionally, these teams should be split across the different campuses in order for them to have to work together remotely. While during their first semester they could be physically on the same campus, during the second semester they should be split across Europe' (Soan).

Corporate social responsibility

The Collins Dictionary (2014) defines the term 'societal' as 'of or relating to society, especially human society or social relations'. Societal management can thus be defined as 'management that takes into account society's overall welfare in addition to mere profitability considerations' (Kaplan 2014, p. 532). Corporate social responsibility (CSR) is described as the 'economic, legal, ethical, and discretionary expectations that society has of organizations at a given point in time' (Carroll and Buchholtz 2003, p. 36). Corporate social responsibility thus embodies the notion that organisations should pursue not only profit but also societal benefit.

Building on the premise that European management is societal by definition, Moore (2004) observes that the European EQUIS policies do not ask for the inclusion of a specific CSR or business ethics course in the respective programmes. This approach can be interpreted as an indication that societal elements should be integrated into all courses, ranging from human resources to finance to business strategy. Indeed, ESCP Europe has adopted this perspective; that is, the school's curricula do not include specific courses on CSR or business ethics, but professors are asked to integrate societal considerations into each of their courses. Moreover, the school itself pursues many societal objectives. For example, ESCP Europe has a clearly defined scholarship policy to enable students from diverse social backgrounds to study at ESCP Europe, and it provides entry examinations designed specifically for candidates coming from disadvantaged backgrounds. ESCP Europe views these policies not only as a means of promoting students from weaker social backgrounds but also as an opportunity for all students to benefit from the experiences and viewpoints of colleagues coming from diverse environments.

While interviewees appreciated the fact that societal notions are integrated into various courses, they also expressed regret that this is not done more often and in a more systematic manner: 'Some professors give this insight but not all of them' (Sixtine); 'Professors in some fields emphasise this at some point in their lectures, though not enough' (Alejandra). Some also noted that ESCP Europe promotes all kinds of professions, not only those that are traditionally associated with business schools, such as consulting or finance: 'ESCP encourages us to do a job that we are good at, not necessarily investment banking or consulting but as entrepreneurs or in the humanitarian sector' (Alberta). In their discussion of societal considerations, several respondents mentioned student societies focusing on humanitarian issues: 'Supporting the student societies who promote societal well-being is a great step too' (Sneha); 'ESCP Europe ensures that future graduates will integrate societal well-being into their management decisions by getting them involved in societies and committees' (Samira). Some interviewees mentioned that they would like to see greater emphasis on companies that take societal notions into consideration when doing business: 'Promote more companies that lead this kind of project, to inspire students; invite them to school' (Sixtine); 'Having case studies on companies that do this, or inviting guest lecturers from such companies' (Sneha).

Contextual diversity

Interdisciplinarity refers to the combination of several distinct scientific disciplines into one domain, thereby creating something new. In other words, as Klein (1990, p. 19) attests, interdisciplinary aspects relate to 'the ideas of a unified science, general knowledge, synthesis and the integration of knowledge'. As noted above, European business schools should educate future managers from an interdisciplinary perspective, both as a means of staying true to their history and to foster their students' adaptability to contextual diversity.

ESCP Europe promotes interdisciplinary aspects through several avenues. First, many of its programmes include courses in humanities and liberal arts, coding, language training, law, mathematics, statistics and economics, on top of courses in business and management. Simulation games incorporated into the various programmes combine multiple aspects into a single task, showing the interdependencies among different domains. Moreover, ESCP Europe's students take part in courses together with students from partner universities coming from other fields than business and management (such as engineering, programming or law), and are thereby exposed to maximum diversity and become familiar with other environments and 'languages' (such as, e.g., the language an engineer would apply). Finally, the school develops and encourages double degrees with partner universities specialised in areas other than management, enabling students to gain a full-fledged second degree in, for example, law or programming, on top of their diploma in business.

Interview respondents diverged substantially in their perceptions of what ESCP Europe does in terms of interdisciplinarity. Some thought that the school does nothing or very little in order to foster interdisciplinary aspects. Simon, for example, stated that, in his experience, 'there is very little interdisciplinary thinking taught at ESCP Europe', and that he was 'personally convinced that strengthening ESCP Europe's interdisciplinary education strengthens ESCP Europe as a school and its students as graduates'. Most interviewees reported that they had learned about other disciplines mostly by joining the various student societies that are run by the students themselves in domains such as arts, sports, politics and professional or humanitarian fields. Thus, both Sixtine and Sneha, for example, described their involvement in student societies when talking about contextual diversity. Some of the interviewees did, however, mention courses in the liberal arts and humanities offered by ESCP Europe, stating that such opportunities should be expanded and made mandatory, with Simon suggesting that 'every student [should have] to choose one out of, e.g., four courses which comes not from a management discipline, but from a different background such as culture, history, art or psychology'.

European culture tomorrow: Minimal diversity – maximum distance?

This chapter looked at the history of business schools and higher education in business and management and compared European education practices to those that are more prevalent in the USA (see also Kaplan 2014). This theoretical and historical analysis was enriched with an empirical investigation of the manner in which a European style of management is taught at ESCP Europe. This comparison aims at evolving towards a theory of European business culture (cf. Ridder et al. 2014).

Future research should broaden the scope of this study and involve a range of different business schools as well as corporations and further types of organisation. In addition to a qualitative research design, a quantitative approach should be undertaken which would allow for a more detailed analysis of the different elements of European business and management. Such a study could involve various stakeholders such as managers working in European organisations displaying experience in international as well as cross-cultural settings.

Notably, cross-culturalism, one of the most prominent components of European management, both in theory and in practice, might actually promote a decrease over time in the high diversity across the European continent. Such a development might be facilitated by initiatives such as the EU Bologna Agreement, which has led to greater similarity among European universities in different countries, or by the Erasmus Initiative, which fosters mobility of students across different countries.

At the same time, researchers and practitioners are increasingly acknowledging that cross-cultural intelligence, societal management and the capacity to adapt to organisational diversity are of vital interest in an era of globalisation and increasing awareness of the need for sustainability, social diversity and inclusion. Accordingly, it seems that the European approach to management, and consequently the way management is taught in Europe, has the potential to become more and more popular. In other words, the 'minimal distance' of different cultures within Europe could be enlarged and interpreted to 'maximum distance'. Indeed, the US-based AACSB (2009) has suggested that its major difficulties are 'differences in organisational and cultural values' and 'cultural diversity among employees and customers'.

If demand for European-style management increases, then how might European management education be made available worldwide, without everybody coming to Europe? Massively open online courses (MOOCs) might be the solution to this challenge. These new tools for distance education make it feasible to teach the same course to several thousands of students all over the world at the same time (Kaplan and Haenlein 2016; Pucciarelli and Kaplan 2016). And while it is theoretically possible that an American university could teach the European approach to management, it seems more likely that such a MOOC will be produced by a business school located in Europe (Kaplan 2016).

The arrival of MOOCS will lead to a more specialised and niche-focused market of higher education. Since the availability of such courses gives students the opportunity to 'strive for the best' and take classes offered by the universities with the highest expertise in particular areas, it is quite likely that several stars will arise who are the specialists in a specific domain. While the best law students might dream of Harvard University, proponents of mergers and acquisitions could strive for the Wharton Business School, and future managers who specialise in European, cross-cultural management might take their chances with ESCP Europe.

Thus, as European management becomes more homogeneous across European countries, it might at the same time be more broadly disseminated all around the world. Accordingly, this chapter's introductory premise of 'maximum diversity – minimal distance' could actually develop somehow into 'minimum diversity – maximal distance'. However, two arguments can be provided to suggest that the first part, at least, will not happen just yet.

First, Europeans speak different languages, which are an expression of cultural diversity and corresponding behavioural diversity across cultures. Given that European citizens will not all begin to speak the same mother tongue in the near future, it is highly probable that distinct approaches to management will persist as well. Second, diversity is considered to provide added value, as expressed through the slogan of the European Union 'United in Diversity'. Therefore, European decision leaders will certainly seek to maintain an environment fostering such diversity and to ensure that Europe will continue to hold 'maximum cultural diversity at minimal geographical distances' (Kaplan 2014, p. 532).

References

AACSB (2009), *Eligibility Procedures and Accreditation Standards*, Tampa, FL, AACSB.

Antunes D. and Thomas H. (2007), 'The competitive (dis)advantage of European business schools', *Long Range Planning*, 40(3), 382–404.

Berger P. and Luckmann T. (1966), *The Social Construction of Reality*, London, Pelican.

Blanchard M. (2009), 'From "Ecoles Supérieures de Commerce" to "Management Schools": Transformations and continuity in French business schools', *European Journal of Education*, 44(4), 586–604.

Calori R. and de Woot P. (1994), *A European Management Model: Beyond diversity*, New York, Prentice Hall.

Calori R. and Dufour B. (1995), 'Management European style', *The Academy of Management Executive*, 9, 61–73.

Calori R., Steele M. and Yoneyama E. (1995), 'Management in Europe: Learning from different perspectives', *European Management Journal*, 13(1), 58–66.

Carroll A.B. and Buchholtz A.K. (2003), *Business and Society: Ethics and stakeholder Management*, 5th edn, Australia, Thomson South-Western.

Collins Dictionary (2014), 'Societal', in Collins online dictionary, Glasgow, HarperCollins Publishers. Available at: www.collinsdictionary.com/dictionary/english/societal. (accessed 8 March 2018).

Donham W. (1933), 'The failure of business leadership and the responsibility of the universities', *Harvard Business Review*, 11, 418–435.

Earley P.C. and Ang S. (2003), *Cultural Intelligence: Individual interactions across cultures*, Palo Alto, CA, Stanford University Press.

Eisenberg J., Lee H.-J., Brück F., Brenner B., Claes M.-T., Mironski J. and Bell R. (2013), 'Can business schools make students culturally competent? Effects of cross-cultural management courses on cultural intelligence', *Academy of Management Learning and Education*, 12(4), 603–621.

Forget E.L. (1999), *The Social Economics of Jean-Baptiste Say*, London, UK, Routledge.

Guest G., Bunce A. and Johnson L. (2006), 'How many interviews are enough? An experiment with data saturation and variability', *Field Methods*, 18(1), 59–82.

Hofstede G. (1980), *Culture's Consequences. Comparing values, behaviors, institutions and organizations across nations*, London, UK, Sage.

Juusola K., Kettunen K. and Alajoutsijärvi K. (2015), 'Accelerating the Americanization of management education: Five responses from business schools', *Journal of Management Inquiry*, 24(4), 347–369.

Kaplan A.M. (2014), 'European management and European business schools: Insights from the history of business schools', *European Management Journal*, 32(4), 529–534.

Kaplan A.M. (2015), *European Business and Management*, London, Sage Publications Ltd.

Kaplan A.M. (2016), 'Academia goes social media, MOOC, SPOC, SMOC, and SSOC: The digital transformation of higher education institutions and universities', in Bikramjit Rishi and Subir Bandyopadhyay (eds), *Contemporary Issues in Social Media Marketing*, Oxon and New York, Routledge.

Kaplan A.M. and Haenlein M. (2009), 'The increasing importance of public marketing: Explanations, applications and limits of marketing within public administration', *European Management Journal*, 27(1), 197–212.

Kaplan A.M. and Haenlein M. (2016), 'Higher education and the digital revolution: About MOOCs, SPOCs, social media and the Cookie Monster', *Business Horizons*, 59(4), 441–450.

Kedia B.L. and Harveston P.D. (1998), 'Transformation of MBA programs: Meeting the challenge of international competition', *Journal of World Business*, 33(2), 203–217.

Kieser A. (2004), 'The Americanization of academic management education in Germany', *Journal of Management Inquiry*, 13(2), 90–97.

Kipping M., Üsdiken B. and Puig N. (2004), 'Imitation, tension, and hybridization: Multiple "Americanizations" of management education in Mediterranean Europe', *Journal of Management Inquiry*, 13(2), 98–108.

Klein J.T. (1990), *Interdisciplinarity: History, theory, and practice*, Detroit, MI, Wayne State University.

LeCompte M.D. (2000), 'Analyzing qualitative data', *Theory into Practice*, 39, 146–154.

Lehmann D.R., McAlister L. and Staelin R. (2011), 'Sophistication in research in marketing', *Journal of Marketing*, 75(4), 155–165.

McNulty N.G. (1992), 'Management education in Eastern Europe: "Fore and after"', *Management Executive*, 6(4), 78–87.

Meyer H.-D. (1998), 'The German Handelshochschulen, 1898–1933: A new departure in management education and why it failed', in L. Engwall and V. Zamagni (eds), *Management Education in Historical Perspective*, Manchester, Manchester University Press.

Moore G. (2004), 'Regulatory perspectives on business ethics in the curriculum', *Journal of Business Ethics*, 54(4), 349–356.

Pucciarelli F. and Kaplan A.M. (2016), 'Competition and strategy in higher education: Managing complexity and uncertainty', *Business Horizons*, 59(3), 311–320.

Pudelko M. and Harzing A.-W. (2007), 'How European is management in Europe? An analysis of past, present and future management practices in Europe', *European Journal of International Management*, 1(3), 206–224.

Renouard A. (1999), *Histoire de l'École supérieure de commerce de Paris*, Paris, Raymond Castell éditions.

Ridder H.G., Hoon C. and McCandless Baluch A. (2014), 'Entering a dialogue: Positioning case study findings towards theory', *British Journal of Management*, 25(2), 373–387.

Sass S.A. (1982), *The Pragmatic Imagination. A history of the Wharton School 1881–1981*, Philadelphia, PA, University of Pennsylvania Press.

Spiggle S. (1994), 'Analysis and interpretation of qualitative data in consumer research', *Journal of Consumer Research*, 21, 491–503.

Taylor F.W. (1911), *The Principles of Scientific Management*, New York, Harper Bros.

Thomas D.A. and Ely R.J. (1996), 'Making differences matter: A new paradigm for managing diversity', *Harvard Business Review*, 74, 79–90.

Tixier M. (1994), 'Management and communication styles in Europe: Can they be compared and matched?' *Employee Relations*, 16(1), 8–26.

Welter F. and Lasch F. (2008), 'Entrepreneurship research in Europe: Taking stock and looking forward', *Entrepreneurship Theory and Practice*, 32(2), 241–248.

West M.A. and Anderson N.R. (1996), 'Innovation in top management teams', *Journal of Applied Psychology*, 81, 680–693.

Wren D.A. and Van Fleet D.D. (1983), 'History in schools of business', *Business and Economic History*, 12(1), 29–35.

PART D

The political economy of doing business in advanced regionalisation

11

REGIONALISATION AND THE EUROPEAN PROJECT

Bruce Wilson

Introduction

One of the remarkable features of the European Union (EU) has been its decision that member states distribute resources across national boundaries, from the wealthier nations to the poorer. The purpose of this distribution has been variously to assist member states to redress regional inequalities, to strengthen competitiveness and to enhance the efficiency and innovative capacity of the Single European Market. While this has been an intergovernmental process, essentially, the progressive development of the policy and its instruments over 40 years has been targeted increasingly at engaging with European business.

Both in its processes, and in its practical impact, the EU's regional policy continues to be a central part of the overall framework of the EU's approach to developing a supranational political and economic entity. It accounts for around one-third of the EU's expenditure and involves complex challenges of focusing and redistributing resources from some member states mostly to poorer regions in other nation states. Since 2014, there has been much stronger linkage between the strategic objectives of Europe 2020, the EU's overarching strategic framework for this period, with a focus on building the 'Innovation Union', and the commitment of the European structural funds, which is the principal means for the implementation of the regional policy (see Foray et al. 2012).

While the commitment of expenditure from the structural funds has been managed through institutional negotiation, the direct and indirect implications for business have been very important. The sums involved have themselves constituted a significant proportion of investment, often leveraging other injections of resources, and the practical project outcomes have provided infrastructure to facilitate business access to markets, improved access to energy, enhanced skills for employees and, more recently, direct incentives and support for innovation (see EC 2014a, 2014b).

This chapter provides an introduction to EU regional policy, its role in promoting a more integrated Single European Market and on developing infrastructure to promote competitiveness, particularly for SMEs. It concludes with an outline of the current emphasis on public-private partnerships to promote innovation.

EU regional policy: The background

The existence of regional inequalities was recognised in the earliest days of the European Economic Community, in the Treaty of Rome in 1957. In 1961, a Conference on Regional Economies prompted investigations which led to the first European Commission Communication on Regional Policy in 1965. The Directorate General for Regional Policy was established in 1968 with the purposes and parameters of regional policy being articulated in European legislation from the 1970s, reflecting a moral imperative to address inequalities. In keeping with the EU's 7-year multiannual financial frameworks, particular iterations of regional policy have been developed for each successive multiannual period since 1975. In 1975, the European Regional Development Fund (ERDF) was established to provide resources for regions to become more competitive, particularly in those areas dependent on agriculture, industrial change or structural under-employment. However, as an indication of the slow evolution of regional policy, member states retained ultimate control of the Fund, choosing themselves how their share of the ERDF would be allocated to the regions (see EC n.d.; Dudek 2014; and also Hooghe and Keating 1994).

This arrangement left room for member states' priorities to intrude into funding decision-making rather than the wider European objectives. In 1985, the President of the European Commission, Jacques Delores reported that disparities amongst regions were widening. This led to a further iteration of policy in 1988, emphasising that redistribution between richer and poorer regions across the different member states of Europe was needed in order to support and to mitigate the effects of the further economic integration that was planned as part of the development of the Single European Market. This led to three major reforms to regional policy:

legally (the use in a Treaty of the specific wording, 'economic and social cohesion');
financing (now three structural funds, with reinforced emphasis on the ERDF's role in addressing regional imbalances); and
regulatory (focused on five priorities, multiannual programming, involvement of relevant regional and local authorities in decision-making within member states, and ensuring that European funds were additional, not used to substitute for member state expenditure).

This was also a period when the administrative dimensions of regional policy implementation were subject to fierce debate (see Dudek 2014). For a start, the determination of regions for policy implementation purposes did not mirror the existing administrative boundaries within member states. Overall, there are approximately 270 EU regions. Far from being self-evident, this has been very much a contested issue. In the first decade or so, member states retained control over the designation of EU regional policy areas. However, in 1988, the European Commission achieved Council support for the determination of regional boundaries at EU level, with consequences for which regions became eligible for one category of support or not. The structural funds regulation, OJEC No. L185 of 15 July 1988, introduced an EU-wide typology of regions (objectives 1, 2 and 5b) using EU criteria and indicators. Objective 1 areas were determined by top-down criteria (EU averages of Gross Domestic Product (GDP) per head) and the Commission oversaw, and intervened in, the selection of objective 2 and 5b areas (Mendez et al. 2006, p. 588).

For the subsequent decade, there continued to be intense struggle over these processes. In the negotiations for 2000–06, the European Commission exercised considerable pressure to limit the scope of regions benefiting from regional funds so as to enhance their impact. Progress was made with this objective, partly because negotiations ensured that the transition would be measured and without unintended impact on regions from which funds were withdrawn.

Further reforms occurred in 1993 and in 1996. The Cohesion Funds were established, and funding was increased considerably. From 1988 to 2005, the Union invested more than €800 billion in the 'less favoured' regions with the main beneficiaries being Greece and Portugal.

In 2004, circumstances shifted considerably with the accession of ten additional member states, mostly from central and eastern Europe (and a further two in 2007). The focus of redistribution shifted, as the formula used to allocate resources put the spotlight on many of the new member states. This formula used the measure of GDP per capita; the regions most favoured in the redistribution were those with less than 75 per cent of European GDP per capita, while those with less than 90 per cent were entitled to a lesser allocation. Since 2006, most funding has gone to the regions in the newer member states in Eastern Europe (see EC n.d.).

A new regional policy agenda for Europe

In 2006, three new objectives were articulated for the new 7-year multiannual financial period, 2007–13: to encourage convergence, regional competitiveness and territorial cooperation. Council Regulation 1083/2006, 11 July 2006, provides general provisions on the ERDF, the European Social Fund (ESF) and the Cohesion Fund. Its aim is to promote the 'harmonious, balanced and sustainable development' of European regions, assisting them to address 'economic, social and territorial inequalities, the acceleration of economic restructuring and the ageing of the population' (see EC 2006). The Regulation goes on to define the context, objectives, criteria for eligibility, financial provisions, and the principles and rules for partnerships. With respect to the latter, specific funding has been established to facilitate sharing about the implementation of regional activities. Overall, these resources were to complement the initiatives taken by individual Member States to address regional issues within their own borders. In keeping with the principle of subsidiarity, the EU could act only in ways which went beyond and added value to the action taken by a particular member state or a subordinate level of government within its borders. For example, member states were restricted from using finances from the regional policy to replace existing expenditure. For example, only a small amount of spending on education has been eligible for funding from the Cohesion Fund. However, the Cohesion Fund does support the training of around 10 million low skilled, long-term unemployed and young people each year through various local development initiatives.

The European Commission, through its Directorate General Cities and Regions, has a key role in implementing the policy:

> EU regional policy is carried out by national and regional bodies in partnership with the European Commission, a system known as shared management. Unlike annual national budgets, the regional policy budget is set for seven years, making it inherently reliable and a valuable resource for private investment to draw upon … The Commission works with the EU countries as they draw up partnership agreements outlining their investment priorities and development needs. They also present draft operational programmes (OPs) breaking down the objectives into concrete areas for action. These can cover entire countries and/or regions and can include cooperation programmes involving more than one country. The Commission negotiates with the national authorities on the final content of these investment plans.

> All levels of governance, including civil society, should be consulted and involved in the programming and management of the OPs. (EC 2014a, c)

Competitiveness was improved, for example, through construction of new motorways, railways or broadband, which facilitated access to markets, and increased speed to market, as well as improving the supply of more skilled labour. Insofar as employment increased from these initiatives, so also did the capacity for local consumption.

The Directorate General manages two of the major funds, the ERDF (easily the largest fund, heavily concentrated in the regions with lowest GDP/head) and the Cohesion Fund (co-finances transport and environment projects in member states whose GNP is less than 90 per cent of the EU average), as well as a fund directed towards candidate countries to develop transport networks and environmental infrastructure. The Directorate General also manages disaster assistance.

Given the scale of resources, and the intentional geographic spread, it is not surprising that there have been large numbers of outputs. Estimates indicate that 400,000 SMEs were supported financially, and that one-third of the 3 million jobs created in the EU between 2007 and 2013 were attributable directly to regional policy expenditure. With respect to infrastructure, one-third of total expenditure went on transport. This included the Trakia motorway in Bulgaria, completing the route between Sofia, the capital, and Burgos, the country's largest port. Other projects focused on urban transport, reducing congestion and increasing efficiency, such as the reopening and electrification of the line between Nantes and Chateaubriant in France (see EC 2016).

For the 2007–2013 period, the Cohesion Fund could be allocated to projects in Bulgaria, Cyprus, the Czech Republic, Estonia, Greece, Hungary, Latvia, Lithuania, Malta, Poland, Portugal, Romania, Slovakia and Slovenia. Spain was eligible to a phase-out fund only as its Gross National Income (GNI) per inhabitant was less than the average of the EU-15.

Hence, this iteration of regional policy encompassed a complex interplay amongst initiatives intended to facilitate economic competitiveness in poorer regions, and improve social cohesion and stronger recognition of territorial connections across borders. The Single European Market benefited from the strengthening of the poorer parts of the EU to both produce and to consume successfully as part of the largest marketplace in the world.

In addition, a major initiative of the Cohesion Fund in this period was to enhance environmental sustainability across the EU and its member states. The Europe 2020 Strategy has a target to achieve 20 per cent of its energy consumption from renewable sources. To achieve this target there had to be significant investment in solar and wind energy in southern Europe, the North Sea coast and along the Atlantic by both private and public sectors. More funding at local and regional levels was required also to facilitate progress in treating waste water in particular in the southern and eastern member states.

When the 2007–13 round of regional policy implementation was launched, there was considerable optimism about the prospect that these initiatives would lead to greater convergence in the economic and social standing of European regions, and of the Single European Market as a whole. These were predominantly public-sector initiatives, but their intent was to stimulate and facilitate business expansion throughout Europe. In this context, regional policy needs to be seen alongside the Schengen Treaty and the Eurozone as a key means of facilitating the conditions for effective European-wide movements of people and goods. To achieve the required outcomes of the Europe 2020 Strategy, there needed to be close coordination between the Europe 2020 Strategy, regional policy and other EU policies so that initiatives were not implemented in isolation. The intention was that, over time, the products and services of poorer regions would be able to compete in the wealthier areas of Europe, the incomes and living standards of their populations would improve and their markets would offer similar opportunities for consumers as in the wealthier regions. By 2020, when Europe was to be 'smart, sustainable and inclusive', it was anticipated that the current disparities revealed in the Fifth Report on Economic, Social and Territorial Cohesion (see EC 2010) should be reduced greatly.

The impact of the global financial crisis

All the hope and expectation of the 2007–13 financial period was dashed by the impact of the global financial crisis. Not only did it lead to deep crisis in the European banking system and to a decade of very low or negative economic growth, it halted and even reversed the progress made towards regional economic convergence. A report released in April 2017 has demonstrated that the crisis has jeopardised almost two decades of progress towards greater EU cohesion, interrupting the convergence process and undermining most of the earlier economic advances (see EC 2017). The analysis has shown that not all the poorer regions of Europe have been affected in the same way, and that structural reforms can make a difference. As in earlier OECD work (OECD 2009), it was found that regions within member states often have greater similarity with regions in other member states than they do with their national macroeconomic profile. However, the capacity for business to work efficiently in some regions is shaped very much by national policies.

There has been some argument that the failure to reduce regional inequality was a result, in part at least, of the design of the policy and its implementation. Some of the criticism has included:

- regional policy was aimed too broadly, a 'catch-all' policy without a clear mission;
- the early focus on transfers had a 'welfare' rather than business development agenda, which meant there was insufficient focus on growth;
- the complex supranational intervention meant that the policy instruments were inadequate to achieve the kind of intervention needed in local economies;
- these instruments meant that the programmes were excessively complex and bureaucratic to administer, compounded by limited capability in the newer member states (especially);
- it was difficult to demonstrate conclusive benefits, particularly to economic growth;
- governance arrangements were often distant from programme implementation, especially in those circumstances where national management committees were not well connected with regional authorities;
- funding opportunities were too complex, illustrated by the number of funds, their distinct yet overlapping purposes, and the requirement for matching funding; and
- it is a challenge to maintain an effective multi-layered intergovernmental, multi-annual, cross-sectoral system of monitoring and accountability (see EC 2017; see also Bachtler et al. 2017; and Fratesi and Wishlade 2016).

This all means that there continue to be significant inequalities across European regions. Even after the decade of growth of the 2000s, the wealthiest regions of the EU had eight times the growth of that of the poorest regions. There is also wide disparity in transport infrastructure across the regions of the EU. Many of the central and eastern member states do not have direct access to motorways, air transport or high-speed rail, which lowers their employment rates and GDP per head as companies struggle to bring their goods and services to market at a competitive price. Broadband has assisted many of these member states to gain access to EU-wide markets and even new global markets. However, broadband across the EU is far from universal, despite the current priority on the implementation of the European Digital Single Market. Some member states (such as Romania) have as few as 45 per cent of their households with a broadband connection, while in the Netherlands, 91 per cent of households have a broadband connection. This has led to calls for more of a coordinated approach to the investment and delivery of infrastructure across the EU (see Bachtler et al. 2017).

The new priority on innovation

In the final years of the 2007–13 EU budget period, there was intense debate over the priorities and focus for the 2014–2020 period. The overall strategy, Europe 2020, continued to set a clear context for these discussions, together with a new urgency about how the structural funds, specifically the ERDF and the Cohesion Fund, could be entwined more closely with other related policy areas, and become integral to stimulating economic growth. A new College of Commissioners and a new EC President, Jean-Claude Juncker, had brought new energy to bear on 'jobs and growth' and, notwithstanding a slight budget cut, the regional policy structural funds continued to be a major source of funding to contribute to these objectives, throughout Europe. As noted by one Member of the European Parliament, 'Cohesion funds will be changing from a compensation or transfer-based approach into a targeted investment instrument based on knowledge, sustainability and jobs' (EC n.d.)

Hence, the conceptual framework for the implementation of the new regional agenda is fundamentally different from that which has been adopted in previous funding periods. The new orientation has been captured in the slogan 'smart specialisation', or RIS3 (regional innovation smart specialisation strategies). Interestingly, the new approach has its origins in the European Commission's Directorate General for Research and its concern to strengthen business investment in research and innovation, well before the urgency of economic malaise had been recognised.

In the mid-2000s, well before the financial crisis, business investment in research and development was 30 per cent less than that in the United States. The Commissioner for Research convened a group of economists to advise on an approach to ensure that knowledge became a critical resource for growth (see EC 2009). However, the agenda quickly became much larger:

> The new situation thus calls for a more complex agenda to address both the new matters at hand (structuring policy response to some urgent and global challenges; managing the new financial constraints) and the original mandate from the Commission (improving general conditions for R&D and innovation). One should note that the various parts of the agenda are completely intertwined: i) only an effective and efficient system of research and innovation would allow Europe to successfully respond to the global challenges posed above; ii) reciprocally, the seriousness of these challenges may foster collaborations between likeminded countries to credibly commit to R&D programs that need to be launched to address the global problems; iii) the mobilization of such resources, however, is likely to be adversely affected by the financial crisis' impacts on the fiscal situation of the EU's Member States. (Foray 2009, pp. 7–8)

The initial work of the EU's science-business group extended quickly into collaboration with the Organisation for Economic Cooperation and Development (OECD). A new policy framework was developed in order to focus European regional authorities on processes for increasing research and development activity, reducing fragmented initiatives across the EU and promoting regional innovation systems. The EU–OECD working party examined both the European experience of place-based innovation systems and the evolving character of global value chains (GVCs) with the conclusion that EU structural fund investments needed to be focused on the application by regional businesses of those knowledge assets within a region that had potential to be successful in global markets.

This was a dramatic shift for the EU. The policy parameters shifted from enabling firms in poorer regions to trade across Europe, to enabling companies from all European regions, including the poorer ones, to be more globally competitive. The sometimes radical, contemporary restructuring of GVCs carries threats but also new opportunities for companies and regions which have seen themselves previously as being tied to a particular sector or phase in the value chain. Whereas value chains used to be relatively linear, through various phases of production and distribution, they are now much more flexible. Specific activities that have been integral to a particular production process (design or component production, for example) can now be applied to the production of other kinds of goods and services. Production processes have become more dispersed internationally because companies relocate activities through a network of their affiliates and independent suppliers. They do this in order to maximise efficiencies, either horizontally or vertically, in the links between various production activities and markets (see OECD 2013).

Hence for 2014–20, the focus on innovation took centre stage. 'Smart specialisation' is central to the new policy approach, its importance reflected in the condition that a Smart Specialisation Strategy be adopted in order for a region to qualify for the structural innovation component of the ERDF. This ex ante conditionality was very effective in that more than 200 regional and national RIS3s were generated in the first 18 months of the programme (see EC JRC 2017).

In this context, smart specialisation becomes relevant as regions can analyse their core assets, specifically those in which they have a comparative advantage, and seek new market opportunities which result from the more dispersed and flexible GVCs (see OECD 2012). In other words, place-based innovation becomes shaped by the emerging global opportunities. Focusing regional knowledge assets (scientific and technological, as well as applied) on emerging global niche markets (specialised 'diversification') is a key objective of the EU's smart specialisation process.

Alongside the requirement that regional authorities develop an RIS3 in order to be eligible for structural innovation funds, the EU has made available a range of resources to assist regions in their development of an RIS3. In summary, this is an engaged planning process which brings together 'entrepreneurially minded public sector officials with business, academic and community participants to examine local (knowledge) assets and identify new opportunities in restructured value chains. 'Entrepreneurial discovery' enables knowledge-based assets (not industries) to be the central focus of analysis (see Foray 2014). While the public sector plays 'a catalytic role' in driving innovation and growth in a particular place (see Mazzucato 2013), the inclusion of companies in a region's entrepreneurial discovery process is crucial. Their intelligence about local production processes and about potential markets is critical to a region understanding where its distinctive knowledge assets are (not always in a science institute), and to identifying the entrepreneurial opportunities (see Foray et al. 2012).

In a number of respects, these reforms were directed at overcoming some of the criticisms of previous iterations of the regional policy. The emphasis on entrepreneurial discovery was a means to put much more emphasis on the insights and role of regional stakeholders rather than national management committees. These processes also required the direct engagement of business ('entrepreneurial') representatives in the development of a region's Smart Specialisation Strategy.

The emphasis on cross-regional collaboration has also been a significant variation from the previous 'vertical' orientation of regions to national management committees or to Brussels. The S3 Platform facilitates peer review workshops in which a number of regions can meet and share insights into the process of implementation. The S3 Platform also facilitates cross-regional collaboration, particularly where regions have similar knowledge assets, and can strengthen the overall European competitive advantage through collaboration rather than competition. Through its various activities, a large network of regions and individuals committed to the successful evolution and implementation of smart specialisation has formed to promote mutual learning and transnational collaboration (see EC JRC 2017).

Considerable effort has been invested in building 'horizontal' linkages with other initiatives, such as Horizon 2020, the work on digital Europe, key enabling technologies, creative industries, green growth, social innovation, regional research infrastructures and science parks. Science parks are seen as a key infrastructure resource for research-intensive enterprises, as well as facilitating interaction amongst firms with similar interests. They play a key role with start-ups and spin-offs in the provision of support services and visibility for high-tech firms, constituting an 'eco-innovation' milieu (see Foray et al. 2012, p. 76).

Universities and R&D centres are integral partners in the entrepreneurial discovery and innovation process. The EU approach clearly acknowledges the increasing intensity of knowledge as a crucial economic resource, and the immense potential of its digitisation for generating new market opportunities. Universities contribute skilled labour supply and research expertise, and also play a part in regional analysis, governance and global connectedness.

While there is a requirement that an RIS3 will be produced, there is very clear acknowledgement of regional differences. Specific issues arise about administrative and workforce capability, the distribution of R&D resources, infrastructure and previous experience with enabling technologies. Wider lessons of EU regional policy underscore the importance of sensitivity to multi-level governance, encompassing not only the EU and member states, but also regional authorities themselves, cross-border authorities and major regional institutions such as supranational regional investment houses. Resources to support initiatives such as clusters, science parks, university–business links, start-up financing, green growth and social innovation are all available, but none is presumed to be integral to an S3 Strategy.

Hence, not all regions are expected to be able to generate strategies with equivalent depths of analysis, nor to demonstrate the same readiness for collaborative leadership or technological advance. The EU has promoted various case studies of particular regions that indicate the value of the smart specialisation process. Flanders, southern Sweden and the Basque regions have all developed smart specialisation strategies which provide road maps both for regional governance and for the investment of funding from the EU's Cohesion Fund.

Ironically, the strong emphasis on sciences, research and innovation can be counter-productive to the wider agenda around regional policy. A region's R&D capability is shaped by pre-existing science and innovation capability, leading in turn to greater disparity. Less developed regions need to build more comprehensive innovation agenda with a primary focus on education and capability more so than on research intensity.

Another challenge for the next iteration of regional policy is the priority that will be placed on cross-border initiatives. Already, regional policy initiatives are presented as key levers for the implementation of the wider 'smart, sustainable and inclusive' strategy. It seems likely that projects that enhance cross-border activity will gain stronger support.

Conclusion

This chapter has suggested that EU regional policy is an integral part of the overall programme of the development of the Single European Market, and hence facilitates the environment for businesses to grow and prosper. This in turn is seen as being central to enhancing the living standards and prosperity of European citizens, not least in those Central and East European nations that have joined the EU since 2004. Since 2014, the regional policy framework has been extended to promote export and trade not only across the 28 member states, but globally, seeking to leverage key knowledge assets to promote regional business engagement with emerging GVCs.

Key features of the EU regional policy model include:

(a) a coherent vision for the economic, social and environmental future of the city regions and other spatial areas which make up the supranational region;

(b) a willingness of wealthier nations to contribute directly to enhancing the well-being of other nations in their region, albeit with a strong element of self-interest;

(c) recognition of the value of international perspectives in building the Single European Market;

(d) the evolution of policy over 35 years illustrates the importance of openness to negotiation and dialogue about both key concepts and implementation, as very difficult tensions can be resolved over time;

(e) the lessons of EU regional policy underscore the importance of sensitivity to multi-level governance, encompassing not only the EU and member states, but also regional authorities themselves, cross-border authorities and major regional institutions such as supranational regional investment houses;

(f) the importance of effective coordination of different authorities in the same geographic space;

(g) the significance of a comprehensive approach to regional development policies, linking economic, social and environmental concerns so that the outcomes in one domain support those of another.

Far from being an altruistic programme of transfers from the larger and wealthier countries to the poorer, regional policy has been driven by a complex mix of economic, social and political motives. While its economic and social dimensions have been crucial aspects of the outcomes delivered for particular regions, it has also played a key role as an incentive for greater economic integration in the EU more broadly. In its current phase, the priority on innovation emphasises regions focusing on their competitive advantages in an increasingly knowledge-based economy, thus enabling them to gain access to new markets, not only in Europe but also strengthening their international competitiveness in global markets.

References

Bachtler, J., Begg, I., Charles, D. and Polverari, L. (2016), *EU Cohesion Policy in Practice: What has it achieved?* European Policies Research University, University of Strathclyde.

Bachtler, J., Martins, J.O., Wostner, P. and Zuber, P. (2017), *Towards Cohesion Policy 4.0: Structural Transformation and Inclusive Growth*, Brussels, Regional Studies Association Europe.

Dudek, C. (2014), *The History and Challenges of Cohesion Policies*, The Jean Monnet/Robert Schuman Paper Series, Jean Monnet Chair of the University of Miami and Miami-Florida European Union Center of Excellence, Florida International University, vol. 14, no. 2.

EC, European Commission (n.d.), *Regional Policy Inforegio – Background*, http://ec.europa.eu/regional_policy/archive/policy/history/index_en.htm (accessed 11 September 2017).

EC, European Commission (2006), *Legislation Summary*, http://europa.eu/legislation_summaries/regional_policy/provisions_and_instruments/g24231_en.htm (accessed 15 February 2017).

EC, European Commission (2009), *Knowledge for Growth: Prospects for Science, Technology and Innovation*, Brussels.

EC, European Commission (2010), *Fifth Report on Economic, Social and Territorial Cohesion*, Brussels, November.

EC, European Commission (2014a), *The European Union Explained: Regional Policy*, Brussels.

EC, European Commission (2014b), 'Investment for Jobs and Growth: Promoting development and good governance in EU regions and cities', *Sixth Report on Economic, Social and Territorial Cohesion*, Brussels.

EC, European Commission (2014c), 'Q&A on the "Partnership Agreements" between the European Commission and the EU Member States on European structural and investment fund investments for 2014–2020', Memo, Brussels, 5 May 2014. http://europa.eu/rapid/press-release_MEMO-14-331_en.htm?locale=FR (accessed 18 March 2018).

EC, European Commission (2016), *Ex post evaluation of the ERDF and Cohesion Fund 2007–13*, Commission Staff Working Paper, Brussels.

EC, European Commission (2017), *Competitiveness in Low-income and Low-growth Regions: The lagging regions report*, Commission Staff Working Paper, Brussels.

EC JRC, European Commission Joint Research Centre Smart Specialisation Platform (2017), 'Activities', http://s3platform.jrc.ec.europa.eu/ (accessed 28 March 2018).

Foray, D. (2009), 'Introduction', in European Commission, *Knowledge for Growth*, Brussels.

Foray, D. (2014), *Smart Specialisation: Opportunities and challenges for regional innovation policies*, London, Routledge.

Foray, D., Goddard, J., Beldarrain, X.G., Landabaso, M., McCann, P., Morgan, K., Nauwelaers, C. and Ortega-Argliés, R. (2012), *Guide to Research and Innovation Strategies for Smart Specialisation*, May, Seville, European Commission Smart Specialisation Platform.

Fratesi, U. and Wishlade, F. (2016), 'The Impact of EU Cohesion Policy in Different Countries', *Regional Studies*, vol. 51, no. 6, June.

Hooghe, L. and Keating, M. (1994), 'The politics of European Union regional policy', *Journal of European Public Policy*, vol. 1, no. 3.

Mazzucato, M. (2013), *The Entrepreneurial State: Debunking Public vs. Private Sector Myths*, London, Anthem Press.

Mendez, C., Wishlade, F. and Yuill, D. (2006), 'Conditioning and fine-tuning Europeanization: Negotiating regional policy maps under the EU's competition and cohesion policies', *JCMS*, vol. 44, no. 3.

OECD (2009), *Regions Matter: Economic recovery, innovation and sustainable growth*, Paris.

OECD (2012), *Draft Synthesis Report on Innovation Drive-Growth in Regions: The role of smart specialization*, December, Paris.

OECD (2013), *Interconnected Economies: Benefiting from global value chains*, Paris.

12

SINGLE MARKET EVOLUTION AND ITS BUSINESS IMPACT

Maureen Benson-Rea and Anna Gerke

Introduction

This chapter builds on the overview of European business (Chapter 2), and on international business theory as applied to the European region (Chapter 4). Those chapters describe and explain theoretically the unique nature of, and context for, business in Europe. This chapter examines a critical component of integration in the European Union (EU), the Single European Market (SEM), which represents the enactment of the EU's economic goals. We review the processes by which the SEM was established, its objectives and how successful the EU has been in achieving those objectives. It provides an evaluation of the SEM's impact on business and future areas for research on business in Europe. We explore what market integration means for EU business and set the scene for the analysis of European business in the world, and international business strategy.

The EU represents the most advanced form of regional economic integration in the world, with its central focus on an integrated market in the SEM (Suder 2011). The SEM is the policy area within the EU integration process with the largest impact on business, putting in place restructuring and change from the late 1980s onwards. Its impact on the economy has been analysed extensively (see, for example, Mikić 1998), though the effects on individual businesses – which vary depending on firm size, location, industry and industry structure – much less so. Initial enthusiasm amongst scholars led to a wave of publications in the early 1980s, mostly on the evolution and homogenisation of consumers in Europe, with a second wave at the beginning of the twenty-first century examining legislation, standardisation and harmonisation issues in the SEM (Apfelthaler 2015). The impacts of the SEM have traditionally been measured at the aggregate level (Mariniello et al. 2015), by trade and foreign direct investment (FDI) flows, and mergers and acquisitions (M&A) (Alhorr et al. 2012; Couerdacier et al. 2009; Zademach and Rodríguez-Pose, 2009), which we discuss below.

There is no doubt, however, of the size and scale of the European market. The internal effects of the SEM mean that business and consumers trade in a single market of approximately 500 million people, with an economic value (GDP) of €14,600 billion in 2014 (European Commission 2014a). There have also been significant FDI inflows (Couerdacier et al. 2009), but the record and the causal attribution on growth, jobs and lower prices (see Table 12.1), and

Table 12.1 Summary of economic evaluations of the SEM

Study	Results	Timescale
Cecchini et al. (1988)	+4.25–6.5% GDP	5–6 years
Baldwin (1989)	+0.3–0.9% long-term GDP growth	Long-term
European Commission (1996)	+1.1–1.5% GDP 900,000 jobs in 1994	Impact to 1994
Minford et al. (2005)	–3% GDP for UK remaining in EU	Forward looking (from baseline status quo)
Ilzkovitz et al. (2007)	+2.2% GDP in 2006	1992–2006
Boltho and Eichengreen (2008)	+2.75 million jobs +5% GDP in 2008	Impact to 2008

Source: Extracted from UK Government (2013, Table 4, p. 72).

whether the full potential of the Single Market has been achieved, are less clear. With a market that generates a quarter of the world's GDP, it is the EU's single biggest economic achievement and any analysis of European business must consider the EU's SEM both as an important driver of Europe-wide strategy and its geo-economic context (Suder 2011).

Analysing the business impact of the SEM is complex (Mariniello et al. 2015; Moschieri and Campa 2014), but particularly for firms, where it is generally done anecdotally or at industry level (Mikić 1998). We begin with a brief overview of the economic integration processes that created the SEM, from its earliest form in the European Economic Community's (EEC) Customs Union through to the EEC Common Market and to the Single Market with Economic and Monetary Union (EMU). The EU currently stops short of full economic (and political) union, although the goal of that ultimate destination recurs on the EU agenda. EU integration has progressed its twin economic and political goals through deepening into more policy areas and widening across more members to the point where the EU is a unique multi-state system. Market integration and deregulation sit alongside the ongoing diversity of Europe, which remains in the structure of its member economies, in domestic regulations, idiosyncratic domestic industry structures and hugely varied levels of competitiveness among EU firms. Country-specific idiosyncrasies of EU markets remain as determinants for many business transactions (Moschieri and Campa 2014).

Whilst there is evidence of EU convergence, much divergence remains – elements of the fundamental values inherent in managing and governing business in Europe may still be guided by local diversity as described in Sapir's (2006) socio-economic models (Nordic, Anglo-Saxon, Continental and Mediterranean). Paas (2003) argues that the rapid and transformative change which the Central and Eastern European countries' (CEEC) businesses went through in preparation for EU entry (2004–07), meant that CEEC businesses were less ready to adopt the prevailing model of socio-economic liberalism and indeed were more neo-liberal and strongly market-oriented. This diversity means that, despite decades of progress, the SEM is not yet complete (UK Government 2013; Mariniello et al. 2015).

The evolution of the SEM

The so-called neo-functionalist compromise establishing the European institutions (1952–57) (Lindberg and Scheingold 1970) was built on an agreement among the EEC founders on the importance of economic determinism, with concessions to federalist political determinism with a long-term view of transcending the nation state. This continued from the Treaty of Paris (1952), establishing the European Coal and Steel Community (ECSC), to the EEC Treaty of Rome (1958). The Treaty of Rome established the Common Market, the Common External Tariff (CET) and a range of common policies and institutions, which set the agenda for the development of the European market into the 1980s.

The Single European Market programme, launched in the late 1980s, was a strategy to achieve complete market integration by removing all remaining physical, technical and non-tariff barriers to intra-EEC trade. The concept of the SEM was built on the so-called Four Freedoms: the free movement of people, goods, capital and services within the EU market (Apfelthaler 2015). From its early stages, the EEC implemented many pieces of legislation to liberalise and deregulate intra-EEC trade through a process of harmonisation of standards and legislation (Suder 2011). Harmonisation implied that all member states would move to adopt the same standards. Because the EEC's institutional decision-making maintained a power of veto by individual members (when initiatives threatened their 'vital national interests') much controversial legislation floundered, unadopted for years (Cecchini et al. 1988).

By the 1970s the EEC was adjusting to major change: enlargement to include much poorer states, the oil price shocks and the instability of currencies after the collapse of the Bretton Woods system (McCormick 2007). Added to this, inflation, unemployment and continuing barriers to cross-border trade led US policy-makers and business commentators (under the Reaganite programme of deregulation) to coin the phrase 'eurosclerosis' (McCormick 2007), which referred to the slowing down of the impetus for European integration and economic growth. The UK Prime Minister at the time, Margaret Thatcher, believed in applying at the European level the same deregulation approach she had adopted at home. So, the UK nominee at the European Commission (EC), Lord Cockfield, led a review of the EEC's progress towards a single market, publishing the so-called Cockfield White Paper of 1985. An economist in the EC, Paulo Cecchini, subsequently co-authored a report on 'The Costs of Non-Europe' (1988) (the costs of not having a truly common market). The report estimated the costs of the remaining barriers to intra-EEC trade (physical, technical and non-tariff barriers) at some £140 billion per year, equivalent to around £414 billion in 2017 prices (Morley 2017). According to Cecchini et al. (1988) the 'costs of non-Europe' were between 4.25% and 6.5% of GDP, and included trade barriers, production barriers (a sub-total of 2.2–2.7% of GDP), economies of scale, competitive effects and reductions in market entry (an additional 2.1–3.7% of GDP) (see Table 12.1). The EC's response was the Single Market Programme to enact the 282-plus pieces of EEC legislation that Cockfield stated were required (at the time) to 'complete' the single market by 1993, to relaunch the process of European economic integration and increase the competitiveness of the European economy and its firms.

The SEM programme was enabled by the Single European Act (1987), which streamlined decision-making through more qualified majority voting, increased the powers of the European Parliament through a 'cooperation procedure' and, most importantly for legislation, enabled mutual recognition and approximation of laws and regulations (using more loosely framed 'directives', which gave member states more discretion around enacting EEC laws into national approaches) rather than attempting to impose a single solution in all members states through harmonisation of laws using regulations (which gave the member states no discretion to adapt laws to the specifics of national contexts) (Suder 2011). Further EU treaties, such as those signed at Amsterdam (1997) and Lisbon (2009) emphasised more political, social, institutional and external policies, and international aspects of EU policy and action, including security and justice, immigration and border controls, environment and sustainable development, health protection, public health and consumer protection.

Table 12.2 Economic benefits of the SEM

SEM dimensions	Key references
Increase intra-EEC trade	Johnson and Turner (2016)
Deregulate public purchasing	Mikić (1998)
Save business costs	Suder (2011)
Lower consumer prices	Johnson and Turner (2016)
Attract investment	Hautz et al. (2013)
Encourage EEC-scale firms through concentration	Johnson and Turner (2016)
Accelerated diversification of EEC firms	Hautz et al. (2013)
Promote international specialisation	Mikić (1998)
Improve EEC competitiveness	Suder (2011)
Boost the EEC's international economic profile	McGuire et al. (2012)
Facilitate EMU	Johnson and Turner (2016)
Intra-EU M&A	Couerdacier et al. (2009)
Internationalisation of traditionally state-owned firms	Kolk et al. 2014

The so-called 1992 programme was one of the three pillars of the 1992 Maastricht Treaty to promote a more federalist agenda for Europe, which were: the completion of the SEM, pursuit of Economic and Monetary Union (EMU) and policies to address cooperation in justice and home affairs. Increased funding to address economic and social cohesion were important to allay any social costs of restructuring and industrial change resulting from the SEM. The SEM reinforced the economic argument for common policies to remove obstacles to factor mobility which would further facilitate EMU, building on what was hoped would be progress towards an Optimal Currency Area – ultimately the euro – through the absence of asymmetric shocks and a high degree of labour mobility and wage flexibility. The broad economic benefits of the SEM are summarised in Table 12.2.

The creation of the SEM

The achievement of the SEM was built on the *acquis communautaire*, the body of policy and laws developed since the 1950s, which together created and maintained the Common Market. These are illustrated in Table 12.3.

The expected benefits of the 1992 programme (Cecchini et al. 1988) identified a range of cost savings, both direct effects – such as the eradication of economic borders – and indirect effects – from economic restructuring, increases in trade and competition, and greater economies of scale. In summary (see, for example, Mikić 1998) these were:

- 'Static trade effects': benefits from allowing public authorities to buy from the cheapest sources;
- 'Competition effects': downward pressure on prices as a result of greater competition;
- 'Restructuring effects': through the reorganisation of industrial sectors and individual companies resulting from greater competition.

Other possible benefits envisaged included:

- Benefits to investment, innovation (encouraging rationalisation, e.g. R&D expenditure) and growth;

Table 12.3 Areas of the *acquis communautaire*

Policy Area
Trade, commercial policy
Competition policy
Industrial policy
Social policy
Environment policy
Agriculture
Special industrial sectors
Structural funds
R&D
Energy
Health
Education and training
Consumer protection

- Savings from the public sector (lower subsidies);
- Capital reallocation through inter-EU M&A.

It was expected that the SEM (Mikić 1998) would contribute to the emergence of virtuous cycles of innovation and competition among firms, which would lead to greater job creation and lower prices for consumers, stimulating consumption and growth. This trend is also evident in the large number of European business research projects on innovation and entrepreneurship (see Chapter 2 by Perenyi in this volume).

Impact of the SEM

The views of economists are mixed (see Table 12.1) but, with the notable exception of Minford et al. (2005), many are positive in their estimations and analyses (albeit with caution about different methodologies and policy motivations).

To analyse the impact of the Single Market on business in terms of what was intended to happen and the actual effect, we draw on the EC's Single Market Scorecard data as well as business reports on investment flows, and M&A data. We aim to assess the achievements of the SEM in terms of its expected benefits, such as those set out in the Cecchini Report (1988). These particularly include industry and market concentration through M&A to achieve economies of scale and rapid market access, and growth through FDI. Mention should also be made of differential rates of transposition and adherence to the Single Market among the member states, which means that benefits may not have been spread evenly across Europe. Mariniello et al. (2015, p. 2) make the point: 'That single market integration generates positive and significant aggregate effects does not imply that its effects are positive and significant for every sector.' While much remains to be done, on trade in services, for example (Coeurdacier et al., 2009), the SEM programme has not been the feared 'Fortress Europe', but rather more a Europe which is 'Open for Business'.

The SEM brought an increase in M&A and joint ventures (seen as 'inevitable' by McCormic, 2007, p. 101), which led to a renewed presence of European firms in the global marketplace. European firms lost national protection under the SEM programme, the euro brought cheaper and more accessible corporate funds, and privatisation and globalisation grew European firms

(McCormick 2007). McGuire et al. (2012) argue that the EU has become a highly attractive destination for FDI from emerging market multinational enterprises to access strategic assets that may not be available in their home countries. McCormick (2007) points to the rise in European firms in the Fortune 500 between 1969 and 2005. In 1969 US firms made up 238 (nearly 60 per cent) and European firms 108 (27 per cent) of the Fortune 500. In 2005, the composition had changed to 176 (35 per cent) and 158 (32 per cent) respectively. By 1993 the EU-15 had outstripped the USA in total trade in services and in goods exports (McCormick 2007). McCormick (2007, p. 87) goes as far as to say that:

'In the space of eight years – from the publication of the 1985 Commission white paper on the single market to the setting of the timetable for the single currency under the terms of Maastricht in 1993 – the European project had been transformed.'

There is no consensus on absolute measures for the effectiveness or impact of the SEM but relative measures are available to assess how it transformed business in Europe. As Mariniello et al. (2015, p. 3) put it, however, 'identifying and quantifying the channels through which market integration is expected to engender growth is methodologically complex'.

Evaluating the SEM

The single market is perceived to have fostered more collaborative, competitive, agile businesses (Gerke and Benson-Rea 2017). It has created new business opportunities for firms of all sizes, from all over the world (Benson-Rea and Mikić 2005). These changes occurred not only via increased market access but through cross-border FDI and commercial integration. Removing cross-border barriers in the single market enabled firms to build economies of scale in Europe-wide production, distribution and brands (Johnson and Turner 2016). It made acquisitions and mergers, and collaboration in joint ventures and strategic alliances suddenly viable and an increase in those internationalisation activities could clearly be observed in the late 1990s and early 2000s (Alhorr et al. 2012; Moschieri and Campa 2014). Firms doing business in the EU market have developed strategies to balance a pan-European approach and single-country localisation. The SEM enables firms to deploy Europe-wide objectives, with market-by-market adaptation and coordination.

Ernst and Young (2015) reports on industry views surveyed in 2010 of Europe's attractiveness as a business location, identifying three key measures for growth: support for small and medium-sized enterprises (SMEs), high-tech industries and innovation. These findings are in line with European business research trends on innovation and entrepreneurship, ethical issues and social responsibility (see Chapter 2 by Perenyi in this volume). Respondents valued the EU's research and innovation capacity, its emphasis on green business, labour force diversity and quality, and its world-class business clusters (Ketels 2015). However, Ernst and Young (2015) reported that 814 global business leaders interviewed in 2010 had found that Europe lacked clarity in direction and the necessary commitment and speed to adapt, necessitating a 'wake-up call'. By the 2015 survey of 808 business leaders from around the globe (Ernst and Young 2015), Europe was finding a path to sustained growth, with investors gaining cautious confidence in Europe once again, although excessive bureaucracy remained an impediment to making the best of Europe's comeback after the recession of the 2000s. The 2015 report (Ernst and Young 2015) also found Europe the most attractive destination in which to establish operations (50 per cent of those surveyed), with 59 per cent of global investors surveyed envisaging an improvement over the next three years (2015–18).

The SEM benefits for business are often seen as favouring multinationals, which have the resources to address the opportunities and challenges of European and global markets, leaving SMEs – firms employing fewer than 250 employees – vulnerable. Mikić (1998) argues that EU enterprise policy evolved to safeguard and improve the environment for business during the completion of the single internal market and beyond, particularly to enable SMEs to exploit the opportunities created by the SEM. European Union SMEs account for some 60–70 per cent of employment and, although traditionally domestically focused, are increasingly international (Mikić 1998). The approximately 20.8 million SMEs registered in the EU represent 99.8 per cent of all enterprises and produce more than a half of European GDP (European Commission 2014b). Between 2009 and 2011, an estimated 56 per cent of all public procurement contracts above the EU thresholds were awarded to SMEs (or groupings led by an SME), 29 per cent on aggregate value (European Commission 2014b). This percentage is, however, 29 per cent lower than it would have been (58 per cent) if SMEs had won the share of public procurement equal to their share of the total gross value added produced in the business economy (European Commission 2014b, p. 5). SMEs, especially the approximately 17 per cent that are sub-contractors (Suder 2011), do not seem to benefit from the SEM in proportion to their importance in the EU economy.

Business Europe (the Confederation of European Business) brings together 40 central industrial and employers' federations from 34 European countries, representing more than 20 million small, medium and large companies (see www.businesseurope.eu). In its policy overview of the SEM, Business Europe (2010) enumerated the benefits of the SEM by stakeholder group as:

- Consumers: lower prices, higher quality and wider choice;
- Economic well-being: between 1992 and 2006 EU GDP grew by an additional 2.2 per cent and 2.75 million new jobs;
- Citizens: live, work, study, retire anywhere in the EU;
- Companies: market access, increased intra-EU trade, up 30 per cent since 1992, cross-border FDI inflows (EU-15) from 53 per cent in 1995 to 78 per cent in 2005.

In one of the few business-oriented studies of the impact of the SEM, Alhorr et al. (2012) conducted an analysis of data on strategic alliances and joint ventures in 29 European countries (1985–2004) and found that closer economic integration had a positive impact on international strategic alliances within the European region. Alhorr et al. (2012, p. 59) point specifically to the adoption of common market policies, arguing that: 'higher levels of economic integration lead MNEs to expand to countries within the economically integrated region and to achieve growth through strategic alliances with other firms in the region'. However, on the other hand, Zademach and Rodríguez-Pose (2009) found that it was 'traditional factors' of access to new and core markets, geographical proximity and internalisation that were the key drivers of cross-border M&A in the EU-25 and the EFTA-4 between 1998 and 2003, and that institutional factors, such as European integration, had less impact. Moschieri and Campa (2014) also find that structural characteristics of the European market such as deal attitude and presence of competitive bids are more important for deal completion in M&A transactions than EU legislation towards market homogenisation. So, evaluations of the SEM vary considerably.

The reality of the SEM

The European Commission's 'Internal Market Scoreboard' was first published in 1997 and is a transparent and detailed contribution to understanding progress and barriers to the ultimate completion of the SEM (European Commission 2016). The Commission places increased emphasis on enforcement and monitoring and the Scoreboard provides information on member states' performance in transposing EU legislation into domestic law, how long the process takes and adherence to timely deadlines. The member states must comply, so non-conformity or infringements are also measured. These legislative gaps, which the Commission refers to as 'fragmentation factors', mean that the European market remains fragmented in places and not 'single'. The transposition deficit, the percentage of internal market measures not yet notified to the Commission via national transposition measures, is another Commission measure of member states' performance. Implementation delays in introducing new and extant legislation into domestic law in the member states can be due to administrative laxity, where national bureaucracies are inefficient or overloaded, or to problems with parliamentary schedules. To address problems with delayed implementation or incorrect application of EU laws concerning the SEM, the Commission established a process for infringement proceedings against individual member states. This amounts to 'naming and shaming' in single market governance (European Commission 2016) and the areas of most infringements show the sensitive areas for individual member states. These delays continue to restrict the SEM.

The Single Market Scoreboard works on a traffic light system (red=below average, yellow=average, green=above average) that indicates the extent to which member states comply with the requirement to transpose EU single market legislation and objectives. This evaluation system is applied under different headings: performance, FDI, legislation, etc. (European Commission 2014c; 2016). To qualify as FDI the investment of one EU member resident (investor) in another EU member resident's business needs to be long-term and exceed 10 per cent of ownership or voting power, across four indicators (change in inward or outward FDI flows; change in inward or outward FDI stocks). Recent indicators vary considerably across member states. Some notable results concern Germany, with a relatively high change in outward FDI flows compared with other EU member countries, and the UK, with a relatively high change in inward FDI stocks (European Commission 2016). The latest Scoreboard (2016) reports Estonia and Finland as the best performing countries, but the aggregate member state performance was below average in 31 areas. However, member states have significantly improved their performance compared with the last Scorecard (European Commission 2016). As to whether and how this translates into performance benefits, Cadman and Tetlow (2017) point to evidence that trade in goods was 73 per cent higher within the SEM than if there had been a free trade area, and 60 per cent higher than if only the World Trade Organization rules had been applied.

Conclusions

The completion of the European internal market was and remains an ambitious programme, but is not yet fully achieved (Mariniello et al. 2015). It remains an ongoing programme as evidenced by the Commission's Scoreboard and new initiatives. Implementation of EU legislation remains patchy but the international competitiveness of the EU economy and its firms remains high on the EU agenda. Despite its policy to leave the EU, a recent review by the UK government recognised that the EU Single Market necessitates legislative and regulatory obligations to make it function effectively. Whilst these had grown in recent years, and were impacting SMEs more than larger companies, the review found that the EU had also been increasing its efforts to reverse that process at EU level. The standard of implementation and enforcement varies greatly across the EU (UK Government 2013) and this may form an ongoing barrier for European business to achieve the full practical benefits of the SEM's opportunities. The trend has been towards deeper economic integration over time, for political as much as economic reasons

(Suder 2011). That integration has brought to the EU, in most observers' opinions, appreciable economic benefits (UK Government 2013). While the SEM process may have spread the Anglo-Saxon approach of neo-liberal policy-making more generally across the EU, it also constrains decision-making at firm, national and EU levels. Some argue that the EU lost its way by enlarging (to include the CEEC countries in 2004–2007) and with the rise of liberal intergovernmentalism (Moravcsik 1993) in which the consensus around rebuilding the European economy and building on its achievement was lost, together with momentum on the SEM.

New areas for the SEM are set out in recent Commission proposals (Johnson and Turner 2016) to prevent unjustified geo-blocking on cross-border parcel delivery services, and to strengthen consumers' rights and guidance in digital commerce (EU Business 2016). Further actions to address remaining barriers to trade within the EU Single Market include trade in services (Business Europe 2010; see also Chapter 25 by Pelle in this volume), financial services, energy and digital business (Coeurdacier et al. 2009). The UK has been pushing strongly for a single capital market, a Capital Markets Union, although TheCityUK, a body representing London financial firms, recognised that this would inevitably require 'strong regulatory coordination at the EU level' (TheCityUK 2014, p. 4). The free movement of goods is still somewhat hindered by national differences in excise duties, taxes and ultimately prices. Taxation remains largely a member state competence, although the harmonisation of indirect taxes across member states could be an essential element for an effective SEM. Unlike most internal market measures, which require qualified majority voting, the harmonisation of taxation is decided by unanimity (UK Government 2013). Other areas for development within the SEM are: the environment, a single market in energy, a single market in transport services and the creation of an integrated transport system. An important new area is a Digital Single Market, a major component of the EC's Digital Agenda. It proposes 'to better exploit the potential of Information and Communication Technologies (ICTs) in order to foster innovation, economic growth and progress' (European Commission 2017). The Digital Single Market Strategy was adopted in 2015 and sets out actions across e-commerce, consumer protection online, copyright, telecommunications, tax, audio-visual media, data protection, cybersecurity and e-government, emphasising access, prosperity and growth (European Commission 2017).

To conclude, SEM benefits have accrued to firms from outside the EU as well as European-domiciled firms. Future developments such as Brexit, further EU enlargement (e.g., Turkey), and the role of Russia, Ukraine, the Neighbourhood policy, and the Middle East, are pressing EU problems which may slow down or even derail the Single Market. Reverberations from Brexit, in which other countries seek to slow down their integration, risk a two-speed Europe. The wider trade issues of the role of international institutions such as the World Trade Organization, trade agreements such as the Transatlantic Trade and Investment Partnership, the role of China and the EU's relationships with these actors and institutions, are important to mention. Current global trends towards economic nationalism, which seek to protect strategic assets from foreign ownership and control as a reaction to Europeanisation/globalisation, may suggest further initiatives to achieve full EU market integration.

References

Alhorr, H.S., Boal, K. and Cowden, B.J. (2012), 'Regional economic integration and international strategic alliances: Evidence from the EU', *Multinational Business Review*, vol. 20, no. 1, pp. 44–66.

Apfelthaler, G. (2015), 'Standardisation versus adaptation of business practices in Europe: 20 years of the Single European Market and two decades of (scarce) research', *European Journal of International Management,* vol. 9, no. 3, pp. 283–287.

Baldwin, R. (1989), 'The growth effects of 1992', *Economic Policy*, vol. 4, no. 9, pp. 247–281.

Benson-Rea, M., and Mikić, M. (2005), 'New Zealand–Europe trade relations: Reconciling hyper-competition with the tyranny of distance', in: B. Luciano and D.G. Mayes (eds), *New Zealand and Europe: Connections and Comparisons. European Studies Series 21*, Amsterdam, Rodopi, pp. 19–34.

Boltho, A. and Eichengreen, B. (2008), 'The economic impact of European integration', CEPR Discussion Paper, No. 6820, May. https://papers.ssrn.com/sol3/papers2.cfm?abstract_id=1143183 (accessed 28 February 2017).

Business Europe (2010), *Go for Growth: An Agenda for the European Union in 2010–2014*, The Confederation of European Business, Brussels. www.businesseurope.eu/publications/go-growth-agenda-european-union-2010–2014 (accessed 28 February 2017).

Cadman, E. and Tetlow, G. (2017), 'The EU single market: How it works and the benefits it offers', *Financial Times*, London and Frankfurt, 1 April. www.ft.com/content/1688d0e4-15ef-11e6-b197-a4af20d5575e (accessed 28 November 2017).

Cecchini, P., Catinat, M. and Jacquemin, A. (1988), *The European Challenge 1992: The benefits of a Single Market*, Wildwood, Hants, UK, Commission of the European Communities.

Coeurdacier, N., De Santis, R.A. and Aviat, A. (2009), 'Cross-border mergers and acquisitions and European integration', *Economic Policy*, vol. 24, no. 57, pp. 56–106.

Ernst and Young (2015), *EY's Attractiveness Survey Europe 2015: Comeback time*. www.ey.com/Publication/vwLUAssets/EY-european-attractiveness-survey-2015/$FILE/EY-european-attractiveness-survey-2015.pdf (accessed 28 February 2017).

EU Business (2016), *EU Targets Geo-blocking to Boost E-commerce*, 25 May. (accessed 28 February 2017).

European Commission (1996), *The Impact and Effectiveness of the Single Market – Communication from the Commission to the European Parliament and Council*, 30 October. http://ec.europa.eu/internal_market/economic-reports/docs/single_en.pdf (accessed 28 February 2017).

European Commission (2014a), 'The economy'. http://europa.eu/european-union/about-eu/figures/economy_en (accessed 28 February 2017).

European Commission (2014b), *SMEs' Access to Public Procurement Markets and Aggregation of Demand in the EU*. A study commissioned by the European Commission, DG Internal Market and Services, PwC. smes-access-and-aggregation-of-demand_en.pdf (accessed 18 March 2018).

European Commission (2014c), *The Single Market Scoreboard*. http://ec.europa.eu/internal_market/scoreboard/ (accessed 26 March 2018).

European Commission (2016), *Single Market Scoreboard 2016*. http://ec.europa.eu/single-market-scoreboard (accessed 28 February 2017).

European Commission (2017), *Digital Agenda in the Europe 2020 Strategy*. https://ec.europa.eu/digital-single-market/en/europe-2020-strategy (accessed 27 February 2017).

Gerke, A. and Benson-Rea, M. (2017), 'The Expansion of the Sport Goods Industry', in U. Wagner, R.K. Storm and K. Nielsen (eds), *When Sport meets Business: Capabilities, challenges, critiques*, London, Sage, pp. 11–29.

Hautz, J., Mayer, M.C.J. and Stadler, C. (2013), 'Ownership Identity and Concentration: A Study of their Joint Impact on Corporate Diversification', *British Journal of Management*, vol. 24, no. 1, pp. 102–126.

Ilzkovitz, F., Dierx, A., Kavocs, V. and Sousa, N. (2007), *Steps Towards a Deeper Economic Integration: The internal market in the 21st century – a contribution to the Single Market Review*, European Commission, European Economy No. 271, January. http://ec.europa.eu/economy_finance/publications/pages/publication784_en.pdf (accessed 18 March 2018).

Johnson, D. and Turner, C. (2016), *European Business*, 3rd edn, London, Routledge.

Ketels, C. (2015), 'Competitiveness and clusters: Implications for a new European growth strategy', *WWWforEurope – Welfare, Wealth, Work*, vol. 84. Vienna, European Union.

Kolk, A., Lindeque, J. and van den Buuse, D. (2014), 'Regionalization strategies of European Union electric utilities', *British Journal of Management*, vol. 25, pp. S77–S99.

Lindberg, L.N. and Scheingold, S.A. (1970), *Europe's Would-be Polity: Patterns of change in the European Community*, New Jersey, Prentice Hall.

Mariniello, M., Sapir, A. and Terzi, A. (2015), 'The long road towards the European Single Market', Bruegel Working Paper No. 2015/01. (accessed 28 February 2017).

McCormick, J. (2007), 'The European Economic Colossus', in J. McCormick (ed.), *The European Superpower*, Basingstoke, UK, Palgrave Macmillan, pp. 84–109.

McGuire, S., Lindeque, J. and Suder, G. (2012), 'Learning and lobbying: Emerging market firms and corporate political activity in Europe', *European Journal of International Management*, vol. 6, no, 3, pp. 342–362.

Mikić, M. (1998), *International Trade*, New York, St Martin's Press.

Minford, P., Mahambare, V. and Nowell, E. (2005), *Should Britain Leave the EU – An economic analysis of a troubled relationship*, UK, Edward Elgar Publishing/Institute of Economic Affairs.

Moravcsik, A. (1993), 'Preferences and power in the European Community: A liberal intergovernmentalist approach', *Journal of Common Market Studies*, vol. 31, no. 4, pp. 473–524.

Morley, S. (2017), *Historical UK Inflation Rates and Calculator*. (accessed 27 February 2017).

Moschieri, C. and Campa, J.M. (2014), 'New trends in mergers and acquisitions: Idiosyncrasies of the European market', *Journal of Business Research*, vol. 76, no. 7, pp. 1478–1485.

Paas, T. (2003), 'The main determinants of transition and competitiveness of the Baltic States', *Journal of East-West Business*, vol. 8, no. 3–4, pp. 25–44.

Sapir, A. (2006), 'Globalization and the reform of European Social Models', *JCMS: Journal of Common Market Studies*, vol. 44, no. 2, pp. 369–390.

Suder, G. (2011), *Doing Business in Europe*, 2nd edn, London, Sage.

TheCityUK (2014), *EU Reform: A view from TheCityUK*, November. (accessed 28 February 2017).

UK Government (2013), *Review of the Balance of Competences between the United Kingdom and the European Union: The Single Market*. (accessed 28 February 2017).

Zademach, H.M. and Rodríguez-Pose, A. (2009), 'Cross-border M&As and the changing economic geography of Europe', *European Planning Studies*, vol. 17, no. 5, pp. 765–789.

13

FREE TRADE AGREEMENTS AND REGIONAL TRADE AGREEMENTS WITH THIRD COUNTRIES AND EUROPEAN BUSINESS

Terrence R. Guay

Introduction

Trade is a central aspect of international business. It also is one of the core economic foundations of the European Union (EU). Cross-border trade, as well as investment, broad economic ties and cultural linkages were viewed by the EU's founders as fundamental building blocks for European peace, political cooperation and prosperity (Dinan 2014). Through the various treaties and agreements since the 1950s, tariffs (or taxes) on the import of goods and services amongst EU member countries have been eliminated, and non-tariff barriers (such as regulatory differences or quotas limiting the quantity of imports) are continuously being identified and eliminated. The 1985 Single European Act (SEA) sought to remove all barriers to the trade of goods and services, and to the free movement of capital and people within the EU (Sandholtz and Zysman 1989). Today, for the most part, operating in multiple EU countries is much easier for business than was the case a few decades ago. A regional trade agreement (RTA) is an accord between two or more countries anywhere in the world to reduce or eliminate tariffs and other barriers to trade on selected goods and services. The EU has become the world's most successful RTA (Katsoulis 2016).

Given the EU's experience with promoting trade ties internally, it is not surprising that the EU has sought to forge closer trade relations with other countries around the world. This chapter will briefly describe how the trade and EU studies literatures explain the EU's involvement in global trade. It then reviews the range of trade agreements the EU has conducted with countries around the world. The chapter concludes by proposing areas where additional scholarly work is necessary.

Trade and the EU

Mainstream economic theory dating to Adam Smith and David Ricardo contends that trade, in the aggregate, creates mutual benefits for the countries involved. The problem, however, is that losses are often concentrated in specific industries and locations where less competitive companies operate (Krugman 2000). This provides incentives for interest groups adversely affected by trade to seek to influence trade agreements and trade policy (Coen and Richardson 2009). One way the EU sought to overcome the political obstacles that can make trade agreements difficult to achieve was to form a customs union. A customs union is one of the most complex forms of RTAs because, not only does it reduce tariffs and trade obstacles amongst its members, but it takes the process one step further by requiring all members to have the same tariffs with non-members (Krueger 1997). This is particularly challenging because a country may prefer to trade with another country outside the RTA for certain goods, but may find it more difficult or expensive to do so upon joining a customs union. For example, one reason the United Kingdom (UK) did not join the EU in the 1950s was out of concern that its trade patterns at the time were heavily weighted toward members of the Commonwealth (Urwin 1995). Joining the EU's customs union would mean having to raise tariffs on products from Australia, Canada, New Zealand and elsewhere to the levels established by the EU. A customs union therefore requires much more political cooperation. Since countries often have to expose less-competitive domestic industries to greater international economic competition for the sake of organisational unity, customs unions impose a more complex negotiating environment among members. For EU members, the reduction in tariffs internally may be offset by higher tariffs on non-member countries, thereby reducing some of the opposition by less competitive industries. But it may also distort global trade, since less competitive companies within the customs union have a tariff cushion, which puts companies from non-member countries at a price disadvantage (Frankel 1997).

Trade policies obviously affect business decision-making. A reduction in trade barriers makes a country a more attractive market for a company's goods and services (Bhagwati 2004). In some cases, companies may try to avoid a country's tariffs by increasing foreign investment. Because the EU is a customs union, such strategies can be very effective. A South Korean company, for example, may choose to build a factory in the Czech Republic to avoid tariffs that would be imposed if automobiles were exported from Asia to the EU. By manufacturing cars in the Czech Republic, the South Korean company can ship cars throughout the EU without facing tariffs or other trade barriers. That is an important reason why the EU's total stock of inward foreign direct investment (FDI) amounts to €4.8 trillion (Eurostat 2017).

Because customs unions require deep levels of political cooperation to face down domestic interest groups and obtain compromise on the level of external tariffs, they are rare. The EU is the most sophisticated customs union in the world. Mercosur (whose members include Argentina, Brazil, Paraguay, Uruguay and Venezuela) is a partial customs union since it includes hundreds of exceptions to a common external tariff. The most common RTA is a free trade agreement (FTA) (Suder 2011). In an FTA, member countries agree to reduce some (but usually not all) tariffs and other trade barriers amongst member countries. But each country is allowed to maintain their own set of tariffs with non-members, and is free to establish their own trade deals with the rest of the world. Because the UK was unwilling to commit to a customs union in the 1950s with the six founding members of the EU, it formed an FTA with Austria, Denmark, Ireland, Portugal, Sweden and Switzerland – the European Free Trade Association (EFTA). For a number of years, EFTA represented an alternative RTA for European countries unwilling to commit to the wider and more political integration of the EU. But, ultimately, the rapid economic growth of EU members in the 1950s and 1960s, as well as shifting trade patterns that made the UK and other EFTA participants more dependent on trade with the EU, led Denmark, Ireland and the UK to abandon EFTA and join the EU in 1973 (Abrams et al. 1990).

FTAs are not nearly as comprehensive as customs unions, but they can serve other purposes. FTAs may be a first step in expanding a range of relationships with other countries. The North

American Free Trade Agreement (NAFTA) covers a range of goods, but also allows Canadian, Mexican and US authorities to cooperate more closely on immigration, drugs and security issues (Hufbauer and Schott 2005). The EU has forged FTAs with the Balkans and North Africa, in part to promote regional stability (Woolcock 2007). FTAs may also represent the extent of what is politically possible and, therefore, viewed as better than no deal at all. Finally, FTAs may be used as a diplomatic tool to nudge countries toward the interests of others. The EU has used FTAs with countries such as Turkey as an incentive to make additional economic reforms and, more recently, with Canada and Japan to put pressure on the United States to negotiate a trade deal with the EU (Sbragia 2010).

Although companies devise strategies in response to the complex global web of trade agreements, FTAs also spawn corporate investment decisions. Since countries that are members of an FTA have different tariffs with non-members, clever managers of companies from non-member countries might try to circumvent relatively high tariffs imposed by one member country (A) by exporting to a second member (B) with lower tariffs, and then shipping the product to country A within the rules of the free trade agreement. But most FTAs contain 'rules of origin' that require a certain percentage of a product's content to be manufactured in a member country to be eligible for tariff-free entry (Chase 2008). As a result, RTAs often shape investment decisions by multinational corporations (MNCs), giving them incentives to have facilities in at least one RTA member in order to have preferential access to other countries. Consequently, many MNCs, including Europe's BASF, Fiat, and Philips, have built factories in northern Mexico to take advantage of lower production costs, while also having tariff-free entry for their goods in the USA and Canada.

Given the size of the EU's market, with a GDP of about €15 trillion and over 500 million relatively rich consumers, the EU can be a formidable negotiator of FTAs. By negotiating on behalf of the entire membership, EU trade officials can obtain terms much more favorable than would be the case if each of the members were left to negotiate on their own. There is some research that contends that the EU is a global 'market power', using access to its market and regulatory impact as leverage with other countries (Damro 2012). Only the USA and China have similar degrees of influence in global trade. Thus, the EU has considerable influence in developing a global trade strategy (European Commission 2015).

Even with these advantages, it can be difficult for the EU to reach agreement on RTAs. One reason is that not all companies gain from trade. As the EU makes market concessions with other countries, once-protected industries become susceptible to more intense competition. These companies and their workers may well lobby relevant EU bodies, as well as their national governments, to block or weaken certain aspects of a deal under negotiation. Environmentalists also are opposed to certain aspects of trade agreements, particularly if they believe governments are sacrificing clean air, water or biodiversity for the sake of corporate interests. As a result, non-governmental organisations (NGOs) and other interest groups have become increasingly important actors in global trade negotiations (Guay 2014).

The EU's trade negotiations are conducted by the European Commission, following general instructions (or 'mandates') given by the Council of Ministers that represents member state preferences. Once the Commission concludes an FTA, the Council of Ministers (and in some cases the European Parliament) must approve the overall terms. On sensitive trade issues, such as audio-visual, health and education, member states must be unanimous in their consent. Business has a mixed record with respect to its influence over the direction and outcome of trade negotiations (Dür et al. 2015; Wilson 1985). Trade associations within the EU are typically two-tiered, with a national association representing the collective interests of a particular industry within a member country, which is then a member in a Europe-wide business group. Consequently, it can be very difficult for such a broad-based organisation to speak with a firm voice about its members' trade preferences (Woll 2009). So, while the Commission does meet and listen to business trade associations and individual companies, it is more important for business to have good communication with national trade officials who ultimately will need to approve an EU-brokered deal (Lawton and Rajwani 2015).

Role of the World Trade Organization

The World Trade Organization (WTO) currently consists of 164 countries and aims to establish rules governing global trade and the reduction of tariffs and other barriers to trade. Established in 1995, the WTO operates under the 'most-favoured-nation' principle, which requires members to offer the same trade terms to all other members without discrimination, although some exceptions (like RTAs) are allowed. RTAs may have the effect of diverting trade from more efficient outcomes. For example, if Argentina and Brazil, both members of the WTO, trade more coffee and beef with each other as a result of their RTA Mercosur, this may come at the expense of Japanese beef and Kenyan coffee producers who face higher tariffs since they are not members of Mercosur. Despite this apparent violation of WTO principles, the WTO recognises the value of RTAs, since such agreements aim to further reduce trade barriers, even if it is amongst a subset of WTO members.

As a result, RTAs have proliferated in recent years, largely as an easier-to-negotiate alternative to a WTO deal. According to the WTO, only a handful of RTAs existed in the 1950s. In the period 1948–1994, the General Agreement on Tariffs and Trade (GATT), which was the predecessor of the WTO, received 124 notifications of RTAs. Since the creation of the WTO in 1995, over 400 additional RTAs have been notified (World Trade Organization 2017). As of June 2017, 279 RTAs were in force (since some of the earlier ones have been reconfigured, and some are not yet operational). The EU is not alone in proactively negotiating FTAs. The USA, Japan, China and other countries have chosen this route, too. Whilst the EU member states mainly do so via their regional association, these countries use their economic clout to obtain greater access for their companies in other countries' markets. This competition to negotiate FTAs puts pressure on the EU member states, represented by the European Commission, to do likewise, so that their firms are not at a competitive disadvantage.

The GATT and WTO successfully completed eight rounds of trade agreements starting in 1947 (Van Grasstek 2013). Each round reduced tariffs on an ever-wider range of goods amongst its members. The most recent negotiations began in Doha in 2001, and thus is known as the Doha round of trade talks. This round is still under negotiation for two reasons. First, earlier rounds focused mostly on manufactured goods. The Doha round sought to make big cuts in the obstacles to the cross-border trade of services, such as finance, retail and transportation, which favoured Western MNCs. But these areas are still heavily protected in many developing countries. The Doha round also aimed to cut subsidies and other obstacles to the trade in agricultural goods. However, this is a sector that is politically sensitive to Europe, Japan, the USA and other richer countries that are not willing to expand access to their markets in this area. Second, the global political economy changed considerably at the beginning of the twenty-first century. The EU also sought to introduce rules governing antitrust (competition) policy and foreign investment, and include safeguards for the environment and labour, but found little support from other countries. During earlier rounds, the USA and EU dominated trade negotiations and could fairly easily persuade other countries to go along with deals that the two heavyweights had hammered out. But the rise of emerging markets in Asia and Latin America, particularly China, India and Brazil, introduced new actors at the international level with different trade interests than the EU

(Woolcock 2010). With their own MNCs and expanding middle classes, these countries could challenge the demands made by the EU and USA. Such countries were unwilling to open their markets to Western service MNCs if richer countries continued to block many agricultural imports from developing countries. The result has been an impasse within the WTO.

The range of European trade agreements

The EU has formed economic and trade agreements with neighbouring European countries with varying levels of cooperation. The closest level is inclusion in the EU's customs union. This is the category for Andorra, Monaco, San Marino and Turkey. The three 'microstates' also forged agreements with the EU to use the euro, and began negotiations in 2012 that could lead to participation in the Single Market. These countries face no tariffs on exports to the EU, and have agreed to a joint customs tariff along with the member countries. A second category includes association agreements, stabilisation agreements, free trade agreements, and economic partnership agreements. The most integrated of these is the European Economic Area (EEA) consisting of Norway, Iceland and Liechtenstein. The purpose of the EEA has been to integrate the EFTA countries into the EU's Single Market, due to their geographic proximity and close economic ties, without requiring EU membership. The EFTA still exists, but has suffered from a loss of members who have migrated to the EU. Today, EFTA members include only Iceland, Lichtenstein, Norway and Switzerland. Swiss voters rejected membership of the EEA in 1992, but a series of bilateral agreements between Switzerland and the EU have effectively replicated most of the EEA's provisions. The third category is partnership and cooperation agreements, which is what the EU has forged with various countries around the world.

For some parts of the world, the EU has viewed trade agreements as an important component of economic development (Suder 2011; Zielonka 2008). This is particularly true for the African, Caribbean and Pacific (ACP) countries, most of whom were former European colonies. The EU has established Economic Partnership Agreements (EPAs) with many countries in this region. Of the world's 49 least-developed countries, 39 are in the ACP – mostly in Africa. While this programme in theory should positively affect ACP countries' economies, the volume of ACP exports to the EU has declined during the more than 30 years of the programme's existence. Another EU programme to facilitate trade with less-developed countries is its Generalized Scheme of Preferences (GSP). There are three main variants of the GSP. The first is the full or partial removal of tariffs on two-thirds of all product categories. The GSP+ scheme removes tariffs completely on the same categories to countries that ratify and implement core international conventions relating to human and labour rights, the environment and good governance. Finally, the Everything But Arms (EBA) arrangement provides duty-free and quota-free access to all products from all least developed countries with the exception of arms and ammunition (Gradeva and Martinez-Zarzoso 2015).

The EU's focus on economic development has occasionally put it at odds with countries that were not party to these FTAs (Alter and Meunier 2006; Josling and Taylor 2003). A controversial case dating from the 1990s challenged tariff preferences that the EU granted to ACP banana exporters. Designed as a way to help banana farmers in ACP countries, the EU granted duty-free access to these producers. At the same time, the EU imposed tariffs ranging from 15 to 20 percent on Latin American exporters on the first 2.5 million tons of bananas, and significantly higher rates above that amount. US MNCs Chiquita Brands and Dole Food Co., who had significant operations in Central and South America, encouraged the USA to initiate a complaint in the WTO, eventually joined by Ecuador, Guatemala, Honduras and Mexico. The case, the first dispute between the EU and USA to be heard by the WTO, began in 1995. The

EU was found to be in violation of WTO rules in 1997 and, after making minor changes to its banana import policy, again in 1999. The USA retaliated, as WTO rules allow, with tariffs amounting to $191 million annually on EU exports to the USA. After more legal wrangling and delays related to the failed Doha trade talks within the WTO, the EU reached an agreement with Latin American banana exporters to reduce import tariffs, while also compensating ACP countries for lost sales (Suder 2011).

The UK and Brexit

The June 2016 referendum in the UK on whether to leave the EU ('Brexit') brought the differences between an FTA and a customs union back into focus. Leaving the EU means that companies exporting from the UK to the remaining member countries will no longer have the same duty-free access to the EU market. This is significant because 51 per cent of UK goods exports go to the EU, while only 7 per cent of EU exports go to the UK (*Economist* 2016). The first phase of Brexit negotiations revolved around the terms of the UK's withdrawal from the EU, which was complicated by the EU's rules allowing the free movement of goods, services, capital and people, as well as budgetary and institutional commitments. This was followed by a negotiation over trade terms for access to each other's markets. It is possible that the UK could eventually develop an arrangement similar to current EEA members such as Norway. However, those countries allow citizens of EU countries to live and work in them, and it was the migration of many Eastern Europeans to the UK in the decade after 2004 (when ten countries joined the EU) that was a major reason why many UK citizens voted in favor of Brexit (Shipman 2016).

Clearly, the negotiations are wide-ranging and complex and will have significant effects on business. As mentioned above, upon the formation of either an FTA or customs union, trade patterns typically change in the direction of greater trade flows between member countries. Both forms of trade agreements can shape foreign investment. Many companies built factories or set up their European headquarters in the UK in the decades after that country joined the EU in 1973. Firms would not only be utilising the UK's attributes of labour force flexibility, English language, access to finance and legal system, but they also could sell their goods to continental Europe without having the common external tariff imposed (Kneller and Pisu 2004). Foreign MNCs have invested a total of $1.2 trillion in the UK – far more than Germany ($771 billion) or France ($698 billion) and almost 16 per cent of the EU's total FDI (UNCTAD 2017). Brexit has required MNCs to rethink their European strategies. While there are a number of reasons why MNCs locate to the UK, including the country's legal system, language and sector-specific strengths, one of the most important advantages of the UK location – tariff-free entry to the EU market – has changed. This is particularly problematic for the financial services industry. Many banks have moved substantial staff and operations from London to EU cities such as Amsterdam, Dublin, Frankfurt or Paris (Goodman 2017). Brexit poses the risk of investment flight from the UK, which could dissuade other member countries from considering leaving the EU (Hobolt 2016; Taylor 2007). More broadly, Brexit represents scepticism and disenchantment with globalisation in all its forms – economic, political and cultural convergence – in the international community (Meyer 2017; Rodrik 2011).

The EU and the USA

The EU and the USA are each other's biggest trading partner. In 2016, almost 18 per cent of the EU's manufactured goods exports, and over 20 per cent of all goods trade (or €610 billion), was with the USA (European Commission 2017). For the USA, the EU accounted for about 19 percent of exports, imports and total trade. Total service trade amounted to almost €240 billion, with similar amounts in both directions. Despite the enormous amount of trans-atlantic trade, non-tariff barriers in the forms of regulations and product standards prevent even greater levels of transactions. Consequently, authorities initiated negotiations on the Transatlantic Trade and Investment Partnership (TTIP) in 2013. Despite the benefits that would accompany an agreement, TTIP proved too controversial on both sides of the Atlantic (Eliasson and Garcia-Duran 2016). Highly secretive meetings conducted during 15 rounds of talks provided an opportunity for opponents to raise concerns about the effects that TTIP might have on public services, the environment, privacy and individual rights, and the ability to devise regulations that reflect local sensitivities and values. Candidate and ultimately US President Donald Trump announced his opposition to TTIP, effectively ending negotiations. Ironically, the EU and USA are participants in dozens of FTAs, but do not have one with each other. Tariffs between these two entities are governed by WTO rules. Brexit complicates any revival of a USA–EU FTA, since the UK is interested in negotiating a bilateral FTA with the USA, which cannot be accomplished until the UK finalises its departure from the EU, leading in all probability to yet another FTA (Oliver and Williams 2016; Wilson 2017).

The EU and Canada and Japan

Despite the inability of the EU and USA to establish an FTA, or perhaps because of it, the EU negotiated deals with two of its most important trade partners: Canada and Japan. Canada, the EU's tenth-biggest trading partner, reached an agreement with the EU in 2016 that would eliminate tariffs on 99 per cent of goods (*Globe and Mail* 2017). The Comprehensive Economic and Trade Agreement (CETA) was approved by the European Parliament, but because of EU rules also requires national parliaments to vote in support of it. Therefore, CETA's terms will be provisionally applied until all parties approve them. European and Canadian officials view CETA as a prominent stand against protectionist and anti-globalisation sentiments in many countries around the world, including opponents of the pact in Canada and Europe. In addition to tariffs, CETA includes other measures, including greater access to sub-national (i.e., provincial and city governments) procurement, pharmaceutical patents, professional certification and the creation of an investor protection court (Hübner et al. 2017).

In July 2017, the EU announced that a trade agreement with Japan, its sixth most important trade partner, was nearing completion (Kanter 2017). The deal would provide European and Japanese automakers greater access to each other's markets, as well as open agricultural markets and government procurement. The agreement could create a bloc to rival NAFTA, currently the world's largest FTA. While the details still need to be worked out, the initiative, when combined with CETA, indicates that the EU is pursuing a global trade strategy that shows a preference for FTAs with select partners rather than a WTO pact, and a willingness to counter current protectionist trends in the USA (Meunier and Nicolaidis 2006).

Emerging markets

With the rise of Brazil, Russia, India, China and South Africa (BRICS), as well as numerous other emerging economies since the end of the Cold War in 1989, the EU has responded to the corresponding changes in the global political economy (Keukeleire and Hooijmaaijers 2014; Renard and Biscop 2012). The EU has identified several countries, including Brazil, India and South Africa, as 'strategic partners' and signed agreements with them based on mutual interests, specific to each relationship. One of the key components of nearly all of these partnership agreements is trade. Total EU–China trade grew from €260 billion in 2006 to €515 billion in 2016 (European Commission 2017). The EU is China's biggest trading partner; only the USA trades more with the EU. But, significantly, China is not one of the countries with which the EU has a formal partnership or FTA (Holslag 2011; Smith and Xie 2011). Like China, India is an increasingly important trade partner, ranking 11th in 2016 (European Commission 2017). Negotiations on an FTA began in 2007, but have yet to yield tangible results (Khorana and Garcia 2013). The main problem is that a comprehensive FTA would challenge India on precisely some of the areas in which it is anxious to retain national control, including investment and the operations of EU companies in India. Yet an FTA with India has the potential to counter-balance the EU's reliance on trade with China and strengthen relations with a key Asian partner on a range of non-trade issues, including security and democratisation. Brazil's situation is similar to India's (Van Loon 2015). Brazil is the EU's 11th-largest trade partner and, while the EU does not have an FTA with that country, it has been trying to form one with Mercosur for some time. Negotiations began in 2010, were put on hold two years later due to disagreements over EU agricultural policies and industrial protectionism by Mercosur countries, and restarted in 2016. An FTA would bolster the EU's already established position as Mercosur's leading trade partner, accounting for over one-fifth of Mercosur's total trade in 2015 (European Commission 2017). EU exports to Mercosur more than doubled between 2005 and 2015 to €46 billion. A partnership with Mercosur would counteract growing Chinese economic relations in the region (Paczkowski 2015). So, a key part of the EU's strategic partnership with Brazil, which is the largest economy within Mercosur, is obtaining greater trade and investment access to the wider region. Although the EU is South Africa's biggest trade partner, the African country ranks only 17th amongst EU trade partners – well behind Brazil, China and India (European Commission 2017). Thus, despite being Africa's biggest economy, South Africa represents only a small part of the EU's global (and African) trade interests. In 2016, the EU signed an economic partnership agreement (EPA) with the Southern African Development Community (SADC), whose current members include Botswana, Lesotho, Mozambique, Namibia, South Africa and Swaziland. Under the SADC EPA, the EU fully or partially removes customs duties on 98 per cent of imports from South Africa, and grants full market access to the other five countries (European Commission 2016). So, like Brazil, South Africa serves as a useful entry point to a wider regional FTA (Fioramonti and Kotsopoulos 2015). The evolving relationships that the EU is experiencing with these and other emerging markets underscores how trade can often be linked to other foreign policy objectives (European Union 2016).

Conclusions

RTAs are an important component of the EU's role as a global actor (Bretherton and Vogler 1999; Soderbaum 2005). The formation of trade agreements with other countries allows the EU to expand liberal economic norms and values, particularly in emerging markets and developing countries with little experience in open markets. With a more protectionist US foreign economic policy under the Trump administration, there are more opportunities for the EU to pursue FTAs with other countries. Negotiations over the EU–Japan trade agreement described above received greater attention from Tokyo once the USA abandoned the Trans-Pacific Partnership – a deal that was completed by trade negotiators but needed country ratification. Absent the USA, the global trade space may provide further opportunities for the EU. Given the impasse within the WTO, and increasing influence of non-Western countries, it seems more likely that the EU will continue its strategy of negotiating FTAs with individual countries. This allows the EU to open other countries' markets for European MNCs, and using the attractiveness of the EU market as a bargaining chip (Suder 2013). Important future research will include examining how the EU chooses where to forge FTAs, and the actors involved in influencing such agreements, including the increasingly important roles of emerging market MNCs (McGuire et al. 2012).

Going forward, there are at least three important research streams for scholars to pursue. The first is to develop a deeper understanding of how the EU chooses which RTAs to pursue. Obviously, there are some two-level game negotiations between the EU and its member states, and the EU and non-EU countries (Putnam 1988). But interest groups, particularly Europe-based MNCs, have preferences based on their global strategies, and the inter-relationships of these groups and their relative bargaining power must be better understood (Dür 2008). A second area that requires deeper understanding is how the 'losers of globalisation' impact trade policy-making. This group includes less competitive industries that face increasing pressure from foreign firms once RTAs come into effect, as well as their supply chains, workers and communities in which they operate. Measuring their ability to resist and shape RTAs, and the various resources at their disposal, will lead to a better understanding of constraints on the EU when negotiating trade pacts (Meunier 2007). Finally, more research is needed on the interests of other countries who seek trade deals with the EU. How, for example, do the strategies of emerging market MNCs seeking to compete in the European market influence their home governments' decisions to pursue FTAs with the EU (Santos and Williamson 2015)? How do countries use FTAs with the EU to leverage wider foreign policy goals with the EU and non-EU countries? These and other research questions will provide plenty of work for scholars to do on the growing importance of RTAs in the global political economy.

References

Abrams, R.K., Cornelius, P.K., Hedfors, P.L. and Tersman, G. (1990), *The Impact of the European Community's Internal Market on the EFTA*, Washington, DC, International Monetary Fund.

Alter, K.J. and Meunier, S. (2006), 'Nested and overlapping regimes in the transatlantic banana trade dispute', *Journal of European Public Policy*, vol. 13, no. 3, pp. 362–382.

Bhagwati, J. (2004), *In Defense of Globalization*, New York, Oxford University Press.

Bretherton, C. and Vogler, J. (1999), *The European Union as a Global Actor*, Abingdon, UK, Routledge.

Chase, K.A. (2008), 'Protecting Free Trade: The political economy of rules of origin', *International Organization*, vol. 62, no. 3, pp. 507–530.

Coen, D. and Richardson, J. (2009), *Lobbying the European Union: Institutions, actors, and issues*, Oxford, Oxford University Press.

Damro, C. (2012), 'Market power Europe', *Journal of European Public Policy*, vol. 19, no. 5, pp. 682–699.

Dinan, D. (2014), *Origins and Evolution of the European Union*, Oxford, Oxford University Press.

Dür, A. (2008), 'Bringing economic interests back into the study of EU trade policy-making', *British Journal of Politics and International Relations*, vol. 10, no. 1, pp. 27–45.

Dür, A., Bernhagen, P. and Marshall, D. (2015), 'Interest group success in the European Union: When (and why) does business lose?' *Comparative Political Studies*, vol. 48, no. 8, pp. 951–983.

Economist (2016), 'A background to "Brexit" from the European Union', 24 February.

Eliasson, L.J. and Garcia-Duran, P. (2016), 'Why TTIP is an unprecedented geopolitical game-changer but not a Polanyian moment,' *Journal of European Public Policy*, vol. 24, no. 10, pp. 1522–1533.

European Commission (2015), *Trade for All: Towards a more responsible trade and investment policy.* Brussels, European Commission.

European Commission. (2016), 'Economic Partnership Agreement (EPA) between the European Union and the Southern African Development Community (SADC) EPA Group', June. http://trade.ec.europa.eu/doclib/docs/2014/october/tradoc_152818.pdf (accessed 8 August 2017).

European Commission (2017), 'Trade'. http://ec.europa.eu/trade/ (accessed 28 November 2017).

European Union (2016), *Shared Vision, Global Action: A Stronger Europe. A global strategy for the European Union's foreign and security policy.* Brussels, June.

Eurostat (2017), 'Eurostat statistics explained'. http://ec.europa.eu/eurostat/statistics-explained/index. php/File:Extra_EU-28_FDI_stocks_by_economic_activity,_EU-28,_end_2014_(billion_EUR)_ YB17.png (accessed 9 August 2017).

Fioramonti, L. and Kotsopoulos, J. (2015), 'The evolution of EU-South Africa relations: What influence on Africa?' *South African Journal of International Affairs*, vol. 22, no. 4, pp. 463–478.

Frankel, J.A. (1997), *Regional Trading Blocs in the World Economic System*, Washington, DC, Institute for International Economics.

Globe and Mail (2017), 'Against all odds, CETA, Canada's trade deal with Europe, moves forward. Now what?' 17 February. www.theglobeandmail.com/report-on-business/economy/against-all-odds-ceta-moves-forward-now-what/article34031523/ (accessed 9 September 2017).

Goodman, P.S. (2017), 'Beginning "Brexit" and bracing for impact,' *New York Times*, 30 March.

Gradeva, K. and Martinez-Zarzoso, I. (2015), 'Are trade preferences more effective than aid in supporting exports? Evidence from the "Everything but arms" preference scheme', *The World Economy*, vol. 39, no. 8, pp. 1146–1171.

Guay, T. (2014), *The Business Environment of Europe: Firms, governments, and institutions.* Cambridge, UK, Cambridge University Press.

Hobolt, S.B. (2016), 'The Brexit vote: A divided nation, a divided continent,' *Journal of European Public Policy*, vol. 23, no. 9, pp. 1259–1277.

Holslag, J. (2011), 'The elusive axis: Assessing the EU-China strategic partnership', *Journal of Common Market Studies*, vol. 49, no. 2, pp. 293–313.

Hübner, K., Deman, A.S. and Balik, T. (2017), 'EU and trade policy-making: The contentious case of CETA', *Journal of European Integration*, vol. 39, no. 7, pp. 843–857.

Huffbauer, G.C. and Schott, J.J. (2005), *NAFTA Revisited: Achievements and challenges.* Washington, DC, Institute for International Economics.

Josling, T.E. and Taylor, T.G. (2003), *Banana Wars: The anatomy of a trade dispute.* Walingford, UK, CABI Publishing.

Kanter, J. (2017), 'The E.U.-Japan trade deal: What's in it and why it matters', *The New York Times*, 6 July.

Katsoulis, S. (2016), 'Multilateralising regionalism and the case of the EU', in D. Anagnostopoulou, I Papadopoulos and L. Papadopoulou (eds), *The EU at a Crossroads: Challenges and perspectives*, Newcastle upon Tyne, UK, Cambridge Scholars Publishing, pp. 163–173.

Keukeleire, S. and Hooijmaaijers, B. (2014), 'The BRICS and other emerging power alliances and multilateral organizations in the Asia-Pacific and the global south: Challenges for the European Union and its view on multilateralism', *Journal of Common Market Studies*, vol. 52, no. 3, pp. 582–599.

Khorana, S. and Garcia, M. (2013), 'European Union-India trade: One step forward, one back?' *Journal of Common Market Studies*, vol. 51, no. 4, pp. 684–700.

Kneller R. and Pisu, M. (2004), 'Export-oriented FDI in the UK', *Oxford Review of Economic Policy*, vol. 20, no. 3, pp. 424–439.

Krueger, A.O. (1997), 'Free trade agreements versus customs union,' *Journal of Development Economics*, vol. 54, no. 1, pp. 169–187.

Krugman, P.R. (2000), *Rethinking International Trade*, Cambridge, MA, MIT Press.

Lawton T. and Rajwani, T. (2015), *The Routledge Companion to Non-Market Strategy*, Routledge, London.

McGuire, S., Lindeque, J. and Suder, G. (2012), 'Learning and lobbying: Emerging market firms and corporate political activity in Europe,' *European Journal of International Management*, vol. 6, no. 3, pp. 342–362.

Meunier, S. (2007), 'Managing globalization: The EU in international trade negotiations,' *Journal of Common Market Studies*, vol. 45, no. 4, pp. 905–926.

Meunier, S. and Nicolaidis, K. (2006), 'The European Union as a conflicted trade power', *Journal of European Public Policy*, vol. 13, no. 6, pp. 906–925.

Meyer, K. (2017), 'International business in an era of anti-globalization', *Multinational Business Review*, vol. 25, no. 2, pp. 78–90.

Oliver, T. and Williams, M.J. (2016), 'Special relationships in flux: Brexit and the future of the US-EU and US-UK relationships', *International Affairs*, vol. 92, no. 3, pp. 547–567.

Paczkowski, M. (2015), 'A Potential Accord: An EU-Mercosur Free Trade Agreement', Council on Hemispheric Affairs, 29 June. www.coha.org/a-potential-accord-an-eu-mercosur-free-trade-agreement/ (accessed 8 August 2017).

Putnam, R.D. (1988), 'Diplomacy and domestic politics: The logic of two-level games', *International Organization*, vol. 42, no. 3, pp. 427–460.

Renard, T. and Biscop, S. (2012), *The European Union and Emerging Powers in the 21st Century: How Europe can shape a new global order*. London, Routledge.

Rodrik, D. (2011), *The Globalization Paradox: Why global markets, states, and democracy can't coexist*. Oxford, Oxford University Press.

Sandholtz, W. and Zysman, J. (1989), '1992: Recasting the European bargain', *World Politics*, vol. 42, no. 1, pp. 95–128.

Santos, J.F.P. and Williamson, P.J. (2015), 'The new mission for multinationals', *MIT Sloan Management Review*, vol. 56, no. 4, pp. 45–54.

Sbragia, A. (2010), 'The EU, the US, and trade policy: Competitive interdependence in the management of globalization', *Journal of European Public Policy*, vol. 17, no. 3, pp. 368–382.

Shipman, T. (2016), *All Out War: The full story of how Brexit sank Britain's political class*. London, William Collins.

Smith, M. and Xie, H. (2011), 'The European Union and China: The logics of "Strategic Partnership"', *Journal of Contemporary European Research*, vol. 6, no. 4, pp. 432–448.

Soderbaum, F. (2005), 'The EU as a global actor and the dynamics of interregionalism: A comparative analysis', *Journal of European Integration*, vol. 27, no. 3, pp. 365–380.

Suder, G. (2011), *Doing Business in Europe*, 2nd edn, London, Sage.

Suder, G. (2013), 'Regional trade agreements and regionalization: Motivations and limits of a global phenomenon,' Australian National University Centre for European Studies Briefing Paper Series, vol. 4, no. 1.

Taylor, P. (2007), *The End of European Integration: Anti-Europeanism examined*, London, Routledge.

UNCTAD (2017), *World Investment Report*. http://unctad.org/en/Pages/DIAE/World%20Investment%20 Report/World_Investment_Report.aspx (accessed 10 October 2017).

Urwin, D.W. (1995), *The Community of Europe: A history of European integration since 1945*, 2nd edn, London, Routledge.

Van Grasstek, C. (2013), *The History and Future of the World Trade Organization*, Cambridge, Cambridge University Press.

Van Loon, A. (2015), 'From interregionalism to bilateralism: Power and interests in EU-Brazil trade cooperation', in M. Rewizorski (ed.), *The European Union and the BRICS*, Cham, Switzerland, Springer, pp. 141–159.

Wilson, G.K. (1985), *Business and Politics: A comparative introduction*. New York, Chatham House.

Wilson, G.K. (2017), 'Brexit, Trump and the special relationship', *The British Journal of Politics and International Relations*, vol. 19, no. 3, pp. 543–557.

Woll, C. (2009), 'Trade policy lobbying in the European Union: Who captures whom?' in D. Coen and J.J. Richardson (eds), *Lobbying in the European Union: Institutions, actors and issues*, Oxford, UK, Oxford University Press, pp. 268–289.

Woolcock, S. (2007), 'European Union policy toward free trade agreements,' ECIPE Working Paper No. 3. Brussels, European Centre for European Political Economy. www.felixpena.com.ar/contenido/ negociaciones/anexos/2010-09-european-union-policy-towards-free-trade-agreements.pdf (accessed 10 October 2017).

Woolcock, S. (2010), 'Trade policy: A further shift toward Brussels', in H. Wallace, M.A. Pollack and A.R. Young (eds), *Policy-making in the European Union*, Oxford, UK, Oxford University Press, pp. 381–400.

World Trade Organization (2017), 'Regional trade agreements and preferential trade agreements'. www. wto.org/english/tratop_e/region_e/rta_pta_e.htm (accessed 6 December 2017).

Zielonka, J. (2008), 'Europe as a global actor: Empire by example?' *International Affairs*, vol. 84, no. 3, pp. 471–484.

14

THE EU'S INSTITUTIONS AND THE BUSINESS ENVIRONMENT

Alan Butt-Philip

Introduction

Business and the various EU institutions enjoy a symbiotic relationship. The EU has multiple responsibilities which affect firms and business, sometimes specific to particular companies, but more commonly shaping and influencing the business environment. Among these responsibilities are competition (anti-trust) policy governing private firms, mergers and acquisitions, cartels as well as state subsidies to private and public sector enterprises; external trade policy and anti-dumping; the running of the customs union and the development of the single European market based on the four freedoms (capital, goods, people and services); health and safety standards; environmental policy and standards; basic employment standards including application of the principle of equal pay for men and women; cross-border research and development policy designed to speed up the introduction of new technology and promote cooperation in R&D between firms; agricultural policy, food and food safety standards; consumer protection; not to mention policies for regional development and vocational training.

The EU does not set economic policy for the bloc as a whole, so member states have formal control over their national budgetary and fiscal policies. However, the European Central Bank in Frankfurt controls monetary policy and sets interest rates for the 19 member states in the Eurozone. In addition, there are norms set for all member states concerning the levels of government debt, the application of which was blown apart by the financial crisis of 2008–10, but which subsequent decisions, such as the Fiscal Compact of January 2012, have tried to resurrect (Intergovernmental Treaty 2012). States that ignore such norms (especially concerning levels of government debt) do so at their peril, as Greece has discovered since 2010. It is clear that the response of the EU to the financial crisis has been to require more economic and financial integration within the Eurozone as the price for guaranteeing the integrity and the stability of the euro, the use of which confers significant advantage for all participating states.

What also needs to be made clear at the outset is that the central EU institutions in Brussels have comparatively little financial power (the EU budget accounts for less than 1 per cent of EU GDP) but they do have significant and often crucial regulatory powers which are of direct concern to most industrial sectors. These include standard-setting (often through the three EU-inspired bodies of the European Committee for Electrotechnical Standardization (CENELEC), European Telecommunications Standards Institute (ETSI) and European Committee for Standardization (CEN)) and the policing of the single European market. There are 37 EU-created regulatory agencies covering policy areas such as the authorising of medicines (EMEA); food safety (EFSA); health and safety (EU-OSHA); employment conditions; environmental policy and standards (EEA); and chemicals (ECHA). These agencies are located in different member states across the EU.

Clearly the EU institutions have a wide policy remit although they are constrained legally by the EU treaty base and, politically, by the appetite of member states for further integration, which often also leads to more centralisation and loss of national government autonomy. The EU is a legal order governed by the terms of successive treaties (Rome 1957, the Single European Act 1986, Maastricht 1992, Amsterdam 1997, Nice 2000, Lisbon 2007 and others) and the interpretations of these by the European Court of Justice. The treaties themselves enable the EU policy remit to be extended, provided key institutions agree, for example using Article 236 of the EEC Treaty (now Art. 352 of the Treaty on the Functioning of the European Union (TFEU)), and the integration process itself can lead to demands for new policy areas to be addressed. A classic example of this was the drive to complete the single market leading to the development of EU policies on aspects of immigration.

A brief survey of the EU institutions

It is beyond the remit of this chapter to look in detail at all the influence of all the EU institutions on the business environment, but some have a more direct impact than others. The European Commission, which has over 30 directorates-general and service departments, is the most significant of all the institutions because of its sole right of initiative, which derives from the EU treaty base, and which makes it the focus of much of the lobbying activity in Brussels. The Commission is a multinational bureaucracy with many very long-serving officials at or near the top of the organisation whose governing ethos is to transcend national interests and to offer truly pan-European solutions to problems. The Commission manages some EU activities directly – the customs union, the external trade policy, the competition policy, and the common agricultural policy, with varying amounts of delegation of responsibility to the member states. More commonly, it is the member states that must deliver agreed EU policies in each of their own territories but they are subject to constant Commission scrutiny (often resented) and they can ultimately be challenged publicly by the Commission for non-compliance with legally binding rules and regulations, even ending up before the judges of the European Court of Justice.

Aside from this executive role, the Commission's exclusive role of initiator means that it is usually the agenda-setter for EU policy. This is a power that the Commission was granted by the Treaty of Rome and it gives a political role to the EU civil service while under the direction of the President of the Commission and his 27 colleagues, who are appointed by the governments of the member states, subject to the approval of the European Parliament. In the development of EU policy, the Commission is usually the starting point, although both the European Council and the European Parliament have ways of prompting the Commission into action. But it is down to the Commission to make policy proposals, and this role in turn attracts representatives of business to make contact with the relevant Commission officials to seek to influence the shape of those proposals before they are more public, or to amend proposals once officially tabled by the Commission.

The Commission is intended to be the 'guardian' for the extensive EU treaty base, both in terms of staying true to the founding purposes of the organisation when bringing forward proposals, and in terms of ensuring that EU decisions are correctly and fully implemented in the member states. Such a role risks putting the Commission into conflict with national governments that the Commission thinks are not meeting their obligations. The Commission has to play its cards carefully and often looks for ways of encouraging national governments to put their houses in order rather than insisting at the outset on its legitimate legal rights. This approach ties in with the final role of the Commission, which is to act as informed 'mediator' between EU institutions that are in conflict over policy (typically the Council and the Parliament) or where member states are in disagreement with each other (Wallace et al. 2015).

From a business perspective, the Commission is much more able to be influenced than the Council of Ministers, because firms and business associations can usually get access to the Commission, whereas access to the Council is usually blocked. Partly this is because of the structure of the Council, which only rarely allows a peak association such as COPA (the European agricultural union created in 1958) or Business Europe to address its collective membership but whose floating composition is a barrier. The Council certainly has most power in the EU but the best place for firms to seek to influence positions taken by Council members is by lobbying activity in the member states (Hayes-Renshaw et al. 2006).

The European Parliament (EP) has become an increasing target for business interests to engage with the EU policy process because successive changes to the EU treaty base have given it more power and leverage among the EU institutions (Shackleton et al. 2011). The EP, which comprises 751 directly elected members from all 28 member states, and in which there is never likely to be a majority for one political tradition, does not have the same level of power as any national parliament as it shares the legislative function with the Council of Ministers and has no say over the revenues flowing into the EU budget. However, it is a crucial player in areas of great concern to the business community such as the detailed functioning of the single market, the setting of environmental standards and other environmental policies, employment regulation and consumer protection. As such there are more than 11,000 individuals who are officially registered by the EU to undertake lobbying activities on behalf of various public and private interests. The EP committees which cover the main subject areas hear evidence and seek above all to call the Commission to account. Since the arrival of the euro, the EP's economic and monetary affairs committee has also sought to examine in public the activities of the European Central Bank on a quarterly basis.

The European Court of Justice in Luxembourg (ECJ) oversees the entire EU legal order – the successive treaties and the application of all the thousands of pieces of legislation that flow from them. The ECJ is in effect the supreme court of the EU and its rulings prevail whenever there is a conflict between national and European law. The ECJ normally takes cases brought to its attention either by the European Commission or by the references from national courts. But such cases often originate because businesses question the application of single market law, or competition rules, or because trade unions are seeking to extend the de facto application of employment or equality law. The case law of the ECJ can have huge commercial implications and has direct effect in all the member states. Examples include the mandatory equalisation of pension ages for men and women in occupational pension schemes (ECJ 1990) and successive ECJ rulings governing the definition of working time.

The European Central Bank (ECB) in Frankfurt was set up following the decisions under the Treaty of Maastricht 1992 to create European economic and monetary union. It is designed to be independent of any political pressures from the participating member states and it decides the monetary policy, in particular the interest rate policy, for the Eurozone as a whole. Although not officially a 'lender of last resort' for the banking systems of the Eurozone states, it has been forced by successive crises in at least six member states to take actions that are analogous to this role. It has instituted several programmes of 'quantitative easing', available to all EU banks, in order to support the banking systems and economic stability in the member states. Despite its restricted legal brief, the ECB has probably done more to support and stabilise the European business environment than any other single actor (Hodson 2012).

The European Investment Bank (EIB) in Luxembourg was set up in 1959 to provide funds, in the form of loans or guarantees, for regional development broadly defined. It is owned by the 28 member states and, by virtue of its AAA rating on the financial markets, it is able to supply loan finance at the lowest possible interest rates. The EIB provides long-term loans especially for major cross-border and infrastructure projects which could struggle to be financed by the financial markets. It provided one-fifth of the funds needed to build the Channel Tunnel. It has provided very large loans to finance telecoms infrastructure, energy-saving projects, the development of renewable energy sources and water supplies, as well as social housing in Northern Ireland. It also provides finance for smaller firms and technological development through intermediaries.

The regulatory agencies referred to above operate under legislation decided by the EU institutions but they are subject to the oversight of the European Commission and the ECJ. They have specific duties that may or may not impact directly on firms and sectors. The European Medicines Agency, at present based in London, licenses all medicines in use in the single market. Its approval enables a drug or other medicine to be sold in all EU member states. Clearly, engagement with this Agency is critical for the pharmaceutical industry and the Agency's rulings control the development of this sector in no small measure. Far less directly engaged with business is the European Environment Agency in Copenhagen. It monitors the environment in Europe generally and specifically monitors and reports on the implementation of EU environmental policies. Its main interlocutors are national environment agencies in each member state, but its assessments of environmental legislation, such as standards for water quality, air quality or vehicle emissions, are significant in the long term for the development of EU policies that directly affect the costs and activities of business across many sectors.

In addition, there is a variety of other EU-created bodies that contribute to the development of policies that affect the business environment. The Committee of the Regions comprises local and regional government representatives who comment on all legislative proposals. Similarly, the Economic and Social Committee draws representatives from business, workers, the professions and other groups from every member state: it too comments on proposals as well as preparing reports on more general issues of interest to businesses. The three standard-setting bodies (ETSI, CENELEC and CEN) have a direct impact on individual sectors when determining European standards. The EU Court of Auditors assesses the value of current policies, their levels of implementation in the member states and draws attention to lapses in the application of EU budgetary and eligibility rules by member states or the European Commission. Their remit thus covers all agricultural, regional development and industrial spending.

Most recently the EU has set up, in the wake of the financial crisis of 2007–2009, supervisory authorities that check for the financial stability of the banking sector and of individual banks.

Key policy areas for business

The EU has general responsibility for controlling the conditions under which businesses operate in the European market but has few opportunities to intervene directly in individual sectors. Even so, the cumulative impact of cross-sector (horizontal) polices and rules can have a huge bearing on what firms on the ground can do, how they behave to consumers and how they compete with other firms. This section will identify how the most critical areas of EU activity can affect sectors and individual firms.

The European economy

While national governments still control some major levers of macro-economic policy, the ECB is now responsible for monetary policy and interest rates in the Eurozone. With other EU bodies, it also sets the framework for the operations of the banking sector. National governments are expected to follow EU rules concerning levels of government debt whether they are in the Eurozone or not. In times of flagging investment and economic growth the EU, through the EIB and other structures such as the European Investment Fund, can borrow on its own account and provide an economic stimulus across the region (see above). The direct interventions of the ECB in regard to Portugal, Spain, Ireland, Italy, Greece and Cyprus since 2010 speak for themselves.

The Single Market

The ambition of the EU from the outset has been to create a fully integrated market, free of internal border controls, where the four freedoms (capital, people, goods and services) could operate seamlessly. This ambition is not yet fully achieved, especially in the field of services, despite a significant relaunch of the project for a single European market in 1985 and the adoption of the Single European Act in 1986. The Commission continues to seek out opportunities to break down barriers to cross-border trade and investment. These could be in the form of different national standards or administrative requirements that inhibit foreign competition. A particular bête-noire is the way that car manufacturers and car dealers have colluded to support differential prices in different national markets for the same model of car. This practice is seen as artificially segmenting the Single Market, as well as exploiting some consumers, and is contrary to EU law. Several car manufacturers have been landed with heavy fines since the case involving Volkswagen in Austria and Italy in 1998. A fine of 90 million euros was eventually imposed after Volkswagen appealed to the ECJ (EU Commission 1998).

The Commission prefers technical standards to be set by the official industry-led bodies (see above) but can also rely on the principle of 'mutual recognition' of standards between member states enshrined in the *Cassis de Dijon* judgment given by the ECJ in 1979 (ECJ 1979). But there are circumstances where the Commission has felt obliged to bring forward legislation itself, as in the case of the Toy Safety Directive 1988. This is to ensure that certain minimum standards are to be relied on wherever certain goods are purchased within the Single Market. Such instances demonstrate that sometimes it is judged necessary for varying national regulations to be substituted by a single EU regulation (re-regulation) which gives both producers and consumers certainty about what is allowed to be bought and sold across all EU member states. The EU, led by the Commission, has also radically changed the business environment in whole sectors, notably telecommunications, waste management and passenger airlines through legislative packages. In the case of financial services, the Commission has preferred to deal with types of financial products case by case.

The customs union and external trade

The EU has jurisdiction over the operations of the customs union although the day-to-day delivery of border controls and responsibility for border infrastructures lies with the member states. Normally it is the EU which determines what can legally be imported into or exported from the Union, and what duties should be applied to either imports or exports, if any. In some poorer member states the EU will even contribute significantly to the costs of new border posts (e.g. Spain, Poland, Lithuania) in order to speed up the movements of goods and people.

As regards the external trade policy of the EU, once again it is the Commission that is in the driving-seat, administering the nearly do trade agreements the EU has signed with other trade blocs or nation states, the latest of these being with South Korea, Canada and Japan. Such agreements determine how far EU firms can access foreign markets and how much access is afforded to foreign competitors in the EU market. But there are some countries, notably the USA, where the EU has yet to reach such an agreement and where WTO rules apply instead to trade. Occasionally the EU will step outside the conventional trade agreement perspective and adopt a 'whole sector' approach. This was adopted in regard to the textile industry in the EU under the Multi-Fibre Agreement (1974–2004) and when the Commission adhered to the 'Elements of Consensus' agreement with the Japanese automobile manufacturers in 1993, which restricted car imports to the EU for the rest of that decade.

The Commission is also the first port of call for those firms or sectors that allege that foreign competitors are 'dumping' goods on the EU market at artificially low prices. WTO rules constrain what the Commission can do but it can impose punitive duties on such imports if there is evidence to justify this. In the long term, such anti-dumping measures have often proved unable to protect sectors (such as photocopiers) where EU industries have been losing competitiveness.

Overall the EU aims for trade liberalisation across the world, and it was a key player in setting up the WTO in 1994. However, its credibility in this regard is challenged by its own somewhat protectionist agriculture policies, although these have been reduced in scale and impact on the world markets in response to international pressure.

The competition policy

The EEC Treaty contains articles outlining the principles governing competition between private sector firms, the behaviour of public enterprises and also the conditions under which state subsidies to firms may be allowed (TFEU 2012, Articles 101 and 102). Because there has been little legislation in this general area, and because for a long time most member states did not have their own competition authorities, the implementation of the rules on competition has been traditionally the responsibility of the Commission itself. It is only since the Modernisation Act of 2004 that substantial powers to enforce the competition policy have been delegated to all individual member states. Even so, the Commission itself still handles the largest cases and it has oversight over the activities of the national competition authorities as well. There is considerable interaction between these various authorities to ensure a consistent interpretation of the treaty principles on competition across all 28 member states.

The EU's competition rules outlaw restrictive practices such as price fixing, market sharing or any other behaviour by firms which has the effect of distorting competition or impeding the functioning of the market. The rules also outlaw any abuses of dominant position by one firm in relation to others – such as loss leading or unreasonable refusal to supply. The Merger Regulation of 1969 also established the right of the EU to control, and on occasion to prevent mergers, acquisitions and business alliances where the combined turnover of the parties is more than 5 billion euros and their business in the EU market is worth 250 million euros or more. Few proposed mergers are outlawed absolutely, and the Commission seeks to balance concerns about the shrinking of competitor numbers with any projected benefit for consumers.

Public enterprises are required to be transparent in their financial reporting, particularly in sectors such as airlines or banking, where they are in competition with privately owned firms.

They must also ensure that their purchasing practices enable cross-border suppliers to bid for contracts.

Finally, the Commission must be consulted about any state subsidies to firms and it defines the appropriate scale of any capital subsidies (according to the level of regional need) that may be allowed. Such 'state aids' (including tax breaks and rent rebates) are broadly defined and permission for governments to pay out such subsidies is frequently refused and illegal payments must be paid back to their donors (EU Commission 1987; 1993).

Agriculture

For over 50 years agriculture in Europe has been dominated by the common agriculture policy (CAP), the EU's first policy programme for a whole sector of business activity. At first some sub-sectors such as 'sheepmeat' were not covered, but now they almost all are. The CAP's original design was to manage agricultural markets day by day in order to support prices and thus to boost production and EU self-sufficiency. Since 2004/5 the method of intervention has changed and individual farms receive payments from the EU budget based on previous payments (but slowly reducing) and cross-compliance with EU environmental policy objectives. So, for most farmers, depending on their sector of activity, their business environment is still dominated by the EU.

The results of the EU's actions are everywhere to be seen in rural areas. Farms have got larger. Farm incomes have risen over time and the rural economy has benefited. Now farmers are being encouraged to diversify their business activities, including into non-agricultural roles, and to become much friendlier to the environment in how they farm – fences being replaced in some areas by hedges, which provide nesting places for birds and cover for wild plants and animals.

At the same time the EU is under international pressure through the WTO to reduce the extent to which agriculture is protected in Europe, as the price for further global trade liberalisation. So, levels of financial support for farms and farmers are falling and this is set to continue. In addition, the EU is reducing export subsidies, which aim to dispose of surplus production at home while, also slowly, opening up more European markets to non-EU produce (such as wine and beef from South America), which is highly competitive.

Regional development and the structural funds

The EU has provided some structural measures (e.g. encouragement of farm amalgamations or investment in land drainage schemes) since the early days of the CAP. Then came grants from the European Social Fund (ESF), which encouraged states and their voluntary sectors to improve vocational training and other labour market skills. Finally, a Regional Development Fund was created in 1975 to provide capital grants for infrastructure projects and long-term job creation in the poorest parts of the EU. These initiatives have been greatly expanded following enlargements of the number of EU member states and as a complement to the competition of the Single European Market and the introduction of a single currency – the euro. Today the structural funds taken together account for over a third of the EU's annual budget – approaching 50 billion euros.

The structural funds concentrate their spending on the poorest parts of the EU, notably Eastern Europe and parts of the Mediterranean coast. Their impact for business can be seen in vastly improved infrastructure – motorways, telecoms upgrades, water and energy supplies – as well as in pockets of industrial development. Modernised airports and urban metro systems (e.g. in Prague and Warsaw) are also testament to these EU funds, and make life easier for the business traveller. The training element of these funds, the European Social Fund, has been important in strengthening national training programmes for those that have difficulty in obtaining employment – i.e. migrant workers, young people under 26 without qualifications, the disabled, and women returning to work after a career break. Generally, the skills profile of those seeking employment has been improved as a result of almost 50 years of ESF funding in the member states.

Environmental policies and standards

Since the 1970s the EU has been the key actor in shaping environmental policies across Europe. This has been made easier by the absence of much interest in such policies in most member states before that time and because of the realistic recognition that pollution, especially air and water pollution, knows no frontiers. Starting with directives concerning air, noise and water pollution, as well as the transport and disposal of hazardous waste, the EU's actions have had a major impact on business activities both on their own premises and in regard to their products and services. From the 1990s the EU has also set standards for waste management and demanded that large sums of public money be invested in major projects, such as the treatment of sewage in all major cities in the name of improving water quality and public health. Such investment inevitably has the effect of raising the cost of water supply and other utilities for business as well as increasing operating costs on sites.

The EU has taken a proactive stance in regard to recycling, requiring all car manufacturers from 2006 to sell only new car models that are recyclable once scrapped. Vehicle emissions for cars and lorries have been legislated since the late 1980s; in 2016, the discovery that Volkswagen alongside many other companies had deliberately and systematically deceived consumers and the official testing bodies for years about the levels of emissions from diesel-fuelled cars came close to orchestrating its corporate collapse. The EU has also tried, rather unsuccessfully, to establish the European Eco-Label as the recognised emblem of good environmentally friendly products and services based on a life-cycle analysis, which can be costly as well as controversial (EC Regulation 2000).

Labour regulation and equal pay

The EU does not have a general remit to bring forward proposed regulations in the field of employment but it does have such powers in specific fields such as health and safety at work (broadly defined to include maximum working hours, and the rights of pregnant women employees), equal pay and anti-discrimination measures.

Much of the impact of the social and employment provisions of the EU treaty base has come about through case law determined by the ECJ. Thus, the definition of equal pay so that it requires equal pay for work of equal value comes from the Luxembourg court. So does the requirement that all occupational pension schemes must have the same benefits and pension ages for women as for men, and the legal demand that part-time workers must enjoy pro rata the same benefits from employment (e.g. holiday entitlements and pension rights) as full-time workers. Where there are genuine areas of doubt over the interpretations of such case law, it can require a new case and a further judgment from the ECJ before clarification can be definitively given.

Industrial policy and research

The EU does not have an industrial policy or an industrial strategy, and only rarely does it have any over-arching plans for particular sectors – the exceptions being steel industry rationalisation and shipbuilding in the 1980s, textiles in relation to the Multi-Fibre Agreement (see above), the long-term investment in the development of telecommunications begun in the early 1980s and the creation of Airbus Industry.

It is also true that a combination of EU measures derived from its roles in regard to external trade policy, the running of the Single Market, the implementation of the competition policy and the setting of environmental standards can have a profound impact on the development, shape and behaviour of all firms in a particular sector – the car industry (manufacturers and retailers) being a case in point. Another important example, where concerted regulatory activity by the European Commission has transformed a sector, is the airline passenger transport market. In 2014, the EasyJet airline told the UK government that without the EU's actions their company would not exist (FCO 2012–2014). A similar story could be adduced in relation to the market for postal services.

The EU has significant funds put aside for research, which are often targeted at key drivers of future industrial and technological development. The mechanisms adopted often require collaboration between several firms and research institutions across borders within the EU. Such activities have seen the development of the GSM standard for mobile phone technology as well as multiple investments in the development of new environmental technology.

Other policies

Sometimes it becomes clear that effective delivery of EU policy in one field demands the development of policy in another field previously untouched by the EU. A classic case has been the need for the EU to propose measures concerning aspects of immigration (e.g. visa issue and the treatment of asylum seekers) in order to deliver free movement of people within the Single Market. Another example, which is also related to the Single Market, are EU measures governing consumer protection and the facilitation of claims and access to justice for consumers across borders.

The EU has found itself trying to assert key principles underpinning the market in the field of sport. This came about as a result of the famous *Bosman* judgment by the ECJ in 1995, which not only established some basic rights for professional footballers, leading to a major increase in their wages at the top of the game, but also decided that football clubs are businesses which must henceforth respect EU rules on competition between firms (ECJ 1995). So, it has to be conceded that the limits to EU intervention as far as businesses are concerned are uncertain and not just subject to the whims of Commission officials. The ECJ can extend the scope of EU oversight to unexpected areas, such as sport and the provision of healthcare services across borders.

Lobbying and representation of business interests

It should cause no surprise that the EU institutions have become major targets for lobbying activity given that they oversee and regulate one of the richest markets in the world, comprising in 2017 some 508 million people. Non-EU governments, trade associations, professional bodies, consultants and individual firms are all involved. As the powers and scope for

EU intervention have increased as a result of successive treaty changes, so has the number of EU lobbying organisations and lobbyists risen, usually, but not always, based in Brussels. At the time of writing the number of lobbyists active in EU decision-making is thought to exceed 20,000 and the number of lobbying organisations targeting the EU institutions around 3,000. Comparisons between Washington DC and Brussels in this regard are appropriate (Coen 2009; Greenwood 2011).

Most lobby groups based in Brussels are very small scale and only become active when proposals are in the air that directly affect them. Otherwise they are mainly listening posts for the national federations who make up their membership. A few groups, however, have a major presence and impact on the Brussels scene – these can be sectoral in composition (e.g. chemical industries, pharmaceuticals or automobile manufacturers) or cross-sectoral such as Business Europe (a peak association representing national employer associations such as the CBI in the UK, the DBI in Germany or MEDEF in France) or AMCHAM's EU committee, which speaks for American businesses located in the EU. These organisations can be very influential because they speak for major business interests and are able to offer creative solutions and informed analysis on a wide variety of subjects under discussion by the EU.

Lobbyists above all seek access to the key decision-makers in the EU institutions (where they will be successful if they can show they are genuinely representative) in order to obtain information about EU thinking and possible influence. In return decision-makers at the Commission and the EP are looking for reliable information about specific sectors, which is not generally available, and for guidance about the possible impact of policy options under consideration.

Occasionally the Commission is prepared to use interest groups or charities as its agents in policy delivery. The rationalisation of the steel industry in the 1980s was mostly achieved through EUROFER, which represented all the major steelmakers. The car and oil industries were similarly privileged under the two AUTO-OIL programmes of the 1990s. In addition, much of the EU's development aid continues to be channelled through charities such as Oxfam, the Red Cross and Médecins Sans Frontières – organisations that both lobby Brussels on policy on the one hand and seek to deliver it on the other.

Business interests dominate the lobbying scene in the EU because they often have direct economic interests at stake and they are prepared to resource such activities adequately. In contrast those organisations at EU level that seek to represent more general public interests – such as consumers or environmental concerns – find themselves at a disadvantage, because of the large number of issues they ought to be dealing with simultaneously while they are greatly under-resourced for this task. The Commission does provide some funding for about 60 such groups, to try to counterbalance the power of business interests, but the more such groups rely on EU funding the more there can be questions about their independence.

Clearly there are issues to be considered in relation to the transparency, accountability and democracy in EU policy-making as a result of the scale and impact of lobbying in the EU. These issues have come to the fore in the twenty-first century and have prompted the Commission and the EP to put in place different schemes to put into the public domain who they are talking to (EU Commission 2017).

Neo-functionalist theorists of European integration foresaw a key role for interest groups in the development and deepening of the economic integration process. New institutionalist theorists in the 1990s also rated the influence of these interests highly in the EU policy-making processes. Intergovernmentalists, however, dismiss the role of interest groups as marginal because they stress the overriding role of national governments in EU decision-making. If the intergovernmentalists are right, it is hard to understand why business interests devote so much time, money and people to lobbying the EU institutions (Coen 2006, Cini and Borragan 2016).

Another critique of the important part played by lobbying in the EU's decision-making is that corporate interests have become so strongly represented at the Brussels level that the necessary components of a truly functioning democratic process – transparency and account-ability – have been sidelined. The analysis above suggests some weight should be given to this kind of criticism, and some moves have been made by the EU institutions to reduce the secrecy that surrounds much of their dialogue with corporate interests. Ultimately, it is both national governments, through the Council of Ministers, and democratically elected MEPs in the EP who make most of the key decisions, and they are only beholden to corporate interests if they choose to be so. On the other side of the argument, it needs to be acknowledged that corporate interests, as much as any others in a vibrant democracy, are entitled to represent themselves and to seek to influence the actions of government, all the more so when the decision-making bodies are geographically so far away from functioning businesses on the ground. It can also be asserted that the EU institutions have so far been the only governmental bodies in Western Europe to have successfully taken on great global multinational companies such as Amazon, Google and Microsoft for anti-competitive behaviour and tax avoidance.

Conclusions

Although the EU institutions are bound by the terms and authorisations granted by the EU treaty base and have inevitably become somewhat rule-bound within this complex legal order, the development of the economic integration process presided over by the EU is still funda-mentally dynamic. This means that as circumstances change and demands for policy adjustments and new initiatives follow, there is still a large capacity for business interests to influence the actions of the EU, and vice versa. It should never be forgotten that while the EU can regulate to open up markets and cross-border competition, it is up to individual firms to decide whether or not to use the opportunities that such economic integration offers. Businesses are as much the agents of European economic integration as the European Commission, and it is not surprising that they do more than just co-exist. This analysis has shown that the EU institutions do indeed have profound impacts on the European business environment at many levels but the separate decisions of business enterprises are also very significant.

References

Cini, M. and Borragan, N. (2016), *European Union Politics*, 5th edn, Oxford, Oxford University Press.

Coen, D. (2006), *EU Lobbying: Theoretical and empirical developments*, Oxon, Routledge.

Coen, D. (2009), *Lobbying the European Union*, Oxford, Oxford University Press.

ECJ (1979), *Rewe-Zentral AG v. Bundesmonopolverwaltung für Branntwein*, C 120/78.

ECJ (1990), *Barber v. Guardian Royal Exchange*, C 262/88.

ECJ (1995), *Union Royale Belge des Sociétés de Football Association ASBL v. Jean-Marc Bosman*, C 415/93.

EC Regulation (2000), European Eco-label Regulation (EC) 1980/2000 as amended by Regulation (EC) 66/2010.

EU Commission (1987), Press Release in regard to the Renault automobile manufacturing enterprise [IP-87–466].

EU Commission (1993), Press Release in regard to Rover (UK) Ltd. [IP-93–405].

EU Commission (1998), Commission Decision of 28 January 1998.

EU Commission (2017), 'Transparency Register'. https://ec.europa.eu/info/about-european-union/principles-and-values/transparency/transparency-register (accessed 17 October 2017).

FCO (2012–2014), 'Review of the balance of competences'. www.gov.uk/guidance/review-of-the-balance-of-competences (accessed 17 October 2017).

Greenwood, J. (2011), *Interest Representation in the European Union*, 3rd edn, Basingstoke, Palgrave.

Hayes-Renshaw, F. and Wallace, H. (2006), *The Council of Ministers*, 2nd edn, Basingstoke, Palgrave.

Hodson, D. (2012), 'Managing the euro: The European Central Bank', in J. Peterson and M. Shackleton (eds), *The Institutions of the European Union*, 3rd edn, Oxford, Oxford University Press.

Intergovernmental Treaty (2012), Intergovernmental Treaty on Stability, Co-ordination and Governance signed by 25 EU member states on 2 March 2012, effective from 1 January 2013.

Shackleton, M. and Jacobs, R.F. (2011), *The European Parliament*, 8th edn, London, John Harper Publishing.

TFEU (2012), EU Treaty on the Functioning of the European Union (Consolidated Version), Official Journal of the EU, C 326, 26 October 2012.

Wallace, H. Pollack, M. and Young, A. (2015), *Policy-Making in the European Union*, 7th edn, Oxford, Oxford University Press.

PART E

Managing people in Europe

15

JOB QUALITY IN EUROPE

Regulation, workplace innovation and human resources practices

Andreas Kornelakis and Michail Veliziotis

Introduction

How do firms manage their human resources to foster workplace innovation and job quality in the European business context? How does the European Union's (EU) integration facilitate these aims and impact the management of human resources? These questions have become all the more pertinent in the current economic juncture, when the European economy is recovering from a deep recession. Yet, the challenges posed by the external business environment continue to threaten the level of job quality in Europe. The world of work in Europe is about to be disrupted by a double blow: a new phase of globalisation and an unprecedented wave of digitalisation. In the face of these challenges, it is important to assess how the macro-level EU regulation responds to these challenges and interacts with national HR practices and strategies.

On the one hand, a new phase of globalisation is best manifested with an intensification of global competition from emerging markets. The global intensification of competition started with the trade liberalisation as part of World Trade Organization agreements, and the entrance of new players such as the BRICS (Brazil, Russia, India, China and South Africa) into global trade. The level of competition has also intensified because of regional market integration in Europe (e.g. the Single Market in the EU), but also in other parts of the world e.g. the North Atlantic Treaty Association (NAFTA) and Association of Southeast Asian Nations (ASEAN). As the markets of BRICS become saturated, new countries such as the MINTs (Mexico, Indonesia, Nigeria and Turkey) are identified as prominent production locations (Forbes 2014). The intensification of competition has led to a vertical disintegration of production in the advanced economies of Europe and exacerbates trends of offshoring and the development of complex global value chains (Gereffi et al. 2005). By implication, the ongoing disintegration of production and offshoring put pressure on the creation of good quality jobs in the European context.

On the other hand, the more recent wave of technological change through the digitalisation of markets, products and processes is challenging the dominance of Fordist mass production regimes of the previous decades. The fourth industrial revolution is reshaping traditional work organisation with the introduction of a wide range of new technologies and innovations (e.g.

the Internet of Things, Cloud Computing, 3D Printing, Advanced Robotics, etc.). Technological change is also manifested with the so-called 'sharing' or 'on demand' economy and is expected to have a massive impact on work and employment (see OECD 2016). In this context, there are several instances of disruption in traditionally sheltered sectors (prominent examples include Uber, which has disrupted the taxi industry, and Airbnb, which has disrupted the hotel industry). More generally, digitalisation and technological change are also expected to disrupt employment relationships and proliferate new forms of flexible work, such as job sharing; casual work; mobile work; portfolio work; and crowd employment (Eurofound 2015a). These new flexible forms of work deviate from the standard full-time employment relationship and some of them might be associated with precariousness and low quality. Indeed, 'bad jobs', especially in relation to low autonomy, is an increasing characteristic of the post-Fordist era (Vidal 2013). Hence, it remains an open question of how regulatory frameworks are adjusted to ensure job quality in these flexible and atypical forms of employment.

The launch of the European Employment Strategy (EES) in 1997 was the first step in a series of coordinated efforts in Europe to address these exact challenges stemming from globalisation, technological change and precariousness (European Commission 2008, p. 147). It aspired to implement policies and actions aimed at boosting labour market outcomes in the EU. Since 2000 the framework of the Lisbon Strategy encompassed not only full employment, but also promoted job quality and productivity, further enriching the EES overarching objectives. Hence, quantitative and qualitative aspects (or 'more and better jobs') were both highly important elements within the EU employment policy agenda (European Commission 2008, p. 147). In March 2010, the EU launched the Europe 2020 Strategy, which replaced the Lisbon Strategy. Under this umbrella, the Agenda for New Skills and Jobs and Flexicurity policies seek to provide Europe's answers to the emerging challenges of globalisation and digitalisation. They shift the attention to policies that encourage lifelong learning to fill shortages in digital skills and also reconcile business needs for flexibility with employees' needs for security. On 17 November 2017, the European Parliament, the Council and the Commission jointly signed the European Pillar of Social Rights at the Social Summit for Fair Jobs and Growth in Gothenburg, Sweden.[1] The European Pillar of Social Rights represents an unprecedented commitment to new and more effective rights for citizens in three main categories (equal opportunities and access to the labour market; fair working conditions; and social protection and inclusion) and includes, for example, rights to fair wages, to healthcare, to lifelong learning, to better work–life balance and gender equality. In this broader context, the interesting tension that this chapter will examine is the potential of EU's regulatory impact to harmonise or converge member states' policies and practices in the areas of workplace innovation and job quality, vis-à-vis the reality of diversity in job quality indicators and outcomes across European countries.

The rest of the chapter is structured as follows. The second section considers the theoretical framing of the chapter grounded in the micro–macro linkages in employment systems. The third section considers the key areas of EU regulation that are likely to have a substantial and direct impact on innovative HR practices. The fourth section examines recent evidence from the European Working Conditions Survey to chart the empirical trends in key areas of job quality across Europe. Particular attention will be drawn to the aspects of HR practice that contribute to job quality outcomes in different regimes in Europe (Holman 2013). Thus, the empirical section examines indicators of skills utilisation and development, task discretion and autonomy, the physical environment, employee participation, absence of discrimination, and working time quality. The final section wraps up the key findings from the empirical section and relates back to the initial questions of how macro-level regulation interacts with workplace-level practices and whether there has been a convergence or 'Europeanisation' of human resources management (HRM) in different countries.

Theoretical frame: Micro–macro linkages in employment systems

One popular strand of the academic literature sought to identify 'best practices' in HRM that deliver high performance; these may appear in 'bundles' and thus have 'internal fit' with the overall business strategy (Macduffie 1995; Huselid 1995; Ichniowski et al. 1997). These practices typically include: job security; selective recruitment and selection; formal job analysis; information sharing; internal promotion based on performance; pay linked with performance; continuous investment in skills and training; autonomy in self-managed teams; formal and regular performance appraisal; and employee participation. Recent variants of this line of research draw on extensive survey evidence to highlight the importance of efficient management practices in human resources explaining variations in productivity across countries (Bloom et al. 2012; Dowdy and Van Reenen 2014).

While this literature usefully attempted to identify 'best practices' for imitation irrespective of local institutional context, another strand of research started on the premise that the best practices cannot be imitated – and if they are imitated they might not work. Instead, the emphasis should be placed on 'external fit' of employment systems and this analysis is couched on the long tradition of the perspective of micro–macro linkages in employment systems (Brown and Reich 1997; Katz and Darbishire 2000; Rubery and Grimshaw 2003; Dobbin 2005; Delbridge et al. 2011). This strand of literature considered the interplay between micro-level practices and macro-level institutions in international and comparative HRM. More recently, research in this strand (Kornelakis et al. 2017) has confirmed that specific practices, such as performance-based rewards, training and teamwork, were very good predictors of productivity improvements in Europe during the financial crisis, but their effects are context-specific. They appear to be more prevalent in specific institutional contexts and less prevalent in others, while their capacity to improve performance is also mediated by the wider employment relations institutions in different countries. Similarly, related research suggests that workplace practices need customisation to local institutional contexts and that multinationals do not standardise practices across countries; instead, hybrids are evolving everywhere (Edwards et al. 2016).

The broad explanation behind the diversity and need for customisation reflects mainly the importance of macro-level institutional contexts and the constraints that these provide to rational business actors. Particularly, labour markets incorporate a wide range of institutions that vary considerably across countries, such as employment protection legislation (EPL) strictness, collective bargaining centralisation and coordination, trade union power, occupational safety and health (OSH) regulations, working time regulations and skills formation systems. These institutions either provide opportunities to business actors to tap into these resources or provide constraints that limit their range of options with regard to strategic or institutional experimentation (Morgan 2009). Hence, several studies have confirmed empirically that workplace innovation and HR practices vary across Europe and there is little evidence of convergence to a European model of HRM (Brewster 2007; Gooderham and Nordhaug 2010; Sparrow and Hiltrop 1997; Lorenz and Valeyre 2005; Stavrou et al. 2010). Similarly, Mikhaylov's chapter in this book outlines the diversity of sub-regional approaches to HRM in Europe. Yet, this appears somewhat puzzling given the breadth of EU regulation that seeks to harmonise some elements of national institutions and HR practices across Europe. The next section considers the key components of the EU regulatory impetus.

The EU regulatory impact on job quality and innovative workplace practices

The EU agenda: From job quality to workplace innovation

The aim of the Lisbon Strategy, launched in March 2000 by the EU heads of state and government, was to make Europe 'the most competitive and dynamic knowledge-based economy in the world capable of sustainable economic growth with more and better jobs and greater social cohesion'.[2] These aims were bundled together with the goals for the earlier agreed EES(Gold 2009) and in 2001 the Commission adopted a communication that provided a broad framework for promoting quality of work (European Commission 2001). Almost in parallel to the International Labour Organization's launch of the Decent Work Programme, the EU began to focus more explicitly on the quality of jobs and to monitor the progress towards the reviewed principles. In 2001, the European Council agreed on a portfolio of 18 indicators (see Burchell et al. 2014, p. 470).

However, the advent of the European crisis hindered progress and the Lisbon Strategy targets were not met (Featherstone et al. 2012). In the fall of 2010 the European Commission effectively relaunched the strategy under a new name: the Europe 2020 Strategy. Europe 2020 is a ten-year strategy for reviving the European economy aiming at smart, sustainable, inclusive growth. One of the seven key pillars (Flagship Initiatives) is the so-called 'Innovation Union', which presents a broad conceptualisation of innovation and represents a breakthrough, if not a policy paradigm shift for European policy, because social innovation, next to technological innovation, is now a key feature of Europe's innovation policy (Oeij et al. 2011, p. 32). The European Commission regards social innovation as a new form of innovation, defined as 'new ideas that meet social needs, create social relationships and form new collaborations'.[3] These innovations are focused on product or services innovation (new products or services), organisational innovation (changes in work flows and production process) or business model innovations (new business models, marketing strategies, service delivery modes, etc.). Other relevant Flagship Initiatives include: 'Youth on the move' (focused on student mobility, higher education modernisation, national qualifications, school drop-outs) and the 'Agenda for new skills and jobs' (focused on Flexicurity, social dialogue, lifelong learning).

The Europe 2020 Strategy signifies some continuity with the earlier Lisbon Strategy, for example the emphasis on innovation, mobility and skills. But it no longer features job quality as a prominent target. Instead, the concept of 'workplace innovation' has become one of the key priorities of the European Commission, for example with the reinforced 2012 EU Industrial Policy Communication.[4] In the European context, the European Workplace Innovation Network, which is supported by the European Commission, has defined workplace innovation as 'new and combined interventions in work organisation, human resource management, labour relations and supportive technologies' (Pot et al. 2016, p. 15).

The EU regulatory impact on workplace organisation and human resources practices

The impact of various EU regulations on day-to-day management of European enterprises is complex and multidimensional and we will only attempt a first approximation here. The EU has multiple direct and indirect tools to influence functional areas pertaining to the management of human resources of European firms (see Table 15.1). For instance, there are 'soft' instruments that may impact indirectly the whole range of HR strategies and functions of European firms, including: training and learning; recruitment and selection; rewards and benefits; expatriate management, and so on. For instance, Flexicurity is a policy model that is related *indirectly* to

Table 15.1 The EU regulatory impact on human resources practices

HRM Functional Area	EU Regulatory Impact (Soft/Hard)
Training and development	Lifelong learning policies, Flexicurity, elearning, higher education, language learning, mobility
Diversity and equality	Anti-discrimination, equal opportunities, gender equality, parental leave, part-time working
Recruitment and selection	Europass CV, mutual recognition of qualifications
Rewards and benefits	Employee financial participation, transferability of pension rights, European health insurance card
Employee participation	Information, consultation and participation of employees, European Works Councils
Health and safety	European Agency for Health and Safety at Work
Technology/ work organisation	Teleworking Directive, Working Time Directive
Expatriates	Posted Workers Directive, transferability of pension rights, European health insurance card
Labour relations	European cross-industry and sectoral dialogue

Source: Authors' elaboration.

skills development and learning practices at the organisational level (Kornelakis 2014). However, this section will focus on reviewing the main areas in which the European regulation has a *direct* impact on the conduct of HR strategies such as: equal opportunities policies; information and consultation (employee participation and involvement); working time; and health and safety.

Equal opportunities

One HR functional area in which EU regulation has had a substantial impact concerns equal opportunities and diversity management policies. At the European level the authority to adopt directives in the field of equal opportunities is enshrined in Article 119 of the Treaty on the Functioning of the European Union (Treaty of Rome). Since the 1970s we have had Council Directives and European Court of Justice interpretations that provide the bulk of regulation in this area.

The relevant equal opportunities legislation concerns: the prohibition of direct and indirect sex discrimination to statutory social security schemes (Directive 79/7/EEC); the Pregnancy Directive (92/85/EEC); the Burden of Proof in Sex Discrimination Cases (97/80/EC); the Racial Equality Directive (2000/43/EC); the Employment Equality Directive (2000/78/EC); the prohibition of direct and indirect sex discrimination in access to and the supply of goods and services (Directive 2004/113/EC); the Recast Directive (2006/54/EC) on equal opportunities and equal treatment of women and men in employment and occupation, which repealed some of the earlier legislation; the Parental Leave Directive (2010/18/EU), which replaced the 1996 Directive; and the prohibition of direct and indirect sex discrimination to self-employment (Directive 2010/41/EU).

This legislation has had indirect effects on pension schemes (equalising the retirement age among men and women) and on companies' pay and recruitment policies (equal pay for equal work). The initial focus on gender discrimination was subsequently extended to cover the grounds of religion or belief, disability, age and sexual orientation.

Information and consultation

The process of information and consultation of employees is a significant part of HR practices concerning employee participation and involvement. The EU has been quite active in this area, starting with the establishment of an innovative new institutional body: the European Works Council (EWC) and then setting a general framework for information and consultation. European Works Councils are bodies representing the European employees of a company. Through them, workers are informed and consulted by management on the progress of the business and any significant decision at transnational level that could affect their employment or working conditions. Member states are to provide the right to establish EWCs in companies or groups of companies with at least 1,000 employees in the EU and the other countries of the European Economic Area, when there are at least 150 employees in each of two member states. A request by 100 employees from two countries or an initiative by the employer triggers the process of establishing the EWC.

The initial EU Directive on EWCs (94/45/EC) goes back to 1994, and was subsequently extended to the UK by another Directive (97/74/EC) and adapted by a third Directive (2006/109/EC) to the accession of Bulgaria and Romania. More recently, political agreement was reached to recast the Directive (2009/38/EC) with the aim to ensure the effectiveness of employees' transnational information and consultation rights, increase the number of EWCs and enable the continuous functioning of the existing ones. The EU Directive established a general framework for informing and consulting employees (2002/14/EC) and plays a key role in promoting social dialogue. Information and consultation are required on: (i) the recent and probable development of the undertaking's or the establishment's activities and economic situation; (ii) the situation, structure and probable development of employment within the undertaking or establishment and any anticipatory measures envisaged, in particular where there is a threat to employment; (iii) decisions likely to lead to substantial changes in work organisation or in contractual relations. The Directive applies only to undertakings employing at least 50 employees, or to establishments employing at least 20 employees, according to the choice made by the member state. Finally, information and consultation is required in the event of collective redundancies (98/59/EC) and also in the event that a workplace is transferred from one employer to another (2001/23/EC) according to the Transfer of Undertaking Protection of Employment (TUPE) regulations.

Working time and atypical work

Another important area in which the European regulations have an impact on HR practices concerns working time. Working time refers to the time that workers spend in paid employment as opposed to personal or leisure time. It is an important aspect of work organisation, as working time arrangements determine the *duration* (total length); the *timing* (scheduling of work time); and *tempo* (intensity with which people work). Working time is also considered as a major source of employment flexibility as manifested in a variety of arrangements (e.g. flexitime, gliding schedule, shift-working, compressed working week, annualised hours, job-sharing, part-time work and overtime). It has also important implications for job quality as different working time arrangements may hinder or enhance work–life balance (Walsh 2013).

The EU activity in this area is grounded in the rationale that to protect workers' health and safety, working hours must meet minimum standards applicable throughout the EU. Therefore, the Working Time Directive (2003/88/EC) amended the previous one (1993/104/EC) and required EU countries to guarantee the following rights for all workers: (i) a limit to weekly working hours, which must not exceed 48 hours on average, including any overtime; (ii) a minimum daily rest period of 11 consecutive hours in every 24; (iii) a rest break during working hours if the worker is on duty for longer than 6 hours; (iv) a minimum weekly rest period of 24 uninterrupted hours for each 7-day period, in addition to the 11 hours' daily rest; (v) paid annual leave of at least 4 weeks per year; (vi) extra protection for night work, e.g. average working hours must not exceed 8 hours per 24-hour period, night workers must not perform heavy or dangerous work for longer than 8 hours in any 24-hour period, night workers have the right to free health assessments and, under certain circumstances, to transfer to day work. The Working Time Directive also sets out special rules on working hours for workers in a limited number of sectors, including doctors in training, offshore workers, sea fishing workers and people working in urban passenger transport. There are separate directives on working time for some other sectors: in mobile road transport activities (Directive 2002/15/EC); civil aviation (2000/79/EC); and seafarers (Council Directive 1999/63/EC).

Furthermore, there is other legislation that regulates provisions in atypical contracts (part-time contracts, fixed-term contracts or agency work) on the grounds of equal treatment. The Part-time Work Directive (97/81/EC), which was extended to the UK by another Directive (98/23/EC), requires that part-time workers' employment conditions may not be less favourable than those of comparable full-time workers, unless there are objective reasons for different treatment. In addition, it exhorts employers, as far as possible, to take account of employees' preferences and their requests to transfer from full-time to part-time employment or vice versa. Employers should also facilitate access to the relevant jobs. Finally, a worker's refusal to transfer from full-time to part-time work or vice versa should not in itself be a valid reason for dismissal. Similarly, the Fixed Term Work Directive (1999/70/EC) forbids employers from treating fixed-term workers less favourably than permanent workers, unless different treatment can be justified on objective grounds. To prevent abuse of successive fixed-term contracts, EU member states, after consultation with social partners, must put in place one or more of the following limits: (i) the objective reasons that would justify the renewal of fixed-term contracts or relationships; (ii) the maximum total duration of successive fixed-term employment contracts and relationships; (iii) the permitted number of renewals. Finally, the Directive on Temporary Agency Work (2008/104/EC) defines a general framework applicable to the working conditions of temporary workers in the EU. The Directive aims to guarantee a minimum level of effective protection to temporary workers and to contribute to the development of the temporary work sector as a flexible option for employers and workers. It lays down the principle of non-discrimination, regarding the essential conditions of work and of employment, between temporary workers and workers who are recruited by the user company.

Health and safety

Although work can be dangerous and a hazard to employee health and safety, HR researchers and managers have tended to neglect this area somewhat, considering it a field for dedicated specialists in occupational safety and health (Clinton and van Veldhoven 2013, p. 370). However, national and supranational regulation in this area may have a substantive impact on work organisation and practice and HR departments need to comply with this legislation in accordance with their duty of care for their employees. At the European level the authority to adopt directives in the field of safety and health at work is enshrined in the Article 153 of the Treaty on the Functioning of the European Union. In the late 1980s and in the run-up to the completion of the Single Market, different regulations on health and safety between member states were widely considered as non-tariff barriers to trade, and this resulted in the European Framework Directive on Safety and Health at Work (Directive 89/391 EEC).

Since then, we have seen a large number of EU Directives, which have sought to regulate aspects of health and safety. There is a wide range of health and safety issues that these Directives regulate: workplace equipment, signs, and personal protective equipment (Directives 2009/104/EC, 99/92/EC, 92/58/EEC, 89/656/EEC, 89/654/EEC); exposure to chemical agents and chemical safety (Directives 2009/161/EU, 2009/148/EC, 2006/15/EC, 2004/37/EC, 2000/39/EC, 98/24/EC, 91/322/EEC); exposure to physical hazards and biological agents (Directives 2013/59/Euratom, 2013/35/EU, 2006/25/EC, 2003/10/EC, 2002/44/EC, 2000/54/EC, 96/29/Euratom, 90/641/Euratom); provisions on workload, ergonomic and psycho-social risks (Directives 90/270/EEC, 90/269/EEC); as well as sector-specific provisions (e.g. Directive 2010/32/EU on the prevention of sharp injuries in the hospital and healthcare sector).

Interestingly, instead of the usual 'lowest common denominator' regulatory approach, standards were raised across the European member states. Labour and business groups participated in policy-making in Brussels and Expert Committees gathered 'best practices', blending together national approaches to health and safety. As Eichener (1997, p. 604) suggests, in occupational health we have a combination of Danish and Dutch approaches (the innovative health concept, the inclusion of work organisation), German approaches (the role of technical standards), British concepts (risk assessment) and French concepts (primacy of inherently safe construction) in almost each directive.

Human resources practices and job quality in Europe
The dataset and variables

This section will examine empirical evidence drawing on the European Working Conditions Survey (EWCS) administered by the European Foundation for the Improvement of Living and Working Conditions (Eurofound). The EWCS started in 1990 and since then it has been carried out every five years: 1990/91, 1995, 2000/01, 2005, 2010.[5] It has been used extensively in recent studies of job quality (e.g. Green and Mostafa 2012; Green et al. 2013). The 2010 wave of the survey covers all EU-28 countries, plus Norway, Turkey, FYROM, Albania, Kosovo and Montenegro. We focus our analysis on the 2010 wave and the EU-28 countries, and include only employees in our national samples, excluding self-employed persons. In total, there are around 31,000 observations in 2010, ranging from 654 sampled employees in Greece to 3,442 in Belgium. In what follows, we construct seven indices of job quality (see Table 15.2), loosely following the work of Green and Mostafa (2012). All indices are normalised to the 0–1 scale (with 0 indicating the lowest and 1 the highest quality). The variables that are included in each index constitute an aspect of work organisation or HR practice. Thus, we are able to gauge the variation and the extent of 'good workplaces' across European countries.

Job quality in Europe

In this section we will map job quality in 2010 across groups of countries in Europe. The grouping follows Holman (2013, p. 492), who identified five regimes: *Social democratic*

Table 15.2 Overview of job quality indicators

Job Quality Index	Aspect of Work Organisation or HR Practice
Skill use and development	Training, solving unforeseen problems, complex tasks and learning new things
Discretion (autonomy)	Able to choose or change order of tasks, methods of work and speed/rate of work
Physical environment	Exposed to vibrations, noise, high/low temperatures, smoke/fumes, chemicals, tiring positions, carrying heavy loads, repetitive hand/arm moves
Information and consultation	Existence of employee representative, management holds meetings
Absence of discrimination	Absence of discrimination based on age, race, nationality, sex, religion, disability or sexual orientation
Working hours	Working less than 48 hours per week
Work intensity	Working at very high speed, to tight deadlines, has enough time to get job done, can take a break when wishes

Source: Author's own representation, based to a certain degree on Green and Mostafa (2012).

(Denmark, Finland and Sweden); *Continental* (Austria, Belgium, France, Germany, Luxembourg and the Netherlands); *Liberal* (Ireland and the United Kingdom); *Southern European* (Cyprus, Italy, Greece, Malta, Portugal and Spain); and *Transitional* (Bulgaria, Czech Republic, Estonia, Hungary, Latvia, Lithuania, Poland, Romania, Slovakia and Slovenia; we also add Croatia to this regime).

The indicator of skill use and development (Figure 15.1) is related to HR practices focused on learning and development and generally human resource development policies. As we have hinted earlier, the EU tends to influence the supply of skills in the labour market through the extensive funding of programmes of vocational education and training and the promotion of life-long learning. The specific indicator is constructed by inclusion of the following variables from the survey: the provision of training in the establishment; the ability to solve unforeseen problems and deal with complex tasks; and the capacity or opportunity to learn new things at work. As such it encompasses both strategic HR practices and work organisation, but also employees' abilities and behavioural aspects of working.

Social democratic countries (Sweden, Finland and Denmark) appear to be at the forefront of skill use and development in 2010. Then the picture becomes somewhat mixed with countries from the Liberal model (UK, Ireland); the Continental model (the Netherlands, Austria, Luxembourg and Germany); and the Transitional model (Slovenia, Estonia, Czech Republic and Hungary). Towards the bottom of the skills use and development appear countries in the Southern model (Spain, Italy, Cyprus, and Greece) and the Transitional model (Romania and Bulgaria).

The indicator of discretion (Figure 15.2) is related to HR practices that are focused on fostering workers' autonomy in work organisation, including decentralised decision-making, flatter management hierarchies and delegating decision-making power to autonomous teams. Teamwork has been identified as one of the key predictors of productivity improvements in Europe (Kornelakis et al. 2017). The specific indicator is constructed by inclusion of the following variables from the survey: ability to choose or change order of tasks, and ability to choose or change methods of work and speed/rate of work. As such it encompasses structural elements of work organisation, but also employees' abilities and behavioural aspects of working.

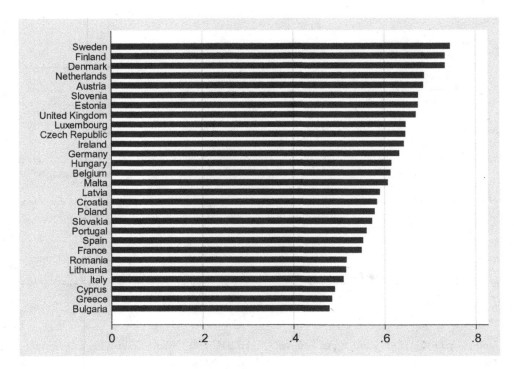

Figure 15.1 Skill use and development index (2010)
Source: Eurofound (2015b) and authors' calculations.

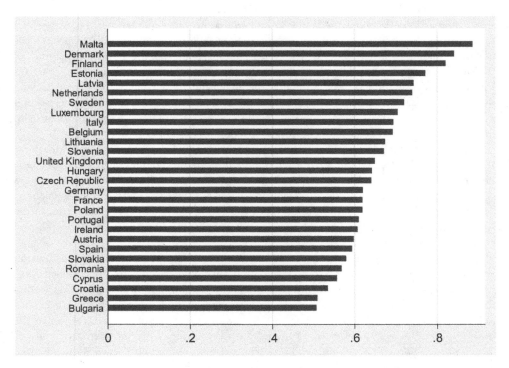

Figure 15.2 Discretion index (2010)
Source: Eurofound (2015b) and authors' calculations.

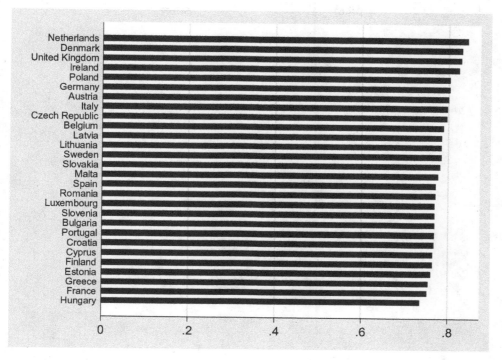

Figure 15.3   Physical environment index (2010)
Source: Eurofound (2015b) and authors' calculations.

Social democratic countries (Denmark, Finland and Sweden) again appear to be at the forefront of discretion in 2010. Then the picture becomes quite blurred with countries from different models appearing close to the top of the ranking: Malta and Italy (from the Southern model); Estonia, Latvia, Lithuania and Slovenia (from the Transitional model), Netherlands, Luxembourg and Belgium (from the Continental model) and the UK (from the Liberal model). Towards the bottom of the discretion ranking again appear countries in the Southern model (Spain, Cyprus and Greece) and the Transitional model (Romania and Bulgaria).

The indicator of physical environment (Figure 15.3) is related to HR practices on occupational safety and health, which tend to affect directly employee health and well-being. As we have mentioned in the earlier section, the EU directly influences policies and practices in the area of health and safety via an extensive regulatory framework that prescribes suitable policies and protections. The specific indicator is constructed by inclusion of the following variables from the survey: exposure to vibrations, noise, high/low temperatures, smoke/fumes, chemicals; tiring positions, carrying heavy loads, repetitive hand/arm moves. As such the indicator encompasses both objective working conditions, as well as aspects of work organisation and the repetitiveness/monotony of work processes.

The picture appears quite different here, as both Liberal countries (the UK and Ireland) appear near the top of the ranking of physical environment quality. Near the top appear also some Continental European countries (the Netherlands, Germany and Austria) and one Social democratic country (Denmark). Towards the bottom of the physical environment quality appear countries from almost all models: Hungary (Transitional), France (Continental), Greece (Southern), and Finland (Social democratic).

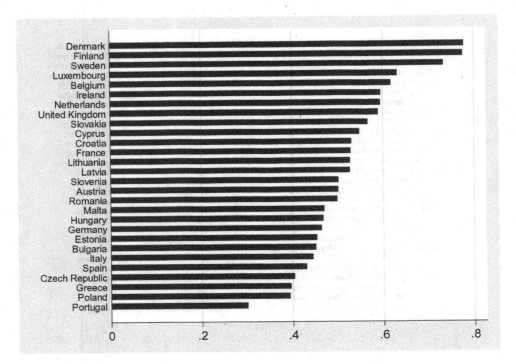

Figure 15.4 Information and consultation index (2010)
Source: Eurofound (2015b) and authors' calculations.

The indicator of information and consultation (Figure 15.4) is related to HR practices that concern employee participation and involvement. As was mentioned in the previous section, the EU has in general been quite active and prescriptive in this area. The index was constructed by inclusion of the following two variables: availability of an employee representative in the workplace; and availability of meetings organised by management in which the employees can express their views about what is happening in the organisation.

The picture here appears similar to the one concerning skill use or discretion. Specifically, Social democratic countries (Denmark, Finland and Sweden) are ranked at the top of job quality concerning availability of information and consultation. Then the picture becomes more mixed with countries in the Continental model (Luxembourg, Belgium and the Netherlands); the Liberal model (Ireland and the UK); and the Transitional model (Slovakia and Croatia), also ranked close to the top. Towards the bottom of the ranking appear countries in the Southern model (Italy, Spain, Greece and Portugal) and the Transitional model (Bulgaria, the Czech Republic and Poland).

The indicator concerning absence of discrimination (Figure 15.5) is directly related to the EU's equal opportunities regulation efforts. It is, however, a more subjective index in nature, since it directly asks employees whether they have experienced any discrimination based on either age, race, nationality, sex, religion, disability or sexual orientation in their workplace. Differences in the cultural understandings of discrimination in the different countries should influence the way employees report such incidents and, hence, they should affect the final ranking of the countries.

The most encouraging finding of the results for this index is the relative absence of discrimination in EU countries' workplaces. Almost all countries score close to 1 (the highest value of

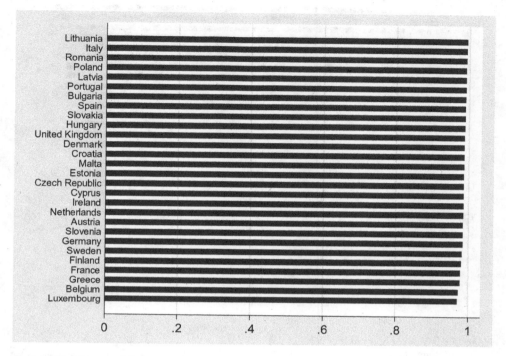

Figure 15.5 Absence of discrimination index (2010)
Source: Eurofound (2015b) and authors' calculations.

the index) and the differences between countries are not substantial (in many cases not even statistically significant). The small differences, however, indicate a relative better performance for the Transitional and Southern countries (with the notable exceptions of Slovenia and, particularly, Greece) than for the Continental, Liberal and Social democratic countries. However, it should be reminded that the sensitivity of employees to incidents of discrimination may be higher in the latter group of countries than in the former, something that may be behind the specific ranking of countries found in the data and observed in Figure 15.5.

The indicators of working hours (Figure 15.6) and work intensity (Figure 15.7) are related to HR practices on working time, which tend to affect directly the duration, intensity and tempo of working. As we mentioned earlier in the chapter, the EU directly influences policies and practices in the area of working time via a regulatory framework that prescribes suitable policies and protections for employees. The working hours' indicator measures working time duration less than 48 hours per week, while the work intensity indicator is constructed by inclusion of the following variables from the survey: working at very high speed; working to tight deadlines; having enough time to get the job done; can take a break when wishes. As such the two indicators encompass both objective working conditions, as well as behavioural aspects of working.

Concerning working hours, the Continental and Social democratic countries appear at the top of the ranking of job quality. After these countries, the picture in terms of regimes appears more mixed. Italy and Cyprus rank quite highly, but other countries from the Southern model (Greece) are located at the bottom of the ranking. Moreover, apart from Estonia and Romania, the rest of the Transitional countries exhibit the worst levels of working hours' quality. From the Liberal model, the UK is also ranked near the bottom.

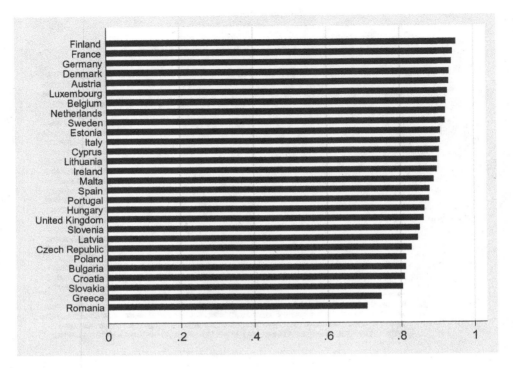

Figure 15.6 Working hours index (2010)
Source: Eurofound (2015b) and authors' calculations.

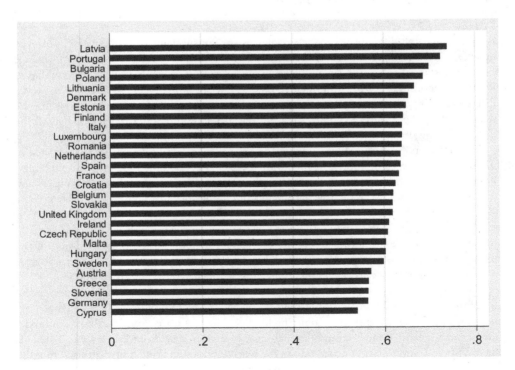

Figure 15.7 Work intensity index (2010)
Source: Eurofound (2015b) and authors' calculations.

The picture appears quite different concerning work intensity, as several countries from the Southern model (Portugal, Italy and Spain), as well as the Transitional model (Latvia, Bulgaria, Poland, Lithuania and Estonia) appear to exhibit much better quality in terms of work intensity. Some other countries such as Denmark (Social democratic) and the Netherlands (Continental) also appear close to the top of the ranking. The worst levels of work intensity appear in some Southern (Greece and Cyprus), Continental (Austria and Germany) and Transitional countries (Hungary and Slovenia).

Conclusion

The chapter set out to explore the interplay between EU regulation and policies for job quality and national HRM strategies and practices. The chapter was framed within the theoretical perspective that suggests that employment systems are characterised by micro–macro linkages, and thus, national or supra-national regulatory institutions provide constraints and resources for HR strategies. We examined the regulatory impact of the EU on job quality through a series of Directives in the areas of equal opportunities, information and consultation, working time and health and safety. Finally, we considered empirically the variation of job quality indicators (skill use and development, discretion/autonomy, physical environment, information and consultation, discrimination, working hours and work intensity) across the EU-28.

The chapter sought to gauge whether the EU regulatory impact provides any ground to think that there has been a trend towards 'Europeanisation' of workplace practice and convergence of job quality levels across European countries. The empirical exploration suggested that there is little, if any, evidence to suggest a harmonisation of European job quality levels. Supranational level regulation may interact with workplace-level practices, however, and mediate through a myriad of national, institutional, cultural and sectoral specificities. In fact, the empirical material suggests that even the traditional clustering of countries into *regimes* (Holman 2013; Green et al. 2013) breaks down. If we wanted to identify a *between-regime* pattern, that would most likely be the higher level of job quality observed in the Social democratic, Nordic countries (Denmark, Finland and Sweden) and the consistently low level of quality in some Southern and Transitional countries (e.g. Greece). However, we also observed that cross-national diversity persists and we also identified some consistent differences in patterns *within regimes*. The prime examples are the Transition countries in Eastern Europe, with a consistently higher level of job quality in Baltic states compared to the countries in the Balkans.

These wide differences in levels of job quality open up avenues for further research. Future work should seek to explain the differences not with reference to 'regimes' or 'models', but consider systematically alternative explanations. These explanations may dwell on the differences in levels of socio-economic development, the cross-country variation in industrial and occupational structures, the within-regimes variation in labour market institutions, historical path dependencies in management practices, as well as cultural variation. Further research in those areas appears even more urgent in order fill the gap in our understanding on how to improve job quality in Europe in light of the wider pressures stemming from globalisation and technological change.

Notes

1 See: https://ec.europa.eu/commission/priorities/deeper-and-fairer-economic-and-monetary-union/european-pillar-social-rights_en (accessed 29 November 2017).
2 See: www.europarl.europa.eu/summits/lis1_en.htm (accessed 19 February 2017).
3 See: https://ec.europa.eu/growth/industry/innovation/policy/social_en (accessed 27 February 2017).

4 See: https://ec.europa.eu/growth/industry/innovation/policy/workplace_en (accessed 11 February 2017).
5 See Eurofound (2015b) for more details. The most recent survey (2015 wave) had just been released as this chapter was being drafted.

References

Bloom, N., Genakos, C., Sadun, R. and Van Reenen, J. (2012), 'Management practices across firms and countries', *Academy of Management Perspectives*, vol. 26, no. 1, pp. 12–33.

Brewster, C. (2007), 'A European perspective on HRM', *European Journal of International Management*, vol. 1, no. 3, pp. 239–259.

Brown, C. and Reich, M. (1997), 'Micro-macro linkages in high performance employment systems', *Organization Studies*, vol. 18, no. 5, pp. 765–781.

Burchell B., Sehnbruch, K., Piasna, A. and Agloni, N. (2014), 'The quality of employment and decent work: Definitions, methodologies, and ongoing debates', *Cambridge Journal of Economics*, vol. 38, no. 2, pp. 459–477.

Clinton, M. and Veldhoven, M. (2013), 'HRM and employee wellbeing' in S. Bach and M. Edwards (eds), *Managing Human Resources*, Chichester, UK, Wiley, pp. 364–388.

Delbridge, R., Hauptmeier, M. and Sengupta, S. (2011), 'Beyond the enterprise: Broadening the horizons of international HRM', *Human Relation*, vol. 64, no. 4, pp. 483–505.

Dobbin, F. (2005), 'Is globalization making us all the same?' *British Journal of Industrial Relations*, vol. 43, no. 4, pp. 569–576.

Dowdy, J. and Van Reenen J. (2014), 'Why management matters for productivity', *McKinsey Quarterly*, September 2014.

Edwards, T., Sanchez-Mangas, R., Jalette, P., Lavelle, J. and Minbaeva, D. (2016), 'Global standardization or national differentiation of HRM practices in multinational companies? A comparison of multinationals in five countries', *Journal of International Business Studies*, vol. 47, no. 8, pp. 997–1021.

Eichener, V. (1997), 'Effective European problem-solving: Lessons from the regulation of occupational safety and environmental protection', *Journal of European Public Policy*, vol. 4, no. 4, pp. 591–608.

Eurofound (2015a), *New Forms of Employment*, Luxembourg, Publications Office of the European Union.

Eurofound (2015b), *Fifth European Working Conditions survey – 2010*, www.eurofound.europa.eu/surveys/european-working-conditions-surveys/fifth-european-working-conditions-survey-2010 (accessed 27 February 2017).

European Commission (2001), *Employment and Social Policies: A framework for investing in quality*, Communication from the Commission to the Council, the EP, the EESC and the CoR, Luxembourg, Office for Official Publications of the European Communities.

European Commission (2008), *Employment in Europe 2008*. Luxembourg, Office for Official Publications of the European Communities.

Featherstone, K., Kornelakis, A. and Zartaloudis, S. (2012), 'Conceptualising the Lisbon Strategy: Europeanisation and varieties of capitalism', in D.Papadimitriou and P. Copeland (eds), *The EU's Lisbon Strategy: Evaluating success, understanding failure*. Basingstoke, Palgrave Macmillan, pp. 50–67.

Forbes (2014), 'After the BRICS are the MINTs, but can you make any money from them?', 6 January. www.forbes.com/sites/chriswright/2014/01/06/after-the-brics-the-mints-catchy-acronym-but-can-you-make-any-money-from-it/ - 292710974ba9 (accessed 17 February 2017).

Gereffi, G., Humphrey, J. and Sturgeon, T. (2005), 'The governance of global value chains', *Review of International Political Economy*, vol. 12, no. 1, pp. 78–104.

Gold, M. (ed.) (2009), *Employment Policy in the European Union*. Basingstoke, Palgrave Macmillan.

Gooderham, P. and Nordhaug, O. (2010), 'One European model of HRM? Cranet empirical contributions', *Human Resource Management Review*, vol. 21, no. 1, pp. 27–35.

Green, F. and Mostafa, T. (2012), *Trends in Job Quality in Europe*. Luxembourg, Publications Office of the European Union.

Green, F., Mostafa, T., Parent-Thirion, A., Vermeylen, G., Van Houten, G., Biletta, I. and Lyly-Yrjanainen, M. (2013), 'Is job quality becoming more unequal?' *Industrial and Labor Relations Review*, vol. 66, no. 4, pp. 753–784.

Holman, D. (2013), 'Job types and job quality in Europe', *Human Relations*, vol. 66, no. 4, pp. 475–502.

Huselid, M. (1995), 'The impact of human resource management practices on turnover, productivity, and corporate financial performance', *Academy of Management Journal*, vol. 38, no. 3, pp. 635–672.

Ichniowski C., Shaw K. and Prennushi G. (1997), 'The effects of human resource management practices on productivity: A study of steel finishing lines', *The American Economic Review*, vol. 87, no. 3, pp. 291–313.

Katz, H. and Darbishire, O. (2000), *Converging Divergences: Worldwide changes in employment systems*. Ithaca, NY, Cornell University Press.

Kornelakis, A. (2014), 'Balancing flexibility with security in organizations? Exploring the links between Flexicurity and human resource development', *Human Resource Development Review*, vol. 13, no. 4, pp. 398–412.

Kornelakis, A., Veliziotis, M. and Voskeritsian, H. (2017), 'How can competitiveness be achieved in post-crisis Europe: Deregulating employment relations or enhancing high performance work practices?' *The International Journal of Human Resource Management*, vol. 28, no. 21, pp. 3089–3108.

Lorenz, E. and Valeyre, A. (2005), 'Organisational innovation, human resource management and labour market structure: A comparison of the EU-15', *Journal of Industrial Relations*, vol. 47, no. 4, pp. 424–442.

Macduffie, J.P. (1995), 'Human resource bundles and manufacturing performance: organizational logic and flexible production systems in the world auto industry', *Industrial and Labor Relations Review*, vol. 48, no. 2, pp. 197–221.

Morgan, G. (2009), 'Globalization, multinationals and institutional diversity', *Economy and Society*, vol. 38, no. 4, pp. 580–605.

OECD (2016), *Automation and Independent Work in a Digital Economy*, Policy Brief on the Future of Work, Paris, OECD.

Oeij, P., Dhondt, S. and Korver, T. (2011), 'Workplace innovation, social innovation, and social quality', *International Journal of Social Quality*, vol. 1, no. 2, pp. 31–49.

Pot, F., Totterdill, P. and Dhondt, S. (2016), 'Workplace innovation: European policy and theoretical foundation', *World Review of Entrepreneurship, Management and Sustainable Development*, vol. 12, no. 1, pp. 13–32.

Rubery, J. and Grimshaw, D. (2003), *The Organization of Employment: An International Perspective*, Basingstoke, Palgrave.

Sparrow, P. and Hiltrop, J.-M. (1997), 'Redefining the field of European human resource management: A battle between national mindsets and forces of business transition?' *Human Resource Management*, vol. 36, no. 2, pp. 201–219.

Stavrou E., Brewster C. and Charalambous, C. (2010), 'Human resource management and firm performance in Europe through the lens of business systems: Best fit, best practice or both?' *The International Journal of Human Resource Management*, vol. 21, no. 7, pp. 933–962.

Vidal, M. (2013), 'Low-autonomy work and bad jobs in postfordist capitalism' *Human Relations*, vol. 66, no. 4, pp. 587–612.

Walsh, J. (2013), 'Work-life balance: The end of the 'overwork' culture?' in S. Bach and M. Edwards (eds), *Managing Human Resources*, Chichester, UK, Wiley, pp.150–177.

16

HUMAN RESOURCES MANAGEMENT AND EUROPEAN BUSINESS

Cordula Barzantny

Introduction

Following Brewster (2007, p. 239) 'Europe offers a wider ranging and more critical concept of HRM.' We are intrigued by the tensions of international standardisation, largely present on the global level, in line with European harmonisation efforts versus still regional, national, cultural particularities and divergences across Europe.

With this chapter, we want to assess the state of the art in the human resources management (HRM) literature across Europe and underline the impact for managers and the influences and requirements for the European managerial mindset. The variety of European businesses requires contextual as well as more global configurations of HRM systems, since Europe is far from being a homogenous group of countries or a region of only (sub-)cultures. The European Union (EU) is striving for common, supranational regulations at the lowest and least intrusive level ('Subsidiarity' principle – for a definition see EU 2017; also Gelauff with Grilo and Lejou 2008; Sinn 1994; Henkel 2002), while considering its countries' differences in the historical, political, legal, social, cultural, economic and ideological environment (Nikandrou et al. 2005; Brewster 1994). Nikandrou et al. (2005, p. 542) state that Europe is 'characterized by internal variation among various clusters of countries and, at the same time, by external uniformity compared to the rest of the world'.

Within the course of discussions centering on the concept of HRM in the nineties, it became clear that this concept is difficult to apply in the same way as it is used in the USA, where the concept has been developed (Brewster 1995; Guest 1994). Guest (1994) argues that the unitarist perspective contradicts the prevailing European tradition of pluralism. Furthermore, the strong individualist orientation inherent in this concept is difficult to realise in societies characterised by a higher degree of collectivism and more emphasis on social welfare and social responsibility for the more disadvantaged in society. Other barriers include differences in the ownership and control systems of organisations in Europe and the strong legal environment in many countries (Guest 1994; Laurent 1983). Limited organisational autonomy is of major importance, too, as suggested by Brewster (1994).

Brewster (1994, 1995, 1999) emphasises the need to pursue a contextual paradigm, i.e. addressing explicitly the external context of firms for defining, understanding and framing HRM. Other researchers have confirmed the impact of the country-specific institutional or socio-economic background (see for example Gooderham et al. 1999; Gooderham and Nordhaug 2010) or of cultural values on HRM (see for example Lindholm 2000; Papalexandris and Panayotopoulou 2004; Cascio 2006). To sum up, it can be said that 'a single universal model of HRM does not exist' (Pieper 1990,' p. 11).

> 'Clearly, the European evidence suggests that management can see the unions, for example, as social partners with a positive role to play in HRM: and the manifest success of many European firms which adopt that approach shows the, explicit or implicit, anti-unionism of many American views to be culture-bound' (Brewster 1994, p. 81; see also Pudelko 2005)

Farndale (2010) examines the possible influence factors on HRM practices leading to differences among European countries in more detail. Consequently, she tests the impact of national culture, national institutions and supranational institutions, such as the Social Charter in the EU. All three variables appear as significant elements of the environment influencing HRM practices in organisations. The unity in diversity of the EU offers a huge cultural, economic, educational, political and social variety in a rather reduced geographical space (compared to the United States or China, for example). The variety of languages spoken linked to a wide array of cultural diversity and the combination of numerous customs and traditions across the Single Market pose the complex reality for European managers as well as managers in Europe overall (for a critical illustration, see Berglund et al. 2009). It is a challenge to be at ease in the diverse European business environment and the effective manager will have to display a quite versatile global mindset for Europe, functional in various European countries and cultural context configurations.

Global mindset

Since we live in a world of global competition, the concepts of cultural intelligence and global mindset have emerged as critical success factors for sustaining the long-term competitive advantage of individuals and organisations in the global marketplace (Gupta and Govindaran 2002; Earley and Peterson 2004; Pucik 2006; Hitt et al. 2007; Javidan et al. 2007a, 2007b; Levy et al. 2007a, 2007b; Thomas et al. 2008); for a systematic review and differentiation of both concepts see Andresen and Berdolt (2017). These authors underline that 'a global mindset becomes highly relevant at the strategic and normative management levels'.

Competition has generated a substantial amount of management literature (Rosen et al. 2000; Earley and Ang 2003; Boyacigiller et al. 2004; Earley with Ang and Tan 2006; Levy et al. 2007a, 2007b; Javidan et al. 2007b; Earley et al. 2007; Ang and Van Dyne 2008; Thomas and Inkson 2009; also Bouquet 2005). Since the 1980s Prahalad and Doz (1987) have underlined the importance of understanding the cognitive orientation of managers, and we observe a re-emergence of management interest in cognitive structures and processes, notably in the cross-cultural context (Smith with Peterson and Thomas 2008; Peterson and Wood 2008; Thomas 2010). With the particular multicultural patchwork of countries and regions in Europe, also facing the global competitive environment, we are inspired to address the contrasting patterns of development of a global mindset for managers in Europe in the context of HRM.

To succeed as a manager in Europe and beyond, the global mindset literature emphasises two constructs described as cosmopolitanism (as an underlying dimension of the cultural perspective) and cognitive complexity (as an underlying dimension of the strategic perspective; see Boyacigiller et al. 2004; Levy et al. 2007a, 2007b). Since it is not only the cultural diversity of Europe that sustains cosmopolitanism, we expect the building of the globally minded manager to be straightforward with basic abilities, requested since a certain time by Adler and Bartholomew (1992) as well as by Roberts with Kossek and Ozeki (1998), by Stanek (2000) and Khilji et al. (2010) to lead the future multinational, global and transnational firms (Begley and Boyd 2003; Beechler and Baltzley 2009a; Beechler and Javidan 2007). Europe offers something of a nursery ground for the truly global manager developing through an HRM leadership approach with a focus on European integration in diversity.

A global mindset for Europe

Even if we have emphasised the countries of the EU, we define Europe mainly accordingly to the geographic continental understanding from the Atlantic shores, the Irish and British Islands in the West towards the Ural Mountains and the Caspian Sea in the East, from Iceland and the Arctic Sea in the North to the Mediterranean shores in the South. Europe has a resident population of roughly 800 million, divided into 51 nation states (including the Vatican City), where about 35 different official languages are spoken but more than 200 unofficial languages, dialects and regionally used languages exist. Two states are geographically Asian but culturally attached to Europe (Cyprus and Armenia) and five countries geographically span the European and the Asian plates (Azerbaijan, Georgia, Kazakhstan, Russia and Turkey).

In the majority of cross-cultural management studies, most often the country is taken as a proxy for culture (Hofstede 1993, 2001; Hampden-Turner and Trompenaars 1993; Leung et al. 2005). This is mainly based on the fact that the legal, administrative, educational and political frameworks arise historically at the nation state level and despite further European (Union) integration, the ultimate official governmental unit is still the *nation* state. Therefore, if we talk about a country, we focus mainly on the administrative state unit, with a dominant (state) culture. Nevertheless, we must keep in mind that in one country various regional cultures can be found, as well as more or less visible 'minority' cultures, which make the overall diversity of cultural heritage far greater than the number of countries may suggest.

Interestingly, Pudelko and Harzing (2007) observed that the general management practice in Europe is strongly influenced by US models. They characterise present European management as showing *continued national diversity with increasing global convergence*, whereas they expect that in the future the European approach might become more important, taking a more 'balanced' approach between economic efficiency and social concerns. A European management model may even provide an additional source of inspiration, both within Europe and beyond, notably in times of shrinking US supremacy and shifting world focus to Asia and emerging powers like China. This results in a more multi-polar world compared to the rather US-dominated one since the beginning of this century. Evidently, this also has an impact on the building and evolution of the global mindset of today's managers.

An extensive body of literature addresses the cultural differences among European countries and the impact these cultural differences have on the various management systems (e.g., Lane 1989; Thurley and Wirdenius 1990; Tixier 1994; Calori and De Woot 1994; Leeds et al. 1994; Propenko 1994; Lessem and Neubauer 1994; Sparrow and Hiltrop 1994; Calori and Dufour 1995; Myers et al. 1995; Schreyögg et al. 1995; Puffer et al. 1996; Lawrence and Edwards 2000; Dülfer 2001; Hofstede 2002; Kets de Vries and Korotov 2005; Larsen and Mayrhofer 2006; Scholz and Böhm 2008). Furthermore, academic research continues the debate about convergence or divergence of European HRM (Sparrow et al. 1994; Claus 2003; Brewster 2004, 2007; Brewster et al. 2004; Mayrhofer et al. 2004; Morley 2004; Farndale 2010; Gooderham and Nordhaug 2010; Mayrhofer et al. 2011). The European mindset may stand as a specific form of a global mindset, since the variety of European cultures can only be successfully addressed by a manager with a truly versatile, multicultural approach. This has also a decisive influence on European HRM.

HRM and European business: State of the art and current debates revisited

With the fall of the Iron Curtain that had divided Europe for more than 44 years, dissolving at least the economic and political gap between East and West, there has now been a rediscovery of the differences between Northern Europe and Southern European countries that finally seem to overshadow the reconnected East and West, also in terms of the global mindset evolutions. This also influences HRM in companies originating from and doing business in Europe. Since EU cooperation and the Single Market have seemed rather successful until recently, representing a powerful economic and moreover political block on world markets and affairs, other countries have applied to join. Turkey started the accession process in 1987; Croatia became the 28th member state in July 2013. Other countries, such as the Former Yugoslav Republic of Macedonia and Ukraine, as future potential candidates will lead, one day, to the EU encompassing most democracies of the European continent. Nevertheless, recent political struggles in Ukraine and Turkey, and also the migrant crisis originating in the Balkans but expanding with exiles from the Syrian civil war, were perceived very negatively by many citizens, notably from Hungary, Poland, Austria. This has led to the regaining of influence for right-wing and nationalistic political forces, which challenge the European democracies and the EU as a whole. Particularly with the UK referendum on Brexit, on 23 June 2016, the EU Exit parties and xenophobia gained momentum and the EU will see its first secession when the UK leaves the bloc in 2019.

All these often-countervailing influences and events challenge the integrated HRM model and add to the genuine European HRM diversity. Mayrhofer and colleagues (2002, 2004, 2011) and Cranet data have offered longitudinal empirical evidence for the contextualisation of HRM practices across Europe. They understate the important differentiation of various national contexts despite some general converging influence through more globalising management. Nevertheless, the more recent political and socio-economic developments are still to be integrated into academic research and will inform future debates. This is certainly true for the impact of Brexit on various aspects of management, society and beyond.

Following Morley (1994) and Morley and Collings (1994) who have offered previous debates on European HRM and industrial relations, present times have seen important changes (Lane 1989; Legge 1995, 2005; Due, Madsen and Jensen 1991; Bartlett and Ghoshal 1992; Stanek 2000; Hyman and Frege 2002; Riby et al. 2004; Rasmussen and Andersen 2006; Bamber et al. 2016). The globalising workplace seems to be a reality around the world (Adler and Bartholomew 1992; Roberts with Kossek and Ozeki 1998; Rosen et al. 2000; Javidan and House 2001; Dalton et al. 2002; McCall and Hollenbeck 2006; 2002; Bird and Osland 2004; Carr 2004; Jokinen 2004; Black 2006; Edwards and Rees 2006; Vance and Paik 2006; Bhagat et al. 2007; Mendenhall et al. 2013; Kaya and Martin 2016) and cross-cultural teams are a genuine continuous challenge, across Europe and beyond (Myers et al. 1995; Earley and Gibson 2002; Athanassiou and Nigh 2002). These teams emphasise interpersonal relationships across cultures into the various contexts (Jackson 1995, 2002, Jackson and Schuler 1995; Bhagat et al. 2009).

Future research agenda for European HRM towards the global mindset

In the face of the present challenges to people management and the European workplace, we expect migration and exclusion–inclusion issues as well as mobility to be the core themes important for HRM managers today and the near future (Brislin 1993, 2008; Brewster and Tregaskis 2001; Kirton and Greene 2005; Ferdmann and Deane 2014). The ever-growing mobility of a globalising workforce will lead to a more culturally mixed workplace than ever before and even local employees who have never left their country of origin will meet the global mix of employees across Europe. However, corporate boards and top management teams of most MNCs remain highly homogenous in their nationalities and are often staffed with home country nationals (Staples 2008; Van Veen and Marsman 2008). This has to evolve if companies want to benefit from the cross-cultural mix and address the multiple stakeholders at the local, international and global level.

This will also enhance the need for proficient global leadership (Davis et al. 2008; Fatehi 2008; Beechler and Batzley 2009a, b; Ng et al. 2009; House et al. 2014) and advanced firms will prepare their employee leadership talent accordingly.

One core purpose of HRM is certainly performance management (Delaney and Huselid 1996), but furthermore, offshoring and rightshoring continue to be important HRM tools. The global mindset coming from European roots will also play a decisive role for global leaders and cosmopolitanism.

Conclusion

This chapter suggests that what can be characterised as a particular 'European' mindset of European managers as well as of successful business managers in Europe may also be an entry point to the global mindset.

To be at ease in the diverse European business environment is a challenge and the effective manager will have to display a versatile global mindset for Europe to be functional in various European countries and cultural contexts. Managers raised in Europe seem to have a 'natural' advantage because of exposure and the prolific context they are exposed to in the comparatively small geographical space that is Europe. This chapter provides insights that this appeals also as a positive base to educate and train future management for a truly global mindset as well as the already very versatile European mindset. This is a core assignment for HRM to be taken up in Europe and elsewhere.

References

Adler, N. J. and Bartholomew, S. (1992), 'Managing globally competent people', *Academy of Management Executive*, 6(3), 52–65.

Andresen, M. and Bergdolt, F. (2017), 'A systematic literature review on the definitions of global mindset and cultural intelligence – Merging two different research streams', *International Journal of Human Resource Management*, 28(1): 170–195.

Ang, S. and Van Dyne, L. (eds) (2008), *Handbook of Cultural Intelligence. Theory, Measurement, and Applications*, Armonk, NY and London, UK, M.E. Sharpe.

Athanassiou, N. and Nigh, D. (2002), 'The impact of the top management team's international business experience on the firm's internationalization: Social networks at work', *Management International Review*, 4(2), 157–181.

Bamber, G. J. with Lansburry, R.D., Wailes, N. and Wright, C.E. (eds) (2016), *International Comparative Employee Relations. National regulations, global changes*. 6th revised edn, London, Sage.

Bartlett, C.A. and Ghoshal, S. (1992), 'What is a global manager?' *Harvard Business Review*, 70(5), 124–132.

Beechler, S. and Baltzley, D. (2009a), 'Leaders with a global mindset'. An ICEDR webinar. 30 June. www.icedr.org/publications/publications.html?q=Global+mindsetandk=. (accessed 5 January 2011).

Beechler, S. and Baltzley, D. (2009b), 'Identifying and developing global leaders', in J. Storey, P. Wright and D. Ulrich (eds), *The Routledge Companion to Strategic Human Resource Management*, London, Routledge, 410–432.

Beechler, S. and Javidan, M. (2007), 'Leading with a Global Mindset', in M. Javidan, R.M.Steers and M.A. Hitt (eds), *Advances in International Management, Vol. 19, The Global Mindset*, Oxford and Amsterdam, Elsevier, 131–169.

Begley, T. and Boyd, D. (2003), 'The need for a corporate global mind-set', *MIT Sloan Management Review*, 44(2), 25–32.

Berglund, S., Duvold, K., Ekman, J. and Schymik, C. (2009), *Where Does Europe End? Borders, limits and direction of the EU*. Cheltenham, Edward Elgar.

Bhagat, R.S., McDevitt, A.S. and McDevitt, I. (2009), 'Cultural variations in the creation, diffusion and transfer of organizational knowledge', in R.S. Bhagat and R.M. Steers (eds), *Handbook of Culture, Organizations, and Work*, Cambridge, Cambridge University Press, 174–196.

Bhagat, R.S., Triandis, H.C., Baliga, B.R., Billing, T.K. and Davis, C.A. (2007), 'On becoming a global manager: A closer look at the opportunities and constraints in the 21st century', in M. Javidan, R.M. Steers and M.A. Hitt (eds), *Advances in International Management, Vol. 19, The Global Mindset*, Oxford and Amsterdam, Elsevier, 201–226.

Bird, A. and Osland, J.S. (2004), 'Global competencies: An introduction', in H. Lane with M. E. Mendenhall, M. L. Maznevski and J. McNett (eds), *Handbook of Global Management*, Oxford, Blackwell, 57–80.

Black, J.S. (2006), 'The mindset of global leaders: Inquisitiveness and duality', in W.H. Mobley and E. Weldon (eds), *Advances in Global Leadership, Vol. 4*, Oxford and Amsterdam, Elsevier, 181–200.

Bouquet, C. (2005), *Building Global Mindsets. An attention-based perspective*, Houndmills, Basingstoke and New York, Palgrave MacMillan.

Boyacigiller, N.A., Beechler, S., Taylor, S. and Levy, O. (2004), 'The Crucial Yet Illusive Global Mindset', in H.W. Lane, M.L. Maznevski, M.E. Mendenhall and J. McNett (eds), *The Blackwell Handbook of Global Management. A guide to managing complexity*, Malden, MA and Oxford, UK, Blackwell, 81–93.

Brewster, C. (1994), 'European HRM. Reflection of, or challenge to, the American concept', in P. S. Kirkbride (ed.), *Human Resource Management in Europe. Perspectives for the 1990s*, London and New York, Routledge, 56–92.

Brewster, C. (1995), 'Towards a "European" model of human resource management', *Journal of International Business Studies*, 26(1), 1–21.

Brewster, C. (1999), 'Strategic human resource management: The value of different paradigms', *Management International Review*, 39: 45–64.

Brewster, C. (2004), 'European perspectives on human resource management', *Human Resource Management Review*, 14 (4), 365–382.

Brewster, C. (2007), 'A European perspective on HRM', *European Journal of International Management*, 1(3), 239–259.

Brewster, C., Mayrhofer, W. and Morley, M. (eds) (2004), *Human Resource Management in Europe: Evidence of Convergence?* London, Butterworth Heinemann.

Brewster, C. and Mayrhofer, M. (2007), 'Comparative HRM policies and practices', in P.B. Smith, M.F. Peterson and D.C. Thomas (eds), *Handbook of Cross-Cultural Management Research*, Thousand Oaks, CA, Sage.

Brewster, C. and Tregaskis, O. (2001), 'Adaptive, reactive and inclusive organisational approaches to workforce flexibility in Europe', *Comportamento Organizacional e Gestão*, 2, 209–232.

Brislin, R. (2008), *Working with Cultural Differences. Dealing effectively with diversity in the workplace*. Westport, CT, Praeger.

Brislin, R.W. (1993), *Understanding Culture's Influences on Behavior*. Fort Worth, TX, Harcourt Brace and Company.

Calori, R. and De Woot, P. (1994), *A European Management Model. Beyond diversity*, New York, Prentice Hall.

Calori, R. and Dufour, B. (1995), 'Management European style', *The Academy of Management Executive*, 9, 61–73.

Carr, S.C. (2004), *Globalization and Culture at Work. Exploring their combined glocality*, Boston, MA, Kluwer Academic Publishers.

Cascio, W. (2006), 'Global performance management systems', in I. Björkman and G.K. Stahl (eds), *Handbook of Research in International Human Resource Management*, Cheltenham, UK, and Northampton, USA, Edward Elgar Publishing Ltd., 176–196.

Claus, L. (2003), 'Similarities and difference in human resource management in the European Union', *Thunderbird International Business Review*, 45(6), 729–755.

Dalton, M. with Ernst, C., Deal, J. and Leslie, J. (2002), *Success for the New Global Manager*, San Francisco, CA, Jossey-Bass.

Davis, E. with Khilji, S.E., Critchfield, A.J., Cseh, M., Yarr, L. and Abou-Zaki, W. (2008), 'Mirror, mirror on the wall; who has the global leadership mindset of them all?' in *Proceedings of the international leadership association conference, Global leadership: Portraits of the past, Vision for the future*, 10th ILA Annual Global Conference, Los Angeles, CA, November.

Delaney, J.T. and Huselid, M.A. (1996), 'The impact of human resource management practices on perceptions of organizational performance', *Academy of Management Journal*, 39(4), 949–969.

Due, J., Madsen, J.S. and Jensen, C.S. (1991), 'The social dimension: Convergence or diversification of IR in the single European market?' *Industrial Relations Journal*, 22(2), 85–102.

Dülfer, E. (2001), *Internationales Management in unterschiedlichen Kulturbereichen*, 6th edn, Munich and Vienna, Oldenbourg.

Earley, P.C. and Ang, S. (2003), *Cultural Intelligence. Individual interactions across cultures.* Stanford, CA: Stanford University Press.

Earley, P.C. with Ang, S. and Tan, J.-S. (2006), *Developing Cultural Intelligence at Work*, Stanford, CA, Stanford University Press.

Earley, P.C. and Gibson, C.B. (2002), *Multinational Work Teams: A new perspective*, Mahwah, NJ, Erlbaum.

Earley, P.C. with Murnieks, C. and Mosakowski, E. (2007), 'Cultural intelligence and the global mindset', in M. Javidan, R.M. Steers and M.A. Hitt (eds), *Advances in International Management, Vol. 19, The Global Mindset*, Oxford and Amsterdam, Elsevier, 75–103.

Earley, P.C. and Peterson, R.S. (2004), 'The elusive cultural chameleon: Cultural intelligence as a new approach to intercultural training for the global manager', *Academy of Management Learning and Education,* 3(1), 100–115.

Edwards, T. and Rees, C. (2006), *International Human Resource Management. Globalization, national systems and multinational companies*, Essex, UK, Pearson Education.

Edwards, V. and Lawrence, P. (2000), *Management in Eastern Europe.* Houndmills, Basingstoke and New York, Palgrave.

EU (2017), *The Principle of Subsidiarity.* Fact sheets of the European Union. www.europarl.europa.eu/ftu/pdf/en/FTU_1.2.2.pdf (accessed 10 March 2018).

Farndale, E. (2010), 'What is really driving differences and similarities in HRM practices across national boundaries in Europe?' *European Journal of International Management*, 4(4), 362–381.

Fatehi, K. (2008), *Managing Internationally: Succeeding in a culturally diverse world.* Los Angles, CA and London, Sage Publications.

Ferdmann, B.M. and Deane, B.R. (eds) (2014), *Diversity at Work: The Practice of Inclusion.* San Francisco, CA, Jossey Bass.

Gelauff, G., Grilo, I. and Lejour, A. (eds) (2008), *Subsidiarity and Economic Reform in Europe.* Berlin and Heidelberg, Springer.

Gooderham, P.N. and Nordhaug, O. (2010), 'One European model of HRM? Cranet empirical contributions', *Human Resource Management Review*, 21(1), 27–36.

Gooderham, P.N., Nordhaug, O. and Ringdal, K. (1999), 'Institutional determinants of organizational practices: Human resource management in European firms', *Administrative Science Quarterly*, 44(3), 507–531.

Guest, D. (1994), 'Organizational psychology and human resource management: Towards a European approach', *European Work and Organizational Psychologist,* 4(3), 251–270.

Gupta, A. and Govindarajan, V. (2002), 'Cultivating a global mindset', *Academy of Management Executive*, 16(1), 116–126.

Hampden-Turner, C. and Trompenaars, F. (1993), *The Seven Cultures of Capitalism. Value systems for creating wealth in the United States*, Japan, German, France, Britain, Sweden, the Netherlands, New York, Doubleday.

Henkel C. (2002), 'The allocation of powers in the European Union: A closer look at the principle of subsidiarity', *Berkeley Journal of International Law*, 20(2), 359–385.

Hitt, M.A. with Javidan, M. and Steers, R.M. (2007), 'The global mindset: An introduction', in M. Javidan, R.M. Steers and M.A. Hitt (eds), *Advances in International Management, Vol. 19, The Global Mindset.* Oxford and Amsterdam, Elsevier, 1–10.

Hofstede, G. (1993), 'Cultural Constraints in Management Theories', Academy of Management Executive, 7(1), 81–94.

Hofstede, G. (2001), *Culture's Consequences. Comparing values, behaviours, institutions, and organizations across nations*, 2nd edn, London, Sage.

Hofstede, G. (2002), 'Images of Europe: Past, present and future', in M. Warner and P. Joynt (eds), *Managing Across Cultures. Issues and perspectives*, 2nd edn, London, Thomson Learning.

House, R.J., Dorfman, P.W., Javidan, M., Hanges, P.J. and Sully de Luque, M. (2014), *Strategic Leadership across Cultures. The GLOBE study of CEO leadership behavior and effectiveness in 24 countries.* Thousand Oaks, CA, Sage.

Hyman, R. and Frege, C.M. (2002), 'Editorial to the special theme: Central and Eastern Europe – Inventing industrial relations, ten years on', *European Journal of Industrial Relations*, 8(1), 6–9.

Jackson, T. (2002), *International HRM. A Cross-cultural approach*, London, Sage.

Jackson, T. (ed.) (1995), *Cross-cultural Management*, Oxford, Butterworth-Heinemann.

Jackson, S. and Schuler, R. (1995), 'Understanding human resource management in the context of organizations and their environments', *Annual Review of Psychology*, 46, 237–264.

Javidan, M., Dorfman, P.W., Sully de Luque, M. and House, R.J. (2006), 'In the eye of the beholder: Cross cultural lesson in leadership from Project GLOBE', *Academy of Management Perspectives*, 20(1), 67–90.

Javidan, M. and House, R.J. (2001), 'Cultural acumen for the global manager: Lessons from Project GLOBE', *Organizational Dynamics*, 29(4), 289–305.

Javidan, M. with Steers, R.M. and Hitt, M.A. (2007a), 'Putting it all together: So what is a global mindset and why is it important?' in M. Javidan with R.M. Steers and M.A. Hitt (eds), *Advances in International Management, Vol. 19, The Global Mindset.* Oxford and Amsterdam, Elsevier, 215–226.

Javidan, M. with Steers, R.M. and Hitt, M.A. (eds) (2007b), *Advances in International Management, Vol. 19, The Global Mindset*, Oxford and Amsterdam, Elsevier.

Jokinen, T. (2004), 'Global leadership competencies: A review and discussion', *European Journal of Industrial Training*, 29(3), 199–216.

Kaya, Y. and Martin, N.D. (2016), 'Managers in the global economy: A multilevel analysis', *Sociological Quarterly*, 57(2): 232–255.

Kets de Vries, M. and Korotov, K. (2005), 'The future of an illusion: In search of the new European business leader', *Organizational Dynamics*, 34(3), 218–230.

Khilji, S.E. with Davis, E.B. and Cseh, M. (2010), 'Building competitive advantage in a global environment: Leadership and the mindset', in T. Devinney, T. Pedersen and L. Tihanyi (eds), *Advances in International Management, Vol. 23, The Past, Present and Future of International Business and Management*, Bingley, UK, Emerald Group Publishing Limited, 353–373.

Kirton, G. and Greene, A.-M. (2005), *The Dynamics of Managing Diversity. A critical approach*, 2nd edn, Oxford, Elsevier Butterworth-Heinemann.

Lane, C. (1989), *Management and Labour in Europe*, Hants, UK, Elgar Publishing.

Larsen, H.H. and Mayrhofer, W. (eds) (2006), *Managing Human Resources in Europe, A Thematic Approach.* London, Routledge.

Laurent, A. (1983), 'The cultural diversity of western conceptions of management', *International Studies of Management and Organization*, 13 (1–2), 75–96.

Lawrence, P. and Edwards, V. (2000), *Management in Western Europe.* Basingstoke and London, MacMillan Business.

Leeds, C. with Kirkbride P.S. and Durcan, J. (1994), 'The cultural context of Europe', in P.S. Kirkbride (ed.), *Human Resource Management in Europe. Perspectives for the 1990s*, London and New York, Routledge, 11–27.

Legge, K. (1995), *Human Resource Management: Rhetorics and Realities.* Basingstoke, Macmillan.

Legge, K. (2005), *Human Resource Management. Rhetorics and realities.* Basingstoke, Houndsmills, Palgrave Macmillan.

Lessem, R. and Neubauer, F. (1994), *European Management Systems*, London, McGraw-Hill.

Leung, K. with Bhagat, R.S., Buchan, N.R., Erez M. and Gibson, C.B. (2005), 'Culture and international business: Recent advances and their implications for future research', *Journal of International Business Studies,* 36(3), 357–378.

Levy, O. with Beechler, S., Taylor, S. and Boyacigiller, N.A. (2007a), 'What we talk about when we talk about "global mindset": Managerial cognition in multinational corporations', *Journal of International Business Studies*, 38(2), 231–258.

Levy, O. with Taylor, S., Boyacigiller, N.A. and Beechler, S. (2007b), 'Global mindset: A review and proposed extensions', in M. Javidan, R.M. Steers and M.A. Hitt (eds), *Advances in International Management, Vol. 19, The Global Mindset.* Oxford and Amsterdam, Elsevier, 11–48.

Lindholm, N. (2000), 'National culture and performance management in MNC subsidiaries', *International Studies of Management & Organization,* 29(4), 45–66.

Mayrhofer, W., Brewster, C., Morley, M.J. and Ledolter, J. (2011), 'Hearing a different drummer? Convergence of human resource management in Europe – A longitudinal analysis', *Human Resource Management Review,* 21(1), 50–67.

Mayrhofer, W., Müller-Camen, M., Ledolter, J., Strunk, G. and Erten, C. (2002), 'The diffusion of management concepts in Europe – Conceptual considerations and longitudinal analysis, *Journal of Cross-Cultural Competence and Management*, 3, 315–349.

Mayrhofer, W., Müller-Camen, M., Ledolter, J., Strunk, G. and Erten, C. (2004), 'Devolving responsibilities for human resources to line management? An empirical study about convergence in Europe', *Journal for East European Management Studies*, 9(2), 123–146.

McCall, M.W. and Hollenbeck, G.P. (2002), *Developing Global Executives: The lessons of international experience*, Boston, MA, Harvard Business School Press.

Mendenhall, M.E. with Osland, J.S., Bird, A., Oddou, G.R., Maznevski, M.L., Stevens, M.J., and Stahl, G. (2013), *Global Leadership. Research, practice, and development,* 2nd edn, London and New York, Routledge.

Morley, M.J. (2004), 'Contemporary debates in European human resource management: Context and content', *Human Resource Management Review*, 14(4), 353–364.

Morley, M.J. and Collings, D.G. (2004), 'Contemporary debates and new directions in HRM in MNCs: Introduction', *International Journal of Manpower*, 25(6), 487–499.

Myers, A. with Kakabadse, A., McMahon, T. and Spony, G. (1995), 'Top management styles in Europe: Implications for business and cross-national teams', *European Business Journal*, 7(1), 17–27.

Ng, K.-Y. with Van Dyne, L. and Ang, S. (2009), 'Developing global leaders: The role of international experience and cultural intelligence', in W.H. Mobley (ed.), *Advances in Global Leadership, Volume 5*. Bingley, UK: Emerald Group Publishing Limited, 225–250.

Nikandrou, I. with Apospori, E. and Papalexandris, N. (2005), 'Changes in HRM in Europe. A longitudinal comparative study among 18 European countries', *Journal of European Industrial Training*, 29(7), 541–560.

Papalexandris, N. and Panayotopoulou, L. (2004), 'Exploring the mutual interaction of societal culture and human resource management practices; Evidence from 19 countries', *Employee Relations*, 26(5): 495–509.

Peterson, M. and Wood, R.E. (2008), 'Cognitive Structures and Processes in Cross Cultural Management', in P. Smith, M. Peterson and D. Thomas (eds), *Handbook of Cross Cultural Management Research*, Oxford, UK, Sage, 15–33.

Pieper, R. (ed.) (1990), *Human Resource Management: An international comparison*, Berlin, Walter de Gruyter.

Prahalad, C.K. and Doz, Y.L. (1987), *The Multinational Missions: Balancing local demands and global vision*. New York, The Free Press.

Propenko, J. (1994), 'The transition to a market economy and its implications for HRM in Eastern Europe', in P.S. Kirkbride (ed.), *Human Resource Management in Europe. Perspectives for the 1990s*. London and New York, Routledge.

Pucik, V. (2006), 'Reframing global mindset. From thinking to acting', in W.H Mobley and E. Weldon (eds), *Advances in Global Leadership, Vol. 4*. Oxford and Amsterdam, Elsevier, 83–100.

Pudelko, M. (2005), 'Cross-national learning from best practice and the convergence–divergence debate in HRM', *International Journal of Human Resource Management*, 16(11), 2045–2074.

Pudelko, M. and Harzing, A.W.K. (2007), 'How European is management in Europe? An analysis of past, present and future management practices in Europe', *European Journal of International Management*, 1 (3), 206–224.

Puffer, S.M. with McCarthy, D.J. and Zhuplev, A.V. (1996), 'Meeting of the mindsets in a changing Russia', *Business Horizons*, 39(6), 52–60.

Ramussen, E. and Andersen, T. (2006), 'European employment relations: From collectivism to individualism?' in H.H. Larsen, and W. Mayrhofer (eds), *Managing Human Resources in Europe. A Thematic Approach*. London, Routledge, pp. 212–236.

Rigby, M., Smith, R. and Brewster, C. (2004), 'The changing impact and strength of the labour movement in Europe', in G. Wood, and M. Harcourt, (eds), *Trade Unions and Democracy: Strategies and Perspectives*, Manchester, Manchester University Press.

Roberts, K. with Kossek, E. and Ozeki, C. (1998), 'Managing the global workforce: Challenges and strategies', *Academy of Management Executive*, 12(4), 93–106.

Rosen, R. with Digh, P., Singer, M. and Phillips, C. (2000), *Global Literacies. Lessons on business leadership and national cultures.* New York, Simon and Schuster.

Scholz, C. and Böhm, W. (eds) (2008), *Human Resource Management in Europe*. London, Routledge.

Schreyögg, G. with Oechsler, W.A. and Waechter, H. (1995), *Managing in a European Context*. Wiesbaden, Gabler.

Sinn, H.-W. (1994), 'How much Europe? Subsidiarity, centralization and fiscal competition', *Scottish Journal of Political Economy*, 41(1), 85–107.

Smith, P., Peterson, M. and Thomas. D. (eds) (2008), *Handbook of Cross Cultural Management Research.* Oxford, UK, Sage.

Sparrow, P. and Hiltrop, J.M. (1994), *European Human Resource Management in Transition,* Hemel Hempstead, UK, Prentice-Hall.

Sparrow, P., Schuler, R. and Jackson, S. (1994), 'Convergence or divergence: Human resource practices for competitive advantage worldwide', *International Journal of Human Resource Management,* 5(2), 267–299.

Stanek, M.B. (2000), 'The need for global managers: A business necessity', *Management Decision,* 38(4), 232–242.

Staples, C.L. (2008), 'Cross-border acquisitions and board globalization in the world's largest TNCS, 1995–2005', *Sociological Quarterly,* 49, 31–51. doi:10.1111/j.1533-8525.2007.00105.x

Thomas, D.C. (2010), 'Cultural intelligence and all that jazz: A cognitive revolution in international management research?' in T. Devinney, T. Pedersen and L. Tihanyi (eds), *Advances in International Management, Volume 23. The Past, Present and Future of International Business and Management.* Bingley, UK, Emerald Group Publishing Limited, 169–187.

Thomas, D.C. and Inkson, K. (2009) *Cultural Intelligence. Living and Working Globally,* 2nd edn, San Francisco, CA, Berett-Koehler.

Thomas, D.C. with Stahl. G., Ravlin, E.C., Poelmans, S. Pekerti, A., Maznevski, M, Lazarova, M.B., Elron, E. Ekelund, B.Z., Cerdin, J.-L., Brislin, R., Aycan, Z. and Au, K. (2008), 'Cultural intelligence: Domain and assessment', *International Journal of Cross Cultural* Management, 8(2), 123–143.

Thurley, K. and Wirdenius, H. (1990), *Towards European Management,* London, Trans-Atlantic Publications.

Tixier, M. (1994), 'Management and communication styles in Europe: Can they be compared and matched?' *Employee Relations,* 16, 8–26.

Vance, C.M and Paik, Y. (2006), *Managing a Global Workforce.* Armonk, NY and London, UK, M.E. Sharpe.

Van Veen, K. and Marsman, I. (2008), 'How international are executive boards of European MNCs? Nationality diversity in 15 European countries', *European Management Journal,* vol. 26, no. 3, 188–198.

17

INTERNATIONAL COMPETENCIES FOR EUROPEAN SME GRADUATE EMPLOYEES

A Dutch experience

Louise van Weerden and Marjo Wijnen-Meijer

Introduction

The globalisation of the world's economy has made it possible for small and medium-sized enterprises (SMEs) to become global players (Oviatt and McDougall 1994; Reynolds 1997). In 2016, non-financial SMEs in the EU-28 accounted for 99 per cent of all business and are considered a major source of economic growth (European Commission 2017). They represent 67 per cent of total employment and create 8 per cent of gross value added (Kalinic and Clegg 2017). Since exporting is the most common mode of SME's internationalisation, export performance is regarded as one of the key indicators of the success of a firm's operations. In fact, SMEs are key generators of export in many EU countries, with medium-sized enterprises (50–249 employees) accounting for the largest average export value per exporting SME (Eurostat 2014). In 2011, almost 81 per cent of EU exporting enterprises outside the EU were SMEs, with Italy, France, Spain and Germany as the leading countries accounting for over 50 per cent of total EU SME exports (Eurostat 2014).

Due to its geographical position and the small home-market of its economy, export is essential for economic growth in the Netherlands. In 2015, 26 per cent of Dutch SMEs contributed to the export income in the Netherlands (CBS 2016). Moreover, 10 per cent of Dutch companies were exporting in 2010, while the European average was between 6 and 7 per cent. In 2015, five EU countries were responsible for 55 per cent of total Dutch exports: Germany (23%) being the most important trade market for Dutch firms, followed by Belgium (10%), the United Kingdom (9%), France (8%) and Italy (4%) (CBS 2016). Export to non-EU countries such as the United States, Switzerland, Norway and Turkey has increased in the past years. The share of exports in the Gross Domestic Product (GDP) of the Netherlands amounts to almost 80 per cent, which is particularly due to the phenomenon of re-exports: goods that are on transit through the Netherlands, are factored into the Dutch trade statistics, and account for about 50 per cent of Dutch exports. By comparison, Germany, one of the largest net exporters in the world, has a share of only 50 per cent.

An important initiative of the EU is The Small Business Act for Europe (SBA), which aims to support SMEs through a set of policy measures ranging from entrepreneurship to internationalisation (European Union 2017). The internationalisation measures, covered by almost all EU member states, involve incentives to stimulate trade missions and export support programmes on specific (e.g. legal, financial, linguistic) issues. An overview of the performance measured by SBA indicators between 2011 and Q1/2016 shows that most policy measures aimed at supporting SME network building (European Union 2017).

Despite the differentiated EU trade policies and export measures (Cernat et al. 2014), only 25 per cent of EU-based SMEs were engaged in export activities and an even smaller share of SMEs (7 per cent) exported outside the EU. Consequently, there are still many SMEs with untapped export potential. Internationalisation poses difficulties for these firms due to, among others aspects, the lack of scalable business models, the financial resources required and the process of selecting international business partners. One SME-specific barrier is the human resources constraint (Hessels and Parker 2013): the lack of requisite managerial skills, employee qualifications, knowledge and time (Cernat et al. 2014). This illustrates that, together with internationalisation, human resource management is becoming more global and complex as well (Schuler 2000).

European companies find it difficult to match their managerial skills with the specific organisational and cultural contexts of foreign companies (see Chapter 19 by Latukha in this book). Given the fact that many SMEs often lack resources for development the talent of their employees, especially in comparison with larger organisations (Hill and Stewart 2000; Chapter 18 by Mikhaylov in this book), it is particularly important that their employees are adequately equipped for carrying out their international duties. The employment of recent graduates, trained at institutions of higher education, allows SMEs to access to young talents (their future export managers) for international starting positions.

One of the goals of higher education is to equip students with the knowledge and skills within the domain of their future profession. Given the growing need of exporting SMEs for graduates with degrees in international business, the preparation of students for their first export job is crucial. Consequently, business educators need to have a clear understanding about the competency requirements that create value in the SMEs' internationalisation processes. A better understanding of these international competencies will facilitate a smooth transition from education to an international starting position.

This chapter aims to describe the international competencies paramount to the starting export professional in his/her first international job. Following a discussion of the relevance of international competencies for European SMEs, it describes an empirical study among Dutch SME employers about their expectations from graduates in their first export job.

Competencies for internationalising SMEs

Empirical studies illustrate the importance of networks for SMEs' internationalisation processes (Ojala 2008; Dragoni et al. 2009; Bucker 2013) as their engagement in long-term relationships provides them quicker access to market knowledge, resources, further alliances and new international markets through a joint marketing infrastructure (Forsman et al. 2002; Lages et al. 2004; Sousa et al. 2008). In order to identify business opportunities in international markets (Chandra et al. 2009), managers require knowledge, attitudes and skills to build and manage cross-border relations with potential business partners (Johansson and Wiedersheim-Paul 1975; Johansson and Mattsson 1988; Myzychenko 2008). Purhonen (2012) contributed to a better understanding of these skills by analysing networking as the interaction between companies globally. Acquiring market knowledge through interaction with other experienced internationalised firms implies that export managers should have a proactive attitude towards networking.

Obviously, a firm benefits from relationships in networks only when its managers can communicate effectively across the globally positioned network partners, which is complicated because of cultural differences (Trompenaars and Hampden-Turner 1998). Therefore, firms need export managers who serve as cultural liaisons (Bucker 2013). According to many academic and business authors, the key success factor of global managers is their cross-cultural competency (Davies et al. 2011; Bucker 2013). While there are a number of definitions of cross-cultural management (Bennett 1984; Phipps and Gonzalez 2004; Sercu et al. 2005; Deardorff 2008), the concept generally relates to the individual's ability to function effectively with people from different cultures (Gertsen 1990) and is summarised by Byram as 'being able to interact with people from another country and culture in a foreign language' (Byram 1997, p. 71). Consequently, the concept of cross-cultural management can be considered as an interdisciplinary human resources field concerned with management and effective communication across borders.

On a European level, too, the interaction between people and their respective cultures is important as the encounter of cultures may lead to misunderstandings, compounded by a lack of foreign language skills, and present an impediment to the economic development of the EU. The exchange of opinions between different cultures, the intercultural dialogue, stimulates a growing awareness of different cultural identities and engenders openness and respect for other people (Council of Europe 2008). This explains why it is one of the main objectives of the EU cultural policy in the field of education, multilingualism, culture and integration.

On the level of enterprises, various studies on the skills of potential new hires have argued that teamwork, effective communication and building interpersonal relationships are among the qualifications that employers value most for future managers (Rodriguez et al. 2002; Hart 2006). In their research, Davies et al. (2011, p. 9) observe that:

> in a truly globally connected world, a worker's skill set could see them posted in any number of locations—they need to be able to operate in whatever environment they find themselves. This demands specific content, such as linguistic skills, but also adaptability to changing circumstances and an ability to sense and respond to new contexts.

Vonk (2006) underlines the relevance of international competencies for Dutch and German exporting companies. In his study, SME directors in the Netherlands and Germany were asked to assess the importance of various competencies for international business graduates in their first international position. Compared to the German respondents who valued highly professional and intercultural competencies, the Dutch respondents considered the social competencies to be more important. This difference may be explained by the focus of German professional education on the acquisition of knowledge and technical skills, whereas Dutch professional education is generally more profession-oriented with a focus on the acquisition of practical skills and experience (Vonk 2006). According to Dutch and German entrepreneurs, export managers must be 'a jack-of-all trades': on the one hand, they must master the basics of business knowledge about marketing and management, write export plans and speak several foreign languages. On the other hand, they must be team players who excel in setting up and maintaining international relationships with potential business partners in other countries (Vonk 2006). Consequently, the success of SMEs' internationalisation depends very much on the quality of its globally competent managers, who must have the required skills, business knowledge and attitudes to adapt quickly to international business and cultural contexts (Hutchinson et al. 2006).

This implies that business educators must train students in a large array of skills, attitudes and relevant knowledge (Laguador and Ramos 2014; Sharma 2015) related to the graduates' effective interaction and personal adjustment in the context of international business (Jackson 2009). Employers expect business educators to provide bilingual graduates with specific social and intercultural competencies for operating in a global economy (Hutchinson et al. 2006; Treleaven et al. 2007). This call for investment in soft skills presumes a disconnect between competencies acquired in school on the one hand and employer needs on the other (Vonk 2006; Jackson 2009), as illustrated in growing research on education and competency mismatch of graduates (Vonk 2006; Green and McIntosh 2007; Islam et al. 2015; Peng et al. 2016).

Competencies for graduates in international business

The success of graduates on the global labour market specifically calls for a greater investment in new basic skills such as digital literacy, social competencies, entrepreneurial skills and language learning in higher education programmes (European Commission 2016). Therefore, the EU has instituted several training programmes (see the New Skills Agenda, 2016) with The Junior Achievement Europe as the largest provider of educational programmes (3.5 million students were involved in 2015). This programme promotes work readiness among students across all levels of education and is designed to forge close cooperation between educational institutions and business communities as well as governments to ensure that students acquire the skills and competencies required to succeed in a global economy. Another leading program is the Erasmus Programme (**EuR**opean Community **A**ction **S**cheme for the **M**obility of **U**niversity **St**udents), a popular student exchange programme launched in 1987 that fosters learning in and understanding of the host country. For many students, participation in the Erasmus programme is considered a great opportunity to study abroad and to socialise with people from other cultures. In so doing, exchange students improve their language proficiency and develop their social competencies as they become more open-minded towards other cultures.

The literature recognises that international competencies and practical experiences are key factors of successful future employability (Stan et al. 2016). Graduate employability can be conceptualised as a set of skills, knowledge and personal attributes that makes a person useful for the labour market (Knight and Yorke 2004). In the case of international competencies, knowledge refers to grasping general international business issues such as export management, marketing planning, financial regulations, cultural values and norms and customer procedures (Ogrean et al. 2009). By 'skills' is meant the behavioural ability to acquire and develop specific skills over time – such as communication, team building and relationship management – to supervise effectively an international team or set up and maintain international business relations. Skills also refer to so-called strategic skills, such as problem solving, analytical thinking and planning (Ogrean et al. 2009). 'Attitudes' refers, for example, to curiosity, taking initiative, open-mindedness, motivation, patience, empathy, respect for others and perseverance (Ogrean et al. 2009). In the next section, we will discuss the conceptualisation of international relations competency as a driver for employability of graduates in international business.

International Relation Competency Model

Based on the literature and empirical studies on relationship management (Bloemer 2009; Kuhlmeijer and Knight 2010; Purhonen 2012), we have developed the International Relation Competency Model, see Figure 17.1, to give insight into the crucial qualifications graduates need to function effectively in their first international job.

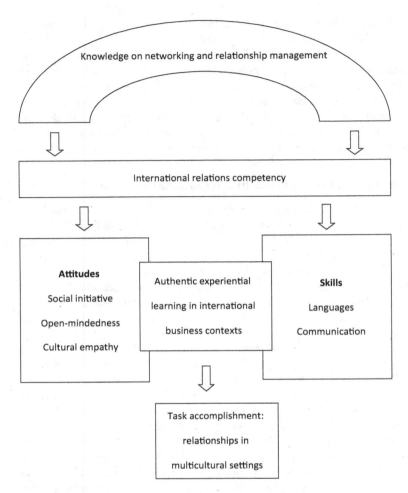

Figure 17.1 The International Relation Competency Model

A major task for the starting export professional is to realise international relationships in multicultural settings, which constitutes the learning outcome of the model. In the upper arch of the model, knowledge on networking and relationship management is presented as the necessary input for relationship building. The first dimension of the International Relation Competency concept is the starting export professional's attitudes, such as social initiative, open-mindedness and cultural empathy. To build relationships, the starting export professional takes the initiative for social interaction with international business partners and has the ability to handle (un)expected differences while engaging with these potential business partners from dissimilar cultures, and negotiate their business motivations, needs and wishes (Davis 1983). These attitudes are also selected from an educational perspective, since business educators want to train students to become competent in building international relationships. We therefore selected only those attitudinal indicators that are trainable instead of predictors that appear to be more stable over experience and time and are therefore less trainable. Some studies on multi-cultural effectiveness empirically demonstrated that 'stable' competencies, such as emotional stability and flexibility, are deeply embedded in the individual personality and hence difficult to develop, which is why they may constrain one's potential to develop a skill (Van der Zee and Van Oudenhoven 2000). The second dimension of the International Relation Competency concept refers to the export professional's ability to communicate in an effective and appropriate way which helps them to realise professional goals and tasks (Purhonen 2012). In their first export job after graduation, young professionals experience the importance of good communication skills as they learn that the same techniques may not work for all people in different cultural situations. Consequently, these communication skills go beyond ordinary foreign language skills and knowledge about other cultures (Knapp-Potthoff 1997). For instance, does the word 'yes' means 'yes' or does it follow the interlocutor's rules of politeness? And how does one interpret non-verbal signals in other cultures? These examples illustrate that good communication skills include the ability to listen, write and understand the specific language of foreign business partners to interpret their wishes as well as read non-verbal signals.

The development of selected attitudes and skills for students during their undergraduate education is enhanced by learning within the work context (Kim and McLean 2014). To prepare students for the global labour market, learning in authentic environments confronts students with realistic situations and tasks in international business settings (Moore 2010). The indicators of international relationship competency form the building blocks for the qualification of international business students. Next, we will further divide these building blocks of international relations competency into specified items in order to collect the views of internationalising Dutch entrepreneurs, as the Dutch traditionally have been successful in international trade and business acumen.

Empirical study

Background, aims and research questions

We expect the International Relation Competency Model to be useful for business educators in teaching students the relevant skills and attitudes. We assume that students with an expanded inventory of these attitudes and skills are more likely to perform well in building international business relationships. To provide a competency match with international business practice, it is imperative that curriculum developers have a clear understanding of SMEs' requirements for international relation competency. Our study was guided by the following aim: to provide insight into the crucial competencies starting export professionals need in relation to their training during bachelor education; a topic that has so far received little research attention.

To define the dimensions of the International Relation Competency Model, we carried out a survey among representatives of exporting SMEs in the Netherlands. The main research question was: which skills and attitudes of the International Relation Competency Model do exporting managers of SMEs consider to be of paramount importance for graduates when they start their first international job?

In order to answer this question, the following sub-questions were addressed:

- How do export managers of SMEs rank the functions of relationship management?
- How do they rate the importance of the selected attitudes and skills of the International Relation Competency Model?
- According to the export managers, which of these selected competencies do graduates need to learn at school and which ones need to be developed in professional practice?
- Do representatives of exporting SMEs consider graduates employable for their first international job?

Methods: Participants and procedure

Participants comprised representatives from SMEs of different economic sectors acquainted with competency levels of starting export professionals. We selected companies with export turnover of 10 per cent or more. All representatives who met this criterion (n = 1670) were asked to participate. In October 2015, we invited the companies by email to complete a questionnaire in an electronic format, accompanied by information about the purposes of the study.

Questionnaire design

The questionnaire focused on international Relation competency and its aspects were drawn from a literature review of selected competency frameworks and empirical studies on international competencies related to international business contexts (Purhonen 2012; Bucker 2013). Three aspects relate to the attitudes dimension and two aspects pertain to the skills dimension.

The questionnaire consisted of five parts. In the first part, the participants were asked about the international activities of their company. In the second part, they were asked to rank both the international tasks of starting export professionals and the function of international relationship management. To evaluate the participants' perceptions on the required attitudes and skills of starting export professionals, participants were asked in part three to rank the relevance of these attitudes and skills on a Likert scale with values from 1 = totally irrelevant to 5 = very relevant. In part four, participants rated their perception of the readiness of graduates for their first international job. Finally, participants gave their views on the role of education in the development of selected attitudes and skills of the international relations competency.

This questionnaire was successfully piloted in a study among directors and export managers of internationalising SMEs from different sectors in April 2015. Nine representatives of SMEs participated in the pilot study. The reliability, calculated by means of Cronbach's Alpha of the components of the pilot questionnaire, varied from acceptable (.73) to good (.86). The participants were asked if they had any questions or ambiguities concerning the questionnaire. This was not the case.

Analysis

We calculated means, medians and standard deviations for all questions. In addition, the skewness of the distributions of the ratings was computed to check on symmetry and to check whether the respondents' judgments tended to be in one direction. Factor analysis (oblique rotation) indicated that the items were divided among three factors, namely 'attitudes', 'skills languages target country' and 'skills English language' (see Tables 17.1 and 17.2). Reliability analysis showed high internal consistencies based on a Cronbach's Alpha of >0.9 for each factor. In addition, the high degree of consistency among participants is reflected in the Jury Alpha of the total questionnaire .97.

Results

Of the 1,670 participants, information was received from 166 respondents, which yielded a response rate of 10 per cent. Despite our careful selection of the participants, 55 of the respondents did not meet the selection criterion on export turnover. Therefore, the results described in this chapter are based on the remaining 111 respondents. Most respondents were

Table 17.1 International Relation Competency Model evaluation: Constructs, measurement items, reliability and validity

Construct	Measurement items	RFL	Mean	SD
General Attitude				
(Alpha = 0.96; AVE = 0.45; CR = 0.95)				
	Understands feelings	0.74	3.93	0.90
	Tries to understand other people's feelings	0.84	4.22	0.76
	Puts his/her own culture in perspective	0.80	3.78	0.87
	Takes other people's habits into consideration	0.81	4.32	0.80
	Knows how to act in social settings	0.42	4.27	0.74
	Knows how to get things done	0.54	4.17	0.79
	Makes contacts easily	0.58	4.25	0.76
	Sees opportunities in other cultures	0.89	4.07	0.88
	Seeks contact with people from a different background	0.75	4.13	0.80
	Waits to judge	0.76	4.14	0.90
	Respects people with other opinions	0.80	4.22	0.86
	Puts his/her own culture in perspective	0.82	3.61	0.92
	Is interested in other cultures	0.96	4.04	0.80
	Is open to new ideas	0.60	4.32	0.72
	Is considerate of other's people's motives	0.38	4.03	0.88
	Takes other people's habits into consideration	0.63	4.08	0.82
	Pays attention to the emotions of others	0.59	3.70	0.82
	Is able to voice other people's thoughts	0.40	4.06	0.79
	Puts others at ease	0.53	3.74	0.92
	Asks questions	0.41	3.97	0.81
	Good listener	0.65	4.60	0.73
	Interprets body language for understanding	0.59	4.04	0.87
	Checks understanding of message with partner	0.56	4.50	0.75
Skills Languages Target Country				
(Alpha = 0.95; AVE = 0.65; CR = 0.95)				
	Masters foreign language other than English	0.54	4.12	0.98
	Solves business problems in language target country	0.75	3.52	1.16
	Negotiates export orders in language target country	0.65	3.59	1.12
	Communicates technological knowledge in language target country	0.90	3.29	1.16
	Communicates market knowledge in language target country	0.93	3.29	1.15
	Communicates marketing knowledge in language target country	0.88	3.19	1.16
	Telephone calls in accurate language of target country	0.95	3.24	1.17
	Formulates appointments in accurate language of target country	0.82	3.66	1.00
	Formulates arguments in accurate language of target country	0.84	3.49	1.03
	Reports market research in accurate language of target country	0.67	3.10	1.08
	Quotations in accurate language of target country	0.81	3.51	1.12
Skills English Language				
(Alpha = 0.93; AVE = 0.53; CR = 0.93)				
	Solves business problems in English	0.93	4.37	0.90
	Negotiates export orders in English	0.89	4.34	1.00
	Communicates technological knowledge in English	0.88	4.23	0.97

(*continued*)

Table 17.1 (Cont.)

Construct	Measurement items	RFL	Mean	SD
	Communicates market knowledge in English	0.83	4.13	0.99
	Communicates marketing knowledge in English	0.66	4.08	0.96
	Translates information into accurate English	0.64	3.93	0.98
	Telephone calls in accurate English	0.60	3.97	0.94
	Communicates and clarifies arguments	0.46	4.15	0.80
	Formulates appointments in accurate English	0.71	4.33	0.85
	Formulates arguments in accurate English	0.71	4.24	0.91
	Reports market research in accurate English	0.44	3.77	1.09
	Quotations in accurate English	0.83	4.42	0.83

RFL = Rotated Factor Loadings (ML, Promax with Kaiser Normalisation).

Table 17.2 International Relation Competency Model evaluation: Descriptives and correlations

		Mean	SD	1	2	3
1	General Attitude	4.10	0.59	–		
2	Skills Languages Target Country	3.45	0.89	.495★★	–	
3	Skills English Language	4.16	0.71	.663★★	.363★★	–

★★p < 0.05; (two–tailed significance tests).

small employers (50.5%; 1–10 employees) followed by employers in medium-sized companies (21.6%; 11–50 employees). The others were employers in companies with 50–250 employees.

The largest number of companies operated within the sector 'Industry, Metal and Plastics' (31.5%) and a sizeable number operated within 'Other' (27%) and 'Wholesale and Retail' (18%). The main activity of these companies was export, followed by import. Respondents consider international sales and export support services to be the appropriate starting positions for international business graduates.

The relevance of training students in relationship management is confirmed by representatives of internationalising SMEs who indicated that building and maintaining relations is the key task of starting export professionals, combined with acquisition. This supports previous studies on international managers' tasks, in which building and maintaining relationships with potential business partners is seen as crucial for the operationalisation of export strategies (Bloemer 2009; Purhonen 2012; Bucker 2013). Employers consider communication skills, including language skills, to be highly relevant, as has been confirmed in many studies on the qualifications of international managers (Laguador and Ramos 2014; Van Heugten et al. 2016). Most of the respondents indicate that attaining a high level of proficiency in English was by far the most important language-learning goal for students. Given the lower ranking of questions about 'the other language' or 'the language of target country', employers favor English proficiency instead of the language of target country. Next, respondents valued the ability to communicate accurately in writing, such as quotations, agreements and confirmations of appointments.

The importance that employers place on the attitude of business graduates (McMurray et al. 2016; Van Heugten et al. 2016) is shared in our study where employers indicate all aspects of the selected attitudes as relevant.

The SMEs' representatives further expect higher education institutions to play a more active role in the development of international relations competency by giving it more focus in the curriculum of international business programmes. In addition, the respondents considered the learning of attitudes and skills to be effectively developed only in the actual working environment (Davies et al. 2011) during bachelor education. Finally, the scores on the views of employability show an unambiguous result: all aspects received a score of 'average', which suggests that there is room for improvement.

Discussion

The survey results reveal a potential mismatch between education and business: our findings suggest that the development of international relation competency is underestimated in business education. This mismatch can also be illustrated from a European perspective. With its high level of policy measures aimed at supporting SME network building (European Union 2017), the EU confirms the importance of relationship building as an internationalisation strategy for SMEs. However, the SBA policy measures for skills and innovation (2011–16) show a significant decrease in the measures that encourage SMEs to internationalise and grow compared to research competency development since 2011 (European Union 2017). In order to strengthen the development of international relation competency within education, closer linkages between institutions of higher education and business may enable the sharing of information and experiences in the training and development of attitudes and skills of students. The strength of this study is that the participants in the survey were SME representatives from different economic sectors. This means that the scores and relevance apply equally to more than one economic sector. For example, all respondents very much agreed on the average employability of recent graduates. A limitation of the study was the relatively small sample size.

Conclusions

The aim of this empirical study was to determine which international competencies directors from internationalising Dutch SMEs considered to be important for their future export managers. The findings suggest that employers highly value the selected attitudes, social initiative, open-mindedness and cultural empathy and the communication and language skills of the International Relation Competency Model. They strongly recommend that business educators strengthen training and development in these aspects within the curriculum of international business programmes, preferably in close cooperation with international business practice. Such improvement will lead to a higher employability of graduates for a starting international position: a serious consideration for institutions of higher education given the growing need of SMEs for graduates for international starting positions. The Dutch success in international trade illustrates the extent to which several industrial sectors (e.g. the dredging industry) depend on internationalisation. Following the Dutch example, the need for international qualifications is apparent. The attitudes and skills of the International Relation Competency Model, valued by Dutch entrepreneurs, will likely aid the internationalisation processes of industrial sectors in other European countries as well.

Acknowledgements

The authors would like to acknowledge Johan Smits (Saxion University of Applied Sciences) for his help with the statistical analyses.

References

Bennett, M.J. (1984), 'Towards ethnorelativism: A developmental model of cultural sensitivity'. Paper presented at the Annual Conference of the Council of International Exchange, Minneapolis, Minnesota.

Bloemer, J. (2009), *International Business en Communication, een kwestie van grenzeloos relatie management,* Inaugural address, University of Applied Sciences Zuyd, Maastricht [in Dutch].

Bucker, J. (2013), *Interacting with Strangers: The cultural intelligence scale: a tool for measuring global management competencies?* Nijmegen, Radboud University.

Byram, M.S. (1997), *Teaching and Assessing Intercultural Communicative Competence,* Clevedon, UK: Multilingual Matters Ltd.

CBS (2016), *Internationaliseringsmonitor 2016, fourth period,* Heerlen/Den Haag, Centraal Bureau voor de Statistiek [in Dutch].

Cernat, L., Norman-Lopez, A.T. and Figueras, A.D. (2014), *SMEs Are More Important Than You Think! Challenges and opportunities for EU exporting SMEs.* No 2014-3, DG TRADE Chief Economist Notes from Directorate General for Trade, European Commission.

Chandra, Y., Styles, C. and Wilkinson, I. (2009), 'The recognition of first time international entrepreneurial opportunities: Evidence from firms in knowledge-based industries', *International Marketing Review,* vol. 26, no. 1, pp. 30–61.

Council of Europe (2008), 'Living together as equals in dignity'. White paper on intercultural dialogue. www.coe.int/dialogue (accessed 28 March 2018).

Davies, A., Fidler, D. and Gorbis, M. (2011), 'Future Workskills 2020', Institute for the Future for University of Phoenix Research Institute. http://cdn.theatlantic.com/static/front/docs/sponsored/phoenix/future_work_skills_2020.pdf (accessed 13 June 2012).

Davis, M.H. (1983), 'Measuring individual differences in empathy: Evidence for a multidimensional approach', *Journal of Personality and Social Psychology,* vol. 44 (January), pp. 113–126.

Deardorff, D.K. (2008), 'Intercultural competence: A definition, model and implications for education abroad', in V. Savicki (ed.), *Developing Intercultural Competence and Transformation: Theory, research, and application in international education,* Stylus Pub Llc, pp. 32–52.

Dragoni, L., Tesluk, P. and Oh, I.S. (2009), 'Understanding managerial development: Integrating developmental assignments, learning opportunities in predicting managerial competencies', *Academy of Management Journal,* vol. 52, no. 4, pp. 731–743.

European Commission (2016), 'Developing future skills in higher education', Directorate-General for Education and Culture: Modernisation of Education II: Education policy and programme, Innovation, EIT and MSCA (2016), ET2020 – Peer Learning Activity (PLA)1, Brussels, 25–26 February 2016. http://ec.europa.eu/education/sites/education/files/2016-future-skills-report_en.pdf (accessed 28 March 2018).

European Commission (2017), 'SME Performance Review 2016/2017'. https://ec.europa.eu/growth/smes/business-friendly-environment/performance-review_en (accessed 20 March 2018).

European Union (2017) Small Business Act for Europe in SME Performance Review. https://ec.europa.eu/growth/smes/business-friendly-environment/performance-review-2016_en (accessed 28 March 2018).

Eurostat (2014), Trade by Enterprise Characteristics Database (TEC), Luxembourg, Eurostat.

Forsman, M., Hinttu, S. and Kock, S. (2002), 'Internationalization from a SME Perspective'. Paper published at the 18th IMP Conference, Dijon, France, September.

Gertsen, M.C. (1990), 'Intercultural competence and expatriates', *International Journal of Human Resources Management,* vol. 1 no. 3, pp. 341–362.

Green, F. and McIntosh, S. (2007), 'Is there a genuine under-utilization of skills amongst the over-qualified?' *Applied Economics,* vol. 39, no. 4, pp. 427–439.

Hart, P.D. (2006), *How Should Colleges Prepare Students to Succeed in Today's Global Economy?* Report based on surveys among employers and recent college graduates, Association of American Colleges and Universities.

Hessels, J. and Parker, S.C. (2013), 'Constraints, internationalization and growth: A cross-country analysis of European SMEs', *Journal of World Business,* vol. 48, no. 1, pp. 137–148.

Hill, R. and Stewart, J. (2000), 'Human resource development in small organizations', *Journal of European Industrial Training,* vol. 24, no. 2/3/4, pp. 105–117.

Hutchinson, J., Quinn, B. and Alexander, N. (2006), 'The role of management characteristics in the internationalization of SMEs: Evidence from the UK retail sector', *Journal of Small Business and Enterprise Development,* vol. 13, no. 4, pp. 513–534.

Islam, T., Ahmed, I., Khalifah, Z., Sadiq, M. and Faheem, M.A. (2015), 'Graduates' expectation gap: The role of employers and Higher Learning Institutes', *Journal of Applied Research in Higher Education*, vol. 7, no. 2, pp. 372–384.

Jackson, D. (2009), 'An international profile of industry-relevant competencies and skills gap in modern graduates', *International Journal of Management Education*, vol. 8, no. 3, pp. 29–58.

Johansson, J. and Mattson, L.G. (1988), 'Internationalization in industrial systems: A network approach', in N. Hood and J.-E. Vahlne (eds), *Strategies in Global Competition*, London, Crom Helm, pp. 287–314.

Johansson, J. and Wiersheim-Paul, F. (1975), 'The internationalisation of the firm – Four Swedish cases', *Journal of Management Studies*, October, 305–322.

Kalinic, I. and Clegg, J. (2017), *SME Internationalization, Public Policy and the Growth Agenda*. Growth Frontiers in International Business, The Academy of International Business, pp. 33–46.

Kim, S. and McLean, G.N. (2014), 'The impact of national culture on informal learning in the workplace', *Adult Education Quarterly*, vol. 64, no. 1, pp. 39–59.

Knapp-Potthoff, A. (1997), 'Interkulturelle Kommunikationsfähigkeit als Lernziel', in *Aspekte interkultureller Kommunikationsfähigkeit* Munich, iudicium, pp. 181–205.

Knight, P.T. and Yorke, M. (2004), *Learning, curriculum and employability in higher education*, London, Routledge Falmer.

Kuhlmeier, D. and Knight, G.A. (2010), 'The critical role of relationship quality in small and medium-sized enterprise internationalization', *Journal of Global Marketing*, vol. 23, no. 1, pp. 16–32.

Lages, L.F. and Montgomery, D.B. (2004), 'Export performance as an antecedent of export commitment and marketing strategy adaptation: Evidence from small and medium sized exporters', *European Journal of Marketing*, vol. 38, no. 9/10, pp. 1186–1214.

Laguador, J.M. and Ramos, L.R. (2014), 'Industry-partners' preferences for graduates: Input on curriculum development', *Journal of Education and Literature*, vol. 1, pp. 1–8.

McMurray, S., Dutton, M., McQuaid, R. and Richard, A. (2016), 'Employer demands for business graduates', *Education and Training*, vol. 15, no. 1, pp. 112–132.

Moore, D.T. (2010), 'Forms and issues in experiential learning', *New Directions for Teaching and Learning*, vol. 124, pp. 3–13.

Muzychenko, O. (2008), 'Cross-cultural entrepreneurial competence in identifying international business opportunities', European Management Journal, vol. 26, no. 6, pp. 366–377.

Ojala, A. (2008), 'Entry in a psychically distant market: Finnish small and medium-sized software firms in Japan', *European Management Journal*, vol. 26, no. 2, pp. 135–144.

Ogrean, C., Herciu, M. and Belascu, L. (2009), 'Competency-based management and global competencies challenges for firm strategic management', *International Review of Business Research Papers*, vol. 5, no. 4, pp. 114–122.

Oviatt, B.M. and McDougall, P.P. (1994), 'Towards a theory of international new ventures', *Journal of International Business Studies*, vol. 25, no. 1, pp. 45–64.

Peng, L., Zang, S. and Gu, J. (2016), 'Evaluating the competency mismatch between Master of Engineering graduates and industry needs in China', *Studies in Higher Education*, vol. 41, no. 3, pp. 445–461.

Phipps, A. and Gonzalez, M. (2004), *Modern Languages: Learning and teaching in an intercultural field*, London, Sage.

Purhonen, P. (2012), *Interpersonal Communication Competence and Collaborative Interaction in SMEs Internationalization*, Finland, University of Juvaskyla,

Reynolds, P.D. (1997), 'New and small firms in expanding markets', *Small Business Economics*, vol. 9, no, 1, pp. 79–84.

Rodriguez, D., Patel, R., Bright, A., Gregory, D. and Gowing, M.K. (2002), 'Developing competency models to promote integrated human resources', *Human Resources Management*, vol. 41, no. 3, pp. 309–324.

Schuler, R.S. (2000), 'The internationalization of human resource management', *Journal of International Management*, vol. 6, pp. 239–260.

Sercu, L., Bandura, E., Castro, P., Davcheva, L., Laskaridou, C., Lundgren, U., Mendez García, M. and Ryan, P. (2005), *Foreign Language Teachers and Intercultural Competence: An international investigation*, Clevedon, Multilingual Matters.

Sharma, E. (2015), 'Role of higher education institutions towards developing the human capital of the world through competency mapping', *Journal of Business Economics and Management Sciences*, vol. 2, no. 1, pp. 1–9.

Sousa, C.M.P., Martinez-Lopez, F.J. and Coelho, F. (2008), 'The determinants of export performance: A review of the research in the literature between 1998 and 2005', *International Journal of Management Reviews*, vol. 10, no. 4, pp. 343–374.

211

Stan, S.O., Butum, L.C., Zodieru, A. (2016), 'New perspectives in developing the relationship between the university and the business environment in the light of the provisions of EU framework documents', Responsible entrepreneurship vision, development and ethics: Proceedings of the 9th International Conference for Entrepreneurship, Innovation and Regional Development, Bucharest, Comunicare.ro.

Treleaven, L., Freeman, M., Leask, B., Ramburuth, P., Simpson, L., Sykes, C. and Riding, S. (2007), 'Beyond workshops: A conceptual framework for embedding development of intercultural competence in business education', *HERDSA News*, vol. 29, no. 3, pp. 9–11.

Trompenaars, A. and Hampden-Turner, C. (1998), *Riding the waves of culture: Understanding cultural diversity in business*, 2nd edn, Chicago, IL, Irwin.

Van der Zee, K.I. and Van Oudenhoven, J.P. (2000), 'The multicultural personality questionnaire: A multi-dimensional instrument of multicultural effectiveness. *European Journal of Personality*, vol. 14, no. 4, pp. 291–309.

Van Heugten, P., Paas, W., Heijne-Penninga, M. and Wolfensberger, M. (2016), 'Characteristics of highy talented international business professionals defined: Qualitative study among international business professionals', *European Journal of Training and Development*, vol. 40, no. 2, 58–73.

Vonk, F. (2006), 'What role for the internationally minded in SMEs? Analyzing the competences of "internationals" in SMEs', *HAN Business Publications*, vol. 2, pp. 45–77.

18

EUROPEAN SUB-REGIONAL APPROACHES TO HUMAN RESOURCES MANAGEMENT

Natalie Solveig Mikhaylov

Introduction

This chapter addresses the development, convergence and divergence of human resources management (HRM)-related practices in Europe, focusing on specific under-researched regions to illustrate and compare employee-related systems, policies and practices applied to European businesses. It demonstrates that while there are clear regional clusters in Europe that develop in similar manners, the questions of complete European conversion is premature. This indicates the relevance of further research into HRM issues in the regional context of Europe and its various forms of market grouping, including the European Union (EU), European Free Trade Association (EFTA) and the European Economic Area (EEA).

The chapter defines human resource management as a distinct method and addresses the current debates in convergence and divergence of HRM policies and practices in Europe. In addition, the role of multicultural companies in the introduction and promotion of HRM in European regions is highlighted. Then it moves to a discussion of European regional clusters, using Central Eastern European and Nordic clusters to illustrate the influence of culture and economic factors on the development of HRM systems. As a conclusion, the possibility of adopting a uniform HRM method in Europe and the conversion of practices are discussed, pointing to further research avenues.

Prior to a discussion of different approaches to HRM, it is appropriate for researchers to properly define it: the term HRM is often incorrectly applied to any practice of employee management and relations. Yet Storey (2007, p. 7) states that 'HR is a distinctive approach to employment management which seeks to achieve competitive advantage through the strategic deployment of a highly committed and capable workforce using arrays of cultural, structural and personnel techniques'. The distinct HRM approach is based on a unitaristic view of the management and employee relationship, where it is expected that all shareholders share the goals and objectives of an organisation and the main purpose of employees belonging to an organisation is to fulfil these goals. Human resources management can be implemented as a 'hard' HRM model, with the goal of the most efficient utilisation of the workforce, or as a 'soft' model, which seeks the commitment of employees (Guest 1987) by an implementation of high commitment work practices (HCWP) (Wood and De Menezes 1998). Both of the approaches were developed in the USA and explored in US-centric contributions to literature.

They mainly illustrate a pragmatic approach to management rooted in the predominantly individualistic and achievement-oriented national cultures of the USA and other Anglo-Saxon cultures (Truss et al. 1997). As such, they are found to be at odds with the rest of the world, including most of Europe, which is more collectivistic and less achievement-oriented than the USA and the UK (Hofstede 1991; Trompenaars and Hampden-Turner 2011).

The discussion of convergence vs. divergence trends in HRM has its roots in the analysis of management practices. A conversion stand is supported by globalisation and growing cooperation among countries, harmonisation of regional labour laws (in Europe) and an understanding of capitalism as the only successful economic system (Drori et al. 2006). The view that there is a diversion trend, however, is supported by a cultural perspective. It states that regional and national differences in norms, practices, values and belief systems result in a different understanding of roles of organisations and management priorities (Hofstede 1991, Trompenaars and Hampden-Turner 2011, House et al. 2004, Hofstede et al. 2004) and thus in diverse approaches to managing employees (Mayrhofer et al. 2004). Mayrhofer et al. (2011, p. 51) suggest that Europe is an appropriate case study for addressing this debate as it 'reflects this peculiar tension between convergence and divergence in a unique way'. Europe combines highly integrated markets including the Single European Market (SEA) and a number of common institutional structures with substantial differences in cultural values, institutions, as well as different but interconnected historical backgrounds and development paths.

Brewster (2007) points out that while management assumptions and behaviour are different from country to country, the management thinking and HRM in particular is heavily influenced by US-style management education and the use of English as the main language in international business. Human resources management is dependent on the understanding of management as a distinctive profession and discipline. In contrast, in Europe, line managers were traditionally promoted from specialists without additional training and the personnel function was considered a clerical, administrative or social service oriented one. Just recently, personnel management was staffed by psychologists and social science professionals, thus putting an emphasis on employee selection, counselling and training rather than managing employee performance and input into organisational strategic plans (Brewster et al. 1992). As personnel management was considered neither a profession, nor a part of the management function, the evidence is mostly anecdotal. For example, the first HR course offered in the Czech Republic took place in 2000 (an undergraduate course of the University of New York and a Thunderbird MBA programme) and even in 2005 all but academic members of the HRM group in Central Eastern Europe (CEE) had non-business-related academic and professional backgrounds. The author's personal contact with HR departments in leading Czech private enterprises and government organisations showed that HR departments were staffed with either psychologists or administrative/secretarial staff. Examples include CEZ (an energy provider), Social Security Administration, the Ministry of Material Resources, Border Guard Authority, as well as various private companies from logistics to food services. The situation was similar in other European countries (see also Hiltrop et al. 1995; Holt Larsen and Brewster 2003).

In the UK, employee-related practices have their historical roots in the social reform movement of the nineteenth century, for example, in the Cadbury model village, where Cadbury Company provided its workforce with housing as well as social and recreational facilities (Cadbury n.d.).

A step back into history illustrates the background to modern HRM approaches. In the 1930s in Central Europe, Jan Antonin Bata, a Czech entrepreneur, had built a model housing project based on the ideal city model for his workers at Bata shoe factories and had plans to expand the model to other European countries (Bata Industrial 2017). In contrast, employee practices at the same time in the USA were based on the scientific management ideas of Taylor, implemented in Ford factories. Scientific management was based on the notion that all large tasks can be broken into smaller ones and that there is a best way to perform them; in addition, workers should be selected based on their knowledge and ability, and should be trained for the assigned tasks and provided with material incentives to achieve the best performance. It is less well known that the same scientific management practices were widely used in the Soviet Union prior to World War II – called the Stakhanovism movement (Bedeian and Phillip 1990). The same methods were applied in the Soviet penal system, with the major difference that instead of rewards for increased production, punishment and reduction of food rations were used for failing to meet production goals (see e.g. Andreev-Khomiakov and Healy 1998). Therefore, we can argue that while Europe has its personnel practices rooted in social welfare and an employee-centred reactive approach, the USA and the Soviet Union developed practices of performance-oriented pragmatic and strategic HRM.

HRM approaches in regional clusters

Holt Larsen and Brewster (2003, p. 12) state that in contrast to the so-called 'universalistic HRM paradigm', practised in the USA, in other countries including most of Europe, 'HRM is understood differently, researched differently and is, in practice, conducted in quite distinct ways'. Consequently, the differences in understanding of the role of managers, their relationships with subordinates and other culturally specific variables determine the implementation of HRM practices in a region (Hodgetts et al. 2006; Hofstede 1991).

On the whole, legislation in Europe, particularly in the EU, shapes the application of HR tools and systems; it prescribes

how employees should be recruited and compensated,
the level of union representation and participation in management and decision-making,
the required notice periods and co-determination required before employee separation,
appropriate qualifications for positions and their documentation.

For example, in France, the vast majority of employees are to work no more than 35 hours a week, and overtime is limited by law, including unpaid time worked by executives and managers. President Macron, when elected in 2017, revised French labour laws to some extent to allow more flexibility in the hiring and dismassal of employees, but his proposals remained unpopular with labour unions and provoked widespread strikes (Vinocur 2017).

Nevertheless, there are significant differences in Europe in the understanding of management's role and, therefore, various ways to differentiate regions based on this shared understanding. One of the approaches is to group the countries according to their prevailing economic system or recent history (Suder 2011). One is the Anglo-Saxon cluster, comparable with stock-market-focused business systems and a liberal market economy. The other cluster is comprised of Germanic states with coordinated market economies, a stakeholder-focused approach to business and legalised employment guidance. The third cluster is South-Western Europe, encompassing Latin countries (Belgium, France, Italy, Portugal and Spain) and the fourth is Nordic economies with a high level of consensus and labour union membership. The next is Southern European or the Mediterranean group (Greece, Cyprus and Turkey), characterised by economies with small firms and mostly family ownership, extensive labour legislation but with general avoidance and noncompliance with such regulation. Finally, there is the CEE with a heritage of centrally planned economies (Parry et al. 2013, p. 18). Another possible differentiation is based on national cultures (Hofstede 1991). A division based on Hofstede cultural dimensions (Hofstede 1994) proposes a clear divide between East and West, as well as North and South and suggests two clusters of North-Western and South–Eastern groups. Austria, Ireland, Finland, the UK, the Netherlands, Sweden, Denmark, Germany and Switzerland constitute the first group, while the rest of Europe falls in the second (Minkov and Hofstede 2014A; 2014B).

In addition, Ignjatovic and Svetlik (2003) propose a different segmentation of countries. In this approach, a Central Southern cluster includes Germany, Austria, Spain, Czech Republic, Slovenia, Italy and Portugal. In this cluster HR managers have strategic responsibility and are management board members. HRM departments here are typically small; employees are not involved in decision-making. The more traditional 'hard' HRM practices are used, aiming at performance management.

The second, Nordic cluster (Norway, Sweden, Denmark and Finland) stresses collaborative decision-making, combined with a greater role for trade unions and co-determination, although its current development is characterised by more individual contacts, a higher presence of MNEs and a lesser role for industry-wide labour agreements. The rules of an organisation are formalised; there is limited emphasis on performance management but an emphasis on employee training and flexibility of employment, which is consistent with family- and education-oriented policies of Nordic welfare states. Employee and union representatives participate in decision-making at industry and organisational levels. HRM departments tend to be small, but professionally trained and well equipped. The authors theorise that a 'small HR department and a highly participative approach increase trust and reduce the need for [formal] appraisal and evaluation' (ibid, p. 31).

In contrast to the Nordic cluster, in the Western cluster, which includes the UK, Switzerland, Belgium, the Netherlands and France, more programmes and initiatives focus on marginalised groups; they use more external services, and attempt to increase the transparency of management and decision-making – employees receive strategic and financial information about the organisation; recruitment, training, and career practices are sophisticated and open. The HR managers tend to be professionals recruited outside the organisation. They play the role of internal consultants with input into strategic plans.

The final 'peripheral' cluster includes Bulgaria, Estonia, Greece, Cyprus, Ireland and Turkey. Its main shared characteristic is the low status and professionalism of HR specialists. While new systems and programmes are implemented, they are reported to be rarely evaluated for effectiveness (ibid). One of the reasons for that might be the small size of firms in this cluster. HRM is not separated from the general management of organisations, with the exception of Greece (Nikandrou et al. 2003; Holt Larsen and Brewster 2003, p. 12).

Influence of MNEs on HRM practices in Europe

Conventional wisdom and existing research suggest that HR-related practices are spread throughout Europe, and specifically to CEE, by MNEs (Buck et al. 2003). For example, in the Czech Republic in 2000, the title of HR manager did not exist, yet with the arrival of international MNEs, including Oracle, Microsoft, IKEA, McDonald's and later Google, and European players, as well an introduction of MBA degrees by internationally accredited programmes, HRM became a clearly recognised profession and HR as a function is present in large and medium-sized organisations. Yet despite a number of scholarly studies on MNEs' HR practices, they are mostly of a quantitative nature (Björkman et al. 2014) and thus rely on a shared understanding of terms, including HRM, rather than a qualitative and more nuanced approach. This assumption of uniformity can be problematic as the understanding of the goals of organisations and management differ among national cultures (Hofstede 1991, House et al. 2004). As the majority of HR-related research has been conducted from so-called 'WEIRD' – western, educated, industrialised, rich, democratic – countries (Henrich et al. 2010), the question of 'how the local context for HRM is influenced by MNEs and MNE subsidiaries, is seldom researched, if at all' (Brewster et al. 2016, p. 28). Clark and Pugh (1999, p. 86) argue that 'if other countries adopt foreign management modes, as they own and expect them to be effective, they must be culturally close to the countries where those theories originated'. Alternatively, the cross-cultural competence of managers and their cultural agility could be a success factor in an adaptation of foreign practices and systems and their implementation in a new environment (Gilbert and Von Glinow 2015).

MNEs that entered the economies of CEE in the early 1990s took with them the HR-related practices that could have been incomparable with the predominant management practices of the local companies as well as the labour law. To avoid potential cultural conflicts with local employees, an MNE would often hire employees without prior experience in the industry, or bring expatriates or third-country nationals to work in a CEE location. They would only gradually recruit local residents, ensuring that recruits were introduced to a strong organisational culture where they were in the minority. In addition, local new employees would undertake a training and socialisation period when they would be immersed in the organisational culture, often at company HQ (Deresky 2017).

The case of Vodafone entering the Czech market in 2005 through a purchase of the Oskar mobile company illustrates intense acculturalisation of employees, including adopting informal business attire and informal communication channels instead of tradition business suits and hierarchy (Čáslavová 2007; Polak 2015). Oracle developed a comprehensive programme of employee engagement in CEE and Microsoft sponsored informal team-building events during the induction period to promote a spirit of entrepreneurship and company loyalty (Manwani and Bharadwaj 2014; Buttyán et al. 2016; Jehanzeb and Bashir 2013).

When HR-related practices are introduced by MNE management, it is unclear how well local employees understand the intention of such practices and how effective, for example, performance management would be in a legal environment where employers are bound by a written employment contract that requires a substantial notice period and in some cases severance compensation. Alternatively, an MNE could recruit and hire foreign employees or relocate them from another country. In this situation employees would depend on the company sponsorship for visa and work permits, being in effect employed at will (e.g., D'Amuri and Peri 2014; Paul 2013). Such practices are used in call centres located in Europe (Breathnach 2000). However, they are unlikely to change the employment-related practices in the host country. Therefore, we can conclude that the influence of MNEs on local practices would be moderated by the business and legal environment, and the cultural distance between the countries, with the North being more likely to adopt the practices, if not the goals, of the HRM, and employees – foreign employees and the less experienced – likely to support and implement HRM practices.

Central and Eastern Europe

Central and Eastern European countries are often combined in a single cluster, based on shared history and economic characteristics. Arguably CEE countries are no longer in a transition from socialist, centrally planned to market economies; nevertheless, the perception of the role and objectives of HRM has not changed that drastically during and since the transition period. One reason is that newly educated managers became familiar with the US-style HRM model, which cannot fully be implemented in Europe. Countries in CEE in the period before the Fall of the Berlin Wall in 1989 had socialist, state-controlled economies with virtually no private ownership (with the exception of Poland and Hungary). In particular, Baltic countries (Latvia, Lithuania and Estonia) were heavily influenced by the Soviet approach to HRM.

As further discussed in the next chapter, in contrast to the supporting welfare and administrative function of personnel management in Western Europe, in the Soviet Union the personnel function was central to an organisation, responsible for vetting existing employees and applicants for security clearance and political trustworthiness. With the majority of industrial production linked to the military and security, security clearance was extensive and, as unemployment was criminalised in the Soviet Union, a department of cadres, as it was called, had power to destroy not only careers but the very lives of employees.

Therefore, there was no enthusiasm for the oppressive human resources-related practices of the Soviet Union in either the conquered Baltic republics or the controlled CEE states. As a 'politically oriented decision-making system' (Garavan et al. 1998, p. 210) personnel practices in the Soviet Union new states and spheres of influence could not get the buy-in of either employees or managers. Although union membership in all socialist states was close to 100 per cent (Kazlauskaitė and Bučiūnienė 2010), employee participation in decision-making was minimal. As promotions and performance bonuses were awarded based on communist party membership and active participation in state-sponsored political and economic campaigns (Karoliny et al. 2010), the department of cadre fulfilled ideological and social (rather than performance-related) purposes. Human resources professionals were perceived by employees as inefficient, bureaucratic and indeed unprofessional (Morley et al. 2016).

It is no wonder that after the disintegration of the Soviet Union and the Soviet sphere of influence, the role of the traditional personnel department had greatly diminished. An additional factor contributing to the decrease of the importance of the personnel function was that the majority of companies in the newly 'turned capitalist' CEE and Baltic States were family-owned micro-companies. In such cases, an investment in specific HRM could be considered too expensive and not conducive to increased productivity. As an example, Kasluskaite et al. (2009) analysed data sourced from Eurostat (2004), which showed that more than 75 per cent of Bulgarian, Slovenian, Czech, Lithuanian and Estonian firms were micro-enterprises. During the socialist period, organisations in the Former Soviet Union and CEE countries applied a uniform mode of personnel management (Koubek 2009), but in the transition period they took diverse paths, returning to their historical economic and cultural backgrounds. Kazlauskaitė et al. (2013) suggested that another reason for decreased HR management involvement in the CEE was a higher level of education of employees and candidates than the EU average, thus there was a reduced need for supervision and management involvement in the work process.

Eventually, the growing popularity of management education in the region and return migration from the USA and UK (Gittins and Fink 2015) gradually introduced western HR methods and practices into the management of these firms. Yet we find that in different countries, different paths to their further adaptation and development are still taken. Morley et al. (2012) suggest that CEE countries experienced diverse trajectories from socialism towards market-oriented economics and thus their HR-related practices and systems differ. For example, the so-called Visegrád Four group, i.e., the Czech Republic, Slovakia, Poland and Hungary, a group aiming to further their European integration, was historically connected with their Western neighbours – Germany and Austria – in particular since Poland and Hungary maintained elements of privately owned enterprises during the socialist regime, and thus used a rapid liberalisation of markets and economy during the transition period (Adam et al. 2009). This model is called by Morley et al. (2016, p. 80)) a 'moderate interventionist model'. On the other hand, Bulgaria and the Baltic states have maintained a closer connection with Russia: Bulgaria and

Russia share the Orthodox religion, their languages are close, and a large minority of ethnic Russians reside in the Baltic States.

The third model that Morley et al. propose is characterised by self-management and personnel decision-making by workers' councils, and this model could be found in the countries of the former Yugoslavia, for example, Serbia and Slovenia.

Interestingly some practices are present in all models:

reliance on a personal interview as the preferable selection method,
training and development focused on managerial and professional employees,
individual-level managerial compensation,
other employees compensated at national levels, and
increasing use of performance appraisal (ibid).

It also appears that while research reports some HR-related practices are adopted in all regions, the objectives of increasing productivity and employee performance are not implemented strategically in any of the models.

The case of the Nordics

All the models discussed uniformly see Nordics – Denmark, Sweden, Finland and Norway – as one specific cluster. It is characterised by high formalisation, high involvement of labour unions in decision-making, both at an industry and individual organisation level, high spending on employee training, which, combined with a high level of education in general, means there is less need for performance management and more for flexibility in working place. Vanhala (2008) postulates that HRM plays a strategic role in Nordic countries, yet without any attempt to influence employee performance, such people-related practices have limited influence on an organisation's strategic results.

Based on Hofstede's (1994) cultural dimensions, the Nordic countries are unique in combining a low masculinity or achievement index with low power distance index and high individualism. Thus, the goals of society and individuals are to maintain their independence, while taking care of vulnerable and disadvantaged members of society in an egalitarian manner. In an organisational context, it is translated into group decision-making, managers as coordinators, not leaders. The focus is on employee-related practices to promote transparency, fairness and benefits to employees and society in general, not increasing company profits or maintaining a market share. Some of these practices, namely job security, merit-based selection of new employees, use of teams and performance-related pay can be found in the high-performance work system (Wood and De Menezes 1998). However, as their ultimate objective is not to increase a firm's performance measured as profit and market share, they could hardly be considered HRM, but rather can be traced to welfare capitalist firms like Bata, Cadbury, IKEA, and Nokia. In comparison with the rest of Europe, the region has relatively low degrees of regulation, a feature that Nordic countries share with the UK and the Netherlands (Mayrhofer et al. 2011). Yet social pressure, including boycotts and media campaigns to adopt the Nordic managerial culture and work practices, can be traced back to MNEs attempting to introduce more performance-oriented techniques and more management control than is customary in the region.

One illustration of the challenges originating from diverging approaches is the practice of hiring unexperienced young local employees, training them at the HQ and socialising them in the company culture. An interesting case was presented by international researchers Skippari et al. (2014), and widely discussed in Finnish official and social media. This case represents deep-rooted differences in the understanding of HR objectives and functions even between Germany and Finland, the countries that can be considered to be culturally close to each other, but belonging to different clusters. Lidl, a German global discount supermarket chain, entered the Finnish market in 2002. Managers were trained in Germany, and the company opted to hire young employees without prior retail experience in Finland. As already mentioned, such practices are common for MNEs entering new markets and attempting to preserve strong organisational culture, which is often is rooted in the national culture of the country of origin (Schneider 1988). Skippari et al. (2014, p. 5) stated that, upon entry, Lidl 'introduced its foreign corporate culture and differing operational practices with little intention to conform to local standards of practice' and then 'tried to transfer its global HR practices … to Finland' (ibid.). As there is no discussion of the appropriate Finnish HR practices in this paper that focused on PR and communications policies (ibid, p. 6), this case reveals possible avenues for additional HRM-centric research. For example, it appears that the company followed all legal requirements for union participation and compensation. While in Finland Lidl followed the employment law, it was not considered to be sufficient from a cultural perspective (ibid, p. 11); one finding makes reference to the acceptability of monitoring employee behaviour on the job, a practice found more acceptable in Germany than in Finland. The case has a happy ending, as, eventually, it is reported, Lidl invested in effective employee training and development conducted by a local Finnish firm.

Thus, using the Lidl case as an illustration, it can be concluded that while there is a definite uniform and consistent approach to employee management in Nordic countries, research demonstrates that it cannot be considered HRM, nor illustrate a Europe-wide HRM approach. While many HPWP features are adopted, the high performance of the firm is not the goal. On the contrary, a firm is expected to fulfil employee needs in terms of income, development and, possibly, social connections. Thus, this distinct Nordic model is not an HRM one within our current research lens.

However, the latest development of Nordic economic and labour regulation point to an increasing degree of flexibility, notable in negotiating employment contracts at an individual enterprise, rather than at industry-wide level, there is more flexibility in using both part-time and limited-term employment contracts, as well as an extension of work hours. Even Iceland is considering abandoning the minimum wage (O'Sullivan and Royle 2014), which could drastically liberalise the labour market. In the case of Finland, the lack of minimum wage regulation had not resulted in low wages due to central collective bargaining, establishing compensation and work conditions industry-wide. Yet as of May 2016 this practice was abandoned and unions ('employee organisations' as they are called in Finland), negotiate sector-specific agreements; this is anticipated to result in more differentiation in compensation and work conditions. Combined with increased labour mobility in the EU and an increased presence of MNEs in the region, we can expect greater flexibility in employment and compensation, which again opens up future research questions.

Would these developments result in a conversion of the Nordic model to other European models? Unlikely, as the basic goals of management and employment are different in Nordic countries than in the rest of Europe. For example, a Social Services (Kela/Fra) initiative in Finland to test a basic income for everyone is a step towards making income dependency on employment obsolete, which will move the employment model even further away from the rest of the world. This chapter argues that the Nordic model is expected to continue to be unique and distinct even when it becomes more flexible. What that means in the future, and how European business opportunities for Nordic firms (and other firms interested in Nordic markets) may be influenced, remains a worthwhile research field to explore.

Conclusion

This chapter has provided an overview of the current employee-related systems and practice in Europe, and concluded that there is no current evidence in literature that organisations in Europe are likely to converge towards one model of HRM that would stress a unitaristic and pragmatic approach (Storey 2007), or focus mainly on performance, profit and return on investment. First, legal barriers to implementation of such a model, in Europe and specifically in the EU, were found; second, the understanding of the role of enterprises in society, the role of management and its responsibilities, and HRM application models are seen to differ throughout Europe. If convergence were to develop, a model of the process of HR practices adoption in Europe – taking the various current models into account – is presented in Figure 18.1, setting a conceptual basis to explore in future research.

Some practices, notably focused on employee development, training and the development of comprehensive and transparent compensation and employment systems are adopted across enterprises that are doing business in Europe. Yet, current literature shows their execution to vary in different regions. In a related matter, Chapter 15 of this book indicates, particularly in the context of the EU and EU regulations that aim at job quality, that there is little, if any, evidence to suggest a harmonisation of European job quality levels.

Unfortunately, there is virtually no comparable data available to date on how HRM practices are enacted by line managers or HR professionals, and qualitative research remains scarce. There is a clear tendency for regional HR systems to develop in a similar direction, which appears worthwhile to explore further. While there is no shared understanding among scholars of how to group different regions using current HRM definitions, the difference between South-East and North-West is shown as pronounced, and a Nordic cluster and CEE countries are taking their own distinct roads. This chapter points to the limitation of extant literature, hence restricting this analysis, and calls for more and more diverse research into the divergence and convergence trends of HRM practices in which European business operates across an integrated marketplace.

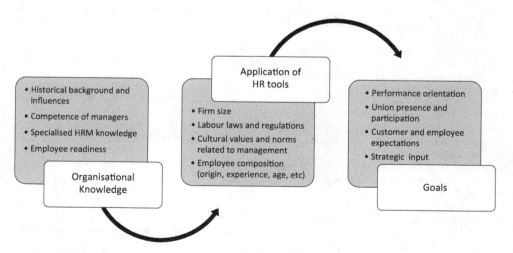

Figure 18.1 Conceptualising a development process of HR-related practices upon European cluster criteria: Strategic or employee oriented goals

References

Adam, F., Kristan, P. and Tomšič, M. (2009), 'Varieties of capitalism in Eastern Europe (with special emphasis on Estonia and Slovenia)', *Communist and Post-Communist Studies*, vol. 42, no. 1, pp. 65–81.

Andreev-Khomiakov, G.M. and Healy, A. (1998), *Bitter Waters: Life and Work in Stalin's Russia*, Boulder, CO, Westview Press.

Bata Industrial (2017), 'Bata Industrials history'. www.bataindustrials.com/about-us/history (accessed 12 January 2017).

Bedeian, A.G. and Phillips, C.R. (1990), 'Scientific management and stakhanovism in the Soviet Union: A historical perspective', *International Journal of Social Economics*, vol. 17, no. 10, pp. 28–35.

Björkman, I., Ehrnrooth, M., Mäkelä, K., Smale, A. and Sumelius, J. (2014), 'From HRM practices to the practice of HRM: Setting a research agenda', *Journal of Organizational Effectiveness: People and Performance*, vol. 1 no. 2, pp. 122–140.

Breathnach, P. (2000), 'Globalisation, information technology and the emergence of niche transnational cities: The growth of the call centre sector in Dublin', *Geoforum*, vol. 31, no. 4, pp. 477–485.

Brewster, C. (2007), 'A European perspective on HRM', *European Journal of International Management*, vol. 1, no. 3, pp. 239–259.

Brewster, C., Gooderham, P. and Mayrhofer, W. (2016), 'Human resource management: The promise, the performance, the consequences', *Journal of Organizational Effectiveness: People and Performance*, vol. 3, no. 2, pp. 181–190.

Brewster, C., Holt Larsen, H. and Trompenaars, F. (1992), 'Human resource management in Europe: Evidence from ten countries', *International Journal of Human Resource Management*, vol. 3, no. 3, pp. 409–434.

Buck, T., Filatotchev, I., Demina, N. and Wright, M. (2003), 'Insider ownership, human resource strategies and performance in a transition economy', *Journal of International Business Studies*, vol. 34, no. 6, pp. 530–549.

Buttyán, L., Félegyházi, M. and Pék, G. (2016), 'Mentoring talent in IT security – A case study', in *ASE@ USENIX Security Symposium*, Austin, TX.

Cadbury (n.d.), 'Our Story'. www.cadbury.co.uk/our-story (accessed 12 December 2016).

Čáslavová, L. (2007), 'Zákaznická loajalita v oblasti mobilní komunikace: Porovnání České republiky a Velké Británie /Customer loyalty in the sphere of mobile communication: A comparison between the Czech Republic and the UK', Doctoral dissertation, Technická Univerzita v Liberci. https://dspace.tul.cz/bitstream/handle/15240/4925/bc_14194.pdf?sequence=1 (accessed 18 November 2017).

Clark, T. and Pugh, D. (1999), 'Similarities and differences in European conceptions of human resource management: Toward a polycentric study', *International Studies of Management & Organization*, vol. 29, no. 4, pp. 84–100. www.jstor.org/stable/40397462 (accessed 15 October 2016).

D'Amuri, F. and Peri, G. (2014), 'Immigration, jobs, and employment protection: Evidence from Europe before and during the great recession', *Journal of the European Economic Association*, vol. 12, no. 2, pp. 432–464.

Deresky, H. (2017), *International Management: Managing across borders and cultures*, India, Pearson Education.

Drori, G.S., Meyer, J.W. and Hwang, H. (2006), *Globalization and Organization: World society and organizational change*. Oxford, Oxford University Press.

Eurostat (2004), Eurostat Yearbook 2004 – European Commission – Europa EU http://ec.europa.eu/eurostat/documents/3217494/5648861/KS-CD-04-001-EN.PDF/05371ffe-c41c-4bec-9093-f507c11cf3ca (accessed 19 October 2016).

Garavan, T., Morley, M., Heraty, N., Lucewicz, J., and Suchodolski, A. (1998), 'Managing human resources in a post-command economy: Personnel administration or strategic HRM', *Personnel Review*, vol. 27, no. 3, pp. 200–212.

Gilbert, G.R. and Von Glinow, M.A. (2015), 'National context and organizational performance across three sectors', *Cross Cultural Management*, vol. 22, no. 3, pp. 356–378.

Gittins, T. and Fink, M. (2015), 'Return migration, informal learning, human capital development and SME internationalization in the CEE region: A systematic literature review', *Journal for East European Management Studies*, vol. 20, no. 3, pp. 279–303.

Guest, D.E. (1987), 'Human resource management and industrial relations [1]', *Journal of Management Studies*, vol. 24, no. 5, pp. 503–521.

Henrich, J., Heine, S.J. and Norenzayan, A. (2010), 'Most people are not WEIRD', *Nature*, vol. 466, no. 7302, p. 29.

Hiltrop, J.M., Despres, C. and Sparrow, P. (1995), 'The changing role of HR managers in Europe', *European Management Journal*, vol. 13, no. 1, pp. 91–98.

Hodgetts, R.M., Luthans, F. and Doh, J.P. (2006), *International Management: Culture, strategy, and behaviour*. New York, McGraw-Hill Companies.

Hofstede, G. (1991), *Cultures and Organizations. Intercultural cooperation and its importance for survival. Software of the mind*. London, McGraw-Hill.

Hofstede, G. (1994), 'The business of international business is culture', *International Business Review*, vol. 30, no. 1, pp. 1–14.

Holt Larsen, H. and Brewster, C. (2003), 'Line management responsibility for HRM: What is happening in Europe?' *Employee Relations*, vol. 25, no. 3, pp. 228–244.

House, R.J., Hanges, P.J., Javidan, M., Dorfman, P.W. and Gupta, V. (eds) (2004), *Culture, Leadership, and Organizations: The GLOBE Study of 62 Societies*, Thousand Oaks, CA, Sage.

Ignjatović, M. and Svetlik, I. (2003), 'European HRM clusters', *EBS Review*, vol. 17, pp. 25–39.

Jehanzeb, K. and Bashir, N.A. (2013), 'Training and development program and its benefits to employee and organization: A conceptual study', *European Journal of Business and Management*, vol. 5, no. 2, pp. 243–252.

Karoliny, Z., Farkas, F. and Poor, J. (2010), 'Sharpening profile of HRM in Central-Eastern Europe in reflection of its developments in Hungary', *Review of International Comparative Management*, vol. 11, no. 4, pp. 733–747.

Kazlauskaité, R. and Bučiūnienė, I. (2010), 'HR function developments in Lithuania', *Baltic Journal of Management*, vol. 5, no. 2, pp. 218–241.

Kazlauskaité, R., Ligthart, P.E.M., Bučiūnienė I. and Vanhala. S. (2013), 'CSR and Responsible HRM in the CEE and the Nordic Countries', in E. Parry, E. Stavrou and M. Lazarova (eds), *Global Trends in Human Resource Management*, London, UK, Palgrave Macmillan, pp. 54–77.

Koubek, J. (2009), 'Managing human resources in the Czech Republic', in M. Morley, N. Heraty and S. Michailova (eds), *Managing Human Resources in Central and Eastern Europe*, London, UK, Palgrave Macmillan.

Manwani, R.K. and Bharadwaj, K. (2014), 'Analysing employee engagement and motivation programmes: A case study in Oracle India's software division', *The IASMS Journal of Business Spectrum*, vol. 8, no. 13, pp. 42–60.

Mayrhofer, W., Brewster, C., Morley, M.J., and Ledolter, J. (2011), 'Hearing a different drummer? Convergence of human resource management in Europe—A longitudinal analysis', *Human Resource Management Review*, vol. 21, no. 1, pp. 50–67.

Minkov, M. and Hofstede, G. (2014a), 'A replication of Hofstede's uncertainty avoidance dimension across nationally representative samples from Europe', *International Journal of Cross Cultural Management*, vol. 14, no. 2, pp. 161–171.

Minkov, M. and Hofstede, G. (2014b), 'Clustering of 316 European regions on measures of values: Do Europe's countries have national cultures?' *Cross-Cultural Research*, vol. 48, no. 2, pp.144–176.

Morley, M.J., Heraty, N. and Michailova, S. (eds) (2016), *Managing Human Resources in Central and Eastern Europe*, London, UK, Palgrave Macmillan.

Morley, M.J., Minbaeva, D., and Michailova, S. (2012), 'The transition states of Central and Eastern Europe and the former Soviet Union', in C. Brewster and W. Mayrhofer (eds), *Handbook of Research on Comparative Human Resource Management*, Cheltenham, UK, Edward Elgar, pp. 550–575

Morley, M., Poor, J., Heraty, N., Alas, R. and Pocztowski, A. (2016), 'Developments in human resource management in Central and Eastern Europe in comparative perspective', in M. Dickmann, C. Brewster and P. Sparrow (eds), *International Human Resource Management: Contemporary HR issues in Europe*, New York, Routledge, pp. 73–99.

Nikandrou, I., Apospori, E. and Papalexandris, N. (2003), 'Cultural and leadership similarities and variations in the southern part of the European Union', *Journal of Leadership and Organizational Studies*, vol. 9, no. 3, pp. 61–84.

O'Sullivan, M. and Royle, T. (2014), 'Everything and nothing changes: Fast-food employers and the threat to minimum wage regulation in Ireland', *Economic and Industrial Democracy*, vol. 35, no. 1, pp. 27–47.

Parry, E., Stavrou, E. and Lazarova, M. (eds) (2013), *Global Trends in Human Resource Management*, London, UK, Palgrave Macmillan.

Paul, R. (2013), 'Strategic contextualisation: Free movement, labour migration policies and the governance of foreign workers in Europe', *Policy Studies*, vol. 34, no. 2, pp. 122–141.

Polák, Z. (2015), 'Public procurement of mobile network operators' services'. Master's Thesis, Charles University in Prague, Faculty of Social Sciences Institute of Economic Studies https://dspace.cuni.cz/bitstream/handle/20.500.11956/67339/DPTX_2012_2_11230_0_387803_0_138183.pdf?sequence=1andisAllowed=y (accessed 16 November 2017).

Skippari, M., Geppert, M., Williams, K. and Rusanen, O. (2014), 'The dynamic interaction between internal and external pressures for MNCs HR management practices: The case of Lidl Finland', in T. Isidorsson (ed.), *Threats and Possibilities Facing Nordic Working Life: The 7th Nordic Working Life Conference, University of Gothenburg, Sweden, June 11–13, 2014. Book of Abstracts and Programme.* Gothenburg: University of Gothenburg.

Schneider, S.C. (1988), 'National vs. corporate culture: Implications for human resource management', *Human Resource Management*, vol. 27, no. 2, pp. 231–246.

Storey, J. (2007), *Human Resource Management: A Critical Text*, London, Thompson Learning.

Suder, G. (2011), *Doing Business in Europe*, 2nd edn, Thousand Oaks, CA, Sage.

Trompenaars, F. and Hampden-Turner, C. (2011), *Riding the Waves of Culture: Understanding diversity in global business*, Boston, MA, Nicholas Brealey Publishing.

Truss, C., Gratton, L., Hope-Hailey, V., McGovern, P. and Stiles, P. (1997), 'Soft and hard models of human resource management: A reappraisal', *Journal of Management Studies*, vol. 34, no. 1, pp. 53–73.

Vanhala, S. (2008), 'Nordic model of HRM? HR practices in the Nordic and other European countries', in *HRM Global 2008, Sustainable HRM in the Global Economy. Conference Proceedings*, pp. 348–356.

Vinocur, N. (2017), '5 key points from Macron's big labor reform', *Politico*, 31 August. www.politico.eu/article/macron-labor-reform-5-key-points (accessed 1 September 2017).

Wood, S. and De Menezes, L. (1998), 'High commitment management in the UK: Evidence from the workplace industrial relations survey, and employers' manpower and skills practices survey', *Human Relations*, vol. 51, no. 4, pp. 485–515.

19

EUROPE AND ITS DIVERSITY

Dealing with human resources management in Russia, Belarus and Ukraine

Marina Latukha

Introduction

Due to the ongoing process of world globalisation, the prevailing majority of the world's biggest multinational corporations (MNCs), including European ones, are opening subsidiaries in the Commonwealth of Independent States (CIS), which was created as a successor entity to the Soviet Union and comprises most of its ex-members. As successors, post-socialist states inherited not only rich resources and large territories, but also the need for transition from planned to open market economies (Altman 2009) that facilitate the interests of European companies in this region, as increasing involvement of European companies in CIS countries means having new markets, customers, labour force and, thus, business development opportunities. The increased economic integration along with the evolution of the important international economic and business organisations has led to a remarkable boost of the world's businesses. The step of expanding companies to the CIS might be considered an inevitable one: while the market niches in these regions are not occupied, the business strategy of market development seems reasonable.

Among other CIS countries, Belarus, Russia and Ukraine are the largest countries of the former Soviet republics strategically linking the fast-growing markets in the East and West. Surprisingly they have not been a very popular setting for management research, but are of high interest to European firms looking to do business in those countries. The best way for CIS countries to transition was to attract MNCs and foreign direct investments (FDI), create institutions that focused on attracting FDI and support the development of human resource management (HRM), needed to manage local employees effectively (Lee et al. 2010; Danilovich and Croucher 2015). However, MNCs faced and are still facing various complications in the adaptation of their management practices to host countries' contexts (Newman and Nollen 1996), due to a poor understanding of HRM specifics and cultural context.

According to recent studies, one of the key success factors for companies' growth is to learn how to manage human capital (Lengnick-Hall et al. 2009; Farndale et al. 2010; Schuler et al. 2011). Aghazadeh (2003) emphasised how important it is for managers to ensure that in the global business environment HRM policies and practices maintain a balance between consistency and the recognition of various differences that occur when doing business. As HRM means a set of managerial practices that aim to attract, develop and retain employees within an organisation, we discuss the most relevant aspects of recruitment, employees' training and development, performance evaluation, motivation and compensation, and career development in Belarus, Ukraine and Russia. Among different well-proven European approaches to management practices, HRM is one of the most crucial elements of a MNC's competitive strategy (Schuler et al. 2002; Liu 2004). When European companies expand to the CIS region, they sometimes face the problem of implementing some of their particular core capabilities, including innovative HRM practices, due to the institutional, business and cultural contexts (Fey and Denison 2003, Novitskaya 2016). The majority of scholars claim that apart from the barriers that are common for underdeveloped countries, such as an unstable political and economic situation, crime and bureaucracy, the weak areas are human capital, in terms of managerial skills (Fey et al. 1999), and organisational structures in post-Soviet countries (Fey et al. 1999; Fey and Denison 2003).

Based on this, we study in this chapter the existing barriers and limitations of HRM in CIS countries related to current HRM conditions that are important to be considered by multinational firms seeking to transfer and adapt their HRM practices to different contexts and in particular here to CIS countries. The chapter discusses the specifics of HRM in Ukraine, Belarus and Russia and highlights both the historical background and the current trends for the implementation of HRM practices. We discuss specifics of HRM in the CIS context in general and in Belarus, Ukraine and Russia in particular, reflecting the main peculiarities of recruitment, training, development, performance management and motivation, allowing us to draw conclusions about HRM orientation and focus in CIS countries.

HRM practice adaptation: From Europe to CIS

Schuler et al. (2011) describe and provide a framework for understanding the linkages of HRM practices with company strategy at an international level. The authors emphasise that it is important to study international HRM in the context of changing economic and business conditions in different countries. In particular, it involves understanding the success factors of HRM practices' adaptation in another country and business environment (Newman and Nollen 1996; Myloni et al. 2004; Gilbert and Von Glinow 2015). Shen (2005) confirms this and adds that the country context is crucial as well. Additionally, Rosenzweig and Nohria (1994) study the effect of a number of factors for successful HRM affiliation with local companies.

Soviet management practices that transferred to a certain extent to CIS countries are described by Vlachoutsicos and Lawrence (1990) and can be considered as barriers for European HRM practices' adaptation. The authors discuss the heritage of collectivist practices in work relations, centralised leadership and hierarchical organisational structure. Additionally, according to May et al. (1998), typical HRM was limited to personnel administration and record-keeping, which was supported by a bureaucratic and exploitative approach used in personnel management comparing to European practices with a systematic and proactive approach to HRM and a focus on innovation. In general, European firms tend to give much more attention to strategic HRM than companies, for example, from Eastern and Central Europe (Mills 1998; Zupan and Kase 2005); in particular, some HRM practices were either weak or did not exist in the Soviet Union. There was no recruitment in Soviet states; in its place was staffing with poor labour mobility, governmental allocation of workers to jobs and the strong involvement of state authorities. Training and employee development were planned and controlled by the government and focused on increasing professional qualifications, without paying attention to the particular needs of employees (Mockler et al. 1996). Compensation management involved low salary differentiation, put high emphasis on non-monetary benefits (such as public recognition), performance appraisals were mandatory, regulated and developed by the state and were considered a formality, which often resulted in a neglectful attitude (Minbaeva et al. 2007; Novitskaya and Davoine 2011). There was no development of organisational culture due to the communist ideology that was integrated into every part of Soviet life. All this resulted in a weak desire for reform and resistance to innovations in management. Many of these Soviet management peculiarities became deeply rooted in the minds of the people and turned out to be significant complications for the adaptation of European management practices in CIS countries.

European MNCs act as a crucial channel through which indigenous businesses tend to adopt new practices (Buck et al. 2003; Novitskaya and Davoine 2011). In some countries, subsidiaries of European MNCs selectively adopt practices or try to develop new ones, especially in training and development. Education and business in most CIS countries were separated and often had weak or no connection between each other (Bruneel et al. 2010; Kaymaz and Eryiğit 2011).

In CIS countries the majority of HR managers play a minor role in business (Croucher 2010). In particular, HRM specialists have a more functional approach and focus more on obtaining, hiring, disciplining and retaining workers. Additionally, widespread scarcity of resources for personal use and a strong communist bureaucratic apparatus made people search for alternative ways of gaining resources or achieving desirable goals and, thus, the role of personal connections increased. Eventually, this led to a rather widespread practice of *blat*, which is defined as the use of personal connections to evade formal bureaucracy. *Blat* is mostly dominant in state and indigenous companies and is used in recruiting, retaining and promoting the 'right' people to the right positions in the company (Wedel 2003).

We see that the adaptation of HRM practices in the CIS context, from one perspective, may serve as a knowledge transfer mechanism that definitely leads to the rise of CIS markets, promotes their growth and pushes the economic, political and social development of CIS countries to be more integrated with Europe. On the other hand, it may be limited by the existing barriers and problems in the HRM area, which need to be identified, noted and overcome in order to help both CIS and European countries to be more consolidated.

Context-related challenges and barriers for European practice adaptation: Current trends and future perspectives

Belarus

Belarus is an Eastern European country, located at the western border of Russia and formerly part of the Soviet Union. It declared independence in 1991 after the dissolution of the USSR. The Belarusian economy largely depends on its ties and links with Russia because of the strong trade and political partnership between the two countries. The overwhelming majority of Belarusian enterprises are (explicitly or implicitly) state-owned, with CEOs appointed by the state. The system of 'ideological control' in enterprises has grown much stronger in recent years, which reflects in HRM policies, which mostly aim to be operational and short term with quite low integration into business (Carraher and Carraher 2006).

Belarus is the only European country with obligatory placement after graduation, which means there are limited opportunities and incentives (Carraher and Carraher 2006; Latukha 2016). Recruitment in Belarus is mostly based on informal connections and networking (HR managers generally refute this statement) (Danilovich and Croucher 2015). Due to the fact that some Belarusian companies are regulated by the government, training provision for the employed workforce has been left, for the most part, in the hands of enterprise management, with governmental and presidential structures controlling only the fulfilment of minimal requirements. This has recently resulted in state-controlled companies shrinking their training budgets to minimal levels and private companies abandoning training altogether to cut costs. Having Soviet heritage, meaning a weak focus on business development, some Belarusian companies still have a lack of business knowledge and language skills, which can explain peculiarities of the training and development system in Belarus (Carraher and Carraher 2006).

Employers are unwilling to support those who engage in full-time study and prefer to conduct in-house training (Danilovich and Croucher 2015), which in many instances brings employees very little or no benefit in terms of wage growth and no visible career progression. Rather than involving employees positively, there has been evidence of training being used as a disciplinary tool (Carraher and Carraher 2006). No company viewed training as a strategic management concern, which, combined with a cost-saving motive, resulted in the prevalence of a semi-informal mode of training: mentoring schemes, which may superficially appear to demonstrate a loosening of the Soviet-style state system of control but are in fact a pragmatic response that leaves some machinery used at less than full capacity (Danilovich and Croucher 2015).

However, European trends in HRM also influence Belarusian firms. The first HR standard for the country, based on an HRM international standard that consists of a balanced scorecard system, was developed in 2015. It includes all the functions of the HR department grouped according to each respective direction: recruitment, adaptation, training and personnel development, motivation, corporate culture, evaluation, development and HRM administration.

Belarus has an annual conference called 'HR-brand Award': awards are given to companies who have performed well in terms of their reputation as a future employer. This ceremony also represents a platform on which to share relevant ideas and projects in the field of HRM. The companies who receive an award simultaneously get recognition of their success in the business community as well as among experts, colleagues, applicants and clients. Each year the 'HR-brand Award' has a newly appointed jury, which gives the event at a high level of professionalism. While choosing the winners, the jury is guided by the following principles: relevance (for the company and the market), methods of implementation (modernity and optimality of selected tools) and efficiency (for business and target audience). The developing conference attracts new participants who in turn are motivated to improve HRM practices and, thus, raises the level of HRM standards in the country.

According to some studies (Carraher and Carraher 2006; Latukha 2016), conducted in several Belarusian companies, the labour market's lack of innovative HRM practices, which are more common in European countries, is the reason some problems may occur. First of all, managers are governmentally restricted concerning the number of benefits they can distribute among their employees. This leads to an inability to stimulate employees' performances through financial incentives. A very common way of hiring employees, for Belarusian companies, is through official job centres, though this method is mostly for low-skilled employees and the allocation of university graduates for internships, who rarely continue their career path at the company to which they have been allocated. Furthermore, recruitment is based on personal connections and relations, which leads to a significant loss of human resource potential (Latukha, 2016). This results in the problem of people who are much more suitable for a job, but are not successful in their application, not finding a way to apply their professional competencies in practice.

Ukraine

As we observed before using the case of Belarus, HRM in CIS countries, Ukraine among them, remains understudied in contemporary literature. Most of the scholars who focus on this particular region identify the heritage of the Soviet Union as a factor that determines the peculiarities of local HRM systems in the most significant way (Vaiman and Holden 2011). In particular, these systems are claimed to be characterised by under-investment in human capital (Alas and Svetlik 2004), poor development of business education in the region and, consequently, a shortage of managers who possess the required managerial competences (Vaiman and Holden 2011); there is an unwillingness among managers to involve their subordinates in decision-making processes and managers perceive young specialists' proactivity as a threat to their own status and authority (Skuza et al. 2015). All in all, this creates a reactive approach in HRM and an orientation towards the short term, where HRM practices are not linked with an organisational strategy.

It is easy to distinguish between two approaches to HRM that have predominated in Ukraine during different periods: Soviet and post-Soviet. The first approach treated human resources as a source of additional cost for the firm rather than a source of competitive advantage (Fey et al. 1999). According to Gurkov et al. (2012), this model first emerged in Russia in the 1970s and later expanded to most Eastern Europe countries (Gurkov et al. 2012). Its core characteristics were: maintenance of zero-level unemployment due to excessive employment creation by the government; low differentiation of salaries with an emphasis on a basic salary; and an active use of non-financial rewards. Dirani et al. (2015) notice that for companies of that period it was not typical to have any kind of strategy with respect to HRM; moreover, the duties of HRM specialists were traditionally limited to paperwork (Dirani et al. 2015).

Despite being very close to CEE countries in its early-1990s HRM-related development, Ukraine did not follow the general trends of the region in later periods. While some European countries, especially the former Czechoslovakia, Hungary and Poland, received huge investments from foreign companies and adopted a West European approach to managing people (Child and Czegledy 1996), Ukraine resembled Russia, more than any other country, in terms of its HRM systems' evolutionary path. The post-Soviet approach to HRM formed in the 2000s, when employment relationships were finally legitimised and new psychological contracts between workers and managers were settled. HRM departments did not significantly differ in terms of structure and tasks in companies with a different competitiveness level and development strategy; at the same time, non-monetary motivation techniques remain underdeveloped (Talaylo 2010). The labour market faced an increasing shortage of highly skilled workers, mostly due to a decrease in the quality of education and a mass brain drain phenomena (Fey et al. 1999). According to Lazorenko (2008), practices that local managers use for managing employees vary depending on the size of the company they work in. For big companies, an autocratic leadership style is typical: managers tend to make decisions on their own without consulting employees and they provide tasks for employees in the form of indisputable orders (Lazorenko 2008). Managers of medium-sized and small businesses, on the contrary, are mostly characterised by a democratic leadership style. An analysis of companies with different ownership structures showed that private entities in Ukraine have more resources for building efficient motivation programmes; at the same time, workers of such companies are less protected with respect to job security compared to those employed by a state-owned company.

Dorofeeva (2012) points out some current problems existing in Ukrainian organisations that substantially influence HRM systems. These are, for example: a mismatch between the organisational structure of companies and their strategic goals and needs; outdated labour-regulating documentation or its complete absence; inefficient motivation systems; and underdevelopment of control systems. Talaylo (2010) emphasises the prevalence of negative-based motivation techniques, e.g. threats, reprimands, penalties, over positive-based approaches (Talaylo 2010). Additionally, Croucher (2010) finds that due to limited business studies on both the country context and language barriers, headquarters of foreign MNCs have significant control over subsidiaries in Ukraine. Thus, they select HRM practices that are specific to the particular subsidiary and track the adaptation process of those practices (Croucher 2010). The author highlights that, among other HRM practices, Ukrainian companies focus on selection methods and have a combination of financial and psychological approaches to motivation. Novitskaya and Davione (2011) find subsidiaries that are rather more autonomous from headquarters' control had the lowest levels of adaptation of HRM practices and were more exposed to national context effects (Novitskaya and Davoine 2011). Companies in which HRM practices were adapted with the assistance of local experts had fewer difficulties with the integration of practices.

A number of researchers (Croucher 2010; Novitskaya and Davoine 2011) highlight the following most common problems, which exist in the majority of companies with Ukrainian origin: a mismatch between the companies' goals and vision and its organisational structure; an absence of modern methods of HRM; an absence of a proper motivational system and performance appraisal system; and the presence of negative motivational methods, such as penalties and threats, which eliminate any possibility of the development of employees' loyalty to a company.

All in all, as in most of the other CIS countries, Ukraine lags behind in its level of HRM development; most companies do not have any opportunity to be competitive due to the absence of proper motivational tools and incentives. This is why adaption to modern HRM practices is an issue of severe necessity and needs to be solved in order to increase productivity.

Russia

Among the CIS states, Russia has received special attention from scholars. Due to Russia's vast natural resources, a large, well-educated population, various business opportunities and the availability of any kind of business, the country is very attractive for different kinds of foreign companies, which means more room for HRM experience and its adaptation. According to Fey et al. (1999), traditionally the Russian attitude towards HRM was: employees were treated as a cost rather than a useful resource; education was considered to be the acquisition of fundamental knowledge rather than the development of skills; limited career progression decreased incentives to work hard; and limited attention was given to motivating employees. As in other CIS countries, the Russian government put a strong emphasis on attracting FDI and, hence, foreign MNCs (Fey and Denison 2003).

Some authors have studied the effects of US and European HRM practices on firms' performance in Russia on the use of major influencing factors such as internal communication, knowledge transfer, employee motivation, training, and job security and so on, and have analysed the adaptability of European HRM (Fey et al. 2000, 2003, 2009; Björkman et al. 2000, 2007). Several works emphasise cultural aspects, considering them as a distinct branch of corporate external environments that came with the managerial tradition of the Soviet organisational system, e.g. strong collectivism, group orientation instead of an individual approach (Fey and Denison 2003), low integration of top management in the development and implementation of an HRM system and a limited stock of executives and HR managers in the labour market in the transition period (Bjoerkman and Ehrnrooth 2000).

Among other barriers is the historically rooted confidentiality, which hinders interactions and coordination between headquarters and subsidiaries (Fey et al. 2000). Attempts to transfer management concepts to Russia that do not take into account Russian managers' values have little chance of success. Previous studies proved the importance of HRM in Russia (Puffer 1993; Fey et al. 1999; Fey at al. 2000) and, compared with HRM practices in other CIS countries, we may see nowadays less of a gap in HRM knowledge in both Russian companies and subsidiaries of European companies operating in the Russian market. The reason is linked to the faster development of the Russian economy, when compared to the economies of Ukraine and Belarus, attracting more FDI from European companies. It is important to mention that in the past and still to a much lesser extent now, many Russian companies have had authoritarian and bureaucratic leadership styles that have limited the responsibility for decision-making, limited employee involvement in decision-making processes. Russian companies have thus been oriented to short-term rather than long-term thinking, affecting the strategic orientation in organisational development, have had a slow rate of innovation and limited initiative taking (Skuza et al. 2013). This can be explained by past experience during Soviet times when managerial education was not of high priority (Holden and Vaiman 2013). Some experts note that most Russians today still lack high-class business experience, which in part may be explained by the relatively young age of Russian business culture and the educational system (Fey 2008; Puffer and McCarthy 2011; Fey and Shekshnia 2011).

Some researchers discuss the key influences on MNC's HRM practices in their foreign branches and identified the following: host country effects, country-of-origin effects, dominance effects and pressures for international integration (Edwards et al. 2010). Novitskaya (2016) discusses host and home country effects during the adaptation of European management practices to Russian and Ukrainian contexts, among them are: transferral of HRM practices from headquarters to subsidiary, management style, control, task fragmentation, delegation, employee discretion, employer–employee interdependence, trade unions and worker–manager separation (Novitskaya 2016). Based on this we can argue that HRM adaptation should happen with the proper monitoring of both host country and country-of-origin effects.

Conclusion

The differences between CIS (illustrated here by Ukraine, Belarus and Russia) and European countries in the HRM area are presented in Table 19.1, which shows the possible challenges in implementing European HRM practices in the CIS context.

We can conclude that, today, HRM practices in CIS countries are in transition from being Soviet-style to European in nature. The major 'providers' of these practices are European MNCs, which, on the one hand, transfer knowledge to CIS countries and, on the other, meet context-related challenges including historical development, norms, traditions, cultures and behaviour. The barriers to European HRM practice adaptation can be divided into three areas: traditional barriers, such as bureaucracy and an unstable political and economic situation; specific post-Soviet barriers – language problems, lack of business education and orientation, authoritarian management style and low integration to global economy; and environmental barriers – aging population, low rate of knowledge transfer and readiness for change in CIS countries.

Our discussion contributes to the previously described factors of adaptation of HRM practices to other contexts (Björkman and Ehrnrooth 2000; Fey and Denison 2003, Novitskaya 2016). By providing analysis of HRM practices in Ukraine, Belarus and Russia we extend the knowledge of HRM in CIS countries, which confirms the former roles of Soviet management practices, organisational culture and norms that are rather strongly rooted in the minds and practices of both managers and employees.

Adaptation of European HRM practices and transition from Soviet management thinking has led to various understandings of HRM practices among managers and may lead to the improper application of those practices. We argue that the specifics of HRM in Belarus, Russia and Ukraine has logically resulted from their Soviet past while some of the practices are a natural response to the economic and political situation in each country. As for upcoming trends

Table 19.1 Comparison between CIS and European HRM practices

Dimension	CIS context	European companies
Approach	Reactive approach that supports more operational and short-term orientation and perspective	Systematic and proactive approach to HRM; building functions based on the strategy used for long-term motivation system
Aim	HRM practice realisation and adaptation of European experience	To contribute to organisational success and provide new innovative approaches to HRM
HRM as a system	Attempts to build HRM system embracing different HRM practices	Interconnection between HRM practices allowing HRM to act as a system
Strategic orientation of HRM	Low integration with business strategy (Russia is an exception because of its more sophisticated experience compared with Belarus and Ukraine)	HRM is integrated in a firm's business strategy
Perception of employees	Cost and investment, human resources for short-term realisation of operational plans and tasks	Investment, human capital for strategic organisational development
Recruitment	Use of personal network, based on professional expertise, sometimes informal	Formal, standardised, based on professional competence
Career development	Depending on position, sometimes informal, based on performance results and usually exists in MNC	Act as a system, linked with training and development, based on performance results
Training and development	Lack of business knowledge and language skills In Russian companies greater attention to training and development compared to Ukrainian and Belarusian firms	Standardisation of training and development programmes, focus on mentoring, feedback, communication and development sessions
Performance management	Formal, based on blurred criteria and sometimes doesn't rely on performance results	Based on feedback and development discussions, performance linked to KPIs
Motivation	Based on short-term tasks, sometimes linked to a position, not competences or results, financial	Based on long-term strategic goals, linked to performance, supporting loyalty and involvement

Source: Developed by the author.

that will form Ukrainian and Belarusian labour markets and, consequently, HRM practices adopted by companies, the most important ones will be a high unemployment rate; an increasing popularity of freelance, remote work and shadow employment (Carraher and Carraher 2006; Novitskaya 2016); a change in the characteristics that companies will require from candidates; and an increase of the minimum salary rate, which will negatively affect small and medium-sized businesses. As for Russia, despite the fact that in many Russian companies HRM is considered a functional area, some of these organisations are now at the stage of transition from a functional approach to one that values partnership with HR departments. The transition is a particularly difficult process, but market trends have forced a move in this direction. The reasons are very similar to those that have led to the surge in interest in HRM: demographic crisis, increasing demand for workers, aging skilled employees, globalisation and inevitable competition with European companies that have more developed HRM practices. We argue that HRM in Russian companies is a step ahead of other CIS countries due to faster economic development and integration with the global environment that in many cases, today, are reflected in well-established and sometimes innovative HRM approaches in Russian companies. But the attitude towards HR practitioners as business partners is still an agenda that can be realised with the help of the adaptation of European HRM practices, especially in Belarus and Ukraine.

References

Aghazadeh, S. (2003), 'The future of human resource management', *Work Study*, vol. 52, no. 4, pp. 201–207.

Alas, R. and Svetlik, I. (2004), 'Estonia and Slovenia: Building modern HRM using a dualist approach', in C. Brewster, W. Mayrhofer and M. Morley (eds), *Human Resource Management in Europe: Evidence of Convergence?* Elsevier, pp. 353–384.

Altman, M. (2009), 'The transition process from alternative theoretical prisms', *International Journal of Social Economics*, vol.36, no.7, pp. 716–742.

Björkman, I. and Ehrnrooth, M. (2000), 'HRM in Western subsidiaries in Russia and Poland', *Journal of East-West Business*, vol. 5, no. 3, pp. 63–79.

Björkman, I., Fey, C. and Park, H (2007), 'Institutional theory and MNC subsidiary HRM practices: Evidence from a three-country study', *Journal of International Business Studies*, vol. 38, pp. 430–446.

Bruneel, J., D'Este, P. and Salter, A. (2010), 'Investigating the factors that diminish the barriers to university–industry collaboration', *Research policy*, vol. 39, no. 7, pp. 858–868.

Buck, T., Filatotchev, I., Demina, N. and Wright, M. (2003), 'Insider ownership, human resource strategies and performance in a transition economy', *Journal of International Business Studies*, vol. 34, no. 6, pp. 530–549.

Carraher, S.M. and Carraher, S.C. (2006), 'Human resource issues among SMEs in Eastern Europe: A 30 month study in Belarus, Poland, and Ukraine', *International Journal of Entrepreneurship*, vol. 10, p. 97.

Child, J. and Czegledy, A. (1996), 'Managerial learning in the transformation of Eastern Europe: Some key issues', *Organization Studies*, vol. 17, no. 2, pp. 167–179.

Croucher, R. (2010), 'Employee involvement in Ukrainian companies', *International Journal of Human Resource Management*, vol. 21, no. 14, pp. 2659–2676.

Danilovich, H. and Croucher, R. (2015), 'Investment in personnel and FDI in Belarusian companies', *International Business Review*, vol. 24, pp. 966–971.

Dirani, K., Ardichvili, A., Cseh, M. and Zavyalova, E. (2015), 'Human resource management in Russia, Central and Eastern Europe', *Handbook of Human Resource Management in Emerging Markets*. Cheltenham, UK, Edward Elgar, pp. 357–371.

Dorofeeva, A. (2012), 'Osobennosti organizacionnogo povedeniya personala promishlennih predpriyatii i osnovnie napravleniya ego regulirovaniya'. http://dspace.nbuv.gov.ua/bitstream/handle/123456789/49454/ST45-34-_59-60.pdf?sequence=1 (accessed 28 March 2018).

Edwards, T., Edwards, P., Ferner, A., Marginson, P. and Tregaskis, O. (2010), 'Multinational companies and the diffusion of employment practices from outside the country of origin explaining variation across firms', *Management International Review*, vol. 50, no. 5, pp. 613–634.

Farndale, E., Scullion, H. and Sparrow, P. (2010), 'The role of the corporate HR function in global talent management', *Journal of World Business*, vol. 45, pp. 161–168.

Fey, C. (2008), 'Overcoming a leader's greatest challenge: Involving employees in firms in Russia', *Organizational Dynamics*, vol. 37, no. 3, pp. 254–265.

Fey, C., Björkman, I. and Pavlovskya, A. (2000), 'The effect of human resource management practices on firm performance in Russia', *International Journal of Human Resource Management*, vol. 11, no. 1, pp. 1–18.

Fey, C. and Denison, D.R. (2003), 'Organizational culture and effectiveness: Can American theory be applied in Russia?', *Organization Science*, vol. 14, no. 6, pp. 686–706.

Fey, C., Engstrom, P. and Björkman, I. (1999), 'Effective human resource management practices for foreign firms in Russia', *Organizational Dynamics*, vol. 1, no. 28, pp. 69–79.

Fey, C., Morgulis-Yakushev, S., Park, H. and Björkman, I. (2009), 'Opening the black box of the relationship between HRM practices and firm performance: A comparison of MNE subsidiaries in the USA, Finland, and Russia', *Journal of International Business Studies*, vol. 40, pp. 690–712.

Fey, C. and Shekshnia, S. (2011), 'The key commandments for doing business in Russia', *Organizational Dynamics*, vol. 40, no. 1, pp. 57–66.

Gilbert, G.R. and Von Glinow, M.A. (2015), 'National context and organizational performance across three sectors', *Cross Cultural Management*, vol. 22, no. 3, pp. 356–378.

Gurkov, I. and Zelenova O. (2012), 'Human resource management in Russian companies', *International Studies of Management and Organization*, vol. 41, no. 4, pp. 66–80.

Gurkov, I., Zelenova, O. and Saidov, Z. (2012), 'Mutation of HRM practices in Russia: An application of CRANET methodology', *International Journal of Human Resource Management*, vol. 23, pp. 1289–1302.

Holden, N. and Vaiman, V. (2013), 'Talent management in Russia: Not so much war for talent as wariness of talent', *Critical Perspectives on International Business*, vol. 9, no. 1/2, pp. 129–146.

Kaymaz, K. and Eryiğit, K.Y (2011), 'Determining factors hindering university–industry collaboration: An analysis from the perspective of academicians in the context of Entrepreneurial Science Paradigm', *International Journal of Social Inquiry*, vol. 4, no. 1, pp. 185–213.

Latukha, M. (2016), *Talent Management in Emerging Market Firms: Global strategies and local challenges*, UK, Palgrave Macmillan.

Lazorenko, L. (2008), 'Osobennosti upravleniya personalom v kommercheskih organizaciyah Ukraini', (accessed 11 March 2018).

Lee, J., Baimukhamedova, G. and Akhmetova, S. (2010), 'Foreign direct investment, exchange rate, and their roles in economic growth of developing countries: Empirical evidence from Kazakhstan', *Journal of International Business Research*, vol. 9, no. 2, pp. 75–90.

Lengnick-Hall, M.L., Lengnick-Hall, C.A., Andrade, L.S. and Drake, B. (2009), 'Strategic human resource management: The evolution of the field', *Human Resource Management Review*, vol. 19, pp. 64–85.

Liu, W. (2004), 'The cross-national transfer of HRM practices in MNCs: An integrative research model', *International Journal of Manpower*, vol. 25, no. 6, pp. 500–517.

May, R., Bormann Young, C. and Ledgerwood, D. (1998), 'Lessons from Russian human resource management experience', *European Management Journal*, vol. 16 no. 4, pp. 447–459.

Mills, A. (1998), 'Contextual influences on human resource management in the Czech Republic', *Personnel Review*, vol. 27, no. 3, pp. 177–99.

Minbaeva, D., Hutchings, K. and Thomson, B.S. (2007), 'Hybrid human resource management in post-Soviet Kazakhstan', *European Journal of International Management*, vol. 1 no. 4, pp. 350–371.

Mockler, R.J., Chao, C. and Dologite, D.G. (1996), 'A comparative study of business education programs in China and Russia', *Journal of Teaching in International Business*, vol. 8, no. 2, pp. 19–39.

Myloni, B., Harzing, A.K. and Mirza, H. (2004), 'Host country specific factors and the transfer of human resource management practices in multinational companies', *International Journal of Manpower*, vol. 25, no. 6, pp. 518–534.

Newman, K.L. and Nollen, S.D. (1996), 'The fit between management practices and national culture', *Journal of International Business Studies*, vol. 27, no. 4, pp. 753–779.

Novitskaya, O. (2016), 'Context effects in the transfer of HRM practices from headquarters of Western MNCs to their Ukrainian subsidiaries', doctoral dissertation, University of Fribourg. http://doc.rero.ch/record/277545/files/NovitskayaO.pdf (accessed 11 March 2018).

Novitskaya, O. and Davoine, E. (2011), 'Transfer Western HR-practices in Ukraine', *Personal Management*, vol. 9, no. 216, pp. 61–65.

Puffer, S.M. (1993), 'Three factors affecting reward allocations in the former USSR', *Research in Personnel and Human Resource Management*, vol. 3, pp. 279–298.

Puffer, S.M. and McCarthy, D.J. (2011), 'Two decades of Russian business and management research: An institutional theory perspective', *Academy of Management Perspectives*, vol. 25, pp. 21–36.

Rosenzweig, P.M. and Nohria, N. (1994), 'Influences on HRM practices in multinational corporations', *Journal of International Business Studies*, vol. 25, n. 2, pp. 229–251.

Schuler, R.S., Budhwar, P.S. and Florkowski, G.W. (2002), 'International human resource management: Review and critique', *International Journal of Management Reviews*, vol. 4, no. 1, pp. 41–70.

Schuler, R.S., Jackson, S.E. and Tarique, I. (2011), 'Global talent management and global talent challenges: Strategic opportunities for IHRM', *Journal of World Business*, vol. 46, pp. 506–516.

Shen, J. (2005), 'Towards a generic international human resource management (IHRM) model', *Journal of Organizational Transformation and Social Change*, vol. 2, no. 2, pp. 83–102.

Skuza, A., McDonnell, A. and Scullion, H. (2015), 'Talent management in the emerging markets', in F. Horwitz and P. Budhwar (eds), *Handbook of Human Resource Management in Emerging Markets*, Cheltenham, UK and Northampton, MA, Edward Elgar, pp. 225–243.

Skuza, A., Scullon, H. and McDonnel, A. (2013), 'An analysis of the talent management challenges in a post-communist country: The case of Poland', *International Journal of Human Resource Management*, vol. 24, no. 3, pp. 453–470.

Talaylo, E. (2010), 'Osobennosti processa motivatcii na predpriyatiyah Ukraini i za rubejhom' (accessed 11 March 2018).

Vaiman, V. and Holden, N. (2011), 'Talent management perplexing landscape in Central and Eastern Europe', in H. Scullion and D. Collings (eds), *Global Talent Management*, London, Routledge, pp. 178–193.

Vlachoutsicos, C. and Lawrence, P.R. (1990), 'What we don't know about Soviet management', *Harvard Business Review*, Nov–Dec, pp. 4–11.

Wedel, J.R. (2003), 'Clans, cliques and captured states: Rethinking "transition" in Central and Eastern Europe and the former Soviet Union', *Journal of International Development*, vol. 15, pp. 427–440.

Zupan, N. and Kase, R. (2005), 'Strategic human resource management in European transition economies: Building a conceptual model on the case of Slovenia', *International Journal of Human Resource Management*, vol. 16, no. 6, pp. 882–906.

PART F

Functional and sectorial perspectives

20

EUROPEAN BUSINESS MARKETING

Elfriede Penz and Barbara Stöttinger

Introduction

The European Union (EU) with its current 28 member states and over 510 million inhabitants offers tremendous market opportunities for marketers around the globe. Among the different trading blocs that were formed in recent history, the EU has definitely reached the most profound regional integration encompassing economic, political and social dimensions. These achievements have spurred practitioners and researchers to discuss pan-European marketing as opposed to country-by-country marketing strategies (Sciglimpaglia and Saghafi 2004).

Companies operating in Europe nonetheless still face a complex international marketing environment. Despite homogenisation efforts within the EU and its institutions, especially with regard to legal and regulatory conditions, considerable economic, social and cultural differences exist among the member states and call for differentiated rather than standardised marketing approaches (Schlegelmilch et al. 2012; Suder 2011). In essence, the EU is far from being a single domestic market for European firms or a single foreign market for non-European companies (Harris and McDonald 2004).

Issues and developments related to marketing in the EU are not only of interest to the business sector, but have attracted ripples of interest in the research community over the years (Apfelthaler 2015). While the practical implications of unified marketing approaches across the EU are huge, research and particularly robust answers to standardisation vs. adaptation requirements for marketing strategies grounded in solid research remain limited.

For our contribution, we have set the following objectives: (1) we aim to embed European marketing in a general framework in order to delineate it from other approaches such as international, global or regional marketing. As has been quite frequently asserted, standardised European marketing strategies are still impeded by the multitude of differences in the institutional environments across EU countries. To evaluate the likelihood that this might change, we (2) highlight the factors of convergence and divergence that are relevant when designing standardised marketing strategies. While legal and economic harmonisation is well on its way (e.g. Aistrich et al. 2006), considerable social and cultural differences remain across the EU (e.g. Harris and McDonald 2004). These differences strongly affect European consumer behaviour as an underlying dimension in business-to-consumer marketing. Therefore, (3) we highlight different facets of European consumer behaviour as important input to pan-European marketing strategies. Last but not least, (4) the status of European marketing strategies is evaluated and implications for their future development within the EU are investigated. While our contribution will not provide a conclusion to the ongoing discussion of standardising marketing strategies across the EU, we aim to achieve a status update and provide a direction for future developments related to this important issue.

Theoretical framework

In categorising the various marketing approaches according to their reach and underlying rationale, different types of marketing strategies have emerged: domestic (oriented exclusively on the home market), international (adapting marketing strategies to the specific characteristics of each market in the country portfolio), regional (marketing strategies adapted to specific regions) and global marketing approaches (a common strategy for the global level as a whole) (e.g. Malhotra et al. 1998, Harris and McDonald 2004). European marketing would reside in either international or regional marketing depending on the degree of standardisation (Harris and McDonald 2004; Figure 20.1).

In this framework, European marketing has a position that exceeds the domestic level, but does not achieve the global level. Global marketing is primarily concerned with developing a marketing programme for the global market, whereby simultaneous coordination and integration of marketing activities is key (Keegan and Green 2013). European marketing may therefore be positioned as either international or regional marketing, as business is done in two or more countries (Bradley 2005). From that perspective, European marketing is a type of international marketing with certain similarities and differences across legal, economic, social and cultural aspects (Harris and McDonald 2004).

Another way of looking at European marketing is to conceptualise it as regional. Regional marketing can be defined by two aspects: (i) the territorial aspect as an area, whose boundaries can rarely be delineated, but instead, are dependent on the purpose for defining the region as such; (ii) homogeneity that unites a region inwardly, while differentiating it outwardly from other regions. Commonalities can be based on political aspects (e.g. Sbragia 2008), or even on historical development (Herrschel 2009).

Perhaps the EU can be seen as a target for pan-European marketing strategies, as it represents a distinct geographic region or segment that differs from other geographic regions. The central concept is segmentation, using national borders as a criterion (cf. Suder 2011).

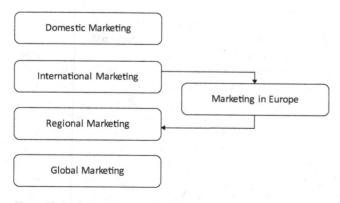

Figure 20.1 Categorising marketing approaches
Source: Based on Harris and McDonald (2004).

In contrast, global marketing treats the world as one segment while international/regional marketing sees the world as distinct country products/markets. Factors supporting the global view can be reduced to two complementary arguments: customer convergence ('the global [or Euro] consumer') and global product efficiencies ('the global [or Euro] product'). Proponents of the global view would imply that the European 'question' is either irrelevant or, at best, a transition from a national to a global approach (Halliburton and Hunerberg 2004).

Clear categorisation of European marketing as either international or regional would be premature at this time. Some researchers point to significant progress towards a more pan-European marketing strategy (Epuran and Tescasiu 2015; Suder 2011) and the emergence of pan-European brands (Eurobrands) (Sciglimpaglia and Saghafi 2004). However, a number of major obstacles to integration, such as deep-rooted consumer preferences, different retail systems, continuing national subsidies and tax differences persist (e.g. Schlegelmilch et al. 2012; Halliburton and Hunerberg 1993, 2004). For example, food products still show persistent national traditions (Steenkamp 2001). Heterogeneity therefore remains prevalent, also given recent political developments (e.g. Brexit, nationalistic tendencies in several markets) (Suder 2011, 2016).

Environment of European business marketing

Every company that conducts business with or in the EU is strongly affected by the activities of EU institutions (Harris and McDonald 2004). In the UK, the job of disentangling these influences is happening at this very moment (Suder 2011). The EU has developed both an advanced regional set of competitive rules and a model of supranational governance through its institutions in which regulatory decisions on competition rest with the EU Commission (McGowan 1998).

For marketers considering an entry strategy into a country or region, cultural and structural issues are commonly evaluated as a first step to assessing market opportunities. At least from a perceptual point of view, the image of the EU has improved recently ('totally positive towards EU': 34% in early 2016, 40% in early 2017). Optimism with regard to the EU has been increasing since late 2016 ('totally optimistic about EU': 50% for 2016 as a whole, 56% in early 2017; Directorate-General for Communication 2017).

An understanding of governmental policy and the process by which it is created is central to effective marketing decisions. Policies that go beyond the economic scope of the EU have been instated to reduce transaction costs and other barriers to business exchange. Thus, the integration afforded by the European multilateral trade agreement represents an enormous opportunity for marketers. Essentially, firms are regulated by the EU and also the member states in which they operate (Middlement 1995). For instance, on a business level, companies must make strategic decisions on operational issues such as pricing, branding and other marketing and business matters (Harris and McDonald 2004). The marketing infrastructure across EU markets displays similarities as to retail structures and media, advertising and distribution networks (Wierenga et al. 1996). Yet, differences, regarding food safety, for instance, are present among EU member states. The majority of EU citizens take quality, price and origin into consideration when buying food, but only a minority are interested in brand information. Overall, on average, more than half of respondents regard quality as a very important consideration. Variation in levels of agreement is high. For instance, respondents in Malta (86%) and Cyprus (84%) consider quality a priority. In contrast, in the Netherlands (52%) and Austria (53%), only a small majority see quality as very important (European Commission 2012).

At the macroeconomic level, the EU countries still display differences in income levels, employment statistics, consumer expenditure and patterns of consumption (Wierenga et al. 1996). Comparing household net adjusted disposable income (i.e., average amount of money a household earns per year, after taxes) in 2015, Latvia had the lowest (13,655 USD) and Luxembourg the highest income (~40,914 USD) (OECD 2017). Regarding unemployment rates, in May 2017 the Czech Republic had the lowest (3.0%) and Greece the highest (22.5%) (World Bank 2017). The final household consumption expenditure per capita (constant 2010 USD) in 2016 was highest in Luxembourg (33,608 USD) and lowest in Bulgaria (5,087 USD). Also, patterns of consumption across member states varied. Household expenditure for food accounted for 12 per cent for the United Kingdom, Luxembourg and Germany but amounted to 37 per cent for Romania (2008); while in Bulgaria, Greece, Portugal and Romania recreation and culture accounted for 5 per cent and in the UK as much as 15 per cent (Eurostat 2017a; Figure 20.2).

Considerable differences are also prevalent in terms of family structures and decision-making processes (Wierenga et al. 1996). Household structures (i.e. number of people, Figure 20.3; share of married couples among families, Figure 20.4) differ across EU member states.

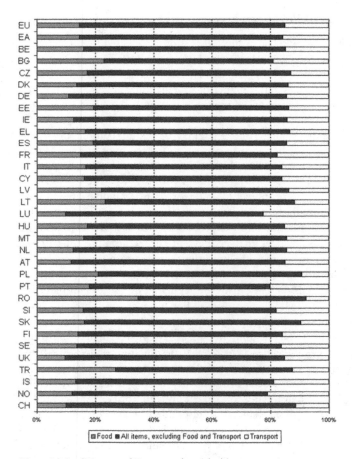

Figure 20.2 Patterns of European household consumption
Source: Eurostat (2017a).

The different decision-making processes and ways in which money is spent can be illustrated, for instance, by Hofstede's (2001) 'long-term vs. short-term orientation' dimension, which influences societies' levels of pragmatism and how they deal with challenges and change. The short-term-oriented Ireland scores 24, while rather long-term-oriented Bulgaria scores 69 (Hofstede 2001). Short-term orientation in a culture leads to more museum visits and sport

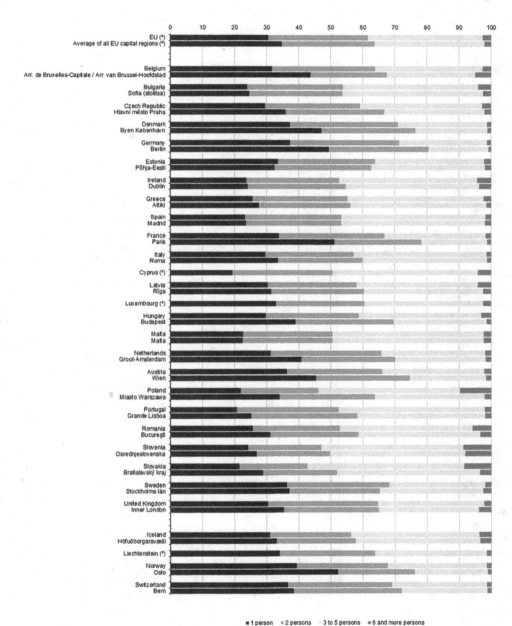

Figure 20.3 Distribution of occupants per dwelling in European capital regions
Source: Eurostat (2017b).

Share of married couples among all families, by NUTS level 3 region, 2011 (¹)
(% of all families)

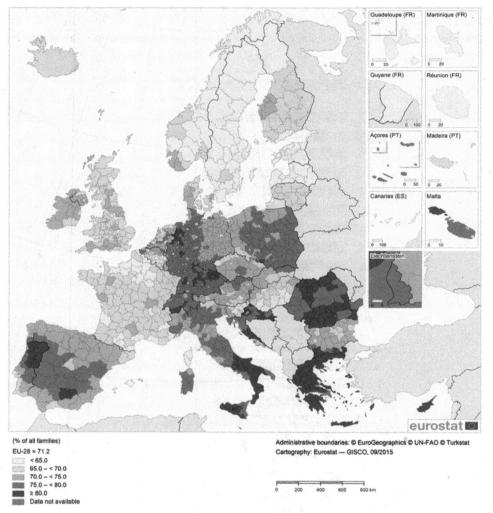

Figure 20.4 Share of married couples among all European families
Source: Eurostat (2017b).

activity while spending money on gardening and plants is related to long-term orientation (De Mooij 2010).

Substantial differences are evident in educational attainment among the EU-28 countries, e.g., between Scandinavia and CEE (in Romania less than 15 per cent are engaged in tertiary education while in Sweden it is over 35 per cent); as well as within countries, for example, among age groups (CIA Factbook 2017).

At the same time, there is some evidence that companies' increasingly 'European' approach, together with advances in European integration, have contributed to a growing similarity in buying habits and demands, and the creation of European country clusters exhibiting similar

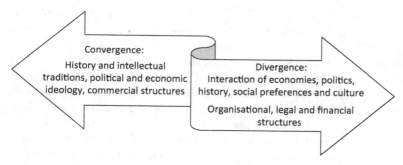

Figure 20.5 Drivers of European convergence vs. divergence
Source: Authors' own representation.

behaviour (Askegaard and Madsen 1998; Halliburton and Hunerberg 2004). In summary, the question of a regional European vs. an international, country-by-country marketing strategy is still open, even though attempts have been made to suggest the supremacy of one over the other (Diamantopoulos et al. 1995). Within the areas of business environment and consumer behaviour across the EU, there are converging factors as well as diverging aspects. Examining the state of divergence vs. convergence, a closer look provides further insights (Figure 20.5).

Convergence in the European business environment

Convergence is most advanced in the political and legal environment. Europe is considered a 'pivotal player in the global economic system as a market, a producer, an exporter and an investor – and is likely to remain so' (Johnson and Turner 2016, p. 4).[1] In order to remain a desirable place to do business, Europe needs to adjust to current issues, expressed by the EU's Europe 2020 Strategy (European Commission 2017). The challenges are expressed in five priority targets that are meant to spur growth in Europe and develop a competitive economy. The identified priorities include smart, sustainable and inclusive growth. The targets are employment, research and development (R&D), climate change and energy sustainability, education, and fighting poverty and social exclusion. Seven initiatives have resulted from this: Innovation Union, Youth on the Move, a digital agenda for Europe, Resource-efficient Europe, an industrial policy for the globalisation era, an agenda for new skills and jobs, and finally, the European platform against poverty (Johnson and Turner 2016).

Industrial areas, such as energy and transport, are subject primarily to the Single Market programme, with resulting Europe-wide competition. However, there are still industries such as defence and pharmaceuticals (Halliburton and Hunerberg 2004) where national regulations apply.

Overall, the economic structure is largely the same in Europe, with agriculture providing a low contribution to the economy (1.7%), industry a moderate contribution (25%) and services a high contribution (73.3%) (Johnson and Turner 2016). The member states are faced with similar domestic and international challenges, e.g., ageing populations, environmental issues related to energy supply insecurity and increased competition from emerging economies in Asia (Johnson and Turner 2016). Companies can benefit from the intra-European networks in various industries created by the institutional environment (Harris and McDonald 2004).

In terms of product regulations, the European Commission's proposals focus predominantly on physical aspects and package labelling. The two most important areas for regulation are technical harmonisation and the regulation of competition (Wierenga et al. 1996).

When it comes to pricing decisions, the removal of fiscal barriers, such as VAT and duties, is of key importance. The European Commission seeks to sustain fair (price) competition across Europe, which might be detrimental for national industries or customers. The EU does not seem to have a substantial effect on companies' profits, although economies of scale can be reaped, and prices thereby reduced (Harris and McDonald 2004). It was found that in many industries prices were converging across the member states, indicating that international markets were becoming more competitive. Nevertheless, in some industries (in particular in areas where large governmental interests are present, such as gas and electricity production and distribution) there was sparse evidence that markets had become more competitive. Those member states that have been members of the EU for a long time provided clearer evidence of greater competitiveness. This indicates that it takes time for companies to rationalise and react to the pressures that emerge from the progress towards free movement (Harris and McDonald 2004).

In terms of the distribution of goods throughout Europe, administrative barriers have been largely removed, with the aim of avoiding local quotas and allowing carriers to operate freely throughout the common market. Last but not least, the aim is to deregulate all modes of transport.

The EU has also instated regulations regarding advertising and promotion, which fosters homogenisation across markets, for instance, regulations regarding door-to-door sales and pan-European broadcasting (Wierenga et al. 1996).

Divergence in the European business environment

Divergence is evident in the interaction of economies, politics, history, social preferences and culture. Different organisational structures are visible in governments (organised along federal lines vs. centralised), and legal and financial structures. The size and role of the welfare state varies within Europe, showing different social protection expenditures as part of GDP (Johnson and Turner 2016).

From a business perspective, the divergence of EU member states can lead to tensions, for instance, in the form of (i) failed cross-border mergers or acquisitions, and (ii) tense or failed business negotiations. The clash of corporate cultures leads to a 70–90 per cent failure rate of M&As (BBC 2007; Christensen 2002). Particularly at risk are business negotiations between negotiators from individualist versus collectivist countries, also due to the negotiators' differing types of negative emotions experienced during the negotiations (Luomala et al. 2015). Hofstede et al. (2012) also emphasise the importance of agents in negotiations displaying culturally differentiated behaviour.

When looking at diverging trends, regionalism must still be considered despite institutional homogenisation at national and supranational levels (Harris and McDonald 2004). Regionalism and the distinct needs and cultures of both separate states and constituent parts of the EU have led to dramatic differences in outlook. Take Italy, for example, where northern Italians see themselves as distinctly different from their southern compatriots, leading to increased regional nationalism. The Lombard League has suggested that the country be broken into two, with the Lombard League state being based in Milan, Bologna, Florence and Turin – the 'Golden Belt' of northern Italy. (Harris and McDonald 2004). These regional forces prevent stronger standardisation within the business environment across EU countries.

Regions across Europe – the case of Central and Eastern Europe

Central and Eastern Europe (CEE) serves as a showcase, where converging and diverging trends are prevalent, displaying how companies are dealing with this in their marketing approach.

For that purpose, the business practices in the CEE region have attracted particular attention regarding standardisation of marketing strategies, as they entered the EU in the most recent accession wave in the early 2000s. What can be observed in a subset of EU countries sharing a great deal of similarities may also have implications for European marketing (Kirpalani et al. 2009). For example, packaging preferences in various regions differ. Consumers in the CEE favour flexible packaging, as opposed to rigid plastic, metal, glass, etc., which is preferred by consumers in Western Europe due to the need for on-the-go products (Euromonitor 2017). There is also a rise of shopping malls in CEE (including Russia and Turkey), while growth in Western Europe has stagnated due to a mature market. Shopping malls are popular as lifestyle destinations, which is accommodated by the rising middle class's increasing disposable income (Euromonitor 2016).

The CEE markets are similar, because these countries had a common political and economic system for many years, which influenced their societies in the same way. However, there is some heterogeneity in terms of consumers' values and preferences (Kirpalani et al. 2009).

Past empirical research highlights convergent as well as divergent tendencies across regions: greater integration into the EU provides the possibility for more standardised marketing strategies. Two-thirds of the exports of Slovenian firms are to the old 15-nation EU, in which domestic economies are stable and markets are relatively homogenous (Kirpalani et al. 2009).

A cross-cultural study in Poland and Romania recommended caution in using a regiocentric (regions that share economic, political, and/or cultural traits) marketing orientation in CEE. Although some commonalities can be observed within economic and social trends, the CEE region is culturally and economically too diversified. Differences are present even inside its sub-regions, for example, the Baltic countries of Latvia, Lithuania and Estonia (Kirpalani et al. 2009). With the shift towards a market economy, CEE countries have been increasingly exposed to modern advertising for such products as Bulgaria's Zagorka Beer, yet the ethical aspects of advertising lag behind Western standards (Kirpalani et al. 2009).

Taken collectively, although EU regulations have led to harmonisation in certain areas of advertising and communications (Okazaki et al. 2007), companies need to consider the differences in their target markets when promoting their products (Berns-Wright and Morgan 2002).

European consumer behaviour

The idea of consumers becoming more alike in their preferences, tastes and standards across regions and nations dates back to Levitt's (1983) seminal article on the globalisation of markets. Convergence in consumer behaviour should lead to standardisation of brands and products on a global scale. Europe-wide availability of similar media, increasing travel within the EU and trade liberalisation expose consumers to lifestyles and brands beyond their national context (Malhotra et al. 1998; Sciglimpaglia and Saghafi 2004; Paliwoda and Marinova 2007). Over time, a so-called Euroconsumer should emerge, a person who has a preference for European products and services and can be addressed by pan-European marketing initiatives (Wierenga et al. 1996). In reality, European institutions have done a lot to support legal harmonisation, rendering the 'Europroduct' within easier reach (Browning 1992, p. B1). Companies operating in the EU should be able to exploit these harmonising consumer preferences by developing and implementing pan-European marketing strategies (Aistrich et al. 2006; Halliburton and Hunerberg 1993).

On a general scale, empirical observations substantiate these normative contentions. What Andreasen (1990) refers to as cultural interpenetration is going on within the EU. Consumers are exposed to a huge variety of local and non-local (EU) products, they have access to media covering regions beyond their home country and are able to move location temporarily for work or study, enabled by programmes such as the EU Erasmus exchange (Cleveland and Laroche 2007). At the same time, substantial regional, country and local market differences prevail (Kaynak 2004).

When it comes to more fine-grained empirical research for convergence vs. idiosyncrasies in EU consumer behaviour, findings remain scarce, scattered and far from being conclusive. Some authors identified similarities in consumer behaviour (Askegaard and Madsen 1998), while others approach convergence from a product category perspective. Steenkamp et al. (1999), for example, pointed out that for many food products national preferences still dominate as represented through local brands. In addition, global companies, such as Coca-Cola, offer some variations in the amount of sugar and carbon dioxide to satisfy local tastes (Harris and McDonald 2004). Such modifications are also made at an EU country level. Usunier and Lee (2013) point out studies (e.g. Clements and Chne 1996) that observe converging consumer behaviour when it comes to wine. While having a stronger tradition in Southern Europe, availability, cultural exchanges and legal frameworks have shifted consumer preferences in Central and Northern Europe away from beer towards more wine.

These diverse findings raise more general questions, such as how consumers deal with the opposing forces of homogenisation vs. the persistence of localness in their consumption. Arnould and Thompson (2005, p. 875) suggest 'that consumption is a historically shaped mode of socio-cultural practice that emerges within the structures and ideological imperatives of dynamic marketplaces.' To operationalise and drill down specific aspects of convergence, Merz et al. (2008) postulate that when consumers across regions or countries share the same categorisations of consumption situations and product choices with fellow consumers in other countries, convergence can take place. If this is not the case, localness prevails.

Penz and Stöttinger (2015) investigated such consumption categorisations for different product categories. It contrasted consumer statements for symbolic vs. functional products (e.g. Ogden et al. 2004). The product category determines the extent to which consumers prefer pan-European products vs. national alternatives. Consumer durables that have a high symbolic value, such as cars, represent a product category where consumers are open to 'European' products and which would thus lend themselves to pan-European strategies. For convenience goods, such as beverages and food, consumers prefer a more personal relationship and thus national alternatives. Findings hold across age, education and nationality, which highlights the customer-driven potential for pan-European marketing strategies (Penz and Stöttinger 2015).

Taking these findings into account, there is still room for greater convergence across EU member states in terms of consumption patterns, values and needs. The often invoked 'Euroconsumer' who prefers European products and services (Apfelthaler 2015; Vandermerwe 1989) is still more of an imagined than actual phenomenon. This also pertains to standardised 'Europroducts' (Browning 1992).

Marketing strategies within Europe

The standardisation vs. adaptation of marketing strategies provides a managerial and research challenge. It can be assumed that standardised marketing strategies are a way to foster trends of convergence and reinforce 'Euromarketing' (Halliburton and Hunerberg 1993, 2004).

In past research, some authors highlight criteria that enable this choice to be made in a more grounded way. Diamantopoulos et al. (1995) point out that the degree of standardisation might possibly depend on the type of product and on the market environment. Specifically, adapting products through basic product platforms, meaningful reactions to legal, economic and cultural differences and the potential to maximise the spread between the price that can be charged in the market and the cost of differentiation are important drivers (Harris and McDonald 2004).

Other authors provide a process for developing European marketing strategies, answering the question of standardisation vs. adaptation along the way. The beginning of the practical process of formulating a European marketing strategy is to assess market conditions. The initial assessment involves screening markets to discover the potential of different countries (Harris and McDonald 2004). Chung (2005) added aspects such as growth rates, technological change creating new opportunities to sell, as well as demographic factors altering demand patterns. Harris and McDonald (2004) thus recommend starting with a small number of countries that are geographically and culturally proximate. Moreover, they suggest starting with simple marketing strategies and then – if successful – moving on to more complex plans. In essence, they relate standardised marketing strategies to a firm's knowledge level and its ability to rapidly adjust its plan to more complex market situations.

Halliburton and Hünerberg (2004) base the degree of standardisation vs. adaptation on a geographic segmentation approach. The most differentiated option would be treating every country separately, which they recommended for the beer market with its strong national idiosyncrasies. In the middleground, their approach would encompass clustering countries or regions that share similarities. Full standardisation would be possible in the case of transnational segments, which they see for certain business-to-business services or automobile brands. For example, BMW or Mercedes Benz aim to sell standardised cars to boost margins. BMW is successively reducing customisation options, e.g., even the i8 hybrid sports car – one of its most exclusive versions – offers only three types of package (Taylor and Preisinger 2014). Other authors also suggest geographic segmentation according to cultural clusters of countries or within/across countries by consumer needs or social and demographic groups (Hofstede et al. 1999).

In practical terms, marketers may refer to the work of market research multinationals, such as Experian (n.d.), which cluster consumers based on demographic data, consumer habits, motivation and feelings and not necessarily geographic location. One example of a convergent, transnational segments could be the group of European Youth. Christensen (2002) states that young Europeans are currently being raised in a multicultural environment, which translates into their travel behaviour, media use and the role communication technology plays in their lives. Young people share similar needs and wants regardless of where they are brought up in the EU, which allows standardised marketing approaches. Moreover, their interconnectedness makes them easy to address.

Baalbaki and Malhotra (1993) state that such transnational segments may also emerge by clustering customers based on their ethnic heritage. Such cultural subgroups exist in every European country. For instance, during Ramadan, certain ethnic communities exhibit specific trends in the use of mobile phones leading to increased traffic in online retail via mobile devices on Ramadan evenings (Criteo 2016).

Conclusion and discussion

In this chapter, our goal was to embed European marketing in a general framework, discuss aspects of convergence and divergence, which are especially reflected in EU consumer behaviour, and evaluate the current status of pan-European marketing strategies. What we experienced is that the discussion on pan-European marketing as a regional marketing approach is far from converging. Existing literature is abundant and examples of business practice even more so, yet no closure can be reached. While the political and legal developments and commercial structures suggest convergence in Europe, divergence results from cultural and social preferences and organisational, legal and financial structures in the environment. This is important to know when doing business in Europe since it forces businesses to constantly monitor regulations and market developments and adapt accordingly.

In addition, CEE regions in Europe have been pinpointed as good candidates for standardisation, which results from their common past. However, even these regions appear similar from the outside only, and more fine-grained environmental analyses point to cultural idiosyncrasies that should be considered in marketing approaches. To this end, some European consumer characteristics based on demographics, such as age ('youth') or income, are useful segmentation criteria when standardising the marketing mix. However, consumer values or identity should be more closely addressed as a basis for developing tailored marketing approaches.

Taken collectively, certain characteristics of Europe and the Single European Market seem to have received some attention in past research, such as the influence of political and legal frameworks on doing business in Europe, and the EU extension with particular focus on CEE. However, there is a lack of research on recent developments and attempts to develop a comprehensive framework that includes aspects of convergence and divergence in the environment. Linked to different industries, this would provide further insights. Finally, these theoretically substantiated frameworks applied to different national contexts would allow for regional segmentation and regional clusters. To advance the idea of pan-European marketing and its feasibility, research can provide support for business practice.

Note

1 Important economies outside the framework are Switzerland and Norway and smaller countries such as Liechtenstein. There are candidate countries, such as Albania and Ukraine and potential candidates, such as Bosnia and Herzegovina. For a current list of EU member states see https://europa.eu/european-union/about-eu/countries_en.

References

Aistrich, M., Saghafi, M.M. and Sciglimpaglia, D. (2006), 'Strategic business marketing developments in the New Europe: Retrospect and prospect', *Industrial Marketing Management,* vol. 35, no. 4, pp. 415–430.

Andreasen, A.R. (1990), 'Cultural interpenetration: A critical consumer research issue for the 1990s', *Advances in Consumer Research,* vol. 17, no. 1, pp. 847–849.

Apfelthaler, G. (2015), 'Standardisation versus adaptation of business practices in Europe: 20 years of the Single European Market and two decades of (scarce) research', *European Journal of International Management,* vol. 9, no. 3, pp. 283–287.

Arnould, E.J. and Thompson, C.J. (2005), 'Consumer Culture Theory (CCT): Twenty years of research', *Journal of Consumer Research,* vol. 31, no. 4, pp. 868–882.

Askegaard, S. and Madsen, T.K. (1998), 'The local and the global: Exploring traits of homogeneity and heterogeneity in European food cultures', *International Business Review,* vol. 7, no. 6, pp. 549–568.

Baalbaki, I.B. and Malhotra, N.K. (1993), 'Marketing management bases for international market segmentation: An alternate look at the standardization/customization debate', *International Marketing Review,* vol. 10, no. 1, pp. 19–44.

BBC (2007), 'Deals fail "after culture shock"', 20 November. http://news.bbc.co.uk/1/hi/business/7104298.stm (accessed 14 September 2017).

Berns-Wright, L. and Morgan, F. (2002), 'Comparative advertising in the European Union and the United States: Legal and managerial issues', *Journal of Euromarketing,* vol. 11, no. 3, pp. 7–31.

Bradley, F. (2005), *International Marketing Strategy,* Harlow, Pearson Education.

Browning, E.S. (1992), 'Marketing: In pursuit of the elusive Euroconsumer', *Wall Street Journal,* 23 April, p. B1.

Cavusgil, S.T., Deligonul, S. and Yaprak, A. (2005), 'International marketing as a field of study: A critical assessment of earlier development and a look forward', *Journal of International Marketing,* vol. 13, no. 4, pp. 1–27.

Christensen, O. (2002), 'Changing attitudes of European youth', *Young Consumers,* vol. 3, no. 3, pp. 19–32.

Chung, H.F.L. (2005), 'An investigation of crossmarket standardisation strategies: Experiences in the European Union', *European Journal of Marketing,* vol. 39, no. 11/12, pp. 1345–1371.

CIA Factbook (2017), 'European Union'. www.cia.gov/library/publications/the-world-factbook/geos/ee.html (accessed 22 March 2018).

Clements, K.W. and Chne, D. (1996), 'Fundamental similarities in consumer behaviour', *Applied Economics,* vol. 28, no. 6, pp. 747–757.

Cleveland, M. and Laroche, M. (2007), 'Acculturation to the global consumer culture: Scale development and research paradigm', *Journal of Business Research,* vol. 60, no. 3, pp. 249–259.

Criteo (2016), 'Consumers turn to mobile spending during Ramadan', press release, 18 May. www.zawya.com/story/Consumers_turn_to_mobile_spending_during_Ramadan_Criteo-ZAWYA20160518095103/ (accessed 27 September 2017).

De Mooij, M. (2010), *Consumer Behavior and Culture: Consequences for global marketing and advertising,* Thousand Oaks, CA, Sage.

Diamantopoulos, A., Schlegelmilch, B.B. and Du Preez, J.P. (1995), 'Lessons for pan-European marketing? The role of consumer preferences in fine-tuning the product-market fit', *International Marketing Review,* vol. 12, no. 2, pp. 38–52.

Directorate-General for Communication (2017), 'Standard Eurobarometer 87 – Spring 2017: "Public opinion in the European Union, First results"', in *Eurobarometer,* European Union.

Epuran, G. and Tescasiu, B. (2015), 'Specific Euro-marketing elements in the single European market. A cultural approach', *Bulletin of the Transilvania University of Brasov. Economic Sciences,* series vol. V, no. 8, pp. 47–52.

Euromonitor (2016), 'The reinvention of the mall: How shopping centres are adapting to global buying habits'. Strategy Briefing, 1 January 2016. www.euromonitor.com/the-reinvention-of-the-mall-how-shopping-centres-are-adapting-to-global-buying-habits/report (accessed 22 March 2018).

Euromonitor (2017), 'Packaging in 2017: Key insights and system refresher', April. http://go.euromonitor.com/EV-WE170911-PETnology_Landing-Page.html (accessed 22 March 2018).

European Commission (2012), 'Special Eurobarometer 389 – Europeans' attitudes towards food security, food quality and the countryside', in *Eurobarometer.* European Union.

European Commission (2017), 'Europe 2020 Strategy'. https://ec.europa.eu/info/strategy/european-semester/framework/europe-2020-strategy_en (accessed 20 November 2017).

Eurostat (2017a), 'HICP – Household consumption patterns'. http://ec.europa.eu/eurostat/statistics-explained/index.php/Archive:HICP_-_household_consumption_patterns (accessed 22 March 2018).

Eurostat (2017b), 'People in the EU – Statistics on household and family structures'. http://ec.europa.eu/eurostat/statistics-explained/index.php/People_in_the_EU_%E2%80%93_statistics_on_household_and_family_structures (accessed 11 September 2017).

Experian (n.d.), www.experian.de/ (accessed 15 September 2017).

Halliburton, C. and Hunerberg, R. (1993), 'Executive insights: Pan-European marketing – myth or reality', *Journal of International Marketing,* vol. 1, no. 3, pp. 77–92.

Halliburton, C. and Hunerberg, R. (2004), 'Pan-European marketing ten years after 1993 – A current appraisal and proposed conceptual framework', *Journal of Euromarketing,* vol. 14, no. 1/2, pp. 15–34.

Harris, P.M., and McDonald, F. (2004), *European Business and Marketing,* London, SAGE.

Herrschel, T. (2009), 'Regionalisation, "virtual" spaces and "real" territories – A view from Europe and North America', *International Journal of Public Sector Management,* vol. 22, no. 3, pp. 272–285.

Hofstede, G. (2001), *Culture's Consequences: Comparing values, behaviors, institutions, and organizations across cultures.* Thousand Oaks, CA, Sage.

Hofstede, G., Jonker, C. and Verwaart, T. (2012), 'Cultural differentiation of negotiating agents', *Group Decision and Negotiation,* vol. 21, no. 1, pp. 79–98.

Hofstede, F.T., Steenkamp, J.-B.E.M. and Wedel, M. (1999), 'International market segmentation based on consumer–product relations', *Journal of Marketing Research,* vol. 36, no. 1, pp. 1–17.

Johnson, D. and Turner, C. (2016), *European Business,* London, Routledge.

Kaynak, E. (2004), 'Euromarketing: An introduction', *Journal of Euromarketing,* vol. 13, no. 2/3, pp. 1–7.

Keegan, W.J. and Green, M.C. (2013), *Global Marketing,* Harlow, Pearson Education.

Kirpalani, V.H., Garbarski, L. and Kaynak, E. (2009), *Successfully Doing Business/Marketing in Eastern Europe,* New York, Routledge.

Levitt, T. (1983), 'The globalization of markets', *Harvard Business Review,* vol. 61, May, pp. 92–103.

Luomala, H., Kumar, R., Singh, J. and Jaakkola, M. (2015), 'When an intercultural business negotiation fails: Comparing the emotions and behavioural tendencies of individualistic and collectivistic negotiators', *Group Decision and Negotiation,* vol. 24, no. 3, pp. 537–561.

Malhotra, N.K., Agarwal, J. and Baalbaki, I. (1998), 'Heterogeneity of regional trading blocs and global marketing strategies: A multicultural perspective', *International Marketing Review*, vol. 15, no. 6, pp. 476–506.

McGowan, L. (1998), 'Protecting competition in a global market: The pursuit of an international competition policy', *European Business Review*, vol. 98, no. 6, pp. 328–339.

Merz, M.A., YI, H. and Alden, D.L. (2008), 'A categorization approach to analysing the global consumer culture debate', *International Marketing Review*, vol. 25, no. 2, pp. 166–182.

Middlement, K. (1995), *Orchestrating Europe*, London, Fontana Press.

OECD (2017), OECD Better Life Index. Available at www.oecdbetterlifeindex.org/topics/income/ (accessed 9 November 2017).

Ogden, D.T., Ogden, J.R. and Jensen Schau, H. (2004), 'Exploring the impact of culture and acculturation on consumer purchase decisions: Toward a microcultural perspective', *Academy of Marketing Science Review*, vol. 2004, no. 3, p. 1.

Okazaki, S., Taylor, C.R. and Doh, J.P. (2007), 'Market convergence and advertising standardization in the European Union', *Journal of World Business*, vol. 42, no. 4, pp. 384–400.

Paliwoda, S. and Marinova, S. (2007), 'The marketing challenges within the enlarged Single European Market', *European Journal of Marketing*, vol. 41, no. 3/4, pp. 233–244.

Penz, E. and Stöttinger, B. (2015), 'Consuming "European": Capturing homogeneity and heterogeneity in consumer culture of five European countries', *European Journal of International Management*, vol. 9, no. 3, pp. 326–341.

Sbragia, A. (2008), 'Review article: Comparative regionalism: What might it be?' *Journal of Common Market Studies,* vol. 46, no. 1, pp. 29–49.

Schlegelmilch, B.B., Bauer, A., Franch, J. and Meise, J.N. (2012), *Diversity in European Marketing,* Wiesbaden, Gabler.

Sciglimpaglia, D. and Saghafi, M. (2004), 'Marketing consequences of European internal market unification: An executive perspective', *Journal of Euromarketing,* vol. 14, no. 1/2, pp. 35–57.

Steenkamp, J.-B.E.M. (2001), 'The role of national culture in international marketing research', *International Marketing Review*, vol. 18, pp. 30–44.

Steenkamp, J.-B.E.M., Ter Hofstede, F. and Wedel, M. (1999), 'A cross-national investigation into the individual and national cultural antecedents of consumer innovativeness', *Journal of Marketing,* vol. 63, no. 1, pp. 55–70.

Suder, G. (2011), *Doing Business in Europe,* 2nd edn, London, SAGE.

Suder, G. (2016), 'Brexit: The European point of view'. https://pursuit.unimelb.edu.au/articles/brexit-the-european-point-of-view (accessed 4 September 2017).

Taylor, E. and Preisinger, I. (2014), 'BMW, Mercedes standardize cars to help buyers and boost margins'. www.reuters.com/article/us-autoshow-paris-standardised-cars/bmw-mercedes-standardize-cars-to-help-buyers-and-boost-margins-idUSKCN0HR1SA20141002 (accessed 7 September 2017).

Usunier, J.-C. and Lee, J.A. (2013), *Marketing Across Cultures*, Harlow, Pearson Education.

Vandermerwe, S. (1989), 'From fragmentation to integration: A conceptual pan-European marketing formula', *European Management Journal,* vol. 7, no. 3, pp. 267–272.

Wierenga, B., Pruyn, A. and Waarts, E. (1996), 'The key to successful Euromarketing: Standardization or customization?', *Journal of International Consumer Marketing,* vol. 8, no. 3–4, pp. 39–67.

World Bank (2017), 'Household final consumption expenditure per capita'. https://data.worldbank.org/indicator/NE.CON.PRVT.PC.KD?end=2016andname_desc=falseandstart=2016andview=mapandyear=2016 (accessed 11 September 2017).

21

EXPLORING THE PREREQUISITES FOR LONG-TERM SURVIVAL OF INTERNATIONALISING AND INNOVATIVE SMEs

The case of the Swedish life-science industry

Sara Melén Hånell, Emilia Rovira Nordman and Daniel Tolstoy[1]

Introduction

Europe's innovation performance needs to be enhanced to master the challenges ahead in a fast-changing global climate (European Commission 2013). There is a specific need to support innovative firms because Europe is suffering from poor productivity performance (Timmer et al. 2010) and its innovation performance has also declined over recent years in comparison to other geographical regions such as the United States and parts of Asia (European Commission 2011). In addition, taken as a share of GDP, venture capital investments in the United States are four times higher than in the European Union (EU) (European Commission 2011). Moreover, the European Commission considers that European investments tend to be spread too thinly as European venture capital funds invest in twice as many companies as their counterparts in the United States (European Commission 2011). If European companies are to remain competitive in the global economy, scholarly literature argues that public policies should focus on creating an environment that promotes innovation, especially for internationalising firms (Nordman and Tolstoy 2016). Increasing the possibilities for innovation is also placed high on the agenda for Europe's leaders and the members of the European Parliament, via the Horizon 2020 initiative which aims to secure Europe's competitiveness. New policies that are being implemented are geared towards increasing the international competitiveness of innovative firms, for example by creating internal markets for venture capital which may enable firms to bring products to international markets sooner (European Commission 2013). One group of firms that often encompasses the innovative features that lay the foundation for export success is international small and medium-sized enterprises (SMEs). This group is defined in this study in accordance with the European Commission definition as enterprises with fewer than 250 employees, with a turnover not exceeding 50 million euros and/or an annual balance sheet total not exceeding 43 million euros (European Commission 2003; Suder 2011). SMEs are particularly important for the growth of the EU region, because they encompass the vast majority of the total number of exporting firms and represent a third of the total export value (Cernat et al. 2014). The EU's dependence on successful innovative and internationalising SMEs is also strong in comparison to other regions of the world. For example, the share of SMEs in US manufacturing activity – and total US exports – is smaller than the share of SMEs in EU manufacturing activity and exports (United States International Trade Commission 2010). Exporting SMEs are often characterised by higher levels of productivity (Adlung and Soprana 2017) and job-creation than other SMEs (European Commission 2010).

Building on these results, the arguments for SMEs to export and internationalise are strong, both from the perspective of individual firms and whole countries. Policy-makers and academic scholars have directed much effort to support and enhance the survival of innovative and exporting SMEs. European policy-makers have in particular highlighted the need to improve the conditions for these SMEs to survive economic downturns and thereby flourish from a long-term perspective (Wehinger 2014). Innovative SMEs often suffer from scarce financial resources, particularly in the time period between the stage of developing a new technology, process, product or service and the stage of exploiting it commercially. Moreover, the European market for financing innovative companies from the pre-seed to expansion stages is still underdeveloped (Lilischkis 2011). The lack of resources during their infancy can affect the long-term economic development of SMEs and the job-creation possibilities within EU. For example, Eurostat (2016) reports that in 2014, there were about 4 million new jobs created from 2.6 million newly born enterprises, whereas 3.5 million jobs were lost due to 2.3 million businesses dying. The one-year survival rate for enterprises created in 2013 was about 80 per cent, whereas the five-year survival rate of enterprises born in 2009 and still active in 2014 was a staggering 44 per cent (Eurostat 2016). Similar numbers, indicating a low long-term survival rate, are reported about newly born firms from the United States, where seven out of ten new firms survive at least two years, half at least five years, and only a quarter stay in business after 15 years or more (Nazar 2013).

The purpose of this study is to contribute to the understanding of how innovative and international SMEs grow and survive from a long-term perspective. To do so, we draw on prior research within the emerging field of international entrepreneurship, which typically focuses on innovative and international SMEs. While previous research within this field has given much attention to small firms' abilities to initiate an expansion abroad, few studies have investigated their survival and development from a long-term perspective. This study contributes to international entrepreneurship literature by presenting a longitudinal study based on data of 26 innovative SMEs in the Swedish life-science industry.

Literature background

International entrepreneurship has emerged as an international business perspective that can capture the subversive elements of internationalisation, i.e. the proactive pursuit of niche business opportunities in foreign markets. International entrepreneurial firms typically internationalise early on in their life cycles and often expand rapidly in the pursuit of growth opportunities by taking advantage of their abilities to innovate (Sapienza et al. 2006). International entrepreneurial firms are typically founded by individuals who are experienced in conducting international business from their previous jobs (Crick and Jones 2000) and have international market experience (Nordman and Melén 2008). Another means by which internationally entrepreneurial firms can overcome the lack of critical resources is to use their existing networks, at both the personal and firm levels (Lindstrand et al. 2011; Nordman and Melén 2008). Collaborative business relationships can enable these small firms to extract value from internal and external resources, which enable them to initiate internationalisation already from inception (McDougall et al. 1994). Even though these firms tend to have limited funds to use for research and development (R&D) or to speed up production processes, their flexibility, rapid decision-making and highly motivated employees can give them an advantage over larger firms (Allocca and Kessler 2006).

Many observations of innovative firms that manage to expand abroad at a relatively rapid pace have been made in previous studies about life-science firms (e.g. Lindstrand et al. 2011; Nordman and Melén 2008). The high degree of innovation in such firms often entails high risks and high costs (Koumpis and Pavitt 1999). One of the largest challenges for these firms has to do with the cost of innovation. Contrary to what might be expected, Raynor and Panetta (2008) suggest that R&D investments made by pharmaceutical firms often do not lead to increases in their innovation pipelines. Research has also demonstrated that life-science firms often experience problems in delivering on their initial promise of launching new products to the market within a reasonable time frame (Pisano 2006).

Method

To conduct this study, a qualitative, longitudinal, multiple-case-study approach was used. The sample was chosen from life-science firms in the Stockholm-Uppsala life-science district. The chosen firms had to satisfy the following criteria: (a) categorised as SME, (b) currently employ their founders, (c) sell at least one product in a foreign (i.e. non-Swedish) market and (d) conduct their own R&D. By serving as sampling criteria, innovativeness is treated as an endogenous variable in this study. Innovative firms face specific challenges e.g. pertaining to short product life cycles and high product development costs, which makes it particularly interesting to study their long-term performance.

Based on these criteria, we chose to contact qualified candidate case firms randomly and stopped after 26 firms had been contacted and visited by members of the research group. More information about these anonymised case firms is shown in Table 21.1.

Data collection

We interviewed the founders and managers who were responsible for each firm's internationalisation process. From 2003 to 2015, a total of 74 face-to-face semi-structured interviews were conducted. To corroborate the tentative results of the study, five final interviews with respondents were conducted in 2016. All interviews ranged from 40 to 160 minutes in length, with an average duration of around 120 minutes. To achieve external validity, we adhered to interview guides. However, we asked follow-up questions when interesting topics arose during the interviews. After the 26 companies had been visited (see Table 21.1), the empirical saturation point had been reached (i.e. the interviews conducted at the last few firms provided us with narratives similar to those we had previously heard).

We used methodological triangulation in our data collection so as to strengthen confidence in the accuracy of the findings and the construct validity of the study (Jick 1979). Thus, multiple data sources (e.g. interviews; annual reports etc.) were used, and data were collected at different points in time. The cross-checking of different data sources increased the reliability of the study. Another test involved receiving feedback on drafts of cases from informants.

Table 21.1 The 26 case companies in the Swedish life-science industry

Firm	Business area	Founded	Number of interviews	Growth*	Survival in original form
1	Detection and monitoring of viral diseases	1984	2	No	No (bankruptcy), product portfolio transferred to another organisation
2	Biological control/plant growth stimulation	1996	2	No	Yes
3	Biochemicals	1995	7	Yes	Yes
4	Bioceramic technology	1987	2	No	Yes
5	Animal vaccine development	1999	3	No	No (takeover)
6	Veterinary medicine and food safety	2001	5	No	No (bankruptcy), product portfolio transferred to another organisation
7	DNA identification and quantification	1990	1	No	No (bankruptcy), product portfolio transferred to amother organisation
8	Arthritic diseases	1998	1	Yes	Yes
9	Genetic analysis	1997	6	Yes	Yes
10	Microfluidic solutions	1999	7	No	Yes
11	Microsystems	1998	12	No	No (takeover)
12	New drugs and dosage forms	1995	3	Yes	Yes
13	Medical devices	1988	2	No	No (takeover)
14	Immunological reactions	1991	1	Yes	Yes
15	Respiratory devices	1997	6	Yes	No (takeover)
16	Bio-detectors	1998	2	No	Yes
17	ECG systems	1999	3	No	Yes
18	Engineered antibodies	1986	4	Yes	Yes
19	Bacteria cultures	1999	2	Yes	Yes
20	Cardiac monitors	1985	2	No	Yes
21	Healthcare products	1987	1	No	Yes
22	Healthcare products	1994	1	No	No (takeover)
23	Biophamaceuticals	2004	1	Yes	Yes
24	Medical technology devices	1968	1	No	No (takeover)
25	Drug delivery devices	1996	1	Yes	Yes
26	Equipment for microvascular diagnosis	1978	1	Yes	Yes

* Increase in number of employees (between 2003/2004 and 2015).

Data analysis

In analysing the data of the 26 cases, our focus was on the firms' survival. In this study, we conceptualise firm survival as sustained firm autonomy by avoiding takeovers and bankruptcies. While takeovers certainly can be beneficial for firms by providing economies of scale and exit opportunities for entrepreneurs, they do also end firm autonomy. Firms that survive these events are therefore assumed to possess certain qualities that make them capable of using their own funds or attracting external capital to stimulate sustained growth and increase the probability of long-term survival. Takeovers are likely to occur when an external actor sees the potential for future revenue generation from products, services or technologies that are developed by a firm, but when it is not likely that the firm itself can generate further revenues (without new organisational and/or financial investments being made). Moreover, bankruptcies occur when costs are larger than incomes and the financiers have lost the inclination to make further investments in a business.

Based on longitudinal analyses of the 26 cases, we determined that the firms could be divided into two groups: survivors and non-survivors. Although the two groups of firms are rather small and unevenly distributed (i.e. 17 survivors and 9 non-survivors), there is still a sufficient number of observations that enable us to make qualitative assessments about them. Statistical assessments are more challenging since groups are small and uneven to fit with parametric statistical tests such as independent samples t-tests. Hence, the analysis of the data in this study is more geared towards observing and finding associations between variables rather than suggesting generalisable relationships.

To provide a more in-depth illustration of the long-term development of survivors and non-survivors, we describe the development of two case firms, where one case firm represents the surviving firms and one case firm represents the non-surviving firms. Single cases can serve as typical or representative cases when they stand as an example of a wider group of cases (Yin 2003). We selected companies 9 and 6, because these firms provided a good representation of the group and could not be considered extreme cases.

Company 9 – a survivor

Company 9 was founded in 1997 around the idea to develop, manufacture and sell tools for genetic analysis on an international market. Since Sweden is such a small market, Company 9 had an international focus from the start. The firm made its first foreign sale within two years from foundation. With the help of investment-capital, the firm could open sales subsidiaries in the United States, the United Kingdom, Germany and the Netherlands soon after its inception.

In 2000, Company 9 was introduced onto the stock market, which generated about 900,000 KSEK. These funds were used to acquire other firms in the life-science industry, which also contributed to broadening the product portfolio of the firm. In 2008–09, the board decided to sell the entire business area in which Company 9 was originally anchored. Sales in this business area had not been as profitable as was first anticipated. In 2010, the CEO said: 'We will never again be so dependent on one segment' (pers. comm., 13 October).

By broadening the product portfolio, the firm also came to focus relatively less on new research innovations and pay more attention to enhancing the pure business aspects of its products. For example, Company 9 shifted to focus increasingly on producing and selling income-bringing consumables. By changing its focus, Company 9 has built up a strong international customer base of industry and academic partners, which include the world's top 20 pharmaceutical companies. Looking back at the firm's international development, the CEO relates that: 'The hardest thing for businesses today is not about developing new ideas or to innovate, but to develop international sales' (pers. comm., 17 May 2016). The group has grown significantly from the start, now employing over 293 people worldwide. With the exception of one year, the firm has been able to make a profit every year since 2006.

Company 6 – a non-survivor

Company 6 was founded in 2001 and was built around research developed within a university-based project. The company was first started with the financial support of a university-based venture capital company. Company 6's business idea was to develop test kits for animal diseases that could speed up test procedures. The tests became popular on the market and the firm started to export within two years of start-up. Because the test kits were user friendly, the employees could manage most of the international sales through email and telephone.

In the beginning, Company 6 experienced an organic growth of about 5–10 per cent per year. Company 6 made a profit for the first time in 2005. The profit was reinvested in new staff and new processes. In 2009, the financial crisis had a negative impact on the firm. In an interview from 2010, the CEO relates that: 'our largest markets are in Eastern Europe today. The animal health programmes that were going on in Eastern Europe were cancelled and the market suddenly died' (pers. comm., 26 October).

Company 6 did not have any significant monetary margins and had to make major cuts in their costs. The management initially tried to cut the employees' work-time down to 80 per cent, but eventually had to start firing people. This was not enough, however, and the firm filed for bankruptcy in 2011. In the aftermath of the bankruptcy, a German multinational took over Company 6's product portfolio. Today the portfolio comprises over 30 different tests that are still supplied to more than 70 countries worldwide.

Survival analysis of the total sample

A majority are survivors

Analysing the total sample of 26 firms, Figure 21.1 empirically demonstrates that during the investigated 13-year period (2003–2015), most firms had survived (17 firms). Six firms have been taken over by other companies and three have been forced to file for bankruptcy.

Figure 21.2 displays the number of surviving firms during the timeframe for our study. We can see that there is no specific time where the hazard of going bankrupt or being taken over by another firm is particularly augmented. Extrapolating from this data, it would not be unreasonable to expect that this hazard rate will continue at a similar pace in the coming years. Even though the firms belong to the competitive life-science industry the survival rate is not alarmingly low.

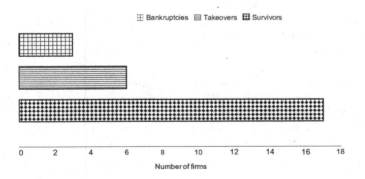

Figure 21.1   Firm survival status per 2015 of case firms in Swedish life-science industry

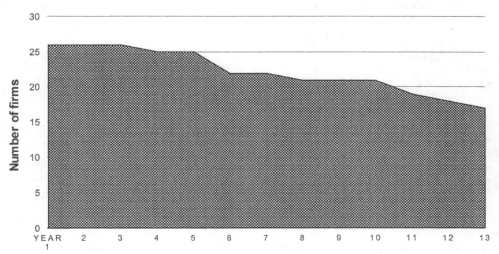

Figure 21.2   Hazard rate of going bankrupt or being taken over by another firm for case firms in Swedish life-science industry

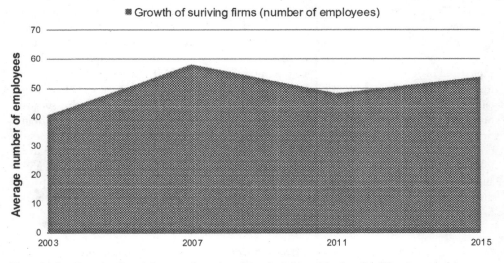

Figure 21.3   Growth of surviving case firms (number of employees) in Swedish life-science industry

Figure 21.3 displays the growth of the surviving 17 firms in our sample. We can see that the growth rate fluctuates over time. Nonetheless at the end of the time-span, firms have grown considerably (by 32 per cent) and have on average moved from the small firm category (with 50 or fewer employees) to the medium-sized firm category (with more than 50 employees). This means that the growth trend is positive among the surviving firms in the sample.

Table 21.2 General comparisons between survivors and non-survivors in Swedish life-science industry

	Survivor (mean)	Non-survivor (mean)	Mean difference
Founding year	1988	1991	2.57
Year of first international sale	1997	1997	-0.66
Number of employees 2003	40	30	-10.373
Size of turnover	38,121	52,292	14,170
Geographical diversification of sales 2003	3.8	4.1	0.287
Revenue 2003	-11,616	-11,420	195.78
Revenue change 2003–2007	39,687	-6,350	-46,038★
Export size 2003	4.1	4.25	0.116
Number of patents 2003	1.765	3.3	1.568

★ Statistically significant at the 10 per cent level.

Mean comparison between survivors and non-survivors

To analyse further the presumptive differences between surviving and non-surviving firms, we analyse the data presented in Table 21.2. Judging from the data, mean differences are usually small and insignificant between the two categories of firms regarding organisational traits such as age, time in foreign markets, size and international strategies (i.e. geographical diversification of sales). There are some noteworthy differences between the two categories of firms in regards to revenue change and number of patents (comparisons are based on the baseline year of 2003). Firstly, the average revenue development is notably higher (and also significant in an independent sample t-test) among survivors. Although this result is intuitive, it confirms that lack of capital and own funds will severely decrease internationalising SMEs' chances of survival. Firms that are able to grow organically, i.e. based on their accumulated profits, will be able to maintain autonomy and present funding for future expansion efforts. We can also see that survivors on average possess fewer patents than non-survivors. This is counter-intuitive since innovative firms are generally hailed as the future of business. The number of patents also influences the possibilities for the non-survivors to either be taken over by another party or be forced to file for bankruptcy in times of economic distress. A comparison between firms that are taken over and firms that file for bankruptcy shows that the bankrupted firms generally held fewer patents than the firms that were taken over. One explanation for this is that access to patents makes firms more attractive to be acquired by an external actor.

Mean comparison between patent holders and non-patent holders in international strategy

Because of the striking differences between number of patents held by surviving and non-surviving firms we probe deeper into the international behaviour of patent holding (patents >0) versus non-patent holding SMEs (zero patents). Table 21.3 compares export volumes and geographical diversification of exports between these categories of firms in the baseline year 2003. It also accounts for changes in these international performance dimensions regarding these two groups of firms over a four-year period (2003–2007). The data reinforces our previous findings by indicating that non-patent holders seem to perform better in their internationalisation endeavours than patent holders. Non-patent holders on average operate on more markets

Table 21.3 Comparisons in international behaviour between patent holders and non-patent holders in the Swedish life-science industry

	Patent holder (mean)	Non-patent holder (mean)	Mean difference
Geographical diversification of sales 2003	3.21	4.75	1.54
Geographical diversification change 2003–2007	0	–0.5	–0.5
Export size 2003	3.91	4.45	0.54
Export size change 2003–2007	0.167	0.636	0.469

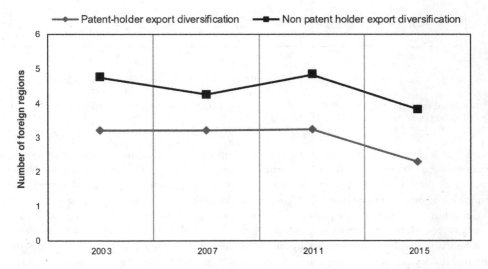

Figure 21.4 Change in geographical diversification* of international sales of case firms in Swedish life-science industry
* Measured in eight regions according to Statistics Sweden's categorisation: 1) Scandinavia; 2) EU; 3) Europe apart from EU; 4) West Asia; 5) Far East; 6) North/Central America; 7) South America; 8) Africa.

than patent holders. In absolute terms, they also sell larger volumes of goods and services to foreign markets.

Figure 21.4 and Figure 21.5 give an overview of the development of export size and diversification of international sales of patent-holding and non-patent-holding SMEs, covering the entire time frame of our study. It is clear that both groups of firms over time move towards a greater level of geographical concentration.

Among patent-holding firms, one reason for this concentration may be that international patent application processes are generally expensive and cumbersome for SMEs (Van Pottelsberghe 2009). Even though firms have the possibility to apply for patents in a number of countries at once (Suder 2011) (at the European Patent Office, which has 35 member states), granted patents still need to be validated (and translated) in each member state, leading to increasing costs (Van Pottelsberghe 2009). Besides this, patent-holding firms need to pay renewal fees in every country where protection is to be prolonged (Van Pottelsberghe 2009).

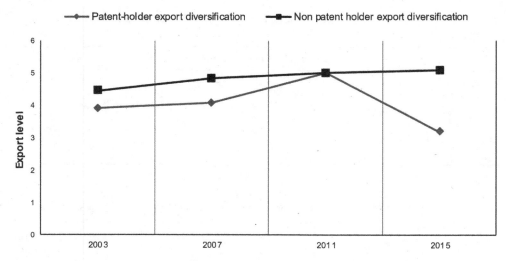

Figure 21.5 Change in export volumes (eight-level scale[+]) for case firms in Swedish life-science industry
+ Measured in eight intervals: 1=≥€1; 2=≥€2,500; 3=≥€100,000; 4=≥€200,000; 5=≥€500,000; 6=≥€1,000,000; 7=≥€5,000,000 8=≥€10,000,000.

Figure 21.5 shows that even though patent-holding firms are catching up with non-patent firms in regard to international sales at one point in the diagram (2011), they are unable to operate at these levels long term. Besides the expense of prolonging patents, this might be explained by other consequences of patent and product life cycles. At the beginning of their life cycles innovative products are protected by intellectual property laws and can be sold at premium prices. However, patents will either expire or the technology on which they are based will be made obsolete by new offerings made by competitors. Hence, dependence on patents and technology are likely to make these firms less able to continually adapt to customers' changing needs, leading to gradually diminishing sales.

Discussion and conclusion

One key result of our longitudinal analysis of 26 SMEs is that most firms in the sample could be classified as survivors. One explanation for so many firms surviving (in comparison to the Eurostat data presented earlier) is that many of the firms that were included in our sample were older than five years at the start of this study (see Table 21.1). These firms had therefore overcome the first critical hurdles that may lead to bankruptcies for newly started businesses. Moreover, the life-science firms in our sample build on technology that was generally well received on international markets. Among the investigated firms we find that the average revenue development is notably higher among survivors than non-survivors. Among the non-surviving firms, we could not find any common explanation for their decline other than that these firms have suffered from a lack of necessary resources. Unlike extant research in the international entrepreneurship research field, this study is not limited to the initial growth patterns of innovative SMEs but instead captures their longitudinal international growth. By doing so, our results can contribute to extending knowledge within the field of international entrepreneurship and European business studies. Extant research has proven that small, innovative firms are able to initiate an international expansion (despite their lack of resources) by using foreign business relationships as gateways into foreign markets (Crick and Jones 2000; McDougall et al. 1994; Nordman and Melén 2008). Even though this study supports these results, its longitudinal perspective highlights that the firms' inability to accumulate necessary resources over time severely decreases the firms' internationalisation and chances of survival. Looking at the case descriptions of Companies 6 and 9, they illustrate that small, innovative firms can internationalise early and yield a profit rapidly by finding and cooperating with customers in foreign markets. However, both firms eventually experienced severe challenges that forced them to adapt to new market conditions. Company 6 suffered losses due to a recession and was not able to accumulate necessary resources to endure the decline in international sales. The managers of company 9 discovered that the original product-portfolio did not bring sufficient income, but that the firm's resources could be used to make changes in the product portfolio and turn business around. In the long term, it was damaging to focus too much on specific customer groups (in the case of company 6) and product areas (in the case of company 9). Company 6 did not have the margins to endure a decline in international sales and change its strong focus on Eastern Europe. Company 9, on the other hand, succeeded in reacting rapidly to changing market conditions, because the firm had the funds to endure the consequences of a disappointing product area. Summarising these findings, SME survival in international markets is greatly influenced by timing and the access to enduring resources.

Our longitudinal case analysis points to two important issues related to the firms' long-term growth and survival. First of all, limited resources continue to be a key challenge for small, innovative firms throughout their internationalisation processes. Second, to manage the situation of scarce resources, it is crucial that these firms are able to stay alert, access and manage new market conditions that emerge and be responsive to a wide array of potential market opportunities. As pointed out by John et al. in chapter 23 of this book, firms and the environments in which they operate influence each other. By being flexible, strategic and adaptive to new environments and new market conditions, firms can make the best use of resources invested in specific market settings. Hence, flexibility, lack of bureaucracy and rapid decision-making are critical prerequisites for innovative SMEs to manage their long-term international growth and survival. Looking specifically at the case of Company 9 (from the group of survivors), it illustrates a firm that focuses on growing organically, and has managed to do so in the long run. The firm was able to change its strategy from focusing less on developing new innovative ideas, to focusing more on developing the pure business aspects of their products to increase international sales.

Another key result from the 26 case firms (measured on an aggregated level), is that the surviving firms on average possess fewer patents than non-survivors. In addition, our results highlight that non-patent holders seem to perform better (sell larger volumes of goods and services) in their internationalisation than patent holders. Moreover, non-patent holders, on average, operate on more markets than patent holders. These findings are counter-intuitive since innovative firms, often measured by their number of patents, are generally hailed as the future of business. Company 9 can give an explanation for these findings. Company 9, which started its internationalisation without holding any patents, eventually decided to focus fewer resources on R&D and instead put more effort into producing and selling more income-generating consumables. This strategy indicates that firms that focus too much on developing patents and new technological innovations may become too product oriented and thereby lose track of foreign customers' needs. Previous studies of life-science firms have highlighted the high risks and high costs involved in accomplishing innovation processes within these firms (Koumpis and Pavitt 1999; Raynor and Panetta 2008). Applications for patents are a time consuming and costly process which balances the efforts of the firm towards engineering and technology. Hence, one reason why non-patent holders are able to internationalise on a larger scale and scope than patent-holders can be explained by the fact that they are not locked in by technology when making strategic decisions related to market selection and pace of internationalisation. On the one hand, firms that have used vast resources to acquire patents can make market decisions centred on this technology. On the other hand, non-patent holders arguably can be more responsive to new market needs and will be more inclined to act on opportunities wherever they emerge.

International entrepreneurship research describes how knowledge about how to do business with foreign customers and partners constitutes the main driver of firms' internationalisation (Crick and Jones 2000; Nordman and Melén 2008). Our study illustrates how critical such knowledge is for the ability of innovative SMEs to survive and achieve long-term international growth. Our study concludes that surviving SMEs are firms that can stay alert and cater to various customer segments throughout their internationalisation, being responsive to a wide array of potential market opportunities. Our study also demonstrates the importance for an innovative SME not to become too reliant on single customer segments and/or product areas, as this can impede the firms' abilities to adapt quickly to environmental changes. Finally, the results highlight the risks involved with investing too many resources in new innovation activities, i.e. developing patents. Too much dependence on patents and technology can negatively affect firms' potential to continually adapt to customers' changing needs, leading to gradually diminishing sales. If the process of taking out international patents was less cumbersome and less expensive, patent-holders would have more incentives to expand their business. Ideally, resource-constrained SMEs should be able to apply for a 'one-stop-shop' patent for any given jurisdiction where protection is sought: national, European or global. With the exception of purely national patents, there is no such one-stop shop at present (Van Pottelsberghe 2009).

Policy implications

A key result of our longitudinal case study is that a vast majority of the investigated firms that we have followed since 2003/2004 still exist in their original form and still contribute tax revenue and create jobs. This result points to the importance for policy-makers within Europe to support internationalisation initiatives, since European national markets are small and successful export is critical (see Mikhaylov, Chapter 18 of this book). To support internationalisation among innovative SMEs, more EU policy initiatives should be directed towards existing, maturing firms and offer support to those firms that have shown they can be internationally successful. Similar to other studies (Lilischkis 2011), we can see that specific policies need to be designed for these 'hampered winners', i.e. firms that need support to grow substantially and overcome temporary market failures. One way to do this is to provide an integrated support system to put entrepreneurs and managers in contact with venture capitalists that can supply both capital and well-founded advice and guidance (Lindholm et al. 2010). This development could be supported by the realisation of a single EU market for venture capital firms. Internationalisation for European firms could also be increased by further movements towards an even more integrated Single Market in the EU and an enhancement of the EU's Enterprise Europe Network (Lilischkis 2011).

New science-based industries (such as life-sciences) were regarded as particularly promising before the turn of the millennium. After the financial crises that followed the dot-com boom, the high expectations for the success of these kinds of firm were significantly lowered, partly due to the high risks and high costs involved in the innovation processes in these firms (Koumpis and Pavitt 1999). Even though the results of this study have highlighted that life science is indeed a risky business, a vast majority of the investigated firms that we have followed since 2003/2004 still exist in their original form. Thus, the long-term survival rate in our sample of investigated firms (of about 65 per cent) is testament to their survival skills. The study highlights the benefits for policy-makers in supporting life-science firms in general, because these firms can create value and enhance the common good. Even those firms in the sample that have not survived have still created value to the new knowledge economy by generating products that are sold by other organisations. Policies aimed at supporting new-science firms are therefore successful not only at the firm-level but also at a national level.

In general there is a lack of scientific work on how to evaluate policy implications (Lindholm et al. 2010). The ideas presented in this chapter may build a basis for how future public policy instruments can be earmarked to support innovative SMEs in Europe, and possibly elsewhere, thus promoting innovation, entrepreneurship and economic growth. Future research needs to explicitly identify what exactly those instruments should be and how public policy can best be deployed to promote these kinds of firm.

Other studies on innovative SMEs have investigated the role that different kinds of SME play in innovation in the environmental sector (Triguero et al. 2016) and the role that family SMEs play in the innovation generation (Classen et al. 2014). This chapter complements previous empirical research, highlighting that aspects such as network access (Nordman and Tolstoy 2016; Triguero et al. 2016) and access to financial resources (Triguero et al. 2016; Classen et al. 2014) also impact the choices that innovative SMEs in the life-science industry make during their internationalisation. However, the scope of this chapter, focusing on life-science SMEs from one European country, does not yet permit broad generalisations to be made. Further research is needed to provide a better understanding of the motivations for innovative and international life-science firms to grow and survive. It would be interesting to extend our analysis using quantitative data, covering larger samples of life-science firms collected from a wider geographical scope. It would also be interesting to investigate the growth and survival patterns of other innovative and international groups of SMEs from a longitudinal research perspective (for example SMEs active in environmental sectors and family-driven SMEs). Such studies could be used to complement and possibly validate the results implicated in this chapter.

Note

1 The authors have contributed equally to the manuscript.

References

Adlung, R. and Soprana, M. (2017), 'Trade policy for SMEs from a GATS perspective', in T. Rensmann (ed.), *Small and Medium-Sized Enterprises in International Economic Law*, Oxford, Oxford University Press.

Allocca, M.A. and Kessler, E.H. (2006), 'Innovation speed in small and medium-sized enterprises', *Creativity and Innovation Management*, vol. 15, no. 3, pp. 279–295.

Cernat, L., Norman-López, A. and Duch T-Figueras, A. (2014), 'SMEs are more important than you think! Challenges and opportunities for EU exporting SMEs'. https://EconPapers.repec.org/RePEc:ris:dgtcen:2014_003 (accessed 13 November 2017).

Classen, N., Carree, M., Van Gils, A. and Peters, B. (2014), 'Innovation in family and non-family SMEs: An exploratory analysis', *Small Business Economics*, vol. 42, no. 1, pp. 595–609.

Crick, D. and Jones, M.V. (2000), 'Small high-technology firms and international high-technology markets', *Journal of International Marketing*, vol. 19, no. 2, pp. 63–85.

European Commission (2003), Article 2 of the Annex of Recommendation 2003/361/EC. www.reach-compliance.eu/english/REACH-ME/engine/sources/regulations/2003-361-EC.pdf (accessed 14 November 2017).

European Commission (2010), 'Internationalisation of European SMEs'. http://ec.europa.eu/DocsRoom/documents/10008/attachments/1/translations (accessed 13 November 2017).

European Commission (2011), *Report from the Commission to the European Parliament, the Council, the European Economic and Social Committee and the Committee of the Region, State of the Innovation Union 2011*. https://ec.europa.eu/research/innovation-union/pdf/state-of-the-union/2011/state_of_the_innovation_union_2011_brochure_en.pdf(accessed 28 March 2018).

European Commission (2013), *Innovation Union - A pocket guide on a Europe 2020 initiative*. https://ec.europa.eu/eip/agriculture/en/publications/innovation-union-pocket-guide-europe-2020 (accessed 13 November 2017).

Eurostat (2016), 'Business demography statistics'. http://ec.europa.eu/eurostat/statistics-explained/index.php/Business_demography_statistics (accessed 30 June 2017).

Jick, T.J. (1979), 'Mixing qualitative and quantitative methods: Triangulation in action', in J. Van Maanen (ed.), *Qualitative Methodology*, London, Sage, pp. 135–148.

Koumpis, K. and Pavitt, K. (1999), 'Corporate activities in speech recognition and natural language: Another "new science"-based technology', *International Journal of Innovation Management*, vol. 3, no. 3, pp. 335–366.

Lilischkis, S. (2011), 'Policies in support of high-growth innovative SMEs', INNO-Grips Policy Brief No. 2. http://innogrips.empirica.biz/fileadmin/INNOGRIPS/documents/01_Policy%20Briefs/IG_PolicyBrief_2_High-growth_SMEs.pdf (accessed 13 November 2017).

Lindholm Dahlstrand, Å. and Stevenson, L. (2010), 'Innovative entrepreneurship policy: Linking innovation and entrepreneurship in a European context', *Annals of Innovation and Entrepreneurship*, vol. 1, no. 1, p. 5602.

Lindstrand, A., Melén, S. and Nordman, E. (2011), 'Turning social capital into business: A study of internationalization of biotech SMEs', *International Business Review*, vol. 20, no. 2, pp. 194–212.

McDougall, P.P., Shane, S. and Oviatt, B.M. (1994), 'Explaining the formation of international new ventures: The limits of theories from international business research', *Journal of Business Venturing*, vol. 9, no. 6, pp. 469–487.

Nazar, J. (2013), '16 surprising statistics about small businesses'. www.forbes.com/sites/jasonnazar/2013/09/09/16-surprising-statistics-about-small-businesses/#3aa830695ec8 (accessed 13 November 2017).

Nordman, E. and Melén, S. (2008), 'The impact of different kinds of knowledge for the internationalization process of Born Globals in the biotech business', *Journal of World Business*, vol. 43, no. 2, pp. 171–185.

Nordman, E.R. and Tolstoy, D. (2016), 'The impact of opportunity connectedness on innovation in SMEs' foreign-market relationships', *Technovation*, vol. 57–58, pp. 47–57.

Pisano, G. (2006), *Science Business: The promise, the reality, and the future of biotech*, Boston, MA, Harvard Business School Press.

Raynor, M.E. and Panetta, J.A. (2008), 'A better way to R&D?' https://hbr.org/2008/02/a-better-way-to-rd.html (accessed 13 November 2017).

Sapienza, H.J., Autio, E., George, G. and Zahra, S.A. (2006), 'A capabilities perspective on the effects of early internationalization on firm survival and growth', *Academy of Management Review*, vol. 31, no. 4, pp. 914–933.

Suder G. (2011), *Doing Business in Europe*, 2nd edn, London, Sage Publications.

Timmer, M.P., Inklaar, R., O'Mahony, M. and Van Ark, B. (2010), *Economic Growth in Europe: A comparative industry perspective*, Cambridge, Cambridge University Press.

Triguero, A., Moreno-Mondéjar, L., and Davia, M.A. (2016), 'Leaders and laggards in environmental innovation: An empirical analysis of SMEs in Europe', *Business Strategy and the Environment*, vol. 31, no. 4, pp. 28–39.

United States International Trade Commission (2010), *Small and Medium-sized Enterprises: U.S. and EU export activities, and barriers and opportunities experienced by U.S. firms: investigation no. 332–509*. www.usitc.gov/publications/332/pub4169.pdf (accessed 13 November 2017).

Van Pottelsberghe, B. (2009), *Lost Property: The European patent system and why it doesn't work*. http://aei.pitt.edu/11263/1/patents_BP_050609.pdf (accessed 13 November 2017).

Wehinger, G. (2014), 'SMEs and the credit crunch: Current financing difficulties, policy measures and a review of literature', *OECD Journal: Financial Market Trends*, vol. 2013, no. 2, pp. 115–148.

Yin, R.K. (2003), *Case Study Research: Design and Methods*, Thousand Oaks, CA, SAGE Publications.

22

FIRM CAPITAL STRUCTURE IN EUROPE

A comparative analysis of CEE firms vs. Western firms in the changing financial environment

Karin Jõeveer[1]

Introduction

The global financial crisis triggered the deleveraging of the financial sector. Capitalisation of the euro area banks has increased. At the same time the total assets of the banking sector declined by 17 per cent from 2008 to 2015 and the share of loans in total assets has decreased from 70 per cent to 64 per cent (ECB 2016). Have these substantial changes in the financial sector had an impact on company finances? This chapter has a deeper look at the capital structure of European firms before and after the crisis comparing the evolutions in both East and West.

The financial sector in Central and Eastern European (CEE) economies is in a different development stage than in Western Europe. The financial sector saw a revival in the 1990s after decades of central planning in CEE. There has been a wave of new and foreign institutions entering the sector bringing along improved methods of allocating credit (Cassano et al. 2013) and increasing the availability of financial sources in the market. Now, foreign financial institutions dominate most of the CEE financial markets (ECB 2016). The global financial crisis and its aftermath have thrown financial sectors into a series of reforms. Basel III regulatory framework requires banks to gradually increase their capitalisation and liquidity. The changes in the financial sector are likely to spill over to the high street as well.

Capital structure research focuses on firm choice between debt and equity in financing investments. Two major competing theories of capital structure are the trade-off theory and pecking order theory. Graham and Harvey (2001) surveyed US chief financial officers and found evidence supporting both theories. Frank and Goyal (2009) show that firm choice between debt and equity may be influenced by many firm-specific features but also by the country's institutional and macroeconomic variables. In the context of CEE economies, the latter are expected to be very important since most of the companies are small, young and therefore more dependent on domestic financial markets.

The structure of this chapter is as follows. First, an overview of the major theories of capital structure and the estimation method is given. Then, firm-level data from nine CEE countries and from five core EU countries is used to show the trends in capital structure and to provide evidence for how well the different capital structure theories work in practice.

Theories of capital structure

The inception of the extensive literature on capital structure theories dates back to a 1958 paper by Modigliani and Miller.[2] Modigliani and Miller (1958) proved the irrelevance of capital structure in perfect and frictionless capital markets. They showed that in those conditions, it does not matter whether the investor holds the shares of a levered company or invests in an unlevered company[3] and uses financial leverage on its own. By using homemade leverage the investor is able to replicate the cash flows of the levered firm. Based on this arbitrage pricing proof the two firms should have the same value. Hence, it does not matter whether the firm uses debt and how much debt compared to equity; the value of the firm is unaffected.

A few years later Modigliani and Miller (1963) relaxed their assumptions, introducing corporate taxes into the model. The asymmetric treatment of debt and equity from a tax perspective[4] reveals large benefits from debt financing. This leads to the prediction that firms should use as much debt as possible. However, empirical findings do not support this expectation.

Trade-off theory

The relatively low actual leverage of the firms compared to the Modigliani and Miller (1963) leverage prediction motivated the further development of the theory. It seemed reasonable to expect that there are some offsetting forces for the benefits of the debt. Hence, firms are balancing the benefits and costs of debt financing. This is the argument laid out in trade-off theory. Among the benefits of debt is notably its tax shield. While among the costs of debt are bankruptcy costs (the higher leverage leads to higher risk and higher likelihood of failure). Trade-off theory argues that there is an optimal combination of debt and equity that maximises the firm's value.

In addition, agency problems may explain the trade-off in debt financing. Conflicts may arise between managers and owners as well as between creditors and shareholders. Jensen and Meckling (1976) show that debt financing can be used to confine managers' self-interested actions. Managers might prefer to keep lower debt levels since this would leave them higher cash flows to manage (giving them more flexibility). Owners can assert control over management and decrease the free cash flow problem by using debt financing. Conflicts between creditors and shareholders rise when the debt is risky. Because the shareholders have a residual claim in the firm, they have a tendency to shift to riskier investments to increase the 'upside' while the downside is limited by the limited liabilities. As creditors realise this problem, the possibility of default will limit the debt usage of the firm. Hence, the debt can mitigate manager–shareholder conflicts but it may increase creditor–shareholder conflicts.

Trade-off theory has several empirically testable predictions:

Companies that are more profitable are expected to have higher leverage ratios. More profitable firms can benefit more from the tax shields and they should face lower default probabilities.

Firm size and asset tangibility are expected to be positively related to leverage. Firms with more assets and with more tangible assets should face lower default risk and should be able to offer more collateral.

Higher-growth firms should face lower leverage. Higher-growth firms are related to increased financial distress and reduced cash flow problems.

Industry median leverage is related to firm leverage. For example, firms in higher-growing industries should have lower leverage ratios.

Higher corporate tax rates should be related to higher firm leverage since the benefits of the tax shields are higher.

Higher expected inflation is related to higher debt ratio since the real benefits of the tax shields are higher.

A weaker institutional environment is related to lower leverage since agency conflicts between the creditors and shareholders are likely to be high. Based on trade-off theory the firm leverage is influenced by the firm-specific as well as the country's macroeconomic and institutional factors. CEE economies have weaker institutions compared to Western counterparts and based on trade-off theory we should observe lower levels of leverage.

Pecking order theory

Another line of thought argues that a firm's capital structure is purely driven by its investment opportunities and the cost of capital. This is known as a pecking order theory established by Myers and Majluf (1984) and Myers (1984). The cost of capital of different sources varies due to asymmetric information. The firm's outsiders (creditors and new equity investors) know less about the firm and its prospects than the insiders do. The bigger the information differences, the higher the cost of external financing. Asymmetric information is most severe for new equity funding and therefore the cost of new equity is the highest. Hence, the firm will observe its investment opportunities and start financing them with the cheapest source – internal funds (so that there is no asymmetric information problem). Next, if the investment opportunities are larger than the internal funds available, debt funding will be used. Finally, once debt funding is exhausted external equity funding will be used. The pecking order theory therefore does not assume any particular target debt ratio.

The pecking order theory also has several empirically testable predictions. Some of them contradict the trade-off theory.

Companies that are more profitable are expected to have lower leverage ratios. More profitable firms have more internal funds and therefore do not need to rely so much on external financing.

Firm size and tangibility of assets are expected to be negatively related to leverage since the larger firms or firms with more tangible assets are expected to face fewer asymmetric information problems. Hence, external equity funding should be relatively less costly.

Higher-growth firms should face higher leverage. Higher-growth firms need more funds for investment (keeping the profitability constant).

Industry median leverage is related to firm leverage. For example, firms from industries that are more dependent on external finance should have higher leverage ratios.

A firm's leverage is negatively related to the business cycle since internal funds increase during economic expansion (all else equal). In CEE economies the asymmetric information is rather severe (e.g. corruption levels are higher) and therefore we should expect to see lower levels of leverage.

Market timing theory

Finally, Baker and Wurgler (2002) offer a market timing theory of capital structure to explain firm leverage. They argue that companies issue equity when the market-to-book ratio is high and buy back shares when the market-to-book ratio is low. By doing this, companies are trying to take advantage of the relative cost of capital. Hence, the capital structure is related to historic market values and is an outcome of attempts to time the equity market. Since few CEE firms are listed on the stock market, this theory is less relevant in the CEE context and so is not further discussed here.

Empirical methodology for analysing capital structure

Shyam-Sunder and Myers (1999) offer an empirical testing strategy to evaluate whether firms are following trade-off theory or pecking order theory. They use a version of the partial adjustment model to estimate trade-off theory. They regress the change in the debt level on leverage gap (deviation from the leverage target). They expect the coefficient in front of the leverage gap to be between 0 and 1 if the trade-off theory holds. Actually, this result should not be exclusively interpreted as the trade-off theory holds and pecking order theory does not because of the mean reverting nature of leverage. For estimating the pecking order theory, Shyam-Sunder and Myers regress the change in debt on external finance needed. They argue that the coefficient on this measure should be close to 1 if pecking order theory holds – the debt financing is moving one-to-one to investment opportunities of the firm (the external equity financing is ignored since this is considered such a rare event).

We start by estimating the leverage regression to see how the different theories hold in practice. First, we estimate leverage on well-known firm- and country-specific factors. This is in the spirit of Rajan and Zingales (1995) except that we pool all firms from different countries into one specification and therefore we can control for the country-specific factors as in Jõeveer (2013a). In addition, we include external finance dependence (EFD) as in Shyam-Sunder and Myers (1999) to our leverage regression. Second, we estimate a partial adjustment model[5] to see what factors explain the changes in leverage and whether we observe a target adjustment behaviour in our data.

Equation (1) is the basic model estimated:

$$Leverage_{it} = \alpha + \beta X_{it-1} + \gamma C_{jt-1} + D_j + T_t + u_{it}, \tag{1}$$

Where i is firm index, t is year index and j is the country index. X is a set of firm-specific control variables – profitability (defined as earnings before interest, taxes, depreciation and amortisation (EBITDA) to total assets), tangibility (defined as tangible fixed assets to total assets), logarithm of total assets, median industry leverage and EFD (defined as (change in fixed assets + change in receivables + change in inventories - change in payables - cash flows) / total assets). C is a set of country-specific variables – ratio of banking sector non-performing loans to GDP, corruption perception index, corporate tax rate, GDP growth rate, inflation index, largest three banks' assets share in the banking market and legal rights index. D and T are country and year dummies respectively, and u is the error term.

The partial adjustment model assumes that a company has a leverage target and the estimation shows how much of the current period's deviation from the target is closed by the change in leverage this period. We follow here Lemmon, Roberts and Zender's (2008) specification:

$$\Delta Leverage_{it} = \alpha + \lambda(\mu_{it}^* - Leverage_{it-1}) + \varepsilon_{it}, \tag{2}$$

Where μ^* is a leverage target and is given by $\mu_{it}^* = \beta X_{it-1} + \gamma C_{jt-1} + \eta_i + T_t$, where η_i is a firm fixed effect and ε_{it} is the error term. We follow Lemmon, Roberts and Zender (2008) who argue that the leverage has a large time invariant component and therefore the target leverage should include firm-specific fixed effects.

Equation (3) is the partial adjustment model estimated:

$$\Delta Leverage_{it} = \alpha + \lambda(\beta X_{it-1} + \gamma C_{jt-1} - Leverage_{it-1}) + \eta_i + T_t + \varepsilon_{it} \tag{3}$$

Coefficient λ is the speed of adjustment parameter – how much of the leverage gap (deviation from the leverage target) in one period is closed.

Leverage ratio may be defined in many different ways (see for example Rajan and Zingales 1995). In the following, we use two measures: total liabilities to total assets (liabilities ratio) and total debt to capital ratio (capital is defined as total debt plus equity) (debt ratio).

Data

Firm-level data (unconsolidated financial statements) are from the Amadeus database provided by Bureau van Dijk. Data cover the years 2006–2014. The firms with total assets less than 1 million euros are left out of the analyses and we also leave out the extreme values (top and bottom 1 per cent for each variable). Table 22.1 provides summary statistics for the sample in 2014. The number of companies covered varies by countries. The largest sample of firms is from Italy – 208,687 firms – and the least from Latvia – 188 firms. Unfortunately, more detailed firm-level data is limited for several countries. Therefore, the debt ratio estimation excludes Hungarian and Romanian firms.

Institutional and macroeconomic variables are from different sources. GDP growth rate and annual consumer price changes (inflation) are from IMF (2017). Domestic credit to private sector to GDP and non-performing loans to GDP are from World Bank World Development Indicators (World Bank, 2017a). Corruption perception index is from Transparency International (2017). Data for corporate tax rates is from KMPG (2017). Index of legal rights of borrowers/lenders in the case of bankruptcy is from the World Bank 'Doing Business' survey (World Bank, 2017b). Financial sector competitiveness is proxied by the asset share of the three largest banks. The World Bank Global Financial Dataset (World Bank, 2017c) provides this measure.

Firm capital structure in a changing financial environment

CEE economies have been catching up their Western counterparts since the fall of the Berlin Wall. Ever since returning to market-based economies the goal has been to reach the living standards of the West. The changes have been apparent in many dimensions. In this section, we present the time dynamics in a couple of financial sector indicators and firms' capital structure.

Figure 22.1 plots the GDP per capita (in constant 2010 USDs) versus the domestic credit to private sector (as a percentage of GDP) in years 2006 and 2014 for selected CEE economies as well as France, Germany, Italy, Spain and the UK. There is a clear positive relationship between the level of per capita GDP and the credit to GDP ratio. Higher economic development goes hand in hand with higher financial development.

In Figure 22.2 we see the time dynamics of the domestic credit to GDP ratio from 2001 to 2014. It has an inverted U-shape. The 2007–2008 global financial crisis has left its mark on the further advancement of the credit to GDP ratio. Still, compared to the early 2000s when the average credit to GDP ratio for the CEE region was 27 per cent the figure in 2014 is sizably larger – 50 per cent. At the same time, the Western countries' ratio went up from 95 per cent to 106 per cent. The gap between the East and West is narrowing but it is still wide and will not be closed any time soon based on the current trends.

In Figure 22.3 non-performing loans to GDP are presented. The impact of the global financial crisis is clear. For most countries in the CEE sample, the share of non-performing loans jumped up significantly. The increase in the Western countries has been at the same time marginal.

Higher levels of non-performing loans might explain the decrease in lending by the financial institutions. Given that CEE financial institutions were exposed to higher levels of

Table 22.1 Summary statistics of firm-specific variables in 2014 across European countries

	Bulgaria	Czech Republic	Estonia	Hungary	Latvia	Poland	Romania	Slovakia	Slovenia	France	Germany	Italy	Spain	United Kingdom
Liability ratio														
mean	0.525	0.517	0.418	0.551	0.533	0.494	0.603	0.668	0.570	0.600	0.605	0.696	0.482	0.573
median	0.502	0.495	0.381	0.551	0.535	0.482	0.600	0.706	0.577	0.619	0.628	0.773	0.480	0.587
st. dev.	0.366	0.322	0.288	0.283	0.329	0.298	0.328	0.325	0.289	0.281	0.258	0.274	0.312	0.304
Debt ratio														
mean	0.319	0.286	0.268		0.355	0.364		0.425	0.518	0.409	0.377	0.434	0.405	0.355
median	0.200	0.181	0.166		0.291	0.304		0.356	0.501	0.368	0.322	0.425	0.362	0.275
st. dev.	0.358	0.314	0.292		0.343	0.301		0.373	0.292	0.297	0.307	0.353	0.309	0.315
Profitability														
mean	0.045	0.047	0.058	0.051	0.048	0.060	0.034	0.023	0.035	0.082	0.114	0.058	0.052	0.064
median	0.025	0.031	0.046	0.035	0.035	0.039	0.022	0.010	0.022	0.071	0.101	0.047	0.040	0.049
st. dev.	0.095	0.084	0.097	0.095	0.087	0.097	0.098	0.084	0.073	0.092	0.093	0.070	0.073	0.094
Tangibility														
mean	0.390	0.428	0.320	0.385	0.533	0.394	0.411	0.453	0.425	0.187	0.323	0.331	0.316	0.226
median	0.343	0.397	0.214	0.351	0.627	0.358	0.395	0.439	0.408	0.071	0.235	0.209	0.220	0.094
st. dev.	0.305	0.311	0.310	0.293	0.310	0.300	0.271	0.322	0.292	0.257	0.290	0.327	0.302	0.279
Total assets (in millions of €)														
mean	8.891	13.000	7.873	15.900	16.300	14.100	37.900	11.300	11.300	20.638	46.020	9.350	12.153	125.894
median	2.461	3.103	2.452	4.138	2.322	3.463	9.741	2.691	2.438	2.815	12.663	2.705	2.560	11.398
st. dev.	54.4	79.7	32.8	262	99.9	125	206	119	91.6	311	250	148	174	1590
number of firms	12,313	17,640	2,988	7,238	188	11,352	4,202	10,733	5,937	83,737	20,506	208,687	121,891	15,813

Note: Liabilities ratio is defined as total liabilities to total assets, debt ratio is defined as total debt to total assets, debt ratio is defined as total debt to capital ratio (capital is defined as total debt plus equity), profitability is defined as EBITDA to total assets and tangibility is defined as tangible fixed assets to total assets.

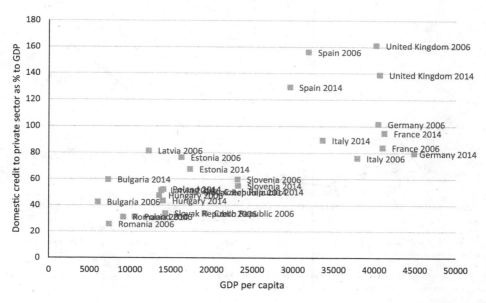

Figure 22.1 Domestic credit to private sector (% of GDP) versus GDP per capita in 2006 and 2014 across selected European countries

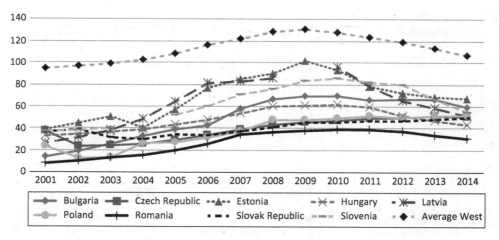

Figure 22.2 Domestic credit to private sector (% of GDP) from 2001 to 2014 across Central and Eastern European countries. Average West is calculated based on data from Germany, France, Italy, Spain and United Kingdom

non-performing loans, it would be natural to expect stronger impact to the corporate capital structures in CEE economies.

In Figure 22.4 the median firm's liabilities ratios over time by country are plotted. For most countries, the median firm's leverage has gone down. Leverage is rather stable for Hungarian, Polish and Romanian samples. In the case of Latvia, we observe an inverse U-shape in leverage and only in the case of Slovakia the increase in liability ratio is observed over time. There is quite noticeable cross-country variation in leverage levels. Western European firms' leverage

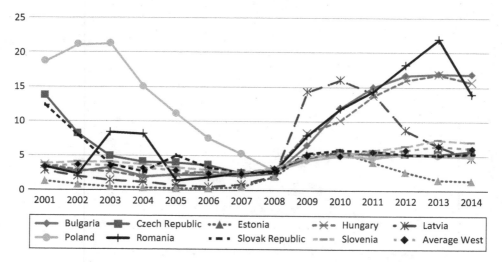

Figure 22.3 Non-performing loans (% to GDP) from 2001 to 2014 across Central and Eastern European countries. Average West is calculated based on data from Germany, France, Italy, Spain and United Kingdom

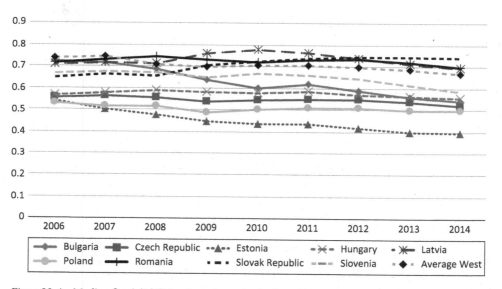

Figure 22.4 Median firm's liabilities to total assets ratio from 2006 to 2014 across Central and Eastern European countries. MedianWest is calculated based on data from Germany, France, Italy, Spain and United Kingdom

has decreased from 73 per cent to 66 per cent while the CEE leverage has gone down from 61 per cent to 58 per cent. Jõeveer (2013b) has shown that the mean liabilities to assets ratio was around 75 per cent in ten Western European countries firms in the year 2000. In addition, Jõeveer (2013a) showed that over the period 1995–2002, the median liabilities to assets ratio increased from 50 per cent to 72 per cent in nine Eastern European economies. Hence, compared to the early 2000s we observe a deleveraging in both East and West.

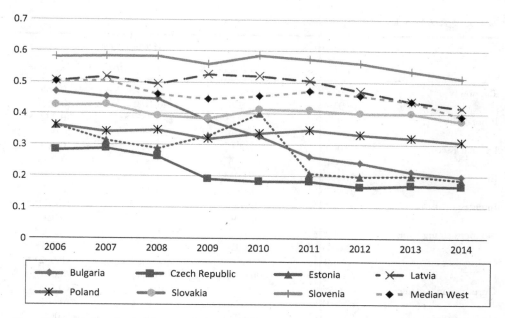

Figure 22.5 Median firm's debt to capital ratio from 2006 to 2014 across Central and Eastern European countries. MedianWest is calculated based on data from Germany, France, Italy, Spain and United Kingdom

Next, in Figure 22.5 the median firm's debt to capital ratios across countries and over time are plotted. The debt ratio has decreased from 50 per cent to 39 per cent in the Western European sample and from 37 per cent to 27 per cent in CEE economies. This ratio varies quite a bit across countries. A noticeable pattern is presented by Estonia, where during the years of the global financial crisis the median firm's leverage went up but it also came quickly down in 2011.

It is interesting to notice the decreasing trends in leverage levels but those changes have not been particularly sharp, and the decreases started before the 2007–2008 global financial crisis and have worsened since. The same trends are visible when the firms are split into size classes. Hence, the decreasing leverage is common for all sizes of firms.

Estimation results

Table 22.2 presents estimation results for equation (1). The first two columns contain the results for the CEE sample and the last two columns the results for the Western firms. From firm-specific variables, profitability is statistically significant in all specifications. It has a negative coefficient confirming the pecking order theory. Tangibility has a negative coefficient, but it is only statistically significant at the 10 per cent level for the liability ratio estimation in the CEE sample. The logarithm of total assets has a negative coefficient but it is not statistically significant. Those results do not support the trade-off theory. External finance dependence enters with a positive and statistically significant coefficient for both leverage measures and samples. This result provides support to the pecking order theory.

From country-specific variables, non-performing loans to GDP enters with an expected negative sign. So worse conditions in the banks are related to lower leverage of the firms. The size of the coefficients are very similar across the CEE and Western European samples contradicting

Table 22.2 Results of leverage regressions across CEE and Western samples

	CEE sample		Western sample	
	Liability ratio	Debt ratio	Liability ratio	Debt ratio
Tangibility	−0.038	−0.052*	−0.094	−0.055
	(0.036)	(0.022)	(0.103)	(0.113)
Profitability	−0.933***	−0.711***	−0.335**	−0.332***
	(0.075)	(0.049)	(0.109)	(0.036)
Ln(total assets)	−0.002	−0.001	−0.007	−0.003
	(0.004)	(0.009)	(0.009)	(0.006)
EFD	0.140***	0.100***	0.138***	0.128***
	(0.017)	(0.015)	(0.008)	(0.005)
Industry median leverage	0.498***	0.443***	0.621***	0.565***
	(0.099)	(0.059)	(0.065)	(0.050)
Nonperforming loans	−0.002**	−0.001	−0.002**	−0.003**
	(0.001)	(0.002)	(0.000)	(0.001)
Corruption	−0.000	0.000	0.002**	−0.002**
	(0.001)	(0.001)	(0.001)	(0.001)
Corporate income tax	0.005***	0.003	−0.002	0.001
	(0.001)	(0.002)	(0.001)	(0.002)
GDP growth	0.001	−0.003	0.000	0.001
	(0.001)	(0.002)	(0.001)	(0.002)
Inflation	0.005***	0.007***	0.004*	0.004
	(0.001)	(0.002)	(0.002)	(0.002)
Bank concentration	0.003***	0.003*	0.002***	0.002***
	(0.001)	(0.002)	(0.000)	(0.000)
Legal rights	−0.016***	−0.006	0.019**	−0.000
	(0.005)	(0.004)	(0.006)	(0.012)
year==2009	−0.020**	−0.060***	−0.017**	−0.012
	(0.008)	(0.009)	(0.006)	(0.018)
year==2010	−0.005	−0.056**	−0.006	−0.002
	(0.009)	(0.022)	(0.008)	(0.023)
year==2011	0.006	−0.032*	−0.011	−0.010
	(0.006)	(0.015)	(0.006)	(0.012)
year==2012	0.000	−0.044***	−0.013	−0.008
	(0.007)	(0.011)	(0.010)	(0.015)
year==2013	0.005	−0.055**	−0.021**	−0.003
	(0.009)	(0.015)	(0.007)	(0.018)
year==2014	0.004	−0.053**	−0.025**	−0.030
	(0.008)	(0.016)	(0.005)	(0.017)
Constant	0.280**	0.180	−0.024	0.294**
	(0.088)	(0.156)	(0.201)	(0.074)
Observations	389,158	312,580	2,524,175	2,344,848
R-squared	0.145	0.112	0.132	0.056

Notes: Liabilities ratio is defined as total liabilities to total assets, debt ratio is defined as total debt to capital ratio (capital is defined as total debt plus equity), profitability is defined as EBITDA to total assets, tangibility is defined as tangible fixed assets to total assets and EFD is defined as (change in fixed assets + change in receivables + change in inventories - change in payables - cash flows) / total assets). Standard errors are clustered by country.***, ** and * denotes significance at 1%, 5% and 10% level respectively.

the expectations that the share of non-performing loans in the financial sector have a larger impact on the capital structure of the CEE firms. The corruptions perception index enters with a positive significant coefficient only for the Western sample. Hence, in less corrupted Western European economies a firm's debt ratio is higher. This is against the expectations that the institutions might affect the capital structure more in CEE economies. GDP growth is not having a statistically significant impact. Inflation is positively related to leverage. This is in line with the trade-off theory. Higher bank concentration is associated with higher leverage in both Eastern and Western samples. Stronger legal rights are related to a lower liability ratio in CEE firms and a higher liability ratio in Western European firms. The CEE sample results contradict the trade-off theory, since based on that theory stronger legal protection should lead to lower bankruptcy costs and therefore to higher leverage. To sum up, the leverage level estimation provides support to pecking order theory and minimal support to the trade-off theory.

Tables 22.3 and 22.4 present the results for the partial adjustment model estimation. Columns one and three contain results of equation (3) estimated with Ordinary Least Squares (OLS) (neglecting firm-specific effects ηi) and columns two and four present results for the firm fixed effects estimations. The latter are preferred and discussed below. The predictive power of the model is substantially better for fixed effects estimation. Lagged leverage enters with statistically significant negative coefficient. It has a slightly larger coefficient compared to the Flannery and Rangan (2006) and Lemmon et al. (2008) book leverage estimations based on US firms. Hence, CEE firms close around 40 per cent of the gap in the total liability ratio in one period and they close around 52 per cent of the gap in the debt ratio in one period (38 per cent and 60 per cent respectively for the Western firms). This finding supports an existence of the leverage target and is consistent with the trade-off theory. Profitability enters with a negative statistically significant coefficient and logarithm of the assets with negative coefficient as in leverage level regressions. Tangibility is now statistically significant and confirms that firms with more tangible assets are associated with increased leverage. This finding is consistent with trade-off theory. EFD enters with positive statistically significant coefficient – higher external finance dependence is related to increased leverage.

To summarise, findings from the leverage level estimations present more support for the pecking order theory but the partial adjustment estimation shows that also trade-off theory forces are in action in determining firm leverage. The impact of the global financial crisis is observed in negative year 2009 dummy (the reference year is 2008). For example, compared to 2008 the liabilities ratio is around 2 per cent lower for both CEE and Western European samples (Table 22.2, columns 1 and 3) in 2009. In addition, we observe more negative effects in subsequent years (in most specifications) confirming the downward trend in leverage since the global crisis.

Conclusions

The global financial crisis in 2007–2008 has had a substantial impact on countries' macroeconomic and financial sector outcomes. The impact has been more severe for the CEE economies, where the GDP growth rates have not yet recovered to the pre-crisis level. In addition, the credit to GDP ratio has decreased after the crisis, while the percentage of non-performing loans has jumped up to a higher level in this region. In light of this, we studied the firms' financing choices. Surprisingly, we do not observe a particular crisis-related impact on corporate leverage ratios. We do observe a decrease in firm leverage but it is rather smooth over time and is not directly attributable to the crisis.

Table 22.3 Results of partial adjustment model for liabilities ratio across CEE and Western samples

	CEE sample		Western sample	
	OLS	FE	OLS	FE
Leverage	-0.040★★★	-0.399★★★	-0.021★★★	-0.385★★★
	(0.004)	(0.002)	(0.004)	(0.001)
Tangibility	0.004★★	0.038★★★	-0.001	0.041★★★
	(0.001)	(0.002)	(0.004)	(0.001)
Profitability	-0.098★★★	-0.061★★★	-0.100★★★	-0.105★★★
	(0.014)	(0.003)	(0.011)	(0.001)
Ln(total assets)	-0.001	-0.026★★★	-0.000	-0.017★★★
	(0.000)	(0.001)	(0.001)	(0.000)
EFD	0.005★	0.013★★★	-0.001	0.006★★★
	(0.003)	(0.001)	(0.002)	(0.000)
Industry median leverage	0.021★★★		0.011	
	(0.005)		(0.009)	
Non-performing loans	0.000	0.000	0.000	0.000★★★
	(0.000)	(0.000)	(0.001)	(0.000)
Corruption	0.000★	0.001★★★	0.000	0.001★★★
	(0.000)	(0.000)	(0.001)	(0.000)
Corporate income tax	0.000	0.001★★★	-0.005	-0.005★★★
	(0.000)	(0.000)	(0.004)	(0.000)
GDP growth	-0.000★	-0.000★★★	-0.003	-0.002★★★
	(0.000)	(0.000)	(0.004)	(0.000)
Inflation	0.001★	0.001★★★	-0.004	-0.003★★★
	(0.000)	(0.000)	(0.006)	(0.000)
Bank concentration	-0.001	0.000★★★	0.001	0.001★★★
	(0.001)	(0.000)	(0.001)	(0.000)
Legal rights	-0.002★	-0.002★★★	0.016	0.024★★★
	(0.001)	(0.001)	(0.020)	(0.000)
year==2009	-0.014★★★	-0.017★★★	-0.018	-0.031★★★
	(0.004)	(0.001)	(0.021)	(0.000)
year==2010	-0.000	-0.009★★★	-0.035	-0.046★★★
	(0.002)	(0.001)	(0.052)	(0.001)
year==2011	0.006★★★	-0.002★★	-0.013	-0.029★★★
	(0.002)	(0.001)	(0.019)	(0.000)
year==2012	-0.003	-0.010★★★	-0.013	-0.030★★★
	(0.003)	(0.001)	(0.014)	(0.000)
year==2013	-0.003	-0.014★★★	-0.022	-0.042★★★
	(0.003)	(0.001)	(0.027)	(0.000)
year==2014	-0.003	-0.015★★★	-0.028	-0.050★★★
	(0.002)	(0.001)	(0.034)	(0.001)
Constant	0.062★	0.546★★★	0.007	0.481★★★
	(0.033)	(0.013)	(0.180)	(0.004)
Observations	384,575	386,280	2,496,477	2,505,410
R-squared	0.023	0.210	0.027	0.221

Notes: Liabilities ratio is defined as total liabilities to total assets, debt ratio is defined as total debt to capital ratio (capital is defined as total debt plus equity), profitability is defined as EBITDA to total assets, tangibility is defined as tangible fixed assets to total assets and EFD is defined as (change in fixed assets + change in receivables + change in inventories - change in payables - cash flows) / total assets). Standard errors are clustered by country.★★★, ★★ and ★ denotes significance at 1%, 5% and 10% level respectively.

Table 22.4 Results of partial adjustment model for debt ratio across CEE and Western samples

	CEE sample		Western sample	
	OLS	FE	OLS	FE
Leverage	-0.112***	-0.526***	-0.108***	-0.602***
	(0.007)	(0.002)	(0.021)	(0.001)
Tangibility	-0.004	0.024***	-0.007	0.031***
	(0.003)	(0.003)	(0.012)	(0.001)
Profitability	-0.091***	-0.069***	-0.063***	-0.121***
	(0.015)	(0.004)	(0.010)	(0.002)
Ln(total assets)	-0.001	-0.020***	0.000	-0.004***
	(0.001)	(0.001)	(0.002)	(0.000)
EFD	0.023***	0.022***	0.037***	0.020***
	(0.004)	(0.002)	(0.006)	(0.001)
Industry median leverage	0.043***		0.062***	
	(0.010)		(0.006)	
Non-performing loans	-0.001	-0.000	-0.002*	-0.001***
	(0.001)	(0.000)	(0.001)	(0.000)
Corruption	-0.001	0.000***	-0.003***	-0.002***
	(0.001)	(0.000)	(0.001)	(0.000)
Corporate income tax	0.001	0.002***	-0.010	-0.005***
	(0.001)	(0.000)	(0.005)	(0.000)
GDP growth	-0.002	-0.003***	0.002	0.002***
	(0.001)	(0.000)	(0.003)	(0.000)
Inflation	0.001	0.002***	0.018***	0.010***
	(0.001)	(0.000)	(0.003)	(0.000)
Bank concentration	-0.002	0.000	0.001	0.001***
	(0.001)	(0.000)	(0.001)	(0.000)
Legal rights	0.002	-0.005***	0.027	0.015***
	(0.005)	(0.001)	(0.017)	(0.001)
year==2009	-0.024*	-0.037***	-0.064**	-0.045***
	(0.010)	(0.002)	(0.021)	(0.001)
year==2010	-0.016	-0.044***	0.006	-0.011***
	(0.014)	(0.002)	(0.017)	(0.002)
year==2011	-0.005	-0.023***	-0.033	-0.035***
	(0.011)	(0.001)	(0.023)	(0.001)
year==2012	-0.011	-0.032***	-0.053*	-0.046***
	(0.007)	(0.001)	(0.023)	(0.001)
year==2013	-0.011	-0.042***	-0.036*	-0.039***
	(0.009)	(0.002)	(0.013)	(0.001)
year==2014	-0.015*	-0.046***	-0.028	-0.049***
	(0.007)	(0.002)	(0.016)	(0.001)
Constant	0.145	0.501***	0.331	0.519***
	(0.076)	(0.024)	(0.162)	(0.010)
Observations	305,044	306,093	2,339,815	2,347,703
R-squared	0.059	0.278	0.063	0.296

Notes: Liabilities ratio is defined as total liabilities to total assets, debt ratio is defined as total debt to capital ratio (capital is defined as total debt plus equity), profitability is defined as EBITDA to total assets, tangibility is defined as tangible fixed assets to total assets and EFD is defined as (change in fixed assets + change in receivables + change in inventories - change in payables - cash flows) / total assets. Standard errors are clustered by country.***, ** and * denotes significance at 1%, 5% and 10% level respectively.

Predictions on capital structure theories are assessed with leverage regressions. We find support for the pecking order theory – profitability is negatively related to leverage and EFD is positively related to leverage. The partial adjustment model confirms also the trade-off theory prediction that firms have leverage targets.

We find that European firms in both East and West are less reliant on debt and use more equity financing. Even though we observe that the leverage levels still somewhat differ across the regions (with lower leverage in CEE) we find that the determinants of the leverage and leverage changes are the same and have similar size impacts in both regions. Based on the analyses the lower share of non-performing loans in the banking sector and a more concentrated banking sector are positively related to corporate leverage. Hence, the financial sector's characteristics have an impact on corporate capital structure and the policy-makers who may want to influence the leverage in a corporate sector may do that through influencing the financial sector.

In addition, policy-makers may want to keep a close eye on the alternative online financial markets (peer-to-peer lending and equity crowd funding, for example), which have popped up in recent years. Those market segments are still in their infancy (crowd-funding amounts to a few million euros in most countries studied here (Crowdfunding Hub 2016)) but are growing at very high speed (achieving 144 per cent growth in the European alternative financial market from 2013 to 2014 (Wardrop et al. 2015)). The emergence of alternative online funding is expected to influence firms' capital structures in the coming years.

Notes

1 This work was supported by Tallinn University of Technology under grant B57 'Efficiency in Financial Sector in Light of Changing Regulatory Environment'.
2 Williams had made a similar argument to Modigliani and Miller as early as 1938, but the research in the field of capital structure theory took off after the Modigliani and Miller 1958 article.
3 The levered and unlevered company are considered to be identical in all aspects except the financing structure.
4 The interest payments to creditors are made from pre-tax profit while the shareholders receive the dividend from the after-tax profit. Hence, the debt has a tax shield.
5 See Flannery and Rangan (2006) for more about leverage estimation with the partial adjustment model.

References

Baker, M. and Wurgler, J. (2002), 'Market timing and capital structure', *Journal of Finance*, vol. 57, no. 1, pp. 1–32.
Cassano, F., Jõeveer, K. and Svejnar, J. (2013), 'Cash flow versus collateral-based credit: Performance of micro, small and medium-sized firms in transition economies', *Economics of Transition*, vol. 21, no. 2, pp. 269–300.
Crowdfunding Hub (2016), 'Current state of crowdfunding in Europe'.
ECB (2016), 'Report on financial structures'.
Flannery, M. and Rangan, R. (2006), 'Partial adjustment towards target capital structures', *Journal of Financial Economics*, vol. 79, no. 3, pp. 469–506.
Frank, M.Z. and Goyal, V.K. (2009), 'Capital structure decisions: Which factors are reliably important?' *Financial Management*, vol. 38, no. 1, pp. 1–37.
Graham, J.R. and Harvey, C. (2001), 'The theory and practice of corporate finance: Evidence from the field', *Journal of Financial Economics*, vol. 60, no. 2, pp. 187–243.
IMF (2017), 'World Economic Outlook'. www.imf.org/external/pubs/ft/weo/2017/02/weodata/index.aspx (accessed 28 March 2018).
Jensen, M.C. and Meckling, W.H. (1976), 'Theory of the firm: Managerial behavior, agency costs and ownership structure', *Journal of Financial Economics*, vol. 3, no. 4, pp. 305–360.
Jõeveer, K. (2013a), 'Firm, country and macroeconomic determinants of capital structure: Evidence from transition economies', *Journal of Comparative Economics*, vol. 41, no. 1, pp. 294–308.

Jõeveer, K. (2013b), 'What do we know about capital structure of small firms?' *Small Business Economics,* vol. 41, no. 2, pp. 479–501.

KPMG (2017), 'Corporate Tax Rates Table'. https://home.kpmg.com/xx/en/home/services/tax/tax-tools-and-resources/tax-rates-online/corporate-tax-rates-table.html (accessed 14 January 2017).

Lemmon, M.L., Roberts, M.R. and Zender, J.F. (2008), 'Back to the beginning: Persistence and the cross-section of corporate capital structure', *Journal of Finance*, vol. 63, no. 4, pp. 1575–1608.

Modigliani, F. and Miller, M. (1958), 'The cost of capital, corporation finance and the theory of investment', *The American Economic Review*, vol. 48, no. 3, pp. 261–297.

Modigliani, F. and Miller, M. (1963), 'Corporate income taxes and the cost of capital: Ac, *The American Economic Review*, vol. 53, pp. 433–443.

Myers, S.C. (1984), 'The capital structure puzzle', *Journal of Finance*, vol. 39, no. 3, pp. 574–592.

Myers, S.C. and Majluf, N.S. (1984), 'Corporate financing and investment decisions when firms have information that investors do not have', *Journal of Financial Economics*, vol. 13, no. 2, pp. 187–221.

Rajan, R. and Zingales, L. (1995), 'What do we know about capital structure? Some evidence from international data', *Journal of Finance*, vol. 50, no. 5, pp. 1421–1460.

Shyam-Sunder, L. and Myers, S.C. (1999), 'Testing static tradeoff against pecking order models of capital structure', *Journal of Financial Economics*, vol. 51, no. 2, pp. 219–244.

Transparency International (2017), 'Corruption Perceptions index'. www.transparency.org/research/cpi/overview (accessed 14. January 2017).

Wardrop, R., Zhang, B., Rau, R. and Gray, M. (2015), *Moving Mainstream. The European alternative finance benchmarking report*, University of Cambridge and EY.

Williams, J.B. (1938), *The Theory of Investment Value*, vol. 36, Cambridge, MA, Harvard University Press.

World Bank (2017a), 'World development indicators'. http://databank.worldbank.org/data/reports.aspx?source=world-development-indicators (accessed 14 January 2017).

World Bank (2017b), 'Doing businesss'. www.doingbusiness.org/rankings (accessed 14 January 2017).

World Bank (2017c), 'Global financial development database'. www.worldbank.org/en/publication/gfdr/data/global-financial-development-database (accessed 14 January 2017).

23

MANAGING CROSS-BORDER M&A

Three approaches to takeovers in Europe

Anna John, Thomas Lawton and Maureen Meadows

Introduction

Since the early twentieth century, there have been seven 'waves' or 'peaks' in cross-border merger and acquisition (M&A) deals in Europe (Fligstein and Merand 2002; Gaughan 2010; Statista 2016). The most recent peaks were due to an increase in deals where domestic firms in the European Union (EU) were targets of foreign firms, either from elsewhere in the EU or from outside the EU (Turvill 2017). Hence, in this chapter, we focus on this type of deal.

Other chapters in this volume consider internationalisation decisions, e.g. the exporting of products and services that presume lower commitment of resources and, therefore, imply lower market and non-market risks. Our chapter adds to these discussions by centring on cross-border M&A, the internationalisation mode associated with higher commitment of resources and hence higher market and non-market risks. A merger may be defined as the combination of two or more companies to create a new entity or form a holding company (Jagersma 2005). By contrast, an acquisition is the purchase of shares or assets of another company to achieve managerial influence (Chen and Findlay 2003), not necessarily by mutual agreement (in this case the acquisition takes the form of a takeover) (Jagersma 2005). Cross-border M&A deals are those between the foreign company and the domestic company in the target country.

As in other parts of the world (Straub 2007; McMorris 2015), cross-border deals in the EU have demonstrated high failure rates (Vaara 2002; Granlund et al. 1998). In this chapter we explore why and how decisions about cross-border M&A are made in an EU context. We consider the underlying value of cross-border M&A, which choices (strategic and organisational) seem to work better for M&A deals and how they take place, that is, the various enablers, or factors – processes and value systems – affecting implementation of the deals.

The chapter is structured as follows. The subsequent sections focus on value, choices and enablers of cross-border M&A within the EU. We explore these themes by looking at three major literature streams, each suggesting its own approach to the successful management of M&A. These are the institutions lens; the resources and capabilities approach; and the firm–environment relations perspective. The chapter ends with conclusions, where we propose directions for future research into failures and successes of European cross-border M&A in the light of recent trends such as integration and disintegration in the EU, devolution of central powers to regional and national jurisdictions in European states and resilience to global recessions.

Achieving value: Why pursue cross-border M&A in Europe?

In this section, we look into why firms pursue cross-border M&A deals in Europe and we explore this issue from the institutions perspective, the resources and capabilities perspective and the firm–environment relations perspective. Table 23.1 integrates this discussion by referring to examples of such deals for the period 2009–2011.

The institutions lens

Some studies of European cross-border foreign direct investments (FDIs) argue that, despite poorer financial performance, M&As are often preferred to joint ventures and greenfield investments because of a number of institutional factors (Nitsch et al. 1996). First and foremost, they may be viewed as better choices for reducing institutional uncertainty (Rui and Yip 2008). This is because they allow the firm to avoid institutional pressures on its existing markets and to create instant institutional embeddedness in new markets. For instance, through M&A, acquirer firms such as Kraft Foods (US) and Abbott Laboratories (US) may reduce reliance on, or even leave, markets with multiple regulatory checks such as the USA and become embedded into the institutional systems of new European markets and the overseas markets of target European firms (Column 'Institutions' in Table 23.1). This rationale for European cross-border M&A deals was confirmed for some Japanese multinational enterprises (MNEs) targeting firms in Europe (Nitsch et al. 1996). For instance, having experienced multiple checks in the market for generic pharmaceuticals in the USA, the Japanese Takeda Pharmaceutical Company had to consider European targets as bridges to new, less-regulated markets in emerging and developing economies (Column 'Institutions' in Table 23.1).

Second, European cross-border M&As may be viewed as responses to isomorphic pressures. For instance, many MNEs have opted for European cross-border M&A by mimicking the strategic moves of leading firms and by replicating their past successful choices (Yang and Hyland 2012). Some MNEs from emerging economies such as China and India (e.g. Bird, a Chinese telecommunications firm) have entered less familiar markets in Western, Central and Eastern European regions by responding to the M&A strategies of leading firms in these markets (Larçon 2008). Likewise, decisions to acquire firms in Europe were stimulated by the rise of initiatives relating to EU integration, when new legislation and professional bodies were created to support M&A activity in the region (Garette and Dussauge 2000). Garette and Dussauge (2000) stress that, until the end of the 1990s, the political environment in Europe had constrained European and non-European MNEs from acquiring market leaders, or so-called national champions in the region. For instance, it had not been feasible for the Swedish firm Volvo to purchase Peugeot and Renault. Chapman and Edmond (2000) observed a similar trend where a significant proportion of global cross-border M&A activity had been focused on the EU, stimulated by economic integration. Likewise, Rui and Yip (2008) showed that Chinese MNEs preferred M&A in Europe due to the greater development of European market institutions.

A resources and capabilities approach

In line with this approach, firms pursue M&A deals to enhance and renew their resources and capabilities (Riviere and Suder 2016) and/or because they have already developed the dynamic capabilities needed to pursue this growth strategy (Teece 2007). Regarding the former case, Anand et al. (2005) show that firms opt for cross-border acquisitions in Europe to gain access

Table 23.1 Illustrative examples of the value of European cross-border M&A

Institutions	Resources and capabilities	Firm–environment relations
The institutions approach suggests that institutional escapism may be one of the reason behind the acquisition of **Cadbury UK** by **Kraft Foods** (now Mondelez International) (U.S.) (2009). Since the mid-2000s the latter had experienced pressures to move into overseas markets to escape multiple checks in the local US context stemming from warnings of voluntary organisations (e.g. Ban Trans-Fat), multiple campaigns and legislative propositions (e.g. Proposition N37 in California) of the US state agencies (e.g. Food and Drug Administration, FDA) against genetically modified foods and trans-fat laden foods (Chopra and Nanda 2012; Jargon and Berry 2012; Eat Local Grown 2017). Targeting a European-based company, such as **Cadbury UK**, with a strong presence in new markets in emerging and developing economies, would help to achieve this goal (Cadbury 2008). Institutional escapism seems to be the motive behind other M&A investments into Europe by firms relying on US markets. Examples include **Abbott Laboratories** (US) (Whalen et al. 2009; Wilson 2009), **Takeda Pharmaceutical Company** (Japan) (Whipp and Jack 2011; Topham and Hirschler 2011), **Johnson & Johnson** (US) (InJ News Media 2012; The Street 2012) and **Teva Pharmaceutical Industries** (Israel) (Biotech 2010; Siebelt and Burger 2010). By acquiring **Skype Technologies** (Luxemburg), **Microsoft Corporation** (US) was responding to competitive pressures in the market environment. The company also had to react to earlier mimetic isomorphism in the market, e.g. attempts by Google LLC to buy Skype Technologies in order to become the market leader for video content and online telephony (BBC 2011; Damouni and Rigby 2011).	Some European cross-border M&As were inspired by the need to enhance resources and capabilities that could help MNEs to improve their competitive positions and open up new opportunities for future growth. For example, the acquisition of **Johnson & Johnson** (US) was motivated by the need to improve its position vis-à-vis key competitors such as Pfizer, GlaxoSmithKline and Merck, whose shares had been rising. In the late 2000s, **Johnson & Johnson** (US) needed to develop expertise in new products and new markets in emerging economies (Das et al. 2011). Similarly, **Takeda Pharmaceutical Company** (Japan) had been slow in entering new markets; hence their interest in the immediate entry into European markets by acquiring a leading firm there (Takeda 2011). Therefore, the acquisition of **Nycomed** (Switzerland) was expected to help develop regulatory expertise and commercialisation capability for new and emerging markets (Whipp and Jack 2011; Topham and Hirschler 2011; Takeda 2011)	Some firms have entered into acquisition deals with European firms in an attempt to reduce their dependence on markets where their bargaining positions were weaker and where ambiguity in relationships with key stakeholders was higher. For example, firms in highly regulated industries such as food and pharmaceuticals have tried to reduce their reliance on the highly regulated US market. In such cases, they were interested not only in less regulated markets but also in those that were highly regulated given the target firm would have the capacity to manage these multiple checks on its home market. Indeed, due to frequent litigation processes and constant checks, the bargaining positions of **Abbott Laboratories** (US) and **Johnson & Johnson** (US) vis-à-vis the US authorities (such as the Food and Drug Administration in the American markets of generic pharmaceuticals and orthopaedic surgery) substantially deteriorated by the end of the 2000s (Rottenstein Law Group 2014; Nussbaum et al. 2011). Likewise, **Takeda Pharmaceutical Company** (Japan) lost its bargaining position in its key market of generic pharmaceuticals in the USA, due to lawsuits filed in response to the company's failure to disclose cancer risks associated with several of its products (Fackler and Pollack 2014). Similarly, **Teva Pharmaceutical Industries** (Israel), specialising in generic drugs, overcame patenting litigations and substantial delays in obtaining patents for one of its leading drugs (Copaxone) in the USA (The Pharma Letter 2011; Grogan 2012). The firms had to consider reconfiguring their resource interdependencies by signing acquisition deals with targets in Europe. Some firms opt for European cross-border M&A to gain fast access to resources that help to rapidly enhance their bargaining power in other markets. Arguably, high-tech leaders such as **Microsoft Corporation** (US) gain additional R&D expertise from European acquisitions, which further enhance their bargaining power in new host markets (Financial Times 2016).

to such an important resource as diversity of markets. For example, the diversity of markets seemed to be one of the key drivers in the acquisition of Synthes (Switzerland) by Johnson & Johnson (US) (Column 'Resources and Capabilities' in Table 23.1). Likewise, they may be interested in M&A deals in Europe as a way to expand brand resources (Capron and Hulland 1999). Furthermore, for acquirers, target firms in Europe may be sources of dynamic capabilities. These may be related to the management of diverse markets in Europe and abroad (Anand et al., 2005). According to Pelzman (2015), these dynamic capabilities come from innovative activity. For instance, unable to induce enough innovation activity internally, MNEs from the People's Republic of China make FDIs by acquiring European firms with high innovative capability (Pelzman 2015).

In the latter case, MNEs opt for European cross-border M&A because they have already developed dynamic capabilities for managing such deals in the European context (Teece 2007; Capron and Hulland 1999).

Firm–environment relations perspective

The firm–environment relations perspective informs us that the major reason for engaging in M&A deals in Europe is the management of resource interdependencies – relationships where both actors depend upon each other in terms of access to critical external resources, such as new markets, raw materials and legal permissions (Pfeffer and Salancik 2003; Hillman et al. 2009). First, such deals help European and non-European MNEs to reduce their critical and ongoing resource interdependencies in existing markets such as the USA and Japan (Walter and Barney 1990; Somlev and Hoshino 2005; Hillman et al. 2009). For instance, as they allow immediate extension of the business resource base to relatively more stable and smaller markets in European countries and to new markets in emerging economies, deals such as the acquisition of Ratiopharm (Germany) by Teva Pharmaceutical Industries (Israel) (Column 'Firm–Environment Relations' in Table 23.1) enhance the overall bargaining power of MNEs, which further helps to negotiate more favourable conditions of access to critical resources in other host markets; hence a possibility of lower resource interdependency (Inkpen and Beamish 1997; Nitsch et al. 1995). Overall, some authors agree that firms investing in European markets would be better off with M&As that offer nearly full absorption of interdependencies than with interorganisational partnerships such as strategic alliances and joint ventures, which offer only partial absorption of interdependencies (Hillman et al. 2009; Harrigan and Newman 1990; Garette and Dussauge 2000; Dussauge 2008).

Second, M&A deals help European and non-European MNEs to reduce uncertainty surrounding their resource dependencies. Through initiatives relating to EU integration, market reforms and privatisation in transition economies in the Central and Eastern European region, the new M&A institutional and regulatory systems in the late 1990s created supportive conditions for cross-border M&A by making this entry mode less risky and by reducing its transaction costs and information assymetries in the European context (Garette and Dussauge 2000). Consequently, many MNEs revised their real options – strategies for progressing from less risky forms of business investments (e.g. alliances/joint ventures) to those with higher risks (e.g. M&A deals) (Luehrman 1998) – in Europe (Garette and Dussauge 2000). The moves to M&A suggested greater absorption of interdependencies due to higher control over resources, easier access to information about potential agents (e.g. host targets, host governments and host deal advisors) and fewer institutional and bureaucratic constraints, leading to lower transaction costs of coordination (Garette and Dussauge 2000; Dussauge 2008; Meyer 2001; Uhlenbruck and De Castro 2000).

Yet, M&As do not always help firms to reduce resource dependencies and to mitigate uncertainty surrounding such resource dependencies. Indeed, instead of strengthening its power vis-à-vis major stakeholder groups in the home market, an acquirer firm may lose its bargaining position there, and may be forced to withdraw from foreign markets. Kolk et al. (2014) discuss one such case by looking at the example of a state-owned energy utility, Vattenfall, which had to return to its three core markets: Sweden, the Netherlands and Germany.

Making choices: Which strategies work better?

The success or failure of a cross-border M&A deal in Europe depends upon the choices (strategic and organisational) underlying the deal. This section explores what these choices are in three approaches to M&A – the institutions approach, the resources and capabilities approach, and the firm–environment relations approach. We provide illustrative examples in Table 23.2.

Table 23.2 Illustrative examples of choices underlying European cross-border M&A

Institutions	Resources and capabilities	Firm–environment relations
Institutional factors can define the choices of specific targets. For instance, by acquiring **Cadbury UK**, **Kraft Foods** (US) did not envisage entry into the UK market as its primary objective; instead, it aimed to use Cadbury UK as a route to becoming embedded into institutionally challenging markets in emerging economies, such as countries in Sub-Saharan Africa (Cadbury 2008). Likewise, other MNEs chose to acquire their targets (e.g. **Solvay S.A.** (Belgium), **Ratiopharm** (Germany) and **Nycomed** (Switzerland)) as sources of fast institutional embeddedness in unfamiliar emerging markets such as India, Brazil, Russia and China (Pharmafile 2010a; Dealbook 2010; Takeda 2011). Apart from their institutional embeddedness, **Synthes** (Switzerland) and **Ratiopharm** (Germany) revealed opportunities for **Johnson & Johnson** (US) and **Teva Pharmaceutical Industries** (Israel) respectively to reduce their tax base (coercive isomorphism) (The Street 2012; Siebelt and Burger 2010).	**Takeda Pharmaceutical Company** (Japan) chose **Nycomed** (Switzerland) as the target of an acqustion because of its large resource base (Takeda 2011). At the time of the acquisition, **Nycomed** (Switzerland) had developed a diversified product portfolio, an extensive European commercial network, strong presence in several rapidly growing and emerging markets, a broad brand portfolio, and R&D capability (Takeda 2011). Similarly, by choosing **Ratiopharm** (Germany), **Teva Pharmaceutical Industries** (Israel) would gain immediate access to a large customer base and become the world's second largest generic producer (Dealbook 2010; Siebelt and Burger 2010)	Emerging economies represent an opportunity for pharmaceutical companies. Their large populations can help to substaintily increase their international customer base. However, most of these markets have become highly competitive, suggesting greater bargaining power of their host governments and greater vulnerability of new entrant firms in applications for patents. Finding target firms to help to leverage bargaining positions is critical in these markets. It would appear that US acquirers target European firms (such as Swiss **Nycomed**, Belgian **Solvay S.A.**, Swiss **Synthes** and German **Ratiopharm**) not only to bargain for access to key European markets but also to bargain for new markets and resources in emerging economies such as India, China, Russia, Turkey and Brazil (Pharmafile 2010a; Dealbook 2010; Takeda 2011).

The institutions lens

In this approach, studies assume that institutions shape the strategic choices of M&A (Akbar and Suder 2006). Multinational enterprises are more likely to fulfil their objectives by selecting targets that can guarantee swift institutional embeddedness, and/or can shape institutional environments to their benefit in new markets (Lebedev et al. 2015). For instance, Takeda Pharmaceutical Company (Japan) chose Nycomed (Switzerland) as an acquisition target, because the latter would guarantee institutional embeddedness into less familiar emerging markets (Column 'Institutions' in Table 23.2).

Furthermore, according to Uhlenbruck and De Castro (2000), the acquisition of privatised firms helps to establish embeddedness into institutional systems and gain access to one of the most critical stakeholders – host governments – in Central and Eastern Europe and former communist countries.

Nonetheless, some studies of European cross-border M&A caution that criteria and approaches to choices of target firms may vary across national systems (Angwin 2001). Differences in softer institutional structures predetermine differences in approaches to managing uncertainty in cross-border M&A in Germany and France (Mayrhofer 2004).

The resources and capabilities approach

In this approach, bidding firms are interested in targets and partners that help to enhance their existing resource base and bring in new capabilities which could not be developed without entering into an M&A deal (Capron and Hulland 1999). For example, Ratiopharm (Germany) appeared to be an attractive target for Teva Pharmaceutical Industries (Israel) due to its large customer base (Column 'Resources and Capabilities' in Table 23.2).

Likewise, whenever possible, target firms will be interested in acquirers and partners having a larger resource base and greater experience in M&A. For example, Forte et al. (2010) conclude that when making the choice to hire a bank advisor, target firms are interested in banks having greater reputational resources (e.g. reputation in M&A and long-term relationships with the target firm) and greater capabilities for managing complex deals (e.g. prior experience in complex M&A).

The firm–environment relations perspective

This approach suggests that, as in other contexts, the success or failure of a cross-border M&A deal in Europe is a function of how strategic choices – such as the choice of a target firm or advisory partner, and decisions about divestments and spin-offs – help to manage resource interdependencies. Multinational enterprises are more likely to fulfil their objectives through M&A if their strategic choices allow them to reduce resource interdependencies and/or reduce uncertainty surrounding these resource interdependencies. For this reason, MNEs tend to target firms that allow greater control over critical resources in the future. Specifically, MNEs may be interested in targets that allow them to absorb direct competitors or supply chain partners in the future (Haleblian et al. 2009; Deng 2009). For instance, Takeda Pharmaceutical Company (Japan) took over Nycomed (Switzerland) as its major rival in the market for generic pharmaceuticals in Europe and emerging economies (Column 'Firm–Environment Relations' in Table 23.2).

Similarly, MNEs tend to choose due diligence advisor partners who can help to reduce uncertainties due to information assymetries in acquirer-target contracts, as well as in negotiations with critical stakeholders such as government authorities and work councils (Meyer 2001; Capron and Guillén 2009).

Finally, MNEs tend to choose payment methods that are more feasible given multiple dependencies upon certain shareholders. For instance, where measures of financial condition weaken, acquirers would prefer stock financing. However, as in the USA, this method of payment in cross-border M&A in Europe may have implications for the future ownership structure in MNEs with highly concentrated shareholdings or many blockholders (Faccio and Masulis 2005). Stock financing may reduce the share of blockholders with voting control and hence control over managerial decisions of acquiring MNEs. Once their control is threatened by stock financing of the new target, blockholders of the acquirer may be interested in preventing stock financing as a payment method. Therefore, where acquiring MNEs have more concentrated control, cross-border M&As are more likely to be financed by cash (Faccio and Masulis 2005).

Managing enablers: How are M&A strategies facilitated?

In this section, we discuss enablers; these are factors such as processes and value systems affecting the implementation of cross-border M&A deals in Europe. How are M&A strategies facilitated? We explore the institutions, resources and capabilities, and firm—environment relations approaches to this issue. Table 23.3 shows some illustrative examples.

The institutions lens

The institutions approach suggests that the success or failure of a particular M&A is a function of organisational arrangements that guarantee continuing embeddedness into the new institutional environment. For instance, successful M&As are those where organisational culture emphasises continuity of managerial teams in targets as a way to maintain successful interaction with key institutions (Lebedev et al. 2015; Angwin 2001). This was one of the reasons why it was decided that Oliver Windholz, CEO of Ratiopharm (Germany), would stay in post for an integration period after the firm was acquired by Teva Pharmaceutical Industries (Israel) (Column 'Institutions' in Table 23.3).

Also, the success or failure of a particular cross-border M&A may be a function of differences in institutional systems. Different norms and expectations of the acquirer and target firms as to what are the right ways of managing the deal may result in the new firm's inability to fulfil its objectives (Björkman and Søderberg 2006).

The resources and capabilities approach

As in other parts of the world, the success or failure of a particular cross-border M&A in Europe is a function of organisational fit and – supporting it – transition-related resources and capabilities (Altunbaş and Marqués 2008). An organisational culture that allows synergies is an important transition-related resource that enhances the performance of M&A at the post-deal stage (Altunbaş and Marqués 2008). For example, the failure of Hewlett-Packard (US) to assess these synergies at the pre-deal stage resulted in the poor performance of its target – Autonomy Corporation (UK) – at the post-deal stage (Column 'Resources and Capabilities' in Table 23.3).

The knowledge of teams managing the transition is another important resource, which acquiring firms use to create value from the deal (Grant 1996; Hébert et al. 2005). Yet, Hébert et al. (2005) caution about using expatriates as sources of knowledge. The authors conclude that expatriation may help an M&A to survive, but this survival depends upon the type of experience and knowledge expatriates have as well as their capacity to lead the transition. Furthermore, some studies point to the problem that ethnocentric views may inhibit knowledge exchange between expatriates and managerial teams in newly acquired firms (Mayrhofer and Brewster 1996).

Table 23.3 Illustrative examples of the enablers of European cross-border M&A

Institutions	Resources and capabilities	Firm–environment relations
M&As have the potential to support organisational arrangements to preserve existing institutional embeddedness and enhance subsequent institutional integration of the acquirer. For instance, the Japanese MNE **Takeda Pharmaceutical Company** adhered to creating a culture such that **Nycomed** (Switzerland) could continue benefiting from its connectedness to market and non-market institutions and Takeda Pharmaceutical Company could learn about the new markets of its target (Takeda 2011). A similar approach was adopted in the acquisition of **Ratiopharm** (Germany) by **Teva Pharmaceutical Industries** (Israel), allowing the latter to benefit from embeddedness into legal and distributional systems created by the Merkle family and the CEO, Oliver Windholz (Pharmafile 2010b).	Examples of the enablers in **Nycomed** (Switzerland) are organisational culture stressing diversified talent and entrepreneurial leadership; and detailed due diligence and assessment of cultural fit at the pre-deal stage (Takeda 2011). By contrast, the impeding factors in **Autonomy Corporation** (UK) were loss of human capital resources, loss of key leaders and lack of capabilities in managing due diligence procedures (Chesters 2012).	An organisational culture with an emphasis on trust and transparency, as well as a commitment to reduce information assymetries, can help to reduce uncertainty in resource interdependency relations between the acquirer's and target's teams. Companies adopt different approaches to enhancing the culture of trust and commitment to mutual goals. For instance, successful acquisitions are supported by similarities in cultures, clear communication of intentions and articulation of mutual goals. These were the principles in the European acquisitions of **Takeda Pharmaceutical Company** (Japan) and **Teva Pharmaceutical Industries** (Israel) (Takeda 2011; Pharmafile 2010b). Alternatively, **Microsoft Corporation**'s (US) experience shows that it may be easier to manage M&A with smaller target companies (Statt 2013). Such companies have smaller teams whose intentions are likely to be more transparent to the acquirer; hence fewer information asymmetries and lower uncertainty in resource interdependencies (Statt 2013).

Likewise, capabilities to redeploy resources such as brands, sales forces and expertise in key areas constitute key transition-related capabilities that lead to cost-based and revenue-based synergies after the deal is complete (Capron and Hulland 1999).

The firm–environment relations perspective

From this perspective, the success or failure of a particular M&A is a function of external and internal interdependencies (Amin et al. 1992; McKiernan and Merali 1995; Norburn and Schoenberg 1994; Angwin and Savill 1997). Regarding the former, cross-border M&As in Europe trigger responses of competitors and other important stakeholder groups in the market and non-market environments (Amin et al. 1992). These responses may have implications for external resource interdependencies and the post-deal performance of these M&As (Amin et al. 1992).

Regarding the latter, the effectiveness of a cross-border M&A in Europe is affected by resource interdependencies in its intra-organisational relationships – those between the acquiring MNE and the target firm. Multinational enterprises manage these interdependencies by reducing information asymmetries with the target at the pre-deal stage (adverse selection) and at the post-deal stage (moral hazards) (Angwin 2001). One way of reducing information asymmetries is by choosing targets the systems and values of which are similar to those of the acquiring MNE (Angwin 2001; Epstein 2004). Some authors stress that, as in other territories such as the USA, cultural incompatibility in European cross-border M&As leads to voids in communication systems, which, in turn, cause information asymmetries and undermine post-deal performance (McKiernan and Merali 1995; Schuler and Jackson 2001; Norburn and Schoenberg 1994). Alternatively, some MNEs (e.g. Microsoft Corporation (US)) reduce potential information assymetries by choosing smaller target firms, as the intentions of such targets are likely to be more transparent; hence, there are fewer information assymetries and lower uncertainty (Column 'Firm–Environment Relations' in Table 23.3). Finally, MNEs may attempt to reduce information asymmetries by thorough due diligence (Norburn and Schoenberg 1994; McKiernan and Merali 1995; Angwin and Savill 1997).

Discussion and conclusions

Academics and practitioners have been relentless in their pursuit of a better understanding of the reasons for the success or failure of cross-border M&As. In this chapter, we revisit this issue by making an inquiry into why, which and how decisions about cross-border M&A are made in the European context. Our analysis suggests that, in most cases, these decisions and their role in failures and successes of European cross-border M&A deals have been addressed by following three major approaches: institutions, resources and capabilities, and firm–environment relations.

Each of these three approaches offers its unique view as to why some deals are more successful whereas others fail to fulfil their objectives. For example, the institutions approach helps to explain failures and successes of European cross-border deals as outcomes of institutional factors, including institutional pressures, institutional uncertainty, institutional embeddedness and institutional configurations. It assumes a passive role of firms in the external environment and argues that decisions about M&A are reactions to institutional and regulatory environments. It suggests that M&As are more likely to succeed in environments with more favourable institutional conditions (such as legislation supporting M&A activity), fewer institutional voids and greater institutional embeddedness. The institutions approach may be pertinent for firms that enter countries whose M&A institutions have formed as protectionist responses to a series of hostile takeovers of national leaders. For instance, this approach may be pertinent to firms interested in M&A in Germany, France and the Netherlands (Barbaglia et al. 2017). Inherent to this approach is becoming institutionally embedded by targeting firms and partners with strong links to the national government.

In contrast, the resources and capabilities approach views successes and failures of European cross-border M&A deals as functions of resources and capabilities. It assumes a proactive role of firms in the environment. It suggests that M&As are more likely to fulfil their objectives where the acquirers are successful in developing and using their resources and capabilities. For example, this approach may be more effective in relation to targets from countries such as the UK, France and Portugal, which, due to their colonial past, enjoy stronger links with new markets in emerging and developing economies, particularly in Asia and Africa. Such targets serve as bridges to new customers, have broader resource bases, stronger brand names and greater commercialisation capacity in these markets.

Finally, the firm–environment relations approach considers the successes and failures of European cross-border M&A deals as outcomes of resources interdependencies. Both firms and environments depend upon and can influence each other. This approach argues that the effectiveness of M&A deals depends upon the management of resource interdependencies. Fewer resource dependencies and lower uncertainty surrounding these dependencies lead to successful deals.

The study of M&A can benefit from each of these approaches; hence, opportunities to combine them should also be considered. Prior research has not explored complementarities among these distinct views. Future studies might address this issue by developing a multi-theoretical framework for the analysis of M&A deals. In this research, several questions may prove to be particularly important. For example, how can firms use their resources and capabilities during M&A to manage their institutional environments and their resource interdependencies? How do institutions shape resources and capabilities as well as resource interdependencies during M&A? How do the resource interdependencies of firms engaging in M&A affect their resources and capabilities and their institutional environments?

References

Akbar, Y. and Suder, G. (2006), 'The new EU Merger Regulation: Implications for EU–U.S. Merger Strategies', *Thunderbird International Business Review*, vol. 48, no. 5, pp. 667–685.

Altunbaş, Y. and Marqués, D. (2008), 'Mergers and acquisitions and bank performance in Europe: The role of strategic similarities', *Journal of Economics and Business*, vol. 60, no. 3, pp. 204–222.

Amin, A., Charles, D.R. and Howells, J. (1992), 'Corporate restructuring and cohesion in the new Europe', *Regional Studies*, vol. 26, no. 4, pp. 319–331.

Anand, J., Capron, L. and Mitchell, W. (2005), 'Using acquisitions to access multinational diversity: Thinking beyond the domestic versus cross-border M&A comparison', *Industrial and Corporate Change*, vol. 14, no. 2, pp. 191–224.

Angwin, D. (2001), 'Mergers and acquisitions across European borders: National perspectives on preacquisition due diligence and the use of professional advisers', *Journal of World Business*, vol. 36, no. 1, pp. 32–57.

Angwin, D. and Savill, B. (1997), 'Strategic perspectives on European cross-border acquisitions: A view from top European executives', *European Management Journal*, vol. 15, no. 4, pp. 423–435.

Barbaglia, P., Wagner, R. and Schuetze, A. (2017), *Germany sets EU tone with tighter curbs on foreign takeovers*. https://uk.reuters.com/article/us-germany-m-a/germany-sets-eu-tone-with-tighter-curbs-on-foreign-takeovers-idUKKBN19W2R6 (accessed 23 March 2018).

Biotech (2010), 'Teva completes acquisition of ratiopharm'. www.fiercebiotech.com/biotech/teva-completes-acquisition-of-ratiopharm (accessed 29 November 2017).

Björkman, I. and Søderberg, A.-M. (2006), 'The HR function in large scale mergers and acquisitions: The case of Nordea', *Personnel Review*, vol. 35, no. 6, pp. 654–670.

Cadbury (2008), *Annual Report and Accounts: Focused on performance and delivering against our plan*. www.sec.gov/Archives/edgar/data/744473/000115697309000187/u06102exv99w1.htm (accessed 29 November 2017).

Capron, L. and Guillén, M. (2009), 'National corporate governance institutions and post-acquisition target reorganization', *Strategic Management Journal*, vol. 30, no. 8, pp. 803–833.

Capron, L. and Hulland, J. (1999), 'Redeployment of brands, sales forces, and general marketing management expertise following horizontal acquisitions: A resource-based view', *The Journal of Marketing*, vol. 63, no. 2, pp. 41–54.

Chapman, K. and Edmond, H. (2000), 'Mergers/acquisitions and restructuring in the EU chemical industry: Patterns and implications', *Regional Studies*, vol. 34, no. 8, pp. 753–767.

Chen, C.Z. and Findlay, F. (2003), 'A review of cross-border mergers and acquisitions in APEC', *Asian-Pacific Economic Literature*, vol. 17, no. 2, pp. 14–38.

Chesters, L. (2012), 'Autonomous once again: The corporate takeover that went wrong', *The Independent*, 24 May. www.independent.co.uk/news/business/analysis-and-features/autonomous-once-again-the-corporate-takeover-that-went-wrong-7786203.html (accessed 29 November 2017).

Chopra, H.K. and Nanda, N.C. (2012), *Textbook of Cardiology: A clinical and historical perspective*, London, UK, JP Medical Ltd.

Damouni, N. and Rigby, B. (2011), 'Microsoft to buy Skype for pricey $8.5 billion', *Reuters Business News*, 10 May. www.reuters.com/article/us-skype-microsoft/microsoft-to-buy-skype-for-pricey-8-5-billion-idUSTRE7490F020110510 (accessed 29 November 2017).

Das, A., Chon, G. and Rockoff, J. (2011), 'J&J to buy Synthes for $21.3 billion', *The Wall Street Journal*, 26 April. www.wsj.com/articles/SB10001424052748704729304576287622474502438 (accesed 29 November 2017).

Dealbook (2010), 'Teva to acquire Ratiopharm for $5 billion', *The New York Times*, 18 March. https://dealbook.nytimes.com/2010/03/18/teva-to-take-over-ratiopharm-report-says/ (accesed 29 November 2017).

Deng, P. (2009), 'Why do Chinese firms tend to acquire strategic assets in international expansion?' *Journal of World Business*, vol. 44, no. 1, pp. 74–84.

Dussauge, P. (2008), 'Alliances, Joint Ventures and Chinese Multinationals', in J.P. Larçon (ed.), *Chinese Multinationals*, Singapore, World Scientific, 9.

Eat Local Grown (2017), 'Blacklisted: GMO supporting food companies to avoid'. http://eatlocalgrown.com/article/11357-blacklisted-12-food-companies-to-avoid.html (accessed 29 November 2017).

Epstein, M.J. (2004), 'The drivers of success in post-merger integration', *Organizational Dynamics*, vol. 33, no. 2, pp. 174–189.

Faccio, M. and Masulis, R.W. (2005), 'The choice of payment method in European mergers and acquisitions', *The Journal of Finance*, vol. 60, no. 3, pp. 1345–1388.

Fackler, M. and Pollack, A. (2014), 'Jury awards $9 billion in damages in drug case', *The New York Times* 8 April. www.nytimes.com/2014/04/09/business/international/japanese-drug-maker-ordered-to-pay-6-billion-over-cancer-claims.html (accessed 29 November 2017).

Financial Times (2016), 'Deep tech ascent: Europe's emerging digital industries'. www.ft.com/content/ad768b58-b64a-11e6-ba85-95d1533d9a62 (accessed 29 November 2017).

Fligstein, N. and Merand, F. (2002), 'Globalization or Europeanization? Evidence on the European economy since 1980', *Acta Sociologica*, vol. 45, no. 1, pp. 7–22.

Forte, G., Iannotta, G. and Navone, M. (2010), 'The banking relationship's role in the choice of the target's advisor in mergers and acquisitions', *European Financial Management*, vol. 16, no. 4, pp. 686–701.

Garette, B. and Dussauge, P. (2000), 'Alliances versus acquisitions: Choosing the right option', *European Management Journal*, vol. 18, no. 1, pp. 63–69.

Gaughan, P.A. (2010), *Mergers, Acquisitions, and Corporate Restructurings*, Hoboken, NJ, John Wiley and Sons.

Granlund, M., Lukka, K. and Mouritsen, J. (1998), 'Institutionalised justification of corporate action: Internationalisation and the EU in corporate reports', *Scandinavian Journal of Management*, vol. 14, no. 4, pp. 433–458.

Grant, R.M. (1996), 'Toward a knowledge-based theory of the firm', *Strategic Management Journal*, vol. 17, no. S2, pp. 109–122.

Grogan, K. (2012), 'Teva shares shoot up after Copaxone lawsuit victory', *Pharma Times*, 25 June. www.pharmatimes.com/news/teva_shares_shoot_up_after_copaxone_lawsuit_victory_977084 (accessed 29 November 2017).

Haleblian, J., Devers, C.E., McNamara, G., Carpenter, M.A. and Davison, R.B. (2009), 'Taking stock of what we know about mergers and acquisitions: A review and research agenda', *Journal of Management*, vol. 35, no. 3, pp. 469–502.

Harrigan, K.R. and Newman, W.H. (1990), 'Bases of interorganization co-operation: Propensity, power, persistence', *Journal of Management Studies*, vol. 27, no. 4, pp. 417–434.

Hébert, L., Very, P. and Beamish, P.W. (2005), 'Expatriation as a bridge over troubled water: A knowledge-based perspective applied to cross-border acquisitions', *Organization Studies*, vol. 26, no. 10, pp. 1455–1476.

Hillman, A.J., Withers, M.C. and Collins, B.J. (2009), 'Resource dependence theory: A review', *Journal of Management*, vol. 35, no. 6, pp. 1404–1427.

Inkpen, A.C. and Beamish, P.W. (1997), 'Knowledge, Bargaining Power, and the Instability of International Joint Ventures', *The Academy of Management Review*, vol. 22, no. 1, pp. 177–202.

Jagersma, P.K. (2005), 'Cross-border alliances: Advice from the executive suite', *Journal of Business Strategy*, vol. 26, no. 1, pp. 41–50.

Jargon, J. and Berry, I. (2012), 'Dough rolls out to fight "engineered" label on food', *Wall Street Journal*, 25 October. www.wsj.com/articles/SB10001424052970203400604578073182907123760 (accessed 29 November 2017).

JnJ News Media (2012), 'Johnson & Johnson Announces Completion of Synthes Acquisition', 14 June www.investor.jnj.com/releasedetail.cfm?releaseid=683098 (accessed 29 November 2017).

Kolk, A., Lindeque, J. and van den Buuse, D. (2014), 'Regionalization strategies of European Union electric utilities', *British Journal of Management*, vol. 25, pp. S77–S99.

Larçon, J.P. (2008), *Chinese Multinationals*, Singapore, World Scientific.

Lebedev, S., Peng, M.W., Xie, E. and Stevens, C.E. (2015), 'Mergers and acquisitions in and out of emerging economies', *Journal of World Business*, vol. 50, no. 4, pp. 651–662.

Luehrman, T.A. (1998), 'Strategy as a portfolio of real options', *Harvard Business Review*, vol. 76, no. 5, pp. 89–99.

Mayrhofer, U. (2004), 'The influence of national origin and uncertainty on the choice between cooperation and merger-acquisition: An analysis of French and German firms', *International Business Review*, vol. 13, no. 1, pp. 83–99.

Mayrhofer, W. and Brewster, C. (1996), 'In praise of ethnocentricity: Expatriate policies in European multinationals', *Thunderbird International Business Review*, vol. 38, no. 6, pp. 749–778.

McKiernan, P. and Merali, Y. (1995), 'Integrating information systems after a merger', *Long Range Planning*, vol. 28, no. 4, pp. 454–562.

McMorris, E. (2015), *Why do up to 90% of Mergers and Acquisitions Fail? Europe Business Review: Finance*. www.businessrevieweurope.eu/finance/390/Why-do-up-to-90-of-Mergers-and-Acquisitions-Fail (accessed 15 June 2016).

Meyer, K.E. (2001), 'Institutions, transaction costs, and entry mode choice in Eastern Europe', *Journal of International Business Studies*, vol. 32, no. 2, pp. 357–367.

Nitsch, D., Beamish, P. and Makino, S. (1995), 'Characteristics and performance of Japanese foreign direct investment in Europe', *European Management Journal*, vol. 13, no. 3, pp. 276–285.

Nitsch, D., Beamish, P. and Makino, S. (1996), 'Entry mode and performance of Japanese FDI in Western Europe', *MIR: Management International Review*, vol. 36, no. 1, pp. 27–43.

Norburn, D. and Schoenberg, R. (1994), 'European cross-border acquisition: How was it for you?' *Long Range Planning*, vol. 27, no. 4, pp. 25–34.

Nussbaum, A., Voreacos, D. and Farrell, G. (2011), 'Johnson & Johnson's quality catastrophe', *Bloomberg Business Week*. www.bloomberg.com/news/articles/2011-03-31/johnson-and-johnsons-quality-catastrophe (accessed 29 November 2017).

Pelzman, J. (2015), 'PRC outward investment in the USA and Europe: A model of R&D Acquisition', *Review of Development Economics*, vol. 19, no. 1, pp. 1–14.

Pharmafile (2010a), 'Abbott completes Solvay acquisition', 16 February. www.pharmafile.com/news/abbot-completes-solvay-acquisition (accessed 29 November 2017).

Pharmafile (2010b), 'Teva to buy Ratiopharm for €3.6 billion', 18 March. www.pharmafile.com/news/teva-buy-ratiopharma-36-billion-euros (accessed 29 November 2017).

Pfeffer, J. and Salancik, G.R. (2003), *The External Control of Organizations: A resource dependence perspective*, Stanford, CA, Stanford University Press.

Riviere, M. and Suder, G. (2016), 'Perspectives on strategic internationalization: Developing capabilities for renewal', *International Business Review*, vol. 25, pp. 847–858.

Rui, H., and Yip, G.S. (2008), 'Foreign acquisitions by Chinese firms: A strategic intent perspective', *Journal of World Business*, vol. 43, no. 2, pp. 213–226.

Schuler, R. and Jackson, S. (2001), 'HR issues and activities in mergers and acquisitions', *European Management Journal*, vol. 19, no. 3, pp. 239–253.

Siebelt, F. and Burger, L. (2010), 'Teva to buy Ratiopharm for nearly $5 billion', *Reuters Business News* 18 March. www.reuters.com/article/us-ratiopharm/teva-to-buy-ratiopharm-for-nearly-5-billion-idUSTRE62H1TS20100318 (accessed 29 November 2017).

Somlev, I.P. and Hoshino, Y. (2005), 'Influence of location factors on establishment and ownership of foreign investments: The case of the Japanese manufacturing firms in Europe', *International Business Review*, vol. 14, no. 5, pp. 577–598.

Statista (2016), *Value of inbound and outbound merger and acquisition (M&A) deals in Europe from 2007 to 2015*. Mergers and Acquisitions in Europe. www.statista.com/study/26388/mergers-and-acquisitions-manda-in-europe-statista-dossier/ (accessed 18 July 2016).

Statt, N. (2013), 'Microsoft's acquisitions: Its biggest hits and misses', *CNET Tech Industry* 3 September. www.cnet.com/news/microsoft-acquisitions-its-biggest-hits-and-misses/ (accessed 29 November 2017).

Straub, T. (2007), *Reasons for Frequent Failure in Mergers and Acquisitions: A Comprehensive Analysis*, Wiesbaden, Germany, Springer Science and Business Media.

Takeda (2011), 'Takeda to acquire Nycomed', 19 May. www.tpi.takeda.com/media/news-releases/2011/takeda-to-acquire-nycomed/ (accessed 29 November 2017).

Teece, D.J. (2007), 'Explicating dynamic capabilities: The nature and microfoundations of (sustainable) enterprise performance', *Strategic Management Journal*, vol. 28, no. 13, pp. 1319–1350.

The Pharma Letter (2011), 'Teva prevails in Copaxone law suit with Mylan/Natco and Sandoz/Momenta', 30 August. www.thepharmaletter.com/article/teva-prevails-in-copaxone-law-suit-with-mylan-natco-and-sandoz-momenta (accessed 29 November 2017).

The Street (2012), 'Johnson & Johnson's Synthes deal revives foreign tax debate', *Forbes*. www.forbes.com/sites/thestreet/2012/06/14/johnson-johnsons-synthes-deal-revives-foreign-tax-debate/#40fd2fc86015 (accessed 29 November 2017).

Topham, J. and Hirschler, B. (2011), 'Nycomed for $13.7 billion', 19 May. www.reuters.com/article/us-takeda-nycomed/takeda-to-buy-swiss-drugmaker-nycomed-for-13-7-billion-idUSTRE74I15620110519 (accessed 29 November 2017).

Turvill, W. (2017), 'Mergers and acquisitions (M&A) activity within the EU reaches 10-year high', 23 May. www.cityam.com/265281/mergers-and-acquisitions-ma-activity-within-eu-reaches-10 (accessed 14 September 2017).

Uhlenbruck, K. and De Castro, J.O. (2000), 'Foreign acquisitions in Central and Eastern Europe: Outcomes of privatization in transitional economies', *Academy of Management Journal*, vol. 43, no. 30, pp. 381–402.

Vaara, E. (2002), 'On the discursive construction of success/failure in narratives of post-merger integration', *Organization Studies*, vol. 23, no. 2, pp. 211–248.

Walter, G.A. and Barney, J.B. (1990), 'Research notes and communications management objectives in mergers and acquisitions', *Strategic Management Journal*, vol. 11, no. 1, pp. 79–86.

Whalen, J., Cimilluca, D. and McCracken, J. (2009), 'Deal opens avenues to emerging markets while adding heart and hormone treatments as well as flu vaccine', *Wall Street Journal*, 28 September. www.wsj.com/articles/SB125411422904045669 (accessed 29 November 2017).

Whipp, L. and Jack, A. (2011), 'Takeda completes Nycomed purchase', *Financial Times*. www.ft.com/content/cf277228-81a1-11e0-8a54-00144feabdc0 (accessed 29 November 2017).

Wilson, D. (2009), 'Abbott in $6.6 billion deal for drug unit', *New York Times*, 27 September. www.nytimes.com/2009/09/28/business/28drug.html (accessed 29 November 2017).

Yang, M. and Hyland, M. (2012), 'Similarity in cross-border mergers and acquisitions: Imitation, uncertainty and experience among Chinese firms, 1985–2006', *Journal of International Management*, vol. 18, no. 4, pp. 352–365.

24

THE FUTURE DIRECTION OF MANUFACTURING IN THE SINGLE EUROPEAN MARKET

A case study

Edgar Bellow and Lotfi Hamzi

Introduction

This chapter makes the case that innovation, entrepreneurship and opportunity for growth within a geopolitically oriented economic policy environment are inextricably linked. While Europe shows specific patterns of highly advanced market integration, due to its geoeconomic and geopolitical position it not only undergoes frequent and rapid change but, in recent years, has been subject to significant shifts due to the eurozone economic crisis. As a result of the contraction in the European economy, therefore, the management of country-based debt has had a negative impact on state-based operations. To this end, it can be argued that the euro crisis has become a matter of solvency linked to overuse of state borrowing, high debt leveraging and substantial fiscal loss over the last five years, and global markets are often targeted as a stop-gap measure in mitigating European geopolitical challenges (Bruno and Shin 2014), which can lead to poor entrepreneurial planning at the firm level (Cowles 2013). This chapter will make the argument that, particularly in European multinational corporation (MNCs), the challenge of balancing planned and divergent strategic behaviour is a major component to innovation and entrepreneurship through diffusion, but structural market context changes linked to geopolitically oriented economic policies can exert a significant influence on the ability of firms to apply divergence and diffusion strategies (Brauer and Heitmann 2013). The focus of this chapter is the manufacturing industry as we see it develop now and into the future. We focus on a company case for illustration.

Approach

The underlying problem that this chapter is trying to solve is that sustainable development, especially in energy dependent industries, requires radical and systemic innovations and divergence strategies (Boons et al. 2013). Specifically, the chapter will consider the role of divergence in sustainable development, which is defined as the deliberate choice made by firms to move away from expected financially oriented standards in order to adopt sustainable development ethics on a fundamental level, either by choice or by political imperative (Brauer and Heitmann

2013; Dominici and Roblek 2016). Chemical and plastics production is highly energy intensive with natural gas and oil accounting for the bulk of consumption, which means that the industry is affected by sustainability risks, but to this end this industry needs to mobilise dynamic capabilities around sustainability (Iles and Martin 2013; Maon et al. 2017), which is why strategy-level divergence from normative values in the industry may be seen as critical to political efforts.

A scenario-based approach to thinking about the European macro-trends that are affecting large energy intensive industries allows for an examination of whether a geopolitically oriented policy environment will have the most significant effect on corporate entrepreneurship and the potential for long-term economic growth in Europe. The question that this analysis asks is whether or not this is the case even for MNCs, using examples from the chemicals industry, specifically BASF SE, a German firm. The method applied to the research detailed in this chapter consists of a qualitative metasynthesis of the literature within a document analysis framework, using BASF as a case study. The rationale for this approach is that qualitative studies using metasynthesis provide a unique contribution to the domain of entrepreneurship within a specific time period and context, which can help generate and test new theories (Hoon 2013; Rauch et al. 2014). Within this approach, data can be seen as a set of constructed entities in which the purpose of the process is to carefully construct ever more informed evaluations and frameworks for the data to finally come to a consensus of how to interpret what has been found by multiple scholars (Hoon 2013). This type of metasynthesis study entails analyses and theory-generating synthesis that remain integral to the interpretive rendering in each study (Bondas and Hall 2007; Sandelowski and Barroso 2007). In contrast to meta-analysis, which uses a quantitative methodology to examine quantitative research studies with an emphasis on the reduction of data, qualitative metasyntheses are integrations of data and theory that offer novel interpretations of findings (Hoon 2013; Sandelowski and Barroso 2007). It is necessary to combine an assessment of epistemological assumptions, theory, and case study work within a metasynthesis of the literature so that there are clear pathways to understanding and integrating data (Bondas and Hall 2007; Rauch et al. 2014). In this case, data from a qualitative metasynthesis of the literature was collated with internal documents from BASF in order to determine a broader assessment of strategic choices for large energy intensive industries within a framework of geopolitical leadership in Europe, taking into account external and internal sustainable development initiatives. Possible scenario outcomes for strategic choices for large energy intensive industries within a framework of geopolitical hegemony are supported by a) geopolitically oriented economic policies, b) regulation, c) industry trends and d) opportunities for growth in different markets (Klein and Welfens 2014; Pisani-Ferry 2012; Popov and Van Horen 2015; Röger et al. 2016), which will be considered in this chapter.

Overview of the industry

The chemical and plastics industry includes research, development and production of both specialised and commodity goods. There is an indistinct connection between purely chemical producers and purely plastic producers because of the fact that the production of one is deeply linked with the other due to both chemical property overlaps and the need for economies of scale in a globalised production environment (Ventrice et al. 2013). Differences in output are most usually tied to innovations in production rather than in product scope, characterised by limited research and development (R&D) expenditure on product development and a more salient emphasis on reducing raw materials, energy and labour costs through engineering process improvements (Lin and Darnall 2015). The business is cyclical in nature; it is capital and energy intensive; distribution methods are varied; and the industry is subject to heavy regulation

(Jernström et al. 2017; Rochman et al. 2013). The primary driving factors for the industry's revenue stream are volume growth and pricing flexibility (Philp et al. 2013). The chemical and plastics industry's health, perhaps not unlike other industries that deal in commodity products and consumable goods, is closely tied to the health of the global economy as reflected by personal consumption, expenditures, retail sales and currency exchange rates (Pettigrew 2013; Valencia 2013).

Europeanisation: Economic and geopolitical factors

The theory that underpins the factors in the case is that the current euro crisis, linked to the geopolitical aims of Germany, has shifted Europeanised macro-trends in business. The reason for this is that investments in R&D in larger organisations in the eurozone, even in strong economies such as Germany, have been slowing (OECD 2016). The strength of the euro, however, has been Germany's greatest stumbling block in terms of managing trade, which has also been complicated by additional sociopolitical challenges in the last few years. What is evident is that there has been a decrease in commodity prices, which affects the chemical and plastics industry, but also, as noted by Heise (2016), an increased interest in shifting towards social security over investment as a policy decision in the Merkel administration. Because of the possible impact of an aging society on the ability of the German government to manage social security outputs, a retrenchment has been perceived as necessary. According to Chu (2015), by 2060, Germany's population could drop from about 81 million today to as low as 68 million, and would most likely be surpassed by Britain and France, potentially changing the balance of power in Europe. Admitting vast numbers of asylum seekers could offset some of these trends, though it could also fuel others. The government's forecast of 800,000 refugees equals 1 per cent of the population.

On a larger scale outside Germany, it has also been noted that globalisation is weakening the grip of individual central banks over the trajectory of domestic real interest rates (Dullien and Guérot 2012). As a result, the movement of business and other societal interests towards the European market, namely Europeanisation, has come under fire due to the fact that internal frameworks for central banks are not necessarily in alignment with EU policy, especially when it comes to business resource development (Hermann 2014). There has been a protectionist policy environment in place in many countries despite calls to regularise eurozone capacity building and resource sharing.

As noted by Simonazzi (2016), there is an implicit assumption within the eurozone that competition, and an austerity regime that is connected to banking and political institutions in more privileged countries such as Germany, can create a positive environment for growth in those countries struggling to manage their economic potential.

What can be gleaned from an assessment of these factors is that an underlying volatility with respect to a lack of equity between eurozone countries is central to the argument regarding the interception of globalisation and fiscal and monetary policy, which has an effect on individual businesses, even MNCs, when they are primarily resident in eurozone countries. It is evident that central banks are beginning to falter in their ability to respond to the demand for depth and liquidity in the global asset markets. These circumstances exacerbate the volatility of the banks' and policy makers' hold on their requisite economies, and thus the propensity of firms to respond with innovative or non-innovative market development trajectories. Although deeper markets allow for greater diversification of risk, investors are still engaged in a learning process regarding the impact of globalisation and of Europeanisation on their corporate decision-making processes (Brauer and Heitmann 2013). The question there becomes: What are the factors that will affect these risks and market development tactics?

Theoretical framework

Five geopolitical variables have been identified as important to the consideration of the effects of the euro crisis on BASF and other MNCs, especially those in the chemical and plastics industries in Europe (Alperowicz 2012; Iles and Martin 2013; Maon et al. 2017; Schönbohm, 2013). These, in no particular order, are as follows.

Destabilisation of trade markets. This factor is the variable connected to the way in which trade markets are changing both within Europe and globally, especially within the context of Europeanisation. Market structures and regulations are shifting, which means that there are issues for individual companies looking at how to mitigate such changes in the short term (Morin and Carta, 2014; Ülkü 2015). These are highly dependent on the way in which regulatory efforts are put into effect by individual countries outside the eurozone and how trade commitments are honoured on a global scale.

Weakening of individual central banks. As noted above, there has been a need to come to terms with the effects of austerity and other measures in order to bring banks in European countries in line with the expectations of the eurozone (Karanikolos et al. 2013). What this means is that these banking crises inevitably weaken country fiscal positions, with government revenues contracting as a result, even though the intention of these protocols is to increase eurozone stability (Reinhart and Rogoff 2013). The result is that business transactions can be deeply affected by these changes.

Evidence of global currency manipulation. Although there has been a shift towards transparency within Europe when it comes to banking and central bank choices, the same cannot be said for the rest of the world. Increasing currency manipulation to engender short-term trade boosts, especially in Asia, has made it difficult for businesses to plan ahead (Gagnon 2012).

Rising European unemployment. Much of the central bank and fiscal reforms, austerity measures and changes in the way that labour markets are structured globally have had an effect on employment levels in Europe (Capaldo 2015). This is leading to increasing insecurity on a political and social level, which has an impact on business development and revenue flows.

Threat of members pulling out of the eurozone. The reality of Brexit is one that may be repeated in a significant way with future elections in the eurozone possibly resulting in similar outcomes. When member countries of a monetary union are downgraded to the status of emerging economies, as well, such as in the recent case of Greece, there is a threat inherent in the possibility that the EU will forcibly remove entities from its collective (De Grauwe 2011). This could not only lead to challenges on a political scale, but also the possibility that a currency crisis could emerge in the eurozone as a whole.

Putting all of these issues into context, the possible positive and negative outcomes of these variables on a broad scale, in either extreme, are illustrated in Figure 24.1. This exhibit demonstrates the range and scope to which it may be necessary to address the variables on a geopolitical scale.

Given the overview of the possibilities that are detailed in Figure 24.1, we can apply these variables to the case of BASF.

Case study analysis

The firm

Just past its 150th year of operations, BASF SE is the largest chemical company in the world, and is resident in one of the strongest eurozone countries, if not the strongest in terms of both fiscal policy and economic viability (Kane et al. 2014). In the 1990s, BASF introduced a radical new

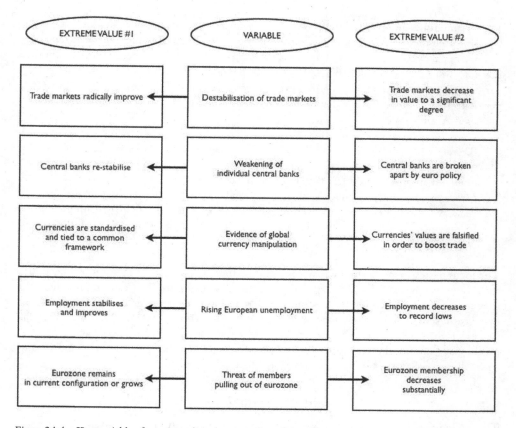

Figure 24.1 Key variables for a geopolitical perspective of manufacturing Europeanisation in context

business model in Germany, converting BASF from a global commodity supplier to a system partner that not only sells chemicals and plastics but services as well (Glückler 2014). One example of this new service orientation can be found in its paint coatings division. Together with Mercedes-Benz, BASF created an industrial-scale production model to offer paint services to car manufacturers globally, and in doing so reduce coating consumption by 20 per cent (Glückler 2014). Beginning with the Mercedes 'A' series, the company reported that:

> Our concept of system partnership, which we initiated four years ago with DaimlerChrysler in Rastatt, Germany, increasingly receives a positive response from other automotive firms. Since then, we have taken on increasing levels of process responsibility at Volkswagen, Audi, Ford and Renault (BASF 2002, p. 32)

This addition of a new level of business led to above-average earnings for the firm over the course of a decade (Glückler 2014), in that:

> BASF is now the leading system supplier for automotive coatings. Twenty production plants operated by eight automotive manufacturers in Europe, the Americas and Japan work with BASF according to this principle, the latest example being VW's facility in Puebla, Mexico. (BASF 2004, p. 27)

At the same time, more recent results from the company suggest that they are not engaging in the same kind of global expansion of their product or service base as in previous years. The most recent annual report states that the Annual Shareholders' Meeting determined that business revenues were down almost 5 per cent over the previous year, with net incomes down 22.7 per cent, but that the company's aim was to increase the annual dividend by €0.10 to €2.90 per share (BASF 2016). This is despite the fact that the company's investment in research has increased. As they state,

> Research and development and thus innovations remain at the heart of our competitiveness. In 2015, we reached our goal of achieving sales of around €10 billion with new and improved products that have been on the market for less than five years. Following a significant increase in research and development spending in the past years, we plan to maintain expenditure at the previous year's level in 2016. Our goal is to convince our customers by continually offering new products and solutions. (BASF 2016, p. 11).

The focus on research within the firm suggests that there is an overt recognition of a need for a focus on research, but the reality is that this has not translated into significant revenue increases in recent years, even looking back at the revenues and net income over the last five years. Year over year revenues and net income are continuing to drop (BASF 2002; 2004; 2016). What this suggests is that there is either an internal or an external set of variables that is having an effect on the company's ability to create new R&D efforts and actualise predicted revenue streams. The following is an assessment of the variables discussed above.

Qualitative variable analysis

The ranking of geopolitical variables related to Europeanisation that can affect the firm's ability to remain entrepreneurial needs to occur in consideration of the nature of BASF as a company and the macroeconomic forces that have an effect on its industry as a whole. The difficulty in identifying what factors are most salient to this case in particular are linked to Germany's comparatively ambivalent position in the EU, in contrast to, for example, France or the UK.

> A somewhat ambivalent position on building a common energy market is represented by Germany. One the one hand, German authorities typically act as advocates of European integration. On the other hand, however, they have usually opposed pro-competition proposals brought forth by the EC, protecting their companies against reforms. Moreover, they have used their strong position in the Union to exempt their important projects from EU regulations – for instance, the OPAL pipeline (which connects continental pipeline grid with the Nord Stream) has been granted exemption from the Third Party Access principle. Meanwhile, most countries of Central and Eastern Europe support the idea of building a single market for energy, since they equate energy security with the notion of European solidarity and securing the supply of energy sources. (Dyduch 2015, p. 199)

Given these findings, the five key variables that have been identified as important to the consideration of the geopolitical effects of Europeanisation on BASF can be ranked in the following way, as illustrated in Figure 24.2 and described below.

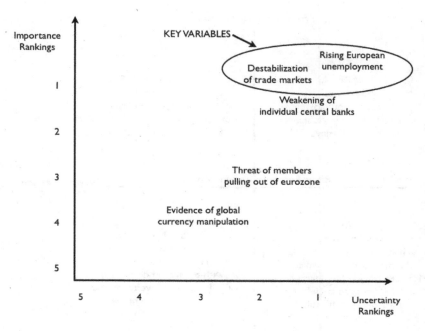

Figure 24.2   Identification of key variables for a geopolitical perspective of manufacturing Europeanisation

Rising European unemployment. The rationale for this variable being identified as first is due to the fact that the chemical and plastics industry relies on a stable consumer base for its clients' products. With employment down, as a whole, the demand for goods in the automobile and construction industries also decreases, meaning that the need for chemicals and plastics decreases.

Destabilisation of trade markets. With the destabilisation of trade markets, the price for natural resources, such as oil, that provide the foundation for BASF's production can fluctuate highly, having a negative effect on the company's cost structure.

Weakening of individual central banks. The natural instability of these banks are problematic for companies such as BASF. Nonetheless the firm also has a responsibility to mitigate these issues through financial strategy building processes.

Threat of members pulling out of eurozone. While this is an important factor to overall geopolitical stability, it is also comparatively predictable, given the long lead time to these decisions, and the fact that changes to eurozone structure also require a great deal of implementation time, which means that companies will have the ability to adapt, even in the short term.

Evidence of global currency manipulation. Again, while this is a salient factor, it is impossible to predict in the short term. While it may have significant effects on BASF as an MNC, a realistic assessment cannot demonstrate how much of a threat global currency manipulation could be.

Potential futures

If rising European unemployment and the destabilisation of trade markets are the primary variables that need to be taken into consideration, there are four potential futures that can

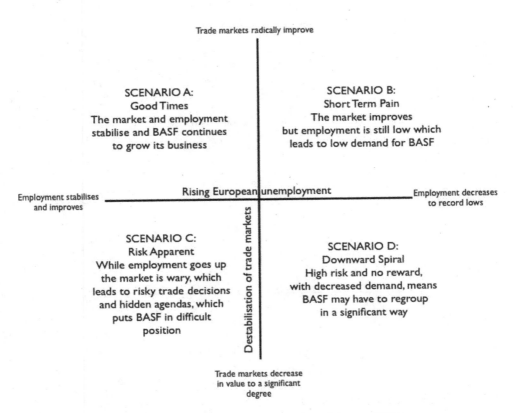

Figure 24.3 Four possible scenarios for effects of geopolitical conditions on BASF

be identified as a result of the development of the importance rankings illustrated in the previous section. The relative challenges and four possible scenario outcomes are illustrated in Figure 24.3.

The scenarios illustrated here demonstrate that BASF is likely to be in a difficult position if and when there are market and consumer reactions to the current geopolitical state, even though the firm is headquartered in Germany, which is relatively stable. Although the German economy, which is the fifth-largest economy in the world in purchasing power terms, 'began to contract in the second quarter of 2008 as the strong euro, high oil prices, tighter credit markets, and slowing growth abroad took their toll on Germany's export-dependent economy' (CIA 2016, p. 8), there has been a shift towards overall leadership in the eurozone and the global product development market in the years since. In the past, a favourable exchange rate and an export equation which is partially dependent on the USA meant that when the US mortgage crisis hit, Germany was heavily affected.

At the same time, it is clear that the bulk of Germany's trade volume resides within Europe, and the recent euro crisis after the challenges that Germany mitigated with Greece, and the increasing destabilisation of France and the UK, have only made the situation more challenging (Dyduch 2015). In addition, these challenges are made more complex by the consideration of the price of oil on BASF's cost structures, and their ability to engage in oil-dependent production. With such a large oil deficit Germany is forced to import both oil and natural gas in order to feed production standards (CIA 2016). This is a risk for both the country and the company;

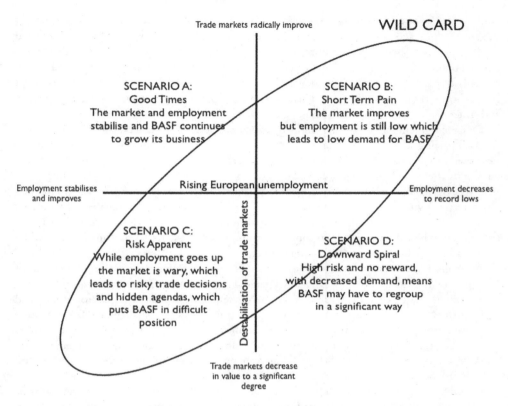

Figure 24.4 Wild card influences for BASF from a geopolitical perspective of Europeanisation

because of the nature of speculation in oil futures, the price of oil could continue to become either more expensive, or unreliable.

To this end, the four narratives present a number of different challenges. While in Scenario A, general conditions for the market and demand increase, Scenario B suggests that there is a possibility for short-term challenges as employment regains parity with positive market forces. It may be that employment continues to suffer, as companies are wary of rehiring after the euro crisis. As well, it is also possible that employment goes up, as in Scenario C, but that the market is fraught with increased and risk-associated speculative futures activity, due to the fact that there has been long-term instability which can lead to more transactions. Scenario D also suggests that neither the market nor employment will increase, which is problematic on all levels due to the fact that the company may neither have buyers for its products, nor stable costs for its key production supplies.

There is one wild card variable which needs to be addressed as well, namely in the case that one or more countries will pull out of the eurozone in the future, and this could affect both trade and employment, illustrated in Figure 24.4. If this is the case, it is possible that BASF will have to deal with increased uncertainty in both trade and employment over a longer term, within the context of unstable policy and a less stable euro, even than the present.

The reality is that the rise of right-wing parties clearly delineates a will against economic integration in Europe, which means that they reject a common currency and foreign policy, and want increased visa restrictions in their states that are different from those of the EU as a whole. It can be said that because the main driving factors for BASF's industry's revenue stream are volume growth and pricing flexibility, and profits are driven by a combination of product mix, raw material costs, capacity use and operating efficiency, the company will be most affected by the euro crisis effects of rising European unemployment and destabilisation of trade markets. The recommendation, therefore, is for the company to support a strong German fiscal policy, create lasting supplier relationships to mitigate shifts in raw material costs, and decrease its prices in the short term to help support and instigate possible increases in demand among its European and American consumer product bases.

One recommendation is for the company to achieve better results on behalf of investors, first, through pricing. Developing volume growth through pricing flexibility, specifically through a decrease in its prices in the short term to help support and instigate possible increases in demand among its clients in Europe and the USA, may be necessary for BASF and other leading companies in Germany and the eurozone. Price is a critical marketing element, especially in markets characterised by monopolistic competition or oligopoly, and perceived-value pricing would be a way for BASF to achieve these goals within all four scenarios to drive down risk. It is also appropriate when the price chosen supports an image of a specific level of quality and when competitors face barriers to entering the market.

A second recommendation is for the company to increase efficiency, creating higher profit through a combination of product mix, raw material costs, capacity use and operating efficiency. The reality is that this approach can only be used when an organisation has data on its demand and cost functions, which is the case for BASF. Firm infrastructure changes, for BASF, require intensive internal controls on research and development and production because of safety issues associated with the products. This new strategy would bring new knowledge management network processes within the firm that would increase revenues, and therefore this approach is best in high-risk Scenarios C and D.

In addition, the company can change financing, sales and marketing costs on a regular basis to test different direct market options. When the objective is to maximise current profits, BASF will estimate what demand and costs will be at different prices and choose the price that will produce the maximum current profit, cash flow or return on investment. As long as their prices cover variable costs and some fixed costs the product offering can survive, but this approach presents the highest risk because it confuses market offerings. This approach is appropriate in low-risk environments such as A and B.

At the same time, these strategic approaches may not be enough to address the fundamental issues at stake. As the company itself reports, its new-found focus in terms of R&D has shifted away from corporate strategy and towards a new interest in sustainable business development. This aim has increasingly been supported in the company since it was taken into account that its 'customers are increasingly focusing on sustainability, [and] we see business opportunities that we want to seize through our innovations. We will further increase the proportion of sales from products that contribute particularly to sustainability' (BASF 2016, p. 11). In energy-dependent industries such as that of BASF, therefore, there may be a different approach needed by both government policy frameworks and by corporate approaches to change.

Strategic initiative recommendations

Given all of the factors and variables reviewed above, what is evident is that with a need for innovation, entrepreneurship and opportunity for growth within a geopolitically oriented economic policy environment, companies such as BASF need to build upon extant policy choices that can support corporate entrepreneurship practices on a broad scale. The circular economy concept being considered by the German government may be able to facilitate such activities in a way that standard policies do not. The circular economy concept is characterised as a 'linkage of the post-use phase with questions of recyclable design and the legal framework for resource-efficient and waste-avoiding production methods' (Wilts 2016, p. 9). Within this framework for understanding corporate growth, German firms would need to be more competitive in their use of secondary materials rather than importing. The ongoing recirculation of these kinds of raw material, such as the chemicals and geological inputs required by BASF, could make Germany more independent from the massive price fluctuations often associated with the import of these commodities (Wilts 2016). In this way, the interests of Germany and that of BASF become linked, and the strategic management of resources can be connected with overall eurozone initiatives.

This is a diffusion strategy. Diffusion, in this way, refers to the internal and external spread of policy innovations that are connected to the needs of a populace rather than to the need for hierarchical instititionalised pressure or collective decision-making (Busch and Jorgens 2012). In this way, Germany's firms, including BASF, can begin to develop capacity-building technologies that lie outside the regulatory aims of the EU and are immune from influence from wild card factors as detailed above. At the micro level, 'diffusion processes involve mechanisms of social learning, copying, mimetic emulation, and political or economic competition' (Busch and Jorgens 2012, p. 70). The benefit to this is, of course, that diffusion techniques, while not necessarily cooperative in nature, tend to align themselves with overarching social and political trends while still remaining innovative.

Rather than becoming constrained by regulatory complications, companies can find real opportunities in diffusion approaches. In the case of BASF, these approaches can be connected back to sustainability initiatives, which are in themselves necessary for the ongoing viability of the firm, but will also be necessary to ensure that the company is able to react to global trends as well as to strictures put forward by the German government within a conservative EU environment, most likely reflecting Scenarios C or D as detailed in Figure 24.3.

The reality is that the factors that are predictive of Scenarios C or D are becoming increasingly apparent in the market as well as the geopolitical sphere in Germany and the eurozone. This is evident in BASF's most recent financial statements and annual report, which suggest that the company's recent downturn in revenues can be connected back to extensive issues within the context of its reliance on oil and gas production and cost structures for its chemical and plastics products:

> In our chemicals business, the oil price initially had a positive impact on margins. Soon, however, it was clear that our customers were becoming increasingly cautious. They held back from ordering – in the expectation of further declines in prices for chemical products. Pressure on margins increased in the course of the year, particularly in the fourth quarter... At the end of the third quarter, we completed the divestiture of our gas trading and storage business to Gazprom. This business contributed approximately €10 billion to sales and €260 million to EBIT before special items in the first three quarters of 2015. In combination with the further fall in oil prices, it became apparent at the end of October that we would probably not reach our annual goals. In 2015, EBIT before special items was 8% lower than in 2014, although we improved earnings in the chemicals business as planned. EBIT fell by 18%, in particular due to price-related impairments to assets in the Oil and Gas segment. As a result, oil prices thwarted our plans in 2015. (BASF 2016, p. 10)

There is a need for BASF, and companies like it, to address this disconnect through divergence strategies (Boons et al. 2013). The interest of the firm in sustainable development needs not to be predicated by complications in the oil and gas sector alone, or in the increasing regulation of the use of oil and gas by Germany, but in the need to divest itself of oil and gas dependency as a whole.

Nonetheless, at the same time, what can also be noted is that divergence may be constrained by current Europeanisation efforts as well as the need for Germany to mitigate the risks associated with Europeanisation and the constraints of the eurozone. The country does not want to expose itself to ongoing risks and relies on companies such as BASF to create a backbone of support for employment and R&D resources, as well as imports and exports (Brauer and Heitmann 2013). While the company has relied on its ability to create an impetus for positive change in terms of overall sustainability, qualifying for the Climate Disclosure Leadership Index for the eleventh time in 2015 (BASF 2016), the current issues around German conservatism in terms of its economic investments may be prohibitive to change. While the EU has made recommendations in this regard, the reality is that there have been few incentives for businesses to change because of a lack of willingness on the part of Germany to invest in infrastructure shifts that will allow for divergence (Brauer and Heitmann 2013; Iles and Martin 2013; Wilts 2015).

Conclusions

BASF needs to mobilise dynamic capabilities around sustainability (Iles and Martin 2013; Maon et al. 2017) in order to engage in the kind of corporate entrepreneurship that will allow them to grow and develop within a conservative eurozone. Particularly in European MNCs such as BASF, the challenge of balancing planned and divergent strategic behaviour is a major component to innovation and entrepreneurship, but structural market context changes linked to geopolitically oriented economic policies can exert a significant influence on the ability of firms to apply divergence strategies (Brauer and Heitmann 2013).

This geopolitical framework, as it stands, will necessarily limit corporate entrepreneurship, and the result will be that large-scale companies such as BASF may need to take a different approach to change mechanisms in order to survive. The company has shown itself to be less than resilient to constrained regulatory and market conditions in which access to resources is limited by both government effects and a need to conserve resources because of nascent difficulties in maintaining a stable eurozone. Although Europeanisation has codified business methodologies and regulatory influences, it has also led to ongoing instability within a number of countries, such as Greece and the UK, either unable or unwilling to align themselves with the standards expected by membership. What this means is that firms are facing an increasing lack of market stability as well as governmental support, in that resources are being shored up in order to offset possible systemic shocks in the near future.

The result is that companies such as BASF need to be able to mitigate these effects and create a new standard for corporate entrepreneurship that bypasses the extant issues illustrated in this case study. These firms may be able to create pricing and cost strategies that can conserve their capital infrastructures, but, ultimately, they need to develop divergence strategies that allow them to bolster their long-term viability in a global but unstable geopolitical market. This industry, in its reliance on oil and gas, is relatively vulnerable. BASF, and other similar firms, must maintain flexible capital budgets for continual upgrading and replacement of existing plants to keep up with changing technologies such as biotechnologies that are informing shifts in the industry on a broad scale, but they must also move outside commodity markets so that they can continue to provide value. This requires looking at their corporate entrepreneurship strategies that are unique as well as organisationally innovative. Sustainable development requires radical and systemic innovations, diffusion and divergence strategies, and this is the likely aim of these firms within the geopolitical environment of Europe at the present time.

References

Alperowicz, N. (2012), 'BASF to restructure construction chemicals in Europe', *Chemical Week*, vol. 174, p. 25.

BASF (2002), *Annual Report 2001*. Ludwigshafen, BASF AG.

BASF (2004), *Corporate Report 2003*. Ludwigshafen, BASF AG.

BASF (2016), *Corporate Report 2015*. Ludwigshafen, BASF AG.

Bondas, T. and Hall, E. (2007), 'Challenges in approaching metasynthesis research', *Qualitative Health Research,* vol. 17, pp. 113–121.

Boons, F., Montalvo, C., Quist, J. and Wagner, M. (2013), 'Sustainable innovation, business models and economic performance: An overview', *Journal of Cleaner Production*, vol. 45, pp. 1–8.

Brauer, M. and Heitmann, M. (2013), 'Antecedents and temporal dynamics of strategic divergence in multinational corporations: Evidence from Europe', *Journal of World Business*, vol. 48, no. 1, pp. 110–121.

Bruno, V. and Shin, H.S. (2014), 'Globalization of corporate risk taking', *Journal of International Business Studies*, vol. 45, no. 7, pp. 800–820.

Busch, P.O. and Jorgens, H. (2012), 'Europeanization through diffusion? Renewable energy policies and alternative sources for European convergence', in F. Morata and I.S. Sandoval (eds), *European Energy Policy: An Environmental Approach*, Cheltenham, Edward Elgar, pp. 66–77.

Capaldo, J. (2015), 'The Transatlantic Trade and Investment Partnership: European disintegration, unemployment and instability', *Economia and Lavoro*, vol. 49, no. 2, pp. 35–56.

Chu, H. (2015), 'For Germany, refugees are demographic blessing as well as burden', *Los Angeles Times*, 10 September. www.latimes.com/world/europe/la-fg-germany-refugees-demographics-20150910-story.html#share=email~story (accessed 2 December 2017).

CIA (2016), *World Factbook*, Washington, DC, Central Intelligence Agency.

Cowles, M.G. (2013), 'The changing architecture of big business', in J. Greenwood and M. Aspinwall (eds), *Collective Action in the European Union: Interests and the new politics of associability*, New York, Routledge, p. 108.

De Grauwe, P. (2011), 'Managing a fragile Eurozone', *CESifo Forum,* vol. 12, no. 2, p. 40.

Dominici, G. and Roblek, V. (2016), 'Complexity theory for a new managerial paradigm: A research framework', in I.V. Raguz, N. Prodrug and L. Jelenc (eds), *Neostrategic Management,* Switzerland, Springer International Publishing, pp. 223–241.

Dullien, S. and Guérot, U. (2012), 'The long shadow of ordoliberalism: Germany's approach to the euro crisis', European Council on Foreign Relations Policy Brief, p. 22.

Dyduch, J. (2015), 'Europeanization of the energy policy within the European Union's system of governance', in: P. Stanek and K. Wach (eds), *Europeanization Processes from the Mesoeconomic Perspective: Industries and policies.* Kraków, Cracow University of Economics, pp. 193–219.

Gagnon, J.E. (2012), 'Combating widespread currency manipulation', *Policy Brief in International Economics*, pp. 12–19.

Glückler, J. (2014), 'How controversial innovation succeeds in the periphery? A network perspective of BASF Argentina', *Journal of Economic Geography*, vol. 14, no. 5, pp. 903–927.

Heise, M. (2016), 'Germany's trade surplus signals trouble ahead', *Wall Street Journal*, 11 October. (accessed 12 March 2018).

Hermann, C. (2014), 'Structural adjustment and neoliberal convergence in labour markets and welfare: The impact of the crisis and austerity measures on European economic and social models', *Competition and Change*, vol. 18, no. 2, pp. 111–130.

Hoon, C. (2013), 'Meta-synthesis of qualitative case studies: An approach to theory building', *Organizational Research Methods*, vol. 16, no. 4, pp. 522–556.

Iles, A. and Martin, A.N. (2013), 'Expanding bioplastics production: Sustainable business innovation in the chemical industry', *Journal of Cleaner Production*, vol. 45, pp. 38–49.

Jernström, E., Karvonen, V., Kässi, T., Kraslawski, A. and Hallikas, J. (2017), 'The main factors affecting the entry of SMEs into bio-based industry', *Journal of Cleaner Production*, vol. 141, pp. 1–10.

Kane, G.C.J., Palmer, D., Phillips, A.N., Kiron, D. and Buckley, N. (2014), 'Moving beyond marketing: Generating social business value across the enterprise', *MIT Sloan Management Review*, vol. 56, no. 1, p. 1.

Karanikolos, M., Mladovsky, P., Cylus, J., Thomson, S., Basu, S., Stuckler, D., … and McKee, M. (2013), 'Financial crisis, austerity, and health in Europe', *The Lancet*, vol. 381, no. 9874, pp. 1323–1331.

Klein, M.W. and Welfens, P.J. (eds) (2012), *Multinationals in the New Europe and Global Trade*, Berlin, Springer Science and Business Media.

Lin, H. and Darnall, N. (2015), 'Strategic alliance formation and structural configuration', *Journal of Business Ethics*, vol. 127, no. 3, pp. 549–564.

Maon, F., Swaen, V. and Lindgreen, A. (2017), 'One vision, different paths: An investigation of corporate social responsibility initiatives in Europe', *Journal of Business Ethics*, vol. 143, no. 2, pp. 405–422.

Morin, J.F. and Carta, C. (2014), 'Overlapping and evolving European discourses on market liberalization', *The British Journal of Politics and International Relations*, vol. 16, no. 1, pp. 117–132.

OECD (2016), *Seminar on Sustainability and the Role of Innovation Policies*. Position paper issued 16 March by OECD, European Commission and Eurostat.

Pettigrew, A. (2013), *The Awakening Giant (Routledge Revivals): Continuity and Change in Imperial Chemical Industries*, New York, Routledge.

Philp, J.C., Ritchie, R.J. and Guy, K. (2013), 'Biobased plastics in a bioeconomy', *Trends in Biotechnology*, vol. 31, no. 2, pp. 65–67.

Pisani-Ferry, J. (2012), *The Euro Crisis and the New Impossible Trinity*. Bruegel Policy Contribution No. 2012/01.

Popov, A. and Van Horen, N. (2015), 'Exporting sovereign stress: Evidence from syndicated bank lending during the euro area sovereign debt crisis', *Review of Finance*, vol. 19, no. 5, pp. 1825–1866.

Rauch, A., Doorn, R. and Hulsink, W. (2014), 'A qualitative approach to evidence-based entrepreneurship: Theoretical considerations and an example involving business clusters', *Entrepreneurship Theory and Practice*, vol. 38, no. 2, pp. 333–368.

Reinhart, C.M. and Rogoff, K.S. (2013), 'Banking crises: An equal opportunity menace', *Journal of Banking and Finance*, vol. 37, no. 11, pp. 4557–4573.

Rochman, C.M., Browne, M.A., Halpern, B.S., Hentschel, B.T., Hoh, E., Karapanagioti, H.K., Rios-Mendoza, L.M., Takada, H., The, S. and Thompson, R.C. (2013), 'Policy: Classify plastic waste as hazardous', *Nature*, vol. 494, no. 7436, pp. 169–171.

Röger, W., Welfens, P.J. and Wolf, H. (2016), 'Overcoming the euro crisis: Medium and long term economic perspective', *International Economics and Economic Policy*, vol. 1, no. 1, pp. 1–3.

Sandelowski, M. and Barroso, J. (2007), *Handbook for Synthesizing Qualitative Research*, New York, Springer.

Schönbohm, A. (2013), *Performance Measurement and Management with Financial Ratios: The BASF SE case* (No. 72), Working Papers of the Institute of Management Berlin at the Berlin School of Economics and Law (HWR Berlin).

Simonazzi, A. (2016), 'Engines of growth and paths of development in the Euro-area', in *Annual Conference of the International Working Party on Labour Market Segmentation* (No. 37a).

Ülkü, N. (2015), 'The interaction between foreigners' trading and stock market returns in emerging Europe', *Journal of Empirical Finance*, vol. 33, pp. 243–262.

Valencia, R.C. (2013), *The Future of the Chemical Industry by 2050*, Weinheim, John Wiley and Sons.

Ventrice, P., Ventrice, D., Russo, E. and De Sarro, G. (2013), 'Phthalates: European regulation, chemistry, pharmacokinetic and related toxicity', *Environmental Toxicology and Pharmacology*, vol. 36, no. 1, pp. 88–96.

Wilts, H. (2016), *Germany on the Road to a Circular Economy?* Wiso Diskurs, FES Foundation, Germany.

25

SERVICES IN THE SINGLE EUROPEAN MARKET IN THE TWENTY-FIRST CENTURY

Anita Pelle

Introduction

The free movement of services is one of the four freedoms forming the basis of the European Union.[1] Over time, the services sector has undergone major transformation. The changes have always been rooted in the sector itself, impacting the EU-level regulatory framework. In parallel, regulation has affected businesses.

In this chapter we first give a short overview of the major advancements in the services sector in the EU from a historical perspective. In the second part of the chapter the single European regulatory framework for the services sector is introduced.

The free movement of services from a historical perspective

The Treaty of Rome of 1957 establishing the European Economic Community (EEC) envisaged the establishment of a common market among the six participating member states.[2] The common market implies that not only the outputs of economic activities (i.e. goods and services) but also the inputs (i.e. capital and labour) move freely across the integrated area. This is how services have from the beginning formed part of European integration and European legislation.

The establishment of the free movement of services

Title III of the Treaty of Rome specifies the provisions on the free movement of services in Chapter 3 (Services). The text talks about progressive abolition of restrictions in a transitional period. A service falls under the Treaty if it is provided for remuneration, and the provider and the receiver of the service are in different EU member states.

According to the rules, businesses may freely provide cross-border services in the EU; no authority or other business entities may impede them in doing so in any way.

Changes throughout the decades of European integration

Since the earliest times, the European economy has undergone fundamental changes, substantially affecting the services sector and the free movement of such activities. Of the major

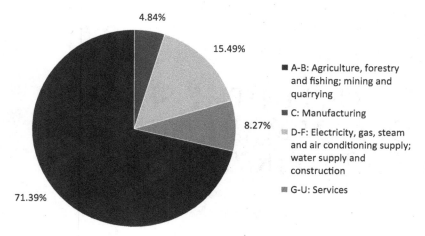

4.84%

15.49%

■ A-B: Agriculture, forestry
and fishing; mining and
quarrying

■ C: Manufacturing

8.27%

■ D-F: Electricity, gas, steam
and air conditioning supply;
water supply and
construction

■ G-U: Services

71.39%

Figure 25.1   Share of sectors (expressed by NACE codes) in employment in the EU-28 (2015)
Source: Author's own calculation based on Eurostat data (Eurostat 2015c).

advancements, the most obvious one is the development of the services sector itself (Orio 1987). By the 1990s, the services sector accounted for as much as 65–70 per cent of EU member states' GDPs (Papp 2003). Of course, this spectacular expansion of the services sector has resulted in the intensification of cross-border service provision in the EU.

Regarding employment and job creation, the share of the services sector is even larger (Figure 25.1): in 2015, 71.39 per cent of all employees in the EU were employed by the services sectors.

Furthermore, unlike manufacturing sectors, services (whether less or more knowledge intensive) have been able to create jobs even in recessions (Figure 25.2). Nevertheless, in the twenty-first century, knowledge-intensive services are creating the majority of new jobs in the EU (EU 2014). Evidently, humans have to possess certain skills demanded by this sector in order to be employable (OECD 2001): digital literacy, the ability to learn and adapt, interpersonal and intercultural communication skills, and a good understanding of the world around us.

Another way of statistically measuring the weight of certain sectors is in their value added (Figure 25.3).[3] We can see that, even if only private services are considered (NACE G-N), the sector generates the most value added in the EU (69.02% in 2013). Moreover, in twenty-first-century manufacturing value added, there is an ever bigger services content (Stehrer et al. 2014) so the indirect effects should not be neglected either. This implies that the share of services in European value added is even larger.

In parallel, technological development has provided ever larger room for the internationalisation of services (Miozzo and Soete 2001), mostly taking the following forms: foreign direct investments, cross-border services and transnational mergers and acquisitions (mainly in the energy sectors upon liberalisation) (OECD 2006; Kacsirek 2007). Examples of foreign direct investment in European services are: mobile phone operators, public utilities companies, banks, business consultancy. Cross-border services (i.e. when the service provider remains in its home country and serves customers of another EU country from home) are most typical in financial services and all types of online sales (general online warehouses, travel agencies, specialised stores such as photography or books).

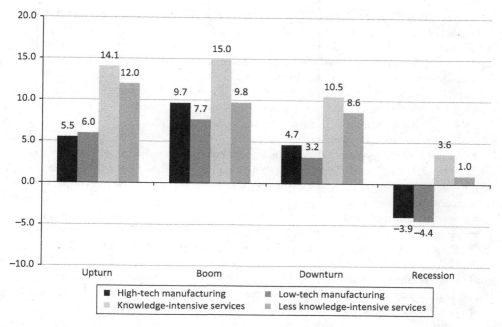

Figure 25.2 Employment effects across sectors in the EU, 1998–2010
Source: Author's own compilation based on EU (2014, p.170).

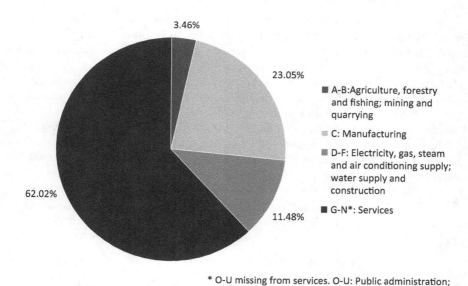

Figure 25.3 Share of sectors (expressed by NACE codes) in value added in the EU-28 (2013)
Source: Author's own calculations based on Eurostat data (Eurostat 2015b).

With the intensification of intra-EU trade, service providers have often followed their clients in support of their cross-border European activities (Molle 2001). It is enough to think about law firms, business consultants or financial service companies going where the clients are active across the EU. With the change of system in the Central and Eastern European countries from socialism to open market economies in the early 1990s, the European services sector gained substantial additional impetus: many giant services sectors were privatised (e.g. public utilities, banking, broadcasting and media, telecommunications) and others developed with the consolidation of the market economy in these countries (e.g. further financial services, consultancy, shared service centres, accountancy).

As regards technology-driven developments, the birth and growth of information and communication technologies (ICT) from the 1990s onwards has been crucial (Sapprasert 2010). ICT has become a new, dynamically expanding services sector in itself. At the same time, ICT has fundamentally revolutionised full sectors – it is enough to think about financial services going electronic, or retail going online. It is not uncommon for individuals or businesses to use a service online without even knowing in which country the service provider is established. In the EU, with the free movement of services, this means in practice that any service company established in one EU member state is immediately free to provide its services all across the EU. Some small EU member states (such as Ireland, Luxembourg, the Netherlands or, most recently, Estonia) take action to attract such service companies to establish their EU-wide headquarters locally. Stemming from the nature of the services sectors, the development of one sector pulls with it further sectors serving it. Attracting EU-wide service providers into a country is thus a means of economic development policy.

Knowledge-intensive services and digitalisation

The knowledge-based economy has definitely gained space in European business by the twenty-first century (Rodrigues 2002; Dosi 2012; Lundvall 2012). In 2015, knowledge-intensive services accounted for more than 56 per cent of all services sector employment (the first four categories in Figure 25.4), which means 87.8 million jobs (EU 2014).

Most recently, digitalisation has been a general trend in Europe, just as worldwide. The services sector is increasingly affected as practically all services can be (further) digitalised. Digitalisation yields higher productivity and thus a competitive advantage.

The Digital Economy and Society Index (DESI) measures the EU's digital performance along five dimensions. Regarding integration of digital technologies by businesses, the overall penetration was at 37.3 per cent in 2017 (Figure 25.5). Nevertheless, there are vast intra-EU differences, ranging from highly digitalised services sectors in Denmark (62.4%), Ireland (55.7%), Finland (55.7%), Sweden (53.8%) or Belgium (51.9%) while considerably lower penetration of such technologies in Romania (18.6%), Poland (21.6%), Bulgaria (22.5%), Latvia (22.7%), Hungary (23.5%) and Greece (24.4%).

The Single Market for services

The Single European Act of 1986 aimed at eliminating the remaining barriers to the free movement of goods, services, persons and capital. Originally, the focus was on goods; services came to the forefront somewhat later (Molle 2001).

The Single Market Agenda of 1992 intended to establish a single set of rules defining the conditions of doing business across the EU. Implementation was first assessed in 1996 and it was found that 'most of the principal obstacles to the integration of product, service and

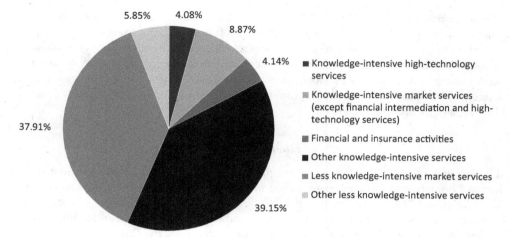

5.85% 4.08%
8.87%
4.14%

- Knowledge-intensive high-technology services
- Knowledge-intensive market services (except financial intermediation and high-technology services)
- Financial and insurance activities
- Other knowledge-intensive services
- Less knowledge-intensive market services
- Other less knowledge-intensive services

37.91%

39.15%

Figure 25.4 Services sectors employment according to knowledge intensity, %, 2015
Source: Author's own compilation based on Eurostat data (Eurostat 2015a, c).

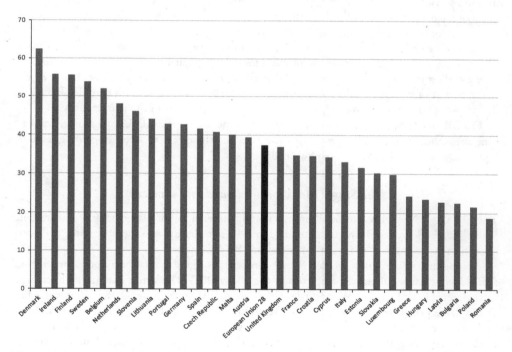

Figure 25.5 Integration of digital technology in the EU and its member states, %, 2017
Source: Author's own compilation using the interactive DESI simulation tool. http://digital–agenda–data.eu/datasets/desi/visualizations (accessed April 2017).

capital markets have been removed' (EC 1996, p. 12). According to the calculations, the Single Market had resulted in an additional 300,000–900,000 new jobs, and extra 1.1–1.5 per cent growth in income, 1.0–1.5 per cent lower inflation, and economic convergence and cohesion, in just four years. This trend has continued since then. In services, a wider range of activities were moving cross-border than before, mainly in transport (especially air transport), financial services, telecommunications and broadcasting. Liberalisation processes have largely supported these advancements.

Liberalisation

The largest services sectors (e.g. transport, public utilities, post) had been segmented along national borders with national, state-owned monopolies dominating these markets (Grabas and Nützenadel 2013). The first case that brought up the idea of the seizure of state monopoly through the unbundling of infrastructure and service was the case of freight services in the port of Rødby, delivered by the Danish railway company, the DSB (Flynn 2002). The case drew attention to the advantages of opening up markets and gave way to a long and ongoing process.

Liberalisation is carried out in a sectorial approach, starting with an investigation, continuing in liberalisation by legislation and, preferably, ending in liberalised markets. First, the telecommunication services sector was investigated, between 2000 and 2002. This market has since become fairly opened up to competition but the role of technology in disrupting established market actors cannot be neglected (mobile phone, VoIP and other internet-based communication technologies). The greatest regulatory success in EU telecommunication markets was the maximisation of within-EU roaming prices in 2007 and then their gradual abolition by summer 2017.

Regarding transportation, the greatest benefit of liberalisation for consumers has been the development of competitive low-cost airlines, eventually bringing about a considerable fall in the prices of traditional airlines (the original national incumbents of the market) as well.

Overall, liberalisation is a continuing process in the EU Single Market, far from complete. One reason for its incompleteness is that the constant changes of markets (including technological advancements) always pose new challenges.

The Single Market scoreboard and services

The EU Single Market was realised through the implementation of a large body of EU law. The Single Market Scoreboard[4] was first launched in 1997 in order to assess member states' performance in the transposition and enforcement of this EU legislation.

Among others, the Single Market Scoreboard assesses the liberalisation of postal services in the EU, which was due to be completed by the end of 2012. The aim is that, in the liberalised market, reliable and high-quality postal services are permanently available throughout the EU at affordable prices (Hermann et al. 2013; Kalevi Dieke et al. 2013). We can see that, in 2015, intra-EU cross-border prices were still considerably higher than domestic prices (except for Finland), indicating that the liberalisation of the sector had not yet been exploited to the full (Figure 25.6). Italian services cost the most in the EU by far, and the gap between domestic and cross-border prices are the largest in the post-socialist new member states – Poland, Bulgaria, Hungary, Estonia and Croatia in particular.

If we take a closer look at countries' performance in the Single Market Scoreboard, we see that they are performing rather well in transposing service-related EU directives. However, the case is not as bright as regards infringement of existing legislation. In particular, sectors

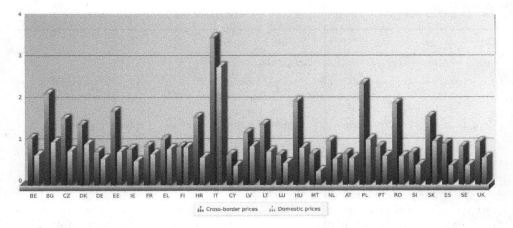

Figure 25.6 Priority mail prices in EU member states, 2015, in purchasing power parity
Source: Single Market Scoreboard, Performance per Policy Area, Postal services. http://ec.europa.eu/internal_market/scoreboard/performance_per_policy_area/postal_services/index_en.htm (accessed 15 September 2017).

with the most infringement cases, as of December 2015 are: transport (especially air transport) accounting for 24.3 per cent of all cases, environment covering 22.3 per cent of all cases (especially water protection and waste management) and taxation at 14.7 per cent. Road and rail transport and transport safety are also among the sectors with a large share of total infringement cases open at the end of 2015 (EC 2016a).

The Single Market Acts and services

There are two packages of measures ensuring the smooth operation of the Single Market: Single Market Acts I and II. The first package was adopted in April 2011 (EC 2011) and encompassed measures along twelve dimensions, including services (fifth dimension) and digital single market (seventh). There are also further, horizontal dimensions that affect the services sector, especially access to finance for SMEs (first), social entrepreneurship (eighth) and business environment (11th dimension).

The objectives in relation to services include the extension of the European standardisation system to services in order to foster their free movement. Standards in services – similar to those applied to products – are guarantees to the consumer that the service coming from another EU member state meets the necessary requirements regarding interoperability (i.e. country of origin of service does not cause any complications), safety and quality.

The smooth EU-wide operation of business-to-business (B2B) services such as logistics or facilities management are of crucial importance to European economic growth. Pelkmans (2011) highlighted the importance of transport liberalisation and the enhancement of the free movement of financial services in this respect, while setting up standards in these sectors would also improve EU-wide market operations.

In October 2012, the second set of regulatory measures was published (EC 2012a). It was presented in the midst of the Eurozone crisis, looking for new growth in the EU. Among others, the continuation of the integration of network industries (rail transport, maritime transport, air transport and energy) was encouraged, together with the dispersion of digital technologies throughout the services sector (Table 25.1).

Table 25.1 Measures proposed by the Single Market Act II concerning the services sector

Lever	Objective	Means	Key action
Developing fully integrated networks in the Single Market			
Rail transport	Improve quality and price for passengers	Open domestic rail passenger services to EU competition	Adopt a fourth railway package (legislative)
Maritime transport	Promote maritime transport	Establish a true Single Market for maritime transport	Adopt the 'Blue Belt' package (legislative and non-legislative measures)
Air transport	Enhance safety, efficiency and environmental performance	Accelerate implementation of Single European Sky	Implement action plan (with legislative measures)
Energy	Further integrate the EU energy market to reduce prices, promote renewable energy and improve security of supply	Improve the application of the third energy package	Enhance implementation and enforcement of third energy package and make cross-border markets a reality
Supporting the digital economy across Europe			
Services	Facilitate e-commerce and online services and therefore consumer choice and convenience	Make EU-wide electronic payment services more competitive and efficient	Revise the Payment Services Directive and make a legislative proposal for multilateral interchange fees
Digital Single Market	Improve availability of high-speed communication infrastructures for citizens and businesses	Reduce the cost and increase efficiency in the deployment of high-speed communication infrastructure	Adopt common rules enabling operators to fully exploit cost-reduction potential of broadband deployment
Public procurement and electronic invoicing	Promote electronic invoicing in order to generate savings for administrations and businesses and to help reduce payment delays	Make electronic invoicing the standard invoicing mode for public procurement	Adopt legislation on electronic invoicing

Source: Single Market Act II Table of key actions. http://ec.europa.eu/growth/single-market/smact/ (accessed 1 April 2017).

The European regulatory framework for services

In the following we briefly review European legislation concerning the services sector. The main piece of legislation covering 46 per cent of EU GDP is the services directive.[5]

The Services Directive

The adoption of the Services Directive was preceded by heated debates. The main underlying conflict behind the debate derived from the Eastern enlargement of the EU: as the new member states were considerably less developed with much lower wage levels, stakeholders in the old member states, including employees' representatives and small business associations, felt threatened by dumping from the East.

The Services Directive (Directive 2006/123/EC), adopted in December 2006, and implemented by all EU countries by the end of 2009, was eventually a compromise among the debating parties: while the principles of the freedom to establish a company in another EU member state and the freedom to provide or receive cross-border services in the EU were reaffirmed, numerous sectors were exempted from the scope of legislation. Major services sectors not falling under the scope of the Services Directive are: services of general interest (regulated under the competition policy of the EU), financial services (regulated separately), certain electronic communication services, transport services (including urban transport, taxi, ambulance, port services), healthcare and pharmaceutical services, audiovisual services, gambling (including lottery and betting), non-profit public and community services (e.g. social and recreational services) and the complete field of the taxation of services.

With these exceptions, the directive aims at further simplifying the establishment of EU-wide service companies, fostering the intra-EU cross-border provision of services while ensuring consumers' rights and their easier access to a wider range of services. Overall, European legislation has been successful and today it has become rather easy to be present in the cross-border services markets of the EU, although there is still room left for further improvement (Monteagudo et al. 2012; Corugedo and Ruiz 2014).

Regulated professions

The free movement of professionals has gradually been extended in the EU. Its basis is the system of recognition of professional qualifications (governed by Directive 2005/36/EC, amended by Directive 2013/55/EC). The system does not only cover the recognition of degrees but also that of professional experience gained in other EU member states. The law covers professions with individual practices, e.g. doctors and architects (Figure 25.7).[6]

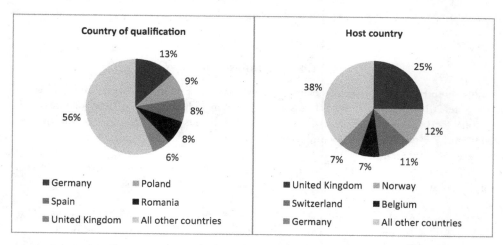

Figure 25.7 Recognition of qualifications in the EU Single Market, country of qualification and host country, 1997–2016

Source: European Commission, Regulated professions database. http://ec.europa.eu/growth/tools-databases/regprof/ (accessed 1 April 2017).

In January 2016, a so-called European Professional Card (EPC) was introduced, currently available in the following professions: nursing, physiotherapy, pharmacy, real estate agency and mountain guiding. With this card, professionals are entitled to offer their services freely in the EU, without any obstacles, and the idea behind the construct is to liberate underlying efficiency capacities across Europe (Barslund et al. 2015).

Retail services

Retail and wholesale services make up 11.1 per cent of the EU's GDP and account for about 33 million jobs (roughly 15 per cent of total EU employment), provided by more than 6 million companies (Eurostat 2015a). Retail and wholesale has been fairly integrated across the EU, thanks to the free movement of goods. Therefore, most recently, EU legislation has focused on the growing sector of e-commerce in order to ensure the safety of both sides of the market. For the time being, domestic e-commerce in EU member states is fairly developed while cross-border e-commerce in the Single Market lags significantly behind domestic online purchasing (Marcus et al. 2017).

Outside e-commerce, the EU-wide regulation of unfair trade practices in the food supply chain has been on the agenda since January 2016 (EC 2016b).

Business services

The size of the varied business services sector is comparable to that of the retail and wholesale services, accounting for another 11 per cent of the EU's GDP (Eurostat 2015a). The importance of this sector lies in several specificities. First, business services are typically knowledge based, thus employing highly qualified people (Di Maria et al. 2012; Doloreux et al. 2016). Therefore, recognition of qualifications is of crucial importance.

Otherwise, business services fall under the general Services Directive, so the free movement and free establishment principles apply. The latest advancements in ICT have further promoted the cross-border business services sector in the EU: it is becoming ever easier to physically be situated somewhere in the EU and cover large geographical areas by service.

Construction services

Unlike business services, the construction service sector's European integration is rather low (Deloitte 2017). There are several reasons for this, including the protection of workers by national legal systems. Nevertheless, as construction accounts for around 6 per cent of the EU's GDP and 7.3 per cent of EU employment (Eurostat 2015b), it is important to find ways to achieve more integration.

In general, the Services Directive applies here. Furthermore, there are initiatives specifically for the construction industry:

In 2011, harmonised rules for the marketing of construction products in the EU were laid down. Also in 2011, a European performance check in construction services was introduced.
In line with the Europe 2020 Strategy, the aim is to enhance the shift of construction in the EU towards more environmentally sustainable solutions.

Posted workers

We introduce here a sector which is working uniquely across the EU: the sector of companies providing posted workers, mainly from Eastern post-socialist new member states to companies in 'old Europe' (Benio 2016), especially in the United Kingdom, which has a highly liberalised labour market (and is still a member of the EU and, potentially, will remain a member of the Single Market even after Brexit takes effect).

The right of companies to post workers temporarily (for a maximum of two years continuously) in another EU member state derives from the freedom of services. Nevertheless, the Posting of Workers Directive (96/71/EC) was adopted in 1996, at a time when intra-EU differences were significantly lower than they have been since the Eastern enlargements. According to this directive, host country rules apply for posted workers in terms of maximum work periods and minimum rest periods, minimum paid holidays, minimum rates of pay, health, safety and hygiene at work, protection of pregnant women, young mothers, children and young people, equal treatment of men and women, and other provisions on non-discrimination. At the same time, home country rules apply in terms of social security and so the posting agency pays social security contributions for the posted workers in the home country.

In fact, the business opportunities lying in establishing temporary agency firms in the new member states which then post workers in old member states for lower-than-average wages in relation to the host country wage levels was gradually discovered by more and more firms on both sides of the market. A thorough investigation of the trends was carried out in 2012 (EC 2012b). Based on the number of issued documents in 2011,[7] the main sending countries of posted workers were: Poland (228,000), Germany (227,000), France (144,000), and then, in smaller but relatively still significant numbers, Romania, Hungary, Belgium and Portugal. The main receiving countries were: Germany (311,000), France (162,000), Belgium (125,000), Netherlands (106,000), and Spain, Italy and Austria still being important receivers of posted workers, especially in relative terms.

The tendencies have continued, which calls for renewed regulation of the field in order to protect workers' rights (Maslauskaite 2014). In 2014, there were about 1.2 million posted workers in the EU (Andor 2014). A new enforcement of the 1996 Posted Workers Directive was adopted in 2014 (2014/67/EU) calling for more exchange of information and control on behalf of national authorities.

Financial services

Financial services make up a considerable part of intra-EU trade in services. The introduction of the euro in 1999 and further countries joining the Eurozone later has fostered the trend.

The two basic principles in relation to the free movement of financial services in the EU are: single passport and home country control. Financial services are economic activities that are subject to permit from the financial supervisory authorities. The principle of single passport implies that, if a company has a permit in one of the member states, it enables them to provide their services across the EU, provided they register at the supervisory authorities of the respective member states. The principle of home country control, on the other hand, says that those activities of the financial services company taking place in other EU countries are supervised by the authority originally issuing the permit.

The need for more harmonisation of rules and activities was recognised in 1999 and the Financial Services Action Plan (FSAP) was adopted (EC 1999). It proposed measures to be undertaken in three strategic areas: wholesale (interbank) financial services; retail (bank–client) financial services; and supervision. Several further areas of strategic importance were added: collective investment in financial companies; distance selling of financial services (online or e-banking); and electronic money.

According to the FSAP, the following areas needed action: barriers to raising capital on an EU-wide basis; securities and derivatives markets still too much segmented across national borders; a single set of financial statements for listed companies to be established; a secure and transparent European business environment for financial services; and an adequate European framework for asset managers in EU-level optimisation of portfolios.

The fundamental approach was to create an EU Single Market as if there were no national borders. One of the first actions in the implementation of the FSAP considered supervision. On 17 July 2000, a so-called Committee of Wise Men on the Regulation of European Securities Markets was set up. The Committee was chaired by Alexandre Lamfalussy and the Committee released its report on 15 February 2001. The 'wise men' suggested that profound change and reform was needed in order to reduce general fragmentation of EU financial markets, further aggravated by additional factors such as multiple clearing and settlement systems, different taxation, cultural approach and regulatory priorities (Lamfalussy et al. 2001). The Committee recommended reforms at four levels:

- Level 1: EU-level framework principles;
- Level 2: the institutions defining, proposing and implementing legislation;
- Level 3: national implementation and cooperation;
- Level 4: the European Commission must be the rigorous guardian of enforcement.

As regards the institutions (Level 2), the Committee proposed the setting up of two new committees, the European Securities Committee and the European Securities Regulators Committee.

The report of the wise men did have some impact but, admittedly, the management of the crisis after 2008 meant much stricter constraints on financial services, so their European regulation today is much more the result of the latter than the former. However, even if out of necessity, a long-sought single regulatory framework for financial services was eventually created in 2014 (Table 25.2).

After 2008, in the first wave of crisis-driven legislation, attention was mainly paid to risks, solvency and prudency. Then, in September 2009, legislation establishing the European Supervisory Authorities was finally proposed. As a result, three European authorities and an independent Board, responsible for the macroprudential oversight of the EU financial system, were created in November 2010:

- the European Banking Authority (EBA),
- the European Securities and Markets Authority (ESMA),
- the European Insurance and Occupational Pensions Authority (EIOPA), and
- the European Systemic Risk Board (ESRB).

Since then, the 2015 Green Paper on retail financial services (EC 2015a) has undergone public consultation. As a result, a truly integrated single market for banking services provided to households and small businesses is to be created, at the same time exploiting the opportunities lying in the digitalisation of financial services.

Table 25.2 EU financial reform – actions taken and related adopted legislation

Date of first proposal by the Commission	Action	Adopted legislation
July 2007	Risk-based prudential and solvency rules for insurers ('Solvency II')	Directive 2009/138/EC
Nov 2008	Credit rating agencies	Regulation EC N°1060/2009 Regulation EU N°513/2011 Regulation EU N°462/2013 Directive 2013/14/EU
Apr 2009	Hedge funds and private equity ('AIFMD')	Directive 2011/61/EU
July 2009	Remuneration and prudential requirements for banks ('CRD III')	Directive 2010/76/EU
Sep 2009	Establishment of the European Supervisory Authorities (EBA), (ESMA), (EIOPA) and (ESRB) regulations	Regulation (EU) No 1092/2010 Regulation (EU) No 1096/2010 Regulation (EU) No 1093/2010 Regulation (EU) No 1094/2010 Regulation (EU) No 1095/2010 'Omnibus' Directive 2010/78/EU
July 2010	Deposit guarantee schemes	Directive 2014/49/EU
Aug 2010	Strengthened supervision of financial conglomerates	Directive 2011/89/EU
Sep 2010	Derivatives ('EMIR')	Regulation (EU) No 648/2012
Sep 2010	Short-selling and Credit Default Swaps	Regulation (EU) No 236/2012
Dec 2010	Creation of the Single Euro Payments Area ('SEPA')	Regulation (EU) No 260/2012 Regulation EU No 248/2014
Jan 2011	New European supervisory framework for insurers ('Omnibus II')	Directive 2014/51/EU
Feb 2011	Interconnection of business registers	Directive 2012/17/EU
Mar 2011	Responsible lending (mortgage credit)	Directive 2014/17/EU
July 2011	Single Rule Book of prudential requirements + stricter rules on remuneration and improved transparency ('CRD IV / CRR')	Directive 2013/36/EU (CRD IV) Regulation (EU) No 575/2013 (CRR)
Oct 2011	Enhanced framework for securities markets ('MIFID/R')	Directive 2014/65/EU (MiFID 2) Regulation (EU) No 600/2014 (MiFIR)
Oct 2011	Enhanced framework to prevent market abuse ('MAD/R')	Directive 2014/57/EU (MAD) Regulation (EU) No 596/2014 (MAR)
Oct 2011	Simplification of accounting	Directive 2013/34/EU
Oct 2011	Enhanced transparency rules	Directive 2013/50/EU
Nov 2011	Enhanced framework for audit sector	Regulation (EU) No 537/2014 Directive 2014/56/EU
Dec 2011[1]	Creation of European venture capital funds	Regulation (EU) No 345/2013
Dec 2011	Creation of European social entrepreneurship funds	Regulation (EU) No 346/2013
Mar 2012	Central securities depositaries	Regulation (EU) No 909/2014
July 2012	Improved investor information for complex financial products ('PRIPS')	Regulation (EU) No 1286/2014

(*continued*)

Table 25.2 (Cont.)

Date of first proposal by the Commission	Action	Adopted legislation
July 2012	Strengthened rules on the sale of insurance products ('IMD')	Directive (EU) 2016/97
July 2012	Safer rules for retail investment funds ('UCITS')	Directive 2014/91/EU
June 2012	Prevention, management and resolution of bank crises ('BRRD')	Directive 2014/59/EU
Sep 2012	Single Supervisory Mechanism (SSM)	Regulation (EU) No 1024/2013 Regulation (EU) No 1022/2013
Apr 2013	Non-financial reporting for companies	Directive 2014/95/EU
May 2013	Access to basic bank account/transparency of fees/switching of bank accounts	Directive 2014/92/EU
June 2013	Creation of European long-term investment funds	Regulation (EU) 2015/760
July 2013	Single Resolution Mechanism (SRM)	Regulation (EU) No 806/2014
July 2013	Revised rules for innovative payment services	Directive (EU) 2015/2366
Sep 2013	Regulation of financial benchmarks (LIBOR, EURIBOR)	Regulation (EU) 2016/1011
Jan 2014	Shadow banking: increasing the transparency of securities financing transactions	Regulation (EU) 2015/2365

Source: Author's own compilation based on: http://ec.europa.eu/info/business-economy-euro/banking-and-finance/financial-reforms-and-their-progress/progress-financial-reforms_en (accessed 1 March 2017).

The digital Single Market agenda

The Digital Single Market Strategy (EC 2015b) was launched in May 2015. The Strategy targets all areas of economic activity, from multi-sided markets (platforms) to personal data protection and copyright. Regarding services, the following are relevant:

- E-commerce opens up opportunities for retail businesses, be they large or small. However, European businesses are not yet able to fully exploit these opportunities, in part due to the fragmentation of the EU retail services market.
- As a competitive European e-commerce market is developing, it is essential that a similarly efficient parcel delivery market develops in parallel.
- Platforms are essential actors in digital ecosystems. They function as a 'meeting place' for the two sides of the market. Thus platforms may easily be the best informed market actors. The opportunities their existence brings should be reaped by European businesses using these platforms.
- Geo-blocking occurs when a digital service is available to its subscribers in a limited geographical area (i.e. in the country where the subscription was made). The aim is to eliminate intra-EU geo-blocking, thus establishing a more integrated market of digitally available services.

There are high expectations surrounding the strategy, which, if certain conditions are met, is likely to bring about the expected upgrading in European markets (Renda 2017).

Conclusion

The chapter provides an overview of services in the EU in the twenty-first century. The sector is continuously improving, changing, absorbing new technologies and discovering new business opportunities.

The latest trends are shaped mainly by technology (ICT, digitalisation, going online) and we can already see that market structures are affected in several ways. Providing services at a European scale is technically easier than ever before and legislation is aimed at keeping it easy while ensuring safety and quality. New powerful market actors have appeared: platforms possess information on both sides of the market and, at the current levels of data analysis, are able to utilise this information for their own benefit.

There are apparent intra-EU differences at the level of development of the services sectors but these differences can actually be beneficial to businesses: low cost in one region can now easily be combined with a developed business environment elsewhere.

Notes

1 For practical reasons, we refer to the European Union (EU). However, for the period preceding the entering into force of the Maastricht Treaty in 1993, the name European Economic Community (EEC) applies.
2 West Germany, France, Italy, Belgium, Netherlands, Luxembourg.
3 Value added represents the difference between the value of what is produced and intermediate consumption entering the production, less subsidies on production and costs, taxes and levies (Eurostat 2017).
4 Regularly updated information and the respective reports are available on the Single Market Scoreboard of the European Commission at: http://ec.europa.eu/internal_market/scoreboard/
5 The chapter relies on information found under the Single Market for Services website of the European Commission at https://ec.europa.eu/growth/single-market/services_en, accessed by the author throughout January–April 2017.
6 For lawyers, there is a different system of recognition as most national legal education in EU member states concentrates on the transmission of knowledge on that particular national legal system.
7 A so-called PD A1 document is issued when a worker or a self-employed person is posted in another European Economic Area (EEA) country.

References

Andor, L. (2014), 'Labour mobility in the EU', speech delivered at the University of Ghent on 25 September. http://europa.eu/rapid/press-release_SPEECH-14-622_en.htm (accessed 17 March 2017).

Barslund, M., Busse, M. and Schwarzwälder, J. (2015), 'Labour mobility in Europe: An untapped resource?' *CEPS Policy Briefs*, 327, Brussels, Centre for European Policy Studies.

Benio, M. (2016), 'Labour costs in cross-border services', Working Paper, November, Cracow, Cracow University of Economics. www.mobilelabour.eu/wp-content/uploads/2017/06/study-UEK-Labour-Costs-in-Cross-border-Services-by-Marek-Benio-2016.pdf (accessed 19 December 2017).

Corugedo, E.F. and Ruiz, E.P. (2014), 'The EU Services Directive: Gains from Further Liberalization', IMF Working Paper, 14/113, July. Washington DC, International Monetary Fund.

Deloitte (2017), *European Construction Monitor 2016–2017: Growing opportunities in local markets*, Deloitte Netherlands. www2.deloitte.com/content/dam/Deloitte/pl/Documents/Reports/pl_European_construction_monitor.pdf (accessed 19 December 2017).

Di Maria, E., Grandinetti, R. and Di Bernardo, B. (2012), *Exploring Knowledge-Instensive Business Services: Knowledge management strategies*, Basingstoke, Palgrave Macmillan.

Doloreux, D., Freel, M. and Shearmur, R. (2016), *Knowledge-Intensive Business Services: Geography and innovation*, London and New York, Routledge.

Dosi, G. (2012), 'A note on information, knowledge and economic theory', in R. Arena, A. Festré and N. Lazaric (eds), *Handbook of Knowledge and Economics*, Cheltenham and Northampton, MA, Edward Elgar, pp. 167–182.

EC (1996), *The Impact and Effectiveness of the Single Market*. Communication from the Commission to the European Parliament and Council, 30 October. http://ec.europa.eu/internal_market/economic-reports/docs/single_en.pdf (accessed 3 January 2017).

EC (1999), *Financial Services: Implementing the framework for financial markets: Action Plan*, Communication of the Commission, COM(1999)232, 11.05.99. http://ec.europa.eu/internal_market/finances/docs/actionplan/index/action_en.pdf (accessed 3 January 2017).

EC (2011), *Single Market Act: Twelve levers to boost growth and strengthen confidence: 'Working together to create new growth'*, Communication from the Commission, COM(2011)0206 final. http://eur-lex.europa.eu/legal-content/EN/ALL/?uri=CELEX:52011DC0206 (accessed 17 March 2017).

EC (2012a), *Single Market Act II: Together for new growth*, Communication from the Commission, COM(2012)0573 final. http://eur-lex.europa.eu/legal-content/EN/TXT/?uri=celex:52012DC0573 (accessed 17 March 2017).

EC (2012b), *Posting of workers in the European Union and EFTA countries: Report on A1 portable documents issued in 2010 and 2011*, Brussels, European Commission.

EC (2015a), *Green Paper on Retail Financial Services: Better products, more choice, and greater opportunities for consumers and businesses*, COM(2015)630 final, Brussels, European Commission.

EC (2015b), *A Digital Single Market Strategy for Europe*, COM(2015)192 final, Brussels, European Commission.

EC (2016a), *Single Market Scoreboard Performance Per Governance Tool: Infringements (reporting period: 05/2015–12/2015)*, Brussels, European Commission. http://ec.europa.eu/internal_market/scoreboard/_docs/2016/infringements/2016-scoreboard-infringements_en.pdf (accessed 1 April 2017).

EC (2016b), *Report from the Commission to the European Parliament and the Council on Unfair Business-to-business Trading Practices in the Food Supply Chain*, COM(2016)32 final, 29 January. http://eur-lex.europa.eu/legal-content/EN/TXT/PDF/?uri=CELEX:52016DC0032andfrom=EN (accessed 1 April 2017).

EU (2014), *Helping Firms Grow: European competitiveness report 2014*, Brussels, European Union.

Eurostat (2015a), 'Services statistiscs'. http://ec.europa.eu/eurostat/data/web-services (accessed April 2017)

Eurostat (2015b), Glossary: 'Gross value added at market prices'. http://ec.europa.eu/eurostat/statistics-explained/index.php/Glossary:Gross_value_added_at_market_prices (accessed 1 April 2017).

Eurostat (2015c), 'Employment and unemployment database'. http://ec.europa.eu/eurostat/web/lfs/data/database (accessed April 2017).

Flynn, L. (2002), 'Access to the postal network: The situation after Bronner', in D. Geradin (ed.), *The Liberalisation of Postal Services in the European Union*, The Hague, London and New York, Kluwer Law International, pp. 181–204.

Grabas, Ch. and Nützenadel, A. (2013), 'Industrial Policies in Europe in Historical Perspective', Working Paper, 15, WWWforEurope project. www.foreurope.eu (accessed 5 March 2015).

Hermann, Ch., Kubisa, J., Gavroglou, S.P., Van Klaveren, M., Vermandere, C., Van Gyes, G. and Haidinger, B. (20173), *The Liberalisation of European Postal Markets and the Impact on Employment and Working Conditions*, Vienna, FORBA.

Kacsirek, L. (2007), 'Nemzetközi szolgáltatáskereskedelem' [International Trade in Services], in A. Blahó, I. Benczes, Á. Bernek, L. Csaba, L. Kacsirek, M. Losoncz, P. Majoros, Á. Mészáros and T. Szentes (eds), *Világgazdaságtan [Global Economy]*, Budapest, Akadémiai Kiadó [Academic Press], pp. 201–222.

Kalevi Dieke, A., Bender, C., Campbell Jr., J.I., Cohen, R.H., Müller, C., Niederprüm, A., De Streel, A., Thiele, S. and Zanker, C. (2013), *Main Developments in the Postal Sector (2010–2013)*, Study for the European Commission, Directorate General for Internal Market and Services, Bad Honnef, WIK-Consult.

Lamfalussy, A., Herkströter, C., Rojo, L.A., Ryden, B., Spaventa, L., Walter, N. and Wicks, N. (2001), *Final Report of the Committee of Wise Men on the Regulation of European Securities Markets*, Brussels, 15 February. http://ec.europa.eu/internal_market/securities/docs/lamfalussy/wisemen/final-report-wise-men_en.pdf (accessed 3 March 2017).

Lundvall, B.-Å. (2012), 'One knowledge base or many knowledge pools?', in R. Arena, Festré, A. and Lazaric, N (eds), *Handbook of Knowledge and Economics*, Cheltenham and Northampton, MA: Edward Elgar, pp. 285–312.

Marcus, J.S., Morales, J. and Petropoulos, G. (2017), 'Strengthening cross-border e-commerce in the European Union', in R. Veugelers, (ed.), *Remaking Europe: The new manufacturing as an engine for growth*, Brussels, Bruegel, pp. 217–251.

Maslauskaite, K. (2014), *Posted workers in the EU: State of play and regulatory evolution*, Policy Paper 107, Notre Europe, Jacques Delors Institute. www.institutdelors.eu/media/postedworkers-maslauskaite-nejdi-mar14.pdf (accessed 19 December 2017).

Miozzo, M. and Soete, L. (2001), 'Internationalisation of services: A technological perspective', *Technological Forecasting and Social Change*, vol. 67, no. 2–3, pp. 159–185.

Molle, W. (2001), *The Economics of European Integration: Theory, Practice, Policy*, Aldershot, Ashgate.

Monteagudo, J., Rutkowski, A. and Lorenzani, D. (2012), 'The economic impact of the Services Directive: A first assessment following implementation', *Economic Papers*, 456, Brussels, European Commission.

OECD (2001), *Education Policy Analysis 2001*, Paris: Organisation for Economic Co-operation and Development. www.oecd-ilibrary.org/education/education-policy-analysis-2001_epa-2001-en (accessed 19 December 2017).

OECD (2006), *How are Services Being Internationalised? And which ones?* STD/NAES/TASS/SERV(2006)14, 1 September, Statistics Directorate, Paris, OECD.

Orio, G. (1987), *The Emerging Service Economy*, Oxford and New York, Pergamon Press.

Papp, I. (ed.) (2003), *Szolgáltatások a harmadik évezredben, [Services in the Third Millennium]*, Budapest, Aula.

Pelkmans, J. (2011), 'Single Market: Deepening and widening over time', *Intereconomics*, vol. 46, no. 2, pp. 64–68.

Renda, A. (2017), 'Will the DSM Strategy spur innovation?' *Intereconomics*, vol. 52, no. 4, pp. 197–201.

Rodrigues, M.J. (2002), 'Introduction: for a European strategy at the turn of the century', in M.J. Rodrigues (ed.), *The New Knowledge Economy in Europe: A strategy for international competitiveness and social cohesion*, Cheltenham and Northampton, MA, Edward Elgar, pp. 1–27.

Sapprasert, K. (2010), 'The impact of ICT on the growth of the service industries', TIK Working Papers on Innovation Studies, 20070531, Oslo, University of Oslo Centre for Technology, Innovation and Culture. www.sv.uio.no/tik/InnoWP/2007%20Koson%20Sapprasert%20-%20The%20impact%20of%20ICT%20on%20the%20growth%20of%20service%20industries.pdf (accessed 19 December 2017).

Stehrer, R., Baker, P., Foster-McGregor, N., Koenen, J., Leitner, S., Schricker, J., Strobel, T., Vieweg, H.-G., Vermeulen, J. and Yagafarova, A. (2014), *Study on the Relation between Industry and Services in Terms of Productivity and Value Creation*, Vienna, ECSIP (European Competitiveness and Sustainable Industrial Policy) Consortium.

PART G

Complex challenges

European society and the natural environment

26

CLIMATE CHANGE, ENERGY AND INNOVATION

Challenges and opportunities for the European Union

Nicholas Parry and Martin Wainstein

Introduction

In one of the most influential reports on climate change published to date, economist Nicholas Stern (2007, p. viii), described it as the 'greatest market failure the world has ever seen'. The report estimated that the costs of climate change would be equivalent to at least 5 per cent of global GDP each year unless action was taken. However, these costs were not directly factored into the practices that cause the problem. Stern made three broad policy recommendations to overcome the failure: price carbon, promote energy efficiency measures and support innovation in low-carbon technologies. This seemingly simple prescription is actually incredibly complex as it entails enormous shifts in our political, legal, economic and social practices, all within an extremely limited time frame. However, amongst the complexities and challenges of climate change, there are economic opportunities for those governments and businesses that respond to these changes and provide innovative solutions.

For the European Union (EU), climate change mitigation and economic opportunity have always been inextricably linked. The EU has long been a leader in international climate negotiations and has often acted as a test laboratory for climate-related policies (Schreurs and Tiberghien 2007, pp. 19–24); however, environmental outcomes have never been the sole driver of EU action. The economic benefits of climate action, particularly as they relate to innovation in clean-energy technologies, are often cited to justify the EU's strong stance. For example, at the beginning of his term as President of the European Commission, Jean-Claude Juncker (European Commission 2014, p. 4), stated:

> We need to strengthen the share of renewable energies on our continent. I want Europe's Energy Union to become the world number one in renewable energies. This is not only a matter of a responsible climate change policy. It is, at the same time, an industrial policy imperative.

This chapter will examine how notions of economic competitiveness feed into the EU's climate policies and how this might influence the ability of European businesses to adapt and grow in response to the problem. It will begin by providing an overview of the Paris climate agreement and the challenge that its objectives entail. It will examine the role that the EU has played in driving international action on climate change, highlighting the importance of economic competitiveness to the EU's position. The second section will then outline the key policies implemented by the EU in relation to climate change, energy and innovation, identifying points of convergence between all three. The third section will place specific focus on the energy sector, examining the ways in which the transition to a low-carbon economy will disrupt incumbent businesses and business models. The chapter will conclude by assessing the EU's progress in meeting its climate and innovation objectives.

The Paris Agreement and EU climate leadership

In December 2015, 196 countries gathered in Paris for the 21st Conference of the Parties (COP21) to the United Nations Framework Convention on Climate Change (UNFCCC). The objective of the meeting was to reach 'a legally binding and universal agreement on climate, with the aim of keeping global warming below 2°C' (UNEP 2015). Although COP meetings had been held annually since 1995, they had only resulted in incremental action that had failed to reverse the growth in global greenhouse gas emissions. The lack of substantive action meant that the window for averting dangerous levels of global warming was fast closing and many saw COP21 as the last chance for the world to establish a mitigation pathway (Christoff 2016). After two weeks of negotiations, agreement was finally reached. At the heart of the agreement was Article 2, which stated that the parties agreed to hold 'the increase in the global average temperature to well below 2°C above preindustrial levels and pursuing efforts to limit the temperature increase to 1.5°C above preindustrial levels' (UNFCCC 2015).

The conclusion of the Paris Agreement was due in large part to the persistence and leadership of the EU over a number of decades (Oberthür 2016; Parker et al. 2017). It had committed to the deepest emissions cuts of all major industrialised economies during the Kyoto Protocol negotiations in 1997, and then engaged in frantic diplomatic efforts to save the protocol when the United States refused to ratify it in 2001 (Wurzel and Connelly 2010, pp. 6–8). It again staked out its position well in advance of the next major round of negotiations in Copenhagen in 2009, committing to a 30 per cent emissions reduction target if an agreement was reached, and a unilateral 20 per cent if no agreement was reached (European Commission 2009). Despite the EU's efforts, the negotiations ultimately failed due to a major disagreement between China and the United States (Christoff 2010; Dimitrov 2010). However, the world finally came to together to conclude the Paris Agreement in 2015.

The Paris Agreement was a remarkable political achievement, but the challenge implied by the 2°C target requires unprecedented levels of international cooperation and action. The Intergovernmental Panel on Climate Change (IPCC) synthesis report from 2014 stated that mitigation scenarios that would likely limit warming to 2°C above preindustrial levels would require the stabilisation of atmospheric CO_2 levels at 450 parts per million (ppm) by 2100 (IPCC 2014, p. 10). At the time the UNFCCC came into effect in 1994, the level was 360ppm, but by the end of 2015 the level had increased to 402ppm (NASA 2017). The global carbon budget, which is the estimate of the amount of carbon that can be emitted from 2015 to avoid breaching the 2°C limit, ranges from 590 $GtCO_2$ to 1240 $GtCO_2$ (Rogelj et al. 2016, p. 251) and based on current trajectories, it could be exhausted within two decades.

If the world is to stay below 1.5°C, or even 2°C, current emissions trajectories must be radically altered. This will require fundamental shifts in policy, economic structures and social practices, all of which will have an enormous impact on the global economy (Dangerman and Schellnhuber 2013; Parrish and Foxon 2009; Unruh 2000).

Climate change and competitiveness

The EU's leadership has not been driven purely by altruism. The climate negotiations in Copenhagen and Paris occurred against a backdrop of economic stagnation within the EU, which fed into long-held concerns that Europe is falling behind other major economies. Debates about economic competitiveness have always been closely tied to questions about the EU's purpose and legitimacy, and have driven significant changes to political and economic structures within the EU.

In the decade that followed World War II, fears that the national markets of Europe were too small to ever compete with the dominant United States created a compelling argument for the creation of a single market (Loth 2008, p. 17). Further concerns were raised following the oil shock in the 1970s and the subsequent stagnation in economic performance. At first, member states turned inwards to protect their own industries, ushering in a period of 'Eurosclerosis' (Jovanović 2013, pp. 515–516), but the adverse economic conditions eventually changed the calculation for member states. The slowing economy, increasing unemployment and concerns about European competitiveness relative to the United States and Japan provided the impetus for a broadening of the EU's powers under the Single European Act (SEA) in 1986 (Egan 2009, pp. 264–266).

The negotiations over the SEA coincided with the development of a concept known as 'ecological modernisation', and a growing awareness of climate change amongst policy elites in Europe. Ecological modernisation saw environmental policy as an opportunity for economic growth rather than an impediment. It first developed in Germany, but quickly became influential within the European Commission and was a key driver in the expansion of the EU's environmental powers under the SEA (Weale and Williams 1992, pp. 42–48; Wurzel and Connelly 2010, p. 14). At the same time, a consensus had formed amongst climate scientists that increasing levels of greenhouse gases in the atmosphere were causing global warming. The European Commission first formally recognised the scientific consensus and the need to take action in 1988 (European Commission 1988), with subsequent communications linking mitigation to economic opportunity, particularly in the development of low-emissions energy technologies (Liberatore 1995, p. 65).

The link between climate change and innovation was reinforced with the onset of the global financial crisis in 2008, which served to highlight the EU's persistent innovation deficit relative to other advanced economies. By its own measures of innovation, the EU lags behind the United States, Japan, South Korea and Australia, with China, Brazil and India also closing the gap (European Commission 2017a, p. 27). While the crisis induced fiscal tightening at the member state level, the EU sought to promote economic growth through innovation, and given the EU's leadership on climate policy, clean energy technologies were seen as particularly fertile ground for development. Strategies to improve economic competitiveness and combat climate change therefore became mutually reinforcing as the EU launched a number of policy frameworks that sought to tackle both challenges simultaneously.

EU climate, energy and innovation policies

The EU first developed an explicit renewable energy policy in 1997 with the release of the 'Energy for the Future' White Paper. The central proposal of the paper was a renewable energy target for the EU of 12 per cent by 2010. The policy aimed to not only reduce carbon emissions, but also improve energy security, and promote innovation and the development of new industries (European Commission 1997). The White Paper led to the implementation of Directive 2001/77/EC in 2001, which established renewable energy targets for the electricity sector in each member state. Although the Directive introduced reporting requirements for member states, the targets were not mandatory and growth in renewables was slower than expected. However, the Directive did establish a framework that was built upon for the post-2010 period (Howes 2010, pp. 122–123).

In 2005, the EU launched the world's first Emissions Trading System (ETS), which is based on the 'cap and trade' principle whereby a cap is placed on the amount of greenhouse gases that can be emitted. The cap is gradually lowered to ensure that emissions fall. Within the cap, companies receive emissions allowances and must surrender enough allowances at the end of each year to cover their emissions or suffer a financial penalty for every tonne of emissions not covered. If they do not have the required allowances to cover their emissions, they can buy them from other companies that have an excess. In its current phase, which runs until 2020, the system is applied to sectors that are responsible for 45 per cent of the EU's emissions, including power and heat generation, domestic aviation and energy intensive manufacturing (European Commission 2016).

A lack of reliable emissions data and an over-allocation of allowances plagued the ETS from the outset, ultimately limiting the efficacy of the programme in relation to emissions reductions (Declercq et al. 2011). However, the ETS did have a positive impact on innovation. Amongst firms directly covered by the ETS, patent applications for low-carbon technologies increased by 36 per cent (Calel and Dechezleprêtre 2016, p. 189).

With the ETS in place, the EU continued to increase its ambition in relation to climate policy. The European Commission released the Renewables Roadmap (European Commission 2007a), and 'An Energy Policy for Europe' in 2007 (European Commission 2007b). The two documents articulated the Commission's ambition to develop an integrated climate and energy package that aimed to reduce emissions, increase energy security and promote the development of new, sustainable technologies. The resulting policy package became known as the '20-20-20 by 20' package due to its three headline targets of a 20 per cent reduction in emissions on 1990 levels, a 20 per cent improvement in energy efficiency, and a 20 per cent share of renewable energy by 2020 (European Commission 2008).

The 20-20-20 proposal was released at a time of heightened awareness of climate change and its impact on energy systems. Record energy prices, the publication of the Stern Review and the need to begin discussions about a global agreement to replace the Kyoto Protocol all fed into a sense of urgency (Howes 2010, p. 118). As a result, the overall targets for the EU were approved relatively quickly by the heads of government in the European Council.

A draft Renewable Energy Directive (RED) was then released in April 2009, which included targets for each member state that ranged from 10 per cent for Malta to 49 per cent for Sweden. There were some misgivings about the targets, particularly from the UK, which was opposed to individual targets in principle, but the momentum behind the negotiations ensured that the Directive was quickly adopted and officially published in June 2009 (Turmes 2017, pp. 27–29). The final Directive (2009/28/EC) again highlighted the centrality of economic competitiveness to climate and energy policy with the first item in the preamble linking renewable energy with 'promoting the security of supply, promoting technological development and innovation and providing opportunities for employment'.

Although innovation is one of the primary goals of the 20-20-20 targets, evidence suggests that demand–pull policies such as renewable energy targets do not necessarily promote innovation, with only a weak correlation between renewable energy deployment and patent applications (European Environment Agency and UNEP 2014, pp. 22–23). Renewable energy targets do have a role in encouraging incremental innovation in technologies that are closer to the market, but in order to promote the development of early-stage technologies, dedicated R&D funding and technology-specific feed-in tariffs are more useful (Johnstone et al. 2010). Public funding is particularly critical for clean energy given the time frame in which the transition must occur, and the fact that it can be considered as a public good. In Europe, public R&D accounts for two-thirds of the total dedicated to renewable energy (Frankfurt School–UNEP Centre 2017, p. 78) and although the bulk of that money is allocated at the member state level, EU programmes have played a crucial role.

The EU supports innovation through the Innovation Union framework, which includes a funding mechanism known as Horizon 2020. The programme will provide 80 billion euros of funding between 2014 and 2020, with 6 billion allocated specifically to non-nuclear energy research (European Commission 2010). A number of other programmes that exist within the framework, including the European Institute of Innovation and Technology, European Technology Platforms and Innovation Partnerships also include specific provisions for clean energy.

Although the EU's overall innovation performance remains poor, it has established a clear leadership position in clean energy. The EU leads the world in renewable energy deployment (REN21 2017, p. 34), R&D expenditure (Frankfurt School–UNEP Centre 2017, p. 78) and the number of patents held for climate change mitigation technologies (CCMT). Europe is particularly strong in high-value CCMT patents – defined as those where protection is sought in more than one jurisdiction – holding 40 per cent of those granted in 2011 (European Patent Office–UNEP 2015, p. 9). Concerns about the EU's competitiveness persist, but by framing the climate challenge as a solution to the economic challenge, the EU has had some success in addressing both.

Energy and opportunity

The EU's policy focus on the energy sector is justified on the basis of its importance to overall emissions reduction, the scope for technological and business model innovation and the underlying need to improve energy security. All of these factors ensure that no other sector will face as much disruption, nor offer as much opportunity, in the coming decades. Energy is responsible for nearly 80 per cent of the EU's total greenhouse gas emissions with electricity and transport the two largest components of that total (Eurostat 2015). This section will examine what the energy transition will mean for businesses within the EU, looking specifically at these two sectors and the related oil and gas sector.

The electricity sector will play the most important role in the energy transition due to its contribution to overall emissions and the fact that least-cost emissions reduction scenarios involve more rapid reductions in the electricity sector than those in the building, industrial and transport sectors (IPCC 2014, p. 38).

The transition within the electricity sector encompasses three related trends: decarbonisation, digitisation and decentralisation (Bumpus and Comello 2017, p. 383). Decarbonisation is driven by the imperative of keeping global warming to below 2°C, which, according to a detailed scenario produced by the International Energy Agency (IEA) will require the effective decarbonisation of the global electricity system by 2050 (IEA 2014, p. 10). Renewable energy, excluding hydro, is expected to be responsible for 45 per cent of all electricity generation by 2050, up from 5.4 per cent in 2015 (IEA 2015a, p. II.5, 2015b, pp. 38–41). There are some positive trends with renewable deployment growing at an accelerating pace. Growth in installed capacity for electricity generation grew by an average of 3.5 per cent per year between 1990 and 2014 (IEA 2015a, p. II.5), but reached 5 per cent in 2015 (IEA 2016a, p. 84). However, emissions from electricity generation actually grew by 50 per cent between 2000 and 2013 (IEA 2016b, p. xvii) and the IEA has concluded that the world is not yet on track to meet the renewable energy targets that would limit warming to 2°C (IEA 2016a, p. 77).

Decarbonisation is already challenging incumbent businesses within the electricity sector. Traditional, carbon-intensive utilities are struggling to transition due to the lock-in effects of existing assets and corporate structures (Dangerman and Schellnhuber 2013; Geels 2014; Unruh 2000). For example, the incumbent utilities in Germany have struggled to find a balance between exploiting existing assets and transitioning to a low-carbon business model. The four largest electricity companies, RWE, E.On, Vattenfall and EnBW, have long dominated the German market, but with the exception of Vattenfall, they have all lost significant market share since 2010 (Bundesnetzagentur 2016, pp. 34–35). The low marginal costs of renewable generation have also driven the wholesale costs of electricity downwards, contributing to a decline in the profitability of the big players (Wainstein and Bumpus 2016). In an effort to improve their competitive position and to build capacity in renewables, RWE and E.On have split their 'new energy' businesses from the traditional, fossil fuel-based businesses, but their embrace of renewables has been slow. Amongst the four utilities, renewables represent about 11 per cent of their total generation, but the market is already nearing 30 per cent (Clean Energy Wire 2017; European Commission 2017b). They are now playing catch-up, but new entrants have already altered the market, utilising renewables to change the way that electricity is generated and traded.

Renewable energy is only part of the equation. Decarbonisation of the electricity system also requires significant improvements in energy efficiency. According to the IEA's 2°C scenario, energy efficiency measures play an even greater role than renewable energy, accounting for 38 per cent of the required emissions reductions. The EU's Energy Efficiency Directive (Directive 2012/27/EU) aims to improve efficiency by 20 per cent by 2020 and includes a specific provision for EU member state governments to carry out energy efficient renovations on at least 3 per cent of the buildings they own and occupy by floor area every year. However, the most substantial improvement in energy efficiency will come from changes in the way that electricity is used. Digitisation will create a smarter grid that allows electricity use to be coordinated on a large scale. Not only will it improve efficiency but also allow for a higher penetration of intermittent renewables such as solar and wind, by better matching demand to supply. This offers enormous scope for innovation as software is applied to everything from household appliances to the grid itself. Investment trends show that early-stage capital investment is already shifting from generation technologies (hardware) to demand-side technologies (software) as the market recognises this potential (Bumpus and Comello 2017, pp. 383–384).

Decarbonisation and digitisation also facilitate decentralisation. Renewable energy technologies challenge the traditional electricity generation and distribution model that has always been supported by large-scale, centralised infrastructure and concentrated markets. A solar photovoltaic (PV) system on a household roof, or a small-scale wind farm, does not require a large capital outlay or long-distance transmission lines to deliver power. This allows for decentralised ownership by individuals or communities, and forms of energy trading that bypass traditional markets (Wainstein and Bumpus 2016). Germany has been at the forefront of this trend with nearly half of all renewable generation capacity being citizen-owned (REN21 2014, p. 27).

The energy transition in the electricity system will also impact the transport sector, which on its own is the second largest source of greenhouse gas emissions in the EU (Eurostat 2015). Under both 1.5°C and 2°C scenarios, the amount of energy generated from electricity in the transport sector will need to grow from 1 per cent in 2015 to about 25 per cent by 2050 (Rogelj et al. 2015, p. 523). The growth in electric vehicles will be achieved in part by tighter vehicle emissions standards, but the competitive nature of the industry is ensuring that innovation is quickly becoming the key driver of growth. The rapid development of battery technology and the associated fall in costs has meant that estimates of the number of electric vehicles on roads are continually revised upwards (IEA 2016a, pp. 104–105; Morgan Stanley 2016).

This transition to electric vehicles is likely to coincide with the development of autonomous vehicles, meaning that the industry is facing disruption on an unprecedented scale. This will challenge an industry that contributes significantly to the EU economy as a whole. Vehicle manufacturing employs over 2 million people within the European Union with a further 10 million employed in related industries (Eurostat 2013). The industry also generates a trade surplus of over €100 billion (ACEA 2016). Traditional automotive states such as Germany, France, the UK and Italy are heavily dependent upon the industry, but as manufacturing has expanded eastward, the industry has become increasingly important to states such as Poland, the Czech Republic and Slovakia.

In the case of the oil and gas sector, its impact will be less severe due to the small number of EU member states with significant reserves and the longer transition time frame required. The EU is dependent on imports for nearly 90 per cent of its oil consumption and nearly 70 per cent of its gas production (European Commission 2017b). Only the UK, the Netherlands and Norway (a non-EU member state) possess significant reserves, and even the UK, which was once described as an 'island of coal on a sea of gas' (McGowan 2011, p. 189) is now a net importer of both fuels (Eurostat 2014). Despite the lack of oil and gas resources, the EU is home to some of the world's largest oil and gas companies, including Royal Dutch Shell, BP and Total. The competitive position of these companies will be threatened in the medium- to long-term as emissions regulations tighten and alternative fuels enter the market. Gas, which is often seen as a transition fuel, has already taken market share from oil and although biofuels have a very small share, production grew by an annual average of over 16 per cent in the decade to 2014 (BP 2016). The EU's big energy companies will have to balance demand for their traditional products with long-term investments in alternative fuels.

The transition to a low-carbon energy system has been under way for nearly three decades, with significant innovations in clean energy technologies already, but it has only just begun. Assuming that the world adheres to the clearly stated objective of the Paris Agreement, the transition will need to accelerate rapidly in the coming decades, creating massive disruption to markets and destabilising incumbent businesses (Geels and Schot 2007). In the electricity sector, technological innovation is already well advanced, but business model innovation is still in its infancy. The increasing use of software provides enormous scope for change by allowing more intermittent renewables to be deployed, improving energy efficiency, and furthering the decentralisation of the grid. The transport sector will also become increasingly electrified, which is likely to coincide with autonomous operation. Large-scale innovation in the electricity and transport sectors will have flow-on effects in the oil and gas sector. The EU has been at the forefront of the energy transition to date, but that position is far from assured. The following section will assess Europe's position and its ability to adapt and benefit from a low-carbon future.

Towards transition – Europe's progress

The EU is likely to meet all of its 2020 objectives. The renewable energy and energy efficiency targets are on track, and the emissions target has already been met with a decline of 22 per cent since 1990 (Eurostat 2017). As demonstrated in this chapter, the targets, combined with direct support for R&D, have also had a positive impact on innovation. However, there are several caveats that should temper optimism. First, although R&D remains strong, overall investment in Europe has fallen by nearly two-thirds since its peak in 2011 (Frankfurt School–UNEP Centre 2017, p. 22). The latest employment figures from the renewable energy sector also show a decline between 2014 and 2015, suggesting that the positive impact of renewables on job creation is weakening (IRENA 2017, pp. 16–17).

Falls in investment and employment reflect uncertainty in climate mitigation and renewable energy support policies. The EU has made a long-term commitment to reduce emissions to 80–95 per cent below 1990 levels by 2050 (European Commission 2011, p. 2). However, the proposed targets for 2030 demonstrate a clear reduction in the EU's ambition (Climate Action Tracker 2017). There is a 40 per cent target reduction in emissions on 1990 levels, a 27 per cent renewable energy target with no binding member state targets and a 27 per cent energy efficiency target that is indicative only. Both the European Commission and European Parliament advocate for stronger targets, but they are effectively vetoed by Poland, which is determined to protect its coal industry and has become more assertive since the 2020 package was negotiated (Skjærseth et al. 2016, pp. 227–232). This highlights how recalcitrant member states can thwart the EU's ambition.

There was also a noticeable shift in the framing of the targets between the 2020 and 2030 proposals with much of the language about economic benefits and a 'green industrial revolution' absent from the latter (Skjærseth et al. 2016, p. 228). More broadly, the rhetoric about the competitiveness of the EU economy has also shifted, becoming less about the development of new industries and more about the protection of the existing industrial base that is threatened by increasing energy prices (Helm 2014).

Despite the obvious appeal of protecting existing economic strengths, it is unlikely to improve the EU's competitive position, nor further the energy transition in the time frame required. The EU's overall innovation performance is poor in relation to other advanced economies and the sectors in which it is strong are unlikely to be at the forefront of the next wave of clean energy innovation. Within the EU, innovation is led by long-established firms that specialise in medium R&D-intensive sectors such as automobiles, industrial machinery and chemicals (Moncada-Paterno-Castello et al. 2010). There are natural synergies between these industries and the renewable energy generation technologies that dominated the first wave of clean energy innovation, thus allowing the EU to establish a competitive advantage. However, the second wave of innovation is being driven by software and the EU is particularly weak in information and communication technologies (ICT) (Veugelers et al. 2015). As new software solutions are deployed across the energy system, the EU's competitive position in clean energy is threatened.

In a transition as complex and comprehensive as the one facing Europe's energy system, it is understandable that the trajectory is not smooth. Unfortunately, however, the carbon budget is fast being exhausted and the EU will have to re-discover its ambition if the objectives of the Paris Agreement are to be met. The EU will also have to overcome structural weaknesses in its innovation systems to ensure that it retains a competitive advantage in the next phase of the transition. The EU has recognised these challenges through policy frameworks such as the Innovation Union, but as the negotiations over the 2030 climate and energy package demonstrate, matching ambition with action is a very difficult process.

Conclusions

Climate change is causing unprecedented change to our physical environment, but it is also triggering enormous changes to the business environment, particularly in energy-related sectors.

The energy transition is already under way and companies that have long dominated these industries are finding that their competitive advantage is being eroded as the response to climate change creates opportunities for new competitors and new business models. Businesses within the EU are well placed to embrace the challenge of climate change and lead the transition to a low-carbon future. The EU's climate policy leadership has created markets for new technologies within Europe and now that many EU policies have been adopted in other parts of the world, the products and lessons developed in Europe can be adapted for international markets.

The EU's leadership on climate action can only be understood in the context of economic competitiveness. A persistent fear that Europe is falling behind the rest of the world has been an important factor in the convergence of climate, energy and innovation policies, enabling the EU to frame climate change as an opportunity rather than a cost. By linking climate action to job creation and competitiveness, it has been able to build support for policy frameworks that support the transition to a low-carbon economy.

However, recent trends suggest that the EU's competitive position in relation to climate change and clean energy innovation is being undermined. The 2030 climate and energy negotiations demonstrate a backsliding in ambition, and the EU's innovation system is currently unsuited to developing the software-based technologies that will drive the next stage of the energy transition. There is some recognition of these problems within the EU, and policy frameworks such as the Innovation Union seek to address these weaknesses, but structural problems run very deep, particularly outside the traditional leaders such as Germany, the Netherlands and Sweden.

It is important to note that innovation alone is not enough to keep global warming to below 2°C. The complexity of the problem requires enormous shifts in policies, laws and social practices, but the development of new technologies and new ways of doing business are an essential component of the response. Europe's leadership in promoting innovation in low-emissions energy technologies has been important to date, but whether it remains at the forefront and benefits from future developments remains an open question.

References

ACEA (2016), 'Trade', ACEA – European Automobile Manufacturers' Association. www.acea.be/statistics/tag/category/trade (accessed 15 September 2017).

BP (2016), 'Statistical Review of World Energy – Underpinning data', bp.com. www.bp.com/en/global/corporate/energy-economics/statistical-review-of-world-energy.html (accessed 15 September 2017).

Bumpus, A. and Comello, S. (2017), 'Emerging clean energy technology investment trends', *Nature Climate Change,* vol. 7, pp. 382–385. https://doi.org/10.1038/nclimate3306 (accessed 9 March 2018)

Bundesnetzagentur (2016), *Monitoring Report 2016.* Berlin, Bundesnetzagentur/Bundeskartellamt (German Federal Cartel Office).

Calel, R. and Dechezleprêtre, A. (2016), 'Environmental policy and directed technological change: Evidence from the European carbon market', *Review of Economics and Statistics*, vol. 98, 173–191. https://doi.org/10.1162/REST_a_00470 (accessed 9 March 2018)

Christoff, P. (2010), 'Cold climate in Copenhagen: China and the United States at COP15', *Journal of Environmental Politics*, vol. 19, no. 4, pp. 637–656. https://doi.org/10.1080/09644016.2010.489718

Christoff, P. (2016), 'The promissory note: COP 21 and the Paris Climate Agreement', *Journal of Environmental Politics*, vol. 765, no. 5, pp. 765–787. https://doi.org/10.1080/09644016.2016.1191818

Clean Energy Wire (2017), 'Germany's largest utilities at a glance'. www.cleanenergywire.org/factsheets/germanys-largest-utilities-glance (accessed 14 September 2017).

Climate Action Tracker (2017), 'EU – Climate Action Tracker'. http://climateactiontracker.org/countries/eu.html (accessed 6 June 2017).

Dangerman, A.T.C.J. and Schellnhuber, H.J. (2013), 'Energy systems transformation', *Proceedings of the National Academy of Sciences of the United States of America*, vol. 110, no. 7, pp. E549–E558. https://doi.org/10.1073/pnas.1219791110 (accessed 9 March 2018).

Declercq, B., Delarue, E. and D'haeseleer, W. (2011), 'Impact of the economic recession on the European power sector's CO2 emissions', *Energy Policy*, vol. 39, pp. 1677–1686.

Dimitrov, R.S. (2010), 'Inside UN climate change negotiations: The Copenhagen Conference', *Review of Policy Research*, vol. 27, pp. 795–821. https://doi.org/10.1111/j.1541-1338.2010.00472.x

Egan (2009), 'The Single Market', in M. Cini and N. Pérez-Solórzano Borragán (eds), *European Union Politics*, New York, Oxford University Press, pp. 255–268.

European Commission (1988), 'The greenhouse effect and the communities – COM(88) 656 final'. http://aei.pitt.edu/5684/1/5684.pdf (accessed 14 March 2017).

European Commission (1997), 'Energy for the future: Renewable sources of energy, White Paper for a Community Strategy and Action Plan – COM(97) 599 final'. http://europa.eu/documents/comm/white_papers/pdf/com97_599_en.pdf (accessed 10 September 2017).

European Commission (2007a), 'Renewable Energy Road Map. Renewable energies in the 21st century: Building a more sustainable future – COM(2006) 848 final'. http://eur-lex.europa.eu/legal-content/EN/TXT/PDF/?uri=CELEX:52006DC0848 (accessed 20 November 2017).

European Commission (2007b), 'An energy policy for Europe – COM(2007) 1 final'. http://eur-lex.europa.eu/LexUriServ/LexUriServ.do?uri=COM:2007:0001:FIN:EN:PDF (accessed 20 November 2017).

European Commission (2008), '20 20 by 2020: Europe's climate change opportunity – COM(2008) final'. http://eur-lex.europa.eu/legal-content/EN/TXT/PDF/?uri=CELEX:52008DC0030 (accessed 28 March 2018).

European Commission (2009), 'Towards a comprehensive climate change agreement in Copenhagen – COM(2009) 39 final'. http://eur-lex.europa.eu/LexUriServ/LexUriServ.do?uri=COM:2009:0039:FIN:EN:PDF (accessed 9 September 2017).

European Commission (2010), 'Europe 2020: A strategy for smart, sustainable and inclusive growth'. http://eur-lex.europa.eu/legal-content/EN/TXT/PDF/?uri=CELEX:52010DC2020 (accessed 28 March 2018).

European Commission (2011), 'A roadmap for moving to a competitive low carbon economy in 2050 – COM(2011) 112 final'. http://eur-lex.europa.eu/legal-content/EN/TXT/PDF/?uri=CELEX:52011DC0112 (accessed 28 March 2018).

European Commission (2014), 'Mission letter to Maroš Šefčovič – Vice President for Energy Union'.

European Commission (2016), 'The EU Emissions Trading System (EU ETS)'. https://ec.europa.eu/clima/policies/ets_en (accessed 4 September 2017).

https://ec.europa.eu/commission/sites/cwt/files/commissioner_mission_letters/sefcovic_en.pdf (accessed 20 March 2018).

European Commission (2017a), 'EU Innovation Scoreboard 2017', DG for Internal Market, Industry, Entrepreneurship and SMEs. http://ec.europa.eu/DocsRoom/documents/24829 (accessed 9 May 2017).

European Commission (2017b), 'Energy datasheets: EU-28 countries'. https://ec.europa.eu/energy/en/data-analysis/country/ (accessed 10 November 2017).

European Environment Agency and UNEP (2014), *Energy Support Measures and their Impact on Innovation in the Renewable Energy Sector in Europe*, Luxembourg, European Environment Agency.

European Patent Office–UNEP (2015), *Climate Change Mitigation Technologies in Europe – Evidence from patent and economic data*, Munich, European Patent Office and United Nations Environment Programme.

Eurostat (2013), 'Manufacture of motor vehicles, trailers and semi-trailers statistics – NACE Rev. 2'. http://ec.europa.eu/eurostat/statistics-explained/index.php/Archive:Manufacture_of_motor_vehicles,_trailers_and_semi-trailers_statistics_-_NACE_Rev._2 (accessed 15 September 2017).

Eurostat (2014), 'Energy balance flows – EU28'. http://ec.europa.eu/eurostat/cache/sankey/sankey.html?geo=EU28andyear=2014andunit=GWhandfuels=0000andhighlight=andnodeDisagg=0101000000andflowDisagg=true (accessed 10 January 2016).

Eurostat (2015), 'Greenhouse gas emission statistics – emission inventories'. http://ec.europa.eu/eurostat/statistics-explained/index.php/Greenhouse_gas_emission_statistics (accessed 12 September 2017).

Eurostat (2017), 'Europe 2020 indicators – Climate change and energy'. http://ec.europa.eu/eurostat/statistics-explained/index.php/Europe_2020_indicators_-_climate_change_and_energy (accessed 3 September 2017).

Frankfurt School–UNEP Centre (2017), *Global Trends in Renewable Energy Investment 2017*. Frankfurt am Main, Frankfurt School/UNEP.

Geels, F.W. (2014), 'Regime resistance against low-carbon transitions: Introducing politics and power into the multi-level perspective', *Theory, Culture & Society*, vol. 31, no. 5, pp. 21–40. https://doi.org/10.1177/0263276414531627 (accessed 9 May 2017).

Geels, F.W. and Schot, J. (2007), 'Typology of sociotechnical transition pathways', *Research Policy*, vol. 36, pp. 399–417.

Helm, D. (2014), 'The European framework for energy and climate policies', Energy Policy, vol. 64, pp. 29–35. https://doi.org/10.1016/j.enpol.2013.05.063 (accessed 9 March 2018).

Howes, T. (2010), 'The EU's New Renewable Energy Directive (2009/28/EC)', in S. Oberthür and M. Pallemaerts (eds), *New Climate Policies of the European Union: Internal Legislation and Climate Diplomacy*, Brussels, VUBPRESS, pp. 117–150.

IEA (2014), *Energy Technology Perspectives 2014*, Paris, Organisation for Economic Co-operation and Development.

IEA (2015a), *Renewables Information 2015*, Paris, Organisation for Economic Co-operation and Development.

IEA (2015b), *IEA Energy Technology Perspectives 2015*, Paris, IEA/OECD.

IEA (2016a), *Energy Technology Perspectives 2016*. Paris, Organisation for Economic Co-operation and Development.

IEA (2016b), *CO2 Emissions from Fuel Combustion 2016*, Paris, Organisation for Economic Co-operation and Development.

IPCC (2014) *Climate Change 2014 Synthesis Report*. http://ar5-syr.ipcc.ch/ (accessed 28 March 2018).

IRENA (2017), *Renewable Energy and Jobs: Annual Review 2017*. Abu Dhabi, International Renewable Energy Agency.

Johnstone, N., Hascic, I. and Popp, D. (2010), 'Renewable energy policies and technological innovation: Evidence based on patent counts', *Environmental and Resource Economics*, vol. 45, pp. 133–155.

Jovanović, M.N. (2013), *The Economics of European Integration*, Cheltenham, Edward Elgar.

Liberatore, A. (1995), 'Arguments, assumptions and the choice of policy instruments. The case of the debate on the CO2/energy tax in the European Community', in B. Dente (ed.), *Environmental Policy in Search of New Instruments*, Dordrecht, Springer, pp. 55–72.

Loth, W. (2008), 'Explaining European integration: The contribution from historians', *Journal of European Integration History*, vol. 14, pp. 9–27.

McGowan, F. (2011), 'The UK and EU energy policy: From awkward partner to active protagonist?' in J.S. Duffield and V.L. Birchfield (eds), *Toward a Common European Union Energy Policy. Problems, progress, and prospects*, Basingstoke, Palgrave Macmillan, pp. 187–213.

Moncada-Paterno-Castello, P., Ciupagea, C., Smith, K., Tubke, A. and Tubbs, M. (2010), 'Does Europe perform too little corporate R&D? A comparison of EU and non-EU corporate R&D performance', *Research Policy*, vol. 39, pp. 523–536.

Morgan Stanley (2016), 'Auto Industry Is Ripe for Disruption'. www.morganstanley.com/ideas/car-of-future-is-autonomous-electric-shared-mobility (accessed 15 September 2017).

NASA (2017), 'Carbon dioxide'. https://climate.nasa.gov/vital-signs/carbon-dioxide (accessed 9 September 2017).

Oberthür, S. (2016), 'Where to go from Paris? The European Union in climate geopolitics', *Global Affairs*, vol. 2, no. 2, pp. 119–130. https://doi.org/10.1080/23340460.2016.1166332 (accessed 9 March 2018).

Parker, C.F. and Karlsson, C. (2017), 'The European Union as a global climate leader: Confronting aspiration with evidence', *International Environmental Agreements: Politics, Law, Economics*, vol. 17, no. 4, pp. 445–461. https://doi.org/10.1007/s10784-016-9327-8 (accessed 9 March 2018).

Parrish, B.D. and Foxon, T.J. (2009), 'Sustainability entrepreneurship and equitable transitions to a low-carbon economy', *Greener Management International*, issue 55, pp. 47–62.

REN21 (2014), *Renewables 2014: Global Status Report*, Paris, Renewable Energy Policy Network for the 21st Century.

REN21 (2017), *Renewables 2017: Global Status Report*, Paris, Renewable Energy Policy Network for the 21st Century.

Rogelj, J., Luderer, G., Pietzcker, R.C., Kriegler, E., Schaeffer, M., Krey, V. and Riahi, K. (2015), 'Energy system transformations for limiting end-of-century warming to below 1.5°C', *Nature Climate Change*, vol. 5, pp. 519–527. https://doi.org/10.1038/nclimate2572 (accessed 9 March 2018)

Rogelj, J., Schaeffer, M., Friedlingstein, P., Gillett, N.P., van Vuuren, D.P., Riahi, K., Allen, M. and Knutti, R. (2016), 'Differences between carbon budget estimates unravelled', *Nature Climate Change*, vol. 6, pp. 245–252. https://doi.org/10.1038/nclimate2868 (accessed 9 March 2018).

Schreurs, M.A. and Tiberghien, Y. (2007), 'Multi-level reinforcement: Explaining European Union leadership in climate change mitigation', *Global Environmental Politics*, 19.

Skjærseth, J.B., Gulbrandsen, L.H., Eikeland, P.O. and Jevnaker, T. (2016), 'Comparative analysis and consequences for EU 2030', in J.B. Skjærseth, L.H. Gulbrandsen, T. Jevnaker and P.O. Eikeland (eds),

Linking EU Climate and Energy Policies: Decision-making, implementation and reform, new horizons in environmental politics. Northampton, MA, Edward Elgar Publishing, pp. 204–240.

Stern, N.H. (2007), *The Economics of Climate Change: The Stern Review*, Cambridge, Cambridge University Press.

Turmes, C.(2017), *Energy Transformation: An opportunity for Europe*, London, Biteback Publishing.

UNEP (2015), 'UNFCCC COP 21 Paris France – 2015 Paris Climate Conference'. www.cop21paris.org/about/cop21 (accessed 2 September 2017).

UNFCCC (2015), Adoption of the Paris Agreement, United Nations. https://unfccc.int/resource/docs/2015/cop21/eng/l09r01.pdf (accessed 12 September 2017).

Unruh, G.C. (2000), 'Understanding carbon lock-in', *Energy Policy*, vol. 28, p. 817.

Veugelers, R., Cincera, M., Frietsch, R., Rammer, C., Schubert, T., Pelle, A., Renda, A., Montalvo, C. and Leijten, J. (2015), 'The impact of Horizon 2020 on innovation in Europe', *Intereconomics,* vol. 50, no. 1, pp. 4–30. https://doi.org/10.1007/s10272-015-0521-7 (accessed 2 September 2017).

Wainstein, M.E. and Bumpus, A.G. (2016), 'Business models as drivers of the low carbon power system transition: A multi-level perspective', *Journal of Cleaner Production*, vol. 126, pp. 572–585.

Weale, A. and Williams, A. (1992), 'Between economy and ecology? The single market and the integration of environmental policy', *Journal of Environmental Politics*, vol. 1, no. 4, pp. 45–64. https://doi.org/10.1080/09644019208414045 (accessed 2 September 2017).

Wurzel, R. and Connelly, J. (2010), 'Introduction: European Union political leadership in international climate change politics', in R. Wurzel and J. Connelly (eds), *The European Union as a Leader in International Climate Change Politics*, Routledge/UACES Contemporary European Studies, Hoboken, NJ, Taylor & Francis, pp. 3–20.

27

BUSINESS AND HUMAN RIGHTS IN EUROPE

Insights from the ILVA case

Chiara Macchi and Elisa Giuliani

Introduction

Seen from elsewhere in the world, the European space, with particular reference to Western European countries,[1] has often been perceived as the stronghold of welfare societies. Despite some economic and institutional differences (Hall 2007), most European countries have often been viewed as characterised by an overall high quality of life, an outstanding level of education and strong national insurance systems for health, pensions and other social commodities (Barcevičius et al. 2015). Historically, moreover, most European governments have afforded, as compared to more liberal market economies, an exceptional level of protection for workers' rights, with labour-related issues being negotiated with governments, rather than with companies, and collective interests being frequently pursued through business associations and unions (e.g. Alesina and Glaeser 2006). Also, some European social programmes have usually been highly redistributive, while European tax systems are more progressive than in other contexts and European countries are known for their strong regulatory systems that are meant to protect the poorest and most marginalised component of European society (Alesina et al. 2001; Majone 1994). On these grounds, the business literature often assumes that European countries possess strong institutions, as compared to other contexts, also due to the convergence pressures at the EU level (see e.g. Matten and Moon 2008; Tregaskis and Brewster 2006, among others).

Although European economic crises undeniably put European countries and their welfare systems under severe pressure (e.g. Engström 2016), the European legal system is viewed as relatively advanced, where human rights (see the next section) are formally afforded protection and promotion. This, among other things, means that business enterprises operating in Europe are expected to conduct business in ways that do not lead to gross human rights infringements, while European governments are expected to be effective in preventing business-related human rights violations, and in remedying them when they do arise. In this chapter we delve into the intricacies of the relationship between business and human rights and contend, using the case of the ILVA steel plant in Taranto (Italy), that European governments may also encounter significant challenges when exercising their political leverage and their institutional role to hold businesses accountable for the negative impacts of their activities. We discuss in this chapter whether the protection of much-needed investments and the maintenance of political consensus in the context of an economic crisis can sometimes take priority over the states' internationally and constitutionally sanctioned human rights obligations. As a result, even in Europe, corporate unethical or even criminal conduct, combined with political weakness or irresponsibility, can still lead to cases of blatant disregard for the rights of workers and of local communities, exacerbating social conflict and, ultimately, harming the economic value of the business activities involved. This chapter outlines, in particular, a case in which different values and interests, among which are development, human rights and environmental considerations, appear to have clashed, posing a challenge to all stakeholders involved. The case study aims to open additional research avenues and thereby extend the European business literature towards more thorough investigations into the conflicts that arise and persist in even in the relatively advanced institutional and policy context of EU countries.

Business and human rights

International perspectives

Human rights are understood as inalienable fundamental rights to which a person is inherently entitled simply by virtue of being a human being.[2] The philosophical foundations of human rights are found in the natural rights thinking of the seventeenth century, with antecedents in the writings of ancient philosophers such as Aristotele, Cicero and Seneca (Fagan 2013). However, human rights gained political authority through the 1948 Universal Declaration of Human Rights (UDHR), which was a response to the atrocities of World War II, and became a milestone document in the history of human rights. The UDHR sets out the fundamental rights to be universally protected, and, in its 30 articles, covers the wide range of civil (e.g. right to life, to non-discrimination on grounds such as race, ethnicity, religion, colour, age, etc.) and political rights (e.g. right to a fair trial, right to vote), as well as economic, social and cultural rights (e.g. right to education, to health, to social security, to work, among others).

The UDHR is formally a soft law instrument, but it set the basis for international human rights law to be developed in the form of binding treaties. These include the 1966 International Covenant on Civil and Political Rights (ICCPR) and on Economic, Social and Cultural Rights (ICESCR), and subsequent covenants and treaties covering the protection of other vulnerable groups such as women, children, migrant workers and people with disabilities, indigenous people, and other specific rights, adopted between 1979 and 2007 (Bernaz 2017). Moreover, a set of treaties has been adopted by states from different world regions. States ratifying the treaties are expected to turn the ratified principles into national laws and ensure their respect within their territory and jurisdiction. If they fail to do so, consequences in most cases will only amount to political condemnation and recommendations by the supervisory bodies that monitor the respect of human rights treaties (such as the UN treaty bodies), but can sometimes entail other types of sanction (e.g. the fines that the European Court of Human Rights can inflict on state parties).

International human rights law was primarily designed to address violations by states, which are direct duty bearers of human rights obligations under international law, while other entities, such as individuals or business firms, are in general not directly bound by its norms. This means that it is the primary duty of the state to ensure that private entities, including companies, respect human rights within their jurisdiction. Businesses, while not generally being bearers of direct international human rights obligations, enjoy some human rights – that they can invoke, for instance, before the European Court of Human Rights – and are also holders of extensive rights under international investment law. Recently, as a result of a world order where business firms, particularly multinational enterprises (MNEs), were on occasion reported in extant literature as enjoying power able to influence and challenge that of states (Barley 2007; Green Cowles 1996; Hillmann et al. 2004; Kapfer 2006; Scherer and Palazzo 2008), a set of initiatives has been promoted to make MNEs and other private firms accountable for human rights violations (Kobrin 2009).[3] To date, the most significant achievement has been reached through a soft law approach, with the adoption of the UN Guiding Principles on Business and Human Rights (UNGPs) and their progressive implementation through national action plans (NAPs). The UNGPs have been adopted in 2011 by the UN Human Rights Council after a long process of elaboration led by the former Secretary General Special Representative on Business and Human Rights, John Ruggie. The UNGPs rest on three pillars. The first is the state duty to protect against human rights abuses by third parties, a well-established principle of international law. The second is the corporate responsibility to *respect* human rights, which means that business enterprises should act with due diligence to avoid infringing on the rights of others and to address adverse impacts linked to their operations. The third is the right of victims to have access to effective remedy, both judicial and non-judicial. While the UNGPs are not legally binding in nature, they have been instrumental in setting an international standard for business practice framed around the 1948 UDHR and subsequent covenants and treaties. The corporate responsibility to respect human rights extends both to the firm's own actions, as well as to its potential 'complicity' in the harmful conduct of its business partners, including governments or suppliers.

The UNGPs have had a significant resonance in the international community. Some states are working to develop NAPs, which will promote the implementation of the UNGPs within their national contexts. Moreover, core elements of the UNGPs were incorporated into the 2011 revision of the OECD Guidelines for Multinational Enterprises (Ruggie and Nelson 2015), while a growing number of MNEs are publicly endorsing the UNGPs as part their corporate social responsibility (CSR) policies.

Business and human rights in the European context

At the European level, the 47 member states of the Council of Europe are bound by the European Convention on Human Rights (entered into force in 1953) and most of them have also ratified the European Social Charter (whose revised version entered into force in 1999). The state parties' compliance with the European Convention, later integrated by several additional protocols, is monitored by the European Court of Human Rights, to which individuals, groups of individuals or other contracting states can lodge applications in cases of alleged violations. As concerns the EU, member states are bound by the Charter of Fundamental Rights of the European Union, which acquired legally binding status with the 2009 Lisbon Treaty. Protection and promotion of human rights are also at the core of the EU's 'relations with the wider world' (Art. 3, Treaty on European Union (TEU), Consolidated version, OJ C 202 (2016)) and of its external action (Art. 21, TEU; Art. 205, Treaty on the Functioning of the European Union (TFEU) Consolidated version, OJ C 202 (2016)).

Concerning business and human rights specifically, the EU, on the one hand, has not endorsed at this stage the project of elaboration of an international binding treaty on business and human rights, currently under discussion at the Human Rights Council (2014). On the other, though, it has actively promoted the UNGPs, calling on member states to swiftly adopt NAPs for their effective implementation (European Commission 2011), an exhortation that has been fully complied with by only eleven EU states at the time of writing (see: Office of the High Commissioner for Human Rights n.d.). Moreover, as detailed by Kornelakis and Veliziotis in Chapter 15 of this book, the EU has put in place an advanced legal framework for the protection of workers' rights in important domains such as equal opportunities and health and safety standards. It has also been rather active in adopting new pieces of legislation tackling the link between business activities and human rights, the environment and conflict (among others, the 2010 EU Timber Regulation (Regulation (EU) No 995/2010), the 2017 EU Regulation on conflict minerals (Regulation EU 2017/821), and the 2014 Non-Financial Reporting Directive (Directive 2014/95/EU)).

Against this background, one of the potentially relevant contributions of the UNGPs is the human rights due diligence, which entails a company's duty of conduct to identify the risks of negative human rights impacts linked to their operations and business relationships, prioritise the most serious ones, take the necessary steps to avoid or mitigate such risks, and provide redress for the negative impacts caused (UNGPs, Principles 15, 17). For businesses operating in European countries this implies, at a minimum, respecting applicable national and European legislation, but it might entail the adoption of additional measures. When the company does not abide by its duties, it is the primary role of the state to enforce applicable laws and regulations, also in line with its international human rights obligations, to prevent or stop human rights abuses. This obligation is not diminished by competing commitments that the state might have agreed under trade or investment treaties or contracts (UNGPs, Principle 9).

Although extant literature reports on relatively strong legal frameworks in Europe, research also sheds light on business activities in Europe that continue to be at the heart of social conflicts and controversies that reveal challenges in the first two pillars of the UNGPs (the corporate responsibility to respect and the state duty to protect human rights), often with grave consequences for the third pillar (the victim's right to remedy). In the next section we discuss a salient business-related human rights controversy in recent Italian history: the ILVA steel plant of Taranto.

The focal controversy: The ILVA steel plant in Taranto, Italy

The case of the ILVA steel plant in Taranto, in the south of Italy, is an emblematic case in which corporate malpractice and the contradictory conduct of local and national authorities have led to a conundrum in which a number of human rights, protected by international legal instruments as well as by the Italian Constitution, have been seriously put at stake. The case is interesting for scholarship as it questions some of the taken-for-granted assumptions about the well-functioning of institutions in advanced countries, and it is particularly relevant for at least two other reasons. The first is the economic and social importance of the plant founded in 1961, which has long represented the largest steel plant in Europe (Cristofoli et al. 2015, p. 103; Ferrante et al. 2015, p. 433). Initially state-controlled and then sold to the Gruppo Riva (in 1995), ILVA came to account for 40 per cent of Italy's steel production (Struggles in Italy 2016; Vagliasindi and Gerstetter 2015, pp. 6–7). In 2013, it directly employed 12,000 workers – today around 10,000 in an area where the current unemployment rate is 16.5 per cent (*Il Fatto Quotidiano* 2017; ISTAT 2016) – and had business relations with around 8,000 contractors (Vagliasindi and Gerstetter 2015, p. 7).

The second reason concerns the extremely serious consequences of the pollution produced by the plant, which has raised concerns since the 1990s, being declared an 'area at high risk of environmental crisis' by a Resolution of the Council of Ministers on 11 July 1997. The pernicious effects of the plant started to be evident when the business, then called Italsider, was still state controlled, as the installations (such as the blast furnace) necessary for production at high temperatures had been built near inhabited neighbourhoods with a view to reducing the costs of transporting materials from the port to the plant (Demurtas 2012). The first investigation against the management of Italsider for dust, gas and fumes pollution was initiated by the Italian authorities in 1982 (Demurtas 2012) and in 1991 the area was for the first time declared at high environmental risk (Demurtas 2012). In the following years, a high number of judicial proceedings were initiated against the management, sometimes leading to convictions. For instance, in the 1990s, the process of asbestos removal from the plant started, together with a long legal struggle of the workers that had been exposed to it for years and wished to obtain compensation and the recognition of their right to an early retirement (Casula 2014a; Demurtas 2012). The insufficient measures adopted to protect the workers from the highly noxious substance led in 2014 to the conviction of 27 former managers of the steel plant by an Italian judge of first instance at the Tribunal of Taranto[4] (Casula 2014a).

In 2005, the section of the plant dedicated to steel production at high temperatures was closed, and two of the managers were convicted by the Supreme Court of Cassation for having provoked and failed to prevent constant and permanent spills of dangerous dusts and minerals from the plant (see Riva ed altri (28 September 2005) Supreme Court of Cassation (Italy), section II, Judgment no. 38936). Four managers were found guilty in 2007 of failing to adopt precautions against workplace injury and the polluting emissions produced by the plant (Tribunal of Taranto, no. 408, 20 April 2007). The judge of first instance noted that the management was fully aware of the structural inadequacy of the production plant, and did not accept the company's alleged shortage of funds as a defence for failing to take the necessary measures (Tribunal of Taranto, no. 408, 20 April 2007).

The controversy concerning the polluting effect of the business reached unprecedented levels when the dimension of the problem was highlighted by a study carried out as part of the court proceedings initiated in Taranto in 2010. The Prosecutor of Taranto, who had started an investigation for environmental disaster, presented a dossier linking the toxic gas and fumes produced by ILVA over 13 years to 386 deaths, 237 malignant tumours, 247 hospitalisations for heart disease, and 937 hospitalisations for respiratory disease (Biggeri et al. 2012, p. 219; Vagliasindi and Gerstetter 2015, p. 13). It also highlighted the disproportionate incidence of tumours, heart diseases and neurological diseases among the plant's workers (Biggeri et al. 2012, p. 221). In addition, the judge who ordered in 2012 the partial shutdown of the plant stressed the obnoxious effects of pollution on livestock and, therefore, on the food chain (*ANSA. it* 2012). Underlining the total disregard for human health and the environment that had characterised the plant's management, she issued an arrest warrant for eight people, including Emilio Riva and his son Nicola Riva (*Il Fatto Quotidiano* 2012). Dioxin emissions, even after the court rulings and despite the national and local authorities' commitment to the clean-up of the area with a 336 million budget, were reported at alarming levels (and even reached a peak in 2016) (Marescotti 2014; Ricapito 2016; Vagliasindi and Gerstetter 2015, p. 14). In spite of ILVA's dramatic impacts, which were confirmed by additional studies (Comba et al. 2012; Pirastu et al. 2011; *Repubblica.it* 2016), its social and economic importance remained such in the Taranto area that eight thousands workers protested against its partial shutdown in 2012 (*Il Fatto Quotidiano* 2012).

The state's duty to protect human rights from infringements by third parties (including businesses) is well established under international law and has been reaffirmed by the UNGPs on Business and Human Rights, which also posit the corporate responsibility to exercise 'human rights due diligence' throughout their operations (Principle 17). The ILVA case is largely considered a case of failure by both the private and public sector to abide by those duties (see, for instance, Greco and Chiarello 2014). The company has often tried to justify its inaction vis-à-vis the well-known inadequacy of its production facilities, pointing at its alleged lack of funds, a thesis that has been more than once disproved by the Italian courts and that, in any case, would not relieve the management from their obligations (Tribunal of Taranto, 2014, p. 203; Tribunal of Taranto, 2007, para 3.2(f)). This inaction – which entailed the failure to stop emissions, but also to inform its own workers, for instance, of the dangers connected to asbestos exposure (Tribunal of Taranto, 2014, p. 205) – is reported in clear contravention to the principle of human rights due diligence, by which the UNGPs mean the corporate duty of conduct to identify the possible negative human rights impacts of their operations and adopt the necessary steps to tackle the risks, prioritising the most serious (UNGPs, Principle 17).

As concerns the state's duty to protect human rights, the Italian government, faced with competing interests – including the rights of the stakeholders involved, but also political consensus and economic considerations –adopted a contradictory attitude that postponed any initiative to stop the polluting emissions. For instance, after the area was declared at high environmental risk in 1991, it took until 1998 to put in place a reclamation plan under the aegis of the Ministry of Environment (Demurtas 2012). After the 2005 final judgment by the Supreme Court of Cassation against the plant's managers, the local authorities decided not to bring a civil action to demand compensation from the company, and instead continued the practice of 'agreement protocols' with ILVA by which the latter repeatedly committed to restoring the safety of the plant, pledges that were regularly disregarded by the company (Crecchi 2012). Given the failure of these agreements, which Judge Todisco defined in 2012 as a 'gross farce' (Repubblica.it 2012), it was nine years after the final judgment that the municipality of Taranto filed a civil lawsuit asking for 3 billion euros in compensation (Casula 2014b). In the meantime, the case had given rise to a clash between state powers, as in 2012 the government issued a decree allowing the plant to temporarily resume operations in spite of the partial shutdown ordered by the court, prompting the prosecutor of Taranto to challenge the constitutionality of the governmental act (Vagliasindi and Gerstetter 2015, p. 14).

Condemnation of the conduct adopted by the Italian public powers throughout the years came both from national and international authorities. The 2014 first instance judgment in the asbestos case underlined the 'inertia of public powers' that failed for decades to exercise their role, directly contributing to the 'disastrous consequences' for the health and life of workers that emerged from the judicial proceedings (Tribunal of Taranto, 2014, p. 206).

The European Commission filed a first infringement procedure against Italy in 2011, which resulted in the finding by the European Court of Justice that Italy had contravened – with regard to ILVA and to other industrial sites – EU norms on integrated pollution prevention and control (Vagliasindi and Gerstetter 2015, p. 11). A new infringement procedure was started in 2013 due to Italy's failure to ensure ILVA's compliance with the EU Directive on industrial emissions (Directive 2010/75/EU), as the company continued to disregard the conditions enshrined in its authorisation to operate issued by public authorities, as required by EU law (European Commission 2014). The Commission noted that dense clouds of industrial dusts and particulate matter continued to be emitted by the plant, causing documented pollution of air, water sources and soil (European Commission 2014). It also found that Italy was failing to respect the 'polluter pays' principle enshrined in the Directive on environmental liability (Directive 2004/35/CE), which prescribes that in the case of dangerous activities (including steel production) a regime of strict liability attaches to the company's conduct, provided that a causal link between the activity and the damage is established (European Commission 2013). Since 2016, the Commission has also been investigating whether the financial support provided by Italy to ILVA is in breach of EU norms on state aid (European Commission 2016), and is closely observing the ongoing process of sale of the plant (*Il Nuovo Quotidiano di Puglia* 2017).

In addition to the controversies linked to environmental and competition legislation, the Italian authorities in the ILVA case seem to have failed to abide by their international human rights obligations. When faced with a difficult balancing task between rights and values protected at the international and national level, states have a duty to recognise the priority of fundamental rights such as the right to life and the right to health. That, as the Tribunal of Taranto underlined, cannot be sacrificed to the freedom of economic initiative (albeit constitutionally protected) of companies (Tribunal of Taranto, 2007, para. 3.2(f)). The state has an obligation to exercise due diligence to protect those fundamental rights even in the face of the competing need to ensure other human rights, such as the right to work protected by the Italian Constitution and by international instruments (e.g. the International Covenant on Economic, Social and Cultural Rights). It is, therefore, unsurprising that alleged victims of pollution in the Taranto area are raising issues under the European Convention of Human Rights. The recent lawsuit, signed by 182 Taranto residents and communicated to the Italian government in April 2016, revolves around the alleged failure by Italy to adopt the necessary legal and informational measures to protect the health of citizens and their living environment (European Court of Human Rights 2016). Pointing to the fact that the government has allowed the plant to continue its activities by means of a governmental decree in spite of the dangers shown by expert studies, the applicants claim their right to life, to private and family life and to an effective remedy (respectively, articles 2, 8 and 13 of the European Convention of Human Rights) have been violated (European Court of Human Rights 2016).

At the time of writing this chapter, the procedure for the initiation of a bid for the acquisition of ILVA is ongoing, while the plant has remained subject to extraordinary administration since the beginning of 2015 (Palmioti 2017) and the future of its 10,000 workers is uncertain (*Il Fatto Quotidiano* 2017).

Discussion

While some European business literature contends that European countries have long been considered a stronghold of welfare societies, this chapter outlines a case illustrating the challenges some countries may face in ensuring respect and promotion of fundamental rights when economic interests are involved, and the challenge that this poses to the European legislator who relies largely on member states' diligent implementation of rules. We note that our critical analysis is in line with earlier views in political science about the development of clientelism and patronage in particular Western European countries, conceived as strategies for the acquisition and maintenance of power by the political parties and actors, and strategies for the protection and promotion of vested interests by other actors including economic ones (e.g. Piattoni 2001). Our focus on business and human rights does not directly address these issues, but it raises similar concerns about the potential failures of existing formal institutions in European countries, and paves the way for further scientific inquiry into the interplay between business, governments and human rights that needs strengthening at the level of the European Union, where the Italian case discussed in this contribution is not an isolated example. In fact, similar controversies exist elsewhere in Italy, as well as in other European countries. Notable cases include protests against the Skouries gold mine in Greece (Meynen and Poulimeni 2016); the new high-speed railway line in Piedmont, Italy (Della Porta and Piazza 2007); the environmental deterioration involved in the Sivens dam project in France (Neslen 2014); the Rosia Montana open pit mine controversy in Romania (Beyerle and Olteanu 2016); and the Shell/Exxon natural gas extraction linked to earthquakes in Groeningen, the Netherlands (Amin 2015), among many others. Moreover, business-related human rights controversies are affecting European decision-makers at large, which makes a strong case for further research and public policy contributions. A recent case in point is the decision by the European Chemical Agency to judge as safe for public use glyphosate, a herbicide that the International Agency for Research on Cancer classified, based on extant empirical evidence, as 'probably carcinogenic to humans' in 2015. Similarly, the European Commission's reactions to the 2015 Volkswagen's emission scandal is reported to have been timid, allowing car manufacturers to take a rather long time to adjust their nitrogen oxide emissions to the limits provided by the law, to the extent that emissions are allowed to be 50 per cent higher than the legal limit from 2021 and much higher than that before then. Given the link existing between the human right to health and nitrogen oxide emissions, questions arise about the capacity of the EU and its member states to ensure respect and promotion of human rights when confronted with pressures from big industry players. These questions warrant further research. Economic crises, as shown in Chapter 15 of this book, could cause a setback for the progress of the so-called Lisbon Strategy and might exacerbate the social conflicts linked to big industrial projects and to business practices perceived as neglectful of human rights and environmental protection. At the same time, they might prompt some governments to relax social and environmental standards, giving priority to investment attraction.

This worrying potential scenario connects to the existing intellectual debate about the normative solutions that can be advanced to prevent business-related harm from occurring. Two intellectual positions are currently dominant in the field. On the one hand, scholars from legal disciplines posit that a hard-law solution in international law could help enhance corporate accountability for human rights violations and overcome the weaknesses of domestic laws (Backer 2014; Bernaz 2013; Bilchitz 2016; De Schutter 2010; Deva 2014; Melish 2014). On the other hand, others fear that embarking on the difficult negotiation of a binding instrument would distract resources from a meaningful implementation of the UNGPs by states and corporations (Ruggie 2013, pp. xxii–xxiii; Taylor 2014) and would not lead to an agreement on a single global corporate liability standard (IOE 2014) or produce tangible effects on corporate conduct around the globe (Rhodes 2014). In a similar vein, management scholars have often invoked the need to convince companies to engage in voluntary self-regulation through the endorsement of soft law initiatives like the UNGPs, the development of CSR policies and firm-level codes of conduct (Rivoli and Waddock 2011), given the failure of many world-wide governments to ensure the rule of law, and the reputational pressures MNEs face when they are exposed to risky institutional environments (Fiaschi et al. 2017). Meanwhile, some emphasise the need for both hard law and voluntary solutions to proceed in parallel (Bernaz 2017), although which normative mix is effective in curbing harmful business conducts is still an open question. Cases such as the Volkswagen scandal demonstrate that even the most frontier companies in terms of their CSR policies potentially enact wrongful conduct while operating in solid institutional contexts like the USA and Europe at large, which in turn suggests that hard law – either at the domestic or at the international level – may not be such a magic bullet.

Conclusion

The existing intellectual debate about the human rights responsibilities of business provides important research avenues for future contributions in this field. First, scholars should make efforts to go beyond anecdotal evidence and case study research, and work at the development of large-scale datasets that codify events of business-related human rights controversies throughout Europe and beyond. This will allow a much more comprehensive look at this phenomenon along with a better understanding of it, especially if human rights data are matched with other business-related data (on financial performance, investments, location decisions, etc.). Second, more data availability would be relevant to answer some of the many open questions in this area of research (for a review and research agenda see Giuliani and Macchi 2014). For instance, we still know very little about the way in which companies' investment strategies contribute to human rights respect or violations, or how these strategies differ depending on the company's country of origin. Are these differences due to their home institutional or cultural context, or to their own internal strategic choices? Do foreign investors in Europe align to European or national standards and, in that case, with what outcomes? How has this changed over time? Does the adoption of voluntary CSR policies across Europe or the endorsement of soft law initiatives contribute to a reduction in business-related human rights controversies? Do European companies sourcing from international suppliers respect human rights of distant constituencies involved in their value chains? How can EU-based approaches strengthen human rights protection and reduce violations in a holistic and comprehensive manner, given the multi-layered nature of multilateral decision-making? These and similar questions are waiting for answers and we hope scholars of different disciplines will contribute further to this research agenda.

Notes

1 We acknowledge that the term Europe is subject to multiple interpretations. In this chapter, we refer to Europe as the European Union (EU), and most of the discussion here is focused on western EU countries, unless otherwise specified.

2 Human rights are understood as universal, indivisible, interdependent and interrelated (Office of the High Commissioner for Human Rights 1993). Our reference here is the 1948 Universal Declaration of Human Rights (UDHR) and subsequent covenants and treaties including the International Covenant on Civil and Political Rights, and the International Covenant on Economic, Social, and Cultural Rights.

3 The complexity of this issue is that MNEs are bound by domestic law, and therefore they are legally liable if they infringe a human right that is protected by the national law of the country where they own a production plant or any other property. However, MNEs do often have operations countries where the judiciary system is poor, and access to justice might be very difficult. In such cases, it is currently extremely complex for the plaintiffs to sue a company and obtain justice.

4 Judgment no. 1431 (23 May 2014) Tribunal of Taranto 2014. www.associazioneitalianaespostiamianto. org/wp-content/uploads/2014/09/26-1.09.2014-Ilva-amianto-motivazioni-sentenza.pdf (accessed April 2017).

References

Alesina, A. and Glaeser, E. (2006), 'Why welfare states in the US and Europe so different?' *Horizons stratégiques*, vol. 2, pp. 51–61.

Alesina, A., Glaeser, E. and Sacerdote, B. (2001), 'Why doesn't the US have a European-style welfare state?' *Brookings Paper on Economics*, pp. 187–278.

Amin, L. (2015), 'Shell and Exxon's €5bn problem: Gas drilling that sets off earthquakes and wrecks homes', 10 October. www.theguardian.com/environment/2015/oct/10/shell-exxon-gas-drilling-sets-off-earthquakes-wrecks-homes (accessed August 2017).

ANSA.it (2012), 'Steelworkers paralyze Taranto over plant shutdown', 27 July. www.ansa.it/web/notizie/rubriche/english/2012/07/27/Steelworkers-paralyze-Taranto-plant-shutdown_7247703.html (accessed April 2017).

Backer, L.C. (2014), 'The Guiding Principles of Business and Human Rights at a crossroads: The state, the enterprise, and the spectre of a treaty to bind them all', Working Paper no. 7(1), Coalition for Peace and Ethics.

Barley, S.R. (2007), 'Corporations, democracy, and the public good', *Journal of Management Inquiry*, vol. 16, no. 3, pp. 201–215.

Bernaz, N. (2013), 'Enhancing corporate accountability for human rights violations: Is extraterritoriality the magic potion?', *Journal of Business Ethics*, vol. 117, p. 493.

Bernaz, N. (2017), *Business and Human Rights. History, Law and Policy: Bridging the accountability gap*, London, Routledge.

Beyerle, S. and Olteanu, T. (2016), 'How Romanian People Power Took On Mining and Corruption', 17 November. http://foreignpolicy.com/2016/11/17/how-romanian-people-power-took-on-mining-and-corruption-rosia-montana/ (accessed August 2017).

Biggeri, A., Forastiere, F. and Triassi, M. (2012), *Conclusions of the Epidemiologic Survey*. www.epiprev.it/materiali/2012/Taranto/Concl-perizia-epidemiol.pdf (accessed March 2017).

Bilchitz, D. (2016), 'The Necessity for a Business and Human Rights Treaty', *Business and Human Rights Journal*, vol. 1, no. 2, pp. 203–227.

Casula, F. (2014a), 'Ilva Taranto, condanna per l'amianto: "Gli operai morti potevano essere salvati"', 9 September. www.ilfattoquotidiano.it/2014/09/09/ilva-taranto-condanna-per-lamianto-gli-operai-morti-potevano-essere-salvati/1114884/ (accessed March 2017).

Casula, F. (2014b), 'Ilva, Taranto chiede 3 miliardi di risarcimento: "Danni da inquinamento"'. 8 March. www.ilfattoquotidiano.it/2014/03/08/ilvatarantochiede3miliardidirisarcimentoperidannidainquinamento/907104/ (accessed March 2017).

Comba, P., Conti, S., Iavarone, I., Marsili, G., Musmeci, L. and Pirastu, R. (2012), *Ambiente e salute a Taranto: Evidenze disponibili e indicazioni di sanità pubblica*. www.salute.gov.it/imgs/c_17_pubblicazioni_1833_allegato.pdf (accessed March 2017).

Crecchi, P. (2012), 'Ilva, i pm: "Ecco le prove"', 30 July. www.ilsecoloxix.it/Facet/comment/Uuid/d8c0e2b2-da0e-11e1-8377-0238be75676d/Ilva_i_pm_Ecco_le_prove_SIMOIlvaprocuravaavanti.xml (accessed March 2017).

Cristofoli, M., Di Pierri, M., Greco, L., Gennari Santori, F. and Greyl, L. (2015), *The Six Legs Dog – An oil corporation under the microscope: The Italian Goliath ENI*. http://cdca.it/wp-content/uploads/2015/03/finalENImarch15_ENG1.pdf (accessed April 2017).

De Schutter, O. (2010), 'La responsabilité des Etats dans le contrôle des sociétés transnationales: Vers une convention internationale sur la lute contre les atteintes aux droits de l'homme commises par les sociétés transnationales', Working paper, UC Louvain. http://papers.ssrn.com/sol3/papers.cfm?abstract_id=2446911 (accessed September 2017).

Della Porta, D. and Piazza, G. (2007), 'Local contention, global framing: The protest campaigns against the TAV in Val Di Susa and the bridge on the Messina Straits', *Environmental Politics*, vol. 16, no. 5, pp. 864–882.

Demurtas, A. (2012), 'Taranto, lavoro e veleni', 27 July. www.lettera43.it/it/articoli/economia/2012/07/27/taranto-lavoro-e-veleni/51187/ (accessed March 2017).

Deva, S. (2014), 'The Human Rights Obligations of Business: Reimagining the Treaty Business'. https://business-humanrights.org/sites/default/files/media/documents/reimagine_int_law_for_bhr.pdf (accessed 23 March 2018).

Engström, V. (2016), 'The political economy of austerity and human rights law', Institute for Human Rights Working Paper, No. 1/2016. https://papers.ssrn.com/sol3/papers.cfm?abstract_id=2734659 (accessed 22 March 2018).

European Commission (2014), 'Environment: European Commission urges Italy to address severe pollution issues at Europe's biggest steel plant', 16 October. http://europa.eu/rapid/press-release_IP-14-1151_en.htm (accessed March 2017).

European Commission (2016), 'State aid: Commission opens in-depth investigation into Italian support for steel producer Ilva in Taranto, Italy', 20 January. http://europa.eu/rapid/press-release_IP-16-115_en.htm (accessed March 2017).

European Commission (2011), 'A renewed EU strategy 2011–14 for Corporate Social Responsibility', COM(2011) 681, 25 October.

European Commission (2013), 'Environment: European Commission urges Italy to bring a steel plant in Taranto up to environmental standards', 26 September. http://europa.eu/rapid/press-release_IP-13-866_en.htm (accessed March 2017).

European Court of Human Rights (2016), *Cordella et al. v. Italy* and *Ambrogi Melle et al. v. Italy*, Apps. no. 54414/13 and 54264/15, 27 April. http://hudoc.echr.coe.int/eng/?i=001-163116 (accessed April 2017).

Fagan, A. (2013), 'Philosophical foundations of human rights', in T. Cushman (ed.), *Handbook of Human Rights*, New York, Routledge, pp. 9–22.

Il Fatto Quotidiano (2012), 'Ilva sequestrata: "Disastro ambientale". Taranto paralizzata da 8mila operai', 26 July. www.ilfattoquotidiano.it/2012/07/26/ilva-sequestrata-disastro-ambientale-taranto-paralizzata-da-8mila-operai/306836/ (accessed April 2017).

Il Fatto Quotidiano (2017), 'Ilva, decreto e legge non coincidono. A rischio la vendita del siderurgico ai privati', 12 February. www.ilfattoquotidiano.it/2017/02/12/ilva-decreto-e-legge-non-coincidono-a-rischio-la-vendita-del-siderurgico-ai-privati/3387025/ (accessed April 2017).

Ferrante, M., Fiore, M., Copat, C., Morina, S., Ledda, C., Mauceri, C. and Oliveri Conti, G. (2015), *Air Pollution in High-Risk Sites–Risk analysis and health impact*. http://cdn.intechopen.com/pdfs-wm/49151.pdf (accessed March 2017).

Fiaschi, D., Giuliani, E. and Nieri, F. (2017), 'Overcoming the liability of origin by doing no harm. Assessing emerging country firms' social irresponsibility as they go global', *Journal of World Business*, vol. 52, no. 4, pp. 546–563.

Giuliani, E. and Macchi, C. (2014), 'Multinational Corporations' economic and human rights impacts on developing countries: A review and research agenda', *Cambridge Journal of Economics*, vol. 38, no. 2, pp. 479–517.

Greco, L. and Chiarello, F. (2014), 'The failure of regulation: Work, environment and production at Taranto's ILVA', *Economic and Industrial Democracy*, vol. 37, no. 3: pp. 517–534.

Green Cowles, M. (1996), 'The EU Committee of AmCham: The powerful voice of American firms in Brussels', *Journal of European Public Policy*, vol. 3, no. 3, pp. 339–358.

Hall, P.A. (2007), 'The evolution of varieties of capitalism in Europe', in *Beyond Varieties of Capitalism*, Oxford, Oxford University Press, pp. 39–88.

Hillmann, A.J., Keim, G.D. and Schuler, D. (2004), 'Corporate political activity: A review and research agenda, *Journal of Management*, vol. 30, no. 6, pp. 837–857.

Human Rights Council (2014), 'Elaboration of an international legally binding instrument on transnational corporations and other business enterprises with respect to human rights', UN Doc. A/HRC/RES/26/9.

International Council on Human Rights Policy (2002), 'Beyond voluntarism: Human rights and the developing international legal obligations of companies'. www.ichrp.org/files/reports/7/107_report_en.pdf (accessed September 2017).

IOE (2014), 'IOE Secretary-General questions Ecuador-initiated proposal for new legally binding treaty on business and human rights', 11 March. www.ioe-emp.org/fileadmin/ioe_documents/publications/Policy%20Areas/business_and_human_rights/EN/_2014-03-11__G-463_IOE_SG_questions_proposal_for_new_legally_binding_treaty_on_business_and_human_rights__1_.pdf (accessed September 2017).

ISTAT (2016), *Province of Taranto*. http://dati.istat.it/?queryid=298 (accessed April 2017).

Kapfer, S. (2006), *Multinational Corporations and the Erosion of State Sovereignty* [ebook], Illinois State University.

Kobrin, S.J. (2009), 'Private political authority and public responsibility: Transnational politics, transnational firms, and human rights', *Business Ethics Quarterly*, vol. 19, no. 3, pp. 349–374.

Majone, G. (1994), 'The rise of the regulatory state in Europe', *West European Politics*, vol. 17, no. 3, pp. 77–101.

Marescotti, A. (2014), 'Taranto, la città della diossina', 8 August. www.peacelink.it/ecologia/a/40487.html (accessed April 2017).

Matten, D.A. and Moon J. (2008), 'Implicit and explicit CSR, a conceptual framework for understanding of corporate social responsibility', *Academy of Management Review*, vol. 33, no. 2, pp. 404–424.

Melish, T. (2014), 'Putting "human rights" back into the UN Guiding Principles on Business and Human Rights: Shifting frames and embedding participation rights', Buffalo Legal Studies Research Paper Series, Paper No. 2014–032. http://papers.ssrn.com/sol3/papers.cfm?abstract_id=2475629 (accessed September 2017).

Meynen, N. and Poulimeni, S. (2016), 'The Greek state has nothing to gain but environmental cost from the investment', 21 April. www.mo.be/en/analysis/greek-state-has-nothing-gain-environmental-cost-investment (accessed August 2017).

Neslen, A. (2014), 'EU takes legal action against controversial French dam', 26 November. www.theguardian.com/environment/2014/nov/26/eu-takes-legal-action-against-controversial-french-dam (accessed August 2017).

Il Nuovo Quotidiano di Puglia (2017), 'All'esame dell'Europa il dossier dell'Ilva. Incontri con le cordate', 20 March. www.quotidianodipuglia.it/taranto/taranto_ilva_europa_controlli-2327625.html (accessed March 2017).

Office of the High Commissioner for Human Rights (n.d.), 'State national action plans'. www.ohchr.org/EN/Issues/Business/Pages/NationalActionPlans.aspx (accessed April 2017).

Office of the High Commissioner for Human Rights (1993), 'Vienna Declaration and Programme of Action, Adopted by the World Conference on Human Rights', 25 June. www.ohchr.org/EN/ProfessionalInterest/Pages/Vienna.aspx (accessed 23 March 2018).

Palmioti, D. (2017), 'Processo Ilva: Per i patteggiamenti udienza fissata al 9 giugno', 19 April. www.ilsole24ore.com/art/impresa-e-territori/2017-04-19/processo-ilva-i-patteggiamenti-udienza-fissata-9-giugno-170633.shtml?uuid=AEOwdu7 (accessed April 2017).

Piattoni, S. (ed.) (2001), *Clientelism, Interests, and Democratic Representation: The European experience in historical and comparative perspective*, Cambridge, UK, Cambridge University Press.

Pirastu, R., Iavarone, I., Pasetto, R., Zona, A. and Comba, P. (2011), 'SENTIERI Project – Mortality study of residents in Italian polluted sites: Results', *Epidemiologia e Prevenzione*, vol. 35, no. 5–6, Suppl. 4, pp. 1–204.

Repubblica.it (2012), 'Il gip: "Ilva mossa da logica del profitto sequestro per tutelare la vita umana"', 27 February. http://bari.repubblica.it/cronaca/2012/07/26/news/ilva_il_gip-39795626/ (accessed November 2017).

Repubblica.it (2016), 'Ilva di Taranto, nuovo allarme del ministero: "Rischi neurologici per i bambini"', 8 December. http://bari.repubblica.it/cronaca/2016/12/08/news/taranto_malatti_neurologiche_ilva-153689013/ (accessed April 2017).

Rhodes, A. (2014), 'The False Promise of an International Business and Human Rights Treaty'. www.huffingtonpost.com/aaron-rhodes/the-false-promise-of-an-i_b_5575236.html (accessed September 2017).

Ricapito, V. (2016), 'Taranto, diossina record al rione Tamburi: I Verdi presentano un esposto contro l'Ilva', 17 March. http://bari.repubblica.it/cronaca/2016/03/17/news/taranto_diossina_record_al_tamburi_i_verdi_presentano_un_esposto_contro_l_ilva-135680234/ (accessed April 2017).

Rivoli, P. and Waddock, S. (2011), '"First they ignore you…" The time-context dynamic and corporate social responsibility', *California Management Review*, vol. 53, no. 2, pp. 87–104.

Ruggie, J.G. (2013), *Just Business – Multinational Corporations and Human Rights*, New York and London, W. W. Norton and Company.

Ruggie, J.G. and Nelson, T. (2015), 'Ruggie & Nelson: Human rights and the OECD guidelines for multinational enterprises: Normative innovations and implementation challenges', *International Law Reporter*. http://ilreports.blogspot.it/2015/05/ruggie-nelson-human-rights-and-oecd.html (accessed 23 March 2018).

Scherer, A.G. and Palazzo, G. (2008), 'Globalization and corporate social responsibility', in A. Crane, A. McWilliams, D. Matten, J. Moon and D. Siegel (eds), *The Oxford Handbook of Corporate Social Responsibility*, Oxford, Oxford University Press, pp.413–431.

Struggles in Italy (2016), 'Workers occupy ILVA steel plant in Genoa', 26 January. https://strugglesinitaly.wordpress.com/2016/01/26/en-workers-occupy-ilva-steel-plant-in-genoaen/ (accessed April 2017).

Taylor, M. (2014), 'A Business and Human Rights Treaty? Why Activists Should be Worried', 4 June. www.ihrb.org/other/treaty-on-business-human-rights/a-business-and-human-rights-treaty-why-activists-should-be-worried (accessed September 2017).

Tregaskis, O. and Brewster, C. (2006), 'Converging or diverging? A comparative analysis of trends in contingent employment practice in Europe over a decade', *Journal of International Business Studies*, vol. 37, no. 1, pp. 111–126.

Vagliasindi, G.M. and Gerstetter, C. (2015), *The ILVA Industrial Site in Taranto – In-depth analysis of the ENVI Committee*. www.europarl.europa.eu/RegData/etudes/IDAN/2015/563471/IPOL_IDA(2015)563471_EN.pdf (accessed March 2017).

28

CONCLUSION

European business – a twenty-first-century research agenda

Gabriele Suder, Monica Riviere and Johan Lindeque

The field of European business research emerged in the late 1980s and early 1990s, setting a basis in literature that, several decades on, has gained significant momentum, especially from the rise of the regionalisation debate in the international business discipline. Valuable research has shown that European multinationals tend to be particularly home-region oriented, and that market integration, even if partial, accelerates trade and investment flows.

At the same time, trends and developments in the international business environment shape the discussion of European business strategy and theory at regular intervals, ranging from economic or financial crisis, to the debate of more or less integration in scale and scope, and from disruptive to constructive events, to complex economic, social, political and environmental issues.

In this book, the main current and future research themes have been revealed, analysed and delivered in a manner that allows for in-depth knowledge acquisition by the reader, as much as providing material to ponder, research and investigate in the future, offering significant opportunities for relevant theory and practice contributions.

Common themes within the chapters in this volume focused on integration and fragmentation, convergence and divergence, harmonisation and complexity. These themes are equally important to consider in European business research and in other regional studies, potentially on a comparative basis.

This is the first single text on the state of research knowledge on European business or that offers a comprehensive guide on the subjects of Europeanisation: a single repository on the current state of research knowledge, current debates, relevant literature and future research agendas. Future research avenues will be built on this basis, to explore further how European business research contributes to the international business field and is a field in itself. Some of the chapters have pointed to the lack of Europe-wide attention, for example in the marketing literature or in human rights scholarship, to the specificities of a potential Single Market-driven approach or to clusters. In some research streams, there may be an assumption that cross-border (bilateral) or global strategy and action would equal those on the European level, but it has been evidenced here that this is not the case. The extant literature points convincingly to a need for further investigation, and this opens up new research opportunities for the coming generations of research publications.

Whilst the contributions already make clear reference to the future research potential, we as editors also feel that more can be done. European business research would be particularly well placed to explore further sub-themes, for example on resilience to terrorism, populism and motions towards pluri- or, at the other extreme, de-integration. Also, there is still a lack of research into the impacts on European business of migration and refugee flows. These are themes that may not be unique to Europe, yet the specificities of the European setting may provide insights most certainly worth bringing together with other regions' findings, to build and expand theory further and strengthen the relevance of international business studies in practice.

Finally, this volume and its contributions support a strong thesis: that research complementing firm- and country-specific advantage literature needs to be furthered, through the development of a region-specific perspective. This strengthens the literature exploring the dependencies of home regionalisation and global internationalisation, whether within the fragmentation of the global value chain, in business-to-business and business-to-consumer transactions. Are there productive capabilities of home-country domiciled firms that aggregate to region-specific advantages of particular host locations, providing MNEs with particular advantage in their regional activity? What distinguishes the advantages gained by firms that operate in advanced market-integrated regions, from others in international business? How do internationalisation strategy, modes and timing evolve in partially integrated regions that encompass developed and transition economies? And how does this extend extant international business theory?

This book has provided evidence for the increasing need of such considerations in future research.

INDEX

Note: Page numbers in *italics* denote figures and page numbers in **bold** denote tables.